Proceedings of the
2nd Seoul International Forum for Literature 2005

Writing for Peace

Proceedings of the
2nd Seoul International Forum for Literature 2005

Edited by Kim Uchang

The Second Seoul International Forum for Literature 2005 was held in Seoul from May 24th to 26th in Seoul, Korea, organized by the Daesan Foundation and the Arts Council Korea.

Publisher's Note: The order of Korean, Chinese and Japanese names are presented in the reverse to the Western format and are transcribed in the following order: surname, given name. French, German and Spanish texts are presented in their original format.

First published in 2006 by Seoul Selection
105-2 Sagan-dong, Jongno-gu, Seoul 110-190, Korea
Phone (82-2) 734-9567 Fax (82-2) 734-9562
http://www.seoulselection.com
email: hank@seoulselection.com

Published in the Republic of Korea by Seoul Selection

ISBN: 89-91913-08-3-93890

Printed in the Republic of Korea

CONTENTS_

foreword_

Presented herewith are the proceedings of the Second Seoul International Forum for Literature held from May 24 through May 26 2005, sponsored by the Daesan Foundation and the Arts Council Korea. Eighty writers and scholars participated in the Forum, among them nineteen writers from abroad representing twelve nations. The scale was roughly the same as the First Forum held in 2000. Yet it was not entirely unjust to say that there was more enthusiasm this time than five years ago. We hope that the participants and the audience returned home from this Second Forum feeling that their time has been well rewarded.

Responsible for the enthusiasm roused by the Forum were no doubt the roster of distinguished writers we had as participants and the importance of the overall theme of the Forum. But it was also the success of the First Forum that redounded from the Second Forum. We feel that the Forum is beginning to acquire some ground as an important institution that brings together writers and intellectuals from all over the world and offers a platform for presenting, sharing and discussing important concerns for themselves and humanity as a whole.

"Writing for Peace" was the official theme of the Second Forum. Peace has been an ideal important in all times, but the selection of the theme was prompted by the condition of our time. The end of the Cold War raised high hopes for an inauguration of a new age of peace for the entire humanity, but they were soon betrayed as wars continued in many parts of the world—civil wars and wars between nations—in Somalia, the Balkans, Rwanda, Sudan and, most significantly, in Iraq. Incidents of violent destruction of life and property have not abated in all the continents of the world. As the papers presented at the Forum testify, we can see that fear of war still reigns high in such a seemingly peaceful area as the Korean peninsula.

The idea of perpetual peace, as envisaged by Kant, was a central point of reference throughout the Forum, but the sense was strong that it cannot be realized without eliminating causes that make, instead of perpetual peace, a perpetual war-like condition a normal state of the world. Many writers also warned in the Forum against the Orwellian inversion of the meaning of peace that could occur in the perverse rhetoric of Realpolitik. As it turned out, the Forum looked more at the causes of conflict than the possibilities of ensuring peace in the present world; clashes of cultures, world poverty, conflict arising along the fissures of gender, race or religion, and ecological catastrophe now threatening life on earth.

The Forum's theme was not only about peace, but also about what the writers could do for it. On this point as well, not too much optimism was voiced, though all felt that it should be part of legitimate concern for the writers. The conference was about writing, but attention was also paid to the significance of media art, such as films and videos, now on the rise, and of new technologies in communication, such as the internet, for the future of humankind.

The papers presented at the Forum, needless to say, do not constitute a systematic treatise on the question of war and peace. Issues raised and the views and interpretations presented are multifarious and diverse refusing to be contained in any constraining scheme; but that is what makes them truly representative. In the Forum's multinational, multicultural, and multiphonal voices run passion and commitment in varying degrees of intensity—memories of wars, testimonials of human suffering in situations of violence, and expression of hopes for the future of peace. There was discussion among participants about finding some way of streamlining the papers presented so that they could be turned into a book easily accessible to a concerned global readership, but the idea was abandoned. Now, the proceedings are being published in all the original multivocal diversity of experiences and views. It is good that it should be so, as this diversity too stands in need of testimony.

In spite of this diversity, there was unity in the universal hope for peace, subdued as it may sometimes sound. All the participants offered their thoughts on how the act of writing could contribute to making the hope of peace come fulfilled. There was then solidarity by the participants in expressing this hope through a public declaration. It is with great pleasure that I note that there was during the Forum one public action the majority of the participants agreed to take together in the form of the Seoul Declaration of Peace they signed, calling for abolition of war as a means of conflict resolution and appealing to the governments and peoples of the world to work towards the elimination of the causes diminishing the bounty of life given to humans and all other living beings on earth. The Declaration was read in one of the last sessions of the Forum meeting by the Hungarian writer Tibor Méray, a veteran witness of wars and violent conflict in Europe, Korea and in the Hungarian Uprising of 1956.

We would like to extend our deepest thanks to all those who made the Forum a great success as we would like to believe it was: first of all the Forum participants; distinguished guests from abroad, participating Korean writers, and the public, who took part in the Forum sessions with more than usual interest and enthusiasm. The members of the Organizing Committee and the supporting staff at the Daesan Foundation worked hard to forestall all the possible thematic and logistical problems in organizing the Forum. Thanks are due to Messrs. Kang Hyung-chul, Kim Dae-young, Kim Hwa-young, Kim Nuri, Yoon Sang-in, Kim Seong-kon, Yu Jong-ho, on the Organizing Committee, and Messrs. Kwak Hyo-hwan, Ahn Young-guk and Jeon Sung-woo of Daesan. All Forum events were underwritten by the Daesan Foundation and the Arts Council Korea. We would like to express our deepest appreciation to Mr. Shin

Chang-Jae, Chairman of the Daesan Foundation, and Mr. Hyun Ki-young, President of the Arts Council Korea. For this volume of the proceedings, we must thank Seoul Selection for undertaking publication. The hard work of copy reading was done by Mr. David Kendall, who made the entire volume more presentable than it would have been with materials translated from the original with varying degrees of skill. I thank him sincerely. Also, we would like to take this occasion to thank Professor Masao Miyoshi of the University of California, San Diego, who spent at our request many hours of labor and thought, trying out more streamlined projections for a possible book that could be worked out of the papers presented, though that book did not materialize.

Kim Uchang
Chair, Organizing Committee
The Second Seoul International Forum for Literature 2005

Session I

Human Values and Political Change

Oe Kenzaburo | We Must Be Still and Still Moving…

Kim Uchang | Politics and Human Values

We Must Be Still and Still Moving . . .

Oe Kenzaburo

I would like to begin by thanking the Daesan Foundation for its kindness and generosity for inviting this Japanese novelist to Seoul, so that he can participate in the "Writing for Peace" conference.

I am delighted to meet and exchange dialogue in Seoul with outstanding literary figures from all over the world, including those from Korean literary circles. In Tokyo, big conferences of this type are no longer held. I am concerned about this, wondering whether it is because Japanese literary figures are preoccupied with their own world, shut off from the outside world. Contemplating this point through dialogue with you is one of the reasons for my coming here.

When I think about it, I am none other than a Japanese man of letters who is preoccupied with his own internal-gazing. I am conscious that I am at a literary turning point – a very critical one at that. I must search for a way to face this turning point or crisis head-on and tackle it by writing fiction, in line with the novelist's "lifelong habit."

Besides, this turning point I am faced with may be the last one for me, because it is related with my old age. I am excruciatingly aware that it is something I have not encountered before. I would like to openly discuss it on the basis of my personal experience.

I am writing a piece of fiction that could be my last. It is divided into three parts, and I am working on my last draft of Part II. Since beginning to write fiction in my youth, the method I have developed in order to remain as a novelist is the continuous revision of a first draft. It is a simple method of revising over and over. I call this process by the English word, "elaboration."

I am currently working on my last elaboration of Part II. When I came to Seoul, I left this manuscript on the desk in my Tokyo library. Upon returning, I will have to complete it and launch into a revision and improvement of Part III, whose images and tone have yet to take clear shape.

This derives from a particular circumstance in which Japan's literary publications find themselves; this revolves around monthly literary magazines. I have already published Part I of *Farewell, My Books*. The title of Part I is *"Let me Rather Hear of Old Men's Folly."* I quoted it from T.S. Eliot's "East Coker" in *Four Quartets.* It goes without saying that my quote comes from the Japanese translation, which was done by Junzaburo Nishiwaki, a modernist poet of Japanese literature who studied literature in England when T.S. Eliot was in his prime.

Do not let me hear
Of the wisdom of old men, rather of their folly
Their fear of fear and frenzy, their fear of possession
Of belonging to another, or others or to God.

My novel is about Japan and the Japanese people of my time. This is no different from most authors who write about their countries and contemporaries. If there is something out of the ordinary in my novel, it is that I narrate it by introducing a character who is almost identical to myself, the writer.

After hearing this, those of you who are familiar with Japanese literature may think of "I-novel *(Shishosetsu)*," a peculiar form of my country's modern literature. The writers insert themselves in their stories, including the details of their everyday lives, to narrate "a story about myself." From the time I first started out as a novelist, I aspired to rebel against the tradition of the "I-novel." My method is introducing into fiction a character who is similar to myself in real life but not exactly as myself.

Several years after I started out as a novelist, a mentally handicapped child was born into my family. Since then, leading a life in my contemporary period has become equivalent to living with a handicapped child. It did not stop there; it became a theme of my literature. Through this process, the characteristic I mentioned earlier began to appear in my stories.

There is criticism that this made my fictional world narrower and the story development limited. I have always felt, however, that by introducing a father who has a handicapped child – the writer himself – as a model, I was able to deal with all the fundamental issues of my contemporaries in Japanese society. To realize this as a conviction in reality, I have sought my own fictional narrative techniques, and my fictional narration has acquired urgent inevitability in my advanced age.

Five years ago, I published a literary work entitled *"Changeling."* I had a friend who deeply influenced me since boyhood. He introduced art, including literature, to me, as we grew up together in a small regional community, and guided me to attend university to study French literature. I married his younger sister, and this friend became a prolific movie director. Some of you here may have watched some of Juzo Itami's films.

That same friend killed himself in his declining years. I attempted to revive what we experienced together for almost 10 years as we were growing up after Japan's defeat in World War II, and "C*hangeling"* was the result. While reexamining my friend and myself, I came across with a new thematic world (thématiques).

I have already written *A Child Who Looks Sad,* a novel that followed "Changeling." By linking these two works, I am working on *Farewell, My Books,* one of my "later works" – I have learned this term from "Thoughts on Late Style," Edward W. Said's last work in his final years before his death a couple of years ago.

I respected and admired him for a long time.

Just like the title of Part I, which I quoted from Eliot's poem, this is about "old men's folly." There are two old men: the author himself and a fictionalized character. Both are a "pseudo-couple," modeled after my thoughts and actions in my declining years.

I can say that I am conscious of myself as an old man while writing this novel. Said concludes "Thoughts on Late Style," which turned out to be his last writing, with:

> This is the prerogative of late style: it has the power to render disenchantment and pleasure without resolving the

> contradiction between them. What holds them in tension, as equal forces straining in opposite directions, is the artist's mature subjectivity, stripped of hubris and pomposity, unashamed either of its fallibility or of the modest assurance it has gained as a result of age and exile.

According to Said, an aged author penning a "later work" reveals a catastrophe by expressing contradictions as they are, in acute tension, without integrating opposing elements, irrelevant of maturity. He refers to it as "late style" and gives as examples outstanding works of Henrik Ibsen, Giuseppe de Lampedusa, and Constantine Cavafy.

I will not say that Said's analysis applies to all aged artists. There are some artists who concluded their full lives in the joy of achieving their long-cherished desires, overcoming the catastrophe through the achievement of maturity and integrity and resolving all contradictions and tensions.

Nevertheless, I admit that at this point, at the age of 70, I get the energy to move forward with my novel-in-progress only through tensions between two contradicting poles. The protagonist, the aged writer, and another character of the "pseudo-couple," who is the mirror image of the writer, are all heading toward the unavoidable catastrophe. I am aware that I have honed my own techniques by setting such a thorough catastrophe as the final goal of narrating a story of contemporary Japan and the Japanese people.

2.

Then why do I want to write about "old men's folly," my own story at that, in the novel I am working on as a "later work?" Why is it filled with old men's "fear of fear and frenzy?" Why does Said's contemplation that sounds like dying words prove to be a correct prediction of my work?

I believe that they are in response to the fact that I, in my old age, understand the direction taken by Japan and that I am fearful of it. A novelist, in his old age, is still a child of the society in which he lives.

I was born 25 years after imperialist Japan annexed Korea. It goes without saying that Japan's defeat in World War II, which I experienced when I was 10, was liberation for you, the Korean people. The memories of my encounters with Korean boys and youths occupy a prominent place in my first novel *Nip the Buds, Shoot the Kids,* which is based on the memory of a child growing up in a remote Japanese mountain village immediately before and after the defeat, and *The Silent Cry (Man'en gannen no futtoboru)*, the work with which I acquired self-awareness as a writer. Besides, the focus is on the tragic relations of tension in a mountainous village between Korean youths and Japanese children, my brothers and I. I cannot say that as a child I was aware of the crimes of Japan and the Japanese in pre-modern and modern history that lurked behind those tensions. When I read my early works, however, I discover that my young self, described there, divined the truth. I believe that a sense of guilt coming from this fact cast a long shadow over my young creative life.

Despite a difficult life after the defeat, I regard the three years between 1945 and 1948 as the most hopeful period of my life. On many occasions, I have defined myself as an "advocate of post-war democracy," triggering mockery and criticism from both the left and the right, but a sense of freedom brought by the new Constitution was indeed refreshing and invigorating.

It was during a 10-year period after Japan's defeat that I began to learn about the atrocities Japan and the Japanese people had committed in Asia during the militarist days – at the time I was certainly a militarist boy growing up on the ideological milk of the imperial emperor system as the absolute. For me, the post-war years were not simply the days when the light of Japan's Peace Constitution began to gleam. I believed that by my middle age, when I would work actively on the foundation of academic learning acquired in my youth, reconciliation would be achieved among Asian countries – although I was not too optimistic to think that it would be easy, I thought it would be possible – and the people of Asia would accept us as new Japanese.

I believed that unless it happened, all the Japanese blood shed in Asia and in numerous Japanese cities, including Hiroshima,

Nagasaki, Okinawa, and Tokyo, would end up meaningless. I felt that envisioning such a future would enable us to grasp Japan's pre-modern and modern periods as a whole and thus accomplish an active integration.

At this point, however, I admit that my life as a novelist was a process in which the most positive vision of the future was breaking down. It has already been 11 years since I delivered the speech "Japan, the Ambiguous, and Myself" in Stockholm, where I had a chance to talk to the world.

It was not simply Japan's political situation toward which I offered self-criticism for being ambiguous. I talked about the cultural ambiguity that Japan faces today. I also mentioned the vagueness of the Japanese language. My literary style, often criticized for being foreign and difficult to understand, has its roots in my wish at the time of my literary debut that I would like to make the Japanese language precise in my own way. As a Japanese who writes fiction and literary criticism in the Japanese language in contemporary Japan, I talked about complex ambiguity harbored by society and individuals.

The person who made an immediate reply to my argument was former Prime Minister Nakasone, who was in charge of the long-term regime in post-war Japanese political history as the head of the conservative right. He emphasized on television that "ambiguous Japan" had to be changed. It is Mr. Nakasone who is currently leading an active movement with regard to the constitutional revision. He intends to make Japan an unambiguous country by removing the renunciation of war and the idea of disarmament, specified in the preface and Article 9 of the Constitution. He nods to the unconstitutional expansion of the Japanese Self-Defense Force, which is vigorously being promoted, and intends to openly reorganize it as an offensive organization.

Needless to say, this right-leaning trend complements Prime Minister Koizumi's persistence on visiting the Yasukuni Shrine. If the Constitution were revised according to what Mr. Nakasone and the ruling party desire, Japan would be completely isolated from Asia because it would become what they call an "ordinary state" that can wage war. The reinforcement of the U.S.-Japan military alliance would be the only thing on which Japan could rely.

It goes without saying that the unambiguous Japan that I had in mind was a Japan on the opposite end of the spectrum. I asked that the current situation be changed to the unambiguous picture of Japan, yearned by the Japanese in 1945 at the time of pledging a fresh start in the aftermath of defeat.

Mr. Nakasone's voice already overwhelmed mine 11 years ago. This trend has expanded and strengthened since then. The time given to me for resistance is limited. Something that can be called helplessness, disappointment, and fear has determined the tenor of my "later work."

3.

In mid-2004, I launched a small political movement. It is an intellectuals' movement I created with the critic Shuichi Kato, the philosopher Shunsuke Tsurumi, and the playwright Hisashi Inoue. We started by holding lectures for a wide spectrum of citizens. The self-reliant intellectuals in other cities have established their own gatherings, and we have joined their rallies, which were organized on their own strength.We have delivered lectures in eight locations during a six-month period, summoning audiences over 20,000. The Tokyo media have ignored our activities, but I believe that before long they will become a foundation on which self-reliant citizens can carry out a larger movement.

The name of our movement is the "Gathering for Article 9." The purpose is to defend the Japanese Constitution, which was drafted on the occasion of the 1945 defeat to regenerate Japan as a state of democracy and peace – in particular that Article 9 declares the renunciation of war.

We have started this project at this particular time because a concrete program to revise the Constitution has blatantly come to the surface, specifically since last year. A motion by two-thirds of the Diet is required for a constitutional revision, but the ruling party and the Democratic Party, the main opposition party, have enough power to do so. Our movement has set course so that people who oppose the constitutional amendment can gather forces for the next stage, a referendum.

I believe that citizens who intend to defend the Constitution's peace article will win in this referendum. The citizens' enthusiastic responses to our small movement support my belief. Even if the constitutional revision is voted down in the referendum, the government, the ruling party, and business circles will never shift their direction. They will more aggressively promote the expansion of the combat power of the Japanese Self-Defense Force, the Japan-U.S. military alliance, and Japan's military show-off in Iraq. Even if the constitutional revision is rejected in a referendum, there will not be a change in the political direction taken by the government and ruling party, and the "ambiguous" Japanese people will not likely continue with the resistance expressed in the referendum. The Asian gaze, far from being ambiguous, will watch the isolation of Japan and the Japanese.

I heard a Japanese political scientist whom I most trusted – I have a happy memory of attending a Seoul symposium with this deceased friend of mine – confess that during his recent visit to Seoul, Korean researchers, who used to ask what Japan and the Japanese could accomplish, said they no longer expected anything from Japan.

4.

This ended up a gloomy speech. As one of the keynote speakers, I reproach myself for failing to fully grasp the nature of this important, big conference. In the aforementioned Stockholm lecture, I said that the desirable image of the Japanese people in the future would be that of "decent people." One of the rich meanings connoted in the English word "decent" is to discern the character of the place one finds oneself in.

I must return to "Writing for Peace," the theme chosen for this gathering. I believe that you can infer that while delivering this somber talk, my mind is constantly on the theme of "Writing for Peace."

I have described the novel I am working on as my "later work." Certainly written here are "old men's folly," fear, and what can almost be called despair. If I may quote another phrase in Said's "Thoughts on Late Style" – which reminds me of his staunchly combative, yet generous and kind character – he wrote as follows:

> . . . he envisages nothing beyond lateness: it is impossible to transcend or surmount it; it can only be deepened.

I cannot transcend fear and despair by writing about "old men's folly," and it is all the more impossible to surmount these emotions. I keep writing it in the belief that it is possible for it to deepen. Now staying at a Seoul hotel, I am thinking about revising and improving the first draft of Part III, which I must start as soon as I return home.

The current first draft has no indication that the protagonist, the old writer, can transcend or overcome fear and despair. My long experience as a novelist tells me that revision, improvement, and elaboration do not entail adding what does not exist in the first draft. For a novelist improving his first draft, deepening is the only way possible.

There is something else, however, that I know from the experience of being a novelist. It is the fact that when I go into the depths of the story through elaboration, I catch a glimpse of a faint glimmer of light from the abyss. I think this is the most mysterious secret to writing. This is why I am encouraged by Said's words.

If I happen to catch that faint glimmer of light in the last part of my "later work," which could also be my "last work," I think I might quote another phrase from T.S. Eliot's "East Coker" in *Four Quartets.*

Before I tell you what this quotation will be, as a long-time fiction writer I would like to briefly talk about something that is related with the theme "Writing for Peace." As I have already mentioned, I do not think that at present Japan is willing to play an active role for peace in Asia and the rest of the world. I do not doubt, however, that many Japanese hope for peace, that they wish to contribute to peace as individual citizens, and that for this goal they long for reconciliation with other Asian countries through sincere atonement. I reconfirm this belief through the meetings of the Gathering for Article 9.

I hope that among those Japanese people, new faces will emerge to deepen the meaning through "writing for peace." New faces, for example, include those who are good at the new form of writing on the Internet. I have a presage that they will act like drills making numerous tiny holes into the deadlocked systems established by various governmental powers. Even when the vision of "peace" is at a stalemate because of politicians and bureaucrats, the "writing for peace" method will be alive and move forward. I think it is a role of an old novelist to "write for peace" and encourage the emergence of the new faces who will deepen and elaborate on it, or at least not interfere with their efforts. We should not give up on this hope. Let me conclude my talk by quoting from the Eliot poem that I mentioned earlier.

Old men ought to be explorers
Here or there does not matter
We must be still and still moving
. . . .

Translated by **Yu Young-nan**

Politics and Human Values

Kim Uchang

1.

The slot I am occupying now was originally planned by the organizers of this Forum for a speaker they would like to invite: a person who had deep commitment to human or humanistic values, on the assumption that they often overlap with values that emerge in literary works—and had at the same time the experience of taking an active part in political action; ideally a writer who had a chance to act in the political arena trying to shape it in accordance with universal human values to which he or she had prior commitment. The plan was to hear a report on his or her experience; what difficulties or disappointments he or she had found, what unexpected chances he or she encountered, and what hopes he or she had come to affirm in the endeavors to make the world commensurate with the promises of human fulfillment, whether they are conceived in personal terms or in terms of collective harmony, thereby ensuring a better chance of peace in the world. We thought, we cannot simply lay down utopian plans for a more peaceful or better future for the world without taking into account what is possible in the reality of the world and within the given of human nature. We would not probably want, even if it were possible to do so, to do away with the reality of earth and humankind as given, in favor of a utopian re-engineering of the world fantasized in the manner of science fiction. And literature—supposing that we are all concerned with the fate of literature in this forum—constitutes, if I may attempt a simplistic characterization of it, a rite of consent to, in the last instance, if not a celebration, of the world as it is, as much as a critique and lamentation over its misery.

Failing to invite a political actor with prior literary experience, I had to fill in the vacancy and the hour with whatever thought I could offer on the ambiguous interface of politics and human values as they come to mind. What I intend to do is to try to reflect on the Korean experience of democracy and whatever is suggested in it of the relationship between politics and humanistic or humane values. Our democracy is relatively new and therefore it can perhaps more easily reveal problems entailed in achieving a pacified condition of existence, which would ultimately constitute the foundation of peace throughout the world. What I am going to say does not derive, needless to say, from a personal experience I have had in the world of Realpolitik but from my life as a student of literature and ideas, which is, however, a life lived in a society where literature has existed in close association with politics—and the close relationship, many would believe, contributed in no small degree to whatever democratic standards of politics that have come to be established in our country, now for more than a decade. In spite of these circumstances that have come to politicize our life thoroughly in the process of this democratization movement, I would be speaking mostly in abstract terms, though they would no doubt reflect the effects of this politicization of life on the country.

Life has existed politicized in Korea from the late nineteenth century as the country had to meet the challenges of Western and Japanese imperialism, but its latest phase, one of the most intensely political phases, is represented by the democratization movement which has continued to agitate people since the beginning of the military dictatorship established in 1961 until it was overthrown to be replaced by a democratic form of government in the late 1980s. I will concern myself in this presentation mainly with the era after the coming of democracy, for it seems to present more vividly than ever problems of symbiotic and antithetical relations existing between politics and human values.

Many Koreans must have expected that with the arrival of democracy the country would enter a stable course of history where there would be change, of course, but within a broad-minded frame of democratic institutions—through rational debate, negotiations and compromises, but not through violence or even by irreconcilable political conflict. Violent conflict has abated, but what reigns on the

Korean political scene after the coming of democracy is not exactly a sense of democratic communality but a deepened sense of divisiveness in the body politic that present day Korea is. It would be naive to expect that democracy would inaugurate overnight an era of brotherly cooperation and peace. There are too many causes in any human society for that, but one would expect that such a basis would be established only if as a vision for the future that would mitigate the present conflicts through its promise of eventual reconciliation. From our experience of democratic politics in the past decade or so, however, it appears that the political process, even a democratic one, contains an unavoidable contradiction that subverts this goal—unless this contradiction is made conscious and deconstructed or a careful equilibrium is achieved between the two poles of the contradiction, the end and the means of politics. For it appears that, even if the end is a communality where there would be reconciliation of enemies in fraternal solidarity, the means for achieving this would inevitably subvert this irenic aim. One can then speculate that this contradiction of course would flow over into the relation among the nations and become one of the causes that aggravate it. In other words, if humane values or, to put them in general terms without really defining them, humanistic values are our aim, they would come into conflict with the means for making them political reality. This is what I would like to think about in the following.

2.

It is not easy, in Korea's long struggle for democracy, to demarcate clearly its inception but it is possible to say that it began in the late 1980s when a series of popular demonstrations, with student activists as the principal actors, forced the military to accept their withdrawal from politics, and set the course of Korean history irreversibly in the direction of democracy. Since then we have had four elected presidents or, if we exclude the transitional ex-general elected by popular vote, three presidents, and there is no denying that the government we have now is indeed a democratic government. However, the fact remains that at present a kind of disenchantment marks the mood of the nation as a whole about the result of democratization, though it is also true that this must be taken within the general affirmative frame of mind people have about the basic institution of governance that has taken root. One latest and dramatic report as of this writing is the Gallup poll that found 74.8% of the polled evaluated the present government as unrepresentative of the will of the people, one of the lowest evaluations among sixty-one countries covered in the poll.[1)] I do not know how representative this view is, and there is certainly some exaggeration to the view, but unmistakable is the mood of disenchantment.

Disenchantment is a word I have taken from Professor Choi Jang-jip, who will also speak at this forum. It is translation of the Spanish, desencanto, which Professor Choi, while assessing the democratic achievement of the last two previous presidencies, in his turn, took over from political scientists who were sounding the temper of people in Latin American countries after the democratic transitions that occurred there almost contemporaneously with the Korean transition.[2)] There are, according to Professor Choi, solid reasons for this mood of disenchantment: policy failures in many areas; in income distribution, welfare measures, education and cultural reforms, and above all in the structural overhaul of the social basis of political power—with the inevitable relapse of democracy into the conservative pattern of politics characterized by deals and negotiations among professional politicos without meaningful popular participation. The last issue formed the focus of Professor Choi's analysis of "democracy after democratization," as he called it. The disenchantment has real causes, as observed, but I think it had better be noted that it has, as it were, a surplus meaning over causes in reality—first, as the expression itself suggests, a romantic meaning, for where hopes are raised too high, disappointments are bound to follow, but it also has a metaphysical meaning, which makes the romantic disillusionment a necessary component of any political endeavor, as it is a result of the ontological make-up of human existence straddling ambivalently between the immediate and

1) *Chosun Ilbo*, February 23, 2005.

2) Choi Jang-jip, *minjuhwa ihuui minjujuui* [Democracy after Democratization] (Seoul: Humanitas, 2002), p. 120.

its transcendence. It is eventually this meaning I would like to think about, for the problems related to it seem to form part of the deeper dynamics of politics in today's world.

The question of disenchantment, while meshing with real topics in the political arena seems to come more to the fore in the present government under President Roh. Professor Choi's diagnosis of the post-democratization malaise concerns the period preceding the present regime of President Roh. But there seem to be reasons justifying the diagnosis of disenchantment for the present government as well, not so much on account of its failures as on the measures it has taken to counter the perceived or potential disenchantment. If conservative relapse gradually brought to stasis the energy for democratic reform in society, what marked the presidency of President Roh was attempts to recharge this energy once again by turning whatever there was in the way of disenchantment into a political passion or a revolutionary élan. This invited much criticism. It was understood in many quarters as engaging in partisan politics, provoking strife everywhere by sharply dividing the politically concerned into progressives and conservatives or more generally, as it was often perceived, into friends and enemies, along the fissures found in generational divides and affinity of personal ties as well as by ideology, though not quite by class. Apart from the divisiveness it seemed to foster in society, some criticism was directed to its practical futility as energy seemed to be spent, instead of on reforms that could be felt in the life of people on the street, on ideological battles or battles of symbols, seen, for example, in campaigns through mass mobilization and legislation for curtailing the power of conservative media or for revising history, which would set right the record of the repression and injustice suffered under the military dictatorship, and instituting criminal investigations into collaboration with the Japanese colonial regime or even restoring honor to the peasant rebels in the Donghak Uprising of 1894.

Some of these political programs were certainly justified, for in the first place there had to be reconstitution of society if the democratic goals of the struggle were to become reality, and in the second place, given our scarred modern history, we needed certain rituals of restitution for wrongs suffered in the past. At the same time, we must say that the criticism is not entirely out of place—criticism that such symbolic warfare produced only divisive effects among the people without any real progress in democratic change. But apart from the pros and cons about the direction Korean politics has been taking under the present government, it says something about the present stage of political development in Korea and by extension the meaning of politics or the political in human life.

Apart from its relevance to the outstanding problems of society in transition, the divisive tactic, intentional or not, can be said as a whole a continuation of the democratic struggle of the previous era. For only a relentless struggle, demanding a large amount of personal sacrifice was a sure way of pushing the nation towards democracy. The struggle clearly called for the militants to draw up the battle-line, distinguish enemy from friend, and march relentlessly toward a life and death struggle. The paradigm forming the political activism was that of revolutionary struggle, if not of military operation. Much of it had Marxist inspiration. The legacy from the militant phase of the democratic struggle lingered on, and is still powerful as a spectral presence behind all political action plans. The habit of thought must be said to remain long even after the use of the thought has passed its moment. The moment can be said to have passed if the goals of the struggle were liberal democracy with political rights and liberties in place. The moment is passed for Marxists or Marxism-inspired political activists, not because the goals have been reached but because they have lost their drawing power with the comparative economic success of South Korea over North Korea, and because the goals simply evaporated from the horizon of conceivable alternative futures with the collapse of the Soviet Union and the socialist bloc as a whole. With the goals gone for different reasons, whatever remained for political activism, if it were to continue, came to look like struggling with symbolic ghosts of the past. But the ghosts were still powerful enough to mobilize people in mass rallies, demonstrations, and denunciatory Internet journalism, whose abundance seemed to mark political activism under the present government. A lot of politics today remains, on the whole, on the plane of symbolic war of words and gestures.

3.

These struggles with symbols from the past may appear exercises in futility along with the divisiveness they create, the betrayal of the original goal of democratic struggle, the vision of a society of fraternal harmony. However, the divisiveness pursued for its own sake seems to confirm the famous thesis of Carl Schmitt that clear distinction of friend and enemy is the determining, almost a priori, condition of the political. But why do we need the political? For Schmitt, there are various positive reasons for it, but most importantly, community is created only through the political. As Schmitt says, "[T]he distinction of friend and enemy denotes the utmost degree of intensity of a union or separation, of an association or dissociation."[3] Thus we must face the deduction that the divisive agency of the political, with its distinction of friend and enemy, is instrumental in the creation of the association of friends, a society of fraternal harmony.

The enemy in the Schmittian community does not, of course, denote enemy in a personal sense; the enemy is a public enemy, and basically an enemy outside, against which the solidarity of the insiders is defined. There is therefore no enemy within the well-defined boundary of a community; nor is there divisiveness in its fraternal solidarity. But to say this is to overlook the complexity of political dynamics involved in the generation of the political. The enemy exists outside the community, but the distinction works tautologically: the community is what remains after any one who is defined as enemy is excluded. From this arises the function that the distinction plays within the community, that is, for spotting internal enemy—the one whose loyalty remains undeclared. There is then the question of decision involved in the distinction of friend and enemy and the definition of community. Abstractly speaking, it is the will of the people as a whole or the hypostatized sovereignty of the state that decides, but it would be in reality the holder of power,

3) Carl Schmitt, *The Concept of the Political*, trans. by George Schwab (University of Chicago Press,1996), p. 26.

the sovereign, the dictator or the vanguard that imposes itself on society as the will of the community as a whole. Any one or group that withdraws from the communal consensus dictated by the sovereign will, whatever this may be in reality, is internal enemy or traitor. In liberal democracy, in contrast, conflict in interests and ideas is recognized and, ideally speaking, must be procedurally resolved. This would give rise to politics—to what Schmitt calls "banal forms of politics" with "all sorts of tactics, practices, competitions and intrigues,"[4] Then there ensues the dissolution of the political.

But even in the politics of the political, there could be internal division that cannot be resolved by the imperative of communal solidarity. It then leads to a civil war,[5] the party politics of internal antagonisms weakens the state as a community of a marked identity. Civil war is a necessity if the state is to be rescued from this weakness, though it too endangers the state's existence. Schmitt's formula of the political assumes the possibility of war, the possibility of the existential annihilation of the enemy. This war could occur for all organized political units, external or internal. "[E]verywhere in political history, in foreign as well as in domestic politics, the incapacity or the unwillingness to make this distinction [i.e. of friend and enemy] is a symptom of the political end."[6] But one can suppose a condition in which internal conflict can become endemic without finding a fast and decisive resolution in civil war. This would justify a prolonged war-like condition requiring the constant, vigilant task of the friend-enemy distinction.

The above seems to be a rough schematization we can apply in our attempt to give a theoretical summary to Korean politics at present. But if we think that Schmitt's idea of the political explains all of it, we would be of course confusing theory and reality. However, when we muse on some of its obscure contour, we cannot help feeling that Schmitt's concept of the political has indeed caught the distinguishing animus of politics, and more generally, the contradiction that seems to be inherent in the political, that is,

---

4) Ibid. p. 30.
5) Ibid. p. 32.
6) Ibid. p. 68.

between the ideal of fraternal communality and the divisive tactic required in political action. It must be squarely faced. Even so, there is of course the possibility that contradiction in it is nothing so irresolvable as it would appear in theoretical reduction. If the inclusive goal, not the exclusive means, is to determine our politics, it is important to watch for the fluctuating fate of this contradiction and remain sensitive to the concrete development of situations that could be considered part of the response to the real problems of society or merely a spectral prolongation of what has past its moment. This sensitivity may be of greatest significance when we consider the question of the relation of politics and humanism.

4.

As observed in the above, there were plenty of psychological resources for the politics of animosity to draw upon: grievances and resentments passed on from the past, calling for redress. Clamor for the identification of the enemy and demand for restitution were bound to rise, But it was also as if there were a theoretical inevitability in politics becoming that of animosity. The distinction between friend and enemy is already there even in the need to face the task to be performed: the task is something that must be confronted and subdued. Leo Strauss, while explicating Schmitt's concept of the political has pointed out that culture is the product of "a harsh and cunning fight against nature."[7] Objectivation, making of the other, involved in culture, must be said to enter a public political task as well; it is part of the work of conquest against the state of nature, and then it is carried over into representation of the task aimed at as well as of what obstructs it as personified enemy.

The work of democratic change requires the political to come into being—a space for common work. The enemy is an indispensable agent for the generation of the political, and this space. Perhaps what is sought after is not so much the enemy as the space of political action where individuals can bond together as a collective through the recognition of a common task, but an enemy is needed. The existence of the enemy becomes more marked when

7) Leo Strauss, "Notes on Carl Schmitt, *The Concept of the Political*," in Schmitt, p.89.

the task to be done is conceived as a destructive work of removing causes of injuries and injustice; moving the objects, constructs and apparatuses at hand into a more or less coherent whole through bricolage, rather than the painful and patient work of building cohesion. There is also an easy commerce between the identification of internal and external enemies: potential external enemies include Japan (as the past colonial overlord who has not quite repented or relinquished its imperialist ambition), China (as a future threat as shown in its attempt to appropriate part of ancient Korean history as its local history), or America (as an imperial power that has lorded over Korea by inflicting division, war and destruction on the nation). These external enemies of course have collaborators or traitors within.

We can explain from this perspective the conjunction of two powerful causes during and after the democracy movement: democracy and nationalism. Democracy was the main political objective pursued in the struggle against the military authoritarian regimes, but nationalism was a motto no less powerful than democracy in mobilizing the masses. The imperative of nationalism, more often than democracy, aroused the ire of the masses against social evils aggravated during rapid industrialization under the authoritarian regimes. The claim of human rights did not have quite as much appeal to the fraternal solidarity of the national community as invoking the defense of national sovereignty from the imperialistic predation of world capitalism. In this combination of democracy and nationalism, the latter was always advanced as having a more justifiable claim on our allegiance. Here once again we seem to see the Schmittian condition for the constitution of the political, that is, a political community faced with a common task.

The alliance of democracy and nationalism has ambiguous implications. It is a necessity as long as there is a political task to be carried out, but it rests on a contradiction that becomes marked sometimes more or sometimes less. The political space born out of the enabling agency of the call for national solidarity against the enemy has difficulty in becoming truly inclusive; it is a space, either divided within itself or closing itself to the outside as a potential enemy. It aspires to inclusiveness, to be sure, but this inclusiveness is delimited insofar as it has to define itself within an actively functioning whole. Democracy, or democracy in the liberal form, defines itself in terms of the rights of the individual which cannot be forcibly subsumed in a social collectivity, while nationalism would claim that these rights could be overridden by the exigencies of the nation as a whole. But, of course, nationalism would claim that its higher imperative really undergirds the interest of the individual, and even in democracy, the individual has his or her rights as long as he or she is recognized as an entity with a proper legal status within the body politic legally constituted. Yet in democracy, the individual is not subjected, at least in principle, to the absolute claims of the collectivity he or she belongs to. If there is to be a collectivity of individuals, it would vaguely extend to humanity as a whole. For the individual can in his or her basic humanity be made into a universality. Needless to say, democratic politics can be considered more open to universal human values while politics of nationalism can run counter to them.

5.

This is again to speak theory. In reality, there is no democracy that embraces all humanity in its promise of universalist empowerment. This is, as we have argued, inherent in the logic of political practice. This is what theory predicts. It conforms to the requirement of political reality that it is always within a community that democracy becomes reality. But there may be many empirical causes, not necessarily stemming from this logic that makes democratic universalism a false promise. Consideration of these causes is in order if we are not to succumb too easily to theory over empirical evidence. What is in question is perhaps the discrepancy between ideal and reality, not theoretical inevitability.

Even in a democratic polity, rights are not always extended to every member that constitutes it; it is taken for granted that convicted criminals have forsaken their rights and so they can be considerably abridged. Rights are valid only within the limits of the laws of the state. Theoretically speaking, the limits can be made more inclusive as the social causes of anti-social behavior are removed by improving the social condition as a whole. Social critics would claim that the rights are defined by the social system, and they would become genuine rights only under a just system; and therefore the system must be changed. This could be done by reforms as well as by revolutions. Marxism long had a formula for overcoming conflict between universal humanistic ideals and the politics of hostility, which it tried to carry to the point of terror and violence; in this formula the latter was a transitional phase in the revolutionary struggle aiming at the realization of the former. This formula of universalism with its temporary suspension during the period of revolutionary change was also extended beyond national communities. Now Marxism has become unavailable, either on account of defeat suffered in the real world of international politics or on account of the discrepancy, confirmed too often in its practical social experiments, between the claim and the reality. What is relevant here is the assumption that the political system can be made to embrace universalism by changing the social conditions. To put the Marxian formula in another way, its theory repudiated universal human values as hypocritical, for it considered them basically as bourgeois values, which the bourgeois class was unwilling to extend to the classes excluded from the benefit of these values—until a revolutionary change occurs. This suspicion of the hypocrisy was confirmed at the international level as colonial experience in the non-Western parts of the world gave the lie to the ideas of civilization, including liberal political values, carried by imperialists. The bitter experience of many subaltern societies, and of all the socially subordinated, was that universalism, considered as instantaneously applicable here and now, is the privilege of the powerful who can support it in the real world. It becomes empty and farcical when claimed by the powerless. We may say that it is the instinctive understanding of the dynamics of ideas and reality that makes it difficult for the subaltern and subordinate to embrace universalism easily. Values without frontiers are not for those who lack the power to cross the frontiers.

Besides these reasons of suspicion and real-political power relations, there are reasons more deeply embedded in the contradictions of traditional societies that make attainment of universalism complicated. Jean-Paul Sartre once remarked that asking Algerians to replace their feudal system with individualistic liberal values would be asking them to expose themselves to the inroad of colonialism all the more defenselessly—that is, even without the protection of feudalistic communality. While this is absolutely true, it draws people into a new dilemma, as that would be like meeting the infamy of today with the infamy of yesterday, that is, if we accept the idea of democracy with the plurality of individuals enjoying equal rights within a common legal framework as a kind of destiny for the political history of humankind. In this case, even if there could be a straight line of development from a limited communal life to universal democracy, complications of history make it difficult to follow this straight line for many societies.

Certainly "infamy" cannot be a proper word for explaining the present condition of Korean politics. However, if there is, in spite of the success of the democracy movement, still remaining repressiveness in Korea, even as a formal democracy, it is not simply because of the unfinished nature of the democratic project in Korea. There is, we must say, entailment from the past to the present in contemporary politics that makes it difficult for Korean politics to extricate itself from the rhetoric of nationalism and to be more receptive to inclusive democratic values. What is most responsible for this entailment from the past is Korea's experience of colonialism and the suspicion of besiegement by imperial forces still troubling the Korean mind. This experience and circumstance makes the more binding the Schmittian condition of the political, expressed in the Korean case, as the imperative of nationalism. Invocation of, or hints at, hostilely defined groups against national identity validates the imperative of national purity and unity. A great deal of the propaganda war relies on an appeal to moral authority, which is usually also the authority of a politically defined collectivity. Appropriation of the moral authority can ensure appropriation of the political authority of the collectivity. This connection is especially strong in a patriarchy that Korea has been for a long time, in which the voice of Father ultimately constitutes the source of all morality. There can of course be struggle against the Father, but it is often only the question of who can speak in his name. The patriarchal legacy from the past has been the easiest resource that could be drawn upon in various political struggles in the troubled modern history of Korea. It was also the case in the democratic struggles of past several decades. Though the idea that mobilized it was the idea of democracy, it is doubtful whether it could have gathered enough strength by itself without the added energy supplied by nationalism. Nationalism was in fact the main mover in the political change that occurred in the recent decades, with democracy riding with it as a fellow traveler. From this composition of political energy at work, it is natural that commitment to democratic ideals in the post-democratic period still remains ambiguous. If we see an old problem in Korean politics today, there is an inevitability which is over determined by various reasons and causes as well as by the demand of the political.

6.

So there is no easy passage from the political to universalist humanism. We must hasten, however, to say that there is no easy passage from humanism to the political, either. Even if our ideal is humanism, inclusively applicable to all humanity, it can be realized, as argued in the above, only through the constitution of the political, which would cement individuals for a common task of humanity; but this would entail division of humanity into friend and foe, whether within a local political community or within an ideal community of humanity as a whole, with the result that this intermediate stage of practical process would defeat the original project of universal communality.

There seems to be no way of escaping from Carl Schmitt's concept of the political with its thesis about the simultaneous foundation of inclusion and exclusion. Jacques Derrida's *Politics of Friendship*, an agonized long mediation on the Schmittian thesis that seems to reveal the original sin of politics, weighs the chance for democracy in today's globalizing world. Derrida's musing on the subject has all the marks of deconstructionist uncertainty and instability, but it is clear that he does not seem to have too much confidence in the possibility of a humanistic democracy without exclusion. However, he suggests that a remedy could be found in a self-critically or deconstructively reflexive democracy which goes beyond itself. For the closure democracy makes inevitable must be broken open continuously.

Much of Derrida's reflection in the book is devoted to the genealogical analysis of community, including democracy, for democracy too is founded, in his view, on the premises of narrow biological origins uncritically accepted—on the "link between [the] isonomic and igonomic, the natural bond between nomos and phusis ... the bond between the political and autochthonous consanguinity,"[8] or, to put it in another way, on the "autochthonous and homophilic rooting,"[9] that is, on the bond of soil and blood. From this originates the idea of country, nation, even state and citizen, all the hostile discriminations necessary for the intensification of the bond of solidarity.

The genealogical analysis Derrida engages in is necessary for the deconstruction of the political—in the interest of the "reconstruction of the political" on a different basis. This reconstruction looks almost like a process of "depoliticization," for deconstructive engagement with the political involves unceasing questioning as to "confidence, credit, credence, *doxa* or *eudoxia*, opinion or right opinion, the approbation given to filiation, at birth and at the origin, to generation, to the familiarity of the family, to the proximity of the neighbour—to what axioms too quickly inscribe under these words." How does one move from this deconstructive work to the reconstruction of the political? Derrida is not clear. He invokes "democracy to come." Democracy as we know it being only a temporary expedience and a passing phase. If the present form of democracy is of any use, it would be so in the form of a deconstructive democracy—democracy as "the *autos* of deconstructive self-delimitation." This delimitation seems to postulate a high idea of democracy, but emphasis is more on the processive nature of democracy's deconstructive maintenance work. For if democracy is to be delimited, it is to be "[d]elimitation not

8) Jacques Derrida, *Politics of Friendship* (London: Verso, 1997), p.99.

9) Ibid. p. 104. Though the entire book is reflection on the genealogy of democracy, Derrida's recommendation, herein discussed, for the procedure involved for the advent of what he calls "democracy to come" would be found in pp.104-106.

only in the name of a regulative idea and indefinite perfectibility, but every time in the singular urgency of a *'here and now.'* "[10)]

However, we must note, as a kind of footnote, the agonizing ambivalence with which Derrida gives his hesitant approval to democracy. What we have just said in the above is the argument we find in the first part of *Politics of Friendship*, but we cannot help but be unsettled once again, as Derrida shows in the last paragraphs ending the book, by the depth of the snarled entanglement of humans in the distinction, if not of friend and enemy, but of "us" and "them," found even in the friendliest declaration of Blanchot for the cause of solidarity with the Jewish people.

It was obviously the Nazi persecution ... which made us feel that the Jews were our brothers and that Judaism was more than a culture and even more than a religion, but, rather, the foundation of our relations with the other [autrui].[11)]

This affirmation of brotherhood and a personal definition of Judaism expressed by Blanchot is troubling for Derrida. When Blanchot says, "our brothers," Derrida asks, who are we that are saying this? And then he says that he could not have written this. What he is implying is that he could not do so, because he is a Jew not included in that "we." He is the other to this "we" even if the declaration is the inclusion of this other in "we." Blanchot's declaration that the French and the Jews are brothers already presupposes distinction between the French and the Jews. The supposition of community is not only operative in politics, but it is ineradicably rooted in our consciousness and in our linguistic habit. In spite of all these reservations and hesitations, Derrida is of course committed to democracy—to the ideal of universal democratic community, that is, democracy to come.

7.

10) Ibid. p. 105.

11) A letter to Salomon Malka, *L'Ardie*, no. 373, May 1988, (emphasis added by Derrida), quoted in Derrida, p. 304.

Self-delimiting democracy—with deconstruction interminable, but we need perhaps analysis interminable—in more than the deconstructive or psychoanalytic sense. For what is in order is questioning the meaning of the political, so indispensable and yet so problematic, from the ontological baseline of human existence. Is the political a condition of work of survival? Is the political truly a necessary condition of human fulfillment? Even if the answer to both these questions is affirmative, is the complete politicization of life a desirable state of affairs? Should not the political be placed better in the complex web of relations constituting the totality of human existence surpassing the political? Perhaps, what is to be pursued is, not the congruence of the political and human values, but their separation or complexly interacting and yet separate co-existence. (Schmitt argues that it is the recognition of the political as an autonomous domain of human activity that would prevent the engulfment of all domains of human activities in politics, which would be the characteristic of "the total state," to which democracy tends.[12)] However, we must say that it is Schmitt's absolutized ideal state that would bring about the total politicization of life.)

When the political is posited, the assumption is its primacy over any other mode of human existence, including that of the individual, though this latter is an absolute empirical given, and forms really the basis of any conception of human values. For when we speak of human dignity, human rights, or human values, we are referring to the individual as their carrier and possessor, including their right to belong to a collectivity born into or chosen. It will at least be fair, in a different tack, to try considering the question of the relationship between the political and human values, not only from the prioritized end of the political, but also from the other end as well. This would be in a way going into the question with more primordial ontological evidence. The question to be asked is: whether the eudainomic fulfillment of humans necessitates political organization of life, whether it calls on the contrary for unfettered freedom, without politics, for the unfolding of individual life, or, supposing this is possible, whether it can be connected to the recognition and promotion of the same eudaimonic fulfillment for

12) Schmitt, pp. 22-23.

all humanity.

A general assumption we have regarding the necessity of political organization of society is that its absence would, as feared by Schmitt or Hobbes, lead to a general chaos of malice, hatred and violence, and the condition of war between man and every other man. However, at the same time, we must note that the emancipatory impulse in the political development of the West in the modern era and also in other parts of the world testifies to the distrust, articulated or unarticulated, of government on account of the threat it poses to freedom. Liberal democracy suggests a compromise between the two possibilities; a form of government that will ensure freedom, largely by substituting a civil organization of collective life for its control by the state. The supposition is that only in this kind of political organization, that is, a democracy, the life of the individual could be led in freedom—freedom, we must say, enjoyed in ordinary life, that is; not necessarily legitimated by divine order or display of virtues of warrior aristocracy (from, which is derived much of the substantive traits of the political).[13)] (The irony is that citizens inspired by revolutionary heroism can establish the polity validating ordinary life, and it would not be easy then for citizen revolutionaries to leave behind the memory of heroism even after the revolutionary struggle is over. This is partly what we see in Korean democracy after the democratization movement.)

However, there cannot be freedom, as observed, without a framing enclosure that supports it. The form of this enclosure delimits human freedom—too often skewed in the interest of the existing form of civil society. It has often been pointed out that the promise of freedom by liberalism, coupled with its twin offspring, capitalism, ends up only as the promise of consumer freedom, with market mechanisms and corporations substituting for the constraint of the political, now seemingly deconstructed. Liberalism or capitalism is only a form of the a-political political, though it often appears to fill the room left by the evacuation of the political and presents itself as the carrier of humanistic values for all the

13) See Charles Taylor, "The Culture of Modernity," in *Sources of the Self: The Making of the Modern Identity* (Cambridge, Mass.; Harvard University Press, 1989).

individuals, now apparently depoliticized—and then adjusted to the system, and in fact supported by a different form of the political which distinguishes friend and enemy in its own way. (This distinction is seen by Marx as that between mutually hostile classes.) Even so, liberalism can be seen on the whole as a way of affirming the worth of individual life, but we must say that it lacks a mechanism by which defense of individual life can be transcended into a universal humanism. It needs a more active moment, the intervention of the political.

8.

What is required is reconsideration of the question of the political that allows us to see it not simply as an onerous burden on human life, as it would appear from a liberal point of view. There is even in individual life a force that impels it beyond the closed circle of individual life. The political responds to this force, a transcendental impulse in humans that would not be laid to sleep even in the pursuit of happiness, if it is to be complete.

For Greeks, for ancient Chinese and also for Koreans under the sway of Confucian social ethic, one of the highest forms of life was public life. Hannah Arendt, following the Greek conception of life which found polis the pivot of meaningful life, thought participation in public life was not merely duty or an occasion for material gain, but a particular kind of activity rewarded with "public happiness": a specially gratifying form of happiness accruing to public action performed in concert with others, unavailable anywhere else. It also elicits and satisfies the "passion for excellence"[14] in humans that lifts individual life to a higher plane. Arendt has certainly marked off by her idea of public happiness an important area of human fulfillment, which can be lost particularly easily in the modern age, owing, in her mind, to the intrusion of social and economic questions into the sphere of politics. Of course, we can say that Arendt's conception of public happiness is too close to the extolment of the political as the arena for realizing warrior virtues,

14) Hannah Arendt, *On Revolution* (New York, The Viking Press, The Viking Compass Edition) 1965 p.115.

often involving a deadly competition. In any case, public happiness is for many too strenuous a form of happiness; its timocratic struggle may destroy the true happiness of the community.

The cost of a politically organized life may make us weigh it once again against the possibility of a fulfilling life lived on an individual basis. The question this time would be whether it is possible to make a retreat from a life of public action and find at the same time a fulfillment transcending the restriction of private life. Arendt's laudation of active public life, vita activa, is an effort of restitution for the higher valuation traditionally put on contemplative life, vita contemplativa as the path of truth, a path lifting individual life to a beyond;[15] In the Confucian conception of life, though public life was considered the most fulfilling kind of life one could lead, yet the pressure and misery of public life was always noted, and the emblematic figure of the solitary hermit in the mountains offered an alternative path of life, equally elevating. In any case, it seems to be entirely anachronistic to conceive of politics as the preserve of noble action. In modern societies, the passion of excellence is often nothing but a sheer drive for power and wealth. Apart from the degraded condition of modern politics, a thoroughgoing politicization of life could be inimical to the recognition of the plenum of human possibilities. That is what we have seen in totalitarian societies. Solidarity is an eminently important social virtue, but solidarity without solitude would be intolerable.

But just as ataraxia is in Stoicism a product of "antithetical energy, antithetike dunamis." Solitary life in nature too represents a strenuous form of life, not simply because the ascesis involved often means rejection of the quotidian life as defined in the dominant value system of the world. More often than not, it is not only the result of struggle against the madding sphere of politics, its lures and snares. It comes into being as the other of the political, agonistically positioned against it. It too is a function of the political obtaining in the age. The struggle is, however, not only with the political but with nature which must be taken possession of as truth. This is usually the case, at least, in the choice of Confucian

15) Hannah Arendt, *The Human Condition* (New York: Doubleday Anchor, 1959), pp. 15-18.

bureaucrat-literati for nature. A Confucian scholar can give up his political career and give himself to a life in nature, in the fields, and in the mountains, but the quest for a holistic vision of nature seldom stops. It is no accident that the title of a study of the lives of scholars of Confucian and other persuasions in China by Pei-yi Wu is *The Confucian's Progress* reminding us of Bunyan's *Pilgrim's Progress*. Theirs was also a pilgrimage into the truth of nature. Life never became complete until there was, to cite a typical passage from the records of the experience of nature, a sense that "Heaven and earth became clear and peaceful, where a vast harmony reigned."[16) The struggle and contest involved here would not have the same aggravating effect as contest in the political arena. The sense of harmony earned in nature had a kind of fullness in it, unlike the perpetual absence created by the interminable process of vigilance or deconstruction involved in political life. There are in nature intimations of a transcendental totality, which could challenge the mind with its unknowable otherness, and seduce it with the possibility of access, but the peculiarity of nature is that it is always fully present to the senses and becomes a source of profound contentment.

There are other totalities that challenge the human mind. The challenge is not simply philosophical or metaphysical. The claim of these totalities, as they are appropriated, can lead to serious social and political consequences, incompatible with democratic values, as we see in theocratic regimes of fundamentalist faiths, This may make us think that all totalities perhaps need to be subjected to an unrelenting process of deconstruction, just like the totality constituted by the political. (Nature would be an exception in this respect, to which we will return later.) But what cannot be simply overlooked is, as we have observed in the above, the impulse towards transcendence. There is an inevitability to it. The individual is constituted as a subject through the interpellation of a larger Subject, an abstracted insurer of the category of the subject.[17) This

16) Pei-Yi Wu, *The Confucian's Progress* (Pricneton University Press, 1989), p. 129. The passage is from the sixteenth century Chinese Confucian, Wan, T'ing-yen, but his is only one typical passage found in many cases Wu discusses.

17) Louis Althusser, *Lenin and Philosophy and Other Essays* (New York: Monthly Review Press, 1971), pp. 171-177.

is what Louis Althusser said concerning the function of political ideology that creates a false sense of empowerment for the individual as a subject, but the interpellation may arise from the ontological makeup of human existence. Human biology is such that humans cannot survive without metabolic exchange with the environment. From this follows their psychic tropism towards the external world, and ultimately the need to establish a relationship with a larger whole which functions as the ground of universal truth and moral imperative, though in another connection the necessity of biological sustenance would underlie them.

If this calling from afar is to be acknowledged and at the same time to be warned against, the contradiction involved can be resolved or confronted only by the operation suggested by Derrida in regard to the closure of democratic community, that it must become a self-delimiting, self-deconstructive democracy. More relevant to our problem on hand, the problem of the call of transcendence as existential necessity, would be his complex pronouncement about negative theology, a discourse on divinity, which tries to communicate the essence of divine being by saying that it lies beyond all predicative determination; its method is to speak and not to speak. Deconstruction may be said in general to stand close to negative theology that tries to approximate ultimate truth through negation, through via negative, but for Derrida, the paradoxical approach of negative theology is not radical enough. For it cannot, in the final analysis, help but posit "the indestructive unity of the world" and "authority of the name" and reaches out to "some hyperessentiality, a being beyond Being."[18] Nevertheless, his criticism is extremely ambiguous: while he seems to repudiate various techniques of apophasic negation, he is not quite resigned to the possibility of negative affirmation, if only in some non-predicative speaking, such as prayer, which is "a pure address, on the edge of silence, alien to every code and to every rite, hence to every repetition,"[19] but which nevertheless gives rise to "writing, the code, repetition, analogy or

18) Jacques Derrida, "How to Avoid Speaking: Denials" in Harold Coward and Toby Foshay (ed.), *Derrida and Negative Theology* (Albany, N. Y.: State University of New York Press, 1992), p.77.
19) Ibid. p.130.
20) Ibid. p.131.

the—at least apparent—multiplicity of addresses, initiation."[20] This latter turn of course marks once again a beginning of hypostasis or reification of the processive event at the edge of being and non-being, and word and silence to be deconstructed.

9.

This is what happens in all cases of totality which responds to the need of humans and at the same time threatens to return as a repressive order. Deconstruction is the final step to take. But as we suggested in the above, our relation with nature as the totality of what there is can be an exception to this reversal, while the possibility is always there that nature as totality can be made into a hyperessentiality, carrying with it political and ethical imperatives beyond what is warranted by life's necessity. Nature is a limit of what there is in totality. As the limit, it is also a challenge to the human impulse of transcendence, but it could also serve as a point of support for a self-reflexive look at the totality of what there is in relation to the sensory manifold of our experience. It is in this respect an infinity beyond all predication and at the same time appears ever-anew to the senses of the human participant as the font of inexhaustible and yet perceivable creativity. Nature as a limit has this advantage, since it is present to us as experience and the environing element of life. It is a totality beyond us but also an ecological totality accessible to life.

This ecological totality I once tried to explain through the idea of landscape; I thought I could abstract from the landscape painting in East Asia. To my mind, landscape painting had a special meaning in the spiritual economy of life in the East Asian traditions as it was given the role of representing the ultimate ground of human existence, mainly understood as the totality of earthly environment. The aesthetic involved can be said that of the sublime, since landscape as a totality is, to borrow the Kantian formula of the sublime, an object distinguished by its boundlessness only present to thought. This boundlessness or magnitude can be quantitative or qualitative. The totality, both quantitative and qualitative in itself is unrepresentable, and it therefore leads to a "supersensible substrate"[21] (ein uebersinnliches Substrat). However, if landscape is seen as a totality in the Asian artistic tradition, it must be said to remain on the quantitative plane, which is experientially accessible to an extent since it is not qualitative, even when it goes over into the supersensible. The idea is perhaps best represented by the title of painting frequently used by artists in China and also in Korea: "Streams and Mountains without End." One of the distinguished participants in our forum, Mr. Gary Snyder, American and yet most Asian of all poets today, has a collection of poetry entitled, *Mountains and Rivers Without End.* Without attempting to expound the meaning of the title of his collection of poetry or, for that matter, the way it might have been understood in Asia, I would like to refer simply to the format of some paintings of this genre: the form of scroll which can be unfolded slowly but continuously as it could go on without end. Mr. Snyder advises us about the proper method of viewing this kind of painting: "Unroll the scroll to the left, a section at a time, as you let the right side roll back in. Place by place unfurls."[22] The format itself suggests how the totality of the earthly environment is conceived—a totality that transcends the limit of human existence, individual, collective or generational, and yet remains accessible to it as sensible reality. The limit helps to see nature in a more enhanced way, for it constitutes, as observed in the above, a point from which human imagination looks back on nature as a totality, as what extends endlessly beyond our sensible experience of it. However, the imagined totality must inform perception, which thus informed would see the sensible more clearly as it becomes a figure against the background of the totality. The totality is of course a supersensible substrate. Perception, turning into philosophy, becomes more vivid. In fact, everything reaching out to a supersensible hyperessentiality aims in a way at intensification—intensification of what is present; only if it overreaches.

10.

What relevance does this contradictory modality of immediacy

21) Immanuel Kant, trans. by J. H. Bernard, *Critique of Judgment* (New York: Hafner Press, 1951), p. 94.

22) Gary Snyder, *Mountains and Rivers Without End* (Washington, D. C.: Counterpoint, 1996), p. 9.

and transcendence bear on the theme of our reflection, the preservation and propagation of human values in general? I would say the above goes to show that human life is open to what lies beyond it, even if one's concern is only to care for oneself or for one's happiness. A fulfilled life calls for relationship to a larger whole surrounding one's life, though it can also lead to a closure on another side as witnessed in many dogmatic forms of commitment as the larger while, the transcendental entity is invoked as the unity of the word, the authority of the name or hyperessentiality. Thus the arduous task of deconstruction becomes necessary to reopen the closure of totality, to return it to what ultimately remains inconceivable and unspeakable. The perpetuity of negation may give a harrowing bleakness to human life. But the ecological totality of earthly life could be something humans can respond to with less danger of becoming dogmatically closed and with a less amount of toils in the bleakness of negativity.

Would the deconstructive move, or the contradictory presence of the transcendental in the immediacy of the senses, as is the case of nature, lead to a general openness to humanity and human values? We note in this connection that if nature is to be seen as a totality, there must intervene a moment of philosophical reflexivity, which transforms the sensible into a supersensible totality. This totality includes of course the individual as the subject of perception and reflection, but it also reveals it as an insignificant finite being pitted against the infinity of nature. The universality of philosophical moment can pave the way for one's recognition of other human beings as standing in the same relation to nature as he or she does. But it is also true that nature is a haven for misanthropes. To be at one with nature is not quite the same thing as to have sympathy for the misery or happiness of fellow mortals. Empathy with nature must be expanded to sympathy with humans and compassion with sentient beings in general. The expansion would require a complex process of sentimental education.

However, the sense of human fraternity, sympathetic generosity and philosophical universalism—these affective arousals do not turn naturally into an effective force of practical action. An impetus from another source is needed, that is, from the political with its contractions. The political calls, as we have observed, for a community of friends as against a common enemy. The archaeology of community reveals that it is based on the autochthonous and homophilic roots of life. It severely delimits its use in affirming the universalism of human values. But it will be unrealistic to deny that blood and soil constitute a primordial anchoring of life on earthly reality—not literally perhaps in this age of universal mobility, but human life is lived here and now, tied to the local condition wherever it happened to be. As long as this is the case, the political cannot be avoided. It must be affirmed but it must be also given over to a care of critical examination or to deconstruction interminable.

But what calls for this deconstruction? What lies under the work of deconstruction? What is the subject of the process, "the *autos*" of self-delimiting democracy? Isn't there something that supervenes in the constitution of the political and senses it as an insufficient form of transcendence? As we have observed, the political is a form of the transcendental upsurge of humans, and yet it somewhat stands apart from other processes of transcendence, more inward-looking and more eudaimonically directed. If the political is not driven by the sense of friend and enemy, it could be driven by justice and anger—both allied to strong thymotic powers, unlike gentler affects arising from the calmer interior of human psyche – and most importantly, from the eudaimonic yearning of humans for fulfillment, at peace with the world and in a fraternal conviviality with all humanity. These gentler and yet more persistent forces of transcendence in human existence constitute the subject behind the deconstructive work on repressive totalities.

I have spoken of the disenchantment in contemporary Korean politics after the democratization. It is a counterpart to enchantment, the enchantment of leaping from one's circumscribed self to a larger whole outside oneself. In modern days, search for enchantment, for élan, is mainly directed to politics, but it is only part of a general movement of the human spirit to self-transcendence and transcendence.

Literature is part of this movement, but it is a somersault always returning to earth, a movement performed while in firm touch with the concrete reality of life here and now. It incites the political and at the same time it objects to the subjection of the individual to the imperative of the community. From this contradiction, it reaches out to universal humanism: it stays in touch to the basal given of life, the individual: it moves to the political, but as the individual and the political come together in a contradictory conjunction, it cannot help but reach out to universal humanism.

Session II

Literature and Human Universality

J.M.G. Le Clézio | Littérature et universel

Yu Jong-ho | From the Scene of Reading: Literature and Universal Human Values

Luis Sepúlveda | Literatura y Universalidad Humana

Hwang Seok-young | Changing Together While Resisting

Littérature et universel

J.M.G. Le Clézio

No people, however harassed by economic need, is without some form of literary art. All people tell tales, presumably for the pleasure of telling them; all people sing and dance; and all people have more or less elaborate patterns of behaviour for public performance. All these activities, besides serving their purpose in the economic and social life of the group, give pleasure by their intrinsic qualities. Wherever these inherent values have been enhanced by formal elaborization we may speak of art.

(Ruth Bunzel, in Franz Boas' *General Anthropology* 1938)

La culture en général, et la littérature en particulier, ne peuvent se concevoir sans le langage ; ils sont, par nature, l'expression d'un particularisme, c'est-à-dire d'un groupe humain, d'une société, d'une culture, avec tout ce que cela signifie de vernaculaire, d'indigène.

Si l'on considère les grands chefs-d'œuvre de l'humanité (ceux qu'elle s'est donnés comme symboles, comme modèles, comme jalons de sa mémoire), il faut y reconnaître la marque du local, du défini. Il en va sans doute ainsi de tout ce qui fait l'humain. En vérité toute histoire est d'abord une micro-histoire. La guerre du Péloponnèse concerne un territoire à peine grand comme un département, et met face à face un millier d'hommes. La prise de Troie par les Grecs est un événement minuscule qui n'excède certainement pas la conquête de la ville de Cuiringaro par l'armée du roi mexicain Tariacuri, au XVème siècle.

On parle de l'un, et l'autre reste aux oubliettes. L'Occident est convaincu de l'importance de la conquête d'Alexandre qui trouva sa fin dans le fleuve Indus. Cinq cents ans plus tard, Attila conduit les hordes des Huns depuis la Chine jusqu'à la Gaule romaine, et son épopée ne laisse dans la mémoire que le mauvais souvenir d'une invasion barbare. Quant au voyage d'Ulysse à travers la mer Méditerranée, malgré l'enjolivure du mythe et la magie de Circé, il n'est qu'un pique-nique si on le compare à l'émigration du peuple maori qui, quelques siècles avant le début de l'ère chrétienne, se lança à l'aventure, remonta les courants et lutta contre les vents et parcourut depuis la Mélanésie jusqu'à l'île de Pâques, sur des radeaux et des canots propulsés à la rame, un océan vaste comme les deux tiers du monde.

Ce qui a donné une manière d'immortalité à l'aventure d'Ulysse ou à celle d'Énée, ce qui a inscrit dans la mémoire universelle la défaite d'un petit royaume d'Asie mineure concurrent de Mycènes, ce ne sont pas les faits, mais la façon dont ils nous sont parvenus, grâce à la poésie d'Homère et de Virgile. Si Attila le Hun avait eu dans sa horde (ce qu'il avait sans doute, mais faute d'écriture nous n'en savons rien) un poète, un aède, un chroniqueur de la valeur d'Homère ou même de Thucydide, sans doute l'Occident n'aurait pas la même idée de son expédition guerrière, et aurait gardé en mémoire son idéal, sa curiosité scientifique, son goût pour la législation et sa vertu morale. Et si l'histoire, par le truchement de la Société Biblique anglaise, n'avait pas décidé d'abolir le prodigieux passé mythique des Maoris de Tahiti, de Hawaii ou de Nouvelle-Zélande, ne laissant que les bribes récoltées et filtrées par le pasteur Henry et sa fille Teuira, peut-être qu'aujourd'hui l'on réciterait dans les écoles du monde les passages des généalogies des rois de Raiatea et les événements merveilleux de la plus grande migration maritime de tous les temps.

J'ai parlé de mythe et non de littérature. Est-ce exagération? La littérature, comme l'histoire, est avant tout liée à un territoire, à un terroir (cela peut être un pays rural comme chez William Faulkner ou Jean Giono, ou bien un pays minéral, urbain, dénué de toute nature comme chez Baudelaire ou chez Juan Rulfo, ou encore un pays intérieur comme chez Proust ou Joyce). La littérature, la langue, cherche sa racine dans ce passé mythique. Ce n'est pas tant le sujet – ainsi Joyce peut appeler Ulysse un Dublinois aussi loin de la Grèce que peut l'être un Coréen – que la filiation qui donne une légitimité, où l'histoire, la fable, et la somme des écrits ont leur part. Si l'on prend l'exemple de Joyce, on constate qu'il n'écrit pas seulement en utilisant le matériau contemporain, mais qu'il puise indifféremment dans le fonds chrétien, dans le roman de Walter Scott ou dans le poème d'Ossian, dans la publicité des journaux, et même dans les refrains de la chanson populaire, comme c'est le cas pour Finnegan's Wake, un roman qui reprend le légende d'un ivrogne ressuscité par une goutte de whisky tombée sur son cercueil.

L'universalité – c'est ici que je voulais en venir au moyen de ce long préambule – n'est donc pas une qualité en soi, mais le produit d'un heureux hasard. Si l'Irlande, au lieu d'être le théâtre d'une histoire tragique, pays colonisé et affamé par les troupes d'Olivier Cromwell, sorte de caldera où la religion catholique, la pensée gaélique et la révolte politique avaient composé un brouet de sorcière, – si l'Irlande était entrée dans le siècle moderne avec le rationalisme prudent de la Suisse – quel écrivain aurait vaticiné sur la marche funèbre de Finnegan ?

Prenons un exemple à rebours.

Au centre du Mexique, dans l'actuel état du Michoacan, a fleuri entre le douzième et le seizième siècle une civilisation exceptionnelle, celle des Indiens Purépecha.

Exceptionnelle, cette civilisation l'était réellement. Sur un territoire grand comme les Pays-Bas, elle avait créé un système de monarchie tempérée par un Conseil élu, dans lequel les corporations ouvrières étaient librement représentées par des syndicats. Cette société avait élaboré un culte au dieu du feu, et luttait contre la corruption par un système de lois. Elle respectait au-dessus de tout la création littéraire, et avait institué une fête de la justice, quand le grand prêtre orateur, durant tout un jour récitait devant le roi et le peuple tout entier l'histoire de ce pays et de sa fondation légendaire.

En 1530, l'arrivée des conquérants espagnols, sous la conduite du psychopathe Nuno de Guzman, a mis fin brutalement à ce règne. Le dernier roi des Purépecha, le Cazonci Tangaxoan Tzintzicha fut torturé, puis condamné à l'issue d'un de ces procès iniques dont les Conquérants avaient le secret, à être brûlé vif et à ce que ses cendres soient dispersées dans le fleuve Lerma. En même temps, tout le pays fut ravagé et pillé, réduit à l'esclavage, décimé par les massacres et les maladies. L'on ne saurait rien aujourd'hui de cette civilisation s'il n'y avait eu un livre, compilé par un moine franciscain du nom de Jeronimo de Alcala, auprès des derniers historiens et poètes de ce peuple, un livre qui constituait à la fois leur testament et leur mémoire, connu sous le titre de Relation de Michoacan. Comme l'Odyssée, comme les sagas des rois de Norvège, ou comme le Samguk Yusa, le livre des anciens Purépecha fourmille de renseignements sur la pensée, le mythe et la façon de vivre des anciens. Mais il touche à l'universel parce qu'il nous touche, nous qui n'avons rien connu de ce peuple. Lorsque nous lisons, par exemple, le récit de l'errance des deux enfants orphelins, Hiripan et Tangaxoan, neveux du roi, réduits à mendier leur nourriture dans les marchés, et que nous suivons les épreuves qui doivent les conduire un jour à hériter du pouvoir, cela nous émeut parce que nous devinons qu'il s'agit d'une histoire aussi vraie et réelle qu'un roman de Dickens, et que ces enfants vivent toujours dans le monde moderne, quelque part à Mexico, à Manille, ou à Marseille.

De même, lorsque nous lisons dans ce livre le récit de la vengeance de roi Tariacuri, qui envoie sa fille pour qu'elle séduise et assassine son rival Cando, nous touchons à l'horreur du crime de Judith dans la Bible, mais aussi à la noirceur réaliste d'un récit policier dans les romans de Flannery O'Connor.

La littérature nous concerne par ce qu'elle a de particulier, le détail, le matériau de la micro-histoire, le quotidien. Et de ce détail, de ce matériau, elle fabrique une substance impalpable et merveilleuse comme un mirage, qui est l'universel.

J'ai parlé tout à l'heure de hasard, parce que la gloire et la lumière de l'universalité ne sont pas données équitablement, selon qu'on écrit dans une langue dominante, en français, en anglais ou en chinois, ou dans une langue dominée, comme le sont les langues des minorités, aïnous, indiens d'Amérique, créole des Antilles ou des Mascareignes, langues d'Afrique.

Cela est tellement évident qu'on hésite à le dire. La poétesse innue du Canada Rita Mestokosho pleure d'avoir à traduire en français ce qu'elle dit à son peuple. Le Créole mauricien Dev Virashawmy, le Créole antillais Raphaël Confiant ne peuvent utiliser leur langue maternelle sans que cela soit ressenti comme un combat.

Pourtant, pour eux, comme pour les romanciers et les poètes des civilisations dominantes, la question de l'universalité ne doit pas se poser. Car elle va de soi, elle est inhérente à toute expression artistique.

Quiconque écrit ou compose, le fait dans la certitude que sa parole sera entendue de tous, et non pas du cercle restreint auquel il s'adresse. Est donc universel qui veut l'être. L'universalité est ce que l'on décide. Si cela n'était pas, comment pourrait-on lire aujourd'hui la chronique de Marcel Proust en ignorant tout de la société petit-bourgeoise des environs de Paris à la Belle Époque? Comment pourrait-on être ému des aventures de Nicolas Nickelby sans connaître le Londres misérable du début de l'ère industrielle, comment pourrait-on s'intéresser au comté de Yoknapathawpa, Mississippi – comté du reste complètement imaginaire – où William Faulkner installe le théâtre de son œuvre, comment partager l'angoisse de Camus sans avoir grandi dans un coin de l'Algérie coloniale, comment pourrait-on lire Marcel Cabon loin de Maurice, Juan Rulfo loin de l'état de Colima, Mexique central ?

Si je tressaille à entendre la sonnette qui résonne chaque fois que Swann pousse le portail du jardin de madame Verdurin, c'est que ce son met en marche dans mon esprit le mécanisme de la mémoire, et que je puis entrer, moi aussi, dans un monde qui ne m'est pas connu. Ce n'est donc pas son altérité qui m'importe, mais la logique qu'il révèle, qui m'aide à mieux comprendre le jeu des sensations et des relations. L'impression de vérité est telle que je puis oublier à quel point l'univers de Swann et des Verdurin m'est étranger. Il m'enseigne à mieux être un homme.

Ce qui nous touche, dans la littérature, c'est donc cette part de quotidien qui nous rend proche des situations et des personnages les plus divers. Nous en retirons l'intuition de l'humain, nous y agrandissons notre connaissance des autres. Non que tout soit semblable, et qu'un homme ou une femme soient les mêmes sous tous les cieux. Non que l'humaine condition soit faite partout des mêmes expériences et des mêmes passions. Mais plutôt, nous y apprenons, grâce à l'art, grâce à la magie de la parole, que nous pouvons être l'autre, que nous devons être un autre.

On touche au mystère. Qu'est-ce qui fait qu'un lecteur oriental, un jeune étudiant coréen, peut être aujourd'hui intéressé et ému par la Princesse de Clèves de Madame de Lafayette, un roman du renoncement janséniste au bonheur et à la tentation qui troublent l'ordre moral du monde ? Dans les romans de Yi Chong Jun, par exemple le Prophète, qu'est-ce qui peut mobiliser l'attention d'un lecteur français, malgré les différences entre les cultures et la méconnaissance des réalités politiques ?

Qu'est-ce qui nous rapproche? Qu'est-ce qui nous divise?

Est-ce l'intuition de l'humain qui nous conduit à reconnaître l'autre jusque dans la différence ? Est-ce un malentendu, et dans ce cas l'universalité de la littérature serait seulement affaire de traducteur ?

La littérature, expression d'un lieu et d'une époque, a vocation à sortir de ces limites. Elle est aussi transgression, passage. Parfois échappée sur un autre temps, sur un autre monde. La littérature puise souvent dans le mythe comme cela a été dit. Mais parfois le mouvement s'inverse, et c'est le mythe qui naît de la littérature, quand la légende s'empare de personnages tels que Don Quixote ou d'Othello, donne une sorte d'intemporalité à William Blake ou à Arthur Rimbaud. D'une certaine façon, la littérature est le contraire de la logique, la négation de la causalité. Sa matière faite du lieu commun des rêves. Comme dans Alice au pays des merveilles, un mot peut s'ouvrir sur un autre.

Pour cette raison, les livres sont ce qui nous procure le raccourci le plus saisissant vers la réalité. Nous y trouvons souvent ce qui va droit au cœur sans besoin d'explication ou de connaissance.

La mort de Tangaxoan, dernier roi des Purépecha, racontée dans la Relation de Michoacan composée en 1540 nous touche parce qu'elle est encore notre actualité, malgré la fracture du temps. La mort du jeune roi, héros malgré lui d'une tragédie moderne, nous touche parce qu'elle est aussi notre mort, qu'elle dit notre fragilité, la vanité de toute prétention à l'immortalité.

Elle nous émeut parce que l'auteur inconnu qui nous parle – un des derniers orateurs du monde indien – voulait que nous l'entendions. Ce cri, cette protestation, c'est à nous qu'il les adressait, à travers les siècles. Sans nous voir, sans rien savoir de l'avenir, mais pénétré de la certitude que, malgré la mort et la destruction de son monde, quelqu'un, un jour, quelque part, dans le futur, un homme comme lui, différent mais semblable, étranger mais familier, connaîtrait son témoignage. Ainsi, en dépit de la violence faite à son monde, une part indestructible, une part réellement humaine lui survivrait. À la fin du récit, lorsque Tangaxoan apprend l'arrivée de ces étrangers barbus, montés sur d'étranges animaux caparaçonnés que les Indiens confondent avec les cerfs rituels messagers du monde de l'au-delà , maniant des bâtons qui imitent le bruit tonnerre, il s'écrie : « Ils arrivent, ils sont déjà là. Devons nous disparaître ? »

C'est ce cri qui émeut notre cœur. Ce cri est l'émotion littéraire par excellence. Dans ce cri réside l'universel de toute littérature.

From the Scene of Reading: Literature and Universal Human Values

Yu Jong-ho

1.

The very title of this talk might seem unfashionable, even anachronistic in this age of "deconstruction" and "theory" when no truism seems safe from being challenged or overturned. The idea it puts forth will probably require a degree of reservation to be accepted now. Redefining literature as "writing judged to be high in value," deconstructionist discourse has countered the view that literature is an enduring entity whose value is inherent and unchanging. It has targeted the concept of literary canon, seeing in its formation the dubious hand of hegemony, and undermined the belief that art appeals and values persist. Indeed, from the perspective that understands literature's mode of existence as a ceaseless process of textual reproduction and contingent replication of meaning, any suggestion regarding continuity or constancy of values is bound to be a conceptual fallacy from the start. Eternal art or works that defy time simply do not exist from this vantage point. Along the same lines, the concept of universality has also come under suspicion. Universality, it is argued, is in point of fact no more than the reverent name forcibly appended to the particularity of the powerful. Given the political, economic and military dominance of a handful of Western nations in the modern world, the idea that universality is the name in which the West's particularity oppresses or suppresses other particularities is widely in currency, especially in the "Non-West." This view cannot be simply dismissed as the posture of self-defensiveness adopted by peoples whose pride has been wounded by the experience of collective humiliation. We must indeed remain on guard against universalism that seeks to reduce everything to the least common denominator. At the same time, however, we cannot deny that humanity's cultural heritage has value that is of a universal character.

Philosophical or ideological attack on literature is by no means a recent phenomenon; one only has to recall Plato's argument in *The Republic* or the closing down of theaters by English Puritans. Against discourses of deconstruction, the defenders of the concept of literature stress that "literature" is not a product of the recent past we call modern society, but a concept with long tradition and history. In the West at least, the position held from classical antiquity onward was that literature referred to writings of fine quality that have certain permanence. To be sure, it was only in the modern period that the notion of literature as verbal art consisting of fictional prose and poetry—a notion that thus excluded works meant to provide information or convey didactic content—rose to prominence. Nonetheless, traditionalist proponents of humanism strongly object to defining the concept of "literature" as a product of the nineteenth century since the claim contradicts a large body of evidence.

It was the humanists, then, seeking to put their faith in the validity of classical education into practice, who proclaimed universal human values to be found in literature. They argued that reading and teaching great literary works refines tastes and character, elevates sentiments, and cultivates moral sensibility. Expanding the horizon of sympathy and understanding, literature both humanizes humanity and helps establish a humane culture. Education of imagination was thus understood as leading directly to the expansion of understanding and sympathy. Underlying these claims was the view that literature embodies universal human values.

Such apologia for literature has sometimes been met with skeptical responses even from humanists. With brutal honesty, George Steiner has examined how humanistic education of imagination failed to translate into practical action where such atrocities as Auschwitz were concerned. Harold Bloom has argued that though literature may be able to give us more refined sensibility, it certainly cannot make us better citizens. It is highly ironic to recall that both Steiner and Bloom are critics who remained faithful to the humanist tradition. Nevertheless, we find ourselves unable to give our unconditional assent to the reign of "theory," its anarchism without alternatives, its rejection of the very notions of literature, canon and human values. Our concrete experiences with how literature is received and enjoyed tell us that the question of universal human values that literature raises is more than a simple idealist invention.

2.

For one of my introductory classes on literature, I once assigned Sophocles' Oedipus trilogy. Students were asked to adopt the persona of one of the dramatic characters and draft a defense on this character's behalf. Contrary to my expectations, more students chose Antigone than any other character, and the majority preferred *Antigone* to *Oedipus Rex* as well. The result was the same when I gave the assignment again the following year. There might have been several reasons for this, of course. Thanks to "Oedipus Complex," even students who had never read a page of Sophocles were already well acquainted with the storyline of the Oedipal myth, and such familiarity could have reduced the shock value and deadened the moving force of Sophocles' text. In comparison, the level of exposure students had to *Antigone* was substantially less, so that the freshness of the text was preserved. Gender may also have played a role: the numbers of female and male students were approximately equal, but most of the female students chose to defend Antigone. These conjectures aside, however, it is likely that students found *Antigone* relevant to their lives; that something in this ancient text resonated with their own experiences of political or social reality. Indeed, many students expressed surprise at the contemporary character of the classical tragedy. They saw the present in the past and confessed that they came to regard classics in a different light.

It is well known that from 1790 to the end of the nineteenth century *Antigone* was the object of much reverence among some of the most accomplished poets, philosophers and scholars of Europe.

Not only was it considered the greatest of Greek tragedies but *Antigone* was also seen as a singular work of art that came closer to perfection than any other created by human mind. Such praise has been frequently explained in connection with the French Revolution. Having experienced the encounter between history and the individual in their own lives, European intellectuals of humanities naturally found much to admire and venerate in *Antigone*'s dramatization of how private life becomes knotted together with public life as well as historical life. Hegel's praise of *Antigone* as "one of the most sublime and in all respects the most perfect of works of art created by man" must be understood in this context. What Hegel saw in *Antigone* was the prototype of a conflict that is properly tragic – a conflict not between good and evil but between two partial and mutually exclusive notions of good.

This substance of Hegelian conflict, however, is not what my students read in *Antigone* when they decide to defend its heroine for choosing to die for family obligation over the imperative of the political community. On the whole, students view Creon's exercise of authority as unjust, arrogant, and despotic, while seeing in Antigone's death the martyrdom of human dignity and justice. It matters little to them that the custom of the times denied proper funerary rites to traitors. Creon's response to his son's plea for mercy on Antigone's behalf—"How, if I tolerate a traitor at home, shall I rule those abroad?"—strikes them as arrogant and absolutist affectations of a despot rather than the internal logic of the political community. In a similar vein, Ismene's refusal to help Antigone, "No sense in starting on a hopeless task," is seen as the action of a craven timeserver. Students also express their agreement with Creon's view on money: "Money! Money's the curse of man, none greater. That's what wrecks cities, banishes men from home, tempts and deludes the most well-meaning soul, pointing out the way to infamy and shame." They tend to consider Antigone's belief that "We have only a little time to please the living, but all eternity to love the dead" as a rhetorical device. For that reason, the chorus's praise of humanity, "Wonders are many on earth, and the greatest of these is man" is understood as a mere aside. In Antigone's final line, students see the end met by a conscience that will brook no compromise: "Go I, because I honored those things to which honor truly belongs." Students thus take the classical tragedy as a modern play that stages the martyrdom of an individual who refuses to conform to society's demands. Although students themselves may not be able to articulate their views in such a clear-cut manner, their reception of the classical tragedy can be summarized as above.

To be sure, a variety of background information provided in the classroom setting enriches the students' understanding of the text. Students learn about the historical rise and decline of Greek tragedies, creative structure of myths, performance of tragedies as part of Dionysian festivities, differences between tragedies and comedies, generic particularities of the Greek tragedy, and the theater's role in the city-state of Athens. Class discussions on the work's perfect composition, which omits nothing that is important and admits nothing that is loose, and on how the resonance of its sublime literary style is apt to be lost in translation further enhance their aesthetic appreciation of the work. Be that as it may, the important fact is that students, even as common readers without prior knowledge or supplemental information, find themselves moved by *Antigone*. The reading experience that the ancient text opens up is both compelling and pleasurable. Perhaps, the text engages students so deeply because they read it as a modern drama at some distance from the original circumstances of its production. One student even wrote that when he opened up a contemporary novel after reading Antigone, he found it trifling and its pages full of "trivial chatter." The classroom experience thus confirms the belief that what we call "classics" are precisely those works capable of giving rise to a wide range of secondary texts and interpretative multiplicity.

3.

Studies on Greek tragedies abound and more are under way. Despite the great variety of studies that have been published over the years, or perhaps because of this variety, there does not appear to be an established theory critically agreed upon regarding the etymological origins of Greek tragedies. Among the most interesting and persuasive of the works that I have read, however, is *Myth and Tragedy in Ancient Greece* by the French classicist Jean-Pierre Vernant. Greek tragedy developed, flourished, and declined in Athens all within the span of a hundred years. According to Vernant, the genre was a thoroughly novel invention in its artistic, social (institutional) and psychological aspects. Building on previous studies that located an intimate link between tragedy and the social philosophy of the city state, especially the legal thought that was developing at the time in Athens, Vernant argues that the use of a technical legal vocabulary by tragic poets clearly reveals the connection between the subject of tragedies and lawsuits under the jurisdiction of the courts. Tragic poets employed legal language, intentionally capitalizing on its ambiguity, variability, and incompleteness. The vague, polysemic, and contradictory nature of this language revealed the difference of opinions that existed within legal thought, as well as tensions between the law on the one hand and religious tradition and moral philosophy on the other. Law, though distinct from moral philosophy, did not yet have a sphere whose boundaries were sufficiently delineated. Greeks did not have a notion of absolute law, a consistent system based on clear principles. Moreover, the meaning of words like justice (dike) and law (nomoi) were highly variable and subject to change. In this context, tragedy staged the tension between justice and law when the latter was not yet securely established. Of course, since tragedy was not a legal debate, the focal point of these works was not the debate itself but the human agent who must make a decision to act in an unstable world where values are subject to radical ambiguity. In short, tragedy was the tribunal and came into being at the same time as the city sate and its legal system.

Vernant further argues that tragedy, at an abstract level of formal logic, represents a passageway between mythic and philosophical thought, or between Hesiod and Aristotle. In the mythic thought, all concepts operate under the logic of variability and ambiguity, while the philosophical thought employs the logic of identity. Between the two lies tragedy. Tragedy's logic is that of conflict between irreconcilable positions and of tension between opposing forces.

Also the logic of Sophists, it grants that two completely opposite views are possible on any given question since there are two extremes in all human problems. In time, however, philosophy's emphasis on the distinction between truth and error triumphed, and tragedy met its end. Vernant highlights Greek tragedy as the product of a particular time in order to stress its role as the bridge between mythic and philosophical thoughts.

If one insists on this analysis of Greek tragedy, which I have selected for my own purposes and adapted from Vernant's extensive study, the way in which everyday readers such as the students in my class approach *Antigone* may very well appear arbitrary and self-directed. One might even argue that these readings are wild misreadings, and that what these students have read has little in common with the play that the ancient Greeks attended. Perhaps such charges can be made in reference not only to classics but to works of art in general. Still, the important fact is that a foreign text, written more than two millennia ago by a playwright who lived at the other end of the earth, continues be read with interest by Korean students; in this ancient text students manage to discover problems that are contemporaneous with their own social reality. If such a discovery is based on a misreading scarred by translation, it is still a misreading that piques interest, produces meaning and pleasure, and leads to greater self-awareness. Historical inquiry into the conditions of textual production or explanations of the social and artistic milieu may supplement this productive misreading but they cannot invalidate or supplant it altogether.

In my class, students engaged in discussions after presenting their defenses. Predictably, heated arguments broke out between those who chose to speak for Antigone and those who embraced Creon's perspective. At one end of the spectrum was the opinion that the legal code of a political community has to be observed if order is to be maintained. At the other end, students questioned the legitimacy of social rules that oppress fundamental human virtue and argued that extenuating circumstances must enter into consideration in every case. Between these poles, there was a range of opinions too, some arguing the validity of both Antigone's and Creon's positions, some negating them both; in either case, students claimed that leniency was in order. Others quoted the chorus to contend that the tragic ending could be prevented only if both sides take a step back from the point of no return. Some were skeptical about whether one position could be espoused over the other, and still others confessed that they were shocked to realize that it was precisely this dimension of indeterminability that made the dramatic situation properly tragic.

The discussion was left open-ended, but the classroom experience demonstrated the power of literature in revealing universal human values. Justice, freedom, equality, conscience, love, sympathy: expounding these universal values plainly is a favored technique of the so-called littérature à thèse. Critics have questioned whether such literature has power to compel the readers; it is true that works which too openly espouse "humanitarian" values can strike readers as being conventional or didactic, losing their appeal as "literature" in the process. To be sure, artists are, and have to be, more aesthetes than moralists. Even though I took my examples from classical theater and did not focus on aesthetic aspects in this talk, it hardly needs to be pointed out that aesthetic qualities common to works worthy of the name of art themselves constitute an important category of universal human values.

4.

In a broad sense, literature is mimesis of life and the world. Even "literature of interiority" which is said to reveal our inner experiences is mimesis of that interior landscape in a strict sense. Because literature is mimesis, it becomes inextricably bound up with social reality, and carries within it the power to induce self-discovery and critical consciousness in its readers. Individual literary works can thus offer a useful frame of reference for social issues. It seems to me, for example, that the literary-historical frame of reference is of great value in laying the grounds for a just and sagacious approach to the question of "rectifying the past," which has emerged as a massive social controversy in recent years in Korea.

This ethical dilemma is reflected with a particular force in the life story of one twentieth-century Korean writer. Cho Myonghui is the well-known writer of *On Spring Grass* and *Naktong River*; his short stories and poems even made their appearance in junior high school textbooks in both North and South Korea after the liberation. In 1928, a year after publishing his major work, *Naktong River*, Cho sought political exile in the Soviet Union. Korea was under the Japanese colonial rule at the time, and Cho's decision became the talk of the town, even occasioning feelings of envy among Korean intellectuals. In the atmosphere of nationalist euphoria following the liberation in 1945, Cho became the object of admiration and homage once again; he was seen as a far-sighted man who chose to go into exile rather than compromise his conscience as an individual and as a writer. In comparison to the careers of Korean writers who stayed behind, most of whom suffered the ignominy, either willingly or not, of collaborating with the Japanese, Cho's exile was seen as a wise and appropriate decision. The following lines in an article written by one prominent critic in 1947, a year before the establishment of the Republic of Korea in the south, allows us to glimpse the reputation Cho enjoyed in the literary world at the time: "A tearful record of Koreans' wanderings as people without a nation, *Naktong River* embodies the incomparable love of one's country, the insuppressible yearning for freedom. Why, then, did the writer of this work exile himself to the Soviet Union?"

Though there were rumors that Cho had become a teacher in a Korean school near Vladivostok, what really happened to him in the Soviet Union did not become known until much later. In his *Travels in the Soviet Union* – after the liberation, Yi Taejoon traveled around the Soviet Union upon the government's invitation – the writer Yi wrote that he tried without success to find out Cho's whereabouts. He ascertained that Cho's family was living in a small farming village in Kazakhstan, about four days by train from Tashkent, but could not confirm what had happened to Cho himself. We now know why Cho could not be located. He was arrested by the Soviet secret police in 1937 and executed the following year in a prison in Havarovsk on charges of being a spy. The fall of 1937, of course, was when 160,000 Koreans living in Primorsky Krai were forced to relocate to Kazakhstan. The relocation to Central Asia was carried out from September to November, with Korean residents in the Soviet Union given just a week to pack up and leave. Until after the *perestroika*, any mention of this relocation was banned in the Soviet Union. Thus, we can see that Cho Myonghui was arrested just before the forced relocation and executed the following year.

At the time of his exile, Cho Myonghui was in his thirties and married with children. In his autobiography, Kim Soun praises Cho's moral rectitude, professing never to have encountered any poet more austere and self-disciplined. At the same time, Kim describes how Cho's family fared after his departure. One of Cho's daughters named Chungnam worked as a bus-girl in Seoul to make ends meet, and Cho's wife, a traditional Korean woman without education, was bowed under the weight of poverty. Surely, from a political perspective, Cho's decision to go into exile is beyond reproach. Who can condemn a man for refusing to submit himself to colonial oppression? We can, however, raise the question of moral responsibility, recalling as we do Kim Soun's description of Cho's family, left behind in Korea without a means of supporting themselves. There has always been a defense for such actions as Cho's, framed in terms of sacrificing one's body to preserve one's dignity, or sacrificing small virtue to preserve a greater one. But can fidelity to the "imagined community" really justify the betrayal of "kinship ethics"? In the name of public good, can we discard that which is personal? We need not be the wife abandoned, the daughter left behind to raise these questions. To be sure, Cho's agony must have been unimaginably intense as he grappled with the conflicting demands of his integrity as a political subject and his responsibility as a family man. Brecht, the poet of "Schlechte Zeit für Lyrik," warned us of too quick a judgment in his "To Those Born Later."

You who will emerge from the flood
In which we have gone under
Remember
When you speak of our failings

The dark time too
Which you have escaped.
For we went, changing countries oftener than our shoes
Through the wars of classes, despairing
When there was injustice only, and no rebellion.

And yet we know:
Hatred, even of meanness
Controls the features.
Anger, even against injustice
Makes the voice hoarse. Oh, we
Who wanted to prepare the ground for friendliness
Could not ourselves be friendly.

But you, when the time comes at last
And man is a helper to man
Think of us
With forbearance.

Cho Myonghui too, perhaps, could have cited this poem and appealed to his family for forbearance, asking them to understand his anguished choice and its unfortunate result. As readers, we sympathize with both the tragic conflict Cho must have suffered and the universal appeal of Brecht's poem. But what exactly is a time in which "man is a helper to man"? If what Brecht had in mind was the realization of a just society to follow the success of socialist revolution, history has shown us the illusory nature of that dream. The poem was written in the mid-1930s; based on circumstantial evidence, we might be justified in reading the poem as a defense of Stalinism. If so, we can say that Brecht's poem was based on an unacceptable double standard, self-righteousness and rationalization. Pursuing this line of thought, we might also ask whether we can unilaterally denounce those Korean writers who stayed behind within the colonial system and tried to adhere to "kinship ethics" rather than show fidelity to "imagined community."

Classical Greek tragedy is an artistic genre that flourished and declined in a particular place at a particular juncture in history. If, however, Vernant's understanding of Greek tragedy as comprising a type of tribunal is correct, Korean society today would benefit from staging a similar type of "tragedy." In so far as *Antigone*, or literature at large, meditates on such questions explicitly or in veiled manner, we can say that universal human values are latent in its pages. As mimesis of humanity and the world, literature possesses a link to this world that is as inextricable as it is inevitable. Nearing the end of the talk, I recall an unforgettable line from a text I encountered for the first time some thirty years ago, *Memoires D'Hadrien* by the French female writer Marguerite Yourcenar: "I don't believe in the afterlife. Because I know all too well the difficulty of rendering judgment." This is a thought befitting an emperor with immense power and responsibility. Through the frame of reference we call literature, we too are reminded ceaselessly about the difficulty of rendering judgment.

Translated by **Yu Young-ju**

Literatura y Universalidad Humana

Luis Sepúlveda

Cuando supe que tenía que escribir un texto sobre este tema, me sorprendí, y no es extraño, siempre me sorprendo, todo me sorprende, justamente porque soy un escritor latinoamericano vivo en un estado de constante sorpresa.

Me sorprenden las palabras y su poder fundador de realidades, soy un hijo de las palabras pues en tanto chileno desciendo de los indios mapuches, de los primeros habitantes de mi país que, si bien es cierto que no tenían escritura, tenían en cambio un desmedido amor por la oralidad, por las palabras que en las frías noches australes ordenaban para contar las cosas del día, para contar la vida y la muerte, las esperanzas y los sueños, y de esa manera, a fuerza de nombrarlas, hacían que todo tuviera vida y fuera real.

Incluso los jefes guerreros de mi pueblo mapuche eran elegidos, no en torneos de fuerza o demostraciones de habilidad física, sino en competencias de oralidad. Debían hablar durante horas, días y noches, manteniendo un discurso equilibrado, coherente y poético. Aquel que mejor lo hacía, era elegido cacique y comandaba los destinos de la nación de los mapuches, de la Gente de la Tierra.

Uno de ellos, según cuenta la historia, habló durante cuatro días con sus noches, y para hacer más difícil la prueba, lo hizo sosteniendo sobre sus hombros un tronco de su mismo peso. Así, cargando su propio peso, el Gran Cacique Caopolicán, señor de las tierras del sur y de las islas, durante cuatro días con sus noches habló, narró, contó los detalles que observa un río en su vertiginoso camino hasta el mar.

Ese antepasado mío, como todos los hombres y mujeres que amamos las palabras, hacía literatura y al mismo tiempo fundaba,

daba razón de ser a todas las cosas que nombraba. ¿Puede haber un ejemplo de universalidad humana mayor?

Cuando los hombres hablamos de la humanidad, nombramos a una gran familia cuyo mayor tesoro es la diversidad de razas, lenguas, color de piel, de costumbres, de relacionarse con la vida y con la muerte. Y esa familia tan diferente tiene sin embargo el componente común que nos hace humanos: la conciencia de los derechos humanos y la acuciante necesidad de que sean estos la única norma que organice nuestras vidas.

Cuando alguien escribe "Derechos Humanos", ya sea sobre el papel, una pantalla de ordenador, un muro o la arena de una playa, está escribiendo el poema de mayor universalidad humana.Y lo mismo ocurre si alguien dice "Derechos Humanos" en una celda, en un país de exilio, en la trinchera de una guerra absurda – y todas las guerras son absurdas e innecesarias-, o en una calle estremecida por miles de manifestantes a favor de la vida. La literatura y su imprescindible mensaje de universalidad humana también se dice en voz alta y con clamor de multitudes.

En mi idioma, el español, que une y da identidad cultural a casi quinientos millones de personas, la palabra PAZ tiene tan sólo tres letras, pero son letras contundentes y graníticas. Es una palabra que amamos pues la hemos dicho y escrito durante siglos sin conseguir, y no por culpa nuestra, que ella, la PAZ sea la luz que ilumina nuestra vidas. Pero seguimos insistiendo justamente porque sabemos que esa palabra PAZ es otra de las grandes joyas de la universalidad humana.

La literatura se hace de palabras y la magnitud de ellas la decide precisamente la humana universalidad del escritor. No es ni la sabiduría ni el acervo cultural lo que da esplendor a palabras breves y bellas como PAN, PAZ, TRABAJO, JUSTICIA y LIBERTAD. Si quien las dice o las escribe no sabe, o no quiere saber que esas palabras son inequívocas en su significado, cualquiera que sea el idioma en que se las diga o escriba, las despoja de esa universalidad humana que tienen esas tres palabras fundadoras de los Derechos Humanos, la gran herencia de todas las civilizaciones.

Yo soy un hombre del sur, Chile es la nación más austral del planeta, y mi país de hombres y mujeres orgullosamente verticales frente a los desafíos de la vida hunde sus raíces en la Antártica. País de Pablo Neruda y Gabriela Mistral, de Salvador Allende y Pedro Aguirre Cerda, de mujeres y hombres que, llegados desde todas las latitudes, junto a los Mapuches, La Gente de la Tierra, fundaron un mestizaje unido por la más esplendorosa diversidad, y por el amor apasionado a las palabras fundadoras de los Derechos Humanos. Los mejores poetas y escritores chilenos han creído firmemente que, o la literatura se basaba sobre los sólidos fundamentos de la universalidad humana, o no servía para nada. Y como los chilenos amamos a nuestros mejores poetas y escritores, les dijimos que tenían razón, y todo el país fue un coro en defensa de los Derechos Humanos. Pagamos un precio muy alto por cantar esos derechos: dieciséis años de oscuridad, terror, miedo, libros quemados en las calles, la más atroz dictadura intentó silenciar nuestras voces que clamaban en nombre de la universalidad humana. Pero no lo consiguieron, y aunque hoy nos faltan tres mil quinientos chilenos que están desaparecidos, seguimos elevando nuestras voces, también en nombre de ellos, para que las palabras PAN, PAZ, TRABAJO, JUSTICIA y LIBERTAD sean los cimientos fundadores del otro

Chile Posible que paso a paso vamos construyendo.

Soy un hombre del Sur, ese es mi mayor orgullo, por mis venas corren los ríos más caudalosos, bajo mi piel se palpa el calor del desierto de Atacama y el filo polar de los glaciares, sobre mi piel llevo tatuados los nombres de las mil islas de Chile, respiro el aroma de sus bosques infinitos, y hablo y escribo y actúo y existo en nombre de los pobres de mi tierra, de los dignos pobres de mi tierra.

Como Chileno y Latinoamericano nací y crecí en la emergencia que nos impusieron. Recitando los poemas de los poetas que nos mataron, como Pablo Neruda y Paco Urondo. Contando los cuentos y novelas de los escritores que nos mataron, como Haroldo Conti y Roberto Walsh. Cantando las canciones de los juglares que nos mataron, como Víctor Jara y Jorge Cafrune. Y son ellos, y tantos otros, los que enseñaron a creer en la universalidad humana de la literatura, porque justamente por eso los mataron.

He escrito muchos libros y en todos ellos están las invencibles palabras fundadoras del mundo posible y fraterno en el que creo. Escribo sobre el papel y sobre los muros PAN, PAZ, TRABAJO, JUSTICIA y LIBERTAD, esas cinco palabras que encierran toda la humana universalidad de la literatura.

Changing Together While Resisting

Hwang Seok-young

The South Korean activists who fought for democracy and reunification against the military dictatorship in the 1970s and early 1980s primarily yearned for freedom of ideology, speech, and election, and secondarily the union of the divided nation. For this reason, they called themselves nationalists.

The rulers of the military dictatorship, who were submissive to foreign powers because they lacked legitimacy within the country, advertised themselves as nationalists as well. As can be seen by the fact that both camps claimed to be nationalistic, the two groups' concepts of the "nation" clashed.

The term "nation" was used without much conflict within the South Korean democratization movement camp until the 1980s. In the 1990s, however, its members found the term unappealing as more people traveled overseas and the world was in the throes of drastic change. With increased exchanges and alliances with civic groups in other countries, the Korean organizations whose titles contained the word "nation" began to change their translated names. Most commonly, "nation" was changed to "people," in view of the fact that nationalism is often associated with fascism in Japan and the West. At the same time, in the ruling capitalist countries, the word "nationalism" is perceived as a backward concept that opposes the global market economic system. In other words, for both ordinary citizens and ruling classes in the West, the term "nation" was suspect.

Korean civic organizations further believed they should clarify their names, for in foreign languages the words "state" and "nation" are often interchangeable. They began to argue that an oppressed people could use the term "nationalism," and that the meaning would change depending on which stratum of society conceptualized it.

Given that the terms "nation" and "nationalism" went through such a convoluted course of change even when our focus is limited to South Korea, it is necessary for us to examine the hypothetical concepts of "globalism" and "universality."

There was a time when the phrase "what is the most Korean is the most global" was in vogue in South Korea. Lurking behind this sentence is the discontent of a country on the fringes of the capitalist world that has been built upon an international hierarchical order and inequality since the modern age, as well as the naïve belief in the concept of so-called global universality.

The hypothesis that modern science and technology advanced by Europe since the Renaissance is universal, and therefore all things European are universal, is a fallacy of Eurocentrism. For this reason, universality is a boundary put in place by those with power. Absorbing outlying areas into its sphere of influence, imperialist Europe beckoned others to "come inside the boundary of global universality." The weaker parties found themselves in a dilemma: rejection of such a proposition would result in the failure of exchange, which would ultimately lead to the loss of existence, whereas acceptance would lead to the loss of identity. A careful look into European history shows that the French Revolution contributed to advancing Europe's belief in universality, and that Napoleon played the role of actually diffusing this belief. Each European country, however, responded in a nationalistic manner from its own particular position. During the period of mercantilism and Enlightenment, Europe shared the concrete meaning of universality, establishing state-level international relations. When Goethe advocated universal world literature, what he meant by the "world," without question, was Europe.

Although Europe advocated a universal world to outsiders, nationalism and internationalism were the internally competing propositions while each country carried out imperialist practices. It was not only the capitalist ruling classes, but also the leftists, from Marxists to Bolsheviks, who denounced or emphasized the two ideologies as a strategic political value depending on the time and circumstance. With European powers' imperialistic expansion, universality and specificity took clearer shape amid conflict and tension between the center and the fringes of power. Even now, such concepts are being reproduced in ever-changing forms in the global market's division of labor. Certain segments in the countries at the lowest rung of the hierarchical order in the global capitalist system are struggling to overcome their alienation by moving inside the fence called universalism – the very fence constructed by European powers. In other words, together with the terms freedom and market, universalism is a slogan put forth by those trying to maintain vested rights and inequality within the capitalist global order. The kind of modernism that was forced upon Asia was Westernization, and it was the only way to be civilized in a "universal" manner.

Therefore, we need to stop and examine humanism, from both the perspective of the universal worldwide ideology and the practical manifestation of it. After the Renaissance, the Western bourgeoisie formed European humanism, which is symbolized as freedom, equality, and civil rights. Europe achieved modernization through citizens' revolutions on the foundation of enlightenment, rationalism, and, above all, science.

At the time when Western European powers were advancing to various continents, including East Asia, indigenous cultures already possessed human-centered ideologies derived from Islam, Buddhism, and Confucianism. The ideology of Westernization, however, put forth the justification that only the West could establish a civilization that had moved from the pre-modern to the modern, and insisted on civilizing "barbarism." In any event, we have found the meaning of "humankind" amid the conflict of the previous century, and even though we have been bruised and covered with blood in the process, we were able to choose and cherish worthwhile values, including freedom, equality, human rights, and democracy.

Eurocentric humanism was of course expressed as disseminating Christian "Good News" or as carrying out civilizing tasks. "Universal humanism," as the Europeans wanted to disseminate it, was based on the premises of prejudice and racial discrimination with the ultimate goal to "enlighten the barbarians." We need not go back far in the past to see how this ideology changed into various forms. If we examine the characteristics of the wars the West has waged in the non-Western world since World War II, we can find that expansionism, the reproduction of capital, and the capitalist system have all been factors as well as prejudices against culture, religion, and race. And a war is still going on in the Middle East. We know all too well what Britons and Americans did to the indigenous populations in India and the Americas in the name of teaching universal human values.

An attendant pushed Mahatma Gandhi, a British-educated lawyer, out of an operating train simply because he was not white. This incident was known to be an unusual occurrence after he became famous, but until very recently non-whites who participated in Western societies all over the world frequently found themselves in similar situations.

There are some jokes on Western civilization and humanism: "No dogs or Chinese" – this sign was posted at the entrance of Huangpu Park in the old Shanghai of the Bund.

A foreign journalist asked the Chinese writer Lu Xun, "What do you think of Westerners and their religion, Christianity?" Lu Xun answered that he was surprised because what their books said was completely different from the goods they used, and that what he had seen together with the Westerners were only guns, tanks, and bombs pouring out of planes.

Someone asked Mahatma Gandhi what he thought of Western civilization. Smiling, he answered that it would be great if something like that ever existed.

An old tribal chief went to see Dr. Albert Schweitzer, who was providing medical care to African natives. This chief was from a region where cannibalism was practiced. After getting treatment, the old man asked, "I heard that a war is going on in Europe these days. Is it true?" Dr. Schweitzer answered affirmatively because Europe was in the clutches of World War I. The chief asked, "How many Westerners have been killed in the war? A hundred?" The doctor answered that more people were dying. "Then a thousand?" asked the old man. "Well, more than a hundred times that," answered the good doctor. The chief was speechless because he had no concept of a thousand times a hundred. He finally managed to say, "You people aren't much, either. Why do you kill so many when you can't eat them all?"

November 9, 1989, Berlin

> I was there at the time. The wall of the Cold War dividing the East and the West was coming down. That day I shed tears standing in front of the Brandenburg Gate. Although people were streaming by to meet those they had not been allowed to see, South and North Korea were still divided, massive state-of-the-art arms and U.S. forces were still stationed on the Korean Peninsula, and 1.7 million young men in the North and the South were pointing weapons at each other.

The first line in my journal entry that day was: "Now the world is changing. Still, I will describe the world through my own methods and means of interpretation that I have formed as a member of the society that I am a product of."

Looking back, Japan forcibly took away the national sovereignty of Korea in the last century, for the leaders during the Joseon Dynasty failed to reform the country and modernize it on its own strength, paralyzed by the politics dominated by elements of the old-guard. In the wake of coerced opening, Japan turned itself into an active tool for Western capital, aiming the muzzle of its gun to its brothers in East Asia. Thanks to the Cold War, after Korea's liberation from Japan in 1945, Japan, the aggressor, went away as it shifted the responsibility for the division of the North and the South to the Korean Peninsula, the victim. The Korean War completed the backbone of the Cold War system throughout Europe and Asia. The United States could conveniently dispose of its surplus weapons from World War II during the Korean War, and practically lay waste to the small Korean Peninsula by pouring down twice as many bombs as the weapons used during the Pacific War. For more than half a century, this division has continued. The entire Korean Peninsula has become an army base on which the United States' political and military strategies are realized.

After the end of the Cold War, the world has become even less stable. Until the last century, it was none other than the West that disseminated the notion that increased productivity through advanced science and technology would boost economic wealth, and that human freedom and equality would be guaranteed. The capitalist and socialist camps each painted a different utopia on the foundation of their respective beliefs. It looked as if the emergence of a new world order was imminent, either an egalitarian community in which differences of class, social status, and wealth would disappear or a world that would be free from the oppression of poverty and disease and human beings could lead more affluent lives thanks to the expansion of capital and technology. At the end of the last century and at the beginning of the new century, we are confronted with bitter disillusionment, as socialism has collapsed and the globalization of capitalism is underway; the new world order is being reorganized around the United States. The environment is mercilessly being destroyed. Civil wars and wars based on religion and race are caused by neo-imperialist powers. Countries on the fringes, which entrusted their futures to modernization and economic development in the aftermath of colonial rule, have endured dictatorships, protests, and frustration, and once again are suffering from poverty, disease, and starvation.

With the collapse of the East European socialist sphere and the dismantlement of the Cold War, the world has been quickly reorganized through the sole hegemony of the United States, but the Korean Peninsula is still divided like a Cold War relic fit for a museum. As Koreans adapt to the so-called era of "globalization" in which neither nations nor borders exist under the strong influence of the United States' hegemony and reorganization of capital, they are weighed down by the vestiges of the past – the division of the Korean nation and its territory. Now, the past ideologies of vague universalism and Pax Americana have been reborn as the term "globalization," and it looks like fancy wrapping paper around the ugly reality of "Americanization."

> More than 1.2 billion people in the world live on less than one dollar a day, and half of the world's population live on less than two dollars a day. The UN budget is $1.25 billion plus the

> necessary finance for peacekeeping per annum. Against this, U.S. citizens spend over $27 billion per annum on confectionery, $70 billion per annum on alcohol and over $550 billion per annum on cars. Who will voluntarily opt for this type of distribution – every day over 50,000 people die of poverty-related causes, such as malnutrition – in which billions of people are victims of serious losses and disadvantages regardless of their intentions and opinions?
>
> While it would take $6 billion to provide basic education, $9 billion to provide clean water and sanitary facilities, and $13 billion to provide basic health care to all the children in the world annually, in the U.S. citizens spend $4 billion per annum on cosmetics, $20 billion per annum on jewelry, and $17 billion per annum on pet food. Who in the world is ready to accept this situation? It will be very difficult to defend that such a person exists through a reasonable argument in a fair court based on ethical reason. Furthermore, given that lifestyles of the world people are visibly transmitted to everyone in the era of mass media like today, it is not surprising that conflicts and disputes are provoked due to global-level inequality. – from David Held's "Globalization after the September 11 Attacks," postscript to the Korean translation of *Global Transformation.*

It is not only recently that the American lifestyle has posed a crisis to the world's peace, a crisis that threatens the world. According to U.N. statistics, until recently the annual U.S. drug consumption equaled the annual Gross Domestic Product of China. Although people are starving in more than 100 countries, the item most traded throughout the world is weapons, not food, and the United States is No. 1 in the sale of arms. This country uses 40 percent of the world's consumer goods, and only one percent of Americans possess half of the nation's wealth. To maintain such a society of maximized production and consumption, it would be necessary to continue plundering other places or sacrificing other people. The U.S. Congress and administration have no choice but to play the role of a spokesperson for corporations and capital. So much so that some Americans lament their government has turned into an organization that carries out the interests of powerful special interest groups. In the past, too, the United States planned and waged war on a regular basis to overcome economic recessions and the Great Depression. This was an unavoidable choice for a country where the military, industry, and politics are thoroughly intertwined.

If people declare the victory of capitalism over socialism, insisting that the era of enlightenment ended with the collapse of socialism in the early 1990s, then they merely attempt to conceal the crisis of capitalism. If the concepts espoused by Karl Marx and socialism emerged as a critical response to the irregularities and corruption of the capitalist world order, and the United States, now the sole hegemonic "empire," can do anything it feels like without anyone's deterrence or criticism, it is indeed a time of danger for the entire world.

After World War II, the United States waged wars in the non-Western sphere, in Korea and in Vietnam. In the name of freedom and anti-communism, it also supported dictatorial regimes in many parts of the world, including those in Asia, Africa, and Latin America, staging coup d'états or overthrowing democratic governments elected by the people after spilling blood. Specifically, in the aftermath of a full-blown war, special operations and large-scale nuclear war exercises continued for half a century in many parts of South Korea under the U.S. Command (until recently, the U.S. forces in Korea called itself the U.N. forces). The resulting wounds still remain in various parts of South Korean society in the form of internal scars.

As was the case in Korea and Vietnam during the Cold War era, the tragic vestiges of rule by partition for the sake of imperialistic interests can still be found in many non-Western regions being devastated by civil wars, including Rwanda, Palestine, Afghanistan, and Iraq. Palestine's long-standing tragedy, in particular, is an example in which the West took advantage of Jewish Zionism in order to transfer its original sin. Israel, though a sacrificial lamb for its own survival, has ended up being the West's advance sentry point imbedded in the Arab world.

With the establishment of the Bush regime, American domestic and foreign policy has been carried out in an ultra-conservative direction, to the point of eliminating the stance of liberal criticism and internal checks and balances that had previously been maintained. The current policy is being switched in the direction of pro-capital and anti-labor, market fundamentalism, racism and white supremacy, anti-environment, and anti-human rights. The United States under the Bush administration seems to have gone to the extreme with the ban on suspicious people's entry into the country, inspections of opposing domestic forces, the Patriot Act, long-term imprisonment of terrorists or suspected terrorists in the Guantanamo naval base, a unilateral war in Iraq despite opposition from the United Nations and Europe, and torture and atrocious acts against Iraqi prisoners-of-war. The most important change is that the United States has completely freed itself from international law, justice, and conventions, and has openly declared and demonstrated that it can wage war anywhere at any time, according to its own will.

On the Korean Peninsula, when it looked as if a peaceful system would be established – the scrapping of the Armistice Treaty and signing a peace treaty seemed imminent in the wake of the June 15 North-South summit talks in 2000 – President Bush, as soon as he took power, declared Iran, Iraq, and North Korea as the "axis of evil," turning North Korean-U.S. relations back to the Cold War era. In the meantime, the United States established a missile defense system and sold a large amount of state-of-the-art weapons to Japan and South Korea. Afterward, the United States heightened tensions in East Asia by openly declaring that it would bring down the North Korean system, thus ignoring the yearning of the South Korean people who want improved relations with the North. South Koreans appealed through various channels that they have the ability to change the North as long as North Korea and the United States improve relations, but this proposition runs counter to American interests. South Koreans, who have lived for over half a century amid the threat of war, say, "Everyday we go to sleep and wake up with our heads on cannons."

According to a U.N. report, approximately 2-3 million North Koreans died during the 1990s because of isolation and embargos.

Needlessly to say, this was not in the African sense in which masses die in a short period of time, but it occurred slowly because of widespread malnutrition and disease resulting from weakened resistance. This has been proven by the death rates of infants and older people. In some sense, the slow process of withering away is the most pathetic of all. During this period, South Korea's food waste amounted to 500-600 million won per year, and at present the amount stands at 1.5 billion won. Against such a backdrop, President Kim Dae-jung's "Sunshine Policy" was introduced, and aid to North Korea was one of the major points in this policy. The United States, refusing to accept even this, is putting brakes on such moves through South Korean conservatives. These acts are tantamount to semi-war tactics, betraying the yearnings of Koreans themselves. Who in the world has the right and justification to keep the Korean people, who have never harmed anyone, as hostages of war for half a century, and continue to threaten them?

I remember that there was a "nuclear crisis" between North Korea and the United States in 1993 when I returned home from the States, knowing that I would be imprisoned. At the time anyone who knew anything about international politics said North Korean-U.S. relations should be improved, and I, too, publicly stated that a peace treaty between the two countries should be signed. In 1994, negotiations between the United States and North Korea broke down, and the United States began a countdown for a war based on the actual scenario of preemptive attacks on North Korea. It came to a halt only moments before the final decision by the Department of Defense and the White House. The U.S. commander, who has the military operation command authority in South Korea, can attack North Korea at any time following the order of his country's president, without any discussion or negotiation with the South Korean government or people. Since the armistice in 1953, such dangerous situations have occurred dozens of times. As if it were not enough, the United States can now wage a war anywhere in the world as it pleases, as we have seen in Iraq. Together with others in the world, we find ourselves worrying about the crisis of American society, which seems to be heading for fascism in actuality, despite its veneer of representative democracy.

I have discussed the reality that seems hopeless, with no good prospect in sight, but if Koreans had not been optimistic, they would not have been able to accomplish this much economic capability amid such life-threatening crises and hardships. It is not mere praise when people say that among the former colonies that recovered independence after World War II, only South Korea achieved both economic modernization and democracy. Via satellite the world has witnessed vivid scenes of Korea's political upheavals, violent suppressions, demonstrations, and tragic crackdowns a dozen of times on their television screens. I have met many international intellectuals who found the emergence of a democratic South Korean government to be a mystery. Whereas Japan, after inflicting all sorts of violence against Asia, joined the ranks of advanced countries thanks to economic booms during the Korean and Vietnam Wars and under the U.S. security umbrella, the modernization and democratization of South Korea, divided from the North, were precious fruits achieved through people's struggle for survival amidst blood and tears.

Then, does this mean that a "universal human value" is non-existent in this gloomy world? It is desirable for a new civilization to gaze upon the world from the viewpoint of the one who went through tragic pain and despair. In East Asia, such a moral decision is called "putting oneself in someone else's place," or to "put oneself in someone else's shoes." It is like role switching in psychodramas or the Korean shamanistic ritual, gut. When I entered North Korea in 1989 as the first South Korean civilian to openly do so after the division, thereby breaking South Korea's National Security Law, I shared a rather serious joke with those who accompanied me. I said, "Let's listen to North Koreans even if they claim that they make light-brown bean paste with red beans." Some people call it an "internal gaze" in a learned way. If we want to discuss universal human values, this act at least must bring forth an action, rather than be a vague, abstract concept.

As for "putting oneself in someone else's shoes," we must demand it of ourselves, not to mention to request that others practice it. For example, as we object to and criticize the South Korean government's policy of dispatching troops to the Iraqi battlefield under American pressure, we are required to criticize the North Korean regime's hard-line militarist stance, which has kept its people in distress for a long time as the country entrenched itself against the U.S. blockade for over 10 years.

Let us stop and think how empty and abstract this conference would have been, had there not been the premise of "writing for peace" while discussing the theme, "literature and universal human values."

I remember an international literature conference in September 2001 in Norway, the country that awards the Nobel Peace Prize. Prominent on the event's poster was the printed word "WAR" while "peace" in small letters was hidden at a corner. At the time, I was a presenter, as was the Israeli writer Amos Oz. It was soon after I had completed my novel *The Guest* and was still engrossed in the book; I said I was against blind adherence to principles or fundamentalism, regardless of ideology, and I remember that Amos Oz expressed a similar stance. Soon after we left that conference, the September 11 attacks took place. Watching the tragic scene broadcast on television, I talked with my German writer friend Hans: "Look, the most dangerous person in the world is George Bush." A war is a product of avarice and exclusive egoism.

Pierre Bourdieu, who attended the first Seoul International Forum for Literature in 2000 sponsored by the Daesan Foundation, died soon afterward, but I remember him saying that we should form a worldwide alliance against globalization while we were in the ancient city of Gyeongju, with a thousand years of history. More than anything else, literature must reach out to universality, namely humankind, while talking about our own experiences in our own tongues. Therefore, the value to be pursued by literature has to be, doubtlessly, "multilateral universalism." Molding varied and universal human values in the world can be a sort of cultural movement against globalization, which opposes any type of hegemony. We can create such an amorphous cultural alliance, and it will be easier and faster than forming any political organization.

I find it is deeply significant that a resolution was passed last year to hold regular meetings by a committee of experts for cultural diversity, where literary professionals from European and Third

World countries would attend, and that the World Culture Open (WCO), an NGO affiliated with the United Nations, was formed last year.

When I was released from prison in 1998, I put forth the "theory on the importance of East Asia." I argued that to overcome Korea's division and find an alternative to globalization, Koreans must break away from the narrow arena – the nation – and find ways to form alliances with civic groups in Asia. I also said that we should reverse the paradigm – "taking what is good from the West while maintaining what we have in the East" – a self-critical stance on East Asia's modernization and a popular ideology of the late Joseon Dynasty (late 19th century). What I meant by this was that East Asians should have resisted the West, thus changing both the West and themselves.

Just because the current American-style globalization is a hypocritical ideology, there is no reason for us to give up hope for an optimistic, peaceful global community. We know that Europe's aspiring values for the economic, social systems are different from those of the United States. We find a possibility of how to view life from the fact that Europe insists on balance and value, telling the United States that economic growth is merely a means, not a goal, and that Europe regards the market as merely a part of the social system. As we prepare to form a progressive alliance with Asian citizens, we must break away from American-style economic management, sharing our beliefs with Europe.

Just as the West has apocalyptic visions, East Asia has the theory of cataclysmic change. While Western theory argues that this scenario will bring an end and ruin to humankind and civilizations around the globe, Eastern belief regards it as the birth of a completely new worldview and the beginning of a new civilization. According to East Asia's ancient astronomy, modern human civilization is at the threshold between summer and autumn. This means humanity is crossing from the conflict of fire or greedy prosperity to harmony, a wrapping-up, or the season of harvest. In a word, the method and content of life will change. It is inevitable because if we stay on the current world capitalist course of infinite consumption and maximum production, humankind and Earth will be completely destroyed.

In the distance, cows moo and the bells on their necks tinkle, and chickens cluck after laying eggs. From the field, people sing as they transplant rice in wet paddies. Floating over the brisk drumbeat of the farmers' musical instruments is the high, cheerful metal clang of a gong. A mother calls out for her children.

Children, Come and eat your meal!

—From Hwang Seok-young's *The Guest*

Civilization or the value of life will be transformed only through the efforts that harmonize nature and people. A peaceful world will appear amid the change initiated by humble, generous actors, not by greedy, selfish movers and shakers.

Translated by **Yu Young-nan**

Session III

Ideals of Peace in the Korean Tradition

Memories, Pain, Doubts and Hopes

Tibor Méray

I arrived in Korea for the first time in my life at a summer dawn. It was in August. It was August the ninth to be precise. It was dark and the air was warm and humid. The stars had begun to fade. I should not forget to add that it was North Korea where I arrived and it was 54 years ago. The year was 1951.

There is no need to remind you: at that time, for more than a year, war had been raging over here. By then the various armies had swept through the country twice. First, down from the 38th Parallel to Busan then up to the Yalu, then back again to the 38th Parallel. However, by the summer of 1951 there was an encouraging sign; armistice talks had begun. I had to leave Hungary in a hurry. The North Korean government had asked the so-called "fraternal people's democracies" in Europe to send journalists to be present at the signing of the armistice. It was a matter of prestige to show that not only South Korea but the North, too, would have on its side non-Asian journalists. I left at one day's notice. I was given high boots from a Hungarian military store and while waiting for the connecting flight in Moscow, I bought a new raincoat there. In Beijing I bought one or two notebooks since, in my haste, I had forgotten to bring any from home. I did not want to be late and I was not late. Afterwards I bought many more notebooks and filled them. I stayed for fourteen months but in that time the armistice agreement had still not been signed.

These fourteen months left an indelible mark on my whole life. Now, as I express my thanks to the Daesan Foundation, whose invitation has enabled me to be here in Korea once again and who has given me the opportunity in the twilight of my life to say farewell to this country where I first set foot as a young man of twenty seven, I am a captive of emotions and memories. I am certain that you will understand why I will not go into some abstract theoretical dissertation but will try to describe my experiences, what I saw, what I felt; what this people, this country and this war meant to me. I am hoping for your understanding so much more because I realize that some of this audience, if not most of you, were not yet born or were children at this time and were growing up in a time of peace, although we remember that on this peninsula, peace is fragile. Fortunately, this generation knows the war only from books, films and stories told by parents and grandparents. For them, some interest might be aroused by an account from an old man who came from a distant place and saw this war, this momentous historical event of yours, with his own eyes.

Let us return to the morning of my arrival. After coming from Andun I crossed the Yalu on a Chinese motorized ferry. There was no bridge; it had been destroyed. We had already tried to cross the night before but either the engine was lacking in power or the current was too strong and we were swept downstream. We were glad to be able to return to the Chinese side of the river instead of drowning. On our second attempt we arrived at Sinuiju. By the time I had found the Soviet-made Pobieda car that was to take me to Pyongyang it was daylight and therefore it was not possible to start my journey. Roads in North Korea could only be traveled with a degree of safety at dawn or dusk. This gave no more than two or three hours for travel per day. During daytime American planes flew unhindered over the roads and machine-gunned every vehicle. We travelers could only hope that during the gray hours, before sunrise and after sunset, the planes could not see us and therefore would not shoot us.

After leaving Sinuiju I examined the map. I wanted to know the names of the towns I was traveling through. But the map was useless; it was not a map but a grammar book that was devoted solely to the past tense of the verb "to be". It read something like this: Anju was here, Sinanju was here; this is where Suncheon was. These towns did not exist. It was impossible to tell them apart. There was not one single building that would have shown that I was in one town or another. There were only ruins and after that, more and more ruins. The houses were demolished to ground level. Had they been homes, schools or public buildings? Who knows? It was as if one was not on Earth but on the moon.

Sinuiju is about 150 kilometers from Pyongyang. It took three days to travel the distance. When I was not traveling I stayed in the homes of farmers, remote from the road. When I reached Pyongyang, in normal circumstances I would have been accommodated in a hotel, but in those days in the capital of North Korea, there was not a single hotel to be found. Therefore the Hungarian Embassy became my host. The word "embassy" sounds grand but it was only a large farm building ten or fifteen kilometers from Pyongyang, hidden among tall trees.

From here, in response to an official invitation, I was taken to a place where there was to be a special celebration. It was arranged by the government of the Republic of the Korean People's Democracy on the evening of August 14 because the next day was a national holiday. On my way, I did not see one intact building in Pyongyang but life was busy: crowds, loud voices, hurrying pedestrians, barbers and markets. Stallholders were squatting on raised boards near their merchandise and market-women were down on the ground selling rice, tomatoes and peppers. There were other things for sale, for example, electric motors, rubber boots, wristwatches and fountain pens.

The scene of the celebration was a huge theatre, at the foot of the Marinbon*.To be more accurate, it was not at the foot but was under the mountain. It was very deep, therefore bomb-proof. We had to walk down at least 200 steps. When I arrived in the hall, having passed through underground corridors, Kim Il-sung was already speaking. I could not have been very late because he continued his speech for hours and hours. I did not understand a word of what he said but at least I had the opportunity to observe the audience. There were several hundred people present. The majority were soldiers: generals, officers, representatives of the various branches of the army. The civilians, who were obviously leading functionaries, were all wearing very neat suits. They were a disciplined array, their eyes glued to the speaker. They stood up, sat down, applauded, stood up, sat down and applauded.

During the speech we could hear noise from above. It was like a drumbeat. After Kim Il-sung concluded his speech a singing and dancing group came on. Meanwhile, the drums were beating above. After the dancers' performance everyone in the audience sang the Stalin Cantata: "Stalin is the battle, Stalin is the peace, with Stalin's name the world is built." The drums continued. Then everyone rushed to the buffet-tables which were laden with everything that could ever have been wished for. The people ate and drank. They drank a considerable amount. Somewhere, high above, the drums continued beating. A group of musicians started to play and people danced. Numerous female soldiers had been invited so that there would be no one without a dancing partner. In a more or less drunken state people did not seem to hear the drumbeat up there. Or they did not want to hear it. They knew what the drumbeat was and they could imagine what was happening outside.

When we arrived up from the depths next morning a sight awaited us that exceeded all imagination. The bombing raid of the previous night had been the most extensive yet on Pyongyang. As far as could be seen the streets were strewn with rubble, bricks, pieces of timber, stones, sheet-iron and torn clothing. There were uprooted trees and bomb craters three or four meters wide. Tram tracks were torn up. Booths were flattened where on the day before people had been selling their wares. Injured people were moaning among the ruins and dead bodies were everywhere, the greatest number of them the corpses of women, children and old men, occasionally a soldier in uniform or a policewoman. Some were torn to pieces, some mutilated, some were charred, some with faces in the mud, some with glassy eyes looking upward. There were some whose faces were burnt beyond recognition and some whose fingers were twisted by napalm.

I knew what war was like. I had lived through the Second World War in Budapest. When the front was approaching and the British, American and Soviet planes began to bomb the Hungarian capital, I was sent from my student desk at university to a detachment that had to go to a scene of bombing after each raid. We had to help the wounded and clear the rubble. I had seen much destruction but never like this in Korea. At the end of 1944 the Soviet army encircled Budapest. The fighting was house to house against the German Nazis and their Hungarian hirelings. I saw many corpses, people shot or frozen to death, but never so many as I saw in Pyongyang on that day. Let there be no misunderstanding: in that other war 350 thousand Hungarian soldiers died and 600 thousand Jews were deported to Auschwitz, most of whom perished in gas chambers. Those Jews whom they could not deport in time were shot by the thousands into the icy Danube River by the Hungarian fascists. Therefore I do not wish to say that the Second World War that was spread over three continents, with its several tens of millions of dead and its destruction, was less horrible than the Korean War. For me, however, the difference between the two wars has three reasons. The destruction of homes and buildings was more total in Korea than in any other country. The ratio of death to the total population was also higher. And, last but not least: Here I saw everything with my own eyes.

There was something else that struck me on the morning of August 15, 1951. This was how the women, the old and other survivors were searching through the rubble. They were not looking only for vanished family members or for the wounded but were picking up scraps of clothing, blankets and kitchen utensils. The market-vendors were trying to re-assemble their small tables and were picking up the remnants of their merchandise. There were some who were straightening pieces of sheet iron and others who were removing fallen power poles from the road. I looked at them and thought that these people could have been lying among the dead and it was only a matter of chance that they were alive. I looked at these hungry, dust-covered women who had not slept the night before and who would try, once again, to cook. I looked at the men who once again would trudge hurriedly to underground factories and offices and at the street-vendors who would once again put out onto the side of the road their meager and shoddy merchandise. Then after today or tomorrow, when the bombing would begin again, I wondered which of them would still be alive. At this horrible dawn, right at the beginning of my assignment, I understood that I was walking among people condemned to death and that I was also one of those condemned. If the armistice was not signed at Gaeseong, in a week's or a month's time a bomb might fall on me, exactly as it had on the corpses lying around me. Might I be among those who were bustling about me and had been treated mercifully by blind fate? The bombs would not differentiate me from those others because of the color of my skin, the shape of my eyes and my light-colored hair. And suddenly I felt, simply, that I was one of them. In this country, where life was hard and dying was easy, among the dangers and privation, in the uncertainty of survival, I also became Korean.

"Bihaengi! Bihaengi!" I learned what Koreans knew already, namely that the biggest danger was the airplanes: the fast flying jets and the slowly approaching bombers. I learned – it was not difficult – the particular sound made by each, either screeching or buzzing. Very little practice is needed to attune the ears to distinguish one from the other at a great distance and to immediately feel a growing fear. Anyone who claims he was not frightened is either not telling the truth or is some kind of Superman. The only people in North Korea who were spared that terror were the highest Party and government leaders and the leaders of the army. These people planned military operations, leaning over large maps, living ten, twenty or thirty meters underground, deep in bomb-proof bunkers. They issued their orders by radio or telephone, commanding when to charge the enemy in a death mission. These orders were given by leaders who had the best of food and drink, dutiful attendants and pretty domestics who saw to their every wish. I wonder how many of these leaders died at the front and in bombing raids.

Fifty years have gone by since then but the sound of those jets and bombers has remained in my ears and my nerves. Fortunately for me, it is prohibited for airplanes to fly over Paris where I live. There is only one exception, the national holiday on the Fourteenth of July. Every year there is a military parade on this day and at noon, jets fly over the Champs Elysées. But if I am staying in the countryside in France or elsewhere and if at night, somewhere far away, an airplane is flying, while everyone else is sleeping I wake up with a start. This sound lives so deeply in my being, under my consciousness, that it interrupts my deepest sleep. On these occasions I tremble: is it death approaching? It takes several minutes for me to become quiet and to fall asleep again. I am convinced that in North Korea there are many among the elderly, those more than sixty years of age, who know this experience of waking up in fear. In this they and I are together.

I don't know how many hundreds of pages I wrote in 1951-52 in Pyongyang and Gaeseong, mostly by candlelight. It would take many hours to give an account of even a fraction of my experiences. Besides tragic events, there were pleasant ones, too. I do not intend to misuse your patience, particularly so, because the topic of this international forum is literature and peace. So far I have only talked about the absence of peace, about war. I might explain this by saying that whatever I have said about my war experiences is about peace as well: I have attempted to make you feel how precious peace is. Perhaps it is not an exaggeration to say that only those who have felt on their own skin what war is like can really value peace. As far as literature is concerned, I met all sorts of people in Korea, farmers, factory workers, printers, journalists, teachers, soldiers and politicians; several of each occupation. However, I met only one writer. If I may, I would like to relate one more of my memories and this will be about this man.

After the bombing on August 14 I arrived at Gaeseong where the armistice talks were held. There were two interpreters with the North Korean delegates. The first was a professor of English and German, about fifty years old. The second was his nephew, aged about forty. I don't recall the name of the first interpreter, it started with T or P. The younger one was called Sul Chung-sik. Well, he was the only Korean writer whom I got to know.

In the beginning we exchanged only a few words. On August 23, less than a week after my arrival, the negotiations were suspended. I traveled back to Pyongyang and at the resumption of the talks, two months later, I went back to Gaeseong. This is when I got to know Sul better. A chance circumstance brought us closer to each other. At the beginning of the war each communist country sent some help to North Korea. Hungary sent a hospital, with full equipment, medicine and fifteen or twenty doctors and nursing staff. Sul had a heart attack in December 1950 and was taken to

Chungwa, where the Hungarian hospital was established and that is where he was successfully treated.

When the doctors found out that this person, wearing the uniform of a major, was not a professional soldier but a poet, they encouraged him to resume writing. This was to help in his recuperation. Let him write anything. Of life, death, the beauty of nature, love. Even short poems, but he should work. Sul then wrote a long string of poems, in 400 lines, and it was about the Hungarian hospital.

I wished to read it. I would have liked to have known at least part of it in English but he did not have the poem with him. He had left it in Pyongyang, with many other possessions, mainly his books. A few months later he received a parcel and the manuscript was in it. I promised him that if he translated it into English I would do my best to have it published in Budapest.

Two communist journalists who were in Gaeseong in the service of the Chinese were English speaking. One was British and the other was Australian. Although Sul knew perfect English he prepared the translation with their assistance. Occasionally they argued about a single word for hours and hours. I sent it to Hungary. There a good poet transplanted it to Hungarian. The publisher had a request, namely that I write an article in my newspaper in which I would introduce Sul to his future readers.

So, we talked a lot in those times. He talked about his life for several days. I don't know how well known is he in South Korea these days. I would like to mention only as much as this: his father was a magistrate of the former Yi (Joseon) Dynasty. He was raised on Confucian classics, studied in China, Mukden and Beijing, at the Protestant university in Seoul and then he studied English literature in Ohio, at Mount Union College and in New York at Columbia University. After the liberation of Korea he was employed by the U.S. Military Government. This is when he joined the Communist Party. He left the excellent American job and wrote poems and novels. Some of them were published, some were banned by censorship. He edited newspapers. But when the North Korean army retreated from Seoul he went with them to Pyongyang. His mother, wife and three sons and his only daughter remained in the

South and he had no news about them whatsoever.

This sketch is too brief. For anyone who would like to know more, I recommend reading the excellent study of him by Professor Kim Uchang.

His poem about the Hungarian hospital had poetic beauty as far as his use of adjectives, images and strong picture-creation was concerned but unfortunately it had a great deal of straight politics. It was published in Budapest in an independent volume in December 1952, with the title of "The Epos of Friendship." I sent a copy to him but I did not receive a reply.

In the summer of 1953, during my second trip to Korea, I was certain that we would meet again. Once more I had to hurry so as not to be late for the signing of the armistice. Once again there was no need for haste: in the last phases of the negotiations a conflict emerged about the prisoners of war so I had to sit around for a month in Mukden and Harbin. The Chinese did not allow me to travel further, saying there was still war in Korea and that they were responsible for my life. It was no use telling them that I had been to war before and as a matter of fact, too much war. I was able to continue my travel only at the last minute. I arrived in Panmunjeom at dawn on the day of the signing of the agreement. This was a moving moment in my life: after all, almost two years beforehand I had been there when the first tent was erected, in this unknown village. (The Western press called it "the village of four mud huts"). And now, on July 27, 1953, I was able to be present in the big tent, at the signing of the armistice, the historical occasion that I had lost hope of ever taking place. The armistice was to enter into effect from ten o'clock that evening and I asked to be taken to the nearby front. I wanted to be present, and I was present when the last shots were fired and when the guns fell silent.

In this hectic situation Sul Chung-sik was not at the center of my thoughts, but I noticed that his uncle assisted at the signing and that Sul was not there in the tent. This appeared natural from the point of view of protocol but in the afternoon I started to ask about him. Where was he? His uncle only said that he had been called back to Pyongyang. The two Anglo-Saxon communist journalists remarked that according to their information there was some problem about him.

It did not take long for me to find out what sort of problem it was. Soon after I went back to Pyongyang I was invited, by the Ministry of Information, to a trial of a group of conspirators. I, being a foreign correspondent, was asked to be there and to write about it.

I went. First the judges entered then the accused were brought in by the guards. They wore crumpled convict clothing and each had a number on his back; they were number One to number Fourteen. Number One was Ri Sung-yup, secretary of the Central Committee of the Korean Workers' Party and minister of justice. The last one, Number Fourteen, was Sul Chung-sik.

I hardly recognized him. His beautiful, tormented face was dulled from exhaustion and resignation. He moved like a robot. I was hoping only one thing: that he did not see me.

The interpreter, who was allocated to me, translated the charges: espionage for the American imperialists, terrorism and murder, treason, conspiracy to overthrow the government of the Democratic People's Republic of Korea. I hardly listened. I knew these charges by heart from the Hungarian, Romanian, Bulgarian trials – not to mention the Soviet show trials of the 1930's.

The whole thing seemed absurd and involving Sul Chung-sik in this trial was even more so. What did he have to do with the higher leadership of the communist party? Nothing, obviously. How could he have conspired with these politicians at Pyongyang when he did not set foot out of Gaeseong, and there his every step could have been scrutinized? What could a poet with an ailing heart have spied upon in Gaeseong and Panmunjeom? Why would he become disloyal to North Korea when he left Seoul for Pyongyang at his own free will? When he even left his family behind and exposed himself to all the risks of the war?

I am convinced that the whole trial was a single lie. The dictator of North Korea, Kim Il-sung, in the same way as his fellow European communist leaders, wanted to eliminate those whom he considered his rivals, first of all those who became Party and government leaders and had come from the South. Sul Chung-sik was but an unfortunate extra in this diabolic stage show: he had studied at American universities; he had a job for a while with the U.S. Military Government. All this sounded excellent and it went down very well with simple folk, it counted as proof for them. It is not impossible that among his thirteen fellow-accused there were many whom he did not even know. In the European show-trials, too, there were persons accused with conspiracy who saw each other for the first time at their trial.

I did not go to the second day of the trial. I was unable to write a report on the so-called conspiracy. I found out only much later, from newspapers back in Hungary, that all the accused were executed. Sul Chung-sik, one of the most original and most talented poets of Korea, was one of them.

Our topic, ladies and gentlemen, is "Writing for Peace". I related the story of a writer who died. Died for what? We could say for peace, after all, Sul Chung-sik was convinced that with his communist belief, with his "Epos of Friendship," he served peace and the unification of Korea. He believed that the opposite side had to be forced to their knees for the sake of peace. In the meantime he was devoured by his own side. This was his fate.

Anyone could say that this was not the typical fate of a writer and he would be right, though Sul was not the only writer who became a victim of dictators. In the Soviet Union and in the People's Democracies thousands of writers and artists died the death of martyrdom or suffered in various Gulags. There is a similar situation, still today, in certain countries in Latin America, Asia and Africa. The fate of Sul Chung-sik, the poet, even though not typical, shows something. It shows how impotent and defenseless an intellectual can be against might, power and politics.

There are counter-examples, too. The influence of the Mind has proven to be stronger, not only in the long run but also in the short term, than arms or the strength of despotism. The most shining example was perhaps the story of the 18th century, leading to the French Revolution. Would absolute monarchy have fallen, would the oppressed masses have gained human rights, could the social order have become more just without Voltaire, Rousseau, Diderot or Beaumarchais? A hundred years later Victor Hugo fought his battle in exile, from a small island, against Napoleon III – the Little

Napoleon – and won.

There was great intellectual enthusiasm against tyranny and the various forms of fascism between the two world wars, too. Malraux and Orwell took to arms to fight in Spain where Federico Garcia Lorca became a victim, just as Sul Chung-sik in Korea, though he became the victim of his enemies and not of his comrades. The Frenchman Julien Benda, with his book that he wrote well before the Second World War, *La Trahison des clercs* (The Treason of Intellectuals) warned the world about dangers lurking. Thomas Mann emigrated from Nazi Germany and he repeated this warning, even more so in the literal sense of the word and more acutely than Benda in his work "Achtung Europa" (Attention, Europe!).

Let us not fool ourselves. These warnings in the last century might have made successful books but they had precious little influence on events. Later on, even the writers' voices became silent. I am thinking back to the Korean War. There were so many world famous writers around. Among others, and mentioning them at random, there was Hemingway, Dos Passos, Steinbeck, Maugham, Evelyn Waugh, T.S. Eliot, W.H. Auden, Dylan Thomas, Graham Greene, Sean O'Casey, Thomas Mann, Brecht, Malraux, Camus, Mauriac, Ionesco. I do not know of a single one of them who raised his voice against the Korean War. (Perhaps Sartre, but only to the effect that at this time he was getting close to the communist "peace movement" which had the hypocritical slogan "Hands off Korea". It was, of course, the Americans' hands in question, not those of the Russians and Chinese.) Korea, a country with a history and culture of several thousand years, was in ruins, the children of an ancient nation were hungry and cold. Millions died and the best known and most prestigious writers of the world were mute. The fact that the guns became silent was not due to the effort of writers, artists and scientists but to the death of one person, Stalin.

I have not noticed any improvement in the situation in the past 50 years. How many writers raised their voices against events in Cambodia or in the Yugoslav republics? And if there had been someone to do so, how large an audience could he have counted on? Truly, let us not fool ourselves about the role of writers. This role is very much diminished compared with the 18th and 19th centuries and even in comparison to the first half of the 20th century. Today, when international organizations look for an artist to raise money for starving children or to create publicity against land mines they look for an actor or a rock star, not a writer. Did this happen because we, the writers, in contrast to our predecessors, have become indolent and indifferent about the world's fate? Or did this happen because in the age of global culture, the world wide web of mass-communication and contemporary technology enables movie stars and glamorous singers to influence people's imaginations more effectively than the words and works of writers? Probably both reasons are true.

We have but one weapon, the word. This Forum may be one of the last opportunities, if not the very last, to see if there is a point in raising our voices. (In the case of writers this decision can only be, naturally, an individual one). If the reply happens to be "yes," then those who respond this way should decide whether they will take up this task. Do they undertake to give a simple, perhaps simplistic reply to the question: do they stand for democracy or dictatorship? For peace or for war? Having decided, do they have sufficient resolution to raise their voice, individually and collectively?

Seoul would be an especially appropriate place for speaking out. Today Korea is a unique country, in several aspects. Of those three countries that were split in two after World War II, two have been reunified, namely Vietnam and Germany. Korea is the remaining one where the same people and same culture are divided in half. This is an unnatural situation. This cannot last forever. There are two ways of reunification, namely the German way or a blood-filled Vietnamese way. Korea has tried one of these ways, the bloody one. We know the result. Only madmen would want to repeat this. The only solution is the one resembling the German example, namely peaceful reunification.

Something emerges here which makes Korea stand out once more as a unique country. The leaders of the United States listed the Northern part of this country, together with Iraq and Iran, as the "Axis of Evil." Out of the three, Korea is the only one where one half belongs to the Good and the other half to Evil. Moreover, North

Korea does not deny that it can develop nuclear weapons but it is even boasting about it. Therefore the Korean Peninsula has an additional reason for being a singular place: here war could break out any time, nuclear war, to boot. Just like fifty years ago, here everyone is potentially condemned to death.

Would it not be natural for the cry for peace to come from where the danger can be the greatest? For this reason I would like to suggest that we, the participants of this forum, draft and publish a manifesto to the world's conscience. Let us make a stand with this Seoul Peace Manifesto against the wars ravaging in the world and demand a quick ending to them. Let us demand effective nuclear disarmament by the nuclear powers and demand that no additional countries have nuclear weapons. Let us demand that every nation be able to decide its own destiny.

I am not naïve and I do not believe that a manifesto like this would change the destiny of the world. But if there is sufficient moral strength, if a possibility for organizing is behind it and if it receives patronage from the Daesan Foundation, then – together with other movements – perhaps it can be broadened and it would not remain ineffective. Whether it is successful or not, it would mean for us, for those who are gathered here, satisfaction that we not only talked but also tried to do something.

Translated by Christine and William Hyde

*Copy editor's note: There is no Marinbon Mountain in North Korea. The author may be confused with Kalinbong, the peak of Myohyangsan, a famous mountain near Pyongyang. In Korean, the pronunciation could sound like Marinbon.

The Search for Reconciliation and Peace on the Korean Peninsula[1]: The Case of Hwang Seok-young's *Guests*

Paik Nak-chung

1.

It is a proposition worth reiterating that overcoming of the "division system" in Korea is not quite the same thing as simply overcoming Korea's division. The latter will be true even of a reunification that devastates the whole peninsula or, while short of war, still proves calamitous to its population, but such a reunification cannot be our goal. We must aim at a unity that results in a better human society than the existing division[2] system.

Yet the reality of the Korean Peninsula is such that we can neither build a decent society of reconciliation and peace while maintaining the division, nor likely achieve reunification by mobilizing the warlike and repressive characteristics of the division system. For any attempt at unification by force will surely lead to war involving nuclear weapons as well; while a project, as in Germany, of "unification by absorption" under the aegis of the establishment interests, would either provoke armed resistance and end up with a nuclear war, or result in chaos and a precipitous decline in Korea's global standing almost equally catastrophic. In this sense, there seems to be little possibility, either, that actual overcoming of division can be any other than overcoming of the division system.

The abolition, rather than amelioration, of a system signifies a

1) In rendering the Korean original into English, I have exercised an author's prerogative and translated with some freedom, cutting or adding details so as to make the text more accessible to English-speaking readers.

2) For an account in English of the sui generis nature of Korea's division, see my "Habermas on National Unification in Germany and Korea," New Left Review 219 (September/October 1996); also Paik Nak-chung, "Coloniality in Korea and a South Korean Project for Overcoming Modernity," interventions Vol. 2 No. 1 (2000), esp. 76-78.

kind of revolution. But in the case of Korea's division system, its overcoming can only be peaceful and long-term, and consequently is in danger of stopping short of real overcoming. Thus, it requires a project of originality and innovativeness far exceeding any revolutionary or reformist strategy in an undivided nation if it is to embrace the possibly oxymoronic "peaceful revolution" or "long revolution" and still achieve a systemic transformation in the shortest possible time, defying the lures of halfway solutions.

Precisely for this reason special stress is placed on the role of a truly creative literature in the process of overcoming the division system. Of course, art has an important role both in the agitation and propaganda of a revolutionary period and in the cultural development of a stable society, but the peaceful yet transformative task of overcoming the division system, more than other historical tasks, calls for the exploration and implementation of the most advanced consciousness and wisdom. I made a similar point in an earlier essay, "The Reunification Movement and Literature" (1989):

> The creative role of literature is vital both in promoting … self-criticism and self-renewal among intellectuals and in activating minjung power. Of course, this is not the exclusive preserve of literature, nor is it the role of our literature alone. But unless Korea's reunification movement is a creative movement of the highest order, it will be difficult to succeed in its aim of overcoming this unprecedented system of division, under which nevertheless both north and south, while being exceptionally brutal and rigid, have borne their respective fruits, to the surprise of the rest of the world. The reunification movement must be pursued as a creative art, so to speak, and all reunification activists must become artists—artists of history-making. Only as one branch of this art can Korean literature bloom to the full; but if the art of the national tongue fails to do its part, it will be vain to expect artists of historical action to turn out for duty without fail.[3)]

3) Paik Nak-chung, "The Reunification Movement and Literature," tr. Kenneth M. Wells, in K. Wells, ed., South Korea's Minjung Movement: The Culture and Politics of Dissidence, University of Hawaii Press 1995, 206-7, (translation slightly revised.)

If we read "the movement to overcome the division system" for "the reunification movement," we may say that demands for the creative role of literature have become even more urgent today.

Literature that contributes in this sense to the overcoming of the division system need not be "division literature" as classified by the subject matter. Even when treating subjects apparently unrelated to territorial partition, national division, or interference by foreign powers, it is sufficient if the work inspires a new awakening and creative response to the current reality dominated by the division system. All the same, Korean literature would hardly be rising to its historic responsibilities if there were no work at all that, based on a knowledge of realities in both north and south, directly addressed problems arising from division. As a matter of fact, the situation that hampers writers of each side to explore the reality across the Armistice Line is precisely one of the conditions enabling the division system to survive to this day.

These restrictions are gradually being loosened with the expansion in legally authorized civilian exchanges between north and south. Thanks to such developments Korean literature, even before the June 15 Joint Declaration (by Kim Dae-Jung and Kim Jong-Il) of 2000, could show a distinguished achievement like Ko Un's verse collection *South and North*.[4)] Not only has the author traveled in both north and south and composed the poems "with the aim of producing a collection that would be read by people on both sides,"[5)] but has in my view actually come up with a volume that would continue to be read even after reunification. But as virtually implied in Choi Won-sik's praise that "if Ko Un's *Ten Thousand Lives* is a glorification [*avatamska*] of people, his *South and North* is a glorification of the land,"[6)] the world of this collection is quite sparsely populated and

4) Ko Un, Nam gwa puk (Seoul: Changbi Publishers, 2001).

5) Ko Un, op. cit., 'Afterword', 253. All translations are mine unless otherwise indicated.

6) Choi Won-sik, "Nawa uri, geurigo sesam: tongil sidae-ui munhak" [Me and us: literature in the age of reunification], Munhak-ui kwihwan [The Return of Literature], Changbi 2001. Characterizing South and North as "the finest collection of verse our age has produced," he goes on to remark, "Even so, his poetry should become more complex. I would like to see a fuller poetic texture which is naturally obtained as the complexity of the process of embodying the ineffable insight and epigrammatic pithiness is brought to agree with the inherent artistic logic of a given work." (Ibid., 85)

gives only a subdued expression to the turbulent conflicts of the age of division. No doubt this accords with the author's intention, but we may also assume that a visit of fifteen days (though longer than average for an ordinary visitor) was not enough for composing a volume of "glorification of the land" that amounted to "a glorification of people" as well; and a certain self-censorship peculiar to authorized visitors may also have come into play.

In that regard, Hwang Seok-young, who since his first unauthorized visit to North Korea in 1989 has probably seen more of the north than any South Korean writer and has paid for it with exile and imprisonment, enjoys a special vantage ground. On that basis, and at a time when that ground was further strengthened by the Pyongyang summit and the Joint Declaration of June 2000, his novel *Guests*[7)] was published. If only because it deals with the North Korean scene (albeit focused mainly on brief periods after the Liberation from Japanese rule and during the Korean War) on the scale of a novel, it deserves special attention in the course of seeking reconciliation and peace in Korea and overcoming the division system.

2.

Not that exploration of a new subject matter could be the main reason why *Guests* deserves our attention. Far more important, the author examines, through his uncovering of the truth regarding the massacre of civilians in Sincheon in North Korea's Hwanghae Province during the Korean War, the process of formation and the constitutive elements of the division system, and evinces in the work a strong wish for "laying to rest by means of this *gut*

7) [Hwang Seok-young], *Sonnim* (Changbi 2001). To my knowledge there is as yet no English edition*; only a French version, Hwang Seok-young, *L'Invité*, tr. Choi Mikyung et Jean-Noël Juttet (Zulma, 2004); and a Japanese one, *Kyakujin (Sonnimu)*, tr. Chung Kyungmo, Iwanami Shoten 2004. All quotations are my translations, and page references, given in parentheses within the main text, are to the Korean and French [abbreviated as F] editions respectively. Unlike the French translators, I have chosen to render the title in the plural, as *Guests*; for what the author has chiefly in mind are the pair of opposing ideologies, Christianity and Marxism, not the fact that Rev. Ryu Yoseop is a visitor in North Korea. (The French title also seems less than felicitous in that both Christianity and Marxism are perceived in this novel as *uninvited* guests; perhaps *Les visiteurs* would have been a better choice. The quotations will also show other divergences between the French version and mine).

(shamanic ritual) performance the war wounds and the specters of the Cold War that still remain on the Korean Peninsula, and of starting a new century of reconciliation and mutual life-giving" ("Author's Words" 262).[8)]

Neither the "Author's Words" nor the novel itself employs the expression "the division system". But I believe there is much in common with that notion in Hwang's pursuit of "a new century of reconciliation and mutual life-giving." North Korea's official position on the Sincheon massacre defines it as "a nefarious crime of the American imperialist aggressors" (90, F 100). Generalizing further, it holds that "our division is basically due to foreign powers; the Japanese and American imperialists have caused this situation" (96, F 105), which does not give sufficient recognition to the internal factors that have enabled the division to set into a kind of system.

Pointing to the responsibility of foreign powers does make sense when applied to the partition of the country in 1945. But the process of the division's solidifying since the Armistice (1953) and its formation of a relatively stable structure that could justifiably be termed a *system* of division has involved various acts of the Koreans themselves, including acts of mutual killing during the war. *Guests*, which reveals that the Sincheon massacre, unlike Pyongyang's official version, was committed chiefly by right-wing Christians, represents the insight that precisely such internal elements went into the construction of the division system and have kept it in existence to this day. It also foregrounds the fact that true reconciliation calls for an effort to ascertain the truth for oneself, unfettered by the official propaganda of either north or south.

The novel, however, is not a one-sided denunciation of the Christians. As a number of critics have pointed out and the author himself states, the "guests" of the title points not so much to the fact that Rev. Ryu Yoseop (or Joseph), a U.S. resident, is visiting North Korea and in that sense is a guest, as that both Marxism and Christianity represent "the modernity that has been imposed on us as we failed to achieve autonomous modernization" (Author's

---

8) The French edition does not include the "Author's Words."
*Copy editor's note: There is now an English version: Hwang Seok-young, The Guest (Seven Stories Press, 2005)

Words 261), hence "two branches from a single root" (262), so that the author "designated Christianity and Marxism as 'guests' … with a view to the fact that ordinary people of pre-modern Korea, conceiving the smallpox as a Western disease and calling it *mama* or *sonnim* (guest[s]) in the hope of guarding against it, produced a form of shamanic performance called *sonnim-gut*." (Ibid.)

At the same time, it is important that the work does not strike a mechanical balance and blames Christians and Marxists equally. Christians themselves are not uniformly portrayed in a negative light, but particularly in the case of Marxism, Hwang faithfully renders the positive and emancipatory functions it exercised in Korean society. This is a worthy achievement in a writer living in the southern half where anti-Communist ideology is still dominant. As many critics have observed, the novel demonstrates that there was a material basis for the adoption of Marxism in Korea.

In fact, both right and left commit atrocities in *Guests*, but at least in Chansaem, Rev. Ryu's home village and the main scene of the novel's action, we can "sense no sign of madness" in the main left-wing characters, as critic Hong Sung-yong observes.[9)] Indeed, Ri Sun-nam and Bak Il-lang are moving figures. The specter of Sun-nam, from the moment it comes to Yoseop together with the latter's elder brother Yohan (John), displays a shrewdness, balanced perspective, and admirable humanity.

> To be frank, didn't your father Elder Ryu In-deok and grandfather Pastor Ryu Sam-seong serve as estate agents for the Japanese colonizers and so come into possession of your fields and orchards? Most of the others who attended Gwangmyeong Church also had lands of their own more or less and didn't have to worry about feeding themselves. … Such people formed most of the members of the Committee for Founding the Nation and went by the respectable name of 'the nationalist camp'. (125, F 137-38)[10)]

---

9) Hong Sung-young, "Mirae -ui jogeon" (The condition for the future), *Jinbo pyeongron*, Summer 2002, 223-34.

10) Much of the novel's dialogue and many of the first-person narrations, including Sun-nam's quoted here, are in the dialect of Hwanghae Province, which Hwang renders with extreme vividness, but which I make no attempt to reproduce.

I am not saying there were no problems on the left, either. Calling themselves communists, they had so many factions, a clodhopper like me couldn't tell which was which. (125, F 138)

You [Yohan's ghost] have said it well. In the Sinuiju uprising both sides were at fault. There are plenty of opportunists in turbulent times who run about on either left or right. (126, F 139)

The poor peasants and masses were, so to speak, these misshapen pots produced by Japanese imperialists. Wasn't it our class position to value them and start with them? You, on the other hand, were all for shattering them. (128, F 142)

And as is revealed later on, Sun-nam dies with dignity, having decided out of love for his family not to run away by himself.

The story of Bak Il-lang, the head of the village People's Committee who used to be a servant laborer and had all his life been known only by the Japanese name "Ichiro," is mostly told by others like Sun-nam and Yohan, except for the scenes of his capture and death toward the end. Yohan targeted him with special hatred because he had used violence against Yohan's parents, his former masters, but his transformation as recounted by his long-time intimate Sun-nam makes the readers reflect on the true meaning of liberation.

Just imagine. This Ichiro you all addressed familiarly and considered a fool with nothing in his head had come to know how to read. He could write his name, Bak Il-lang. Isn't this what liberation is supposed to be? While you guys were eating white rice, sleeping under warm covers, and taking lessons in schools so you could read the Bible and pray and sing hymns in churches, Comrade Il-lang who would be schlepping wood bundles and working like an ox had managed to read and write the words 'land reform'. (138, F 153)

Il-lang is dragged away with a wire run through his nose and dies an atrocious death, burned in a gasoline fire along with others who were confined in an air-raid bunker. But his last narration is deeply impressive with its genuine pride and advancing consciousness:

> Ah, yes, throughout my life with not even a family or given name, I, Ichiro, labored and labored with my back always bent, yet for the past several years it's been worthwhile. ...
>
> I have never hated anybody in my life. On some special day when they would give out a big bowlful of rice, I would keep on digging the field so they shouldn't call me a good-for-nothing. But when I saw my family being killed before my eyes, I knew: you are no better than an animal unless you've woken up inside yourself. (224-35, F 247)

In the background of such authorial sympathy with characters like Sun-nam and Il-lang lies the recognition that the question of land reform above all else constituted the key agenda and the focus of conflict in their time. As Yohan's ghost recounts the tremendous shock of having the land confiscated (123-24, F 136), the beginning of the "madness" lay precisely there. (It was in the course of demanding that Yohan's father give up the land that Il-lang came to hit him in the face.) This point, too, has been made by a number of critics, among whom Yi Chaeyeong, noting that "not the repression against Christianity but the land reform provided the decisive occasion for the massacre of the population,"[11)] concludes that "the choice of Guests as the title of this work does not seem to correspond to its actual content."[12)]

We probably need not take such a conclusion as a negative criticism. A title that does not accurately summarize the content could add to the attractions of a work. Only, the author's own words telling how he "designated Christianity and Marxism as 'guests'" (262) do involve a certain danger of limiting the work's relevance; perhaps this is another instance where we should trust the tale rather than the artist. If we look at the work itself, there is indeed

11) Yi Chaeyeong, *"Chinsil kwa hwahae: Sonnim ron"* (Truth and reconciliation: On Guests), in *Hwang Seok-young ui munhak segye* [The world of Hwang Seok-young's work], ed. Choi Won-sik and Im Hong-bae, Changbi 2003, 109.

12) Ibid. 114.

corroboration of the "Author's Words" in the protest by Yoseop's great-grandmother: "You deserve the name of a human being only if you properly respect your ancestors. This country has gone to the dogs because we worship spirits of foreigners" (39, F 45); and again, "they would tell me the smallpox was originally a Western disease, that it came from the barbarians of the West. Isn't it clear it came from countries where they believe in the Western evil spirits?" (43, F 50) But whether, taken in their dramatic context, that these remarks legitimately apply to the ideology behind land reform as well as to Christianity is by no means clear.

The contending theoretic claims of the "guests" and the land question as the primary cause are further complicated by the presence of An Seong-man, Yoseop's maternal uncle. He is a devout Christian but also supports land reform: "It was good even in light of Jesus' life that the poor were given land and enabled not to starve. It was proper, too, that landless peasants came to possess lands previously owned by churches and temples" (176, F 194-95). But while his criticism of "new learning" has something in common with the notion of the "guests," it does not postulate a dichotomy of the indigenous vs. the foreign.

> I think at that time we were immature on both sides. We needed to grow up more and realize that human affairs were complicated and called for much more mutual understanding. As far as affairs on this earth are concerned, the main thing after all was to labor hard with a full respect to material things and to share them equitably so as to enjoy them together. Only if such justice is done can your faith as regards heaven be honorable. It was less than a full generation since we had accepted either Protestantism or socialism as new learning, and on each side there were only zealots who had forgotten about the ways of human living that had gone on from the old days. (176, F 195)

The implication is that, given more time and effort, the 'guests' could have settled down as "hosts," and the way to reconciliation of Marxism and Christianity is left open as he finds material equality and social justice agreeing with both "Jesus' life" and socialism.

Only the general immaturity that prevented the realization of this possibility gave rise to the madness and murder.[13)] Here we find another reminder that we need a complex vision of both the internal and external factors that have gone into the formation and reproduction of the division system.

3.

But what kind of response to actual reality would have resulted from a more mature understanding of human affairs? Starting from a fundamental recognition of the legitimacy and practical necessity of land reform, what kind of agrarian policy, for instance, would have done justice to "the ways of human living that had gone on from the old days"? The policy of "confiscation with compensation and distribution for value" later adopted by South Korea would have failed to meet the needs of most peasants and fallen short of social justice. Yet the "confiscation with compensation and free distribution" not only would have overburdened state finance, but would have still left the question unanswered as to the precise level of compensation—or the precise range of uncompensated confiscation—that might have succeeded in both mitigating the landowners' resistance and carrying out an effective reform.

Of course, it isn't incumbent upon An Seong-man to answer that question—nor on Hwang Seok-young, either. It is enough if an author through his work raises the right questions in good faith and makes the reader think for oneself. But it is part of the good faith that his raising questions should be so passionate and thorough that the reader cannot rest content with answers that are not real answers. If we are to criticize Seong-man's pronouncements in *Guests*, it is not that they fail to amount to correct answers, but that Seong-man is portrayed like a man who has arrived at correct answers to most questions in life.

13) The madness in the novel isn't uniform, either. As the incidents in the town of Chaeryeong demonstrates, both sides fell victim to madness, yet the main left-wing characters in Sincheon, as indicated above, remained free of it. In the case of right-wing youth group, too, we may observe a distinction between the early days when, though enflamed with a sense of the Holy Ghost entering them and full of hatred for the Satan, they still maintained a certain discipline, and the final stage when, according to Yohan's own account, they "were no longer crusaders crushing the Satan" (246, F 269).

The novel clearly shows that Seong-man's has not been an easy life. But by the time Yoseop comes to him, all his conflicts are over and he has in his way achieved reconciliation. Referring to the day when the Sincheon massacres reached their height, he says, "I almost abandoned my God. The following night came to shake terribly fifty years of my faith" (210, F 231), but he gives no account what he saw that night nor any further mention of the trials he subsequently went through as a believer. It is not out of character that in talking to his nephew he should be reticent about his inner life, but the writer could easily have chosen to convey it, say, in the form of silent recollection.

Though a pastor's son and recipient of infant baptism, Seong-man, who even as a youth was more drawn to (the presumably non-Christian) Gang seonsaeng and furthermore experienced that 'fiery hell' during the war, must have needed a rare spiritual experience in order to remain a Christian to this day. Conflict with a communist system, too, must have been considerable. But the friction caused, for example, by his insistence on observing the Sabbath while on duty at the iron factory of Hwangju is resolved all too smoothly thanks to the enlightened attitude of the director (178-82, F 197-201). In short, he is now living as both a Christian and a party member highly regarded by the authorities, a man who has lived through all sorts of tribulations in a long life, and as such can pronounce authoritative statements such as: "We needed to grow up more and realize that human affairs were complicated and called for much more mutual understanding," or, regarding the visits of the specters, "Maybe because the world is ripe for a change, their appearances have recently become quite frequent. … It shows time is ripe for those who went through those events. I mean it's ready for them. So—they appear for their salvation" (174-75, F 193), and, after they have gone, "Those that are to go away must go away; now the living must start their life anew" (251, F 276).

It is not easy to date exactly these scenes where "time is ripe." Seong-man, who is reported to have been thirty-five about the time of Liberation in 1945, says he is eighty-five now, which should make the year of Yoseop's visit 1995.[14)] On the other hand, if we take his "fifty years of my faith" literally, the time would be more like 2000 or thereabouts, when Hwang was writing the novel and the Pyongyang summit meeting took place—a date more becoming as a time of change. But whether 1995 or 2000, it would postdate the death of the North Korean leader Kim Il-Sung (1994), yet the novel provides no indication of the fact. We may find this vagueness regarding the time appropriate in a work that, while utilizing memories from the author's visits in 1989 and 1990, also intends to embrace the spirit of "a new century of reconciliation and mutual life-giving." It must be judged a technical flaw, however, that, by specifying Seong-man's age as eighty-five, the novel invites readers to conjecture the precise date.

It is due to flaws like this that the reconciliation portrayed by *Guests* comes across as, in the words of one critic, "somewhat sudden and forced."[15] This is not, if I may repeat myself, to demand a concrete alternative or answer from either the author or a given character, but to insist on the need to scrutinize the artistic realization that is to ensure the importance and intensity of the work's questions.

I have noted that Yoseop's uncle Seong-man had virtually achieved reconciliation prior to his meeting with his nephew, but in fact Yoseop's sister-in-law presents a similar case. Regarding the harsh and harrowing years she must have suffered through as wife of the murderous reactionary Yohan, a wife moreover abandoned by her husband the moment she had given birth to a son, the white-

14) The fact that Seong-man is mentioned as being "less than forty" in October 1950 when the massacre took place would in that case either represent a minor error or indicate that, born in 1911, he was then less than forty and had been thirty-four in 1945, i.e., thirty-five only by the Korean (and East Asian) way of counting.

15) See Cho Seongmyeon, "Ch'ŏnch'ing, kwangki ŭi yŏksa wa haewon ŭi riŏlijm" [An insane history and realism of resolving grudges], Chakkadŭl, Winter 2001, 324: "The ending where Yohan, Sun-nam, Il-lang and so many aggrieved spirits are presented as having achieved deliverance together after only affirming their different positions and showing no other conflict among themselves, and where all their tense antagonisms and past wounds are brought to a close with only a recitation of a portion of the jinogwi gut (shamanic ritual of appeasing the dead), is too unreal and amounts to a letdown." The same critic, however, proceeds to argue that this is not so much a fault in the work as indicative of "our remaining tasks": "For, to be frank, what other way and option can there be for us? In a sense, the very demand for and expectation of a meaningful alternative or perspective is a delusion. Shouldn't we be looking for a way to reconciliation and mutual life-giving even in such an inadequate manner as the novel's? The rather sudden and forced reconciliation at the end, which can be interpreted as lack of alternative and perspective, is not the author's limitation alone but that of all of us, a phenomenon inevitably imposed by current historical reality." (214)

haired sister-in-law (who must be over eighty-five since she is Seong-man's elder sister) offers only a single quiet remark: "Remaining here alone as a culprit—having lost the daughters because I wasn't able to feed them properly, and living with that single surviving child [her son Danyeol (Daniel)], I kept thinking: God, too, is guilty." (152, F 170) But she also managed to come to terms with such a life before Yoseop's arrival.

> "I used to think God, too, was guilty because he remained silent while looking down on those hellish scenes. But recently I came to change my mind. It's a long time since I read the Bible. I've forgotten most of it. But I do remember Job. ... As a matter of fact, everybody is born into the world with his share of suffering. All those your brother killed had souls. They weren't devils. Ryu Yohan wasn't a devil, either. Only his faith was distorted. Now I know God isn't guilty."
>
> "What is your wish now, sister?"
>
> "I hardly have any wish. Maybe peace on earth and glory in heaven, something like that. Even though the world may be full of evils, those of us living should go on living by working to remove them." (153, F 170-71)

And when Yoseop has finished his brief sermon, she murmurs to herself, "I already knew it..." (155, F 173)

Seen in this context, Yoseop's receiving from her Yohan's clothes with which the newborn baby had been wrapped and later burying them along with Yohan's remains is no more than a ratification of the peace she had achieved on her own. Potentially more controversial is her remark, "There is no such thing as God of Israel or God of Korea. God is simply God" (157, F 174), for it sounds like a refutation of Il-lang's dying cry, "Believe in the God of Korea!" (17, F 22)[16] But this remark, too, is only given out as a sign of the sister-in-law's recovery of faith through her meeting with Yoseop, and does not lead to any serious exploration of the conflict and possible reconciliation between "God of Korea and simply God," or between "God of Koreans and God of Americans."

Probably the decisive reason for the less than fully convincing nature of the reconciliation in *Guests* is because Rev. Ryu Yoseop himself, who returns to his native village for the purpose of apology and reconciliation, does not experience any serious new conflict in the course of the visit. The initial discord and embarrassment upon meeting his nephew Danyeol are soon worked out with little real problem. More importantly, Yoseop is in possession of the main facts of the Sincheon events before he undertakes the journey, and has more or less settled views regarding them. When he visited his brother for the last time and held a prayer service, he preached, "Jesus taught love and peace. Those who have remained in our native village and have possession of it, I repeat, have souls like us. We must repent first" (15, F 18); and, upon meeting Danyeol, tells him, "In those days we hated and killed each other. But those people, too, are passing away, one by one. If we don't forgive each other, we'll never be able to meet again." (94, F 104)

The accuracy of his diagnosis is another matter. For instance, this is his answer to the nephew's protest, why did he have to come and rake up bygone matters:

> "There is an old proverb about how it begins with pulling out a hair and ends up with killing somebody. Also, they say it takes two hands to clap. It wasn't some others who committed those crimes, it was us—those of us who had lived amicably in the same village."
>
> "The superstitious wretches did it, I am told."
>
> "No, it was Satan who did it."
>
> "Which evil spirit is that one, now?"
>
> Rev. Ryu Yoseop answered, "It is something dark that always accompanies us in our hearts." (116, F 126-27)

16) This cry is repeated later in Il-lang's first-person account of the same scene (214, F 235). The French edition renders the two remarks differently: "C'est aux dieux de la Corée qu'il faut croire…"; and later, "Croit plutôt au dieu de Chosun!" The second is obviously correct, although even here "dieu" should be rendered in the upper case to indicate the God of Christianity, who, it is being urged by Il-lang and elsewhere by a party cadre (190, F 210), needs to become rooted in the reality of Korea (or Chosun). It must be noted, however, that the cadre's remark on God is rendered still differently by the French version: "Même si vous êtes croyant, vous devez prendre le parti du people. Ce qui veut dire qu'il faut croire aux dieux des Coréens, pas à celui des Américains." But the admonition to believe in "the gods of Koreans" would agree neither with Seongman's remaining Christian (which is being assumed) nor with the Party's policy of eradicating native superstitions.

The statement that it was us and not some others undoubtedly comes closer than the official propaganda of "the crimes of American imperialists" to the truth as the novel presents it. But it focuses almost exclusively on domestic factors, and is liable to the charge of blaming the victim and the victimizer in equal measure. His gloss on Satan derives from his somewhat idiosyncratic view of God and salvation which, after reading from the Book of Job for his sister-in-law, he expounds in his short sermon: "This passage shows that the Almighty and All-knowing God, too, is a Being who has internal conflict like us. To say so isn't sacrilege. God becomes a perfect Being only through the faith and decision of human beings" (155, F 172). This thought offers a sharp rebuke to the habits of demonizing other people, but also runs the danger of making vague and abstract the real conflicts *between* human beings such as those surrounding land redistribution.

Perhaps a statement like this by Yoseop works to draw attention to the limitations of a character born into the landowner's class and currently residing in America as a Christian minister. The author's question, "Now I look at it, isn't the U.S. as a matter of fact still the really fearful 'guest'?" (262), hardly seems adequately realized in the novel itself, but could it have been his intention to bring in the problem of the U.S. by noting the limitations in Yoseop's thinking? In order to succeed in such a project, however, not only should the work show a greater distance between the author and the character, but Yoseop should have been delineated as a character who, as the rest of the story unfolds, is brought to face his own limitations, experiences certain inner changes through which some of those limitations are overcome, and so helps open the way to a genuine reconciliation.

To the contrary, the problem in the characterization of Yoseop seems precisely to result from lack of authorial distance. Despite the fact that Rev. Ryu Yoseop is quite a different person than the writer Hwang Seok-young, he often functions—as do his uncle and sister-in-law—as a device to convey what the author's own message to the reader. Moreover, the implicit projection of the author's own patently different circumstances in the representation of the character's sojourn in North Korea tends to diminish the reality of the work. To cite an obvious example, the North Korean authorities not only grants him permission to visit his home village, for which he had not applied beforehand, but also many other privileges as well. This cannot be explained merely by the Party's expectation that Yoseop, a pastor in the U.S., would "work actively for the reunification of the fatherland" (117, F 128). It would have been quite different with Hwang Seok-young, the renowned South Korean writer who had braved the Natural Security Law to come north: granting him extraordinary privileges would have been natural enough, and plausible, too, would be the expectation that, on a visit to his native Sincheon, he would be impressed by and help to publicize the crimes of Americans. But what chance was there that Ryu Yoseop, who as a boy of fourteen had been an eyewitness to the scene, would come to agree with the Party's propaganda line by visiting the museum in Sincheon or the site of massacre in Wonam-ri and by talking to surviving relatives?

In terms of characterization Yohan is a far superior achievement. He is a criminal who murdered not only the activists on the other side but the unarmed and innocent girl soldiers and, at the last moment, the mother and six younger sisters of his friend's fiancée; and, even in the final phone conversation with Yoseop, yells at him, "Why should I ask for forgiveness? We were a crusading army. The Reds were children of Lucifer. Satan's host. I was on the side of Archangel Michael and they were the beasts of the Apocalypse" (22, F 26). But by the time the narrative of Guests is over, we come to agree with his wife's remark, "Ryu Yohan wasn't a devil, either," and to accept him as a human being.

That he must have committed heinous acts is implied at the very beginning of the novel in Yoseop's dreams, and in the first of his first-person narrations he reveals, albeit fragmentarily, that he had dragged away Ichiro by a telephone wire run through the nose or, of Sun-nam, "I do away with him that winter" (20, F 24). When the full story of his atrocities is at last revealed in Chapter 8, they quite boggle the mind. But it isn't a story of unmitigated inhumanity, either. Against Il-lang, it was quite a studied revenge, but the killing of Sun-nam, although hanging him on a wire didn't lead to a quick death and thus produced a rather symbolic scene reminiscent of the killing of a dog, was an act of consideration to spare him the pain of being taken to town for torture and eventual death; and so was the pistol shot that put an end to Sun-nam. The shooting of the female schoolteacher in the recreation center, too, contrasts him favorably with his fellow Youth Association members who enjoy gang raping her; Yohan, as a matter of fact, was always vaguely attracted by her. Much less forgivable is his murder of the girl soldiers in clear breach of his promise to his younger brother, or the slaughter of Bak Myeong-seon's mother and sisters. But in the former case, he was affected by the instance of an Association member who had just been arrested for harboring a "Red," and in the latter, it was revenge for the killing of his elder sister (whose husband had joined the Party for self-protection) by his friend Sang-ho, Myeong-seon's fiancé.

In view of these facts, we may conjecture that Yohan's exclamation, "We were crusaders. The Reds were children of Lucifer. Satan's host," represented not so much his full conviction as an exaggerated cry arising out of a conviction shaken or destroyed. As a matter of fact, he had observed when he learned how his sister had died, "I thought that our days of representing the righteous side were over. We were no longer the crusading army of the Lord crushing the Satan" (246, F 268); and just before his death, he was planning to look up Bak Myeong-seon now living in Los Angeles. We might regret that the novel does not give us more of his inner conflicts while he was alive—by rendering, for instance, the scene of his first encounter with the specters or of the time when he began to see them again after the death of his second wife—but there is little doubt that, along with Sun-nam and Il-lang, he remains one of the most vivid characters in *Guests*.

4.

The author himself has stated that the novel *Guests* utilizes as its basic formal frame the twelve scenes of the jinogwi gut from Hwanghae Province, and this choice has been acclaimed by numerous critics. Adoption of an indigenous popular form accords well with the theme of the 'guest;' the jinogwi gut is a ritual for resolving old enmities and promoting mutual life-giving. At the same time, the familiar experience of hearing through the shaman the voices of the deceased provides a device for the now mostly dead participants of the Sincheon massacre to join in the narration.

To regard this as some extraordinary achievement "going beyond realism," however, would be an arbitrary appraisal based on an unduly narrow conception of realism. As Hong Sung-yong points out, "We have no reason to get confused meeting specters as characters in a realist novel of the twenty-first century," and since before this century, too, "realism has been understood with considerable latitude."[17] If we thus recognize the formal and technical multiplicity of the realist novel, not only is there no need to regard as a departure from realism the use of the jinogwi gut form in order to enable the dead to speak, but one could also accept first-person accounts by the dead without necessarily resorting to that form.

The important thing, however, is not to classify the achievement of Guests as realism or post-realism, but to see and evaluate how its narrative strategy actually contributes to the novel's effect. For one thing, the experience of a living person's encounter with ghosts is something that a natural scientist or the strictest naturalist writer could accept. It is another matter how faithfully that experience has been rendered; and how far the pronouncements of the ghosts agree with the truth, and to what extent such agreement would win the reader's approval, are different questions still.

In the case of Guests, it is obvious that the words of the ghosts are far from groundless claims by unreliable specters, but rather the truth as perceived in their respective situations. We know this in part because the numerous first-person accounts by both the deceased and the surviving join together, particularly in the climactic eighth chapter, to form a coherent and overwhelming picture, but also because the writer, when he briefly returns to third-person narration, makes a statement in an authoritative, objective-

17) Hong Sung-young, op. cit., 226-27. He cites the example of Bertolt Brecht, to which we may add that Georg Lukács himself, nowadays often viewed as an old-fashioned proponent of realism, included E. T. A. Hoffmann's fiction as a fine achievement of the nineteenth century realist literature.

sounding tone, directly contradicting the official line and supporting the testimonies of the ghosts:

> They [the American forces] stayed in the town of Sincheon for only two hours. ... Regular troops, whether American or South Korean, marched on northward and would not be seen again until their retreat in winter. As soon as the welcoming rally was over, the right-wing youth association and the militia were organized at the county Party office, the members congratulating themselves that reunification through the crushing of Communism had been achieved. The next day the ceremony of launching the militia and police forces was held in the yard of the Party building. Then begin the killings in air-raid shelters and bunkers. (223, F 245-46)

Actually, if we are to find a problem with the novel's ghosts in artistic terms, it must be the fact that they are not sufficiently ghost-like. Not only do they never behave like evil spirits that deceive or lead astray the living, but they hardly show any deep rancor or frighten the beholder even though they died unreconciled. Nor do any of them, including Il-lang, who was burned to death after being dragged by a wire through his nose, show up in the bloody and disfigured shape in which they must have died. This is no doubt due to the novel's peculiar conception that "all the right and wrong in one's life disappear" (194, F 214) the moment one dies, and the living characters too, except in their initial encounters, relate to the ghosts as though they were living people. Indeed, the ghosts, when they assemble for the last time in Chapter 8, behave like ordinary folks in a village gathering. Being specters, they could have appeared before Seong-man separately or chosen a moment when he and Yoseop were together, but instead, "Turning around at the sound of the words, 'Why don't you come out, too, Seong-man?', Yoseop saw Sun-nam at the door of his uncle's room summoning him, and Seong-man sauntered out to the living room" (194, F 214). Moreover, this scene is conveyed not by Yoseop in the first person but by the third-person narrator.

Of course, the novelist is free to utilize the ghosts as no more than a narrative device, instead of vividly reproducing the experience of seeing a ghost in real life or the voices of the dead heard during a performance of a *jinogwi gut*, and such a narrative strategy would not necessarily diverge, either, from realism in a wider sense. Yet the impression of a rather forced reconciliation at the end must have something to do with the fact that the specters, who play such a large role in the novel, come across as so little like 'real' specters and wrongfully murdered ones at that. A genuine reconciliation calls for not only the uncovering of the facts in the Sincheon massacre, but also requires determining precisely which among the original conflicts that caused the tragedy are to be taken over as their share by the living generation. The specters in *Guests*, however, have virtually accomplished reconciliation at the moment of their deaths and make a collective departure, declaring that their pacification has been completed through Yoseop's visit and through their comparing of notes with Yohan's ghost. But is there no necessity, for example, for confrontation and reconciliation with Sang-ho who is reputed to have killed more people than Yohan and who, unlike the latter, has chosen not to emigrate but to remain in South Korea. And can the spirits be unconcerned about the reality where the authorities are loudly and daily repeating a version of the story that negates the specters' heartrending case?

One final remark on the ghosts: while both male and female spirits make their appearance, not a single female is allotted a first-person narrative of her own, whether in the form of a dramatic monologue or private reminiscences. For instance, the two girl soldiers who used to sing and play the violin are characters that the reader would love to meet again even in a spectral form; and if any of even the more briefly introduced characters—from the schoolteacher Yun (killed in the recreation center) to Bak Myeong-seon's mother and six younger sisters to the wives of Sun-nam and Ilang—had given us her story from her own mouth, the memory of the massacres would have been far more shocking. It may have been more difficult, too, for the male ghosts to agree amicably among themselves to forget everything and go away.

These observations may seem ungenerous, directed as they are at a work which represents a remarkable achievement of Korean literature in the new century; a unique novel that directly addresses the reality of division and searches for reconciliation. But if we define our task as the overcoming of the division system, literature that rises to that world-historical task must have a vision fully as complex as the self-reproducing process of that system, and must include not only a desire for national reconciliation and universal peace but an educated awareness of the workings of various contradictions such as those involving class, gender, and ecology.[18) The awareness naturally must be one *embodied in the work*, which entails a corresponding technical innovativeness and meticulous execution. Reading *Guests* is a rewarding experience for anyone seeking reconciliation and peace in Korea, for even its shortcomings provoke fresh reflections on the nature of the division system, while its solid achievements provide the reader with considerable immediate pleasure and enlightenment.

18) Regarding the possibility of class, ecological, and gender discourses being combined in the context of the movement to overcome the division system, see Paek Nakch'ŏng (Paik Nak-chung), "Pundan ch'eje kŭkbok undong ŭi ilsanghwa rŭl wihae" [Toward Making the Movement for Overcoming the Division System a Daily Practice], Hŭndŭlinŭn bundan ch'eje bundan ch'eje [The Shaking Division System], Changbi 1998, esp. section 4 (pp. 35-52).

Literature of Memory Struggle

Hyun Ki-young

1.

While war and peace are on the opposite ends of the scale, a void of war does not necessarily translate into peace – cold war, another form of war, is rarely regarded as peace. Korea, a nation that has sacrificed tremendous human lives during the Korean War, was pegged at the forefront of tensions during the Cold War era and has lived as a divided nation representing both sides in one nation. While Americans enjoy the status of the top manager of the Cold War as liberalists pursuing freedom, small and weak nations that have been incorporated in America's plans have ubiquitously suffered under dictatorship. A prominent example is none other than Korea. An ironic situation unfolded in Korea - it was included as one of the 'free nation league' led by the U.S. but at the same time was forced to accept life in total lack of freedom.

Korea, a minor power, has historically suffered from great pain caused by foreign powers. The Koreans, who have never invaded a foreign country, are peace-loving people. Nevertheless, Korean contemporary history is characterized by the tremendous sacrifices of life, which were brought about by the Japanese occupation, the Second World War, the 6/25 War*, and the great massacres between the two wars. Among them the Jeju Massacre is the most remarkable, which has been my life-long literary subject. Last spring when I visited Germany, on the Rhine I happened to see an epigram inscribed on the relics of an iron bridge destroyed by air raids. "Peace without freedom is not peace."

A new government was established based on true democracy after the student-led revolution in 1960 in protest against the corrupt dictatorship of the Liberal Party which had witnessed the Korean

War. The new government, however, was short-lived and was crushed by a military coup d'etat after only one year of existence. The military dictatorship employed ever more brutal and systematic methods to remain in power. The establishment of the so-called October Revitalizing Reform, or Yusin, in 1972 was the harbinger of a dark period comparable to the Medieval Age due to its oppressive rule. Military rule wielded its powers relentlessly against its people, unchallenged for nearly a quarter of a century until its demise in face of strong protests from the people in June 1987.

Under the pretext of ensuring national stability and growth, the Yusin system degenerated the status of freedom into something to be protected rather than to be enjoyed. Such freedom demanded that the people put their lives in danger to protect "freedom for display" and to put on hold the freedom for the majority of the general public to guarantee the freedom of a handful of the privileged.

The intellectuals had to undergo hardships in face of the ruthless and systematic destruction conducted by the ruling power. A considerable number of intellectuals succumbed to self-effacing pressure and turned into collaborators. They researched and provided method-of-governing techniques bordering on witchcraft for the ruling power and cast a web of false propaganda around the people for the purpose of maintaining the dictatorial regime. Another group of intellectuals which existed during the Yusin period resorted to indifference, or neutrality according to their terms, standing awkwardly somewhere between the dictatorship and the people. Such groups of literati included those insisting on the artistic value or purity of literature no matter how severe the adversity that lies before them. They chose to stay silent in the face of the catastrophe, Yusin. They failed to protest against the wrong and looked the other way from the truth. There must have been those among them who agonized over the fact that silence meant consent. With the help of those unprincipled intellectuals, the despotic regime enabled its false propaganda to sound like truth to the people; truth became falsehood, and in turn, falsehood became truth.

Under such circumstances true intellect meant resistance not submission. As darkness grew deeper, a flickering light of resistance lit up. Those were the seeds of creation, of life amid absolute darkness. The creators were survivors of the destructive force which deprived liberty, the essence of life and the plot to sap life out of the people across the nation. The sporadic act of resistance took on a more systematic approach and grew into a formidable body of resistance. Arrests, torture, and imprisonment which ensued only added fuel to the fire which spread like wildfire among students and intellectuals who became bolder, oftentimes sacrificing themselves.

Yusin also inflicted great tribulations to me at the time. I was a fledging writer who believed history progressed, albeit in a painstakingly gradual pace. I was aghast at the regression of history. Yusin declared the invalidity of the ideals and dreams of a liberalist instilled in me through an education based on curriculum influenced by the U.S. Freedom; a freedom monopolized by the ruling class and merely put on display for the common people.

While I am currently categorized as a so-called activist writer, my origin is pure literature. As an English literature major, I set my model for literature as English/American literature, hoping that my novels would be regarded as unique and experimental inventions of aestheticism. Once I had entered the literary circle, however, my thoughts began to change. Yusin left little room for the luxury of singing lullabies to the public under the name of pure literature. It was not the time for writers to appease the wrath for justice with sweet lullabies, not at a time when the call for justice should be expressed. Writers are probably a group most sensitive to freedom and oppression. Is it not that freedom is the essence of being a writer? The so-called "voluntary depravity" is so willingly accepted by writers because of this very freedom. I therefore decided to postpone my pursuit of the aesthetics that had been inculcated upon me through my education in English/American literature and pure literature.

2.

Many writers have unbearably painful or tragic memories as youths and choose to become writers as if ordained by fate. Such memories still lingering in the writer's mind, residue of oppression and the resultant chronic depression probably had a decisive influence in choosing their occupation. Literature is equal to freedom or liberation. The writer creates novels to liberate the oppressed self and to provide an escape route by transforming oneself into one of the characters in the novel. If, for example, our psyche is distorted through oppressed concepts of sex, it should rightfully be liberated through incarnation of sex in novels. The memory of a tragic incident which I experienced as a child was oppressed within me. It was the memory of the massacre that resulted from the April 3 Insurrection in 1948. The brutality of the experience had once made me stutter and I suffer till this day from chronic depression. The pain of the massacre still persists among all Jeju islanders, including myself. The collective inferiority complex suffered by most Jeju islanders and myself simply had to be relieved through literature. I felt that I had to somehow break away from the bondage of the massacre to unfold my career in the literary circle – literary spirit could be achieved only when my spirits were free from all forms of subordination.

So I decided to write a novel on that very subject, to relieve myself from the oppression and pay my debt. I had at the time been away from my hometown ever since I left for Seoul to attend college. There I was able to gain a better picture of my hometown, just as one gets a better view of the forest only when away from the trees. For nearly thirty years the massacre was the worst taboo in Korean modern history. Only when I was able to maintain a distance from the source of the oppression I had felt was I able to witness my feelings toward the incident surface from obscure subconsciousness. The massacre, a taboo that no one dared to speak of, took the form of a gray cloud in a gloomy winter day, just like those that pressed down hard from the skies of my hometown. Sometimes, it would look like that dark spot blotted out of the map, just like the 130 villages and hamlets burned down to the ground and turned to ashes after the raid from the military and police. I felt the sorrow and wrath inside me twitching and coming to life. I could not disassociate my hometown with the feel of hurting. My hometown was a prison floating on the dark sea at the end of the world. A brutal massacre of unseen and unheard scale was taking place on an island isolated from the world by a sea blockade. Islanders were dying under false charges that they were insurgents or communists.

Those who barely survived became blinded by fear. The massacre was a taboo no one was to speak of. Their lips froze at the mention of the incident. They were victimized so severely that the incident was internalized and rooted as second nature. The islanders fostered a sense of inferiority, defeatism and self-deprecation as well as blind terror towards authority, and ironically, an absolute envy towards the central government. I myself was feeling similar oppressed sentiments. In my short story "Tale of the Sea Dragon" I write,

> The scene of the nightmare, the years of haunting dreams, those were his hometown. It represented everything he yearned to forget and discard. It was understood as the direct opposite to happiness or making his way to the world.

Once I set my mind on the theme, it seemed like a crime trying to write about something else. I planned to write four or five short or medium-length stories on the massacre before I returned to pure literature. I thus looked back to my hometown with a different perspective and I realized that it was not that different from assessing myself in an objective manner. To set my hometown and its tragic incident as a subject matter was none other than to place myself, a particle of the scene, under intense scrutiny. It was a whole new look towards my hometown as well as myself.

So I finally set myself in the realm of the taboo. I was only a child of six or seven years and thus had limited memory of the incident when it had occurred. I had my work cut out for me. I needed to conduct extensive research, which I found quite challenging. I looked for data at the National Library only to find records that were either unreliable or severely geared to the extreme right. I could not repress the sadness I felt when one day I found two years amount of newspaper articles omitted from the Jeju Daily rack. It seems that the massacre was brutally deleted from modern history. Korean modern history is a record of the winners who put on memories that pleased them only while stifling or crossing out those of the losers.

I concentrated on collecting witness accounts in search of the truth, which was distorted as a pro-communist revolt. This was not as easy as I had thought. The collective memory of the people seemed shattered ruthlessly by a policy designed to obliterate the memory of the incident from the people's minds. Nearly three decades of policies to deliberately crush memories of the massacre by dictatorial governments have frozen the lips of the islanders. The majority voluntarily killed the memories themselves since it was virtually impossible to live on without deliberately trying to erase the brutal scenes from one's mind.

I was working as a high school teacher at the time and visited my hometown every vacation for two years. I had such a hard time gathering information from the witnesses (survivors) who obstinately refused to recount the memories. Even my close relatives chided me for opening an old wound and hesitated to cooperate with my research. One old lady couldn't stop shedding tears as she held my hand, telling me how I resembled her son who had died in the massacre. She too, however, did not disclose her story kept deep in her heart till the end. I had no other choice but to go back, sharing the tears with her. As I built my story I had hoped that I could deliver the entirety of the unconsolable resentment, wrath and fear of the survivors who lowered their voices stammered and laid out a deep sigh in tears. In the process of materializing the heartbeats, blood and sweat I had a peculiar feeling of being able to identify with the victims, as if the tribulations the protagonist in my story had to endure were mine. Many times I sat in front of the desk at night alone writing with tears flowing. I realized first-hand that literature is the only way one can obtain indirect-experience.

There was a photograph taken from the Cambodian civil war in which a young boy is staring into the camera on the top of a staircase in front of the front door. The house was half destroyed with bodies lying on the ground. Roland Barthes made an annotation to this photograph, stating that the look on the eyes of the boy is what the dead had endowed the boy to display to the outsiders who have no idea what it is like to be on the scene.

Through the eyes of the boy the outsiders are able to witness the tragedy and the dead bodies. I was the boy. It was the obligation of the survivors to tell the story on behalf of the dead. As a survivor of the massacre, I was obligated to look at the world with the same expression of the boy in the photograph.

To my surprise, my first work to deal with the massacre, *Uncle Sun-i* published in the summer of 1978, was well received. Writers are affected not only by works of others but by his or her own work. This is because the statement made through one's work cannot be taken back and has a certain force that has a firm grip on the author. A writer who has made a strong impression on the reader can seldom be free of the expectations or demand of his/her readers. Readers rooted for me and my efforts and I answered by producing three more short stories on the subject. Then came the unbearable anxiety. Will I be able to remain unscathed after having written such a provocative message? I thought I was ready to face whatever it took, but the fear became real once I had done it. I secretly prayed that the authorities would let it pass just this once, and I'd never deal with that topic again.

But they would not. The publication of *Uncle Sun-i*, a compilation of short stories on the subject seemed to have been the last straw and they snatched me away to the military secret service. In the basement of the headquarters, I was treated no different than a dog. The caning turned my body black and blue. My heart still beats at the haunting memory of torture. My body still recalls well the fear and pain. The torture made it clear that the massacre which took place thirty years before was still an important issue and I felt like the last victim of the incident. The bruise from the caning disappeared about two weeks later but the mental scar still lives on, victimizing me until this day.

I was tortured for three days, day and night, incarcerated and released after 25 days. I was arrested again several months later, this time, by the police. About twenty days before the arrest, I knew I was being watched. Thereafter, until the arrest, I felt like a sitting duck waiting to be caught. I was so anxious and fearful that I lost almost 8 kilograms. It seemed the police originally planned to press formal charges against me. However, the massacre was not such a small issue and they feared they might attract unwanted attention by presenting the case in front of the court. So I was released and my book was banned from circulation.

After the incident, I became depressed and unsure of myself. I stopped writing for more than a year, relying on alcohol to soothe the pain and despair. Then one night I had a dream. A woman in mourning clothes appeared admonishing me to get up and rise above the weight of despair, and continue the mission I was ordained to complete. The woman was none other than the protagonist in my own creation I realized that the fictional figure was alive within me. Rather, the woman had already been transformed into an entity in reality. Amazingly I was able to regain the strength to write again after I had awoken from the dream.

3.

The premise of the massacre is not limited to the armed uprising which took place on April 3, 1948 in protest of the establishment of a government in South Korea without including the north. It includes the process of suppressing the uprising and the resultant massacre of at least 30,000 civilians by the military police. The national goal of foremost and imminent importance at the time was the abolishment of the demarcation line and the clearing away with the past evils during the Japanese colonial rule. Liberation from the Japanese, however, brought about another kind of occupation. The general sentiment among the people was that a united government, not separate governments built in South and North Korea, should establish a new nation. If Jeju Island was ever culpable it was perhaps that it was the most aggressive in expressing its opposition to a separate government.

Before the massacre struck the island, there was the March 1 Protest a year before which was in a way a precursor to the massacre. On March 1, 1947, an outdoor rally by the people demanded the pull-out of American and Russian troops from the peninsula to achieve true independence. The police, under U.S., control fired at the protesters, killing six people and hurting ten others. The general strike launched by the islanders in protest of such atrocity was met by brutal oppression, not an apology. The entire island was accused of holding a pro-communist stance. It is well known that the police roundups, terror and torture committed by the American military government police resulted in many deaths, which triggered the April 3 uprising.

The general strike in which almost all islanders joined speaks volumes of the communal nature of the island. The cohesiveness of the island community stems from a long history of fighting against outside forces that harmed the community. Jeju is a rocky island formed in the middle of the ocean from the ashes of volcanic eruptions. Its inhabitants are as strong and willful as the deep root of the weeds. Its barren soil forced all residents, including the upper class and the literate, to labor in the fields in order to have three square meals a day. It was a poor community but equal. This is how all islanders built a strong sense of community; that they were in the same boat. The islanders who lived in a tight-knit society like the weeds intertwined in the barren soil faced two kinds of outside intrusions. One was the foreigners that invaded the island – the Mongolians, Japanese pirate raiders, imperialist France and Japan. The other was the central government, which had nothing to provide the islanders but seized every opportunity to take away from the island. The politicians in exile banished from the central government also played a role in this anti-central government sentiment: The island was the disposal site for fallen politicians whom the central government wished to isolate. So the island has had a long history of small and large-scale resistance against the central royal government, which exercised severe discriminatory policies against the island while imposing an inordinate amount of tribute and harsh military obligations on it.

Those who are oppressed and exploited tend to resort to messianism. They long for a savior or a hero who will come to their rescue and save the people from misery with a vision of new life. Islanders referred to such a hero as Jin-in, or true man. Crying lips of at least 10,000 were thought as necessary for the far-away royal government to hear them out. This required an extraordinary amount of bravery since leaders of such an insurgency were invariably decapitated. The birth of a hero in the remote island suffering from discrimination, in other words, meant nothing more than an insurrection that always ended in the execution of the hero accused of treason. The heroes whose lives ended in death were "true men" who sought to save the people by sacrificing themselves.

The massacre, therefore, was an extension of the island's characteristic tradition of resistance, not, as the ultra-rightists claim, a communist proletariat insurrection. The island, painted red by the extreme right wingers, became the stage of indiscriminate carnage. What the islanders thought of as resistance in the traditional sense produced a totally different result from the past. Unlike the past where the heroes' lives were sacrificed in return for the deliverance of the people, the leaders in the April 3 uprising faced a tragic situation where they not only found themselves killed but also the people. The islanders were in a state of total shock as they were unsuccessfully trying to make sense of the unfamiliar scene of massacre unfolding before them. At the time the massacre was under way, the president of the U.S was Truman and Korea's ruling group tried to deceive the people into thinking of Truman as Messiah by translating literally the name Truman into Jin-in (眞人).

The impact of the incident seemed as grave as the atomic bomb explosions on Nagasaki and Hiroshima. The magnitude of the violence was such that at least 30,000 civilians, or one-ninth of the total population, were brutally murdered and 130 villages scorched. The massacre took place as part of the strategic framework for the U.S. Can the U.S. profess innocence simply because they didn't bloody their hands? The fact that the scene of genocide was void of U.S. presence and committed by Korean soldiers in American military uniforms and boots does not excuse the U.S. of the crime. War inevitably makes humans act more impulsively and instinctively. The U.S. has taken full advantage of such human nature and granted a so-called "license to kill" even to the lowest-ranking snipers, raising human savagery to its maximum. Under the cloak of the Military Advisory Council, the U.S. remained invisible throughout the massacre, hidden inside the warships that formed a blockade around the island, inside the landing ship tanks and the CIC offices in Jeju County. They understood perfectly well that the most efficient way for the occupiers to quell an insurrection is to create a war among those under subjugation and to refrain from direct involvement in the bloodshed. The following is an excerpt from "Steel and Flesh":

> Whose crime is this? The machine gun? The shooter pulling the trigger? The officer making the orders? The battalion commander who handed the down the decision through the walkie-talkie? The regimental commander? Or the U.S. military advisory council? Someone in the higher ranks? Who stands at the top of the commanding pyramid? Was Truman really a 'True man'?
>
> Orders from the top were mechanically delivered to the lowest level. Mechanical thinking was void of any human element and everything was alarmingly simple – The mid-mountain areas were the base camp for human and resource flow for the guerrillas. Therefore, everything including human lives had to be completely destroyed. Cold harsh steel machine automatically moved at the press of a button. Fingers that press the button need not bloody their hands. To them, the death toll is merely a statistic with hardly any scent of blood involved.

On the battlefield, it is impossible to disobey orders from the top. Under the circumstances that even innocent people such as children, old men, and women were the target of indiscriminate killing, the solders might control the guilty conscience by saying to themselves, "Exactly so, they are reds. They are but reds."

It was actually quite simple – the massacre which killed at least 30,000 innocent civilians, erupted in the process of eliminating 200 or so young men who revolted without any proper weapons, having to rely solely on insuppressible wrath. There was at the time a saying "kill a hundred with one culprit" which meant if you kill one hundred civilians there's bound to be at least one guerrilla among them. So is it that 30,000 civilians were brutally murdered to get rid of 200 guerrillas?

The U.S. and the ruling government colored 80% of the island as red and called it the "Red Island." Red at the time meant death. When I was tortured at the military secret service, they too called me a “red writer,” trying to frame me as pro-communist. But the only red they saw was the blood clot in my mid finger crushed by the torture. Had such an incident taken place in 1948, I would surely have been shot.

So many civilians were killed, branded as pro-communist during the massacre which was dubbed the “Red Hunt.” This wasn’t necessarily limited to “hunting down the communist.” As was the case in the massacre, it is somewhat an ironic term, which refers to framing innocent people as communists. The term borrows its form from the “witch hunt” during medieval times during which a huge number of women were branded as evil witches or having communicated with witches and were sacrificed in the name of religion. Modern times saw history repeating itself by once again sacrificing numerous civilians in the name of ideology, falsely charging innocent people as communists.

Truman was head of the U.S. administration both in 1948, the year of the massacre and in 1950, the year of the 6/25 War. And it was also in 1950 that “McCarthy’s tornado” took place in the U.S. It seems that the term “Red Hunt” was frequently mentioned during the period of intense anticommunism called McCarthyism. Hundreds of civil servants lost their jobs, while writers, artists and intellectuals were branded communist sympathizers by ultra-rightists. But how different the ‘Red Hunt’ in the U.S. was from that that had unfolded on Jeju – indiscriminate massacre of innocent lives.

“Hunt” is a term used on animals not on humans. “Rabbit hunt” or even “‘witch hunt” might make sense because a witch is not human. “Red hunt” must operate under the premise that communists are not human. When the Spaniards ruined the Maya civilization in the 16th century and slaughtered the Mayan people, the Catholics granted themselves an indulgence in the heinous killings by deciding that the indio were non-human and that they were closer to animals than mankind. To kill without any sense of guilt, the target must either be an animal or an inferior human, in other words, a savage. Such logic is behind the carnage of Native Americans committed by the pioneers in the U.S. while expanding its frontier to the west, the Pacific coast.

The equation that communists were non-human was behind the

massacre. Communists were not "people of leftist ideology," but inferior beings, or savages. Those who killed such "savages" were exonerated of any sin. The problem was, however, that out of the 30,000 victims, only a small number were pro-communists while the majority were innocent civilians. Atrocity was committed under the name of civilization. In my short story "Steel and Flesh," the following appears:

> Oh, how mysterious, unbelievable, incomprehensible. It is truly a tragedy, unseen nor unheard of. How can humans crush so brutally fellow humans? Animals are rarely slaughtered in such manner. (.................) To destroy evidence they poured gasoline and burned the bodies which, they said, smelled much like burning pork. So did the murderers, through the familiar scent of burning meat, confirm once again that what they had slaughtered were indeed not human but animal? No, not at all. They left the scene in haste, covering their noses with queasiness.

I had employed harsh terms to describe the cruelty of the massacre: the beauty of camellias whose flowers fell on the snow, for example, is represented in a distorted manner to bring about the image of decapitated heads soaked in blood tossed on the snow. Narratives of the documentary kind were used instead of the traditional method of writing novels. It was my hope that I would be able to share with my readers the indirect experience with the utmost urgency I had acquired while conducting research and compiling notes.

4.

My exploration into the massacre which started with a novel later continued through participating in organizations and campaigns. The quest for truth with regard to the massacre was a part of the democratization movement during the 1980s. The quest which continued under intense fear was a struggle against conspiracy of concealment, denial, and distortion committed by the ruling government and against indifference and cynicism by the general public. The democratization movement finally claimed victory in the 1990s after a long and difficult struggle. The campaign to shed light on the truth of the massacre also bore fruit – the Special Law on the Massacre was ratified by the National Assembly five years ago. It was truly a feat, a miracle for Jeju residents. The massacre is currently under investigation by the government. A collection of witness statements, much like the Recovery of Historical Memory of Guatemala, is currently underway. The memory of Jeju residents, suppressed for so long a time, is beginning to raise its voice.

This is, however, just the beginning. While discussing the memory of the losers and victims is now allowed, it will take much longer to quell the protests from the opposition and to replace the official memory with the truth. It is one thing to accommodate the memory of the innocent victim, but quite another to reinstate the memory of the loser, perhaps impossible for the time being. This is precisely why the struggle to remember the massacre must continue. Unfortunately, the massacre is fading away from the psyche of the general public too soon. No sooner had the incident recovered its shine from darkness than it lost its glitter. Just as the buzzwords of the 1980s such as "history," "people," and "the populace" faded away, the massacre also faces the danger of disappearing from the people's minds amid a short-circuit, materialistic society. The atrocities committed during the incident have yet to be identified before fading into oblivion.

The entrance at Auschwitz still bears the following message: There is one thing more fearful than Auschwitz. It is that mankind might forget. It is an epigram warning of the possibility of history repeating itself for those whether it be individuals or the entire society that choose to forget. In "Beloved" by Toni Morrison, a term "rememory" appears. Rememory is a word to emphasize the meaning of memory, or the behavior of continuously trying to remember. Seth, an escaped slave and mother, lives with the ghost of her dead baby daughter, Beloved whose existence signifies the importance of reremembering the painful past, the racial discrimination and cruelty. The ghost and its character have enabled such an intense subject matter to be presented in the form of art. I remain envious of Morrison for possessing such extraordinary powers for artistry.

In retrospect, the sorrow of the massacre was far from the delicate and profound sadness often expressed through pure literature but rather a fierce and painful sorrow amid heaps of bodies, blood, and crying. One can easily understand why Theodor Adorno argued that "writing poetry after Auschwitz is barbaric." Literature has a bad tendency of evading social issues and harsh reality in favor of fantasy, romance and fiction. Literature favors melancholic sadness which humans can tolerate. It is therefore difficult to find literature that deals with dead bodies, blood, screaming, cries or formidable pain. Readers also instinctively shun away from such novels. Sorrow and misfortune in a novel are allowed only when they are part of overall happiness in a novel. Daniel Defoe shied away from the plague and the dead bodies he witnessed and wrote fictional tales such as Robinson Crusoe, as did Pascal who was able to concentrate on his Pensées without uttering a word on the religious wars which entailed merciless slaughter. Then again isn't it human nature to try to look at the bright side? Who wants to deal with a world of dead bodies anyway? Isn't it a fact that the survivors of the massacre themselves keep trying to forget the dreadful memory?

Even if this is the case, it would be impossible not to mention such horrific incidents in literature. As Roland Barthes said, this is because the living are endowed with the inevitable responsibility to reveal the truth by the dead, no matter how painful and fearsome the experience is. The living owe it to the dead to make way for the dead to declare their bitter grief. The responsibility lies especially heavily on writers. Literature should not look the other way from blood, crying, dead bodies or sheer hell simply because they represent a world totally different from the world of art and beauty. So what if our work becomes non-literature, even anti-literature? If we as writer share the view that the pen is an obligation as well as a right, the survivor of the horrible incident and outsiders observing the scene alike shall not hesitate to speak their minds and show interest in the hidden truth.

Bloodshed continues well into the 21st century. Evidently it is barbarism, not civilization. The wars are of the conjunction of high technology of complete accuracy with the complete barbarism and complete blindness. Small and weak nations are crushed by strong nations which possess hi-tech destructive force. While one side is in a 'safe' war without casualties relying on sophisticated missiles and bombers, the other is pounced on beaten down and destroyed. Wars in the Gulf, Afghanistan, and Iraq are some examples. One side easily wins the war by pressing the button of a missile, without having to bloody one's hand while defeat and casualties await the other side in a losing battle.

Strangely though, reports on war never show bloody corpses. The trace of fire blaze, red flame, and black smoke are all that are seen, but none of the horrifying scene of bodies. The mass media simply refuses to show such sights. It would be a terrible sin for outsiders to feel a sense of thrill at such a scene; a sensation we feel while watching firework displays or online games. Unfortunately, however, not many feel such guilt. Hollywood blockbusters and online games have rendered banality and routineness to the images of war. War has become nothing more than just another form of entertainment minus its gruesome reality. If the truth about the massacre couldn't come out at the time of its outbreak due to insufficient telecommunications technology, it is still muffled by the distorted coverage of the mass media. How should we deal with the innocent deaths and the bloodshed excluded from airtime and paper space and thus unrecognized by the world community? Shouldn't that role be assumed by literature? Whether be it inside or outside the scene, silence shall not be allowed to writers who live in the world of language.

No nation can be guaranteed safety simply because it is not included among the so-called "Axis of Evil." Humans tend to hypnotize themselves that war may break out anywhere but their homeland. September 11, however, is proof that no country can proclaim safety. Like Tolstoy we appear more accustomed to saying "War and Peace" rather than "Peace and War." War may erupt anywhere, anytime. History has been a succession of wars, while peace appears to be an insertion between numerous wars on a temporary basis. Are wars indeed inevitable? Is it impossible to reverse the order from "War and Peace" to "Peace and War," if not a complete stop to war? If peace is what we truly hope for, we need to be able to see eye-to-eye the brutal reality of destruction by war or those in power. This is where the mission for writers lies. We need to recreate the atrocities for the world to feel, to appeal to human emotion and sentiment and concretize the image of war. Writers must strive in search of artistic expression through language beyond literature relying heavily on rage, blunt rhetoric and slogans. As in the rememory strategy introduced by Toni Morrison, the discovery of new language plays a pivotal role. The language must be able to face head-on with language used for the purpose of commercializing war and turning it into a form of entertainment. I sincerely believe literature has the capacity to imbue the sorrow and terror of war in the human heart and to transform such great pains into the ability to organize campaigns for peace.

Translated by **Kim Hye-young**

*Copy editor's note: Koreans often refer to the Korean War by the date it started 6/25; yuk-i-o, literally six-two-five.

Session IV

East Asian Ideas of World Order

Hasumi Shigehiko | The Temptation of "Red"

Bok Koh-ill | The Ideal International Order in East Asia

The Temptation of "Red"

Hasumi Shigehiko

Conflicts and Disorder

I am well aware that the theme of this forum is "Writing for Peace." And of course I know that I have been asked to speak at the session on "East Asian Ideas of World Order." Nevertheless, I would like to begin my talk not with peace nor with order but with their opposites: conflicts and disorder. This does not mean that I am questioning the issue of "Writing for Peace," nor do I intend to criticize, through the relations between East Asia and the world, the arguments of Samuel P. Huntington in *The Clash of Civilizations* that are little more than crude entertainment for globalized mass consumer culture. Rather, my focus on conflicts and disorder comes from a simple principle of language: that the majority of people should not share in advance the same interpretation of a difficult-to-define concept. In literature in particular, I believe, the only truly creative concepts are those that give rise to inconsistencies because of the many diverse interpretations that they inspire. And only if we struggle our way through such creative inconsistencies will the concept of peace become more than an abstraction.

I would like to confront the semantic disorder and interpretive conflicts surrounding a single word that touches the very core of literature. That word is "fiction," and what draws my attention to it is the massive inconsistency in its meaning. I am sure that everyone here—writers, critics, philosophers, the entire audience—have said the word "fiction" more times than we can count. It is widely used as part of our everyday vocabulary. But once we begin to examine its structure and meaning theoretically, the rivalries and mutual indifference between scholarly fields create discord and confusion. In philosophy and literary theory, the semantic disorder of this word has collapsed into a state of anarchy.

The semantic inquiries into the word "fiction" that stimulated Twentieth Century thought in so many ways have not yet taken firm intellectual root in East Asia. Universities in this region have creatively absorbed the works of poststructuralism and produced significant results in areas from postcolonial studies to gender studies. But in the field of fiction studies, almost nothing of note has been accomplished here despite the active work elsewhere in the field over the past three decades. As Plato and even Aristotle did not know what fiction was, fiction seems to be an illegitimate child in the context of the Western thought on which today's theoretical analyses are built. What brought me to my topic today is irritation that, while non-Western thought should be able to contribute greatly to the clarification of the meanings of fiction, in fact very little has been done.

Chaotic and Perverse

The anarchistic confusion over the interpretation of the word "fiction" has been pointed out by many writers. At the beginning of *The Distinction of Fiction*, Dorrit Cohn writes, "Divergences in the significance of the term are plainly visible from dictionary entries under fiction. Their only common denominator, it appears, is that they all designate 'something invented.'" If almost all Western dictionaries disagree about the meaning of "fiction" other than that it is "something invented," then it is not surprising that people use the word to refer to completely different things. To show that the confusion about this word's meaning has a history stretching back nearly a hundred years, Cohn, an American literary theorist, quotes the 1911 work *Die Philosophie des Als Ob* by the German philosopher Hans Vaihinger as follows: "As ... Vaihinger remarked almost a century ago, 'The word "fiction" is subject to chaotic and perverse linguistic usage: even logicians employ it in different meanings, without taking the pains to define the term or to distinguish among its different meanings. "' (p. 1)

As shown by Vaihinger's subtitle—*System der theoretischen, prakitschen und reilgiösen Fiktionen der Menschheit*—his work examined the concept of fiction not in literary theory but in human thought in general. In this regard, Professor Cohn writes, "Thus Bentham calls the juridical term *right* 'a fiction,' Kant explains that the products of our intellectual intuition (notions like time and space) are 'heuristic fictions,' and Nietzsche tells us that an individual's sense of existing as a unified subject (of having a unified self) is 'the fiction that many similar states in us are the effect of one substratum.'" (p. 1)

This quotation is enough to remind us that fiction was a philosophical concept before it was a literary one. If we extend Newton's statement that gravity is fiction, then everything else—from Rousseau's state of nature to Freud's unconsciousness—must also be called fictional. For Philippe Lacoue-Labarthe, whose *La Fiction du Politique* was written after Professor Cohn's book, even Nazism is fiction. Gilles Deleuze, the author of *Différence et Répétition*, wrote that philosophical writings must be science fiction; Roland Barthes declared in *The Pleasure of the Text* that ideological systems are fiction; and Michel Foucault wrote that his own philosophical-historical works are fiction. Thus the meanings of this word are expanding steadily beyond literature.

The first serious literary examination of fiction as a philosophical topic was Käte Hamburger's 1957 *Die Logik der Dichtung (The Logic of Literature)*. This German literary theorist pointed out that, while the structure of the "as-if" proposed by Vaihinger is suitable for mathematics, physics, jurisprudence, and other abstract systems, it is not appropriate for literary fiction. Writing that "Schiller did not form his character Maria Stuart as if she were the real Maria," Hamburger defines the fiction of literature to be "as-structure" rather than "as-if," and she criticizes Vaihinger for failing to distinguish between the feigned and the fictive.

Professor Cohn accepts the main thrust of Hamburger's position. Cohn emphasizes the auto-referentiality of literary texts and defines fiction as "non-referential narrative." In contrast, Hamburger defines fiction only as a "third-person narrative," and she focuses on genres such as epics or drama in the tradition of Aristotelian aesthetics. But of course neither "non-referential narrative" nor "third-person narrative" is a necessary and sufficient condition to define "fiction."

While mentioning Gérard Gentte's *Fiction et Diction* and other works written in the latter half of the Twentieth Century, Professor Cohn deplores the increasingly "chaotic and perverse linguistic usage" of the word "fiction" in recent works of literary theory. I have no reason to argue with her position, but it is also difficult for me to avoid the conclusion that her own writings, despite their well-intentioned attempt to be rigorous, themselves reinforce that chaos and perversity. After all, there are many third-person narratives and non-referential narratives that are not fiction. Thus even incisive new works in this field add even more new meanings to the word "fiction."

But this dilemma—into which the author of *The Distinction of Fiction* fell unaware while endeavoring to "take the pains to define the term" and "to distinguish among its different meanings" as Vaihinger had—is the result not of confused thinking by individual critics nor of insufficient theoretical care nor of methodological flaws. Rather, the problem is that fiction is a concept utterly removed from essential substance and has no pure state of its own. This uncategorizable power of fiction resists synthesis and analysis, and inquiries about the meaning of fiction are doomed to failure. My position then is that the "chaotic and perverse linguistic usage" of the word "fiction" should not be feared by those of us who discuss fiction.

Factual / Feigned

In "The Logical Status of Fictional Discourse," John R. Searle writes that "there is no textual property, syntactical or semantic, that will identify a text as a world of fiction." This linguistic philosopher describes this paradox as follows, "...how can it be both the case that words and other elements in a fictional story have their ordinary meanings and yet the rules that attach to those words and other elements and determine their meanings are not complied with: how can it be the case in 'Little Red Riding Hood' both that 'red' means red and yet the rules correlating 'red' with red are not in force?" (p. 58)

This assertion has connections to so-called speech acts theory. The creation of J.L. Austin, speech acts theory became widely known due to Professor Searle and his book *Speech Acts*. Searle regards the "assertions" in fictional discourse to be parasitic relative to the "factual assertions" in "normal real world talk." What Austin called "parasitic" is further described as "feigned" by Searle, who himself asserts that authors of fiction pretend to be making factual assertions. As Richard Rorty points out sarcastically in his paper "Is There a Problem About Fictional Discourse?," the analytical philosophy of language expounds on the problem of fiction and reality with absolutely no reference to literary theory and has failed to separate semantics and epistemology. If, with regard to Bertrand Russell's discussion of "reference," we accept the "axiom of existence" that "whatever is referred to must exist," then all assertions that refer to Sherlock Holmes as a character in fiction must be errors.

To resolve this conflict between the "axiom of existence" and references to "fictional (and also legendary, mythological, etc.) entities," Searle introduces the concepts of "parasitic" and "feigned." He concludes that such a resolution is possible by using the concept "exist-in-fiction" for fictional characters such as Sherlock Holmes in contrast to expressions such as "the Gold Mountain" or "the Rectangular Circle," which, he says, are not references because they do not exist in the real world. We do not need even Professor Rorty to point out that Searle's argument is a muddled compromise that raises doubts about his real intentions. To explain the concept of "feigned" that he introduces to distinguish fiction from lies, Searle uses some awkward comparisons: "One can pretend," he writes, "to hit someone by actually making the arm and fist movements that are characteristic of hitting someone.... Similarly, children pretend to drive a stationary car by actually sitting in the driver's seat, moving the steering wheel, pushing the gear shift lever, and so on." (p. 68) But authors of fiction do not pretend to make serious utterances with the intention of eventually actually making serious utterances, so Searle's comparison to pretend-driving by a child fascinated by cars is clearly inappropriate.

Sharp criticism of speech acts theory appeared in 1971 in Jacques Derrida's paper "Signature Événement Context." The author of *L'Ecriture et la Différence*, Derrida directed his critique at Austin's *How to Do Things with Words*, but his focus was actually

Searle, who had incorporated Austin's "parasitic" concept and extended it to "feigned." I do not have time to go into detail here about the well-known debate between Derrida and Searle, but let me quote what Derrida wrote regarding what he saw as one flaw in Austin's argument, that is, Austin's failure to distinguish between written and spoken communication:

> For the written to be written, it must continue to 'act' and to be legible even if what is called the author of the writing no longer answers for what he has written, for what he seems to have signed, whether he is provisionally absent, or if he is dead, or if in general he does not support, with his absolutely and present intention or attention, the plentitude of his meaning, of that very thing which seems to be written 'in his name.' (p. 316)

These characteristics of *écriture* that Derrida identifies clearly render invalid the concept of the agent of enunciation, which Austin regarded as responsible for the construction of context, as well as Searle's idea of the writer as the source of "illocutionary intentions." In the eyes of Derrida, who discussed the drifting of *écriture* from the viewpoint of the absence of the agent in written texts as opposed to the agent's presence in spoken language, the concepts of "parasitic" and "feigned" were meaningless, because, as Derrida wrote, "a written sign carries with it a force of breaking with the context" and "that force of breaking is not an accidental predicate, but the very structure of the written" (p. 317). In his "Les Actes de Fiction," the French literary theorist Gérard Genette regards many of Searle's points in "The Logical Status of Fictional Discourse" as *désisif* contributions and generally accepts the concept of feigned assertion, but he also states that there is no need to introduce the "exist-in-fiction" concept and suggests that the following is sufficient: "la capacité manifeste (et largement exploitée hors fiction) du langage ordinaire à entendre plus, moins, ou autre chose qu'il ne dit." In this case, meanings different from the "illocutionary intentions" of the writer are formed, and thus in a sense Genette's position can be said to be close to Derrida's.

But Searle is confident that the intentions of the writer are invariable, and he states, "If I say now, 'I am writing an article about the concept of fiction', that remark is both serious and literal." Searle's intention does seem clear, for his purpose is, he says, "to explore the difference between fictional and serious utterances." He adds, "it is absurd to suppose a critic can completely ignore the intentions of the author" (p. 66). But even when a "serious utterance" is in the form of written signs, the agent responsible for creating the context is, as Derrida points out, absent. And as Genette shows, a single text can mean not only what it says but something more, something less, or something different. So let's try analyzing the "something more," "something less," and "something different" in Professor Searle's text.

Little Red Riding Hood, the Red Shoes, and the Reddish-Brown Stocking

I would like to begin by analyzing what would seem, at first glance, to be a rather minor question. That question is why Professor Searle referred to "Little Red Riding Hood." The answer is that, as we saw earlier, he says that the word "red" means the same thing in fiction and in daily life. He states, "'Is red' can be predicated only of objects which are colored (or colorable)" (p. 316). Because hoods are objects that are colorable, the red hood works for him as an example. This example is related to the statement by the Japanese literary theorist Toshihiko Miura that the following proposition is true: "In the fictional story 'The Red Shoes,' the girl Karen danced in red shoes." According to Miura, this proposition is true because the story "The Red Shoes" encompasses a world in which the shoes of the girl protagonist are red. But in his book *Metaphysics of Fictional Worlds*, Miura states that the same cannot be said with certainty to apply to colors such as "reddish-purple" that straddle the color category boundaries. Thus Miura, in contrast to Searle, mentions the incompleteness of fictional worlds. This comment is reminiscent of the position of Erich Auerbach, who analyzed Virginia Woolf's novel *To the Lighthouse* in the last chapter of his book *Mimesis*, which he titled "The Brown Stocking." This chapter title ignores the vague boundary-region colors mentioned by Professor Miura, for the stocking mentioned in Virginia Woolf's beautiful text is described much more often as "reddish-brown hairy" than as merely "brown."

Why did Auerbach ignore the word "reddish" that Woolf used so many times? This question leads us as well to the question of why Professor Searle mentioned "Little Red Riding Hood" in his paper "The Logical Status of Fictional Discourse" and why Professor Miura referred to "The Red Shoes." From the logical context of their papers, they did not have to refer to "Little Red Riding Hood" or "The Red Shoes" at all; had they mentioned any other color – Bluebeard, Snow White – their arguments would have been the same. In fact, when Searle applies his analysis of fiction to Iris Murdoch's *The Red and the Green*, he says, "This and other examples of fiction used in this article were deliberately chosen at random, in the belief that theories of languages should be able to deal with any text at all and not just with specially selected examples." But was "Little Red Riding Hood" really "deliberately chosen at random"?

Several objective facts show that this "serious utterance" by Searle is not true. First of all, his statement that the "red" in "Little Red Riding Hood" means red is a quotation from his own book. In the chapter "Reference as a speech act" in *Speech Acts*, Searle wrote, "...it is essential to realize that even in 'Little Red Riding Hood,' red means red. The conventions of fiction don't change the meaning of the words or other linguistic elements." (p. 79) This repetition between two different parts of his text proves that "Little Red Riding Hood" was not "deliberately chosen at random." And the word "red" appears again in the *Speech Acts* chapter "Deriving 'ought' from 'is'." When criticizing the concept of descriptive judgment of R.M. Hare, the author of *Freedom and Reason*, Searle quotes Hare's statement that "If a person says a thing is red, he is committed to the view that anything which was like it in the relevant respects would likewise be red" and writes several propositions that include the word "red." There is no avoiding the conclusion that Searle was forced to choose red by some intertextual necessity.

A significant repetition of "red" is found as well in "The Logical Status of Fictional Discourse." Immediately after Searle states, as I mentioned earlier, that the "red" in "Little Red Riding Hood" means red, he begins contrasting Iris Murdoch's *The Red and the Green* with a newspaper article "deliberately chosen at random." What matters here is that Searle, rather than quoting from the text of this fictional work, repeats the word "red" in his own text. While this repetition is unlikely to have been intentional, meaning can be read into the coincidence. After all, in our literary intertextual memories the title *The Red and the Green* immediately recalls Stendhal's *Le Rouge et le Noir*, and in our philosophical intertextual memories it draws us to the problem of red-green colorblindness raised in Wittgenstein's *Remarks on Colour*. Many will also recall that this same relation between red and green was discussed by Paul Valéry in his *Poétique* lectures at the Collège de France. One is also reminded of Jean-Pierre Richard's splendid interpretation in "Géographie Magique de Nerval" of how the theme of the green of vegetation eventually arrives at *rouge*: "achèvements logiques de la végétalité flamboyante de Nerval." In line with Marcel Proust's analysis that finds "ce rappel du rouge" in Nerval, the French critic Richard concludes: "Le vert aboutit donc à du rouge" (p. 42). Perhaps Professor Searle would say that such conclusions are unrelated to the context of his own writings. But the written text is constantly exposed to unlimited intertextual temptations that transcend the intentions of the writer.

The Thematics of Red

It is fascinating how analytical philosophers of language develop their arguments with such frequent references to red. At the beginning of *Linguistic Categorization*, for example, John R. Taylor writes, "In many respects, colour terminology provides an ideal testing ground for theories of categorization," and he begins his arguments with reference to the phonetic form of "red." In the chapter "Phenomenalism" of his book *Science, Perception and Reality*, Wilfrid Sellars mentions red several times in examples backing his statement "physical objects are patterns of actual and possible sense content," including "Jones sensed a red and triangular expanse," "There exists a red and triangular expanse," and "A red and triangular sense content exists." Willard Quine begins the first chapter, titled "Language and Truth," of his book *Word and Object* with a consideration of "ordinary things." He mentions "Ouch," a subjective one-word sentence that expresses pain, and then begins analyzing red as a more objective example in which "a nearly uniform stimulatory condition is shared by simultaneous observers." Starting with the problem of how color-blind people identify "lobsters only after boiling" as red, Quine goes on to state that "Vagueness is of the essence in the first phase of word learning" and that "Stimulations eliciting a verbal response, say 'red,' are best depicted as forming not a neatly bounded class but a distribution about a central *norm*." In the chapter "Prospects for a Theory of Projection" in his book *Fact, Fiction, and Forecast*, Nelson Goodman, examining whether the statement "Everything in bag *A* is red" can be "a presumptively projectible hypothesis" under all conditions, begins with the statement "All the marbles in bag *B* are red" and lists various cases of "red" and "not-red." And even Jean-Paul Sartre, whose philosophical stance was different from Goodman's, states the following in *L'Entre et le Néant* as an example of how motion does not change the quality of an object but does change its manner of being: "This red ball which rolls on the billiard table does not cease *to be* red, but the ball is not this red which it *is* in the same way now as it was the red when at rest. The red remains suspended between abolition and permanence.... Thus through abolition it escapes being, and through being it escapes abolition. Therefore a category of 'thises' is encountered in the world which have the peculiar property of never being without thereby becoming nothingness." (pp. 289–290)

What matters here is that Sartre also refers to red. One philosopher after another mentions red in his text almost as if this proved the legitimacy of his argument. These many examples thus give us reason not to believe Professor Searle's statement that the red of "Little Red Riding Hood" was "deliberately chosen at random."

Critics discussing fiction also put red into their arguments. The French literary theorist Michael Riffaterre, who discussed the problem of reference in poetry in his provocative book *Fictional Truth*, quotes in *Semiotics of Poetry* the following line from a novel by Alphonse Allais as an example of how far literary fiction can be from mimesis: "Récolte de la tomate par des cardinaux apoplectique au bord de la Mer rouge." In this quotation, the word "red" appears only in the place name of the Red Sea, but the other adjectives and nouns are known culturally to be red. Similarly, "Little Red Riding Hood" is frequently quoted by theorists as if to add even more to this deluge of red. For example, in *Explaining Culture: A Naturalistic Approach (Contagion des Idées)*, Dan Sperber builds his anthropological theories in part on a reference to "Little Red Riding Hood." Applying Richard Dawkins' immunological concept of memes to the transmission of culture, Sperber believes that, during transmission, ideas not only replicate themselves but also change themselves, and he discusses how the stories collected by Charles Perrault had changed as told from person to person and therefore were categorized by Perrault into different versions. The standardized parts are replicated easily, while the incomplete versions are revised by the listeners and gradually approach standard versions.

Jean-Marie Schaeffer's *Pourquoi la Fiction* deals with fiction more directly, and once again "Little Red Riding Hood" appears right from the start – this time, though, in an analysis of Mercel Aymé's short story "Loup," a parodic variation of "Little Red Riding Hood" in which the wolf is the protagonist. In that story, two young girls are visited by a wolf while their parents are away. The wolf pretends to be gentle and peace-loving, and he is welcomed and soon becomes the girls' friend. The girls suggest playing Little Red Riding Hood. The wolf doesn't know the game, so the girls tell him the story of the brutal wolf. I won't tell you the end of the story except to say that a complicated situation develops in which the real wolf plays the wolf of the fictional story. The French literary theorist Schaeffer extracts from the development of this children's game a number of the components of fiction, including resemblance, imitation, feint, and fascination. By referring to this parody of "Little Red Riding Hood," Schaeffer excites the reader with the suggestion that Searle's theory itself has been parodied, but that does not seem to have been Schaeffer's intention. In any case, most of what are said to have been "deliberately chosen at random" form accidental coincidences beyond the intentions of the writers.

What deserves notice here is that so many people who have discussed fiction bring up red or "Little Red Riding Hood" as if that reference is a condition for guaranteeing the legitimacy of their theoretical arguments. The color creates an intertextual realm that has no relation to the intentions of the authors, and in that realm a meaning forms that ignores the contexts of the individual texts and is not shackled by the semantic, syntactic, or grammatical logic of the writers' theses. I use the word "theme" to describe this suction that draws together similar linguistic symbols transcending the logic of arguments and that forms outside those different systems, because thematic decoding that is suitable for the analysis of fictional texts appears to be applicable to theoretical texts as well. After all, Searle and Miura and Auerbach and Schaeffer are all bound by the thematic system of red through no conscious choice of their own. In the realm of themes that are beyond the reach of the writers' intentions, even theoretical discussions of fiction seem to approach fiction.

The Red Monster

Auerbach's *Mimesis* begins with a reading of Homer's *Odyssey* and ends with a reading of Virginia Woolf's *To the Lighthouse.* Though separated by thousands of years, these two works are intimately connected through their depiction of a woman bent over at a man's feet. In his first chapter, "Odysseus' Scar," Auerbach analyzes what he calls the "well-prepared and touching scene" of Euryclea bathing Odysseus; when she touches his leg, she realizes from the scar on it that he is her former master. In his final chapter, "The Brown Stocking," Auerbach notes that, while knitting a stocking for the lighthouse keeper's son, Mrs. Ramsey tries to judge the length by repeatedly holding an unfinished "reddish-brown hairy stocking" up against her own son's legs, which are a similar size. But the son is not happy about being the model for another person's stocking, and he ignores his mother's entreaties. The boy's silent refusal of his mother closely resembles Odysseus's silencing of Euryclea as she is about to let out a cry of welcome on learning from his scar that her master has returned home. Just as Mrs. Ramsey never finishes knitting the stocking, so too did Penelope never finish her weaving as she waited for her husband's return.

The images of women crouched at men's feet is sufficient to highlight the thematic similarities between these two works. Although Auerbach shows no awareness that, at the beginning and end of his book, he has analyzed in detail two works that share the same theme, the readers of *Mimesis*, when encountering at the end a scene similar to one seen at the beginning, experience an excitement similar to that felt when reading a work of fiction. This surprise shows the significance of reading theoretical works thematically. Auerbach, who shortened the phrase "reddish-brown hairy stocking" that had appeared in the original novel to just "The Brown Stocking," is unaware that his own criticism can thus be functioning as fiction. The expression "reddish-brown hairy stocking," which Auerbach also quotes, is brought back to life by the reader within the thematic system of red.

This thematic perspective has not been adopted by the fiction theorists who take narratological approaches. The concept of *mise en intrigue* of Paul Ricouer, the author of *Temps et Récit,* begins with Aristotle's aesthetics and includes narrative structural analyses from Propp to Genette but expels completely any thematic meaning from fictional discourse. But just as with Auerbach's *Mimesis*, my position is that, regardless of whether utterances are serious or fictional, we can awaken to meanings of linguistic symbols that slumber within contexts that are limited by the intentions of the writers. To do so, we must reconsider from a thematic perspective the "red" to which so many different theorists have referred.

From that reconsideration three different themes emerge. "Little Red Riding Hood" is a metonymic reference to fiction itself, but it also links to the theme of the hood as covering the body. Next, there is the theme of things such as marbles that can be manipulated with the hands. And finally there is the theme of images such as "red and triangular sense" that contribute to conceptualization. This last red, which appears in Quine, Sellars, Taylor, and Goodman, can be replaced by other colors. When we exclude that last theme, there appears a strange entity dressed in red that combines the first two themes. This entity is an image that resembles a human being, with head and legs and hands and brain.

This is only a fictional image, of course; its identity is uncertain, and its gender and age are unclear. But a red hood covers the upper part of the body, and red shoes enclose the body's lower part. And the feet inside those shoes are wearing reddish-brown stockings. The body's vertical axis creates a fictional image modeled on a human being. The body is draped in red cloth like a cardinal's robe, and the face peeking out with indistinguishable features is apoplectic red. The image picks bright red tomatoes near the Red Sea and checks whether or not all the marbles in the bag are red and has hands agile enough to roll red balls across a billiard table. Its brain is wise, and even if colorblind it can judge that lobsters only after boiling are red. In works of literature, red aspires to arrive at green.

Let us refer to this strange red image depicted in the philosophical and literary intertextual network as a "thematic Monster." Works of fiction contain no characters or other elements that are so dominated by exaggerated redness. This Red Monster becomes visible only through reading theoretical studies, but the theoreticians themselves are unaware that their own texts lead to the appearance of this odd image. In fact, this image that suggests a human being springs from no proper source such as a writer, and it was born with neither a father nor a mother. The ephemeral image is a thematic Monster created accidentally through serious factual utterances in theoretical writings with no connection to the intentions of the agents of its enunciation. Because this reading is made possible only by ignoring the logical contexts of the individual writings, some people might say that accepting this Monster requires a schizophrenic attitude. Some might even insist that this type of reading is so anarchistic as to be unacceptable in any academic field. But even without following Derrida, we can remember that written linguistic symbols experience an essential, irresponsible drifting. And as Derrida himself wrote in the paper "Signature Événement Context" from which I quoted earlier, "This essential drifting, due to writing as an iterative structure cut off from all absolute responsibility, from *consciousness* as the authority of the last analysis, writing orphaned, and separated at birth from the assistance of its father, is indeed what Plato condemned in the *Phaedrus*." (p. 316)

While I do not belong to Derrida's camp, I sympathize deeply with the concept of "writing orphaned, and separated at birth from the assistance of its father." Of course, Derrida did not think that something like this Red Monster would appear when the drifting of written words is examined closely. I want to dedicate this Red Monster that my speech puts before our vision to the memory of Jacques Derrida. To me, peace is, like this Red Monster, a schizophrenic, anarchistic concept. Neither synthesis nor analysis will draw forth its definition. Rather, peace is a concept filled with semantic conflicts and interpretive disorder. And what have created that disorder are the feigned intentions for excessively exclusionary rigor by researchers who discuss fiction only in their separate, isolated academic fields.

Ka no Yô Ni

Finally, I would like to touch briefly on an East Asian topic: *How Hans Vaihinger's Die Philosophie des Als Ob*, which Käte Hamburger and Dorrit Cohn both mentioned, was received in the intellectual climate of Japan. Only a year after the book was published in Leipzig in 1911, a literary work was written in Tokyo making use of Vaihinger's philosophy. That work was a short novel by Mori Ôgai titled *Ka no Yô Ni*, a Japanese phrase that corresponds to "Als Ob." This story was probably the earliest positive reaction anywhere in the world to *Die Philosophie des Als Ob*. Such a speedy response might be expected from Mori Ôgai, who had lived for several years in Germany in his youth, but it is the essential drifting of its written linguistic symbols that allows it to create this unexpected coincidence. That Käte Hamburger and Dorrit Cohn are able to quote Vaihinger and discuss fiction without even momentarily suspecting the possibility of East Asian contributions makes me, as a Japanese critic, uncomfortable.

Japan embarked on the road to modernization in 1868, and Mori Ôgai was one of its first real novelists. In his fictional story *Ka no Yô Ni* appear a young historian who has just returned to Japan from Germany and a young artist who has lived in France. These two fervently discuss *Die Philosophie des Als Ob*, which the historian spent most of the previous night reading. The historian explains the title using the French phrase *comme si*. He interprets it to mean "a conscious lie" and says that this philosophy suits him now. When he says "Points and lines do not exist. They are conscious lies. But if we cannot think that points and lines exist, then geometry is impossible," he is quoting Vaihinger's book nearly exactly. The historian says that reality is built upon this "as-if" and so is literature. "Novels are lies in the sense of whether they present facts as true," he says. "But they never try to show facts. They are created and distributed with awareness that they are lies, and therein exists life and value."

The historian's view of fiction anticipates in a sense Professor Searle's concept of "feigned," but the historian's comment that "therein exists life" is fundamentally different from the position that views fictional assertions as parasites on factual assertions. It was possible for Vaihinger's philosophical work to be thus discussed in Japan's capital in 1912 so soon after it was published in Germany only because the characters in this fiction belong to a privileged class. The young historian, the son of a viscount, spends his days immersed in books, and his father fears that he will succumb to "extreme liberal attitudes."

Into this story intrudes a nonfictional event. A few years before "Ka no Yô Ni" was written, a plot had been uncovered to assassinate the Japanese emperor. The conspiracy shook Japan, as the nation was being modernized on the foundation of the emperor's authority. The conspirators were tried in a secret tribunal, and some were immediately executed. An influential political figure who was a patron of Mori Ôgai demanded that novels be written to dispel the "dangerous thinking" that was spreading among young people, and it has been widely believed that "Ka no Yô Ni" was written in response to that demand. The concept of "conscious lies" has been taken as if it were what Ôgai himself thought, and the story has been interpreted to be a call by Ôgai to avoid social turmoil. Critical evaluations of the story have therefore been generally negative.

Taking the words of characters in fiction to represent the thinking of the writer should, of course, be avoided in the reading of fiction. But then what is the proper way to read "Ka no Yô Ni" as fiction? Here we should focus on a third character who appears in the story but who says almost nothing. It is a young woman who works as a maid in the historian's home. As can be seen by the very first sentence of the story, which begins "In the morning, when Yuki the maid came in to light the charcoal brazier," the main role of this maid is to "light the flame" of the heater. Her job is also to enter the historian's bedroom early in the morning to light the gas heater while he is still asleep, but one morning she notices in the darkness the "redness" of the flame of his cigar, so she quickly leaves. The historian has been awake all night, reading Vaihinger's book until dawn. At this point, it becomes clear that Ka no Yô Ni should be read in conjunction with the theme of "red."

The maid also appears in the parlor where the historian and the artist are eagerly discussing Vaihinger's philosophy. First, when she places herself at the historian's door to tell him that his friend has arrived, the artist pushes her shoulder away with his "red hand" and jokes to her that she shouldn't gaze so lovingly on her master. She turns "bright red" and runs away. The historian is annoyed by his friend's joke, and it is clear that the maid is an erotic presence that cannot be dismissed as a "conscious lie." The artist, too, as he discourses on the philosophy of "as-if," sips at the tea that the maid has brought and mutters, "When that proven fact named Yuki comes in, my thoughts get all confused." The maid disturbs the men's abstract discussions about "as-if." The story "Ka no Yô Ni" is thus clearly not defending "conscious lies"; rather, it is a work of fiction on the theme of the difficult-to-resolve conflicts between "conscious lies" and "proven facts."

The maid who exists as a "proven fact" also, as the "woman who lights the fire," arouses the men with "red." The "redness" that fills her "bright red" cheeks as she runs away infects the men arguing about the philosophy of "as-if." When the historian declares that "there is no position other than mine of respecting the 'as-if', ... the edges of his eyes in his pale face blush red, and a light flares deep in those eyes like the flame of fanaticism." When the artist rejects his friend's words, "his eyes flash in an instant like steel." The historian notices this, and "once again the edges of his eyes turn red." Clearly the maid "lit the fire" with "redness." Thus *Ka no Yô Ni* is fiction that should be read within the thematic system of red, beginning with the temptation of red in the flame of the cigar in the darkened room and ending with the corresponding red arousal. How does this "red" filling the viscount's house in Tokyo in 1912 interact with the Red Monster? For this question to be discussed, a new theory of fiction must be conceived with Mori Ôgai's story *Ka no Yô Ni* as its starting point. I am now writing about this, and what I have presented here is only part of that theory.

To close my speech, let me read a marvelous passage that refers to red in *The Pleasure of the Text* by Roland Barthes: "We read a text (of pleasure) the way a fly buzzes around a room: with sudden, deceptively decisive turns, fervent and futile: ideology passes over the text and its reading like the blush over a face (in love, some take erotic pleasure in this coloring); every writer of pleasure has these idiotic blushes (Balzac, Zola, Flaubert, Proust: only Mallarmé, perhaps, is master of his skin)." (p. 31)

What constantly seizes hold of us in works of fiction is this "coloring" of "idiotic blushes," but I declare that we should not turn our faces away. Mallarmé's complete mastery of his skin is the terrible temptation that draws people to fiction's Degree Zero.

The Ideal International Order in East Asia

Bok Koh-ill

1. Need for a Common View on History

East Asia is an important region. Nearly one-third of the world's population lives there. In terms of economy, its importance is still greater. The region's economy has grown fast and its two major countries, Japan and China, are respectively the second biggest economy in the world: Japan is the second biggest economy in terms of total value of goods, China by Purchasing Power Parity (PPP). And the region's cultural contribution has been substantial and steadily increasing.

On the other hand, it is one of the most dangerous regions in the world. The two Koreas are technically still at war, having failed to conclude a peace treaty even after a half century of armistice. China regularly threatens to invade Taiwan if the latter proclaims independence. The territorial claims for islands in the East China Sea and the South China Sea might ignite military clashes that would involve almost all the countries in the region. And religious strife and massacres are continuing. After all, the two major wars after the Second World War – the Korean War and the Vietnam War -- were waged there.

Regrettably, there is no regional supra-national organization that would deal with the regional affairs. And it is not likely that one will come into existence in the near future. This lack of political coordination sharply contrasts with the voluminous and ever-increasing trade in the region. So it is meaningful to deliberate on the ideal international order in East Asia. A regional order, of course, should be dealt with in the context of the world order, especially in the age of globality. This condition puts a severe limit on the scope and depth of the deliberation.

The word "ideal" here actually means "the best possible in the present conditions." This article is not a place to think of designing an ideal international order of the region in the manner of John Rawls's "original position." Such attempt is futile for two reasons.

First, history puts fundamental boundary conditions on the matter. The history of the peoples and countries of East Asia would limit the scope of possible orders and fundamentally influence the shape of the future order. Second, the international order, like other social orders, is to a large degree a "spontaneous order" as Friedrich Hayek said. It grows spontaneously out of the trade of goods and exchange of ideas. The ideal international order of the region we should deliberate on, therefore, is of necessity the best order permitted by the history of East Asia.

Naturally, it is essential for the peoples and countries of the region to reach a consensus in their interpretation of the region's history. Only on that foundation any meaningful discussion for the ideal or best possible international order for the region could be conducted. As the "History Questions" that plague the relations between Japan, Korea and China painfully show, however, such consensus is very difficult, if not outright impossible, to achieve. So great is the gulf between the view of Japan who was the aggressor in the modern era and that of the rest of the region's countries who were its victims that they could not agree on even small matters in the historical assessment. And without narrowing such difference in the view of history, any substantial improvement in the relations between countries in the region, let alone design of a new international order, is not likely. A consensus on this matter, therefore, has practical urgency as well as intellectual value. So I will attempt to offer an interpretation of the modern history of East Asia that might narrow the difference.

2. Influence of European Civilization

The primary theme of the modern history of the world is the conquest of the world by European civilization. As Paul Kennedy succinctly described, the ascendancy of the European civilization over other civilizations of the world was sudden and unexpected.

In the year 1500, the date chosen by numerous scholars to mark the divide between modern and premodern times, it was by no means obvious to the inhabitants of Europe that their continent was poised to dominate much of the rest of the earth. The knowledge which contemporaries possessed about the great civilizations of the Orient was fragmentary and all too often erroneous, based as it was upon travelers' tales which had lost nothing in their retelling. Nevertheless, the widely held image of extensive eastern empires possessing fabulous wealth and vast armies was a reasonably accurate one, and on first acquaintance those societies must have seemed far more favorably endowed than the peoples and states of western Europe. Indeed, placed alongside these other great centers of cultural and economic activity, Europe's relative weaknesses were more apparent than its strengths. It was, for a start, neither the most fertile nor the most populous area in the world; India and China took pride of place in each respect. Geopolitically, the 'continent' of Europe was an awkward shape, bounded by ice and water to the north and west, being open to frequent landward invasion from the east, and vulnerable to strategic circumvention in the south. In 1500, for a long time before and after that, these were not abstract considerations.

[...]

Unlike the Ottoman and Chinese empires, unlike the rule which the Moguls were soon to establish in India, there never was a united Europe in which all parts acknowledged one secular or religious leader. Instead, Europe was a hodge-podge of petty kingdoms and principalities, marcher lordships and city-states. Some more powerful monarchies were arising in thewest, notably Spain, France, and England, but none was to be free of internal tensions and all regarded the others as rivals, rather than allies in the struggle against Islam.

Nor could it be said that Europe had pronounced advantages in the realm of culture, mathematics, engineering, or navigational and other technologies when compared with the great civilizations of Asia. A considerable part of the European cultural and scientific heritage was, in any case, 'borrowed' from Islam, just as Muslim societies had borrowed for centuriesfrom China through the media of mutual trade, conquest, and settlement. In retrospect, one can see that Europe was accelerating both commercially and technologically by the late fifteenth century; but perhaps the fairest general comment would be that each of the great centers of world civilization about that time was at a roughly similar stage of development, some more advanced in one area, but less so in others. *(The Rise and Fall of the Great Powers)*

Thanks to the scientific revolutions and the subsequent Industrial Revolution, European civilization quickly acquired ascendancy over other civilizations in nearly every field. Its ascendancy was greatest in industrial power and military might. And the rest of the world could not offer any effective resistance to its conquering armies.

Its conquest, like others, could not be otherwise than violent, brutal and destructive. But because of the great gap in the level of development between European civilization based on modern science and technology and other civilizations, its conquest had another dimension. The intellectual tradition of European civilization proved so much superior to that of other civilizations that it replaced almost entirely the indigenous ones. And the whole world has been integrated into one global civilization centered round the European intellectual tradition.

The above fact indicates that we should pay more attention to the role of knowledge in modern history, especially in the conquest by European civilization. Interactions between civilizations are essentially flow of knowledge. Nothing is more valuable or influential than knowledge. While the most visible part of interactions between civilizations involves trade of goods, the essential element there is also the knowledge contained in the traded goods. Naturally, in the intercourse of civilizations, extensive exchange of knowledge in the form of goods, services, contracts, ideas, ideologies and institutions occurs.

When the two interacting civilizations are similar in the level of development, the flow of knowledge would be a two-way process. But when the gap in the level of development is substantial, knowledge would mostly flow from the superior civilization to the inferior one, replacing the knowledge of the latter with the superior knowledge of the former. That is what happened when European civilization met others. The gradient of knowledge was so steep that knowledge from European civilization flowed ferociously into the indigenous civilization and soon flooded it. The process was inevitably violent, confusing, and destructive. War, conquest, subjugation, colonization, exploitation, and destruction of traditions followed. Though such violent events were unprecedented calamities to the victimized civilizations, they were parts of the process of the flow of knowledge from the advanced civilization to the less developed ones. It could become a normal flow of knowledge only when the gradient of knowledge became not so steep.

In the intercourse between European civilization and others, another factor aggravated the already dire situation. The essence of life is information processing. Growth, metabolism, and reproduction of an individual involve enormously complex and admirably accurate information processing.

> The central insight of the Santiago Theory [of Cognition] is the identification of cognition, the process of knowing, with the process of life. Cognition, according to [Humberto] Maturana and [Francisco] Varela, is the activity involved in the self-generation and self-perpetuation of living networks. In other words, cognition is the very process of life. The organizing activity of living systems, at all levels of life, is mental activity. The interactions of a living organism – plant, animal or human – with its environment are cognitive interactions. Thus life and cognition are inseparably connected. Mind – or, more accurately, mental activity – is immanent in matter at all levels of life. (Fritjof Capra, *The Hidden Connection*)

Naturally, an individual's body embodies a vast amount of knowledge. One kind of such biological knowledge is that for immunity. Our body has a great amount of knowledge for immune responses to germs. And such "immunoknowlege" is of critical importance in the intercourse of civilizations.

The majority of mankind have lived in the Eurasian continent and enjoyed civilizations more advanced than those of the people in the other continents. Extensive animal husbandry and urbanization there provided a good environment for germs and the Eurasian people had many diseases and in time developed immunity to them. But the aborigines of Africa, the Americas and Oceania lacked immunity to many diseases brought by the Europeans. And the epidemics inflicted fatal calamities upon them.

> [A]rchaeological excavations, and scrutiny of descriptions left by the very first European explorers on our coasts, now suggest an initial number of around 20 million Indians. For the New World as a whole, the Indian population decline in the century or two following Columbus's arrival is estimated to have been as large as 95 percent.
>
> The main killers were Old World germs to which Indians had never been exposed, and against which they therefore had neither immune nor genetic resistance. Smallpox, measles, influenza, and typhus competed for top rank among the killers. As if these had not been enough, diphtheria, malaria, mumps, pertussis, plague, tuberculosis, and yellow fever came up close behind. In countless cases, whites were actually there to witness the destruction occurring when the germs arrived. For example, in 1837 the Mandan Indian tribe, with one of the most elaborate cultures in our Great River Plains, contracted smallpox from a steamboat traveling up the Missouri River from St. Louis. The population of one Mandan village plummeted from 2,000 to fewer than 40 within a few weeks. [...]
>
> The historical importance of animal-derived diseases extends far beyond the collision of the Old and the New Worlds. Eurasian germs played a key role in decimating native peoples in many other parts of the world, including Pacific islanders, Aboriginal Australians, and the Khoisan peoples (Hottentots and Bushmen) of southern Africa. Cumulative mortalities of these previously unexposed peoples from

Eurasian germs ranged from 50 percent to 100 percent." (Jared Diamond, *Guns, Germs, and Steel*)

3. East Asia's Relative Advantage

East Asia's history since the overseas expansion of European civilization followed the same pattern as that of other civilizations. The countries in the region tried to accommodate the new civilization with far superior military might and scientific and technical knowledge. But they were soon overwhelmed by European civilization and eventually integrated into a new global order centered round it.

But there was a substantial difference between the fate of East Asia and that of other regions. The gap in the level of knowledge between East Asia and Europe was not as great as in other cases. After all, the Chinese civilization that encompassed China, Korea, Vietnam, Mongolia, and Japan was well advanced and still vigorous when the Europeans reached East Asia. This relatively small gap in the level of knowledge gave East Asia relatively large room for adaptation to the changed environment due to the sudden appearance of a superior civilization.

It should be noted here that one factor conferred a critical advantage to the East Asians largely denied to other peoples in their dealings with the Europeans. The "immunoknowledge" of the East Asians was quite similar with that of the Europeans. Situated at the western and eastern end of the Eurasian continent, respectively, the European and Chinese civilizations have had continual intercourse and, naturally, most of the germs carried by the Europeans were known also to the East Asians. In actuality, many germs originated in East Asia ravaged Europe rather than the other way around.

> [W]e cannot specify where within the Old World most major diseases of Old World origin arose. However, European writings from Roman and medieval times clearly describe the arrival of bubonic plague and possibly smallpox from the east, so these germs could be of Chinese or East Asian origin. Influenza (derived from pigs) is even more likely to have arisen in China,

since pigs were domesticated so early and became so important there. (Jared Diamond, *Guns, Germs, and Steel*)

The most famous case is the Black Death, the plague that ravaged Europe between 1347 and 1351 and proved to be the greatest catastrophe experienced by Europe up to that time. It has been since firmly established that it had come from the east.

> The Black Death came from Asia, where it had already wrought havoc in China and in Turkistan. It decimated the armyof the Kipchak Khan Janibeg, while he was besieging the Genoese trading port of Kaffa (now Feodosiya) in the Crimea (1347), and by catapulting plague-infested corpses into the townthe khan contrived to infect his enemies. From Kaffa Genoese ships carried the epidemic westward to the Mediterranean ports, whence it spread inland. ("Black Death," *Encyclopedia Britannica*)

Then, the recent outbreak of avian flu has merely followed the ancient pattern. So the East Asians had nothing to fear from the Europeans as far as germs are concerned.

Such a relatively small gap in the level of knowledge and full sufficiency in "immunoknowledge" against the European germs gave the East Asians a respite in the accommodation of the ascendant civilization. Fully availing themselves of such a respite, they attempted to incorporate the superior knowledge of European civilization in a more or less orderly fashion. It is significant that China and Japan, the two major countries in the region, managed to keep their political independence and cultural identity intact.

It was evident from the first that the East Asian countries should absorb the knowledge of the ascendant civilization to survive or else be totally subjugated by the Europeans. On the other hand, since absorption of foreign knowledge takes time and resources, it was necessary for them to decide what among the vast European knowledge should be brought in and allowed to replace the traditional knowledge while others were earmarked for later introduction or to be rejected outright. The rational attitude in such a situation was to selectively accept material things in foreign civilization that were evidently better than the traditional ones but keep the cultural and moral system more or less intact. Only in that way a society could keep functioning and maintain its identity. At stake was nothing less than one's identity and the loss of one's identity was the ultimate defeat.

It is not surprising, therefore, that the strategies adopted by the various East Asian countries were practically identical. They all tried to keep the traditional world view and value system as the foundation of society and adopt useful things of the ascendant civilization in support of such traditional world views and value systems. In China, the "Theory of Chinese Body and Western Tool (中體西用論)," which argued that China should keep its traditional disciplines, knowledge and value system as the social foundation and adopt only those things from Western civilization that proved to be superior as tools, emerged as the orthodox theory. In Japan, the "Theory of Eastern Morals and Western Art (東洋道德西洋藝術論)" argued that the traditional moral system of the East should not be discarded but reinterpreted and such a reinterpreted moral system could be the foundation for the absorption of superior Western technology. In Korea, the "Theory of Eastern Morals and Western Tools (東道西器論)," similar in outlook and prescriptions to the other two, soon emerged.

Actually, this kind of policy was, at least in theory, adopted in nearly every country and civilization. When the coming of an evidently superior civilization suddenly destroys the traditional frame of reference, the most natural and rational attitude is to keep the traditional value system as the foundation and selectively adopt the evidently superior tools and technology from the foreign civilization. It was a sensible strategy. Sadly, it turned out that such strategy was not adequate. It certainly would be insufficient simply to adopt new industrial technology and military equipment to meet the crisis. It would also be not enough to adopt political, social and economic institutions. Ultimately, it was neither feasible nor meaningful to separate tools or institutions from the value system that produced them. To adopt, copy, adapt, and improve on the technology and institutions of the superior civilization, it was necessary to understand the essence of the civilization. The essence of European civilization was its scientific attitude. So it was inevitable that East Asian countries were eventually forced to abandon their traditional systems and adopt European ones almost entirely. Through that inexorable process, East Asia was integrated into the new global civilization centered around European civilization.

4. Two Questions: Why not China? and Why Japan?

The modern history of East Asia from its first encounter with European civilization to its eventual absorption into the new global civilization is a large subject that cannot be properly dealt with in an article like this. Fortunately, there is a convenient way to delineate the core seams of the region's modern history. We can ask two questions that admirably illuminate those core seams. One is "Why not China?" and the other "Why Japan?"

The former refers to the famous question about the Scientific Revolution: "Why, in Eurasia, was it the European civilization rather than the Chinese civilization that discovered scientific methodology and achieved the Scientific Revolution?" Once the Europeans achieved the Scientific Revolution, it was inevitable that their civilization based on ever-rapidly accumulating scientific knowledge would conquer the whole world, and East Asia would suffer the fate of a subjugated civilization. So the question "Why not China?" is the most profound question to be answered in the study of the modern history of East Asia.

The question "Why Japan?" addresses the fact that among the many non-European countries so far, only Japan managed to successfully absorb the superior knowledge of the European civilization and modernize itself. It is truly remarkable that, since European civilization expanded over the globe five centuries ago, only Japan has boosted itself into the rank of advanced countries. All others that have done so are offshoots of European civilization, like the USA, Canada, Australia, and New Zealand. (Though Hong Kong and Singapore also have managed to do so, they are city states and in reality were overseas territory of the British Empire for the critical first part of their history. So they can be disregarded in connection with this discussion.) Japan's such unique achievement is interesting and important in itself. After all, all the less-developed countries of the world have been trying to emulate Japan in that regard. But to the rest of East Asia Japan's success had fateful implications. Through successful modernization Japan became the region's hegemonic power and the other countries have suffered from Japan's aggression and dominance ever since.

The two questions, "Why not China?" and "Why Japan?", therefore, neatly illuminate the core seams in the modern history of East Asia and offer convenient focus for the arduous task of summarizing it for the discussion.

5. China's Failure to Discover Modern Science

Yes, "Why not China?" During the Middle Ages, Chinese civilization apparently had a better base for the discovery of scientific methodology than other civilizations. Joseph Needham averred, "Apart from the great ideas and systems of the Greeks, between the first and the fifteenth centuries the Chinese, who experienced no 'dark ages', were generally much in advance of Europe; and not until the scientific revolution of the late Renaissance did Europe draw rapidly ahead."

It is well known that only from the base of advanced technology can science arise. And what China achieved in technology is really impressive.

> In technological influences before and during the Renaissance China occupies a quite dominating position. In the body of this contribution we shall mention among other things the efficient equine harness, the technology of iron and steel, the inventions of gunpowder and paper, the mechanical clock, and basic engineering devices such as the driving-belt, the chain-drive, and the standard method of converting rotary to rectilinear motion, together with segmental arch bridges and nautical techniques such as the stern-post rudder. The world owes far more to the relatively silent craftsmen of ancient and medieval China than to the Alexandrian mechanics, articulate theoreticians though they were.

(Joseph Needham, *The Grand Titration*)

Then, what is it that the Europeans achieved and the Chinese failed to achieve? Why is it so important?

> When we say that modern science developed only in Western Europe at the time of Galileo in the late Renaissance, we mean surely that there and then alone there developed the fundamental bases of the structure of the natural sciences as we have them today, namely the application of mathematical hypotheses to Nature, the full understanding and use of the experimental method, the distinction between primary and secondary qualities, the geometrisation of space, and the acceptance of the mechanical model of reality. Hypotheses of primitive or medieval type distinguish themselves quite clearly from those of modern type. Their intrinsic and essential vagueness always made them incapable of proof or disproof, and they were prone to combine in fanciful systems of gnostic correlation. ... In the West Leonardo da Vinci, with all his brilliant inventive genius, still inhabited this world; Galileo brokethrough its walls. This is why it has been said that Chinese science and technology remained until late times essentially Vincian, and that the Galilean break-through occurred only in the West. (Joseph Needham, ibid.)

What is the fundamental reason for this different outcome? What attracts one's attention in the search for an answer to this important question is the contrast between China and Europe in the effect of technology and science on the structure of society. It is interesting in itself and offers an important clue to China's failure to achieve a scientific revolution. Major technology that fundamentally disturbed European societies had had negligible effect on Chinese society. Needham succinctly describes this point in *The Great Titration*, a work that explicitly attempted to 'titrate' the great civilizations against one another.

> The development of gunpowder weapons was certainly one of the greatest achievements of the medieval Chinese world. ... For

decades, indeed for centuries, from Shakespeare's time onwards, European historians have recognized in the first salvoes of the fourteenth-century bombards the death-knell of the castle, and hence of Western military aristocratic feudalism. … In one single year (1449) the artillery train of the king of France, making a tour of the castles still held by the English in Normandy, battered them down one after another at the rate of five a month. Nor were the effects of gunpowder confined to the land; they had profound influence also at sea, for in due time they gave the death-blow to the multi-oared slave-manned galley of the Mediterranean, which was unable to provide gun-platforms sufficiently stable for naval cannonades and broadsides.

[…]

Here the contrast with China is particularly noteworthy. The basic structure of bureaucratic feudalism remained after five centuries or so of gunpowder weapons just about the same as it had been before the invention had developed. The birth of chemical warfare had occurred in the Thang but it did not find wide military use before the Sung, and its real proving-grounds were the wars between the Sung Empire, the Chin Tartars, and the Mongols in the eleventh to thirteenth centuries. There are plenty of examples of its use by the forces of agrarian rebellions, and it was employed at sea as well as on land, in siege warfare no less than in the field. But as there was no heavily armoured knightly cavalry in China, nor any aristocratic or manorial feudal castles either, the new weapon simply supplemented those which had been in use before, and produced no perceptible effect upon the age-old civil and military bureaucratic apparatus, which each new foreign conqueror had to take over and use in his turn.

[…]

[T]he magnetic compass, or more broadly speaking, the knowledge of magnetic polarity as well as magnetic attraction, had also its sociologically earth-shaking character in the Western world. The part which it played in the nascent phases of modern science would be sufficient justification for this in itself, but there

> was more; for in the hands of the European sea-captains of the fifteenth century the compass crowned a whole period of navigational science which had been inaugurated in the thirteenth, and made possible not only the circumnavigation of the African, but the discovery of the American, continent. How profoundly this affected the life of Europe, with the influx of vast quantities of silver, the marketing of innumerable new kinds of commodities, and the opening up of colonies and plantations, hardly requires elaborate emphasis here. ... But again there is the other side of the picture. Chinese society was not upset by the knowledge of magnetic phenomena; the geomancers continued to advise families upon the siting of houses and tombs with ever-increasing refinements of their baseless art, and the sea-captains continued to find their way to the East Indies or the Persian Gulf in a trade that was peripheral to China's main economic life.

We can easily discern the same pattern in all the other major inventions – printing, hydro-mechanical clock, astronomy, foot-stirrups and efficient harness for equine animals, rotary-milling, driving-belt, stern-post rudder, and fore-and-aft sails.

As seen above, China should have achieved a scientific revolution long before Europe. All three inventions cited by Francis Bacon as discoveries that "have changed the whole face and state of things throughout the world," namely printing, gunpowder, and the magnet, were first discovered by the Chinese. But the social impact of such inventions was not great enough to begin a revolution of any kind. While China experienced endless social upheavals of foreign invasion, dynastic change and rebellion, "the basic forms of its social life remained relatively constant." The conventional view of "stagnant China" is largely true. And it was European civilization that eventually achieved the crucial intellectual breakthrough. Why Europe? Why not China?

Needham said that the key to the question might lie in four factors: geographical, hydrological, social and economic. He ruled out at the start all explanations in terms of the dominance of Confucian philosophy on the ground that they would only invite the further question, "Why was Chinese civilization such that

Confucian philosophy did dominate?"

> Economic historians ... tell us that though Chinese and European feudalism were not unlike, when feudalism decayed in China, it gave place to an economic and social system totally different from anything in Europe; not mercantile, still less industrial, capitalism, but a special form which may be called Asiatic bureaucratism, or bureaucratic feudalism. ... [T]he rise of the merchant class to power, with their slogan of democracy, was the indispensable accompaniment and sine qua non of the rise of modern science in the west. But in China the scholar-gentry and their bureaucratic feudal system always effectively prevented the rise to power or seizure of the State by the merchant class, as happened elsewhere.
>
> On the geographical side, China is a continental country, bound to agriculture, not an archipelago teeming with maritime mercantile city-states, as Europe always was. China's rainfall, moreover, is highly seasonal, and highly variable from year to year; this necessitated works of irrigation and water-conservation, river control, drainage and inland navigation, far greater than anything which had to be done in the West. Some have seen the origin of the Asiatic bureaucracy in the necessary control of the masses of manpower which were required to construct these great works, but perhaps it is more probable that an irrigation-civilization impinged upon feudalism because the great engineering works transcended the boundaries of the lands of individual feudal lords. Their power thus inevitably became absorbed by the imperial power, and after the union of the countryunder the first Chin Emperor in the late third century B.C., the feudal lords steadily declined until they lost all importance. Correspondingly the imperial bureaucracy gained in importance, and while on the one hand it prevented any recrudescence of feudalism, it also absolutely prevented the rise of the merchants and the coming into being of capitalism.

Jared Diamond in his *Guns, Germs, and Steel* argued that geography and ecology offer the ultimate answer to the question.

> I suggested that the underlying reason behind Europe's overtaking China was something deeper than the proximate factors suggested by most historians (e.g., China's Confucianism vs. Europe's Judeo-Christian tradition, the rise of western science, the rise of European mercantilism and capitalism, Britain's deforestation coupled with its coal deposits, etc.). Behind these and other proximate factors, I saw an 'Optimal Fragmentation Principle': ultimate geographic factors that led to China becoming unified early and mostly remaining unified thereafter, while Europe remained constantly fragmented. Europe's fragmentation did, and China's unity didn't, foster the advance of technology, science, and capitalism by fostering competition between states and providing innovators with alternative sources of support and havens from persecution.

As is now widely recognized, competition is crucial for progress. As Friedrich Hayek aptly remarked, competition is a 'discovery process.' Diamond supported his convincing argument with a similar view by Graeme Lang.

> Differences between Europe and China in ecology and geography helped to explain the very different fates of science in the two regions. First, [rainfall] agriculture in Europe provided no role for the state, which remained far from local communities most of the time, and when the agricultural revolution in Europe produced a growing agricultural surplus, this allowed the growth of relatively autonomous towns along with urban institutions such as universities prior to the rise of the centralized states in the late Middle Ages. [Irrigation and water-control] agriculture in China, by contrast, favored the early development of intrusive and coercive states in the major river valleys, while towns and their institutions never achieved the degree of local autonomy found in Europe. Second, the geography of China, unlike that of Europe, did not favor the prolonged survival of independent states. Instead,China's geography facilitated eventual conquest and unification over a vast area, followed by long periods of relative stability under imperial

rule. The resulting state system suppressed most of the conditions required for the emergence of modern science. The explanation outlined above is certainly oversimplified. However, one of the advantages of this kind of account is that it escapes the circularity which often creeps into explanations which do not go deeper than social or cultural differences between Europe and China. Such explanations can always be challenged with a further question: why were Europe and China different with regard to those social or cultural factors? Explanations rooted ultimately in geography and ecology, however, have reached bedrock. (Graeme Lang, "State Systems and the Origin of Modern Science: a Comparison of Europe and China")

Needham's and Diamond's views are essentially similar and supplement each other. So we might regard them as having enunciated at least an important aspect of the matter. But we cannot expect a definitive answer to this important question to emerge soon. Since controlled experiment is not available to historians, the verification of historical hypotheses cannot be rigorous. Furthermore, a scientific revolution belongs to those events that can take place only once. Once a civilization achieves a scientific revolution, it would become so ascendant over others that it would rapidly conquer others and replace the indigenous traditions with their own. In the real history, European civilization rapidly overwhelmed others and there really was no chance for another civilization to achieve a scientific revolution by itself. Unlike other historical questions, therefore, the question about the origin of scientific revolution cannot even resort to "natural experiment."

6. Japan's Achievement

Japan's experience in its encounter with European civilization was remarkable and exceptional. And unlike the question "Why not China?" its relevance has not diminished with the years. If anything, it has acquired global relevance while the whole world searches in earnest for the causes for economic and social development.

Though it permitted limited trade with Westerners for centuries,

Japan was the most closed society in East Asia. But it was forced to open its harbors to the West by the military might of the United States of America under humiliating conditions.

> Perry duly returned with seven ships in February 1854. … Perry remained firm in his attitude to the Japanese, not hesitating to utter threats at appropriate moments in the negotiations, which indeed were not long drawn-out. Finally, on 31 March, 1854, at a little fishing village called Yokohama, a treaty was signed. This agreement, known as the Treaty of Kanagawa, opened the ports of Hakodate and Shimoda to American ships for supplies and for trade, subject to local regulations. Shipwrecked mariners were to receive help and protection. An American consul was to be allowed to live in Shimoda. (Richard Storry, *A History of Modern Japan*)

Only half a century later, another treaty, which was very advantageous to Japan, announced that Japan had emerged as a global power. It had won the Russo-Japanese War.

> The Treaty of Portsmouth (New Hampshire) which concluded the war was signed on 5 September, 1905. The Russians agreed to recognize Japan's 'paramount political, military, and economic interests' in Korea, and to transfer to Japan the lease of the Liaotung peninsular and the railway connecting Port Arthur and Mukden as far north to Ghangchun, beyond Muckden. Russia also ceded to Japan the southern half of the island of Sakhalin together with special fishing rights. (Richard Storry, ibid.)

It is not easy for us now to imagine the shock Japan's victory over Russia gave to the contemporaries. But the shock was felt all over the world and affected the course of history in many ways.

> More important than these tactical changes were the influences of Japan's victory on world affairs. It disrupted Russia by stimulating the virus of revolution which for long had eaten into

her bowels. By liberating Germany from fear of war on her eastern flank it freed her to concentrate on her western border, and thereby upset the balance of power in Europe. This caused Great Britain to abandon her policy of isolation, which had been the backbone of the Pax Britannica, and, in order to re-establish the balance, it drew her away from Germany toward France. Further, by challenging the supremacy of the white man over the colored, it awakened Asia and Africa and dealt a deadly moral blow to every colonial empire.

[...]

In Africa the influence was equally profound. Dicey, an Englishman, who had lived in that continent for 40 years, writes: 'Suddenly and unexpectedly, the conviction that native forces, however brave, were bound to be worsted by Europeans, was shaken to its base by the discovery that Russia, which was regarded in the East as the greatest military power in Europe, had been driven from pillar to post by the victorious Japanese, that her armies had been put to flight, her navy destroyed, her fortresses captured by a comparatively diminutive and feeble Power, whose people, whatever else they might be, were certainly not Caucasians or Christians.

[...]

But it was in India – the pivot of British imperial power – that this world revolution took surest form. There 'a stir of excitement passed over' the northern provinces, writes C. F. Andrews. ... 'Asia was moved from one end to the other, and the sleep of the centuries was finally broken.'

In corroboration of this, Mr. Prahan writes: 'It is impossible to exaggerate the effects of the Japanese victory on the Indian mind.' Indian students began to study the history of Japan to discover what had enabled her to wound so deeply one of the greatest European Powers. They found the answer in Japanese patriotism, self-sacrifice and national unity. Here were miraculous powers beyond the might of armaments. ... Indian students flocked to the Rising Sun, and in the years 1907, 1908 and 1909 they returned haloed with knowledge, both true and spurious, to take part in the 'Swadeshi' movement, and to help a cause which the Japanese

> victories had endowed with a vigour undreamt of before the war.
>
> All these stupendous happenings were fertilized by this conflict, fought on the far eastern flank of Asia, as over 450 years before an equally great conflict had been fought on the far eastern flank of Europe. The fall of Port Arthur in 1905, like the fall of Constantinople in 1453, rightly may be numbered among the few really great events in history. (J.F.C. Fuller, *A Military History of the Western World*)

The Russo-Japanese War made clear to the whole world the successful metamorphosis of Japan from a feudal state to a modern state. Such metamorphosis was, of course, a gigantic effort, involving a myriad of projects that demanded a high degree of devotion, determination, ingenuity, and luck. We can see how difficult each of such myriad projects really were and how admirably the Japanese managed to overcome the obstacles in railroad construction, the symbol of modernization.

> There were no railways at the time of the restoration. The British minister, Sir Harry Smith Parkes, recommended the building of railways when the southern Japanese island of Kyushu suffered from famine in 1869, while there was a surplus of rice elsewhere. Neither the state treasury nor private capitalists were willing or able, at first, to finance railway construction. But an Englishman, Horatio Nelson Lay, offered to find the necessary funds and a loan of 1 million pounds was floated on the London market. Great Britain supplied some of the engineers and material for the first lines, which connected Tokyo with the neighboring port of Yokohama, and Osaka with its adjacent port of Kobe. There had been opposition to the railway project in some circles, persons occupied in other forms of transportation fearing ruin, while extreme nationalists feared the loss of independence through the flotation of a foreign loan. However, the leading statesmen of the restoration, Ito Hirobumi and Okuma Shigenobu, carried through the scheme, and the presence of the emperor at the opening of the first line, between Tokyo and Yokohama, in 1872 silenced all opposition. The Osaka-Kobe line was completed in

> 1874 and extended to Kyoto in 1877. While British engineers surveyed the routes and supervised the work during the first few years, the Japanese showed themselves as apt pupils in railway construction as in other industries and trades which they learned from abroad, and they were soon able to dispense with foreign assistance. ("Japan," *Encyclopedia Britannica*)

The Japanese, "apt pupils" of Western civilization, boldly attempted in their turn railroad construction in Korea and Taiwan in 1899, a mere 25 years since they had constructed their first railroad with the help of Westerners. And they completed the railroad line that crossed the Korean Peninsula from south to north in 1906 and the one that crossed Taiwan in 1908. Adoption of technology from foreign civilization this successful was unprecedented.

Then, what is the secret of Japan's success? It is certainly difficult to answer the question "Why Japan?" Though the adoption of European civilization and modernization was amazingly brilliant and successful, there was little in the Japanese society before the opening of the ports that indicated such success for Japan. If the contemporaries had been asked about it, most would have regarded China as the likely candidate for successful confrontation with the superior European civilization. Why Japan, indeed?

Many answers have been offered to this vital question. And certainly many more shall be offered in future. It is not likely that a definitive answer will emerge in the near future.

One interesting fact is that the 'Optimal Fragmentation Principle' proposed by Jared Diamond fits remarkably well to Japan. Among the East Asian countries, only Japan was fragmented for the most part of its history. Such unique features have undoubtedly influenced the course of history, especially in the crucial juncture when the countries had to cope with the advance of a superior civilization.

First, unlike China, Korea, and Vietnam, each with an undivided land mass as territory, Japan has been geographically fragmented from the first. Kyushu Island has been the center of Japan in ancient times and in later times it maintained its role as a counterweight to the much bigger Honshu Island. Actually, the political groups based in Kyushu, especially the Satsuma clan, played a role against the central power in Honshu, and still do even in modern times. So the control of the Honshu-based powers was never absolute.

Second, Japan maintained a system of fragmented political power. Japan claims that it was founded by Jimmu Tenno in 660 B.C. While most scholars doubt the authenticity of such official claims, which are based on the legends in *Kojiki* and the *Nihon Shoki*, it is certain that the imperial system was very ancient, and, more remarkably, the imperial dynasty continued unbroken for two millennia. But in the late 12th century Minamoto Yoritomo grabbed power and established the Kamakura Bakufu and ever since the political power was divided between the imperial court and the bakufu. The emperor and his court retained the symbolic role and the source of legitimacy, while the shogun and his bakufu wielded the real power and administered the country. Moreover, the Shogunate system itself was not monolithic but extensively fragmented. Though in theory, the Shogun had nearly absolute power and control over the daimyos, in reality, daimyos had authority of their own and substantial room for discretion.

Third, unlike the other East Asian countries, Japan fostered commerce and the Japanese merchant class had enjoyed substantial freedom and power. Urbanization also progressed prominently, so there was to some degree social fragmentation.

Such multiple fragmentation in Japan certainly helped it in the efficient absorption of European civilization and rapid modernization. The emperor offered an alternative political institution around which the radical forces could rally. And the prospering clans of the western part of the countries commanded enough resources for the overthrow of the shogunate system.

7. Two Problems of East Asia

Japan's successful adaptation to the new environment that led to its rapid modernization was a great achievement. But to the rest of East Asia, Japan's success had fateful implications. Once an ascendant civilization comes with its superior knowledge, institutions, and products, the traditional order of the indigenous civilization is subject to fundamental changes. Now the factor that comes to have the paramount importance is the absorption of the ascendant civilization. Those who successfully absorb the superior knowledge and follow the new ways, both at the level of individuals and of societies, would prosper and become the dominant members, while those who failed would become weaker members. And in the critical last decades of the 19th century, Japan suddenly became the hegemonic country in the region, even stronger than China, the traditional hegemonic country, and began to pursue aggressive expansion policy. And the other countries had to suffer.

So the two questions, "Why not China?" and "Why Japan?" well delineate the crucial factors in the modern history of East Asia. The fact that the Scientific Revolution arose in Europe instead of China made the subjugation of East Asia by Europe inevitable. Also, it made the absorption of the superior knowledge of European civilization the crucial factor in the emerging order of the region. The fact that only Japan managed to successfully finish that task made Japan the region's new hegemonic power, and Japan indeed played the dominant role in the evolution of the region's history.

As seen above, the modern history of East Asia, like that of other parts of the world, was in essence the history of the introduction of the superior knowledge of European civilization and the replacement of traditional knowledge with it. The process of absorption of new knowledge was very much confused, complex and violent. It could not have been otherwise. Though the gap in the level of knowledge between the European and Chinese civilizations was relatively small, it was still very great in absolute terms. And down the steep gradient of knowledge, the superior knowledge of European civilization fell upon the region like a cataract.

Faced with such a bewildering and fearsome situation, it was only natural that in East Asian societies violent clashes of views regarding the best way to deal with the crisis arose. In general, those in power of necessity adopted policies of accommodation, if not enthusiastic embrace, of European civilization. But it was also inevitable that more conservative elements would refuse to accommodate it. Such differences in attitudes and policies often led to violent clashes and sometimes developed into a full-blown civil war. The Taiping Rebellion in China, the protracted civil war between the pro-Bakufu armies and the pro-Emperor armies and the later Satsuma Rebellion in Japan, and the Donghak Rebellion in Korea were all essentially such clashes. Even the calamitous struggles between capitalism and communism that engulfed the region in the 20th century – the Chinese civil war between the Kuomintang regime and the Communist regime, in a sense still being waged between China and Taiwan, the Korean War between the capitalist South and the communist North, that still continues technically, and the Vietnam War between communist North Vietnam and the capitalist South – were in essence clashes between different views regarding the knowledge pouring in from European civilization, and without taking into consideration that fact, they could not be fully understood.

In the international arena, Japan's aggressive overseas expansion dominated the region's history. It colonized Korea, practically annexed Manchuria, occupied a large part of China, and during the Second World War occupied the entire region. Only with Japan's defeat in the Second World War was the region relieved of Japan's oppressive dominance.

Such experiences shaped the modern history of East Asia and still exert powerful influences on the relations between the countries in the region. They are the proximate reason why relations between these countries are so cool and distant and why there is no active supra-national body, even while the rivalry-ridden European countries succeeded in forming the EU from a small body after the Second World War.

So the modern history of East Asia could be seen as the flow of knowledge from the superior European civilization into the region. Such a view not only succinctly delineates the history but also brings into focus the primary problems the region must deal with for the emergence of a new order. The first problem is the communism system still in place. The second problem is the recent history poisoned by Japanese aggression.

8. Dismantling of the Communist System

The dismantling of the communist system is East Asia's most urgent task. Socialism became the most attractive ideology in Europe in the 19th century. Communism founded by Karl Marx became the mainstream among various socialist doctrines in the last decades of the 19th century and after the Russian Revolution its attraction and credibility greatly increased. So it is not strange that communism held sway over the intellectuals of East Asia and succeeded in grasping the power in many countries in the region after the Second World War. But it proved to be an erroneous ideology that, once put into practice, would inevitably lead to misery and oppression. And it met bankruptcy in the last decade of the 20th century.

Unfortunately, the great debacle of communism, which toppled all the communist regimes in Europe in the 1990s, did not remove the communist regimes in East Asia. China, North Korea, Vietnam, and Laos are still ruled by communist regimes.

The problem posed by communism is grave indeed. Communism is not only inefficient and oppressive, it is also by nature militant.

> In the only extant letter to his father, written when he was 18, [Marx] shows himself as an unsure youth, his breast, like Swift's, lacerated by savage indignation, searching violently for guidance through the maze of problems and ideas which he had encountered at the university. Thirty years later he had become the cocksure writer of the preface to *Capital*. In this interval the revelation had been received and it had been enshrined in doctrine. Looking at this development, I conclude that the first and most potent ingredient in the attraction of Marxism is that it offers the certainty of dogma. Offensive though this might be to true believers and to Marxists alike, I must, therefore, class it with the religions. Like them, it not only gives certainty of a final destiny but it imposes upon the follower a duty to make his own contribution to this end and it lays down a clear line of conduct. 'The philosophers', quotes the inscription of Marx's tomb at

Highgate, 'have only interpreted the world in different ways: the point is to change it.' This then is the kernel of a militant faith. Like others, its initial appeal tends to be mainly in the young. Like others, it has readily bred bigots and fanatics; and it has, in the end, increased rather than diminished the sum total of human misery which, at its origin, it had set out to abolish." (Eric Roll, "Marx's *Capital* - An Assessment")

Such militancy of communism as well as the misery and oppression it brings make it nearly impossible to improve the international order as long as the majority of the East Asians live under communist rule. So the dismantling of the communist system is the foremost precondition for an improved international order in East Asia.

The communist regimes will disappear in time, of course. Communism unequivocally lost in the bitter competition with liberal democracy and capitalism. But the aftermath of communist failure will pose its own grave problems. Even when the communist system is dismantled and replaced with the capitalist system, the power structure may remain intact. Such a situation is more likely to occur if the dismantling is carried out by the ruling groups themselves. In such cases, the former rulers will still rule, but they will lack legitimacy. They will have lost even the halo of socialism. So they will search for something that might give their rule a semblance of legitimacy and the ideology most convenient for such a purpose is nationalism. It is almost inevitable, therefore, that in formerly communist countries virulent nationalism replaces the decrepit communism as the dominant ideology. Nationalism, of course, will not be conducive to amicable relations between countries and harmonious international order.

Here we should note that nationalism in its present aggressive form is an ideology originating from European civilization. The reach of European civilization is long indeed and other civilizations could never manage to step out of its influence. Now East Asia defines itself with the views and ideologies of the ascendant European civilization.

9. Detoxification of History

Compared to the dismantling of the communist system, the detoxification of the modern history of the region poisoned by the Japanese aggression is a much smaller task. But it still is a very difficult task to carry out. To leach the poison out of the history, it is necessary first of all for East Asians to reach a consensus on the causes, nature and effects of the Japanese aggression. And such consensus can be achieved only when the modern history of the region is viewed in a broad context at the level of civilization. The national histories currently taught in the countries' schools are written under the overwhelming influence of nationalism and cannot provide a frame for such consensus.

In this matter the historical view described above could be of help. Such a view regards knowledge as the essential element in history and studies the intercourse of civilizations in terms of the flow of knowledge. The gap in the level of knowledge between two civilizations takes the primary importance in such a view, and the modern history of the region is regarded largely as the process of the introduction of the superior knowledge of the ascendant European civilization down along the steep gradient of knowledge. It offers a perspective quite different from the conventional ones and provides a better explanation of the causes, nature, and effects of the Japanese aggression.

What should be pointed out first is that Japan was the conduit through which high-pressured knowledge of European civilization came into East Asia. Japan absorbed the superior knowledge and adapted it into forms more congenial to its traditions. And such knowledge adapted by the Japanese was also more congenial to the other East Asian countries than the original knowledge and thus more easily absorbed by them.

This point is well illustrated by the fact that most of the abstract words in the countries where neologism had been based on the Chinese characters, that is, China, Japan and Korea, were coined by Japanese scholars through translation of the European concepts. In broader context, it may be argued that the translation of the Western books and the accompanying neologism by the Japanese "Dutch scholars" during the enlightened administration of Shogun Tokukawa Yoshimune in the late 18th century was the most important cultural event in East Asia since the translation of the Buddhist Scriptures and the accompanying neologism by the Chinese Buddhist scholars of Tang Empire in the 7th century.

Astonishingly, Japan still plays the role of conduit for introduction of knowledge from the West into the region after nearly two centuries. Western science and technology usually come to East Asia through Japan. Japan first absorbs the latest technology and adapts or improves upon it. Since such technology already transformed to fit the Japanese society is much easier and efficient for the other East Asian countries, they prefer Japanese technology to the original Western technology. So Japan keeps on playing the role of conduit. The enormous and ever-increasing trade deficit Korea has with Japan attests to this fact. For technology-hungry Korean firms, Japanese firms are a convenient source of advanced technology. The same for Chinese firms, except that, due to the lag in development, Chinese firms often prefer technology adapted and improved upon by Korean firms.

Then, this is the great benefit conferred to East Asia by Japan. By its success in the absorption and adaptation of the superior knowledge of European civilization and in the transformation of itself from a feudal state to a modern state, Japan contributed to the modernization of the other countries in the region. And its contribution still continues and will do so in the foreseeable future. This is a dimension of the modern history of the region that has been usually hidden from view but should be made explicit for a balanced evaluation.

In this perspective, the fundamental condition in the modern history of the region was the introduction of European civilization's superior knowledge along the steep gradient of knowledge and both the contribution and aggression of Japan were secondary effects. Once this fact is accepted, the Japanese aggression takes a meaning subtly different from the conventional evaluation. When there is a gap in the level of knowledge between two civilizations, such a gap acts as the pressure that pushes the knowledge of the superior civilization into the inferior civilization and the pressure will exist till some sort of equilibrium is reached. Since the gap was great in this case, the pressure was great and the process of inflow of knowledge was inevitably violent. And the Japanese aggression was a part of such violence. Even if the Japanese aggression had not happened, the process would have been still violent, probably taking the form of military conquest of the region by the European powers. We should remind ourselves of the fact that in the 19th century the European powers did not hesitate to use military power to acquire territory and interests in East Asia. Russia's behavior was especially threatening. Somewhat crudely speaking, due to Japan's victory in the Russo-Japanese War, the role of expansionist Russia was replaced with that of expansionist Japan. Despite the reversal, Russia managed to retain the vast area that it had taken from China in the Far East. And it is not unreasonable to conjecture that the total violence would have come out more or less similar.

The planetary heat balance would provide an apposite analogy. A hurricane is one of the most violent physical phenomena on the planet and inflicts great misery to mankind. Its violence is due to the thermal imbalance between tropical and polar regions. The tropical region receives a far larger amount of heat from the sun than the polar regions and there exists a great thermal imbalance between them. A hurricane is one of the processes through which such great thermal imbalance is corrected. As long as the thermal imbalance is great, hurricanes will be there. A hurricane is a calamity to those who happen to be in its path, but without hurricanes, the planet would be a place less hospitable to life. Japan's modernization was a hurricane. It emerged from the great imbalance in knowledge between European civilization and East Asian civilization. So it could not be otherwise than violent. And from its violence East Asians, including the Japanese themselves, suffered much. But we should not let the violence blind our eyes from the underlying cause or the ultimately beneficial effect.

The above statement is not intended as a defense or justification of the Japanese aggression, of course. Nothing can justify the unprovoked aggression of Japan and the atrocities perpetrated by the marauding Japanese armies and carpetbaggers. And the rigorous verdict on their guilt cannot be challenged in any way. The above statement merely points out that the Japanese aggression was an aspect of Japan's modernization and that Japan's modernization itself was a part of the process through which the imbalance in knowledge between the two civilizations was steadily decreased.

The historical view described above might help in achieving a broad consensus on the modern history of the region, freeing the East Asians from the stifling intellectual straightjackets imposed by their nationalistic history textbooks. And such broad consensus might encourage the arduous and time-consuming process of detoxification to begin. The countries that have suffered from the Japanese aggression would recognize the more fundamental and impersonal dimension in addition to the moral dimension and begin to better understand the causes, nature and effects of the Japanese aggression. Also they would appreciate the great contribution Japan has made and is still making by its successful absorption of superior knowledge from European civilization and modernizing itself. We can hope that such understanding would make it easier for them to deal with Japan and eventually to forgive its wrongdoings.

Then, a more balanced view of Japan's achievement and contribution to the introduction of European civilization's knowledge would give the Japanese much needed psychological balance and confidence. The Japanese feel that they have too long been vilified but lack the confidence to fully accept the responsibility for their wrongdoings. So they were niggardly in apology and reparations that are due the other countries. The historical view that gives credit to Japan's role as the conduit of Western knowledge would give the Japanese the psychological foundation for a mature response. It is time for the Japanese to discard the worn-out shield of nationalism and to free themselves of the politicians seeking cheap political assets through shameless chauvinistic stances.

This point is well illustrated by the "Question of the Yasukuni Shrine," a small matter that never fails to muddy the water in the region's international relations. As its name indicates, the Yasukuni Shrine is a place that commemorates the soldiers who had died for the "peace and security" of their fatherland Japan. The shrine was erected by Emperor Meiji in the 1870s and has commemorated the

Japanese war-dead ever since. By the treaty concluded between the Allies and Japan after the Second World War, the ministers of the Japanese cabinet were forbidden to pay a visit to the shrine. In 1985, the then Prime Minister Yasuhiro Nakasone paid a visit to the shrine in violation of the treaty. At that time, he argued that Japan had a right to commemorate its war-dead just like other countries. He is right. The Japanese should be able to commemorate the soldiers who had sacrificed their lives for their fatherland. But he turned his eyes away from a plain fact. At the cemeteries commemorating the war-dead of other countries there is no place for those sentenced to death for war crimes. The Yasukuni enshrines those criminals found guilty of war crimes. Commemorating General Iwane Matsui, who was ultimately responsible for the infamous Nanjing Massacre, is like commemorating Heinrich Himmler or Karl Adolf Eichmann and commemorating Prime Minister Hideki Tojo is not so different from commemorating Hitler. It does not serve the memory of millions of dead soldiers that Yasukuni enshrines Class-A War Criminals together with those soldiers. It is very hard to understand such an attitude on the part of Japan. It is not that those guilty of war crimes should not be commemorated. It is only that they should be commemorated in other places so that the spirit of the international treaty should be kept alive. In actuality, it has been repeatedly suggested that Japan should provide a separate shrine for the war criminals. But the Japanese government does not heed such eminently sensible suggestions.

The question of the Yasukuni Shrine is ultimately a matter of political calculation. The major reason why Japanese ministers keep on worshipping at the shrine in contravention of the international treaty and why they do not heed to the sensible suggestion of separating the war criminals from the war-dead is that they believe such action is politically advantageous to them. Sad to say, their calculation is right. The passionate support of the extreme nationalist elements is politically more valuable than the tepid approval of ordinary citizens who are not greatly interested in the matter. As long as such political calculation is realistic, Japan's attitude with regard to the question of the Yasukuni Shrine will not change.

Now the historical view described above might improve the

situation. The Japanese would realize that their aggression was a grave blemish on their solid achievement and such realization would give them a psychological foundation to fully admit their fault. Then the political clout the extreme nationalist elements have enjoyed so far would be dwarfed by the more sensible attitude of ordinary citizens. And the citizens of other countries would be more ready to acknowledge Japan's great achievement and contribution and to absolve its fault. Only then, the modern history of East Asia poisoned by the Japanese aggression would be free of the poison and become healthy again.

10. Concluding Remarks

As pointed out at the beginning, international order cannot be designed. It is to a large degree "a spontaneous order." The primary factors that shape it are the trade of goods and exchange of ideas.

What we can do about the international order of East Asia, therefore, is to understand the forces that shaped the modern history of the region, identify the obstacles that might harm or pervert the relations between the countries in the region, and find prescriptions to remove or diminish such obstacles. It is a modest assessment of our ability but also a realistic one that might actually contribute something concrete. For that reason, the historical view that focuses on the flow of knowledge, as described above and epitomized by the two questions, "Why not China?" and "Why Japan?" is relevant to the discussion about the desirable international order of the region and might provide some small but real contribution.

Session V

Power, Human Values and Political Order: Dictatorships, Wars and Peace

Traffic, Religion and "We"

Orhan Pamuk

The car we were riding in was passing by a certain place in the southern part of Teheran. Many bicycle shops and auto-repair shops could be seen from the car window. As it was Friday, all the shops were closed. The streets, pedestrian roads and teahouses were all quiet. Our car was entering a huge and empty plaza. Among such plazas that you find here and there in Teheran, there are often round-shaped rotaries to help keep traffic flowing. For our car to enter the left-hand road, we would have to go to the right side and turn around the plaza.

I could see that the driver of our car was thinking of entering the left-hand road directly instead of taking the circuitous route, because I noticed that he was carefully looking right and left to see whether there were other vehicles coming to the plaza. He seemed to be debating whether to observe the traffic regulations or act by applying a practical mind.

I could understand this state of mind, because I had experienced driving on the streets of Istanbul when I was young. I had tried to keep the traffic rules while driving in the central part of a city, which was crowded with "traffic in a state of anarchy," according to the term used by the newspapers. However, I used to drive my father's car at will, ignoring the traffic rules on side streets paved with regular square stones where nothing was to be seen. It seemed to be a matter of form neither practical nor reasonable to follow a "No Left Turn" sign at a back street where no cars were to be seen, or to wait with patience until a red light changed to green at a quiet plaza late at night. It seemed the people who observed all taboos and rules to the bitter end were not wise, creative nor characteristic. I thought only those who squeeze toothpaste from the bottom or read the directions for using medicine to the end followed the traffic regulations on an empty plaza when there were no vehicles around. I remember reading about this mental symptom, myself dubious and against the rules, from a Western magazine in the 1960s, like the cartoon where a driver by himself waits for a green light on an endless road in the American desert.

In the lowest stratum of the attitude of ignoring the traffic rules in Istanbul from the 1950s through the 1980s was the notion that opposition against the West, rather than disobedience, was "refinement" for us. This included the practical intelligence that the past was still going on and the nationalism that "WE are by ourselves." Making a broken down radio work, which even the German maker could hardly repair, by beating it with a fist, or making a buzzing telephone work properly by driving a small nail into it endowed the "practical" people living in Istanbul with national pride in the 1960s and 1970s. Of course, in the lowest stratum among these, we had a mind to remind ourselves that we were intelligent people with practical minds, standing face to face with the Western people who had been thought to be superior over us in terms of technology, culture and rules, a notion we had felt in our daily lives.

When I was young, I also used to feel excited at the spirit of "WE," which all Turkish people had felt about Western technology and cultural superiority. A part of my rationality was open toward the power, attraction and flash of wit of Western civilization. With regard to this, I was also one of the Kemalists[1] like all the children of this country. However, with a feeling eager to envy and imitate the West in mind, I had another idea that "WE are different from them." "WE" surely wanted to be Westerners; nevertheless, we had to remain as "WE" were. I think even nowadays after a lapse of forty years, the clash between the desire to be a Westerner and that to remain as "WE" is expressed in the culture of Turkey as well as mine. At the same time, I guess it is essential for us, living all over the world other than in the West, to understand the clash properly in order to arrive at democracy, tolerance and a culture of peace.

---

1) This refers to the people who support the inclination of Westernism of Kemal, who was the first President of the Republic of Turkey.

First, I would like to mention the cultures of peace and tolerance. The word "peace" has been used too often in our daily lives and in international political speeches and it has almost lost its persuasive power. What I mean by "peace" does not mean that the people, who have hostile and aggressive thoughts, temporarily give up a war due to the drying up of their fountainhead. Rather, it is the thought which Kant defined as an "eternal peace." The "eternal peace" explained by Kant has not yet been realized, but I still believe in it. I don't mean that the hostility existing between two parties is discontinued temporarily but that I am dreaming of the state of peace that resists all the imaginable possibilities of wars permanently.

Today, what makes such a peace impossible in the world is not the excessively aggressive militarism of the American empire or the imperative attitude of the Bush government alone. Another factor that threatens the peace of the world is radical nationalism, namely, an anger like "WE-ism" which exists outside the Western world. At the lowest stratum of the radical religionists and nationalists, the thought "WE are different; WE will never become like them" lies just as I moderately experienced in my childhood.

For the last forty years the great change brought on by technological and economic development, especially communications technology, television, journalism and the Internet, has made it difficult for the thought "WE" to be preserved in a pure form. Unfortunately, the thought "WE" no longer speaks for the pure and childlike anger and the understandable identity which I experienced in Istanbul in my childhood. The central mass media of America like Fox TV, which advocates the militaristic aggressiveness of the Bush government, are well aware of the "WE" spirit of local democracy and are using it as a pretense of attack by severely exploiting it. At the same time, these mass media employ other spiritual materials like democracy other than the West's own, human rights, women's rights and the rights for the minority in the conservative battle with other nations. All my literary works are a response to those spiritual materials of solidness, wrath, internal conflict and history. Perhaps I also might be composed of these materials and I would like to talk about the

"WE" spirit a little more.

To begin with, since we live and feel the "WE" spirit as a part of the national education program of a country, the "WE" spirit justly endows us, the nations other than the West, with a strong dependent spirit of the plain people, the consciousness of history, right or wrong, and a stronger sense of pride. This spirit in Turkey comes to possess the stories or legends that "WE" are different from other people in our daily life, at home and on the street, just like the pride of the history of the Osman Empire. In connection with these legends, when German, American or Japanese products were out of order – there was no Korean technology when I was young – we used to obtain strength from the skills of our people in making the broken device work by beating it with a fist. Nobody other than "WE" could be practical, honest, right or smart. To become one among "WE" automatically bestows these necessary virtues on us.

In the 1970s and 1980s Turkish intellectuals, who tried to move the fruit of thoughts such as the Western principle of quality, democracy, and women's rights to Turkey, attempted to prove that such seeds of thought had already existed in the Osman Empire, namely, in the history of Turkey. Today, we may possibly think that the attempt was reasonable due to the affirmative political result of those days. A number of drivers on the Teheran streets, however, did not observe the modern traffic rules due to Iran's own kind of "WE," just like myself in Istanbul in my childhood. While I was in Iran, I heard that many intellectuals who protested against the order of Islam tried to coincide their sincere ardor with the Koran in order to realize democracy, human rights and women's rights. The radical and egalitarian Western thought might have sprouted among us only when its origin began from "WE." This "WE-ism" (or nationalism) based on thought, which coincides with a group other than individual conscience or freedom, is useful mostly in the suppression of political movements like peace, equality and women's rights and for the reinforcement of local dictatorships. We all know that the "WE-principle" or nationalism which stands against the demand for Westernization is a strong supporting base of wrath.

But I could see that for our conflicted driver's observing the traffic rules at an outer village of Teheran was one thing and his response, pretending to be a nationalist, was another, because I knew who he was. What he was worrying about was something more worldly. As we were in a hurry, for us to make a round of the plaza seemed to be a waste of time. On the other hand, on the grounds that he was in a hurry, his eyes wide open, he was attentively watching other roads leading to the plaza lest he should collide with other vehicles.

However, on the previous day when we were walking around the city in the fearfully congested traffic, he complained with a smile that no one keeps the traffic rules in Teheran, the many vehicles like entangled thread. When we saw vehicles bumper to bumper or the drivers of vehicles of Iranian make, the sides of which bore the scars of accidents, shouting to each other, their vehicles entangled, we smiled bitterly as if we had been moderners observing the traffic rules properly. On the face of our driver, who was trying to take a short cut against the red light, uneasiness was suffused together with the smile of that time.

As I had experience as a driver in the congested traffic of Istanbul while young, I felt that the uneasiness was a kind of loneliness. Our driver, ready to give up the usefulness and observance of universal traffic rules, supposed to solve the problem by himself. He had to calculate quickly all the possibilities, watch every road and make a quick decision. He might have felt a great sense of responsibility, because the lives of himself and many other people in his company depended upon his driving.

The driver of our car may have thought that he himself chose this loneliness and freedom without observing the traffic rules. But he knew well the habits of other drivers in Teheran and was aware that he was always lonely in the traffic of Teheran, even if he had not chosen this loneliness and freedom himself. Even if you kept the modern traffic rules, others might not observe the rules on account of practical reasons. All the drivers in Teheran should pay heed to the traffic signs and rules at intersections as well as at the huge plazas. This situation is quite different from the easiness which modern drivers experience on the traffic lanes of the Western world, enjoying music. This is a free state with some uneasiness.

Whenever I saw confusion and accidents caused by the drivers in Teheran last May, who adhered to their own free zone outside the traffic rules, I felt a strange contradiction between the individual "freedom" of petty outlaws and the religion suppressing and pressing Teheran. Under the dictatorship of mollahs[2], women had to veil their faces, publications had to be inspected, prisons were full of prisoners and the huge walls of the cities were filled with the pictures of martyrs who had died for religion and Iran in order to show that all the people had thoughts in common at public places or on the city streets. Owing to the freedom of the outrageous drivers of the cities, the existence of religion on the major streets is distorted and assumes a strange form. When the government forces the people, who do not know the general rules of religion and the Scripture, to keep the rules or when the general rules force all the people to be united, it is almost impossible for them to rise against the religious taboos without going to prison. Nevertheless, no one observed or followed the traffic rules and they only regarded them as a category beyond their own freedom, creativity and thinking. At public places, on the roads, on the markets and on all the streets of a city, the Iranian intellectuals, whom I respected and whose freedom was restricted by the government's forcible demand of religion, preserved their self-respect. This showed me that the people could talk freely at home and put on whatever they wanted to wear and could drink home-made wine as much as they wanted in order to prove that the place was neither Germany under the reign of Hitler nor Russia under the rule of Stalin. In other Islam countries under dictatorship as well as in Iran, they believe that democracy will be settled by the people of an opposing group who are free only at home. People like us in the Islamic countries, who hope for democracy to be realized, are supposed to support these intellectuals. The aggressiveness of the American militarism isolates these intellectuals and suffocates them in the wrath of nationalism.

The following words are added in order to remind people of the fact that the nationalism of other empires as well as America can be very hostile to peace and democracy when they criticize local

2) High-ranking muslim judges

nationalism. We have recently seen in the Iraq War the phrases of democracy and human rights used by America in order to justify nationalism and the politics of world domination. We are all conscious that American nationalism carries doubts and abasement of the people "who are not like us" and that it is very convenient for people to use violence.

As a literary man, I would like to mention a novel with regard to this problem. At the final part of Lolita, Humbert is going far from the site where he killed Quilty. He begins to drive his car, about which every reader knows well, on the left traffic lane. As the people who are fond of modern literature know, the novel Lolita is the story of a middle-aged European intellectual who is in love with a young American girl. The sneering description of Humbert, who pretends to accept American rules in order to approach the young girl, can be said to be the power of this novel, although he does not believe in the rules. Humbert, who hides the soul of the outlaw in his own mind, liberally shares the darkness, the desire of crime and the growing sneers in his mind with the readers, while observing the plain rules of the world. The readers can notice from this wonderful novel that he does not believe in any traffic rules but pretends to believe in them so that the trace of his crime may not be detected. After Humbert kills the girl, namely, breaks the laws of society, he never hesitates to violate the traffic rules. The mask of the outlaw with which he had hid his mind is removed. Even if he violates other laws, the situation cannot be different. As all of us who are living in modern cities know, traffic rules are the universal codes which exercise the modernity and its endless rules before us in the stream of our daily lives, and at the same time they are the rules which least reveal taboos and political characters. The sneering protagonist, Humbert, having committed murder, immediately clarifies for fear of the readers' misunderstanding that his driving in the left lane is neither resistance nor a symbolic action. He already has proceeded contrary to morality by killing a young girl while falling in love with her. The readers, however, can notice from the beginning that what makes this novel and the story of Humbert so cutting is the sense of guilt and the loneliness of a criminal.

We writers know that the rules we violate are the traffic rules and laws of "WE." Violating the regulations of society and modern rules liberates us. But what is important is that we do so without being based upon "WE." All my books are made of something that connects "traffic and WE." Of course this is not my own. That is the very good reason of literature. This good reason makes us free.

On the outskirts of Teheran, our driver, having hesitated for a moment, went into the wrong lane, chose a short cut and proceeded to the road which we wanted without any accident. As I did while young in Istanbul, we looked at each other smiling, thinking of ourselves as being "clever" with the delight that comes from violating the rules. However, what makes us sad is that there are only traffic rules that we can violate outside and on the street like the people in Teheran, who can violate rules only at home between close friends, or like Humbert who can be clever only "in secret" when he talks to himself, having the crime in common with Lolita in a secret language.

Translated by **Moon Jung-il**

Peace, Violence and Literature

Ko Un

There are times when the question as to what literature truly is cannot be restricted to a concern with literature as such. Perhaps what turns literature into a form of servility is the way it fails to oppose a war while the war is being fought, only opposing it once it is over. In spite of that, any literary activity primarily demands a sense of duty – we must do everything to restore to life that peace which dies whenever there is a state of war.

In 1936, in the midst of Japan's colonial oppression of Korea, Hong Myeong-Hui published his "War Reflected in Literature." This is the moment when Japanese imperialism, having taken control of Joseon (Korea) by force and still not satisfied, is initiating a war in the Manchurian territories to the north. This text, which expresses an awareness that the "Manchuria Incident" of 1931 represented a grave risk for all of East Asia, since it might well lead to an invasion of China proper, begins with the thought that "war begins with civilization and progresses with civilization," before going on to point out that the disastrous effects of war are growing increasingly severe as the development of weapons follows the development of capitalistic states, and finally foretells that as a result the second world war would be a correspondingly immense tragedy. Moreover, he claims that the sudden emergence of anti-war writing is the most significant aspect of war literature following the First World War. He stresses that the disaster of the First World War marked the end of earlier kinds of war literature that had been an officially sanctioned song in praise of heroes, great generals and early death. He even goes so far as to introduce the impact of such European anti-war works as Remarque's *All Quiet on the Western*

Front, which certainly required immense courage in times such as his. At the same time, he writes in enthusiastic support of the peace movement represented by the writers assembled in Paris in June 1935 for the First International Congress of Writers for the Defense of Culture, intent on promoting peace and preventing a return of war in the face of the rise of fascism.

Immediately after this article was published, the Korean novelist Yi Kwang-Su, in his "A Novelist's Attitude in Wartime" expressed a directly opposite opinion to Hong Myeong-Hui's pacifism. He insists that the ambitions of Japanese imperialism toward the Korean Peninsula and the mainland are completely justified and he is impatient to embellish the Japanese invasion, praising their victory in advance.

With the newspapers at that time producing emergency special issues with a whole series of articles on "War and Literature," the two writers' views on war, the current situation and even literature were bound to be as radically opposed as they were. When they were students in Japan, they had been the closest of companions. Hong Myeong-Hui gave almost every book he had finished reading to Yi Kwang-Su. Returning to their homeland in the 1920s, Yi Kwang-Su adopted an ideology of "gradual national development" and an attitude of unbridled devotion to Japan while Hong Myeong-Hui became involved in the domestic Joseon Independence Movement, composed as his major work "Im Kkeok-jeong" characterized by Korean popular feelings and traditions and lived a life marked by imprisonment and poverty.

Just when the Japanese were at the height of their occupation of Manchuria and invasion of China in 1936, the novel *Funnyotan* (A Story of Shit and Piss) by the Japanese writer Tamai Katsunori (penname: Hino Ashihei) was awarded the prestigious Akutagawa Award. He was serving as a corporal in China at that time; he later composed *Mugi to Heitai* (Barley and Soldiers) about life in the army during the campaign. The influential Japanese critic Kobayashi Hideo was a leading member of the jury for the Akutagawa Awards; he visited the battle lines in China to bring the award to Hino Ashihei. And in a subsequent essay he wrote: "Once the battle has begun. ... I shall be glad to take up arms on behalf of our country.

But to write is wholly to work for peace, so that it is absurd to say that I am carrying a gun as a writer. Fighting means fighting with the status of a soldier. If the time comes for me to bear arms, I can abandon writing immediately. … It is meaningless to ask a soldier what he thinks as a writer when he is setting off to war."

Utterances of that kind by Kobayashi, who was one of the most important figures in modern Japanese literary criticism, and the theory of war literature formulated by Yi Kwang-su, one of the leading supporters of the Japanization of Joseon, continued until the end of the war. For myself, the background of such colonial literature, together with the "literature of ruins" that survived in the wake of the Korean War during the 1950s, served as the womb for my birth as a poet. The splendor and shame of those two senior writers, Hong Myeong-Hui and Yi Kwang-Su, makes me ponder deeply on the form of relationship existing between peace and literature, war and literature.

It is now more than fifty years since the Armistice brought the Korean War to an end. An "armistice" in terms of international law is a part of war, psychologically it is a state of quasi-warfare. Concretely, Korea's long-drawn-out insecurity, with the concept of peace dependent on an armistice, that is to say a momentary interruption of hostilities, goes hand in hand with an agonizing experience of the constant question of how true peace might ever be possible.

In this situation, society is bound to become fixed in antagonistic relationships. Then inevitably the meaning of that most frequently used word "peace" becomes increasingly degraded by its triteness. In a situation such as that of the division of Korea into North and South, the shared agenda of peace and literature is likely to end up as just another cliché as that reality grows stronger.

In the autumn of 2004, 300 writers from the two sides of the divide, two hundred from the South and one hundred from the North, had agreed to hold a six-day literary festival in Pyongyang, Myohyang Mountain and Diamond Mountain (Geumgang-san). This was to have been the first literary event of its kind, almost 60 years after the division of the country, and 52 years since the Armistice was signed. But a variety of factors at home and abroad blocked this project and the event had to be postponed. With that festival now due to be held in March 2005, it promises to be a moment allowing us to search for ways of transforming the "literature of division" into a "literature overcoming division." In addition, it offers a chance to share ideas on the role of literature in bringing about peace in order to put an end to this division that is now the only relic of Cold-War ideology left in the world.

Apart from this literary festival, a joint South-North editorial committee has been established for the compilation of a full-scale *Pan-Korean Dictionary of the Korean Language*. This is a large-scale project, the first since the division, bringing together some two hundred thousand words of the standard vocabulary and dialects used in South Korea, North Korea, and among other Korean-speaking ethnic groups. This focus on our Korean language, designed to encourage peaceful coexistence and ultimately peaceful unification between South and North, should be completed in five years' time.

Together with the above two projects, last year South Korean writers participated in demonstrations against the sending of Korean troops to serve in Iraq and against the American invasion of Iraq. The "Korean Literary Peace Forum" established in this connection has also been making visits to regions affected by the heaviest fighting during the Korean War, regions within the Demilitarized Zone, regions affected by the nuclear problem, regions with American bases and firing ranges, etc., to denounce the destruction of peace and the environment with the affected citizens.

Peace is a pan-human value inspiring a universal desire, whatever the region affected. In regions of conflict or those constantly under threat of war, it is a direct question of having food to eat, not just a value or a moral duty. In the cultural zone employing the Chinese characters in North-East Asia, China, Korea and Japan, the currently-used word for peace is *Pyeong-hwa* (平和) but in former times the word employed reversed the ideograms to give *"Hwa-pyeong"* and that form is still frequently used in China and in Vietnam.

The character *pyeong* signifies balance or equality, the value emerging from an essentially negative scale of every kind of human inequality. It takes as its basis a scale that is not biased toward any one side. At times, *pyeong* can be used in the sense of "pacification."

But fundamentally *pyeong* indicates a fully achieved realm of stillness. In that sense it may have some kind of relationship with the despair Rousseau felt when he wrote about the fundamental theory of human equality or the theory of the social contract. He arrives at a concept of Order achieved by people's voluntary acts, which can be achieved by rejecting civilization and society, corresponding precisely to *pyeong*. So the predicament in which Rousseau found himself when Voltaire railed that he meant "a return to the state of a quadruped" perhaps underlies the more advanced discourse of later days.

The second character, *hwa*, is formed by a combination of the characters for "grain" and "mouth," indicating the situation when food enters the mouth. Thus *hwa* expresses the way people become gentle and attain harmony with others, reaching a "model state," where "concord" and "optimal relations" are realized.

What we see in peace is humanity's long-nourished dream of a state in which are resolved the material and class-based contradictions of society. Thus peace does not signify a state of absence of war or the silence of a society ruled with an iron fist but should properly begin by signifying a state in which no one is starving, no one is naked.

But peace cannot be found when there is warfare, even though people have food to eat. Its definition begins first with a state of no warfare. Therefore strictly speaking, the character 武(meaning militarism in the act of war) represents constraint and limitation regarding weapons, not the use of them. It indicates a restriction, involving the non-use of weapons if it all possible, rather than the ready use of them. Early Confucianism termed weapons "means of murder" and this likewise indicates an ethical eschewal of weapons.

But the real world is far more accustomed to arguments that take no notice of that kind of consecrated definitions. Thus when we are defining power, power is a matter of being on the offensive and not on the defensive. The pre-emptive strikes of a Hitler or a Bush or the wars of aggression of unilateralism come under that heading.

While George Orwell was living in Burma, then a British

colony, he was able to experience the close connection existing between imperialism and colonialism. He points out that the colonial exploitation of states is inevitable to preserve the standard of living enjoyed by the middle classes back in the homeland at that time. Scott Nearing, who withdrew from society to live in a remote village of the eastern United States, says the same, being ultimately confronted with the fact that American society with its inflation and over-consumption requires the colonialization of other regions.

In the real world, with its active recourse to aggression and exploitation, the power of arms is almost absolute. What of the reality in which the response to the power of Israel's new weapons is suicide-bombing by young Palestinians?

Ancient Israel was dominated by a memory penetrated by a religious faith in the need for peace. David, the great hero of wars, was not permitted to construct the Jerusalem Temple. One with blood on his hands did not have the right to erect the sanctuary of God. But his son Solomon, king in times of peace, was asked to build it.

It is very obvious that Israel, nowadays confronted with Palestine, and the United States behind it, are not following the model offered by the *"Shalom"* respected by the Jews when they endured great suffering under Roman rule. The heads of Jewish families and their rabbis cry *"Shalom!"* lifting up their hands to Heaven as they bless their family or congregation. That is "peace" as a righteous blessing of the Lord shared equally over all the twelve tribes of Israel: "Peace! Peace!"

That is not the same as the "Pax" of Rome. The *Pax Romana* is far from the peace of the Jews enduring patiently the pain of being subject to other rulers. *"Shalom"* is a threatening thing to the Roman Empire, while to the Jews it is the name of the highest form of peace. Today in Gaza and the West Bank, the reality of that *"Shalom"* is nothing more than a conventionalized habit of repetition for the Jews.

If we take today's *Pax Americana*, modeled as it is on the *Pax Romana*, I suppose that no one will deny that that peace is just another name for aggression and hegemony. Indeed, it is a matter of fact that at the top levels of the American government and among the assemblies of the ruling intellectuals, it is becoming day by day more a habit to refer to America, not as a democracy but as an empire. The overinflation of "freedom" together with "peace" is part of the logic that claims that things American alone are right and the only means to American-style peace and freedom everywhere. In particular, the peace advocated by American Christian fundamentalism does not accept anything but a state where their own fundamentalism reigns supreme. Today the American democracy that Tocqueville praised so highly is extinct. The meaning of peace, one of the basic words of the American system, has changed to an amazing degree from the original sense.

It is essential that the true definition of peace should survive as we advance through times like ours. And that definition should be free to vary widely from one region to another. For example, whereas in ancient China, *Heiping* (和平) means harmony as order, in India *Shanti* is peace seen as cosmic awakening. Yet despite this plurality of interpretations of peace, the communality and mutuality that embody the union between you and me together with the difference between you and me must remain the fundamental basis for peace.

Peace is not a totalitarianism regimenting uniformly every region and every organization, but a culture of life resulting from authenticity for each and all. Still, when this individual interpretation of peace is exported to another region, it invariably becomes distorted. Indeed, when one place's peace is exported and extended to another place, that can go so far as to result in war. That is the world of the *Pax Romana*.

Regarding this, Ivan Illich's claim that "peace is a method of living" is intensely suggestive. He stresses that we must rescue the meaning of peace from the way of talking that justifies and authorizes aggression, protecting its meaning in the original languages employed in each region and country, and calls our attention to the fact that the ultimate meaning of peace can never be translated. So peace is as hard to translate as a poem is.

Historically speaking, the word "peace" was not originally a state of absence of war between one lord and another, one king and another; it meant protecting people's life and belongings from the violence of war, it meant ensuring complete security for grain-stocks and seeds, working oxen, and fields prior to harvest. In short, peace meant "the peace of the land." This makes it clear that the so-called peace that signifies a suspension of hostilities between enemies is a mere lack of peace.

At this point, we are obliged to investigate to what extent such a consciousness of peace is contained in the canons of literature. Put bluntly, the main subject matter of classical literature, of classical epic poetry, is mostly warfare. Probably the sublime structures of epic narrative would never have come into being without the violent acts of what is known as war.

The *"Mahabaratha"* and the *"Ramayana"* of India, together with the Greek epics of warfare, with their militaristic myths and stories of feats of arms have come to be considered the classic models of literature. This is a very different world from the world of the peaceful joys and sorrows of people or of mankind's inner melancholy, of the Chinese "Book of Odes", the "Songs of Chu," and other folk tales. Of course, it is true that later in China the success of the "Romance of the Three Kingdoms" proved that the dramatization of warfare was a fundamental element for the de.velopment of narrative literature to make a book become a must-be-read book among the masses.

As Hong Myeong-hui pointed out, most classical epics focus on scenes of combat by heroes, great commanders and brave warriors. In the case of the *Iliad*, we cannot imagine the epic world the poem represents without Hector, Prince of Troy, and those come to destroy his city – Achilles, Odysseus, Aias and Agamemnon. It is very odd that from one bizarre incident of a pretty married woman's kidnapping and the most shameful thing that could happen to a married man, people made absurd pretexts for total war; that serves to manifest the true character of classical epic. There is no justification for war there, beyond getting back a woman, taking revenge for the kidnapping of that woman. Of course, behind the outlines of the epic itself, it seems certain that strained relationships of interests and imbalances of power around the Ionian Sea must have played a role in its composition.

What is clear is that there was no need for heroic wills set on conquest or lofty intentions of holy war for one's motherland. Now it was precisely this kind of epic literature that the Greeks took as their schoolbooks, so that even Plato grew up being educated by the epics. Homer's main aim in writing was not necessarily the praise of war; he shows not the least sign of distancing himself from the classical view of war, according to which people's heroic and destined deeds are only possible in warfare. After all, the *Iliad* begins: "Sing, O goddess, the anger of Achilles."

After that, the literary consequences of war and conquest were often at the level of the frontline correspondent or the wartime writer. Then Hong Myeong-Hui found himself with the task of raising questions about this issue with his theory of an anti-war literature formulated in the 1930s, in the thick of frenzied enthusiasm for war. That is why it was possible for the meaning of peace to be deeply inscribed in the works he wrote in his native Korean language, with its representations of the popular, indigenous life of traditional Korean society.

We have grown accustomed to the term "Lord God of Hosts (Armies)" in the Christian Old Testament. It is a traditional expression that appeals to the masses, arousing a strong emotion. And in such terms we are enabled to sense how militaristic is the ideology behind the rhetoric of the Bible. It is virtually indistinguishable from the way in which contemporary politicians and general culture employ such terms as "strategies" and "tactics", without being aware that they are warfare terminologies.

Aristotle wrote that war is a natural phenomenon of human society and that, together with the fact that he was tutor to Alexander, only adds another positive affirmation to the history of human warfare. The war-centered idea that the history of humanity has been nothing but a history of war and that human civilization has mainly developed through warfare and must presuppose that there is a daily life, or a daily sense of peace and daily habit of peace. This is not to overlook the fact that the nuclear power-station is related to nuclear weapons, or that mobile telecommunications have evolved out of means of close communications under battlefield conditions.

Probably, in human history, times of war have exceeded times of peace in length. Peace has always been an insecure state, and that is where the meaning of peace and the meaning of insecure coexist. In any case, it might be possible to say that what we are calling peace is merely the valley lying between one war and the next, or the time of respite before provoking the next war. The way in which the more than eight thousand peace treaties ending more than eight thousand wars on this planet have all been in vain is another indication that one war presupposes a following war. So war came before war and war also followed war. From that emerges the anguished view that peace is merely a waiting-period before war.

Actually, the creation myths of some of humanity's aboriginal peoples seem to find it natural that war plays a major role. There are not a few cases where the climax of the myth has the gods snatching victory, leading the fight in the field. The Germanic peoples, after victory in battle, used to hold a victory celebration before Odin, their god of war, where they drank from the skulls of the enemy soldiers; feasted on their cattle, and massacred enemy troops who had been captured alive. A similar bellicosity can be found among the Brahmans of ancient India. They record wars involving men and monkeys and other animals. In their sacred wall-paintings they portray in detail grim scenes of gods riding in chariots in the course of murderous warfare.

In the myths of Greece, Zeus with other gods battles against the Titans, and even against his own father god. Mars, the god of soldiers, is proud of the title "the Murderer." Even Apollo is equipped with arrows. Plato and other thinkers stress that all wars, both defensive and offensive, on behalf of the polis are justified. The *polis* as such was a defensive structure, a military structure. In Assyria, Egypt, and among the Aztecs too, we find celebrations with tens of thousands of prisoners of war being thrown to their deaths from cliffs amidst clouds of incense and cries of victory. The heaven of Islam is likewise a paradise for those who die fighting. This is seen in the suicide bombers of the current Iraq resistance campaign. The Japanese *kamikaze* squadrons during the second world war, before taking off drank wine which was a gift from the emperor and performed their own funeral ceremony, before dressing in white, the color of death, renouncing all earthly attachments and desires.

This artificially constructed sacredness of war, which has continued from ancient times to the present age together with its tragic character, has still not reached an end. Yet while people endured the tragedies caused by innumerable wars with lives brought to their last extremity and death, that has in fact served to deepen the significance of peace as never before. Mencius says: "Adopting a policy using military power is to be a tyrant; and a tyrant must possess a wide territory. But one who pursues a policy of virtuous acts is a monarch; a monarch does not mind if his territory is not so large," and this expresses the clearest political philosophy of the rejection of war in the whole of North-East Asia.

But a clearer conception of peace can be found in Kant's "Perpetual Peace." That is rightly admired for the way it goes beyond the aphorisms of the middle ages to propose a truly creative theory of peace. He fully recognizes how difficult the practice of peace is. He realizes that peace is not a matter for a single nation but is only possible through an international solidarity. It might even be that this theory underlies the establishment of the League of Nations after the First World War and of the United Nations after the Second World War.

Regarding Napoleon's words that "the founder of an empire does not view people as human beings but as tools," Hegel celebrated him as "a world spirit on horseback." He goes so far as to declare that "war is the divine goal," and "the providence of God can only be sensed in war." We cannot help having doubts about the world spirit as post-Kantian metaphysics.

This approval of war develops further, with the appearance of Nietzsche, into a war instinct. He says that "a war opposed by reason must be conducted in the name of instinct [...] for instinct draws humanity into a front line in making human life more complete."

These positive expressions in praise of war ignore completely the way in which every generation's war games have inflicted ruthless violence on the lives of ordinary people. There we realize that the logic of conquest and domination contained within those theories of war goes hand in hand with a logic dominated by the superiority of the upper classes. This is where Hitler's Heidegger and Stalin's Union of Soviet Writers emerge.

Now we must set out on a practical quest for a peace arising from the new human mind, putting an end to the intellectual annals of theories in candid praise of war, a peace that has been universally desired from the very beginnings of human history. In actual fact, an intense awakening to peace arises not from a superior mind but from a sincere heart. The time has come to see that peace is first and foremost not an inferior aspect of human systems but a value emerging on the horizon of the most sublime human existence. We might say that it coincides with what is meant by being in interrelationship in the worlds of what Buddhism calls "conditioned arising" *(pratitya-samutpada)* or "Indra's Net," or relational being as an innumerable host of blossoms according to the world of the *Hua-yen (Avatamsaka)*. Perhaps it is the realization of such a world that will in the future come to form the finest discourse pointing toward a universe of peace.

Paradoxically, I would affirm that the disastrous wars the world has seen, or the way human life and culture have been preserved through those wars, denotes a great change in human history, whereby the meaning of war is no longer able to outdo the meaning of peace. That might signify a change from the inborn world designated by the Korean method of interpreting the *Book of Changes* to an acquired world view.

From now on, popular wisdom is required in order to bring an age of new harmony and vitality after an age of warfare and violence. A natural logic of peace is strictly required against the violence, which is, as someone has pointed out, immersed in the English word "peace," against the way war has a tendency to try to unify every culture as one, against the way capitalism ends up leaving nothing but a market of cultures.

Peace does not appear everywhere wearing the same armor. The Korean coat with many-colored sleeves, the Japanese *haori*, the drums of the African bush, indeed the motions of poetry and all forms of culture in every place are all forms of peace. The peace talked about in the Pentagon is a very different thing from that of Basra. There is also a great difference between the concept of peace held by Ito Hirobumi as he prepared the annexation of Korea by

Japan early in the 20th century and that of the Korean patriot An Jung-geun who demanded Peace in Asia. It would also be possible to find a routinizing of peace in the "*Hwa*" (和) thought of the Korean philosopher Choi Han-gi.

Truly, the inherent qualities of the life of people in every part of the world and the integrity of every particular custom is the starting point of peace. It is what brings life to the destruction of individual existence by the market-oriented forces of capitalism.

Peace is also a matter of practice. Once peace ends up being a mere discourse about peace, the seeds of warfare get skillfully sown. In this sense it is very important that, as Kant says, if everlasting peace remains at the level of words, the result is nothing more than slogans from the grave. What he particularly fears is the heroism that claims that a single state will bring peace to the world. The six preliminary conditions for peace that he lays down are far more realistic. First he states that the republican quality of a state is a basic requirement for putting the conditions into practice. This serves to remind us that today American republicanism has been transformed into imperialism both within and without.

Noam Chomsky has argued that since 1945 the United States, having won the Second World War, has engaged in war or aggression somewhere in the world once every two years. In addition, there have been constant cases in every part of the world where it has been deeply involved in subversive acts and coups d'état designed to eliminate regimes that were seen as an obstacle to American interests.

In the 1970s, the White House undertook a secret research project assembling representative experts from every sector of American society. Those experts included writers. The conclusion of their report was that the United States could not survive without war. Therefore the United States finds itself obliged regularly to provoke war, and that war enables it to safeguard Christian democracy, open markets and resources, all of which facilitates the use of the weapons that the United States unceasingly produces.

Despite constant red figures in trade and finance, the United States endlessly interferes with world prosperity, manipulating financial markets behind the scenes, and operating an all-direction, all-weather military system. American capitalism runs and consumes the whole world. Likewise, the world consumes America. Every kind of symbolic product – jeans and fast food, media, ideas, CNN News, music, language – is daily consumed. The aggressive quality of American football is no longer only American, it is repeated as the aggressiveness of each and every nation. The American right to possess firearms is inspiring armed crime in other parts of the world. In addition, America's democracy is undermining its own economic democracy.

Nowadays, systems of language and symbols have become immensely powerful in the world. Last year, one American newspaper reported that "English is contemporary Korea's religion." That is not only true of Korea. Even in France, one newspaper devotes a regular special column to articles from the American press.

The one-way equation of globalization with Americanization tramples on the definition that true globalization means a situation in which all the world's variety of multi-polarity and pluralism opens up to one another. That is why it is hard to find the oriental virtue known as "Hwa-i-bu-dong" (和而不同), one but diverse, "we are together but we differ." After all, following the 9/11 incident, the United States welcomed that event as a fine opportunity to wage war on Afghanistan, then Iraq. Yet today even a majority of Americans seem to have turned against those wars.

"The world generally speaking is now drifting on a more and more devastating course towards the absurd target of extermination … The distressing situation of our era is rising from a clearly irredeemable misconception, viz. that the use of weapons, *violence*, can lead to *victory* …" These words from the speech with which Alva Myrdal accepted the 1982 Nobel Peace Prize long ago fell on the deaf ears of those now pursuing war.

How is it possible for literature to preserve a *raison d'être* in the midst of such a heartless state of affairs with its calls to globalization and warfare, with every kind of constraining relationship in and out of reality? How can literature detach itself from the literature of former times marked by bourgeois purism and complacency and find its own living form full of peace and lively self-identity through union with the popular masses?

Indeed, a shift to opposing warfare lies before us as the main topic for literature at present. After the end of the Second World War, such works as *The Naked and the Dead*, *Young Lions, From Here to Eternity*, *The Blood of Others*, went in quest of humanity through the subject-matter of war and embodied the distorted inner depths of the human environment.

Such works, unlike the great war dramas of classical literature, draw conclusions favoring peace. In our Korean literature too, we have many works of fiction, both long and short, devoted to war, such as the medieval epic *"Dong-myeong-wang-pyeon"* by Yi Gyu-bo, or the 16th century's *"Im-jin-rok,"* and *"Im-gyeong-ob-jeon"* which belong to war literature, as well as such modern novels as Hwang Sun-won's *Trees on a Slope*, Choi In-hun's *Square*, Pak Kyong-ni's *Marketplace and Battlefield*, Hong Song-won's *North and South*. These mostly expose in various ways the inhumanity and blindness of war and so in conclusion tend to sow seeds of peace. But in spite of the achievements of these, I consider that we only now stand at the starting point of a Korean anti-war or pro-peace literature of quality.

But what must come first is a new, spontaneous, subjective sense of war and a sincere experience of peace thought. Literature must no longer serve as war's cleaners-up, and after a war is over its task will not be to depict that war but it will find itself obliged to play an active role, directly confronting it by having a serious feeling that war is a logic of power that devastates the whole of human life and culture.

In addition, literature must take the lead in showing that peace is not simply a gentle image of a rural landscape. For until now, literature, as an easy-going peacetime activity merely depicting in many small-scale works a simple war-abhorring sentiment, has been unable to reach an intense level of awareness in response to violence.

We are familiar from Darwin's theory of evolution with an ecosystem's "struggle for survival" or the "survival of the fittest." Practically, the survival of an animal or plant through the course of a fierce struggle is a possibility. It is only too easy to perceive human warfare as some kind of life-system, similar to such ecological systems.

Only this world is not something that came into being on the basis of "I" being able to live by having "you" die. Unlike the ecology of the past, today's life sciences are much more concerned with the principles of symbiosis than of competition. That is to say, they are discovering that the power of an ecosystem with symbiosis in mutual interdependence in the relationships of flowers with butterflies, small animals with large animals, plants with other plants, insects with insects, is far more predominant than hostile ecosystems.

It seems possible to derive the principle of symbiosis from the Buddhist theory of consciousness where the subject of *samsara* (reincarnation) is not a "self" but a "knowing" or a "storehouse of consciousness" *(alaya–vijnana)*. This latter is a state of "that which is unrecordable" which cannot be classified in terms of good or evil. Corresponding to the practice of symbiosis is a fundamental act sublimating a bi-polar system of principles in opposing relationships – is it this or that, I or you? – into a field with a triple set of principles – something neither this nor that.

The term "symbiosis" employed in speaking of relationships between living creatures in ecology is nowadays often employed by futurology as embodying peace in human society. But in Korea there has recently been a tendency to prefer the term *"sang-saeng"* (相生, mutual life) and this is somehow different from the Buddhist term "sang-jeuk" (相卽, phenomenal identity) where water is wave, wave water.

In the ancient Chinese Theory of the Five Elements (五行說), as opposites in the concept of "mutual incompatibility" we see what is meant by "sang-saeng," a chain-like world phenomenon where water emerges from metal, wood from water, fire from wood, earth from fire, metal from earth. But rather than this natural definition of "mutual life," the concept of symbiosis in human society may prove more effective in yielding a culture of peaceful symbiosis, peaceful coexistence, peaceful sharing.

Once the age of politics and the age of economics are past, an age of culture is bound to come. In order to welcome such an age, literature must cultivate the power of a peace literature capable of transforming the aggressivity that is spread across the whole of human history as a fundamental trait of human nature. It requires not the object of life welcoming peace as something given, but a subjective agony that encompasses thought and feeling and draws peace toward a world where it is practiced.

Literature must look further for more languages of peace and make it an important, motivating issue by discovering anew the true qualities of peace long transmitted within the lives of the world's peoples. Now is the time when we have to invoke the spirit of peace-literature contained within the collective and individual ideals of the common folk, not the literature of heroism and feats of arms. A literary revelation, an apocalypse, must publicize forcefully the ways in which humanity's sacred everyday lives and the true meaning of life have been violated by war – the greatest of festivals for which human beings have been used – and also by the theatricality of militarism as the most splendid decoration of war while performing it.

The Second World War took twenty million lives. The Korean War too robbed three million people of life in the course of its three years. By the Vietnam War, other genocides and now the killing in Iraq, the task of living literature must be to denounce the manipulated reality of those events and put an end to such inconsistencies.

We have to liberate people from too many war memorials and the natural religions of memorial ceremonies. Rejecting any attempt to use literature in the service of war, literature must not be permitted to remain a passive spectator when faced with the logic of war, to take to its heels in flight, to remain turned in on its inner world, or to prescribe prizes in the rear of the battle zone. There is a widespread, mistaken notion that war is supposed to be dynamic, peace static, but it would be intolerable for peace in literature to remain dormant.

Peace is a phenomenon of life, demanding fervor in incarnating the mind of life. Therefore the peace depicted in literature should be extraordinary and vibrant with life. Perhaps the ultimate finality of peace is nature. That non-artificial nature continues in unceasing action. Perhaps the ultimate phase of poetry is the vitality which will be in union with nature. In that case, the literature of peace will need to gain its own momentum through literature's active desire.

This will be made visible if the writers of every part of the world establish an organization of solidarity in support of peace. Last year's large-scale anti-war movement by poets all across the United States was marvelous. The sight of poets from all across the United States at a moment when it was bogged down in individualism gathered together as an anti-war *locus* was a rare thing in the present state of America. It so happened that just then the First Lady had invited the poets of America to the White House. Faced with such a large-scale event, many poets turned down the invitation in protest against the invasion of Iraq; others instead of refusing, declared that they would attend wearing the anti-war ribbon, at which the pretentious event that had been designed to enhance the public image of a poetry-loving presidential couple was, inevitably, cancelled.

This reminds me of how in the summer of 1945, the coded message indicating the successful dropping of the atom bomb on Hiroshima, that reduced in a flash some 200,000 people to ashes was, "The baby was born." Truman was overjoyed to receive such a message. Such is the extent to which warfare grows drunk with victory, warfare that murders even language, heedlessly committing literary blasphemy by employing such a poetic expression to indicate the fact that huge numbers of people have died.

Nowadays, most of the world's writers consider it normal that literature be separated from politics. In many different places we can find literature imprisoned within its own games of awareness. The self in contemporary literature has become an honorable emblem of humanity as a whole. The speaker of contemporary poetry has come to occupy a position identical with that of God. But that self is enclosed within its own limitations and the ultimate result is that it turns into an embodiment of selfishness. I would go so far as to say that within literature such a self, with such a restricted set of desires, is today diminishing the stature of literature itself.

Regarding this, Susan Sontag's literary self-exploration *Regarding the Pain of Others*, in which she reflects on human egoism and selfishness, is particularly meaningful. "I" am the other's other who cannot exist without another. The desire of each "I" is a matter of desiring the desire of another. Here can be glimpsed in an epoch-making manner the mutual exchange of "I" and other, the high synthesis of ego and alter ego.

Peace literature is also the literature of a life in which the dialogue between "I" and others is constantly pursued, in a normal way or a dramatic way. Through that unending construction of the relationship between peace and literature, writers must never in any way cease their sincere protests against the war-mongers who destroy both humanity and nature, whether in writing or beyond it.

The way in which Tolstoy wrote that "seen in the oriental sense, Koreans are extremely civilized people" and scathingly criticized the imperialistic policies and aggressions of his own nation, Tsarist Russia, along with the great powers of western Europe and then, immediately after the Russo-Japanese War disavowed both Russia and Japan together, saying that he only took the side of the peoples who had suffered on account of the war, helps us all realize more clearly what the mission of literature is. More than that, by denouncing Hito, the first Japanese Resident-General after the annexation of Korea, as "a madman," he bequeathed us a literary Bill of Rights by showing how very dynamic East-West reciprocity and populist pacifism can be.

Concerning war and state violence, and the peace that absolutely must be sought beyond them, literature elicits by metaphor and reflection bright alternative topics in every age. Beyond that, the crisis of literature, even the death of literature sees literature surviving, transformed by the paradox that ensures the enduring meaning of literature. Homer's *Odyssey* concludes with the affirmation that it has "brought war to an end for ever." If that can be affirmed in poetry, how little literature need bother itself thinking about the next war.

Here, literature begins again.

Translated by **Brother Anthony of Taizé**

Unwegsame Wege

Wolf Biermann

Schmerzlicher als die meisten Deutschen in Ost und West im Kalten Krieg auf den Fall des Eisernen Vorhangs hofften, sehnen sich viele Koreaner in Süd und Nord nach einer Wiedervereinigung ihrer Heimat. Wann wird diese schwärende Wunde am 38. Breitengrad heilen? Keiner weiß es. Aber ich vermute: Früher als manche denken, früher als die einen hoffen, früher die anderen fürchten.

Als Motto für das Meeting in Korea steht auf meiner Einladung: Writing for Peace. Als ich das las, wollte ich im Affekt die Reise in den fernen Osten lieber gleich absagen. Seit dem Streit um die beiden letzten Irak-Kriege hat es sich in Deutschland herumgesprochen: Wolf Biermann ist ein Bellizist. Und auch wenn ich ein einfältiger Friedensapostel wäre: Man fliegt doch nicht Tag und Nacht rund um den Erdball, nur, um irgendwelchen netten Leuten mitzuteilen, daß man Frieden schöner findet als Krieg. Ich denke, die Veranstalter, die meine teuren Flugtickets und mein Hotelzimmer zahlen, hätten ihr Geld rausgeschmissen (und ich würde meine knappe Lebenszeit vergeuden), wenn ich in der rasenden Blechdose über Sibirien und China um den Globus bis nach Seoul flöge, nur, um Friedensfreunden in Poesie und Prosa mal wieder genau das mitzuteilen, was sie selber wissen: daß auch ich für den Frieden bin. Ich lag im Juli 1943 – da war ich sechs Jahre alt – unter dem Bombenteppich in Hamburg. Schon darum bin ich – automatisch wie Luftholen - ein Writer for peace. Aber was sagt das schon. Genau so gut schreibe ich for fee, for vanity, bin ein writer for fame and for enjoyment, ich bin ein writer for hate and for love. Das sind alles wahrhaftige Phrasen. Ich schrieb ja immer auch für den Krieg. Ich muß auch für den Krieg sein, für den Krieg gegen Völkermörder und Tyrannen. Ich bin nur am Leben geblieben, Kommunistenkind in Nazideutschland, weil die Mörder meiner ganzen jüdischen Familie endlich mit Waffengewalt gestoppt wurden. Ich verdanke mein Leben den amerikanischen und russischen und britischen Soldaten, die für mich kämpften und starben.

Nicht Krieg und Frieden – nein, die Hoffnungen und Ängste in Bezug auf die Wiedervereinigung Koreas sind das peinliche, das eigentliche Thema hier in Seoul. Und weil der gescheiterte Bruder im Norden nun dem reichen und freien Süden sogar mit Atomraketen droht, ist der uralte Konflikt, ob Frieden mehr wert ist als Freiheit, ob also Krieg schlimmer ist als eine Diktatur, dramatischer als noch vor ein paar Jahren.

Ich kann mir denken, daß die meisten von Ihnen inbrünstig hoffen auf genau das, was sie zugleich am meisten fürchten ... will sagen: fürchten müssen: Die koreanische Wiedervereinigung.

Ich weiß, wovon ich rede, denn ich komme aus Deutschland. Die Ausgangslage ist gewiss nicht gleich, aber doch vergleichbar: Ein totalitär verelendetes halbes Volk soll mit seiner wohlstandsverwüsteten Hälfte nach Jahrzehnten der Trennung wieder zusammen leben. Unser sozialdemokratischer Politiker Willy Brandt prägte beim Fall der Berliner Mauer den polit-poetischen Satz: „Jetzt wächst zusammen, was zusammen gehört!". Da witzelten die Spötter in Deutschland: die Banane soll mit der Bockwurst zusammenwachsen. Für Korea würde diese sarkastische Metapher nicht passen, denn die Nordkoreaner sind nicht so verfettet vom vielen Bockwurstfressen wie es die Ostdeutschen waren. Alles ist anders hier. Und dennoch: Trotz aller Unterschiede - es müssen ja die Koreaner auf nichts so neugierig sein wie auf die Erfahrungen der Deutschen mit der Wiedervereinigung. Und dieses Interesse ist doch auf den ersten dummen Blick verständlich und sogar vernünftig: Die Koreaner wollen aus deutschen Fehlern womöglich lernen. Fragt sich nur, ob man überhaupt aus Fehlern anderer Leute was lernen kann, das gilt fürs Private wie fürs Historische. Ja, man vermeidet die schlimmsten Fehler der Anderen, aber doch nur, um noch viel schlimmere eigene Fehler zu machen.

Um es also gleich zu sagen: Es wird schrecklich. Und Sie werden es dennoch wagen müssen. Es wird für den freien Süden nicht nur teuer, sondern ruinös. Alle Beteiligten werden am Ende unzufrieden sein, das ist dann der neue Friede. Beide Seiten werden sich betrogen fühlen. Die befreiten Sklaven des Nordens werden sich nach den bequemen Wassersuppen der Diktatur zurücksehnen. Die Südkoreaner werden sich mißbraucht und ausgeraubt vorkommen.

Nix da! mit dem Lernen von den Deutschen. Die Umstände, die Vielzahl der wirkungsmächtigen Vektoren in solch einer geschichtsmächtigen Rechnung sind unberechenbar. Sicher ist nur das Unsichere, klar erkennbar ist nur unsere brachiale Blindheit in jeder neuen historischen Konstellation.

Unser Philosoph Georg Wilhelm Friedrich Hegel verfaßte als Professor und Staatsbeamter im Dienste des Königs von Preußen eine Geschichte der Philosophie, in der er die einzelnen Philosophen, von Anfang an, seit der Antike, so aneinander reihte, daß ihre verschiedenen einander widersprechenden Lehren die aufeinanderfolgenden Schritte des dialektischen Erkenntnisprozesses formulieren. Diese Metamorphose der philosophioschen Begriffe liefert uns den logischen Denk-Prozess des homo sapiens auf dem endlosen Wege von einer unvollkommener Erkenntnis zur nächst höheren Vollendung der Unvollkommenheit. Das ist bei Hegel ein Fort-Schritt.

Dieser geniale Philosoph verfaßte aber nicht nur eine dunkle Geschichte der Philosophie, sondern auch eine hellsichtige Philosophie der Geschichte. Und darin beschreibt er den Geschichtsprozess wie ein Naturwissenschaftler die Braunsche Molekularbewegung aus der Perspektive der Thermodynamik. Der Fortschritt, was immer das bei Hegel sei, ergibt sich als Summe aller divergierenden Kraftvektoren, die im Lebensprozess der Menschen zur Wirkung kommen, kleinste und größte, privatestes Tun oder Lassen und politisch gebündelte Aktionen bunt durcheinander, miteinander, gegeneinander, nebeneinander. Kein kluger Mensch, keine hochgebildete Schicht, keine revolutionäre Klasse kann die Wechselwirkungen der Elemente erahnen, kein kluger Kopf kann die Resultante der verschiedenen Aktivitäten berechnen, geschweige denn voraussagen. Alle, auch die Gebildeten, sind in diesem Sinne dumm, auch die Sehenden handeln blind. Ja - und die Ungebildeten sind sogar oft um Einiges klüger als die Intellektuellen, weil sie nicht ganz so viel ideologische Bretter vor der Stirne haben.

Wir alle wühlen also im Gewusel nach den eigenen Interessen, jeder entscheidet in Aktion und Reaktion nach der eigenen bornierten Urteilskraft.

Dabei foppt uns der Weltgeist damit, daß grade die weitsichtigen Weltverbesserer meistens grauenhafte Wirkungen provozieren. Und nach dem mephistophelischen Gesetz, wie Goethe es in seinem FAUST formulierte, ist es grade der kurzsichtige Bösewicht, der langfristig und unfreiwillig oft das Gute schafft oder wenigstens befördert.

Viele kommen aus dieser Einsicht zum trübsinnigen Schluß, daß aus der Geschichte nur das Eine zu lernen ist: Die Menschheit kann nichts lernen aus ihrer Geschichte. So denke auch ich. Und bin dabei, grade in diesem Punkte, meistens nicht meiner Meinung. Immerhin verhindert das Studium der Geschichte, daß wir immer wieder die genau gleichen Fehler machen. In jedem wirklich neuen Irrweg aber steckt die latente Chance eines unerwarteten Auswegs aus einer auswegslosen Misere. Die Weltgeschichte der Menschen kommt mir vor wie eine Wundertüte, manchmal wunderbar und meistens grausam.

Und das ist der Grund, warum es echte Propheten nie und nimmer geben kann. Ich wußte 1988 ganz genau, daß die DDR länger halten wird als ich. Allerdings haben meine Lieder und Gedichte einiges dazu beitragen, daß ich am Ende mit meinen hochintelligenten Voraussagen dermaßen glücklich im Irrtum war.

In Korea können die deutschen Erfahrungen mit der Wiedervereinigung auch deshalb nicht viel hergeben, weil die totaltäre Deformation der Untertanen im kleinen kommunistischen Nordkorea offensichtlich viel brutaler und gründlicher verwirklicht wurde als seinerzeit in der größten DDR der Welt. Die Versklavung bis tief ins Gehirn und bis in die Seele und ins Gemüt hat sich in Nordkorea in den Jahrzehnten des Kalten Krieges viel ungestörter verfestigen können. So unbekümmert wie Kim Il Sung und sein schwachsinniger Sohn mit dem Volk umspringen konnten, war es den Quislingen Ulbricht, Honecker und Krenz nie erlaubt. Der Viermächtestatus von Berlin, die Präsenz der amerikanischen Armee, das grenzüberschreitende Radio, das Fernsehn, die Rentnerreisen. Auch das minderte die totale Totalisierung: Die totale Niederlage Nazideutschlands 1945. Die zerbombten Städte. Das Elend der Flüchtlinge aus Ostpreußen und Pommern. Die unleugbare Schande des Völkermordes an Juden und Zigeunern. Deutschland war als Missetäter erkannt, ertappt und erschlagen.

Korea dagegen war im II. Weltkrieg ein Opfer der japanischen Großmachtpolitik geworden. Und Erinnerungen an Erfahrungen in der Demokratie konnte es nicht geben. Korea hatte kein liberales Kaiserreich, keine Weimarer Republik erlebt.

Zudem war die arme DDR niemals so ein total verarmtes Land wie Nordkorea, das seine Bewohner durch die schlimmste Massenfolter chronisch quält, die es wohl gibt, denn schlimmer als Meinungsterror und Spitzelei ist für Massen: Hunger und Kälte. Im Gegenteil, diese arme DDR war mit ihrem materiellen Lebensstandard in den Zeiten der Teilung Deutschlands das reichste Land im gesamten Sozialistischen Lager. In diesem verrotteten Ostblock war die DDR fast schon ein Wohlstandsparadies. Wenn wir damals in Ostberlin witzelten, daß Ungarn hinter dem Eisernem Vorhang die lustigste Baracke im Sozialistischen Lager war, dann war die DDR die ordentlichste, sauberste und gemütlichste Baracke in diesem Lager.

Das stimmt: die Schurigelung der Jugend war widerlich, die lähmende Angst vor der Gesinnungsschnüffelei war groß und begründet. Der VEB-Knast war grauenhaft. Aber gemessen an Nordkorea war die DDR ein fast schon freies Land.

Und ich vermute, die Lage der Nordkoreaner wurde sogar noch verzweifelter seit dem Zusammenbruch der Sowjetunion. Und dieses Nordkorea muß ja noch elender abgesackt sein, seit der rote Riese China mit Siebenmeilenstiefeln in den gleißenden reißenden Konzentrationslager-Kapitalismus marschiert. Es gibt einen Grad von Schwächung, die jedes Aufmucken, jede Rebellion fast unmöglich macht.

Dennoch könnte es passieren, durch die dialektische Zauberhand des Hegelschen Weltgeistes, daß anders als wir alle denken, die Widervereinigung auch in Korea passiert. Eine der Optionen wäre allerdings auch die apokalyptische Wiedereinigung unter den radioaktiven Rauch-Pilzen eines Atombombenhimmels über Süd- und Nordkorea. Das wäre des nordkoreanischen Diktators einzige Chance: Er einigt die Koreaner, indem er sie alle in den atomaren Abgrund reißt.

Nehmen wir aber mal an, das freie Südkorea gewinnt diesen Bruderkrieg und ebnet den Weg des Nordens in die Demokratie. Reden wir also konkret vom schnöden Mammon. Das kann ich kolportieren: Die USA pumpten von 1945 bis 1953 insgesamt etwa 13 Milliarden Dollar in das verwüstete Europa. Das war der berühmte Marschallplan: eine Soforthilfe. Das Geld wurde einigermaßen gerecht aufgeteilt, den größten Brocken kriegten die schwer verwüsteten Engländer. Die Gesamtmenge teilten sich außerdem die okkupierten Franzosen, die halb besiegten Italiener, die Belgier und Holländer. Das faschistische Spanien kassierte keinen Penny. Und die ganz besiegten Deutschen? Ab 1949 flossen in die Bundesrepublik immerhin 1,5 Milliarden US-Dollar, das waren nach damaliger Währung 4,5 Milliarden Deutsche Mark.

Ein Haufen hartes Geld! Und das will ich in der Hektik der Maulschlachten nie vergessen: marxistisch gesprochen bedeutet diese Geldsumme eine gewaltige Menge geronnener menschlicher Arbeit. Die Finanzmittel wurden den Europäern in den verbrannten Hintern gesteckt, in den zahnlosen Mund geschoben, in die taubgebrüllten Ohren gestopft, in die löchrigen Taschen und in die gerümpften Nasenlöcher, egal. Jedenfalls war es gedacht und funktionierte als Startkapital, um die Trümmer des Krieges zu beseitigen und eine Landwirtschaft und Industrie wieder aufzubaun: Es war eine großherzige und weitsichtige Hilfe zur Selbsthilfe. Und natürlich war es auch eine kluge Strategie im Kalten Krieg zwischen den Alliierten von gestern. Eine aufblühende Wirtschaft sollte die freien Westeuropäer davon abhalten, den kommunistischen Tierversuch am lebendigen Menschen unter der Peitsche der Genossen Stalin & Co zu machen.

Das ist lange her, aber gut zu wissen. Und heute? Die reiche alte Bundesrepublik hat inzwischen jedes Jahr seit der

Wiedervereinigung etwa 100 Milliarden D-Mark in die ehemalige DDR gepumpt. Also seit der Wiedervereinigung etwa 333 mal so viel wie der Marschallplan. Und der Erfolg? Sehr groß, sehr klein. Die verrotteten Häuser sind saniert, volkseigene Industrie-Dinosaurier wurden weggerissen, mehr neue Shopping-Paläste als neue Fabriken wurden aus dem Boden gestampft. Und das neue Straßennetz verhält sich zum alten wie eine Rennpiste zum Schützengraben. Den tiefsten Schaden aber kann kein Geld so schnell reparieren: die Verwüstungen im Seelenhaushalt der Untertanen am Ende einer totalitären Diktatur.

Und in diesem wunden Punkte haben es die Polen und Tschechen und Ungarn und sogar die Russen besser getroffen: Sie haben keinen superreichen Bruder, der ihnen beisteht. Sie taumeln also nicht von einer politischen Unmündigkeit in eine ökonomische. Die schlimmste Verwüstung aber ist die tief eingefressene Unmündigkeit. Man ist für nichts verantwortlich, das ist ein herrliches Sklavenleben, das sind die Bequemlichkeiten der strengen Erziehungsdiktatur.

*

Ein ökonomisches Problemchen, an dem das System sozialer Sicherheit in Deutschland krankt, wird Sie beim Gedanken an die Wiedervereinigung Koreas interessieren. Millionen DDR-Bürger haben natürlich auch gearbeitet und damit ihr Geld zum Leben verdient. Aber in die Rentenkassen der Bundesrepublik Deutschland konnten sie ja keinen Pfennig einzahlen. Im Deutschen gibt es die Redewendung: Der Teufel sitzt im Detail. Die heikle Frage also: Aus welchem Topf bezahlt die Gesellschaft die Renten nun für die Millionen Rentner im Osten. Im Einigungsvertrag von 1990 wurde festgelegt, daß diese Gelder aus den gefüllten Rentenkassen der reichen Bundesrepublik einfach mitbezahlt werden. Die Folge: der riesige Topf hat sich in 15 Jahren katastrophal geleert. Die Fachleute, zu denen ich gewiss nicht zähle, sind der Meinung, das war ein vermeidbarer Fehler. Die Renten für Menschen aus der DDR-Zeit hätten besser aus höheren Steuern bezahlt werden sollen. Vor dieser Lösung hatten aber alle Politiker Angst, weil sie bei den nächsten Wahlen auf Teufel komm raus gewählt werden wollten. Und so kam der Teufel dann auch raus.

Aber egal, aus welchem Topf gegessen wird - das pekuniäre Problem hat außerdem eine moralische Seite. Grade weil Ihnen hier in Südkorea eine Wiedervereinigung mit einem totalitär ruinierten Land bevorsteht, will ich anmerken, daß auch alle Offiziere der Nationalen Volksarmee der DDR, daß alle Bonzen im Staats- und im Parteiapparat aus diesem Rententopf gefüttert werden.

Sogar die Offiziere des Ministeriums für Staatssicherheit, die zum Beispiel zehntausende DinA4-Seiten allein schon über Wolf Biermann in ihren Archiven angehäuft haben, also: tausende Spitzelberichte, Zersetzungsmaßnahmen, abgehörte Telefongespräche, Tonbandaufzeichnungen der Abhörwanzen in meiner Wohnung – all diese hohen Offiziere, deren Namen ich kenne, gelten jetzt als pensionierte Beamte des Staates Bundesrepublik Deutschland. Sie beziehen eine viel höhere Rente als ihre kaputtgemachten Opfer, die nicht so gut davonkamen wie etwa Wolf Biermann, der mit seinen Liedern immer mehr Geld verdiente als er brauchte.

Nach meiner Ausbürgerung im Jahre 1976 lebte ich in meiner Vaterstadt Hamburg. Auch im Westen wurde ich intensiv vom Staatssicherheitsdienst der DDR beobachtet und operativ „zersetzt". Westliche Agenten des MfS kontrollierten im freien Deutschland lückenlos meinen Telefon- und Briefverkehr, man registrierte meine Kontakte zu Menschen in der ganzen Welt. Meinen ersten Manager im Westen fand ich nach der Öffnung der Stasiakten wieder als IM „Willy", meine Finanzen, meine Steuerabrechnungen, mein juristischer Stoffwechsel mit der bürgerlichen Gesellschaft wurde vom MfS in Ostberlin kontrolliert und manipuliert. Und der Chef dieser Spionage-Organistion gegen den Klassenfeind in der Westlichen Welt war der Sohn des antifaschistischen Dramatikers Friedrich Wolf, die gefürchtete Graue Eminenz unter den Geheimdienstkrokodilen, der MfS-General Markus Wolf. Dieser parfümierte Menschenfresser suhlt sich seit dem Zusammenbruch der DDR in Talkshows und lebt von seiner Rente, die ihm zusteht als hoher Beamter der Firma „Horch & Guck" (das war der populäre Spottname für den aufgeblähten Geheimdienst der DDR)

Was macht man am Ende einer mörderischen Diktatur, einer verhaßten Schreckensherrschaft mit all den professionellen

Canaillen des gestürzten Regimes? Was soll man mit all den Folterern und mit den Massenmördern machen, die die blutige Schmutzarbeit verrichteten? Und was soll geschehen mit den gekauften Intellektuellen, die mit Lügen und Heuchelei die große Menschen-zerbrech-maschine konstruiert und repariert und geschmiert haben? Und was soll man machen mit denen, die die Befehle zum Morden und Foltern gaben, die darüber entschieden, wer hinter Stacheldraht, Minengürtel und Selbstschußanlagen verfault.

Ich sage es Ihnen kurz und klar im Vorübergehn: Das befreite Volk sollte die entmachteten Massenmörder in Uniform und in Zivil, die Spitzel und Denunzianten, die Propagandamonster des zusammengebrochenen Regimes erst mal alle töten.

Nachdem die Bastille gestürmt war, vor über 200 Jahren, da tanzte das Volk von Paris durch die eroberte Hauptstadt und gröhlte ein neues Lied, geschrieben von einem Straßenmusikanten mit Namen M. Ladré zu einer Melodie von M. de Bécourt:

Ah! ça ira, ça ira, ça ira!
Les aristocrates à la lanterne.
Ah! ça ira, ça ira, ça ira!
Les aristocrates on les pendra.
Si on n' les pend pas
On les rompra
Si on n' les rompt pas
On les brûl'ra.
Ah! ça ira, ça ira, ça ira...

Es lohnt sich, die französisch zusammengereimten Knüppelzeilen in platte koreanische Prosa zu übersetzen: An die Laterne! Hängt sie auf, die Aristokraten! Jetzt gehts los! Jetzt gehts ran! Und wenn sie nicht hängen, dann solln man sie rädern, sie sollen zerbrochen werden und zerrissen, und wenn das nicht funktioniert, dann wolln wir sie brennen, verbrennen, braten, rösten – so etwa sollten wir uns das Verb „brulér" übersetzen.

Und diese peinliche Mordlust-Arie ist das berühmteste, das bis heute populärste Lied der Großen Französischen Revolution. Diese

Muster-Revolution begann mit dem noch harmlosen Sturm auf die Bastille, erhitzte sich mit dem Völkermord in der Vendée bis zum Terreur, und sie kochte über mit der Hinrichtung des Jakobiners Maximilien de Robespierre 1794. Die heiße Blutbrühe erkaltete dann und erstarrte mit der Kaiserkrönung des Revolutionsgenerals Napoleon Bounaparte im Jahre 1804. Als der kurzbeinige Kanonenoffizier sich eigenhändig die Krone aufsetzte, da hatte die große französische Revolution sich trotz dieser absurden Inszenierung vollendet. Mit dem Wort Vollendung meine ich nicht ironisch die Machtoperette in der Kirche Notre Dame auf der Ile de la Cité in Paris, nein, die tatsächliche Vollendung der französischen Revolution war der so genannte Code Napoleon, also das Bürgerliche Gesetzbuch. Das nämlich war und blieb trotz des feudalverkitschten Mummenschanzes im Kaiserkostüm die revolutionäre Substanz: Die Behauptung bürgerlicher Eigentums- und Freiheitsrechte gegenüber dem Regime des Feudalismus. Und nun kommt die blutige Gretchenfrage: Wäre den frechen Franzosen all das gelungen ohne diese blutrünstige Orgie des Pöbels, der erstmal nichts anderes wollte, als Rache, nichts anderes als munter aufhängen, fröhlich zerfleischen.

Elf Jahre nach dem Zusammenbruch der DDR schrieb ich mal wieder eine Bilanzballade:

BIERMANNS BILANZBALLADE IM ELFTEN JAHR

Der Moloch krepierte wie nebenbei
Stocknüchtern und kreuzbrav vernünftig – so haben
Wir ohne Pogrome und Weltkrieg III.
Den Kommunismus zu Grabe getragen
Die sanfte Spaziergänger-Revolution
In Leipzig gelang ohne Re-vo-lu-tio-näre
Werweiß, wenn bei unserer Ost-Rebellion
Das Blut in Strömen geflossen wäre

Ein lachender Racherausch war einst, mein Gott!
Der Sturm auf die Bastille dagegen
Da tanzte der Pöbel um das Schafott

Besoffen vom blutroten Frühlingsregen
Mir reicht es als Rache, wenn alle die
Uns quälten, bald auch in der Hölle braten
Mir reicht eine mausgraue Demokratie
Schön bunt brauch ich nur unsre Demokraten

All meine treuen Todfeinde sind
Mit blauem Auge davongekommen
Die jungen Partei-Kader sind geschwind
In stinkenden Geldflüssen mitgeschwommen
Die haben sich clever widervereint
Und machen den Reibach beim Wiedervereinen
Sie sühln sich im Bett mit dem Klassenfeind
Und lachen sich eins ins Fäustchen beim Greinen

Marxistisch verklart, ganz ohne Krampf
Im alten Jargon kann ich singen und sagen:
Das Volk, jawohl! hat im Klassenkampf
Historisch den Sieg davongetragen!
Im Übrigen weiß ich: Kein Racheakt
Könnt Jürgen Fuchs mir lebendig machen
Ich lebe! und stehe nun splitternackt
Mal wieder am Anfang und weine beim Lachen

Das sollen Sie wissen in Korea: Keiner der großen Schinder wurde nach dem Sturz des DDR-Regimes ermordet, hingerichtet, zusammengeschlagen oder auch nur mit einer Mistkarre von wütenden LPG-Bauern in die Jauchegrube geschmissen. Und es war dennoch eine echte Revolution! Oder etwa nicht? Der Sturz der totalitären Monopolbürokratie im gesamten Sozialistischen Lager war doch viel mehr Revolution als das anarchische Gebrüll und Gemetzel auf den Straßen von Paris genau 200 Jahre vorher. Das war viel mehr als nur ein blutiger Rülpser der besoffenen Weltgeschichte. 1789 und 1989 - beides waren radikale und plötzliche Umstürze, es wurde die Struktur etablierter Macht- und Besitzverhältnisse zerschmettert. Und solche tiefen Brüche nennt man im politischen Jargon halt eine Revolution.

So weit – so gut. Es bleibt aber die Frage: Was wird aus einer Revolution ohne Revolutionäre? Ich befürchte: Es wird daraus eine Demokratie ohne Demokraten. Ein dermaßen radikaler Machtverlust ohne auch nur einen Hauch von Racheorgien in den ersten Erschütterungen, ist ein Seelenkrüppel von Anfang an. Ganz ohne Plünderungen staatlicher Magazine, ohne spontane Raubattacken, ohne die Raserei des befreiten Pöbels gegen seine verhaßten Unterdrücker, ohne das blinde Wüten der gequälten Menschen gegen all die Spitzel und Denunzianten, ist es eine Mißgeburt der Weltgeschichte.

So passierte es in Deutschland: Die Kader des alten Regiemes verbündeten sich noch im Sturze akrobatisch mit den Rittern von der Schnellen Mark aus dem Westen, mit Bankrotteuren aus München und abgebrannten Halunken aus Hamburg. Mit schmalem Hintern verdrückte sich das privlegierte Personal der Diktatur in seinen Villen. Die schuldbeladenen Funktionäre der SED, allerhand geistlose Blutsäufer mit Sektglas, die herzlosen Schreibtischtäter, die verachteten Apologeten des alten Propaganda-Apparats, die verfetteten Klassenkämpfer hinter den Bankett-Barrikaden – sie alle haben sich auf leisen Sohlen in ihre Datschen verpisst und warteten auf die Resignation ihrer Opfer und auf bessres Wetter für Cretins ihrer Art. Was soll man also machen mit all diesen Samt- und Seide-Lumpen, was können die befreiten Menschen tun gegen die kleinen Büttel und die großen Nutznießer der entmachteten Allmacht.

Sie werden es ja erleben: Die gestürzte Elite des totalitären Machtapparats liefert meistens auch das Personal für die neue Elite. Die ostdeutschen Parteikader haben sich - automatisch wie Luftholen - sofort in Seilschaften organisiert. Die SED wurde umgetauft in PDS (Partei des demokratischen Sozialismus) Die Milliarden des SED-Parteivermögens auf ausländischen Banken sind unauffindbar gewaschen. Der Immobilienbesitz im Lande selbst und auch rund um den Erdball ist privat verstreut. Verdeckte Beteiligungen an Konzernen in der ganzen Welt wurden so über zuverlässige Einzelpersonen verschachtelt, daß der Deutsche Staat nie mehr an diesen Raub aus Jahrzehnten herankommt.

Der Leiter einer Gedenkstätte in der ehemaligen Untersuchungshaftanstalt des MfS in der Bautzner Straße in Dresden, der DDR-Bürgerrechtler Lothar Klein, fand in den Akten der Stasi ein streng geheimes internes Dokument aus dem Jahre 1988, es wurde also verfaßt ein Jahr vor der sanften Spaziergänger-Revolution. Da steht schwarz auf Weiß in knallhartem Bürokratendeutsch:

> **Für den Fall des Untergangs der DDR sollten bewährte Genossinnen und Genossen so viel wie möglich an sozialistischem Eigentum übernehmen in private Verantwortung, um die materielle Basis für die Weiterarbeit unter veränderten Bedingungen zu sichern.**

Und genau das haben sie getan, die Erben der Nomenklatura. Und sie fühlen sich bei dieser Orgie der Bereicherung nicht etwa wie gemeine Diebe, sondern wie die tapferen Kämpfer in einer vom imperialistischen Klassenfeind aufgezwungenen Illegalität.

Das befreite Volk wird diese Kader des totalitären Regimes in Nordkorea im ersten Affekt wie tolle Hunde erschlagen müssen.

Aber genau dieser Massenmord geht eben leider nicht. Das Christentum verbietet es den Menschen im fernen Europa. Und ich Gottloser weiß auch ohne Religionsunterricht, daß ich an solchen gestürzten Mördern nun nicht selber zum Mörder werden darf. Wir müssen den Teufelskreis der Gewalt und des Unrechts durchbrechen. Wenn es wahr ist, was unser Gotthold Ephrahim Lessing in seinem Stück Nathan der Weise über die berühmte Ringparabel erzählt, daß nämlich die humane Substanz aller Religionen die gleiche ist, dann wird das auch für Sie hier in Korea gelten. Ja, ich denke auch so: Jede Religion, wenn sie nicht demagogisch verfälscht und terroristisch mißbraucht wird, predigt dasselbe nur in verschiedenen Variationen: Der Mensch soll gut sein, freidlich, er soll gütig und hilfreich und wohlwollend sein gegen alle Mitmenschen, er soll den Teufelskreis der Rache tapfer durchbrechen, er soll den Fremden beherbergen und tolerant sein gegen Andersdenkende. Schöne Wort, nicht wahr? Aber trotzdem wahre Worte. Es wird auch in Ihren religösen Ideengebäuden im

Korea ein Verbot gegen den heillosen Rausch der Rache geben. Nein, wir können, wir dürfen und wir wollen nicht sein und nicht werden wie dieses totalitäre Pack.

*

Vor zwei Jahren besuchte mich ein koreanischer Dichter bei mir zu Hause in Hamburg-Altona. Da ich nichts von ihm kannte, nichts wußte, sagte man mir, ich solle ihn unbedingt treffen, denn er sei der singende Poet des koreanischen Widerstandes.

So trafen wir zusammen. Er saß mir mit seiner Übersetzerin gegenüber am Kamin. Sie machte ihre Transportarbeit genau und elegant. Aber was soll man reden mit solch einem Menschen vom anderen Ende der Welt? Ich weiß ja dermaßen wenig über Korea, daß ich nicht mal kluge Fragen stellen kann. Also fragte ich ihn, halb aus Verlegenheit: Herr Kim Ming´Gi - was ist Ihr Hit in Korea? Ich meine wie geht Ihr bestes Gedicht, was ist ihr populärstes Lied dort im eigenen Volk. Die Frage war ihm peinlich. Wer spreizt sich schon naiv mit seinen eigenen Schlagern! Aber ich fragte weiter: Mit welchem ihrer Verse haben Sie am meisten bewirkt in Korea? Sowas muß es doch geben in Ihrem Werk. Ich zum Beispiel habe auch solch ein Lied. Es ist nicht mein bestes, aber doch eines, das für viele Menschen in Deutschland immer wieder ein Stück Seelenbrot war, besonders für Menschen, die in derr DDR im VEB-Knast saßen. Das Lied heißt Ermutigung. Und dann gab ich seiner Übersetzerin den Text und sang es ihm vor zur Gitarre.

ERMUTIGUNG

Du, laß dich nicht verhärten
In dieser harten Zeit
Die allzu hart sind, brechen
Die allzu spitz sind, stechen
Und brechen ab sogleich.

Du, laß dich nicht verbittern
In dieser bittren Zeit
Die Herrschenden erzittern

- sitzt du erst hinter Gittern -
Doch nicht vor deinem Leid

Du, laß dich nicht erschrecken
In dieser Schreckenszeit
Das wolln sie doch bezwecken
Daß wir die Waffen strecken
Schon vor dem großen Streit

Du, laß dich nicht verbrauchen
Gebrauche deine Zeit
Du kannst nicht untertauchen
Du brauchst uns. Und wir brauchen
Grad deine Heiterkeit

Wir wolln es nicht verschweigen
In dieser Schweigezeit
Das Grün bricht aus den Zweigen
Wir wolln das allen zeigen
- dann wissen sie Bescheid.

Nun hatte sich die Hemmung gelöst, und er sagte lächelnd: Ja, ich habe auch solch ein Lied.

Wir verbrauchten eine ganze halbe Stunde dafür. Er zitierte Zeile für Zeile. Die Übersetzerin diktierte mir Wort für Wort. Ich schrieb mir alles genau auf, auch die Doppelbedeutungen mancher Wörter, auch den gemeinten Hintersinn, die literarischen Assoziationen in der koreanischen Literatur, die historischen Hintergründe, ein ganzer Komplex aus Buchstaben, obwohl der Text nur zwei mal acht Zeilen hat.

Er hatte eine Kassette mit CDs dabei, auf denen ich mir dann auch diesen populären Titel anhören sollte. Ich revangierte mich mit einem Packen meiner digitalen Tonkonserven und meiner Bücher mit Poesie und Prosa. Als er wieder gegangen war, zog ich mir die Melodie rein, die mir gar nicht so exotisch asiatisch vorkam. Und dann machte mich an die vertraute Arbeit.

Morgentau

Wach wach lag ich die Nacht
Auf Gräsern glänzt der Tau
Der Morgentau glänzt nobler noch
Als alle Perlenpracht
Todtraurig schlägt mein Herz
Am Hügel hinterm Haus
Probier ich trotz der Kümmernis
Ein kleines Lächeln aus

Blutrot steigt der Sonneball
Vom Friedhof. Doch erst dann
Zeigt die Mittagshitze an
Ob ich widerstehen kann
Der Weg ist voll Gefahr
Wird wüst sein, hart und weit
Und doch: Jetzt laß ich hinter mir
Mein elend altes Leid

Dieses Lied könnte eine zweite Welle der Popularität erreichen. Der harte lange Weg ins Ungewisse, von dem der Liedermacher Kim Ming´Gi da singt, der beginnt abermals, wenn Korea wiedervereint ist, wenn diese verfluchten Menschenfallen am 38. Breitengrad nur noch ein Museumsstück für zahlende Touristen sein werden.

Die Wege zur äußeren und zur inneren Freiheit sind immer unwegsam.

The Shadow of War Cast in Me

Oh Jung-hee

Dictatorship, war, and peace—at first the issues feel large and most appropriate for a political discussion. Resolving the problems posed by these topics is a difficulty as old as history, an everlasting dilemma, and a pursuit that has no culmination. To attempt to resolve the problems is to grope at ways to avoid violence, suppression, and destruction—the things that prevent a life worthy of men and their ideal pursuits. Because I am a writer and not a politician, historian, or sociologist, I think what I can do to enhance the conversation in a truly meaningful way (including social, political, and cultural points of view) is to present how my own experience and the effects of war and dictatorship have influenced my writing. In this way, I would like to discuss briefly the close relationships between my individual life, my personal observations of my life, and my writing.

There has been no era or region without war in human history. Generally speaking, it would not be an exaggeration to describe human history as a history of wars. War has divided regions and moved boundaries, separated and brought together ethnic groups, disrupted societies, and changed populations of lives against their wills. War has had a particular presence in Korean history. The Korean Peninsula has endured invasions, revolts, and civil war since the founding of its first dynasty; challenges to governance and sovereignty in Korea have occurred every seven to eight years, on average.

I grew up listening to old stories and songs about the regrets and hardships of war refugees—their wandering in unfamiliar lands or how they tried to establish new homes. These were oral histories marked by the intangibility of human memory. Retracing the oral histories of families by means of war—for example the Korean War, or Chinese and Japanese invasions—demonstrates the powerful influence war plays in changing the lives of families.

My grandfather was orphaned in the nineteenth century Sino-Japanese War of 1894, which mostly took place on the Korean Peninsula. His bitter hardships had a profound effect on the lives of his descendents.

I first learned of the Sino-Japanese War in an elementary school textbook. Later, I read Lee In-jik's novel *Tears of Blood* in middle school; the novel is a literary account of the war. To this day, I remember a sentence from the novel's description of a certain battle: "The civilians, running for their lives, were scared to the point of insanity by gunfire." I would learn from my parents that this battle described in Lee's novel was the battle that orphaned my grandfather. I came to realize history was not an impersonal collection of events in a book; history had played a direct role in my life. Novels like Lee's introduced me to the idea that I was a living participant in the flow and whirl of history.

My parents were born during the Japanese colonization of Korea. They lived through the Manchurian-Japanese War, the Pacific War (World War II), and the Korean War, which in Korea is called *yuk-i-o* (6/25)*, somewhat near to the date of Korean independence from Japan. These three great wars that they experienced in their not long lives thoroughly shook their minds and destinies.

One of my uncles returned alive from the Pacific War. He had been drafted as a student soldier. Though my uncle survived the Pacific War, he returned disabled and endured a miserable life.

The facts of history place little value on speculation. There is no doubt, however, that without war, my grandparents, parents, and uncle would have lived different lives with different fates.

The Korean War began soon after my second birthday, near when I was to begin speaking and walking. My first memories of childhood are of confinement in a dark cave with others. I remember the choking sensation of a thick, sticky hand on my mouth, the sight of a big dog hanging from a pole, and the features of my mother, screaming and convulsing in a gloom-filled room.

These images have remained with me since my youth, like vivid but unreal pictures. I once considered them to be like scenes in a dream, or perhaps a product of childish imagination. Later, I learned these images actually occurred during that summer to autumn under the rule of the enemy. When the city was under siege, many times a day I ran into a ditch with my neighbors to hide from bombing. Dogs were hung from poles to prevent their running mad from the sound of bombs, and my mother gave birth to my brother in these hard times.

The war, which began in 1950, lasted three years and one month. The land was entirely reduced to ashes, and over five million people died. I was a lucky child. I was not abandoned, did not fall from a refugee train, die of a cold, starve to death, get lost, or die from bombing. I was a child who possessed the rare luck to live. I have never been a victim of a real bombing or seen people dying from war, but my first memories and impressions of the world are very unpleasant, grotesque, and inflicted years of anxiety upon me.

Any object or event may grow larger than reality. This happens when rumors or differences in individual perception play upon fears of imagination. The unconscious memories of war and the desolateness of Korean postwar society dominated my early formative life with an insidious force.

The memories and emotions I once held of my toddler years spent as a refugee were filled with hunger and anxiety. In those days, my tragic awareness of life was that the world was neither bright, warm, nor a shelter. Finally understanding this may provide the reason why I am a writer. I have been forced to look at weakness instead of strength, the shade rather than light, psychological scars, and the primal nature of human fear and torment. I was not an active adult participant in the so-called "postwar generation," but I do not hesitate to take my beginnings as a writer and my sensibilities in literature from my memories and emotions of hunger and disquiet caused by war.

Even after the war, life itself was a battle for survival. Children in my youth used to love pretending to be soldiers on one of two sides: either the National Army or the People's Army. They used to sing depressing funeral marches mourning the flower of fallen youth killed on the battlefield. Everywhere there were war orphans, widows, and severely disabled veterans. The adults who suffered from the war were rude, harsh, and sometimes neurotic. Their coarse words and physical abuse hardened children's survival skills, even though the children's practices of stealing, robbing, and begging followed laws of the jungle.

In those days, Koreans of all ages used to name Switzerland as the best place to live on Earth, or perhaps a country of paradise. Almost none of them had ever been to Switzerland or met anyone from Switzerland. Koreans did not think Switzerland afforded its citizens a good daily life, that it had a good welfare system, or that the Swiss landscape was unusually beautiful. Koreans believed Switzerland was so wonderful because the country is forever neutral and had never participated in war. Switzerland is a place of peace. At that time, Koreans dreamt about and wanted to live a tradition and faith that people could live safely from yesterday, to today, and tomorrow in peace.

A friend from my youth, who at the time was aged ten in elementary school, said she witnessed the bombing of her parents on the way to shelter. She became a war orphan and the bomb blew one of her hands off. My friend then lived in a home for orphans, and she told me her dreams. She would dream of the days with her parents, but she would always wake, crying in fear that the scenes in her dream were real, while her sleeping with children in a cold dark room was a nightmare.

When one experiences unexpected horror and life is thrown into chaos, that person may feel reality is actually a dream. Based on these thoughts, I wrote a short story, "The Tale of the Hand." This somewhat ridiculous and strange story is about my friend's missing hand hopping around to find its body on a vast, snow-covered field. It was composed by the creativity that resides in a child's imagination. Children perceiving horrors of reality as a dreamed nightmare suggested to me that my own childhood traumas were carved indelibly into my mind. This understanding gave shape to my adult novels.

There was a "Mother's Home" in my neighborhood. It was a community of war widows managed by a Christian organization.

They were reclusive and poor. They labored in a factory run for the sake of charity, and held services to God in a brightly-lit church on a hill. Their prayers were always full of sorrowful appeals, resentment of their daily difficulties, and endless grief. The widows' tears and prayers moved the whole town.

The church was lit so bright on the hill it was like a raised lamp. I used to creep around the shadows outside and look in, curious as to what was taking place inside. Sometimes I cried along with their long endless lamentations to God, who always remained invisible. On those occasions, I seemed to experience a mystical inspiration along with them. It was as if I were raised above the widows' valley of tears by a graceful arm.

I was about twelve when I began to read Korean novels by writers classified as "Postwar Generation." These novels began to appear five or six years after the Korean War had ended. Thematically, they deal neither with vivid accounts of war nor war itself, but are about people who physically or psychologically endure a loss that makes one wish to die, among other forms of suffering. These books of skeptical and despairing stories typically portray the squalor and misery of human beings. The novels question what humankind truly is, whether humanity deserves to go on, how permanent the world is, and what the changes of fortune and pain imply about the human condition. The internal and external landscapes of individuals dominate the themes of this postwar literature.

I received these novels in my sensitive youth without any censorship or criticism. War was an important word to me. It required explaining, understanding, and analysis of the people and the time. I read many books during this period of my youth.

We cannot talk about life or literature without also talking about war. I learned from the eloquent books I read that literature should naturally include themes of war, poverty, disharmony, loss, a lack of material goods, and despair. Even in my own childish ways, I observed, experienced, and came to have an understanding of the world and its people through the novels I read. The powerful impression these novels made upon me became part of my literary practice.

The intensity of positive and negative experiences on human beings is the challenge a writer must aspire to create through his or her writing. The duty to shape the writing is enticing to a writer. War—such a powerful experience—informs the writer that he or she must be in the awareness of the process of history, a social being, and a witness to the naked core of humanity, whether willing or not. Hence, the confession by a senior colleague of mine that he began to write to testify to the misery and tragedy of war, and that he could not be a writer without war, carries significant meaning. Writers cure their pains and expand their worlds only by writing. To a writer, seeing and writing are, in the simplest of terms, speculation and act. It is usually true that writing begins with comprehending one's own identity and pain. The act of writing is not different from questioning who I am, what life is, and what life means.

Sometime after I began to write with confidence, I came to understand that describing people in the situation of war is quite reasonable and natural for a story. Families are torn apart and destroyed by war. A family's child being hurt and suffering endless thirst (thirst for food, affection, protection) is the central theme in a novel I wrote, *The Garden of Infancy*. The novel recalls my earliest childhood memories of another friend of mine. This friend would have grown up a naive girl in an ordinary family, had it not been for the corruption of the war. She endured her father's conscription, her mother's work as a bar hostess, and a fear of her brother as he became mentally unstable; he grew mean-spirited and violent from pressures of rage and sorrow. Early on, she understood the dark, incomprehensible side of life. Those memories inspired me to fictionalize women's suffering from their bitter struggles for survival and sending their men off to war. Fundamentally, *The Garden of Infancy* is about a woman's life of serious hardships.

I wrote *The Soul of Wind* in 1982. In the novel, a woman is the lone survivor of the killing of her entire family by a robber. The novel plots the struggles of this woman's family life after marriage, which are caused by her psychological traumas.

Another novel I wrote on a similar theme is *A Hill in the Distance*. The male protagonist is a soldier during the war. After his company is massacred, he becomes a radical nihilist who masochistically wastes his life.

The novels I have so far described are records of my growth in a chaotic and dissolute period of war, the ceasefire, and reconstruction. They are records of my witnessing of people, family, and neighbors as they traveled through the space-time of postwar difficulties they could only endure.

Half a century has passed since the ceasefire. A generation that vividly recalls those times has almost disappeared, and a generation that has known no battles on the scale of war has grown. This new generation knows no fear, destruction, starvation, or war that has forced them to lose their human dignity. Yet, Korea is the only divided country on the earth, and war has not ended; a truce keeps the peace. Like layers under the earth's surface, a hidden current of water, or an invisible stream, the dangers of war still encircle us. Regardless, the old recollections of war hold no interest to the younger generation, and the literature of war and division is being pushed aside.

Occasionally we hear news of a farmer plowing his field, and then finding the skeletons or fragments of war dead under his shovel. We still hear reports of old POW's not allowed to return home. It is easy to witness the one hundred fifty-five mile ceasefire line running through the peninsula.

Marked by stone obelisks in the north of Gangwon Province near the 38th parallel, the DMZ is two kilometers wide. It is lined with red triangular landmine warning signs hanging on barbed wire. Animals continue to die from the landmines.

I see that the traces of war have not simply passed. I think about how unsafe the basis for our stable and orderly daily life is. We live the reality today.

Though we forget or conceal these matters, they are not so easily remedied or made to disappear. Issues emanating from past wars simply become more deeply concealed or obscured as old wounds.

What is considered ended or resolved may in fact be the beginning of a new journey. In this situation, what was once deceptively concealed must be fully explored. The exploration may lead to a hard fought but more genuine conclusion.

I found a rusty canteen on the desiccated floor of Lake Pahro a few years ago. The lake is famous for a hard-fought battle during the Korean War, and the canteen surely belonged to a Chinese soldier. I remember a sense of changeability and forlornness there. I heard wind over the enormous empty field as a lamentation of the long dead; several tens of thousands of Chinese soldiers were buried under the water. That place is where literature begins.

Being a writer, I constantly consider what literature is, why I write literature, and what literature should be devoted to. These questions sometimes force such an excessive self-consciousness upon me that they hinder my ability to write, or conversely, fill my heart with a confident sense of purpose. The more I realize my social circumstances as crisis and pain, the more I have these feelings of doubt and confidence.

I began writing at a very young age. The motivation and starting point for my writing arose from personal desire and the traumas of my life. Over the course of my life as a writer, I have adopted the attitude that literature is not a way to serve a sense of purpose—for example an ideology, justice, or even enlightenment—but to illustrate and deal with the aesthetics of literature and human life.

When military dictatorships and outright suppression arose during my thirty years as a writer, I was never free from self-questioning, doubt, or obstacles I had no control over. I have seen people from a variety of societal backgrounds, such as writers, intellectuals, and students become fighters for freedom and peace, then lose their lives or suffer tremendous privation. I bore the conflict of testifying against and responding to the oppression and injustices we all experienced.

Part of my response to these troubles was writing novels like *Winter Watercock*. Calling upon my childhood memories of society after the war, the novel is about children denied the opportunity to live normal lives because they grow up in a postwar society. The outcome is they all become degenerate. A college instructor, one of the main characters in *Words of Farewell*, loses his life, and suicide is suspected. His death happens because of being attacked for his anti-government writing and actions as a freedom fighter. Another novel I wrote during this period, *Lake Pahro*, is about a lie. A teacher pretends to be a freedom fighter, and through his pretense loses everything. As a writer and average person of that time, my novels explored the anger and depression from my weaknesses.

A writer is a person who comprehends and questions his or her contemporary moment in crisis. The writer should be a person in an uncertain location, on a boundary, orphaned, and lost. The end of dictatorship, war, and conflict, an abundance of compromise, hope, peace, and a beginning of happiness—these are not for literature or a writer. The pain endured for the sake of these achievements—this is the duty and purpose of literature and writers.

Sympathy, to me, means feeling another's pain in my heart. How deep and sympathetic the heart is a starting point for literature, and only a writer can show it. A writer has no ability to show or execute a practical solution to systematic or structural problems that cause suffering, prevent human happiness, or an ideal way of life. A writer's only weapon that has power is writing.

Writing is also a coping mechanism. The fate of a writer is to be on the side of dark instead of light, to portray the disfigurements of life instead of honor, defeat instead of victory, and pain instead of joy. Writing shows the depths of life, reveals the natural forms of oppression that destroy, and causes people to stop and look at what they thoughtlessly pass by. Writing introduces people to the absurdity of the world they live and think in. This awareness shows the reader that there is a concrete meaning and purpose to life besides it being a simple random lot. The reader's new understanding reveals a portrait of dignified life, which inspires the person to strive for the dream.

Translated by **Heo Tae-young**

*Copy editor's note: *In Korea, "World War II" is referred to as "The Pacific War," and the Korean War by date started in 6/25; yuk-i-o, literally six-two-five.

Session VI

The Idea of Perpetual Peace

The Idea of Perpetual Peace

Robert Hass

I need to begin by saying that, when I received from Mr. Ahn Young-guk a letter proposing that I speak for forty minutes of the idea of perpetual peace, my heart sank, partly because it is an idea particularly difficult for a citizen of the United States to hold in mind in the year 2005, two years after the current government stampeded the country into acceding to the invasion of Iraq. Though the claims made to justify the invasion by the American government were known, by any reasonably well-informed person, to be manifestly false, and though millions of people all over the world demonstrated in the streets against the invasion, though popular support for the invasion in the United States was never much more than half of the adult population and far less than half among U.S. allies, like England, Poland, Spain, Italy, and Korea, which had been persuaded to give some military support to the adventure, the invasion occurred anyway. The television newsreaders dutifully read the government's propaganda on the air, the TV screens were full of images of rippling American flags and rolling tanks accompanied by the strains of stirring martial music, and official opposition to the war, even official caution about its prudence, was limited to a single elderly senator in the opposition party.

The U.S. military and its civilian administrators had learned from the experience of the Vietnam War that one key to civilian support for a war was control of the press. In the intervening time they had come to understand that the best way to control journalists was to give them what they wanted. And what they wanted was "hot news," not background briefings, not statistics designed to maintain the morale of troops, officers, and civilians on the home front, not ideological reiterations of the justifications for the war or the war strategy, and not reminders, in the face of apparent setbacks or atrocities or local civilian suffering, of the officially rosy larger picture—these had been the style of the entirely misleading military press conferences for journalists in the Vietnam War, in which communications officers from the commanding general's staff read fictional numbers of enemy dead to skeptical reporters who then went into the combat zones to report for themselves apparent facts that tended to undermine the official story and also to be visually compelling.

But in the twenty-five or thirty years since Vietnam, American television had also changed. Cable television had created the twenty-four hour news channels familiar to the world from CNN and the many channels were engaged in intense competition for the advertising dollars that produced their income. What was required were vivid and exciting images that made viewers feel good about the war and the American young who were fighting it. This was achieved by embedding journalists in military units where they were more or less compelled, by their angle of vision and by the men around them who were protecting their lives, to take the American combat soldiers' view of the experience and to have as little access as possible to the point of view of the enemy or of the helpless civil society of Iraq which was caught in the crossfire. In return the employers of the reporters got what they needed, television images which made war seem heroic, young Americans brave and heroic. The military, as a matter of policy, released no statistics on Iraqi civilian casualties and forbad any photographing of the care or transportation of the bodies of American dead. So the American public was more or less insulated from the horror of war. It has been a stunning and appalling public relations victory for the war party in Washington D.C., and profoundly dismaying to observe for people of my generation who had some memory of the journalists of the Vietnam era some of whom allowed one to believe in the survival of an occasional respect for facts, even in wartime.

Seeing how easy it was for the administration to persuade the American people to give up some of their sons and daughters to this war and to shut out of their conscious knowledge the suffering they were inflicting, seeing how easy it was for whole classes of journalists, military men, intelligence officers, politicians, diplomats, and academics to be silenced, intimidated or marginalized so that the fictitious reasons for the war could be floated is one of the reasons why I felt my own imagination shrinking from the idea of perpetual peace.

"We had fed the heart on fantasies," the Irish poet William Butler Yeats once wrote, and

"The heart's grown brutal from the fare." It seemed to me, in my dismay, easy to think of perpetual peace as one of those sentimental ideas that bred brutality. The only way to maintain wholly unreal ideals is to make sure that the right hand never knows what the left hand is doing, which is, of course, a knowledge of one's own behavior that breeds cynicism about the behavior of others and makes brutality possible by making it seem inevitable. One comes, thinking this way, to very dark conclusions, even before one has turned to the question of the role of literature in assessing issues or war and peace.

I have also a second confession to make. When I read Mr. Ahn's letter, I was unaware of Immanuel Kant's great essay, *"Zum Ewigen Frieden,"* which is entitled in English, "On Perpetual Peace." So I wondered what Korean phrase the two words translated and whether the originators of this idea for a panel understood the principal connotations of the words in English. They called to my mind two phrases from the Mass for the Dead in my Roman Catholic childhood. One was, of course, *Requiescant in pacem*, "May they rest in peace." The other was "May the perpetual light shine upon them." I thought, somewhat bitterly and ruefully, that these echoes were entirely appropriate, and that the idea of perpetual peace was not only naïve, it was, as an ideal, undesirable—undesirable because life is conflict. One might speak of non-violence as an ideal, or pacifism as a philosophical or even a tactical relation to human violence; one might speak of peacefulness as a social habit or tranquility as a spiritual one, but, I thought, if those ideas are worth valuing, they are worth fighting for, and some great lines from William Blake's poem "Jerusalem," came to my mind:

Bring me my Bow of burning gold:
Bring me my Arrows of desire:
Bring me my Spear: O clouds unfold!
Bring me my Chariot of fire!

I will not cease from Mental Fight,
Nor shall my Sword sleep in my hand,
Till we have built Jerusalem
In England's green & pleasant Land.

Blake believed that the human imagination was born from conflict. Limitation, against which it must always rebel, brought it into being. And I am inclined to agree. So, I wanted to say, as to the idea of perpetual peace, forget it. The only people who are fully at peace, as the Korean phrase translated into English unconsciously suggested, are the dead. It turns out, of course, that this was exactly Immanuel Kant's joke. Or rather the joke of the Dutch shopkeeper whose sign he had glimpsed sometime toward the end of the 18th century and its interminable small wars. There was a picture of a graveyard printed on the shop sign and "To Perpetual Peace" was the inscription. So might a harried shopkeeper nod sardonically toward his final reward. And thus was the phrase translated from Dutch into German, from German into Korean, and from Korean into English, so that I, remembering the Church Latin of my childhood, could misunderstand it. But my misunderstanding was good preparation for the surprise and the nobility of Immanuel Kant's essay. Against common sense, against the sound skepticism of Dutch shopkeepers and the cynicism of "heads of state who can never get enough of war," Kant had taken up reason, philosophy's bow of burning gold, and tried to see what a sane and reflective intelligence could say about the dream of an *ewigen Frieden*. (You see that I say it this time in German, so that it sounds to my ear more dignified and less hopeless.)

It is the example of Kant, his refusal to give in to despair or cynicism that made me think that a talk like this might be possible. What Kant proposed was six preliminary articles for peace among nations and three definitive articles. Reading them, these few pages with their list of eight ideas seemed to me a remarkable moment in the relatively brief history of human consciousness (2,600-5,000 years that we have even the skimpiest human records of, 10,000 years to the Neolithic, perhaps 100,000 to the beginnings of symbolic behaviors among hominid species, all these a blink of the eye by the measure of geological or even biological time scales). Someone had proposed the idea of thinking through in a reasonable way, outside the context of any particular religious or tribal ideal, how one might go about eliminating or at least minimizing warfare among peoples. His ideas, of course, reflect the historical experience of the European 18th century. One of his preliminary propositions addresses war as a habit of mind: "No treaty of peace that tacitly reserves issues for a future war shall be held valid." It is less a legislative proposition—intention is next to impossible to regulate—than a definition. Two of the remaining articles are, in effect, counsels for disarmament: "Standing armies shall be gradually abolished" and "No national debt shall be contracted in connection with the foreign affairs of the nation." The other two define sovereignty: "No independent nation, be it large or small, may be acquired by another nation by inheritance, exchange, gift, or purchase" and "No nation shall forcibly interfere with the constitution and government of another." A final article address means of waging war that make future wars more likely; it is a start on international conventions for the regulation of warfare.

And just as the final preliminary article anticipates the Geneva Conventions, which my own government has felt justified in selectively ignoring in its treatment of prisoners during the wars in Iraq and Afghanistan, Kant's three definitive articles imagine a global structure of governance that would tend toward the establishment of peace. First, he says, the civil constitution of every nation should be republican. Secondly, the rights of nations shall be based on a federation of free states. And finally there should exist among states a right of what he calls "universal hospitality." This implies the free circulation of peoples and ideas: the right of aliens not to be treated as enemies in another's country and the right of all humans to associate "by virtue," he says, "of their common ownership of the earth's surface." The rest of the essay is a reflection on how, practically, these propositions might be first instituted and secondly guaranteed. I will not attempt to summarize his thought, but only to remark that the definitive articles themselves are so far-seeing that we are still trying to establish the ideals he proposes and find the grounds for their guarantee.

I rehearse them here, really, out of wonder. They were produced in the same century that produced *Candide*, that famous cure for innocence. And "To Perpetual Peace" is not innocent exactly. It insists, in fact, that violent war and its expectation are the natural condition of man, and that the state of peace is unnatural and must be struggled toward. Its nobility is its rebellion toward innocence and against the brutality of things-as-they-are. The essay is one of the most admirable documents of the European enlightenment. It is an act of imagination that issues from an impatient hope that human beings can eventually be led to what is both prudent and good through the use of reason.

2.

This is peroration, a way of saying that reading Immanuel Kant led me to wonder, if his essay embodies what reason brings to the idea of perpetual peace—though two still more violent centuries intercede between the composition of his essay and the present, during which technologies have increased immeasurably the human capacity to destroy not only human lives and cultures but much of the rest of the biological life on earth—what the literary imagination has had to contribute.

But I am not quite done with casting doubt on this enterprise. We do not know, in the first place, how old literature is, in the sense of song-making and story-telling. We get our first glimpse of it at the horizon of literacy, which even in the most precocious cultures occurred only two or three thousand years ago—and the record in all of those cultures is that the story-telling, singing, and myth-making begins with some form of the glorification of a masculine warrior ethos. There are evolutionary reasons for this, no doubt, rooted in hunting cultures and in the allied skills necessary for self-defense in times when the relation of each tribe to every other was, as the earliest records suggest they were, piratical at best. We can see the instinctual mechanisms of it in male competition for dominance across the mammal species. Also in human and other animal territoriality, especially as it exists among children and in adolescents and young adults as strategies of violence and affiliation in our crowded cities. It is there in the *Iliad* and the *Odyssey*, in the apotheosis of the warrior Arjuna in the *Bhagavad-Gita*, in *Beowulf* and the *Niebelungen* tales, and in the countless Chinese and Japanese tales of noble warriors and self-immolating retainers. It finds its smooth and half-ironical summing up in the verses of Horace: *Dulce et décor est pro patria mori*. And its evocation of loyalty to political authority in the sijo of Chong Mongju.

Of course it has been argued that the poems of Homer convey a tragic sense of war. And so they do: the death of Hector and the grief of Priam and the ruin of Troy, the death of Patroclus and the death of Achilles have been deeply imprinted in the world's imagination, and so also the wanderings and suffering of Odysseus. And it has been argued—though no one is quite sure how Virgil intended to conclude the *Aeneid*—that its concluding image, the moment when Aeneas hesitates and then plunges his sword into the gut of his rival and enemy Turnus, is an emblem of the violence of war as original sin, of the founding act of Roman power—and by extension all earthly power—as an act of violent usurpation. And it has been observed that *Beowulf*, indeed all the oral poems in the old Germanic languages, are profoundly elegiac. And it has been argued that in all these ancient poems war itself is a kind of metaphor for nature, which takes us from us all, eventually, our youth and our strength and our beauty, so that war has the special beauty of taking these things from us while we still have them. And it seems to me that it is for this reason that, even though the evocation of war in the greatest of our early literature is tragic, it makes the meaning conferred by the tragedy of war immensely attractive—so that over and over human beings have made the choice of Achilles. They have preferred the dead lion to the living lamb.

Perhaps the sense of the tragic in these stories, a sense that we might imagine would cause some humans to pause longer at the threshold of violent behaviors, reaches deeper into some minds and hearts than others. For it is not only the case that these stories are so attractive and so memorable because they are war stories, everybody knows, for example, from the history of film that it is practically impossible to make an anti-war film that does not at some level make war seem attractive. It is not just the hugely popular fantasies that celebrate violence and killing and the taking of revenge against a usually faceless (but racially coded) form of evil, as in the films of Sylvester Stallone, or the comic fantasy violence of the brilliant upstart in the films of Jackie Chan or the dream of murderous violence as a form of balletic, even supernatural grace in samurai films and Hong Kong thrillers. These are the films that the world's audiences pay billions of dollars a year to see and see again. They seem to be what the human heart craves. But the films of more complicated moral intent can make war seem equally attractive. The American writer Anthony Swofford in his book *Jarhead* describes his experience in a platoon of U.S. Marine snipers in the first Iraq war. And one of the stories he tells is about the leisure time of the warriors in training. Together they watched all the anti-war films that had been produced by the Vietnam War, films like *Platoon* and *Full Metal Jacket*. They watched them, he said, to feed a kind of warrior lust, a sense of exhilaration at the root of their training. Even if the heroes of those films came to a solitary understanding of the horror of war, what made them attractive was that they had to go through the war to acquire that understanding. The sort of moral orphaning, the loneliness in the universe that those young men acquired and that Swofford's recruits in the desert recognized, was a gift that war gave them. And if anti-war films have this effect, we do well to wonder how deeply the tragedy of war ever penetrates human consciousness.

The truth is that we have no control for testing the proposition that literature or philosophy, or religion for that matter, has had any mitigating effect on the violence of human behavior. This is the only world we've had and it is an exceedingly violent one, made more violent in the last hundred years by the enormous inventiveness of human technology and the greater ability of nation states to mobilize vast populations for the purposes of war. And we know that the human heart loves images of superior strength, loves especially the combination of superior physical strength with superior agility of mind and nobility or gracefulness of demeanor. It loves vengeance, though there is some hope in the fact that, through some scruple in our natures, it loves vengeance against those who have done harm to the innocent and the weak, and it constructs plots, just as nation-states construct ideological justifications for war, that allow for this moral gratification of the love of violence and vengeance. Would some better and more powerful act of imagination make the world any better than it has been? Is the world better than it would have been had there been no songs or stories that rebelled against the violence in our natures and mirrored it back to us in a way that might have made us, or some of us, hesitate? We have no way of knowing.

Except that we know, perhaps, that it is better to speak then not to speak. One of the twentieth century's instructors in this fact has been Czeslaw Milosz. Here are some lines that come to my mind in this context from a poem of his called "The Spirit of the Laws." It was written in Washington D.C. in 1947, where he found himself in the wake of the destruction of Warsaw:

From the cry of the children on the floors of stations beyond time,
From the sadness of the engineer of prison trains…

With the silenced memory of dead friends,
And the silenced memory of towns and rivers,
I was ready to tear out the heart of the earth with a knife
And put there a glowing diamond of shouts and complaints,
I was ready to smear the bottom of the roots with blood
To invoke the names of their leaves,
To cover the malachite monuments with the skin of night
And write down with phosphorus Mene Tekel Upharsin,
Shining with the traces of melting eyelids.

It is better to speak than not to speak, even if our speech is violent resistance to violence.

The first anti-war speech in the European literary tradition is the one delivered by the bandy-legged Thersites in the second book of the *Iliad*. He is presented as an ugly little man, a cynic, the stomach's response to the heroic ethos, and Odysseus promptly beats him down. But he spoke up, and his voice has echoed through the centuries. The next reframings of the heroism of war that I'm aware of both came from 5th century Athens. And they take quite different approaches. Euripides in *The Trojan Women* wrote the first searingly angry depiction of the horror and senselessness of a war. And Aristophanes in *Lysistrata* was the first to teach us to laugh at the absurdity of it. It is not without meaning that both of these plays were written by men from the point of view of women. It seems that they needed to step outside the male ethos in order to speak their thoughts.

3.

So I can think of three ways in which literature has resisted the imagination's love of war. The first, though not the earliest in the history of literature, is to imagine peace. The second is laughter. The third is witness. There are probably others. I wish I knew enough about the Korean, or about the Chinese and Japanese literary traditions, but perhaps my listeners will be thinking of instances of their own.

After I thought about the war in Iraq and the ease with which Americans recently undertook the invasion of another country, and the Latin root of the idea of perpetual peace, and how the imagination of William Blake would have resisted the idea, I did think about the ways in which poetry, or at least some poems I loved, embodied the idea of peace so that humans could hold it in mind. The poem that leapt to my mind was a haiku by Basho, because it is one I often say to myself as a sort of mantra, a way of calling myself to calm or to evenness of temper. It is a poem that appears in his *Narrow Road to the Far North*, and it begins with a note, indicating it was written at a hermitage where the travelers had stopped for the evening and done some work in exchange for their dinner. It reads in English translation:

> A cool fall night—
> getting dinner, we peeled
> eggplants, cucumbers.

It seemed, it still seems, a joke, like Kant's joke at the expense of philosophy, to hold this small poem up to the whole history of human violence, and yet there are powerful reasons for doing so. It is not an accident that the poem takes place at a hermitage or a monastery. It is not an accident that it is almost ridiculously simple, too simple to be a poem at all. Nor is it an accident that it is about paying attention to the most ordinary human experiences, or that the *kigo*, the seasonal reference in the poem, "a cool fall night" is by its association with the change of seasons signaled by a new sharpness in the night air a traditional figure for awareness of mortality. This is a poem about the preciousness, the almost silly preciousness of the most ordinary experiences and about the fact that we are all going to die some day. Its aesthetic and its spiritual tradition is specifically Buddhist. The hermitage in which the poem is set implies a withdrawal from worldliness, from the violence of the world.

There are, so far as I know, in the history of the world two figures who have stood powerfully against its history of violence. They are Christ and Buddha. Christianity, of course, is hardly a pacifist religion. It has had, like Islam, a history of zeal for conversion by the sword and for the warrior ethos. But there is explicitly in the teaching of Jesus of Nazareth and occasionally in the history of Christianity a profound resistance to violence against life. I have a less clear sense of the history of Buddhist civilizations, and I am sure that pious Buddhists have also found ways to pick up the sword, but respect for life seems to have been nearer the center of Buddhist practice than of Christian. I could be wrong about this and merely idealizing a tradition I understand less well. Nevertheless it is from these traditions, I think, that resistance to violence and the embodiment of an idea of peace in literature have principally drawn.

Though perhaps there is, in the European world, one earlier tradition. I am thinking about a phrase of Ezra Pound's, "Mediterranean sanity." Pound associated the Christianity that he knew with an unhealthy dualism about the body and the soul and an unhealthy devaluing of the soul, nature, and the natural world. In his early poems he tried to reimagine, as many other aesthete-poets did at the turn of the twentieth century, the terms for a viable revival of paganism. Part of what I think he had in mind was a sort of realistic pastoralism in the Greek and Roman admiration for abundance and good order, for fields of ripe grain and for grape harvests and for the loveliness of winds whitening an olive orchard. It is from both Buddhist and Christian points of view, I think, a secular and a worldly tradition, though a very rich one. One embodiment of it is in this wedding song from one of the plays of Aristophanes. In English translation it reads like this:

It's time to say words of good omen
And to bring forth the bridegroom and the bride.
It's time to raise torches and dance and rejoice.
We can take harrow and plow and our sharp scythes back to the fields
Once we have danced and poured wine and chased out bad luck
And after we've prayed to the gods of the earth, sea, and sky
To help us to an ample life, to grant us a good crop of barley
And plenty of wine and the sweet meat of figs,
And that we bring forth children, supple limbed, loud at their play,
And that all the good things we lose by war
Are returned to us when we gather ripe fruit for the wedding feast
And the fiery sword has been put away.

If this is the worldly tradition of resistance to violence, the other poem that came to my mind, quickly, on the heels of my thought of Basho, was a very famous poem about peace by William Butler Yeats. It is "The Lake Isle of Innisfree":

I will arise and go now, and go to Innisfree,
And a small cabin build there, of clay and wattles made.
Nine bean-rows will I have there, a hive for the honey-bee,

And live alone in the bee-loud glade.

And I shall have some peace there, for peace comes dropping slow,
Dropping from the veils of morning to where the cricket sings;
There midnight's all a glimmer, and noon a purple glow,
And evening full of the linnet's wings.

I will arise and go now, for always night and day
I hear lake water lapping, with low sounds by the shore;
While I stand on the roadway, or on the pavements gray,
I hear it in the deep heart's core.

I think I thought about this poem in connection with Basho's because they are both poems of retreat. Students of Yeats know several things about this poem. One is that Innisfree is a place in the west of Ireland where the Irish language was still spoken and which therefore was considered after centuries of brutal British colonial occupation a purer and truer Ireland and nearer to the ancient essence of the Irish national character. Another is that Yeats was inspired to write this poem by his reading of Henry David Thoreau's *Walden*. So Thoreau's record of his withdrawal to a hermitage near Walden Pond near Concord, Massachusetts, a record from which the American environmental movement may be said to have begun, also sparked the Irish poet to imagine a similar withdrawal. Yeats lived in London. He was sociable, a man of the theater, and in his later life a politician. As beautiful as it is, I have always thought of this poem, therefore, a bit skeptically; it seemed a busy man's daydream, which perhaps it is, and deficient as a work of art for that reason. But I have come to see that there is another way of thinking about this poem. It is deficient perhaps as a description of a realizable place on earth, but it is not deficient as a description of a place held close to the heart.

It is not irrelevant that the Henry David Thoreau who wrote *Walden* is also the man who invented non-violent civil disobedience when he refused to pay a tax to support the Mexican War of 1846, like the Iraq War one of America's adventures in invading another country to liberate it from tyranny. Thoreau went to jail for his refusal and wrote an essay about it. Thoreau's essay was read by the South African lawyer Mahatma Ghandi who put Thoreau's idea into practice in India on a national scale to resist British colonialism, and Martin Luther King studied Gandhi's example and forged a Christian form of non-violent civil disobedience to help African Americans to resist and overthrow the American system of apartheid. It is a strange mix of cultural traditions: something flinty and individualist in New England Protestantism and the deep streak of asceticism in the Hindu Ghandi, and the powerful millenarian longings stirred in the African American Christian churches by the Biblical story of the Jewish people freed from Egyptian bondage. There was in each of these traditions, and perhaps a weaker though not less real one in the aestheticism of the Irish poet, sources for resistance to the world and its instinctual violence.

4.

War and laughter. The laughter comes in two forms: the satiric and the comedic.

One of the interesting facts about the history of war in Europe and the United States has to do with the ways wars have been commemorated. I have read that the practice of publicly honoring fallen soldiers is a relatively recent innovation and that it was brought into existence by the plebiscite. Before the advent of democratic elections, victories were honored by statues of generals or the public display of some sort of war loot, e.g., an Egyptian obelisk set down in a square in London or Paris, or by the creation of some ceremonial arch that dignified imperial power. Only when heads of state became accountable to the citizenry for the fates of their sons did nations begin to find ways to memorialize the ordinary soldier and sailors who had, previously, though the historians do not exactly say this, been either mercenaries or a drafted peasantry and hence either cannon fodder or assumed to be included anonymously in the gesture of national greatness. Thersites would no doubt have his say about this late onset of public piety from the tombs of the unknown soldiers in France and the United States to the simple and eloquent listing at the Vietnam

War Memorial in Washington D.C. of the names of the 55,000 American dead. (It would have taken more space than a public park could accommodate to name as well the two million Vietnamese dead) .

And Thersities does not have his say in these memorials. The common soldier is remembered there as mute and a hero. Thersities is another matter. He is the bottom-up view of the world, the one that sees Agamemnon as a blowhard prince who sends other men to their doom. He is the one who thinks that the male virtues of courage and loyalty are for idiots. In the history of European and American literature, at least, he has his say in comedy and satire. He is, for that reason, dangerous. He often shows up in literature paired with his opposite: Don Quixote and Sancho Panza, Prince Hal and Falstaff. One of the rich sources of all humor is discrepancy, but the distance between the ideal and the real, between war rhetoric and the actuality of war may be too painful in its consequences to be mined very directly. Perhaps that's why these classic pairings have a way of showing up in the literary imagination. The ways in which Falstaff and Panza subvert the warrior ethos would be too threatening if they appeared on the stage by themselves. They need to be measured against some idea of the nobility and attractiveness of the ideals human beings imagine and then imagine themselves killing and dying for, just as the madness of Quixote and the mix of courage, privilege, and calculation in King Henry V need to be measured against Sancho and Sir John.

There is some hope for an understanding of peace in this dialectic of the imagination. Just as there are heroic and tragic ways of presenting images of war, there are satiric and comic ways of calling warrior virtues into question. Satire in that way opposes romance; it is the enemy of idealization. Whenever it hears ideals of self-sacrifice being evoked, it asks who is doing the sacrificing and—to use a pungent term from the habits of European tables—it asks whose bread is being buttered. Satire is the instrument of Thersites. It was also the instrument of Karl Marx when the spirit of invective moved him. Its power, always, and its threat is to ask, from the bottom up, who pays? who profits?

Comedy, which is sometimes satiric and sometimes not, has the same contentious relationship to tragedy. I have in mind here the connection in the European tradition between comedy as a genre and fertility ritual. If tragedy is an autumnal rite that emerged from the exhausted end of the agricutural cycle, comedy belongs to rituals of spring and the rebirth of things. Classic comedy like Shakespeare's celebrates the victory of the young over the old, the agile over the rigid, simplicity over cunning. Clowns are an important element in comedy. They represent the normal, the normally silly, the unheroic dailiness of life and its wisdom. Comedies end with marriage: they are about—to paraphrase Aristophanes—the goodness of life once we have put the flaming sword aside. Eros and thanatos. Comedy is on the side or eros as a subverter so long as it returns life eventually to the norm of social order. It is against thanatos in almost every circumstance. I think of thanatos not as an instinctual drive toward death in human beings. I doubt there is such a thing. Thanatos is the imaginative conception of death as escape from nature, death as glorious transformation. We feel its presence in the stillness at the end of a tragedy, in our awe at the power of death and the struggle of life. Martyrs love thanatos. The appeal of death in war must certainly lie in part in its escape from the tedium of a normal life and from age and change. The beauty in youthful death lies there; it lies in the choice made by Achilles to be a dead hero rather than an ordinary old man with liver-spotted hands. And comedy has no use for this view of the world.

I grew up in the years immediately after the Second World War. It was a time in the United States when movies were the central ritual of American popular culture. So I grew up on a steady diet of heroic and patriotic movies. And also on a diet of comedies, including what were called "service comedies," movies in which the protagonists were in the armed forces It is one of the interesting facts about the era that produced John Wayne as an international archetype of the genial, easy-going, and relentless American warrior that it also produced as a second feature on almost every program comedies whose protagonists were lovable cowards. Often, usually, they behaved bravely when the moment required it. Often they did the right thing or triumphed by accident. Usually the forces they were pitted against were large and stupid. Sometimes they survived by wit, sometimes by innocence. Almost always they acknowledged fear. And they would always rather play than fight. In almost all of the films I can remember, they would eventually back into the warrior ethos, but their glory was the way that they called it into question.

Commercial film could probably not carry this subversion very far. It found its way into modern literature and into the landscape of mechanized and almost inconceivably destructive war in figures like Hsaek's Good Soldier Schweik and Joseph Heller's Yosarrion in Catch-22. Yossarion's dilemma probably captures as well as anything the paradox at the center of the heroic ethic. Yossarion can be excused from his duties as a bomber pilot only if he is insane. And the fact that he wants to be excused is proof of his sanity. And it is part of the richness of Heller's book that our laugh at this impossibility contains the responses evoked by both satire and comedy.

Another way of thinking about it is to consult thinkers on the psychology of humor—its sources in human life and its uses. One psychoanalyst who writes about this subject has distinguished among three connected forms of pleasure that get expressed through humor and he connects them to stages in human development. The three kinds are the smile of happiness, the belly laugh, and the laughter that responds to wit. The smile of happiness has its origins in the smile of the infant who gazes into the full face of the mother. It belongs, for the psychologist, to Freud's oral stage of life where we receive nurture and learn trust. The belly laugh belongs to the toddler phase of development. There is apparently a moment in development when a child, seeing a man in a film slip on a banana peel and fall down, does not cry, but laughs, and laughs richly. This change, they speculate, is connected to self-mastery. The child who can walk, who has begun to have autonomy by mastering his bowels and using the toilet, can laugh from a feeling of confidence and a perception of absurdity. This is the territory of slapstick comedy. The comedy based on verbal wit is associated with the acquisition of language (and, for the psychoanalyst, the Oedipus complex). It is the intellectual equivalent of what the belly laugh is the physical model for, but it is a more aggressive version. It sees through things; it gets the ridiculousness of pretension, of our vanities, blindnesses, benighted idealizations. It may see them sweetly or harshly, but it sees them. And perhaps these three impulses, laughter at the goodness of existence, laughter at its ridiculousness, and laughter at its pretensions, are all in the service of an imagination of life that has some power to hold at bay, or at least mitigate, the power in us of the imaginations of violent triumph and destruction.

5.

War and witness. Human beings seem unable to hold in mind the enormity of their violence or the damage it has done. They seem not, as T.S. Eliot observed, to be able "to bear very much reality." And so the function of witness has been to try to see what's there. It is apparently the most difficult act of imagination, to see through the acts of imagination, the pictures of the world, that desire and ideology are always constructing.

I have only a few more minutes and not a great deal needs to be said about this function of the imagination of peace. And the examples are not difficult to point to. *The Trojan Women* is probably the earliest effort and a rare one to create an entirely tragic and unredeemed vision of the violence of war, and its achievement was, as the tragic poetry of Athens sometimes did, to step outside the point of view of the male warriors. In the twentieth century Erich Maria Remarque's *All Quiet on the Western Front* is often described as the great depiction of the horror of war. It was published in 1926 and the events in Europe that followed are not an argument for the efficacy of literature. But perhaps Immanuel Kant's essay is a counsel of patience. Realism, as a literary movement, is two centuries old. It was born, in part, out of *Don Quixote*, and it staked its claim as anti-romance. Perhaps the battle scenes in *War and Peace*, a hundred years into that project, were a first attempt to de-mythologize warfare, that is to say, neither to exalt nor attack the warrior ethic, but to describe what war is like from the perspective of ordinary soldiers, one on which Remarque's novel and other books of that genre have built.

This struggle of the literary imagination became acute in the twentieth century. "Reality," Czeslaw Milosz asked in his "Six Lectures" of 1985, "what can we do with it? Where is it in words?"

Just as it flickers, it vanishes. Innumerable lives
Unremembered. Cities on maps, only.
Without that face in the window, on the first floor, by the market,
Without those two in the bushes near the gas plant.

It is one of Milosz's themes that we cannot grasp our most ordinary experience, let alone our most violent and terrible. The value of the passage that follows is not perhaps that it 'witnesses,' in the English language sense of 'bearing witness' to, a life and a death, but its anguish at the limits of witness:

While here, I, an instructor in forgetting,
Teach that pain passes (for it's the pain of others),
Still in my mind trying to save Miss Jadwiga,
A little hunchback, librarian by profession,
Who perished in the shelter of an apartment house
That was considered safe but toppled down
And no one was able to dig through the slabs of wall,
Though knocking and voices were heard for many days.
So a name is lost for ages, forever,
No one will know about her last hours.
Time carries her in layers of the Pliocene.
The true enemy of man is generalization.
The true enemy of man, so-called History,
Attracts and terrifies with its plural numbers.

Milosz's power as a poet of witness comes from the fact that he despairs of its possibility. A realist by temper, and by philosophical conviction a believer in the uniqueness and singularity of every mortal life, he has a keen sense of the inadequacy of language to its task and the necessity of the task. His greatest poems push language to the place where language, the linguistic enterprise, wavers.

Another European poet of witness to the horror of the European wars was Paul Celan, a Romanian Jew and German poet who had to make an account of his experience in the language that had forged the rhetoric that had sentenced his parents to death. Celan was an artist driven to tear apart and reconstruct the language he worked in. That is one form the impossibility of witness takes. It seems to me that Ko Un's remarkable *Ten Thousand Lives* is another form of the impossibility of the realist project and another defiant assault on generalization. In the versions available in English, *Ten Thousand Lives* is, as it were, Euripides' *Trojan Women* fused with Aristophanes's *Lysistrata*—an accounting of the tragedy of war exploded out of the unities of drama into the individual lyrics of countless lives, comic and tragic, terrible and kindly.

Milosz's lecture ends this way:

History is not, as Marx told us, anti-nature,
And if a goddess, it is a goddess of blind fate.
The little skeleton of Miss Jadwiga, the spot
Where her heart was pulsating. This only
I place against necessity, law, theory.

Ko Un in *Ten Thousand Lives* has placed against them the peasant women from a far village whom a boy, almost asleep on a Saturday night, hears returning home from the market town where they spent the day. Dogs bark as they pass. He can hear the murmur, but not the content of their talk, about their day, and their children, and what they have seen and what they bought and sold.

6.

I'd like to end by returning for a moment to Kant's essay. It requires an emendation. As much as Kant foresaw, he did not see the technical advances that would make war so much more lethal than it had ever been. Or that the same technological advances would have made the ecosystems of the earth so fragile that every human war is now, automatically, a war against the earth. So that our understanding of war requires at least two more preliminary articles.

7. No nation at war shall employ weapons systems or combat strategies whose most substantial impact is suffered by civilians.

8. Nations at war shall be financially responsible for the ecological consequences of their methods of warfare, the value of which to be determined by a disinterested international tribunal.

While we are smoking the Dutch shopkeeper's pipe and smiling the German philosopher's rueful smile, we may as well make these two more offerings at the altar of reason and imagination.

The Conditions for Peace in the Korean Peninsula: From the Perspective of Kant's 'Perpetual Peace'

Choi Jang-jip

Introduction

At the present moment, the problem of North Korea and its associated nuclear problem (the North Korea/nuclear problem) is, together with the issue of Iran's nuclear ambitions, one of the most dangerous issues in international politics. From the point of view of international politics, the Korean Peninsula has become the most dangerous region, as a focus for world conflict, after the Middle East. It is a great tragedy that the Korean Peninsula, which once before became the seismic center of world conflict in the course of the Cold War that followed the Second World War, with the Korean War, should now again be subjected to the threat of becoming the site of world conflict in this post-Cold War period. It is very hard to evaluate positively the current international political scene developing in East Asia, so far as securing a stable peace not only in the Korean peninsula but in North East Asia as a whole is concerned. The problem of how to solve the North Korea/nuclear problem and achieve peaceful coexistence between North and South Korea has emerged as a vital challenge for international politics that has to be tackled for the sake of peace in the Korean peninsula, indeed for the sake of the peace not only of the East Asia region but of the whole world.

The crisis involving the North Korea/nuclear problem is manifesting itself in the form of two opposing attitudes that admit no easy compromise. On the one side, there is the strategic choice by North Korea, the very survival of whose system is hanging by a thread, of using its nuclear capacity as a weapon to ensure its security. On the other hand, there is America, that does not recognize the North Korean system, and that is pressing them to give up their nuclear program, uncompromising in a hardline policy. If this is seen as a crisis, it is because North Korea, before endangering peace by pursuing its nuclear program, can also end up in a situation where it threatens peace in the process of trying to solve the problem. A top priority in America's overseas military strategy is a policy of preventing the proliferation of nuclear weapons and especially of obstructing the flow of nuclear technology or nuclear weapons from so-called "rogue states" such as North Korea to terrorist organizations. As the Bush regime has repeatedly declared, North Korea is viewed as one of the states forming the nucleus, together with Iraq and Iran, of the "axis of evil" or "outposts of tyranny." In one section of the American government, as hardline as that view of North Korea is, there are indications of ultra-hardline solutions such as a "surgical strike," "regime change" or "regime transformation" to the problem of nuclear facilities that North Korea considers integral to its very existence. The six-party talks seeking a solution to the North Korean nuclear problem may serve as a starting-point for the resolution of the nuclear issue and ensuring the peace of East Asia, but should they fail, it could easily provoke a hardline policy relying on America's use of force or coercion which might create a situation on the Korean Peninsula that could lead to a new war.

This paper intends to view the situation from the viewpoint of the local region, the Korean Peninsula, in which this conflict has arisen and discuss in what ways peace can be established securely in the whole area. To do this, three main levels of discussion and debate will be needed. The first and broadest level is the dimension related to the direction of America's policy toward North Korea and East Asia as a whole. The second involves questions concerning the possible contribution that could be made by the South Korean government and society toward peace on the Korean Peninsula and East Asia. The third concerns what efforts the various nations of the region should make to secure a stable peace in East Asia.

2. Why is the end of the Cold War a problem?

The North Korea/nuclear problem is basically a product of the Cold War. Above all else, the division and confrontation found on the Korean Peninsula were not only the result of confronting forces that provoked division just between North and South Korea; those forces maintained confrontation between rival factions on a worldwide scale and throughout the whole of East Asia. Fundamentally, it is because those former Cold War structures could not be reorganized that the North Korea/nuclear problem, which has them as its core, could not be solved but continues and has grown into a major issue. Of course, on the worldwide level and across the whole of East Asia, the ideological confrontation between two polarized sides represented by capitalism v. communism has effectively been resolved. In particular, by an explosive growth far exceeding all expectations, China has become the main partner in investment and trade of America, Japan and Korea, dramatically increasing the region's economic mutual interdependence. China has now become indispensable for those nations' economic development and has taken its place as a central figure in the ordering of the world's markets. Moreover, after the fall of the Berlin Wall, on the Korean Peninsula too, that was once termed "the Cold War's desert island," the confrontational relations between North and South have been conspicuously reduced with the ongoing process of détente. Recently, in Japan, China and Korea, nationalism has produced widespread popular fervor, rapidly taking the place of the ideological confrontation (capitalism v. communism) of the Cold War days. Definitely the former Cold War order of things has greatly changed and is still changing. Nonetheless, even though I claim that East Asia's Cold War has come to an end, it is still true that the structures that sustained the Cold War's confrontations remain as before, because forces intent on maintaining those structures control international relationships not only on the Korean Peninsula but in all of East Asia.

The Cold War structures that were rapidly coming apart from the late 1980s began to revive with the installation of the Bush government. At the heart of this revival is the reinforcement of the

American-Japanese alliance. Beginning with the National Defense Program Guidelines (NDPG) and the law on peripheral situations (LMEPSJ) of 1995, and continuing with the emergency legislation (TAASRL) and the law providing financial support for the reconstruction of Iraq (LSMHRAI) of 2003, a series of measures covering the execution of America's defensive strategy in the world and in East Asia have included America's policy of reinforcing its alliance with Japan, designed to bestow on Japan a greater partnership role than during the Cold War years. The Armitage Report of the year 2000 demanded that the American-Japanese alliance should be developed to the level of the "special relationship between the U.S. and the U.K." This policy shift, challenging the Geneva Agreements signed in 1994 and urging a comprehensive solution involving not only the nuclear problem but also missiles and conventional weapons and even economic reform, for which diplomatic negotiations and military confrontation should be applied simultaneously, is in harmony with the hardline approach to North Korea found within the Republican Party (Seo Jae-jeong 2005). Unfortunately, this reinforcement of the American-Japanese alliance coincides with a right-wing shift in Japan's domestic politics. Moreover, that results in an increased risk that the stale confrontational relationships of the Cold War era will be revived, with the American-Japanese alliance on the one side, and China on the other.

The reinforcement of the American-Japanese alliance might easily become a source of instability and tension in the relationships between the nations of East Asia. Above all, because America is at the same time adopting and pursuing in practice a hardline policy toward North Korea, the stronger that alliance becomes, inevitably the space available for the South Korean government to establish a relationship with the North with peace-oriented structures will become far more restricted. Clearly, in addition, that will also serve to introduce greater tension in the relations between Japan and China. The result is the nationalistic fervor currently on the rise in both countries. Today in Japan, the mobilization of conservative populism in support of reinforcing the American-Japanese alliance and a swing to the right combined with, in China and Korea, demands for an apology for the imperialistic invasion and colonialist oppression by Japan during World War II and the dispute between Japan and Korea concerning sovereignty over Dokdo are all shrouded in a storm of nationalistic sentiment. What is interesting is the fact that, although the ideological basis for a Cold-War-style international confrontation in the competition between capitalism and communism has greatly weakened, the nationalistic outpouring in all these societies takes its source in a condition in which the basic framework of confrontation between different states remains intact. That is to say that we have a situation in which, while at one level hostile structures have been maintained, at another level existing forms of ideological confrontation have grown weak or ceased to exist. There are constant attempts to integrate South Korea as a main axis of the American-Japanese alliance. At the same time, the Cold-War pattern of confrontational relations is preserved further by the way the Chinese-North Korean alliance is being maintained. Yet, again, since ideological patterns of confrontation have weakened or vanished, Cold-War patterns of confrontation no longer exist, and all these nations are engaged in a new process of increased regional rapprochement through economic exchanges and increasing investment. Most problematic is that, within Japan, the political and social foundation for the American-Japanese alliance is a strengthening of the conservative shift to the right. Because the conservative shift to the right in Japan has its historic basis in Japan's invasion and colonization of it neighbors, it is bound to provoke a nationalistic response in Korea and China. In the present situation, the nationalistic response in Korea and China has served in turn to provoke a yet stronger move to the right in Japan. In this kind of environment, the response of South Korea policy-wise, directly confronted with the North Korean problem as it is and with it being a direct topic it is obliged to solve, is bound to grow increasingly schizophrenic on account of that additional set of ideas and emotions. The North-South policy centered on reconciliation, co-operation and peaceful coexistence that the democratic governments of South Korea have pursued since the presidency of Kim Dae-Jung cannot fail to come into conflict with the hardline policies of the Bush administration and the hostile policies of the Koizumi government toward North Korea, as well as with the goals of the American-Japanese alliance. In contrast, South Korea and China, given that they share a common historical experience as targets of Japanese imperialistic invasion, and on account of expectations that the role of China can be a positive aid in assuring peaceful coexistence between North and South Korea, have come to a much greater sense of emotional affinity. However, unlike changes in the emotional dimension, in the dimension of practical politics the relationship of South Korea with China is not one that can claim the same standing as that with America or Japan. In this situation, particularly, the initiative or space available for South Korea to make progress toward a peaceful relationship between South and North Korea has been reduced until inevitably it retains only a very limited effectiveness in finding a peaceful solution to the North Korea/nuclear problem.

In the historic-institutional approach found in economic history, there is a concept known as "path dependence." It is a theory regarding the constituting of historical causation, according to which major decisions on a specific point are not complete in themselves, but rather a series of choices following on from them create a result that sets history on a trajectory that is sustained by a specific reproductive mechanism (Katznelson 2003, 290). The current state of affairs in East Asia is in that precise situation. The American-Japanese alliance, one of the main axes of confrontation in East Asia during the Cold War years and now once again growing stronger in the course of the reorganization of things in East Asia in the post-Cold-War period, is faced with the danger that it may provoke a process by which the relationships between the nations of the region might easily be reborn as something similar to the confrontational pattern found during the Cold War, rather than moving in the direction of cooperation and peace. This would increase the risk that international relations in East Asia (the region including the Korean Peninsula and the North Korea/nuclear problem) might move in directions that would threaten peace, the complete opposite of the direction pursued so far in the post-Cold War period.

3. The importance of an approach directed toward peace

The question of what policy America adopts toward the North Korea/nuclear problem is of decisive importance. Because America is the only superpower, hard to challenge in every domain – be it in military power, politically, economically, culturally or ideologically, worldwide, and particularly in East Asia – it exercises the most significant influence on the behavior and policy choices of other nations. In the case of a confrontation of forces in the domain of international politics, or competitive relationships, those involved have a choice of policies; they have reasons and justifications corresponding to their own standards. In the momentum of a shift from competition and confrontation to dispute, from dispute to war, it is extremely rare to find a case in which one of the parties is clearly right and has justice on their side. To view critically the Americans' hardline countermeasures to the North Korean nuclear program does not mean that one considers the reasoning put forward by North Korea to be right. What is important is the fact that America is a superpower, and that therefore the range of choices available to America is incomparably wider than those of North Korea, and that as a result America's policy cannot be content with being merely based on a realistic logic of force. Powerful states dispose of a wide range of choices that exercise direct influence on the conduct and policies of the rest, and since as powerful states they dispose of relatively superior power they can act with established authority toward others. Therefore, it would be very wrong for a powerful state not to exercise a political and moral responsibility as great as the outcome of the policies decided on by them.

Serious doubts arise as to whether America's policy toward the North Korea/nuclear problem is sincerely oriented toward peace. That is closely related to the ways in which the high-level policy makers in the Bush administration perceive North Korean issues. The North Korean problem has its origins for a large part in a fundamental perception; the policy measures based on it aiming at a collapse of the North Korean system or its total isolation, are the result of a policy whereby America does not recognize the existence of the North Korean system, in an extension of the Cold War's structures of confrontation. The realistic alternative, seen from the viewpoint of peace on the Korean Peninsula, is a policy of acceptance toward the North. That means recognizing North Korea at the political level so that it can become a normal player in East Asia, while providing aid to allow its economic survival. American policy does not opt for the latter alternative, but remains fixed on the former one, making it very difficult to solve the problem, and so long as that remains unclear, I think that the North's nuclear program will continue and there is a strong possibility that the crisis on the Korean Peninsula will continue in a lasting manner. It may be that America is deliberately sabotaging any prospect of a negotiated settlement. Even if we set aside as irrelevant the claims of critics of Bush's diplomatic policy inside and outside of the United States, those people who either have been directly involved in diplomacy toward North Korea or have closely investigated that whole process openly say that in fact "America does not want a peaceful solution" (Jeong Se-Hyeon 2005; Seo Dong-Man 2005; Bak Chan-Su 2005). The hardline policy toward North Korea has as its starting-point a way of defining the North Korea/nuclear problem. That involves regarding North Korea as a key trouble-making nation, a threat to peace on a worldwide scale, therefore identifying North Korea with similar nations in the Middle East, and therefore as an enemy state in America's declared War against Terror.

Obviously, the causes for the conflict America is confronting with the Islamic states of the Middle East and for the conflict with North Korea here on the Korean Peninsula in East Asia are fundamentally different in character, and as a result the solutions are bound to be different, too. While the Middle Eastern problem is deeply linked to the problem of Israel and to the problem of oil resources, the North Korea problem, an unsolved question of the post-Cold-War era in East Asia, involves the survival of a system resulting from isolation. In American eyes, the fundamental issue in the Middle East is how to assure lasting stability and peace for an Israel besieged in the midst of the vast Islamic region. What makes it so difficult to find a solution is that this besieged Israel is supported by an alliance with America and has an overwhelming superiority in military and economic terms, while on the other hand there is an extreme imbalance of power with the Islamic nations behind Palestine, that surrounds Israel, unable to modernize their military capabilities and kept in economic poverty. Such a situation serves as a hotbed for terrorism. In comparison, the North Korea/nuclear problem is giving rise to an extreme imbalance between a North Korea that is besieged militarily and alienated economically as one of the poorest nations, unable to gain recognition as a player in normal international politics in the East Asian international order under American leadership, and those states intent on maintaining the status quo. That in turn gives rise to an extreme resistance in order to survive, a so-called "brinkmanship diplomacy" using the nuclear program as a weapon. The Middle East situation and the North Korea problem are made similar by an imbalance of power. Yet compared with the problem of the Middle East, it is relatively easy to solve the Korean problem. Regarding North Korea, an end to isolation, recognition of its right to exist, an internal unification of systems offer a way of solving the problem logically and at the least cost. It is possible to think that the North Korea problem is a far simpler one than that of the Middle East, unless the American policy-makers do not want a solution to the North Korean/nuclear problem but a continuation of it, judging that to be more advantageous either because unstable security in East Asia can encourage a build-up of such strategic space defense systems as TMD or NMD, or because it allows the continuing existence of a strong political and strategic military leverage over the other states of the East Asian region. In short, America's hardline policy toward North Korea, unwilling to take seriously the difference between the North Korea problem and the Middle East situation, makes it hard to accept the rightness of their diagnosis of the situation, while it is also not an economic one given the excessive costs it involves.

The countries included in the list of "rogue states" are some of the poorest and most backward in the world. Once having assumed their existence, superpower America undertook the Iraq War, which has all the characteristics of a preventive war, while arming itself with weapons using the most advanced technology and planning a new space defensive system at astronomical expense. Walter Russell Mead, the international political theorist, has said that under the Bush administration the fundamental contradiction America is faced with is the tension between the rapid increase in American power by an acceleration in globalization and technological development and the demand that every state should have an equal voice on the basis of sovereign equality. He has also said that, by a loss of balance because of this contradiction, a "secession of élites" is occurring within these states, with the result that there has been a great loss of support from friendly nations. Speaking of Korea, he says that is reflected in a difference of outlook between the generations (Mead 2004, 150; 160).

Despite Mead's acute observations, when we consider the North Korean/nuclear problem from within South Korean society's viewpoint, it seems necessary to add one other fundamental contradiction. That is the fact that the excessive use America makes of the logic of ostentatious power in pursuing its foreign policy comes into collision with the values of peace and morality. That is linked to the problem of American hegemony. During the Cold War, as far as weaker nations such as South Korea were concerned, America strove to show that its power went hand in hand with maintaining peace and democratic values, manifesting a moral effectiveness ensuring that it was always accepted freely and spontaneously. What is problematic today is the question why America, despite the fact that as a superpower a diplomatic space is open for it to manipulate in favor of peace, is so intent on employing displays of overwhelming superior power. The cognitive discrepancy between this logic of power and state of crisis suggests that American foreign policy is domineering and aggressive, with no interest in peace. Instead of America's present policy toward North Korea, pressuring them and talking of the possible use of force including preemptive strikes, incentives supporting their modernization and providing economic aid would render them less inclined to violence and offer an effective course at lesser cost. Of course this does not only apply to North Korea, it applies to the American approach to all the rogue nations. Besides, this approach is supported by the "engagement policy toward North Korea" of the Americans in the post-Cold War period before the inauguration of George W. Bush as president as well as the experience of détente with the North made by the South Korean government with its "Sunshine Policy." The process of democratization that accompanied détente in South Korea dramatically expanded the influence of popular opinion on and popular control over foreign policy, including policy toward North Korea and that of relations with America, in the sense of supporting peace-oriented policies. Since the people of Korea have experienced the Korean War, their understanding of peace and veneration for the values of peace are especially deeply rooted. In South-North relations, with the exception of the extreme belligerence shown by extreme right-wing groups, veneration for the values of peace is shared by the majority of South Koreans, whether conservative or progressive. This can be considered the greatest positive outcome of the Korean War.

The concept of republicanism based on Kant's theory of perpetual peace pays tribute to a system that gives priority to public advantage and popular control of foreign policy (Kant 1991, 930130). In this respect, the theory of Kant the philosopher has much in common with the theory of democracy exposed by Robert A. Dahl, the political scientist. Dahl used to consider that possessing an alternative source of information, being capable of an enlightened understanding and a rational judgment of issues, was an essential condition of democracy; likewise, Kant clearly understood that if such a condition is satisfied, democratic citizens are capable of controlling foreign policy and in such a case, it will be peace-oriented. (Dahl 1998). Kant's theory establishes a mutual relationship between a nation's ability to realize peace and its internal forms of government. The way in which South Korea's policy toward North Korea has consistently pursued collaboration in reconciliation and peaceful coexistence, despite instances of conflict between the Korean governments after democratization and the fundamental American policy line toward North Korea, corresponds to Kant's thesis that the fundamental characteristic of a government possessing a republican (democratic) constitutional system will be peace-oriented. Whereas, regarding the qualitative change in the international political order and democracy centered on America, Kant's theory of perpetual peace makes the three following strong reservations. We need to consider further Kant's thesis that wars do not occur between democratic states.

First comes the problem of the imbalance of power between superpower and weaker nations that Meade pointed out as a basic contradiction. Even if its government is democratic in form, a superpower is able to impose its own policy on weaker states on a global scale exceeding even the difference in territorial size, and that at the possible expense of peace, contrary to the peaceful orientation hoped for by those states. Kant's theory of peace was constructed at the time of the French Revolution, when the political system was overwhelmingly one of enlightened despotism, and when international relations meant a limited number of European states of similar power establishing a balance of power by means of a power struggle. England's constitutional monarchy or America's and France's republican constitutions manifested the rationalism of the Enlightenment, and could be considered an institutionalization of it. It is therefore difficult to apply Kant's theory of peace to the present day's international relations when America stands as the only, central superpower.

Second, today the idealism of the neoconservatives can be seen as an inverse form of Kant's notion of perpetual peace. The decrees of reason and the moral code within the human person are the source of the urge to put into practice that form of justice we are calling peace. With its rejection of utilitarianism, Kant's rationalism has peace as its goal and its means. The logic of Fukuyama's "end of history" comes into conflict with the idealistic foreign strategy of the "neocon" with his active planning of a "regime change" toward democracy by using arms. According to Kant's thesis, if the world can at some point be unified as a single free, democratic state, the generalization of peace will follow automatically. In such a case, it is possible to argue logically that even the use of military power is justified to spread freedom and democracy across the whole world. That is what Emmanuel Kant called "democracy as threat" (Todd 2003, 45-47). But using the logic of destroying peace now in order to achieve the goal or ideal of peace later cannot but be the inverse of Kant's thought.

Third, today's democracy is utterly different from the ideal of republicanism reigning at the moment when Kant expounded his theory of peace. Kant defined a republic as a political order possessing a civil constitution embodying an inner morality and the rule of reason, and reckoned that when republics possessing that kind of constitutional system came together to form a federated system in support of peace, perpetual peace would be attained. There is obviously something idealistic about the notion that reason can be materialized in the form of a constitution in the world of Realpolitik. As Dahl says, just as all modern democracies are incapable of attaining democracy in reality, so equally the functioning and practice of the democratic system are being perverted and weakened through the overwhelming influence of large-scale capital and mass media. In his "On Perpetual Peace," Kant says that probably "of the three powers within a state—the power of the army, the powers of alliances and the power of money—the third is probably the most reliable instrument of war" (Kant 1991, 95). The same is applicable to today's situation. Only today, the power capable of engaging in war is manifest in such a magnified form as to be capable of changing the very character of a democratic system. A number of American scholars stress that during the Cold War the fundamental character of the American state changed greatly in its quest for victory over the USSR. The increase in the American military budget and the resulting overinflation of the function of the Pentagon in the structures of the state, with the subsequent military Keynesianism, transformed America's state structures and its economy. The state-run sectors of security and technology produced the momentum for industrial development (Gourevitch 2002). Today, America's industrial sector is closely linked to the military, and as Chalmers Johnson has said, the state has been transformed into a "Pentagonized presidency" (Johnson 2004, 285). After the fall of the USSR, the defense and industrial systems were obliged to reinvent themselves. This structural change indicates the importance of the problem of internal conditions in obliging America to select an aggressive foreign policy. For rather than a policy aimed at developing social security and the service sector, it suggests an increase in constraints from within American society rendering peace-oriented approaches difficult, a system demanding the prioritizing of an aggressive foreign policy.

4. Two notions of peace in Korea

When it comes to finding a solution to the North Korea/nuclear problem and establishing peace on the Korean Peninsula, the role of the United States is decisive. But that does not mean that America should solve everything. Since South Korea is confronted with the North Korea crisis but is also on the other hand its partner, and is therefore most directly involved in the problem, it occupies a position just as important as that of the United States. South Korea is consistently insisting to America that there should be peace on the peninsula, and it would be very wrong if South Korea did not have such a North Korean policy in order to create the conditions needed for America's policy to turn in a peace-oriented direction. But what should be its contents? That is deeply linked to the sense of the word unification on the Korean Peninsula. It can be claimed that the most recent statement concerning this problem or indication of a direction in North Korean-directed policy is to be found in the so-called "four-stage unification" to which President Roh Moo-hyun referred during his recent visit to Germany (*Hangyeore sinmun* 2005/04/15). Prior to this, while the process of intellectual discourse planning peaceful coexistence was focused on the pending issues that the two Koreas had neglected, there was a tendency that seemed to make this easily vanish from the foreground of the issues. From that point of view, President Roh's reference to a "four-stage unification" is highly significant in the light of the current ongoing crisis regarding North Korea's nuclear capabilities, and in a situation in which such hardline policies such as "regime change" and "North Korean regime collapse" and an aggressive discourse are so influential, evoking once again as a topic the question as to how he plans to pursue long-term coexistence with North Korea.

There is a need to make a distinction between a maximalist

vision/idea of unification and a minimalist vision/idea. The former signifies a South Korea intent on imposing its own ideology and system on the North, or on the contrary North Korea wishing to impose its own ways on the South. The latter involves establishing a process of long-term peaceful co-existence, while moving toward eventual unification. While the former supports a hardline policy or goes well with it, the latter prefers a moderate or comprehensive policy. If we take a long-term view of events from the Cold War period until the post-Cold-War present, attitudes toward unification in South Korea have shifted from maximalist notions of unification to minimalist ones. But even if we make a distinction between the two, notions of unification are still notions of unification. In other words, whereas there may exist a notion of unification, no notion of peaceful coexistence exists as yet. Maximalist or minimalist notions may differ in method, still the goal of both is unification. I believe that the time has come to distinguish clearly between notions of unification and notions of peaceful coexistence when it comes to dealing with relations between North and South Korea and establishing long-term goals. That is to say that when it comes to the goals and means required to establish peaceful relations between North and South Korea, overall priority has to be given to the value of coexistence. That requires a shift from minimalist notions of unification to notions of peaceful coexistence. One possible practical model for this is found in the "Ostpolitik" of West Germany's Chancellor Willy Brandt establishing the theory of "one people, two states" in the late 1960s. That established the special relationship between the single people of East and West Germany, which were not foreign countries to one another although each possessed sovereignty and existed independently.

The reason for speaking negatively of notions of unification is that fundamentally, be the approach maximalist or minimalist, at its core is an approach aiming ultimately to attain peace through a merging into a single system and set of values of two very different political entities. That is quite different from an approach based on notions of peaceful coexistence achieving peace by acknowledging those differences and coexisting with them. Moving toward unification, in the process of merging the two different realities, the competing entities each try to come out on top, and since the balance between the two is always unstable, it is very easy for the stronger entity to fall into the prideful temptation of trying to achieve a hierarchical merger with the weaker one. In the process of unification, violence can easily erupt, and unification can easily come to mean imposing order on differences by hierarchy. That does not only apply to unification by force. Today, East and West Germany have accomplished peaceful unification in a peaceful manner at the political and military levels, but it can be thought that at the economic level it has been at the cost of East Germans merging with West Germans as second-class citizens. By contrast, the approach with coexistence as the goal, not the merging of differences, may prove to be a more truly peaceful one, the process toward a goal of coexistence being shared by all concerned. Of course, once peaceful coexistence has become the goal and the means, there would be no need to reject unification if that should turn out to be the result of the long-drawn-out process of peaceful coexistence. The unification of the two Germanys, rather than being the intended goal or result of an eastward policy was the unanticipated outcome of a process of peaceful coexistence. In other words, the ideal form for relations between North and South Korea is not to have as ultimate goal a single system and to set out preparing for that to happen, but rather to concentrate every effort on establishing as the primary goal ways in which the systems of North and South Korea might peacefully establish coexistence, when for over fifty years since the Korean War they have developed hostile relations marked by hatred and confrontation. If unification is taken as the goal, how on earth can there be a merging of the totally divergent histories South and North have experienced, including the ideological tensions and war of the past? If we make unification the central value, that will give rise to endless tensions. Because coexistence is possible while acknowledging the tense history of the past, the ideal and practice of peaceful coexistence is capable of reducing the cost of the discord caused by past history and differences, hard to anticipate in advance. It is peaceful coexistence, not unification, that is best able to maintain peace. When it comes to the peaceful coexistence between North and

South Korea, democracy does not have much meaning. Not that democracy as such is a problem, but the segmentation of democracy between right and left is problematic. As the experience of the Korean War shows, it is a fact that democracy, far from being able to prevent the division of Korea and the war, constituted one of its causes.

In the light of this, another category of concept becomes necessary. If we consider that positing a democratic unification as the ideal form for relations between South and North Korea is a maximalist form for relations between the two, then taking peaceful coexistence as our goal can be seen as a minimalist form for those relations. Since this minimalist form of relations recognizes differences, takes difference and coexistence as value and norm, it rejects any temptation or attempt to impose on North Korea any such values as those termed democracy, freedom, or human rights. Otherwise, any system or group convinced of possessing superior values on a hierarchical scale will be able to justify intervening in North Korea's internal problems for the sake of "humanitarian interventions" or "regime change." But to say that is not to prevent North Korean society from becoming democratic in its own way, adopting a market economy, developing and changing into a system that takes seriously and respects human rights. The essential thing is that they should do this for themselves. Kant's theory of perpetual peace is potentially useful here, too, because with an increasing number of states uniting around their sovereign interests and becoming a republic with the result that they come to form a "universal community," the perpetual peace he referred to is a crystal forming through cumulative, lengthy and voluntary efforts. Peace, then, is not the result of any external force, but is something that sovereign states can achieve on their own. There lies the reason why today we should reject any form of vision, expression or policy that plans to achieve a change of system through the use of force and then impose democracy on top of that.

5. An East Asia Peace Community by Social Imaginaries

Even if South Korea sets about developing relations of peaceful coexistence between North and South, if international relations in East Asia do not develop in the direction of peace-oriented relations supportive of that, there will be serious limits to the extent to which peace can be implemented securely in the Korean Peninsula. Moreover, when we consider today's conditions, where with South Korea's democratization the democratic governments have been consistently pursuing peace-oriented relations with North Korea since the later 1990s, we see that when East Asia's international relations have been peace-oriented, optimism has been possible about the construction of a peaceful order on the Korean Peninsula. As I wrote earlier, I consider the North Korea / nuclear problem to be a residue left over from the Cold War. And I noted that the post-Cold-War period's reinforcement of the American-Japanese alliance made it all the more difficult to contribute to developing the order of things in East Asia in a peace-oriented direction. That can be seen as the expression of a hegemonic project based on a reinforcement of power, and within that framework the North Korea / nuclear problem is approached through the use of force or coercion. This approach reflects the standpoint of Thomas Hobbes who advocated the establishment of a strong authority, as represented in his Leviathan, capable of bestowing peace and order by means of a "war of all against all." Such an approach toward peace takes as its basis a Realpolitik founded on a kind of physical conception, establishing overwhelming power externally to restrain lesser powers by warfare or else intent on ensuring peace through a balance of existing powers. With the end of the Cold War, the possibility of any great dispute was removed and in its place a variety of new forms of small-scale disputes are arising world-wide; that is the reality of today's international politics. In such an environment, theories of "realism" or "neo-realism" can be considered a method of understanding international politics well suited to America's main view of the world order, with America performing the role of "the world's policeman" pursuing the War against Terror or preventing nuclear proliferation even by means of "preventive war," intervening actively in local conflicts intent on dominating the world order. At the present time, there can be no denying that this is a dominant method of understanding the realities of world politics. But one of the biggest problems with this approach is the way in which the nations of East Asia, in order not to be placed in an inferior position in the power competition, are pursuing a Realpolitik, planning an expansion of militaristic strength while encouraging nationalism, and running an increasing risk of turning the region into an arena for a trial of strength. A situation where a build-up of strength on one side provokes a corresponding build-up of strength on the other side is bound to be a situation that most directly threatens peace.

To my own way of thinking, one of the main points in Kant's notion of perpetual peace is precisely, as he says, the need to create a peace that is lasting, secure. As he says, peace is "not a mere truce, a suspension of hostilities. Peace means an end to all hostilities …" (Kant 1991,93). Since a Realpolitik-style of approach assumes a balance in relation to an external power that is constantly in a state of perpetual flux and change, the peace obtained by such means will always be insecure and temporary. Kant's notion of perpetual peace involves a longing for peace, which discovers the source of peace in an inner craving that sets out to practice justice as a value originating from the reason and moral standards within us, functioning as a power making possible the institutionalizing of force in the service of peace. Therefore, since human reason exists, lasting peace is a practical possibility. That is why he was deeply skeptical about any diplomacy that relied on diplomatic intrigues and secret treaties, and stressed the importance of conscience and openness. People of a realistic frame of mind are going to reject as impossible any idea that so-called international politics can understand or solve problems by the use of reason or the imagination. That is right, but it is not always right. The founding of the League of Nations, mother to today's UN, can be seen as a practical application of his notion of enduring peace. Then, when Jean Monet advocated the establishment of a federation of European states by a Federated European Constitution, that was at that point of time clearly a matter of "social imaginaries" (Taylor 2004). Today peace in East Asia, or an East Asia Community as an alternative to the American-Japanese alliance in support of a hegemonic project, can be seen as one of those "universal communities" that Kant conceived of. Because a union of republics capable of achieving perpetual peace would be a gradual, cumulative process, it can be considered an intermediate form leading to the constitution of a universal community on a world-wide scale.

In that case, why is there so little being done on an institutional level in the East Asian region to come to a collective decision that would make possible a peace and security that could cope with disputes and tensions between states and territories, and offer a common security? It is hardly necessary to say that when common security and peace are under threat and incapable of stability, the economic exchanges and integration in this region, rapidly growing with globalization, encounter severe handicaps. Why is East Asia taking a course so different from the union displayed by the EU? A number of major factors can be indicated for this. The most significant one is the fact that, although in the Cold War both regions were similarly under American hegemony, they developed differing systems, with Europe developing its community while Asia evolved a system that kept to a structure of one-to-one alliances with America. Yet in spite of that difference, it cannot be said that the path leading to the establishment of a community in Asia has been closed off. Since the later 1980s, the East Asian region has rapidly developed relationships of economic union, investment, commerce etc., with rapid economic growth as the basis, and that has in turn become a foundation calling out for discussion of an economic unification in this region. Today, in East Asia a sudden rise in regionalistic discourse is a very natural outcome related to various forms of economic union. Clearly the development of economic union is capable of becoming the socio-economic basis that can serve to develop a peace community of political significance.

It is worth drawing attention to recent debates among critical intellectuals from Korea and Japan concerning approaches to a regional union of East Asia centered on the North Korean problem and the question of peace on the Korean Peninsula, as a starting point for the peace of East Asia. This has produced a variety of perceptions such as "North-East Asia a Shared House,"

"Discovering East Asia," "Ideas about a North-East-Asian Age." Broadly speaking, I share in these discussions and outcomes. (Wada Haruki 2003; Gang Sang-jung 2002; Baik Young-seo 2000; Choi Won-sik 2004). But regarding these discussions, it is necessary to mention the problem of nationalism that is the main hindrance when it comes to the formation of any kind of East Asian Community. Most of the participants in these debates, estimating that nationalism is the gravest obstacle, in order to break it down show a great interest in discovering an "East Asia Community" or an "East Asian authenticity" either by the development of economic and commercial relations or by transcending the region's national frontiers by history through the Confucian culture that was once common to the whole region, or by developing a theory of Post-nationalism, which they then project into the future. This results in a logic moving in the direction of a wider-ranging community for the East Asia of the future, freed of tensions either by avoiding or transcending the tensions of the present.

We may be better able to envisage this difficulty through Ralf Dahrendorf's conflict theory. According to him, when conflict is suppressed it can cause greater harm to a society, so that rather than avoiding conflict, it is better to institutionalize it. In other words, a realistic approach to conflict is not to try to abolish the conflict or try to move toward a state without conflict, but to exhaust it by externalizing it (Dahrendorf 1998). To my way of thinking, East Asian nationalism has evolved in the process of modernization in China and Korea in confrontations and conflicts resisting the domination they were under, unable to achieve their own modernization on account of the spoliations of Japan that had the lead in modernization. Therefore the nationalism found in these nations coincides with such resistant ideas and attitudes as National Liberation, Right to National Self-Determination, National Sovereignty in reaction against foreign domination. Although such ideas can today function in a reactionary direction, provoking tightly-closed, collective nationalistic fervor, that is in reality a major force, and on that account, the problem of Japan's past history is something hard to ignore even though the quest is for some kind of East Asian Community. In other words, this process is not a matter of moving beyond confrontations over past history, it demands making them a basis for something better.

Just as Germany's role was central in the process of constructing the European Union, so too, in order to build up any kind of community in Asia Japan's role is central. It is precisely because of the importance of the role of present-day Japan that it finds itself saddled with a moral responsibility for the question of its past history. In this process it is important to strive to create an "overlapping space of meaning." This overlapping space of meaning is going to have to abandon the Cold War legacy of seeing regional international relations in terms of ideology, give up considering others as rivals or potential enemies, and take as its foundation a realistic appraisal of what are the dangers and interests common to all in the region. For then it will be possible to realize that peace, far from being an ideal, is in reality the value that most fully satisfies the interests of each and every state. It can be claimed that the creation of this overlapping space of meaning is primarily a task for political decision and leadership, rather than for society at large. For if the creation of a community for East Asia's defense and peace is not subject to a political decision, when enlarged relations occur at the level of the economy and society, of culture, East Asia being as it is, it will be hard to adapt a kind of functionalistic theory of union, viewing that as the starting-point with a political promotion of relations following later. The relationships between South Korea and Japan, Japan and North Korea, are identical with those between Japan and South-East Asia, capable of focusing purely on economic relations (Sakamoto 2003). What makes a space of meaning important in the East Asian region is that, although there is a growing network across the region on account of the development of economic relations, with increasing cultural exchanges, South Korea, Japan and China need a separate dimension, capable of realizing that the region's community needs a collective solidarity for security and peace.

Personally speaking, I do not see the way in which Japan is striving to become a "normal" state through the legalization of a military capacity and rearmament, and the conservative rightward trend in Japanese society, as signs of a revival of an earlier Japanese militarism, as many people with a simple nationalistic viewpoint do. Likewise I do not consider the conservatism of present-day Japan and the rearming of its military as being identical with the expansionist, imperialist militarism that claimed hegemony over East Asia, as the militarism of the past did, and neither do I think that it is moving in that direction. But in so far as the path of Japan's rearming combines with militarism through the framework of the American-Japanese alliance, I fear that there is a great possibility that it will have a negative effect when it comes to solving the North Korean nuclear problem, and, beyond that, building up peace and a common security throughout East Asia. Here again, we see the importance of a space of meaning. That demands action based on a know-how concerning the demands and value of peace, and at the same time means that all the nations involved in East Asia must show a readiness to shoulder the expenses involved in putting it into practice. In the present situation in East Asia, to permit a change of course in this direction Japan should be the first to indicate a readiness to shoulder expenses. Once it does that, efforts for the establishment of an East Asia Peace Community will not only be more justified, they will correspond better to today's post-Cold War reality and offer a realistic prospect of better corresponding to the demands of security and mutual prosperity. The East Asia Peace Community is not something created in a void; despite the violence of current reality and efforts to conquer a dominating position, and the uncertainties of the future, it requires a resolve ready to make sacrifices because it is a matter of justice and morality.

Translated by **Brother Anthony of Taizé**

Works Cited

Dahl, Robert A. 1998. *On Democracy*. Yale U. P.

Dahrendorf, Ralf. 1998. *The Modern Social Conflict: An Essay on the Politics of Liberty. U. of California Press.*

Gourevitch, Peter A. 2002. "Reinventing the American State: Political Dynamics in the Post-Cold War Era." in Ira Katznelson and Martin Shefter eds. *Shaped by War and Trade.* Princeton U. P.

Johnson, Charlmers. 2004. *The Sorrows of Empire: Militarism, Secrecy, and the End of Republic*. Henry Holt and Company, LLC.

Kant, Immanuel. 1991. "Perpetual Peace: A Philosophical Sketch" and "Appendix." edited by Hans Reiss and translated by H. B. Nisbet. *Political Writings* (second, enlarged edition). Cambridge U. P.

Katznelson, Ira. 2003. "Periodization and Preferences: Reflections on Purposive Action in Comparative Historical Social Science." in James Mahoney and Dietrich Rueschemeyer eds. *Comparative Historical Analysis in the Social Sciences.* Cambridge U. P.

Mead, Walter Russell. 2004. *Power, Terror, Peace, and War: America's Grand Strategy in a World at Risk.* Alfred A. Knopf, pp.150,160.

Sakamoto, Yoshikazu. 2003. "Envisioning a Peace on the Korean Peninsula: Can Japan Do It?" Jang jip Choi ed. *Post-Cold War and Peace*. The Asiatic Research Center.

Taylor, Charles. 2004. *Modern Social Imaginaries*. Duke U. P.

Todd, Emmanuel. 2003. *After Empire: the Breakdown of the American Order.* Columbia U. P.

강상중 저, 이경덕 역. 2002. 『동북아시아 공동의 집을 향하여』. 뿌리와 이파리.

박찬수. 2005. "부시의 김정일 혐오, 북핵 해결 막는다." 『한겨레신문』4월 4일.

백영서. 2000. "20세기형 동아시아문명과 국민국가를 넘어서." 『동아시아의 귀환: 중국의 근대성을 묻는다』. 창작과 비평사.

서동만. 2005. "단독 인터뷰." 『신동아』 48권 4호(통권 547호).

서재정. 2005. "일본의 篤돼幄린逆 과 미국." 『한겨레신문』 4월 2일

연합뉴스. 2005. "윤곽 드러낸 노대통령 4단계 통일방안." 『한겨레신문』4월 15일.

Wada Haruki 저, 이원덕 역. 2003. 『동북아시아 공동의 집』. 일조각.

정세현. 2005. "단독 인터뷰." 『신동아』 48권 3호(통권 546호).

최원식. 2004. "천하삼분지계로서의 동아시아론." 한국동북아시아지식인연대 편. 『동북아공동체를 향하여』. 동아일보사.

Session VII

Varieties of Modernity in the World

Bei Dao | Modernity and the Country Mouse

Hwang Ji-woo | Stigmata of the Modern Circulation, Function, Style of Korean Poetry Today

Kim Yeon-soo | Clock, History and Fate of Individuals

Modernity and the Country Mouse

Bei Dao

1.

The children's story goes like this: A country mouse invites a city mouse to visit him in the country and feeds him corn, potatoes and grain. After eating, the city mouse doesn't say a word except to invite the country mouse to visit him in the city. One day, the country mouse goes to the city. He is surprised to find that the city mouse eats ten times better than he does: cheese, butter, ham, cake and such fare. But right in the middle of stuffing themselves, the city mouse cries out, "Run for your life! It's the cat!" He scrambles away, but having escaped that danger, he is almost crushed beneath one of the many cars flying back and forth along the street. Finally, panting for breath, the country mouse says, "I am better off with my peaceful life in the country. Here you may eat well, but you fear for your life all the time."

I am like a country mouse, looking up at the blue sky and white clouds all day. But I was a city mouse for many decades before this, wandering all over the world: "At forty, I was no longer confused." Five years ago, I finally moved to a small town in California and settled down. Every time I go back to the city, I eat and drink well, but I still miss the quiet of the country.

Compared to Beijing, our little town is the countryside. There are fifty thousand or so people, with no industry except for a tomato processing plant. Surrounded on all sides by fields, you'd ride a horse to death before reaching the distant mountains. The agricultural school of the University of California at Davis is ranked number one or two in the U.S., but because the university uses animals in experiments, it is frequently attacked by the local Greenpeace group. Bicycles are the main means of transportation in town. There is no news in the local paper, and the daily air pollution index is so low that it creates the illusion that I'm living on another planet.

Every day I wake up to the calling of birds. Listening carefully, I can make out the exaggerated flirting of two red-billed tits; a magpie chatters away in a one man talk-show; a flock of sparrows acts like a bunch of unruly fellows, afraid they won't get the attention they deserve.

In Paris, I woke at exactly 2:00 a.m. every night when the bar across the street closed and tossed out the drunks who moaned and howled in the street. At 6:25 a.m., I was awakened by the garbage truck, and though I would immediately cover my ears with the pillow, it was no use. The truck was as heavy as a tank, making noises that shocked me into panicked wakefulness, crashing around as if it was trying to come directly into my bedroom, pack me in, and take me away. It reminded me of when I was a child living in Sanbulao Alley in Beijing, across the street from a textile plant. In the summer, all the windows of the plant were opened like a hundred loudspeakers shouting at us in some monotone language. The factory closed on Fridays, the silence unbearable. At night I would toss and turn, wishing they would hurry up and get back to work.

But this was nothing compared to the noise in New York. I once stayed at a friend's house in downtown Manhattan. In the middle of the night, there was the crisp, clean sound of gunshots, closely followed by the approaching howl of sirens. The next morning I read in the newspaper that it had been an exchange of fire between some gangsters—one dead and two wounded. When you bring this up with New Yorkers, they complain you are overreacting.

But don't forget that New Yorkers have grown up in a hail of gunfire which has toughened their nerves. They say that when someone fires a gun on the street, most New Yorkers, with as much experience as any guerilla, will just lower their heads, crouch slightly, and step clear of any possible danger. Then they might curse a little, brush the dust off their clothes, stand up straight, and rush back to their own battlefields.

One night in Paris I was robbed. It was after eleven in the

evening. A friend dropped me off at the place I was staying near the Gare de l'Est. I noticed two men following me—one tall, one short. The short one scuttled forward a couple of steps until he was at my side. In halting English he said, "Money! We have guns." I cast a glance behind me, the big one put his hand inside of his jacket, but it didn't really look like he had a gun, it could just as well have been the stump of a broom. I fumbled around and dug out one hundred fifty francs. They snatched the money and ran off. The next day, I passed by a bar in the neighborhood and saw the two off-duty thieves drinking with my francs.

On his first visit to New York, a Danish sinologist I know was standing on a street in Manhattan holding a map, looking around him, when suddenly a large black man put a friendly arm around his shoulders and the point of a knife in the small of his back. Trapped, he could only pull some money out of the pocket of his shirt. At first he thought he could get rid of him by just giving him five or ten dollars. But he accidentally pulled out a one hundred dollar bill. The man seized his wrist. The dire circumstances inspired my friend to rail bitterly about racial discrimination in the U.S. The man was pleased and gave him a discount, lowering his price to eighty dollars. Then my friend started cursing President Reagan, calling him all manner of foul names. The black man clapped him on the shoulder—"Brother, you're cool, just give me fifty." The sinologist and thief shook hands, parting reluctantly.

Running into a mugger with such good sense was a stroke of luck, though naturally it is best not to run into them at all. Starting in the 80s, students from China surged into big American cities in great numbers. Poor, they could only live in the worst areas. When faced with danger, they each developed their own clever stratagems. I met a foreign Chinese student in New York who would dress in a very special way: black wool overcoat, sunglasses, black fedora pushed down over his eyes, cigarette hanging askew from his mouth. With both hands in his pockets, he'd skulk crabwise down the street—a typical FBI agent from a Hollywood movie of the thirties or forties. Even though the outfit was a little out of date, it still struck fear in the hearts of evildoers, who did their best to keep their distance.

Dali was my classmate in high school. He has studied in New York for four years and lives in Harlem. I asked him how he was able to survive the constant warfare without having so much as a hair on his head harmed. "You must have extraordinary kung fu skills," I guessed. He shook his head mysteriously, spread out his fingers, and summarized three things he had learned: "First, when you see a group of suspicious-looking figures, adopt a cowering attitude, cross the street and go around them. Second, if you can't avoid them, look right into the face of the one who looks like he might be the leader, and let him know you will remember him; this will reduce the impulse to commit a crime. The third, and most crucial, is that whenever somebody is following you, you must head to the nearest garbage can and start rummaging around in it." I didn't comprehend this final point. Dali said with a chuckle, "If you are poorer than him, why would he rob you?"

2.

The famous Russian cellist Mstislav Rostropovich once said that city people are in a race toward death. This is a sensible observation. City mice are exhausted every day from being constantly on the run, as if they're wound up on a spring. Except for sleeping, when do they have time to rest? Actually, life is a kind of experiencing—if there's no time for leisure, how can one's experience deepen? Time filled compresses. A year seems as short as a day and rushes by.

But we have entertainment, say the city mice. But entertainment is empty. Like work, it fills time and cannot bring true leisure. People get together because they are afraid of loneliness. And besides, nowadays, if you want to see a movie, you don't have to live in the city. A lot of people, trying to appear sophisticated, go to great lengths to see the first showing of a new movie so as to have some conversational capital when they see their friends at work the next day. But what I really don't understand is why city people get so meticulously dressed up to go listen to classical music. After all, they aren't going to a wedding reception. And then once there, you pay for your own punishment—stifling coughs and holding bladders, not even daring to breathe too loud. If you're not careful and doze off, you'll be wakened by the applause. Then you stand up with everyone else and cheer without stopping until the musicians come back out for an encore. Isn't this ridiculous? Listening to music is a private affair. It's better to stay at home and not make such a big fuss.

But we country mice …

My New York friend Eliot teases me right back saying, "Country mouse? What you are is a suburban mouse."

Generally speaking, suburban mice work themselves to death, drive Camrys, eat fast food, tighten their belts so they can afford to live in a good school district, borrow money to buy a house, cut grass and tend flowers, go running and walk the dog; behind closed doors they watch TV, argue, and burn themselves out, then spend money to see a psychiatrist.

After careful consideration, there aren't many real country mice in the United States. Most are suburban mice, workaholics really not much better than city mice at all. According to recent statistics, Americans work the longest hours in the world, even surpassing the Japanese who are notorious workaholics. What people call the wealth of America seems to me to be nothing but a number; all day Americans are pointlessly busy; butts in the air chasing their own shadows. After they earn all that money, what then? When is there time to enjoy any of it?

The layout and structure of a house in some ways determines how people live. Gazing out over the suburbs, most of the houses look like they've been formed from the same mold. Over time, the people living inside also become exactly the same as each other. When I taught at a university, I found that many American kids all thought in more or less the same way, which surprised me. But then staring at row after row of standardized houses in the suburbs, I suddenly understood why. Sometimes I think this kind of modernized brainwashing is more frightening than authoritarian brainwashing because people lose any awareness of resistance and think everything is exactly as it should be.

Americans are in love with the idea of space, the bigger the better, from big houses, big cars, and big television sets, to eating big, drinking big, and getting big because of it. There are many fat people in the suburbs, directly related to the piles of junk food. Every weekend I drive my car and join the ranks of American shoppers. Chain stores like Costco are as large as an airport, the goods inside look like they've just been unloaded from an airplane. All the food comes in bulk packaging: ten pounds of beef, five dozen eggs, thirty cans of beer. Cars are stuffed full, each person goes home overflowing with happiness.

A South African friend of mine visited the U.S. and said to me with surprise, "Americans are so poor they are fattened to death." Mulling over this comment, I realized it had two implications: first, American obesity, in general, is a result of the wide ranks of the working people who are too hungry to be picky; second, it refers to the coarseness of the culinary culture in the United States. This must have something to do with the traditions of the Puritans whose descendants happened to become wealthy very rapidly, wanted more and more faster and faster, so they made processed junk food wrapped in commercial packaging and then spread it all over the world along with their advertising. When American monsters like McDonalds and KFC can gain a foothold in China—where people never tire seeking the most exquisite kinds of food—you can see just how formidable they are.

The worst are American-style buffets in small towns that draw fat people in droves. I think this is one of the most fiendish parts in the plot of commercialization. Like opium, it makes people who like to eat unable to stop even if they want to, fattening them until it kills them.

Writing this, I cannot suppress a shiver. Is suburban life really so horrible? I think suburban mice at least put on the appearance of civility. In the morning, when you go out for a walk, people wave and greet you with endless hellos and good mornings. After all, this is better than city mice with their cross faces and cold manners, always ready to draw knives on each other. They say that if a child from the country first visiting New York gets off the bus and greets each passing pedestrian, no one will pay any attention and before going very far, the child will give up. Maybe in the big city people have a deeper understanding of loneliness and don't need to pretend otherwise. If not, then they're nothing more than Giacometti's statues—people as thin as bamboo rods set in the metropolis.

New York City is a lunatic asylum. I was in New York two days ago staying with a friend who lives in Greenwich Village. It was the middle of the night when we went out and New York's nightlife had just begun—the throngs of traffic and blazing lights and colors made me gape. A young woman was shouting in the street, talking to a man over the cars parked by the side of the road; an old man, most likely just out of jail, was running laps in the same place; a half-naked drunk stood muttering in the street; a tall, wiry black man walked along, swinging his hips, moving his hands to some interior rhythm.

While writing this, I'm suddenly aware that I've most definitely become a country mouse and it would be very difficult for me to readjust to city life. But then new changes have also happened in my life. This country mouse has no choice but to move back to New York, that most odious of places. I must prepare myself for air pollution and noise, fear and the art of survival.

Stigmata of the Modern Circulation, Function, Style of Korean Poetry Today

Hwang Ji-woo

Republica Poetica

Korea is a peculiar country where poetry is still alive and thriving—as far as I know, an unprecedented phenomenon in civilized societies today. Needless to say, the abundant life of poetry in Korea owes its existence to not only the number of good poets we have but also to the number of highly literate readers who have good sense in poetry. And, I suggest that this is deeply related to the tradition of poetic literacy unique in Korean history.

The illiteracy rate in Korea is today close to zero; it is, one can say, a result of the Korean's high, perhaps often pathologically high, desire for education. The cause of the low illiteracy rate may also be attributed to the Korean phonetic system, developed by an enlightened king in the 15th century; it is, according to linguists, one of the most scientifically devised languages, of which syllables are composed in such a digital way to learn it with great ease. However, be that as it may, one must distinguish literacy in general from one's ability to read poetry. It is one thing to have the competence to read documents from public offices and newspapers, or even to comprehend legal documents and court rulings. But the literacy of poetry is quite differential and very special, because, ultimately, when we talk about poetic literacy we must return to the issue of the reader's taste, an ability to recognize and judge the essence of poetry, or 'what poetry is.' As can be inferred from the famous maxim, *de gustibus non est disputandum*, the sense and appreciation of what is good and bad in poetry are matters of individual taste; it is different among individual readers, and it cannot but be subjective.

At the same time, however, the reader's ability to distinguish what looks like a poem from what is poem — for example, an ability to say "this is, at least, not poetry," looking at what is written like a poem in verses and rhymes, and conversely, an ability to say "this, at least, contains what poetry is" even as to what is written in prosaic form — makes it possible for us to posit the existence of a certain standard of taste that "postulates everyone's consent," in Kantian phrase; the readers also depend on such a standard for developing their taste. In other words, literacy of poetry cannot but presuppose a certain shared universal taste that works as *sensus communis* within a linguistic community. I think here we had better perhaps blur the universality of taste as a matter of degree, because no one can have the last word on what is an absolutely fine poem. The degree of literacy, the ability to read poetry and even enjoy *plaisir du texte*, differs among individuals. Is there not such a difference even within an individual, depending on the period of one's life cycle!

Nevertheless, where there are, as in Korea, social networks of poetry as mentioned above, they could be formed because of, and only when there are, avid exchanges and distribution of the affective contents of a shared poetic literacy that has a certain degree of universality. In other words, the fact that poems are widely read in Korea and that there are intensively activated networks of poetry signifies the presence of a relatively prevalent literacy about poetry within the Korean language community. Of course, the cultivation and propagation of such literacy are channeled through education at school, in particular through studies of the liberal arts and the literature major in colleges and universities, i.e., the cultural institutions of poetry. Undeniably, the knowledge of history and theory of poetic works and traditions does provide us an ability to read and interpret poems. However, some readers, though never taught of how to see them, can respond affectively to what is really poetic on a certain level of aesthetic enjoyment they share; they have, somewhat, intrinsic sensors to sensitively be transmitted and reacted by a poem and make themselves tightly held by the electric current in what poetry is;

they buy poetry books for gift exchanges; and they form informal social nets and build the webs on-line where the spider, poetry, dwells. This kind of literacy is not something that can be learned by simply studying; it is beyond what institutionalized education can afford. In fact, the circles through which poetry travels in Korea today weave a web of literary network made of various social and economic classes, away from the hallowed towers of academia. For example, in 1980's the poet Park No-hae, a factory worker himself, stood for a kind of literary syndicalism that the working class should be no longer a passive reader but a subject of writing about themselves; recently a woman in her 50s, who has worked all her life in one factory after another, debuted as a poet through a newspaper's call for poetry submission and is currently active in poetry circles. Literacy itself in poetry gives us a chance to be a poet.

What then is the cause, or the source, of such a poetry boom and the abundance of poetic life in Korea? The answer to it seems to lie in the special background and circumstances of Korean history, throughout which the social function of poetry was positively and actively embraced.

In Korea, its five thousand year old history was traditionally led by the politics of civilian literacy, unlike in Japan where traditionally the Samurai ruled with "politics by sword." From early on in history, government bureaucrats in Korea were selected based on a system of civil examination. The system was borrowed from China, but the examinations in Korea were quite different from those administered in China. The Chinese examination focused mainly on the knowledge of sacred texts of Confucianism and legal codes, while in Korea the focus was on creative writing of odes. In other words, the Joseon Dynasty, which ruled the country with relative political stability for 500 years, was in short *republica poetica* in which intellectuals with distinguished poetic literacy were in charge of politics as bureaucrats.

"What is political is also poetic, and vice versa" was a proposition that was all too fitting for the poet-politicians of the Joseon Dynasty. For them, poetry was the fastest conductor for communication. It was their poetic sensibility that made it possible for them to sharply read the hidden or untalkable desire of *minjung*, the people, and they tried to reflect such an insightful reading in politics. They possessed the distinctive ability to select and tune language, "a mirror held up to world," and to put it in the best possible form; ultimately, they knew how to maintain harmony between the world and I as a speaker.

Plato argued for the banishment of poets from his ideal state. Unlikely, the Joseon bureaucrats, on the other hand, despite the limitations posed by the historic condition of being part of a Confucius monarchy, dreamed of an ideal state where a certain spirit of poetry would permeate the social order and where a certain *poesie* would replace the frigidity of reason or logos; moreover, throughout the different periods of the Joseon Dynasty's history, which ended in the early 20th century, there were attempts to realize such a dream during their life time.

But before Korea could internally unravel itself from its historic feudal fetters, modernity arrived from without, through the cracks of history, and it meant a loss of history for Koreans. The country was lost, the culture prohibited, the names confiscated, and freedom absent. What modernity brought us were the nightmare and the stinging trauma of Japanese colonialism (1910-1945) and following dictatorship (1948-1992). From this alien and horrible reality of modernity, and from the nadir of the deprivation and void brought on by it, a bonfire that was poetry, with all its striking and splendid tower of light, was ignited; in the long historic shadow, poets in Korea transposed what was deprived and void, and, through poetry, they became instead ardent longings and aspirations. During the 20th century, they have been positioned to function sometimes as the spokespersons for the people dreaming to take their nation back and reunite it, and sometimes as the spokespersons for the yearnings of the citizenry for democracy and freedom.

It is not surprising then, that modern literature in Korea, by its very nature of birth circumstances, could not but be conspicuously involved in clearly political and social projects, longings based on strong expressions of the collective unconsciousness of the society with a relatively high degree of homogeneity. Poetry was at the vanguard of this *telos* and expression. Here, in 'the sad Arctic' of our modern, it carried out its role beyond what was asked of it and performed almost all forms of cultural work: identity formation, community formation, nationalism, and revolutionism. Think about it! When the nation was confiscated and the Japanese language was imposed as the one and only official language, the very act of writing a lyric in Korean, regardless of what it wanted to convey, could not but be a political one; it was a threadbare act at worst, but nevertheless a heroic one for clinging on to the minimum thread of national identity. The Japanese militarists came back victorious from bombing Pearl Harbor and took away the family names of Koreans[1)], traditionally the strongest symbol of self-identity in Korea. At that time, the very act of writing a poem under one's own name connoted a political message that was as strong as any conveyed by the revolutionist literature of KAPF[2)], which advocated national liberation and class struggle under colonialism. Furthermore, taking the poems back to the historic backdrop of young women—sisters and lovers—being shipped away as a slavish prostitution army for the Japanese soldiers raiding China and Southeast Asia, the messages contained in the popular lyrical poems of the period such as the following leave long echoes of emphatic political statements more mesmerizing and scathing than any agitation-propaganda literature.

Thou, pass by in serene blossom
With thy flower-juiced step by step airily
Treading azaleas that I scattered around
On the path thou go through soon
—Kim So-wol, "Azalea"

Or,

Oh, my beloved's lost into shade of fall mounts!
Still never do I let thee be gone.
—Han Yong-un, "Beloved"

---

1) Japan carried out a policy of assimilation in which Koreans were forced to change their names, including the family name, to Japanese early in 1940's.

2)Korea Artista Proletaria Federario is abbreviated to KAPF, which was connected with NAPF in Japan under the same Marxist-Leninist aesthetics in the 1930's to 1940's.

Here, we have to pay attention to the femininity of the lyric speakers common in these poems, to their women-like appealing, weak and depressed voices, because the feminine could be perhaps the most meaningful antithesis and at the same time most potent antibody to the cruel masculinity of the colonialist rulings.

In any case, modern literature in Korea grew up in an environment where writing even a lyrical poem, though dealing with the most trivial, private, and intimate, would still have a political ramification. From the 1930s to the 1980s, this situation created the basic relationship of tension between poetry and politics in Korea. Moreover, under the military dictatorship, whose state authority lacked in legitimacy due to its governing without the consent of the governed, poetry in particular became the womb mothering the political unconscious. Korean modern poetry was, and has been excessively under the weight of reality, and at the very pressure point of that overloading, the proposition that "what is poetic is political, and vice versa" came true. As a consequence, poetic literacy in Korea provided moments of socially critical epiphany, regardless of what the poets intended; in the era when one could not speak freely, poetry was a language in silence, immediately recognizable upon sight like a body gesture of pantomime; it became the voices of the short-wave radio heard from far-reaching distances. Poets were the keepers of the conscience out of which one could "look up to the stars at night without a shame."[3)] Many poets were imprisoned. Among them, Yoon Dong-ju, who died in a jail in Fukuoka, Japan, and Kim Ji-ha, who was imprisoned in the 1970s, are legendary poets in Korea; they were those who turned the cells of the state penal institutions into sanctuaries with mortgages on *Zeitgeist*. The harsher the deprivation became in our brutal times, the clearer the visions poets projected to us by dint of their idealizing what was lacked and absent in us. Holding the lamp that they fueled, we could look around the lost horizon of our modern history. At last, they have made their country in age of need into a 'land of poetry,' well-webbed on its networks, rich in its literacy, and alive in its circulation.

3) Yoon Dong-ju's "Prelude"

My era: Modernity's Sentence Distorted

I was born during the Korean War (1950-1953) and spent most of my formative years under military dictatorship. During the 1960s and 70s, the military dictatorship compressed the 300-year history of the modernization in Europe into a 20-year process in Korea; in fact, the soldiers carried it out, as if it were a military exercise, in advance before the civilian forces started to rise by themselves in growth In the process, I witnessed the two inevitable faces of our modernity; those of the terrifying and the kitsch.

In the construction of our modernity's sentence, the subject was the military, which inherited the colonial military legacy[4)], while we were merely the predicates subjugated to it. The *"Nihongo"* was gone, but we were still those who suffer the sentence of history under the long shadow of colonialism, not yet and never liquidated within the state apparatus. For us, in short, this wrong written sentence meant nothing more than a *fascism from within*, unlike what Europeans experienced from a similar sentence in the 1930s. The fascism of General Park had no manifest exterior for expansion. In actuality, its center was at a tangent of a fascism that had expanded into our interior. General Park turned the periphery from without into a central locus of internal oppression, mastering its use as an absolute apparatus of masochistic power, and mobilizing the entire population, whose sovereignty was suspended, for his modernization project. What came out of this plan was, shall we say, a "contramodernity," an irony of history similarly witnessed in other regions such as Africa, Asia, and Latin America during their de-colonial/post-colonial eras.

Whereas in Europe modernity projects had been based on faith in the reason of the 18th century enlightenment thinkers, and then subsequently, out of fierce criticism of the reasons, resulted in the ramification, compartmentalization and articulation of a whole social world, in South Korea, the military, who jumped into the civilian domain with the remnant forces from the Korean War, became the commanders-in-chief of the modernity imperative; "Do that, then done!" What the fascists had was such blind passion for a "can-do" spirit: They suppressed the natural stirring of the reason in our own brains; the soldiers terribly disliked the critical mind. And they soon turned every sector of the society into army barracks; the parliament was shut down, the press thoroughly controlled, and the arts and literature censored. They themselves planned the economy, raised selectively a few of great enterprises, *jaebeol*, with the milk of special favor of monopoly capitals, and kept the conglomerates subordinated under them in close contact. The routine of everyday life was almost petrified in the chilly fear of chronic marshal law. Needless to mention, indispensable in the center of execution of this state project was the infamous KCIA[5)], which took its panoptic surveillance of the population. The military thus had a monopoly on the power to rule the country and had a near-complete control of the nation. As for the virtues of democracy, all of South Korea was close to a big "gas chamber" in which all forms of freedom were doomed to be suffocated to death.

In short, the modernity I witnessed had the face of terrorism in its nature. It was a "terrible and terrifying" modernity[6)] The Gwangju Uprising of May 1980 was a gruesome mise-en-scène in which the genuine face of this terrible modernity was exposed in the eyes of the entire world. For ten days, the military isolated a city that was demanding freedom instead of marshal law, and highly trained special national troops were dispatched to massacre and humiliate the citizenry. The soldiers who fired the guns turned inward at the time were forever the alienated "other."

From the time I was in elementary school to when I was a graduate student, the general urged a ceaseless assault on the fort, i.e., modernization. Over the years, he left in me an indelible image of himself as a stepfather, the unfamiliar and repressive "Other." My work came into being at a point where my Oedipal relationship began with that paternal power. In a similar manner, I believe that in the cases of my contemporaries, such as the poets Yi Song-bok, Choi Seung-ja, Kim Chong-hwan, Choi Seung-ho, and Kim Hye-sun, their work is also directly or indirectly prompted by an anti-

4) General Park Chung Hee was once an officer of the Japanese army.

5) Korea Central Intelligence Agency.

6) My essay, "Terrible Modernity," 1992.

paternal iconoclasm, repudiating any authority the state might claim as the father.[7)]

One of the most well-known Korean phrases worldwide is *bballi, bballi*.[8)] Hastiness, haphazard administration, and illegal construction practices are the inevitable by-products of the militaristic code for compressed modernization. The rivers became polluted, and the air was replaced by smog. A bridge would suddenly fall down and a large department store in a posh neighborhood would collapse for no apparent reason. Nevertheless, the apartment complexes that began lining both sides of the Han River in Seoul in the 70s spread rapidly throughout the country; smoke belched non-stop from the chimneys of the steel mills coast to coast; and the automobile industry, once thought impossible to build in Korea, began to see manufacturing plants coming up one after another, in competition. It seemed as if the mammoth pulse of the heavy industries were finally supplying the blood of modernity uniformly and rapidly, finally taking a full charge of shaping and regulating our form of life. Apartments and automobiles are probably the two most significant symbols of the modern modus vivendi. They effectively articulate space and add speed to the movement between the spaces. In this sense, they are the executors of modern values.

For a period, the images of our modernity we saw in the contorted mirrors held up by colonialism and military dictatorship had given us the shudders; we were ashamed of what we saw. We lived with this inferiority complex for some time. Whether it was an apartment building or an automobile, what we made seemed to be a tacky imitation, clumsy, vulgar, crass, and crude. In fact, our modernity was all kitsch, whether it was a school, a hospital, a church, a theatre, or a factory.

However, if an unskilled mechanic tinkered around with a broken automobile, taking it apart and putting the parts together in a repeated manner, he would eventually come to understand the "language" of an automobile. In the same manner, in Korea, it was

---

7) My essay, "A Leaf on the Rapid," 2000.

8) "Bballi" is an adverb that can be used as an imperative. It is often meant as in this case to be emphatic, and it means, "Hurry up!"

as if we took apart the syntax of modernity, reshuffled the different parts of it, tried inserting a new phrase or a word, and suddenly we started to recognize the mechanism of its signification. In other words, the Korean automobiles started to become “automatically mobile,” i.e., to work. The language of that car began to make sense. In the act of uttering the sentences of modernity, what was previously nonsensical, polluted, coarse, and shoddy, i.e., all that belonged to the kitsch were cast away. I had called it a “sedimentation of modernity.”[9)]

The phenomenon clearly meant modernity being internalized in Korea; our modern was no longer unfamiliar, awkward, or extraneous. People slept in an apartment, drove their own cars through rush hour traffic to get to work, to earn a living, to incur debt, or to invest in stocks. Should there be a traffic accident, the victims were taken to a hospital, and the surgeries they would have were identical to what one might see in hospitals in New York or Tokyo. The internalization of the modern modus vivendi is criticized by some critics as being a subjugation to the distant origin, or the “other,” that had dispatched or inserted the first sentence of modernity among us. It was either that, or a deepening of uneven development caused by the dependence, they argued.

I believe such a criticism is biased in postulating that what we have is a simulation model between what is original and what is a copy, its double. I agree that the phenomenon appears as such. But I cannot agree with the dichotomy that presupposes superiority of the original. Human history is a history of endless reproduction of copies, and if we were to distinguish the copy from the original, we might as well reduce the civilization back to the Stone Age, or beyond. The language of a Korean automobile might look like a somewhat blurred copy of that of a Western car. But the signification of the Korean car industry started to work, and through the sedimentation process, it now clearly makes sense; Korean cars started to actually run on the streets of South America and Eastern Europe. The Korean shipbuilding industry has closed down the historic shipyard of Göteborg in Sweden. *Hyundai* Automobile started to even compete with major industry brands in the West.

9) Ibid.

And later, in semiconductors, mobile communications, and IT industries, Korea started to catch up with and bypass Japan.

In short, in my generation, the modernity that was internalized through repression, distortion, and refraction began to operate of its own accord. My poetry was energized, whether positively or negatively, precisely by this modernity *in action*. It came from and was, directly related to the political, economic, and cultural dynamics of the predicates of our historical sentences changing them into the possibility of the subject, under the modern conditions that influenced, in its last instance, the very basis of our lives. In particular, the 80s were the time when such dynamics exploded in Korea. It was our modern time, tragic and violent; we were easily hurt and restless with ideals.

The Institution and Function of Poetry, Its Style, and the Osmosis of Tradition

In the 1970s I was an aspiring poetry student, deeply immersed in its spirit. The cognitive map for the literary world at the time was provided by a topographical chart containing mostly *Creation and Criticism* and *Literature and Intellect*, two quarterly literary journals, each representing a coterie of critics, and each having different aesthetic position and attitude. Both journals attracted major writers in their publications, and they became two literary "schools" unto themselves. If the former emphasized the social responsibility of literature, then the latter stressed the inherent autonomy of literature. Their difference provided a fine balance to the overall landscape of Korean literature. These two literary base camps in Korea, today recognized by their initials CC and LI, each have their own publishing houses; they have become cultural institutions, exercising power of literary criticism that has much greater influence than any college lecture halls do. It was through their journals that major writers of our times were published; new poets and fiction writers were discovered through them; and through their publishing houses the writings of such writers were circulated. What is interesting is that the readers are also aware of the difference among them and are divided accordingly, along the line of their preferences for the two camps. In other words, the readers who buy fiction or poetry books from LI tend not to buy those from CC, and buyers of CC books have tendency to ridicule LI readers as having bourgeois tastes.

It is understandable that in the distribution channels of literature, readers are divided into this or that group, according to the social strata to which they belong. It is an example of how "the institutions of various literary activities have differing impacts on the way in which fiction or poetry is consumed." In the case of Korea, it is also true that the different institutions have differing impacts on the way in which fiction or poetry was written. There was a close relationship between literary institutions and the aesthetic styles of the works they published. For example, the works published by CC clearly shared a distinct style, and it could be roughly categorized as that of "critical realism" in a broad sense. The LI style, on the other hand, could be said to have more diversity, but still the different styles had a family-resemblance that emphasized personal introspection and the play of the imaginary. Between these two institutions of literary tendencies, in some cases, a writer would publish a work of one style in CC and of another style in LI, each in accordance to the known style of the journal. Here, clearly, the discursive power of critics was in operation. The writers, who could not but pay attention to how their work will be evaluated by critics, wrote, consciously or unconsciously, according to the known standards of the critics, and the result was certain literary stereotypes and clichés. I could not stand such state of affairs.

The modern Korean literary landscape, from the time it was first introduced in the colonial era, carried with it a mixture of critical trends and literary styles of the West, from realism to modernism, even before the modern conditions for such works were hardly mature in the basis of our social formation. Nevertheless, in the process of going through a series of historic controversies over the roles, functions and their resultant styles of literature—the debate was prompted by KAPF in the 30s, by the proponents of *"engagement literature"* in the 60s, and the coterie of CC and LI in the 70s—a dichotomous distinction between social and autonomous aspects of literature has been maintained to this day.

In 1980, when I began formally publishing my poems, my poetic strategy and style were to dismantle and blur this distinction. Although most of my poetry books were published by LI, if I must declare an allegiance of style for myself, it belongs to neither LI nor CC. Nor does it lie anywhere in the middle of the two.

Just in time, the new military regime of Chun Doo Hwan & Noh Tae Woo came back to Seoul from having suppressed the uprising in Gwangju and consolidated newspapers and broadcasting companies. In the process, CC and LI were both closed down. In the state of such vacuum, I was engrossed in the fundamental proposition that "what is poetic cannot but be political, and what is political needs to be poetic." However, what pumped poetic blood directly into my whole body of poetry was a personal trauma related to my Gwangju experience. That shaped the style of my poems.

I was tortured in prison, and I came to thoroughly understand the incredibility of language itself. Those of you who have been tortured would know, torture is an unremitting and desperate game of language between the torturer, a fucking asshole, and the tortured, who turns into nothing more than a lump of meat. The text of the dialogue between the torturer and the tortured, constructed in a form of painstakingly monotonous Q&A, is a concoction extracted from the painful *signifiants* pressing and twisting the body; the text is hidden from, or absent in, the one-to-one correspondence with the *signifié*; it is a false parchment. It was this language, the text of torture that controlled, ordered, and determined my body and reality. [10)]

After being released from the prison, the reality I had to face as a poet was being enunciated through the very same grammar of torture I had experienced. Amazingly, the party of evil, the new military regime that had saturated itself with the blood of its own people, called itself *Minju jeong-ui-dang*, "The Party of Democracy and Justice." From that very moment on, all discourse of the regime became a grotesque comedy of paradoxes and ironies. The regime had a tight reign over the press, took away the freedom of expression and freedom to think, and thoroughly censored literature and arts.

10) My paper, 1992.

If by fate, I had to live in the same linguistic community and share the same native language with them, the military, the question was "How could I write poetry?" How could I do that when the language, the *langue*, I had to share with them was pre-emptied as an instrument of lies, hypocrisy, disguise, and symbol manipulation?

At least during colonialism, when the very existence of the language and our personal identities were threatened, writing poetry in Korean was a reason enough for it to exist, without having to consider its function "to purify the dialect of tribe." But now I found myself in an era where there was language but no "meaning." 'Noisy silence" controlled all discourse. I asked myself, "Can I write poetry? How?" If "European and American poets have traditionally recognized the link between the clarity and sharpness of public language and the accuracy and credibility of poetic language," in Korea there was now a physiological antagonism between the political and poetic within the same language.

I could not but distrust all forms of public language, and I despaired at the meaning arising out of them. My poetic strategy was to stop, deconstruct, and interrupt the instrumental usages of language, the "source of all kinds of misrepresentation and duplicity." In other words, my strategy was to rupture and to split into pieces the ideological syntax of the public language; by quoting the splinters of the sentence trunk and making them look out of place, I wanted to stop the incredibility of the language turned into an instrument.

For example, using a razor blade, I would randomly cut out newspaper articles and connect together the cut-off sentences from different articles. Sentences thus constructed lacked any context or framework. A space of absence was created on paper, filled with such disjointed sentences. The absence thus created on paper was my poem and its function. I would also take non-poetic speech acts and dress them with poetically charged magnets. Or, I would strip all meaning out of words, put them together in a certain geometric pattern, and create a poetic space with only the reverberation of the sound quality of the words within the given space. I suppose I can say I was somewhat abusive with the use of language. Because what I wanted to express was not allowed to be expressed, I demolished the standardized forms of speech in the narratives of the public sphere, such as the news, advertisements, official statements, notices of reserved army training, epitaphs, almanacs, etc., In turn, I stylized the forms of my destruction. My deconstruction strategy implied on one hand, a momentum to resist and to criticize and, on the other hand, a will to communicate, whatever it took to do so, with those on the other side of the language wall.

And the disfigured form of poetry, under the condition of extreme limitation of expression, was surprisingly quickly communicated to the reader. Poetry was the volatile inflammable, which ignited at the slightest suggestion of a symbol. In return for the historic misfortune of the nation, poetry was blessed in Korea, more than any other genre of literature, in terms of its function, the speed of distribution, and the scope of literacy. And people called the 80s the "era of poetry." Some critics call my poems of the period "disfiguration poetry," or "deconstructionist poetry." Putting aside the issue of whether or not it is appropriate to name my work using such terminology, I must speak on my own behalf that, whatever style my poetry may be called, for me, the inner necessity to write poetry came from the two faces of modernism I witnessed in the 1970s and 80s in South Korea. But, certainly this cannot be true of my poetry only.

My poetry, even in my own eyes, is full of controversies. It looks hypermodern at times, and at other times, protomodern. In September of last year, I had an opportunity to read my poems at *Frauenfelder Lyriktage* in Switzerland, along with Mark Stand from the U.S. and Inger Christensen from Denmark. I noticed that my poetry, translated and read in German for the occasion, passed through the audience, creating a resonance of a certain degree of universality of poetic literacy between the audience and my poetry. On the other hand, when I read my poems here in the U.S. and in South America, some poets have remarked that my poems remind them of haiku. It seems to me that such a comment may come from a misunderstanding caused by the fact that since the Impressionist time Japanese culture has monopolized the landscape of Orientalism for East Asia in the West. My generation in Korea is almost completely ignorant of the Japanese language and culture, since they have been strictly cut off from us since national independence in 1945. Quite on the contrary to what the haiku commentators have said, there is in Korea sijo, a short, standardized form of poetry that perhaps precedes, or even directly or historically influenced, the writings of haiku in Japan. Sijo is still written in Korea. In any case, if one insisted on finding the origin of my poetry among the traditional forms of Korean literature, then I should think that it would be found in *Zen* poetry, rather than in *sijo*.

It is in fact true that, in Korea, the modern literary forms were notably disjointed from the traditional forms of literature, in the process of modernity going through a historic spasm in the country. A number of Korean poets and critics who had a modernity neurosis even argued for a consciously active separation from tradition. On the other hand, some emphasized a creative adaptation of the traditional forms as a means to resist against the neo-colonial reality. For example, the epic ballads of Kim Ji-ha, which frightened the wits out of the military regime, were masterpieces that consciously and purposely embraced the narrative style of pansori, a form of musical story telling in monologue, as dramatic as an opera, both in musical and theatrical aspects. Tradition cannot be wished away, because it permeates through the very biorhythms of our lives. Even in the moments of the last instance of the modern conditions taking root in the foundation of our lives, tradition osmoses in our life forms.

My deconstruction strategy met, in the end, with *Zen* spirit. This is to say that, it is evidence on which one can say that the *Zen* mind itself is deconstructionist. In *Zen* discourse, what is spoken before now is endlessly eradicated and transcended. My poetic deconstruction project, which was to inevitably threat or undermine the existing forms of poetry, always left me one problem; instrumental language must be reduced to its elements and at once what remains must be at least poetic. Then, the question on their residues was "what makes something poetic?", and "what makes language poetry, and how?" After much pondering, I reached a conclusion; what makes poetry is what is poetic.

Tautology voids content. In the same manner, what is poetic is also void of its contents. However, this void is not nothingness. What is poetic does exist in its action. Of course it exists in all good poetry. But the existence of what is poetic is not limited to only poetry. It exists in paintings, in music, in photographs, in figure skating, and in gambling. A music critic has commented that a Debussy played by Baek Geon-woo, a Korean pianist living in France, is "so poetic." The films by Tarkofsky are distended with fully blown expansions of what is poetic. What is poetic exists both inside and outside of language. It appears with ubiquity in the world, with certain suggestions or hints, certain symptoms or gestures, and the flickering of signals. Poetry stands, leaned into a linguistic medium. But, I do not believe that a linguistic creation is in itself poetry. Nor do I believe that a certain mental state—joy, anger, excitement, sadness, and pain—is the seat of poetic appearances. Such mental indexes are merely a response to, or an effect of, what is poetic. What is poetic is not limited to what is emotional. Therefore, what we can say to aspiring, would-be poets today is to first be awaken to what is poetic before attempting to write poetry. Again, poetic literacy is not a linguistic competence but, ultimately, an "awakening" to what is poetic.

In this sense, what is poetic has certain similarities to Zen. First of all, although there is a degree of difference, neither poetry nor Zen entirely trusts language. Of all other forms of art, poetry uses the poorest medium; poetry barely speaks. Meaning in poetry radiates from silence, i.e., from the blank space of what is unspoken, rather than from what is spoken. In Zen meditation, countless thoughts, i.e., concepts and sentences, that occur during the meditation are deleted through a method of "language under erasure"; it endlessly deconstructs language. In Zen, monks use language to grasp the truth in silence, to show what, in fact, cannot be told in language. Poems are then recited as an ending, to wash away any residue from such a preaching. And yet, for meditation, Zen still depends on hwadu, or "meditation topics," certainly a linguistic concept.

There is perhaps a difference of degree, but whether it is poetry or Zen, it throws away the ladder once it reaches the rooftop where the *unspeakable* has a seat. In the lightening rod of that pointed rooftop, a high-pressure electric current flows; a spirit, like a bolt of lightening. The rod would burn us black at contact, radiating a blinding white light of the moment; it is the conductor of celestial flash to the earth, and that perhaps is what poetry is. Whether we call it nirvana or freedom, it is perhaps to reach the unwieldy spirit that makes a leap of consciousness possible, that we, 2,800 years since Homer, continue to read and write poetry, and to even saw boards of poetry out of a seminar such as this.

ENGLISH: A New Babel Tower

Ladies and gentlemen, I've written an impromptu paragraph, which I would like to read to you in Korean. Listen carefully to these strange sounds. Perhaps you may even recognize a few words.

미스터 김은 와이셔츠 칼라 단추를 끼워주려는 아내의 손이 다가오자 얼굴을 돌리며 짜증스럽게 내뱉었다. "아, 냄새."
"어머, 미안해요. 방금 마늘을 만졌더니..." 아내는 곧장 싱크대로 갔다.
그의 돌려진 얼굴을 향해 텔레비전은 텍사스 산 원유가 배럴 당 50달라로 급등했다는 뉴스를 쏴댔다. 그는 소파 위의 노트북을 챙겨들고 현관으로 갔고, 거울 앞에서 넥타이를 바르게 고쳐맸으며 주방 쪽을 향해 큰 소리로 "오늘 좀 늦을 거야." 하고는 아파트를 빠져나왔다. 단지 내 주차장으로 가는 사이, 놀이터 한 켠 물 웅덩이에 역광의 아침 햇살이 눈부시게 빛나는 걸 보면서 호주머니를 뒤지다가 자동차 키를 두고 나왔다는 걸 깨달았다. 그는 핸드폰을 꺼내 들었었다.

Mr. Kim turned his face away from his wife's hands as she tried to button the collar of his shirt. "You smell," he said irritably.

"Oh, I'm sorry. I was chopping garlic," she said and went straight to the sink.

The TV shot the news toward his averted face that Texas crude was approaching $50 a barrel. He gathered up his notebook on the sofa and headed for the hall door. Straightening his tie in the mirror, he shouted toward the kitchen, "I'll be a bit late today" and left the apartment. On his way to the parking lot, the morning sunlight flashing in a puddle in a corner of the playground dazzled him. He felt in his pocket for the keys of the car and suddenly realized he had come out without them. He took out his hand phone.

This paragraph describes a typical scene from a man's daily life in Korea. It contains no less than 14 English words. Some of them can be translated into Korean, but most of them, words like "white shirt," "television," "apartment," "sofa," "notebook," "key" and "hand phone" are used unconsciously; they are part of ordinary language. In a way these words transcend language; they have become part of the fabric of life. In the name of the "modern," they have penetrated into the core of our lives; they wrap our bodies; they have their own mass and heat; we touch them, see them, hear them. No matter how one insists on the purity of the language of the tribe, it is difficult to escape from the power of the sign when it comes to naming things and giving things signification. Whether we want it or not, as long as the basis of our life is controlled in its last instances by such modern conditions, it seems inescapable that spotted sentences and mottled paragraphs made of hybrid words should dominate the language of everyday life. Purists may moan the loss of the national language, but English words are so much a part of the language that newspapers, magazines, and textbooks all use moth eaten ragged draperies. Korean literature today is no exception. The works of our young writers give the impression that they are almost translations. This translationality does not come simply from word hybridization. I have to confess as a writer myself to being disturbed by a strange feeling that when it comes to developing and expanding an idea my sentences are only a shell written in Korean while the inner core is not my own language. Ideas that at one level are clear and refined seem to follow Western patterns so that I feel I am translating rather than writing. These days I deliberately employ archaic styles from pre 19th century times that I detested as a young man, but I cannot evade the impression that I am organizing the writing by unconscious premises.

In 1980 I went to jail during the Gwangju Uprising, and when I got out, I described the experience in a poem called "A Swarm of Flies" which begins:

Parineun nabiga anida

Twenty years later, I wonder if that Korean sentence was not controlled by the English translation:

A fly is not a butterfly

Some years ago I read a piece by Homi Bhabbha in which he describes postcolonial realities by the very interesting coinage *"transnational and translational."* Without the "transit" experience of either study abroad or emigration, I wonder if my cultural location here in Seoul thousands of kilometers from the U.S. is not postcolonial in character?

In autumn 2002 I attended the International Writers Program in Iowa University. Twenty-seven writers from various countries met for two months on a daily basis, discussing fixed themes, engaging in free talks, and reading from their own works in a carnival of literature. These priests in their own native tongues had English as a common language. All spoke fluent English. Without taking into account the Irish writers, there were writers from Israel, Argentina, Brazil, Nigeria, India, Singapore and Russia. All were able to express their ideas and feelings in the new Esperanto called English. They did not appear to be translating; they already were at the heart of the English language experience. The young Nigerian writer not only swayed his shoulders with Anglo-Saxon swagger, but he was able to joke and entertain the crowd, obviously intoxicated by his mastery of the language. I may have felt him to be a little glib but as I listened I couldn't help the absurd feeling "That damned colonialism had its value too." English had become a tower of Babel risen again on the wreck of tribal languages.

Four language heretics sat on the fringe of the tower, either pretending to understand or sitting there with non-plussed expressions: two women novelists from Vietnam and Myanmar, a literary critic from Poland, and me. The Pole seemed very intelligent. Why he could not speak English, or whether he chose not to speak English, I cannot say. We sat at the back at every literary gathering; we grouped together at every party. At a gathering of world writers where English was the only means of communication, not to be able to speak English was like being retarded. Whether from embarrassment or shame we quickly became friends; we had a camaraderie that came from the recognition of common purpose. Ironically when we met we tried to express ourselves in faltering English.

Literacy in English is a mark of status and privilege not just in Korea but throughout the world. The Internet is increasing the imperial power of English. I have studied English since I was thirteen. I suffered under Korea's harsh educational system. In high school the teacher made us memorize the dictionary and conducted word tests on a daily basis. I was beaten for every word I got wrong. Studying philosophy and aesthetics at undergraduate and graduate level, I read in English the works of Wittgenstein, Frege, Quine, Putnam, A. Danto, and G. Dickie. But under Korea's flawed educational system I read these works for the English; it was a deaf-mute system without room for personal thought. In recent years with greater opportunities to meet foreign writers, I feel the need of a greater elegance of expression in speaking with them as a poet. The more I feel this need, the more clotted my English becomes. I am caught in a tangled mass of English nerves.

At the end of the IWP when it was my turn to make a presentation, I said the following: Like Catholicism in the Middle Ages, English has become the universal vehicle of communication. It will be a terrible day if as a result of entering the broad network of communication we allow English to become one dominant super plant that covers the face of the world. A writer may seek to communicate universality with his or her many readers, but there are times when a writer says, "I don't want communication; I have something no one understands and I want to guard it." Just as wild flowers that have not been given a name have the right to exist, so also languages in remote parts of the world that have not a hundred speakers must have their right to be, respected. Every writer has the obligation to make the veins of the language of the tribe stand out and live.

Clock, History and Fate of Individuals

Kim Yeon-soo

1.

Modernity always reminds me of the department store in my home town in the 1970s. I come from a small town called Gimcheon in Gyeonsangbuk-do (Province) in the southeast of Korea. Department stores in those days were found in large cities like Daegu, about an hour travel by train. Everybody has different ideas in what qualifies as department stores. One indicator comes from the reform plans laid out by Dakahashi Yoshio who was appointed as the director of the Japanese department store, Mitsukoshi in 1895. Yoshio who carefully studied the management system of American department stores changed the display method, created a fashion trend for women's apparel, hired employees with high education background and launched active advertisement schemes. Mitsukoshi's management style was introduced to Korea almost in its entirety and what we saw in Korean department stores in those days weren't that different from the Japanese version.

But we kids had our own rule to apply when it came to deciding those that met our standards and those that failed - escalators and elevators. Those that had them were department stores in its own right, those without simply weren't. The latter would fit more into the category of variety stores. So we were dying to find out whether the so-called department store under construction in our hometown really fit the category. The department store which stood right across the street from our home was three stories high and one-level underground. It wasn't gigantic but not bad for a small town. Rumor had it that the department store would have an escalator linking the first and second level and no elevators. I guess the owner of the department store also had the idea that department stores must have escalators, which is why an escalator was installed as an insignia, running only between first and second level too but the other floors.

As Takahashi Yoshio had emphasized, advertisement was the key and the department store had a truly grandiose opening ceremony. The organizers called in entertainers and singers and because of the huge crowd gathered at the store I couldn't even get near the scene and had to listen to the voice of the entertainers shouting through the amplifier at home. The entertainers who came later than scheduled left the scene after about an hour but the crowd remained. The next day and thereafter the department store became our playground. I have to confess that that was the first time I had laid my foot on an escalator. It was pure shock to actually see stairs move. The escalator only moved up from the first to the second level so we had to walk down the stairs next to the escalator. Now the department store management probably was at its wit's end with kids going up the escalator and storming down the stairs all day long (another reason why they should have installed another set coming down!).

After a while, a security guard was hired to guard the escalator. His mission would be to ward off people who came into the store just to ride on the escalator without any intention of buying products. Since grown-ups rarely idled their time riding on escalators, his target was, of course, kids in the neighborhood. So we would ride on the escalators when he was out of sight but would run away when he showed up. At first he didn't take us seriously just feigned to come after us but got annoyed when this routine repeated and would sometimes chase us until he actually caught one of us. Things got so out of hand that the whole neighborhood block often rattled with chase scenes between the guard and the kids. What role did the escalator assume? Was its duty simply to deliver customers from one level to the other? The elevator which gave me my first ride employed a security guard who made kids cry when they were caught which made parents angry enough to protest to the department store. The elevator had several additional functions, so to speak.

As my childhood experiences show, all modern products performed additional roles in addition to its original purpose. And such additional features often played a much more important part in our lives than its intended role. That escalator in my hometown introduced us to department stores. The security guard let us know that people who are eligible to ride the escalator were customers. Being a sensitive child, I understood such rules quickly. I realized that the guard could not chase me out of the store if I looked and behaved like a customer. I had to learn to get on the escalator as gracefully and elegantly like the rich kids who were more than qualified to shop at department stores. The security guard gave me a suspicious look but as long as I did not run down the stairs and take the escalator again, he could not turn me away. I was labeled as a customer.

So I came to be acquainted with window shopping for the first time. There were so many things displayed in the department store, mostly men and women's apparel, accessories, toys, etc. Once as I was going around the corner I came across a sweet scent. It smelled like tropical fruit or a scent of perfume of a young female. I headed towards the source of the aroma and found myself at the imported goods section. Most were from Japan and America, most fascinating nonetheless. One of the merchandises I remember was the sculpture-like pendulum that had a tiny steel rod with steel beads at each end. I would pull one end of the rod upwards and let go and it would spin as if there was no stop. I realize that the law of physics would stop the movement at some point but at that time it looked like it would last forever since it was repeating the same movement. Perhaps the exotic scent and the repeated movement lasting an eternity were my first brush with modernity.

2.

Let me continue with the Mitsukoshi story a bit further. Mitsukoshi had numerous gadgets and facilities to hold customers longer in the department store, one of which is a restaurant inside the department store, a feature seen only in Japan. Exhibitions and lectures were also held. Such features turned department stores into a space representing modernness. A garden on the rooftop of the store is another example. The so-called 'mid-air garden' was first open to the public in 1907. A document on the mid-air garden explains as follows:

"The garden is about 200 square meters located on the roof top of a western architecture and has a pond, a fountain, and plants. A merry-go-round and telescopes were installed to create an atmosphere of a small amusement park."

Mitsukoshi Department Store opened its Seoul branch in 1930. The four-story, one-level underground structure still stands under a different name, Shinsegae Department Store. Mitsukoshi also had an elevator. There was a 'mid-air' garden too. Matsuzakaya Department Store's Asakusa branch in Tokyo which opened around the same time had a small zoo and rides for children and was called "Sportsland." Compared to what Matsuzakay had, pictures of a Mitsukoshi's 'mid-air' garden in Seoul in those days look more like a street café. But as with the experience I had, people in Seoul in those days must have been exposed to a facet of modernity with, of course, a strong aroma of coffee.

Yi Sang, a Korean poet in the 1930's during the modernism era, was fascinated by this new space called department stores and left many pieces related to them. He was especially impressed by its rooftop garden which became an important motif for his writings. One of which is a poem titled 'Exercise.'

> I go up to the rooftop garden perched on the third level which sits on the second level which sits on the first level. I look to the South and North but fail to find anything interesting. So I go down to the third, second, and first level to find the sun fall on the west from the east, coming up again from the east and setting in the west, again coming up again from the east and setting in the west, and when the sun rose again from the east and stood right in the middle of the sky I pulled out my watch which told the accurate time. No matter how hard I tried to convince myself that the watch is not younger than me or that I am not older than the watch, I simply couldn't and thus I ended up smashing the watch on the ground.

I don't know how our invited guests from overseas appreciated this poem but we all admit that it is extremely difficult to grasp the full meaning of Yi Sang's poems. Against the danger of offending those who do not particularly take the liking for Yi Sang's poems, I dare to take another example from his works. This is a poem by Yi Sang titled "AU MAGASIN DE NOUVEAUTES" published in *Joseon and Architecture* in July 1932. It is a widely known poem, famous enough to become a motif for a movie. A part of it goes as follows:

> Autumn in the Orient greeted by the Coty perfume containing the Spring in Marseille
> The zeppelin floating in the clear sky says 'roundworm medicine.'
> Demoiselles mimicking the monkeys in the rooftop garden.
> Rides that race through the round line in a straight line
> A sunset inundated on the number 12 of the watch plate.
> [...]
> Those coming down from above and going up from beneath and coming down from above and going up from beneath are those not going up from beneath and not coming down from above and not going up from beneath and not coming down from above.

The "zeppelin," or an air balloon, is advertising medicine for roundworms. Monkeys indicate that they might have been on display at Mitsukoshi's rooftop garden shortly after. An interesting item in the poem is the Coty perfume and the elevator which are the items that fascinated me in the imported goods section on the second level of my hometown department store. One more example: You need not worry because this time it's a part from his novel *Wings*, not a poem.

> I have no idea where I've been, only that it was broad daylight by the time I reached the rooftop of Mitsukoshi department store several hours later.
>
> I plumped down on the ground and looked back on the twenty six years I have lived. I couldn't give a title to it.

Next is where the protagonist is looking into a gold fish inside a fish tank. So this comes to show you that there was also a fish tank at the rooftop garden. There is one common item that appears in the three examples - the clock. On the rooftop garden Yi Sang invariably looks at that the clock. 'Wings' concludes its story with the following passage.

> Then came the siren announcing the time - high noon. Everyone is flapping their four wings. The glass, steel, marble walls, bank notes and ink all boil excitedly. It is truly the epitome of confusion.
>
> My armpit itches, ah, where my artificial wings were budding. Wings I do not have today, the missing pages of hope and ambition suddenly flashed by like the pages of a dictionary.
>
> I wanted to stop walking and shout,
> Fly again wings.
> Let's fly, fly, fly. One more time.
> Let's fly just this once.

I believe that the clock Yi Sang looked up at the garden was like the ornamental pendulum that repeated its movement at the imported product section on the second level of my hometown department store. It was like the clock that moved according to a set rule. Yi Sang's poems on the rooftop garden at Mitsukoshi tried to tell us that the core of modernity lay in repetitive movement. The siren announcing the arrival of the high noon is its symbol. The siren signals the end of morning work shift. People go out for a meal at the siren. Yi Sang, in other words, was waiting for a new siren that would grant him budding wings which he does not have.

3.

Longitude by Dava Sobel shows well how the invention of the clock opened a new era of exploration overseas. In explaining how he came to write the book, Sobel mentions his childhood experience with the sculpture of the Atlas installed at the Rockefeller Center International Building on the Fifth Avenue in New York City. Atlas holds a sphere with imaginary lines indicating the equator, the zodiac, the Tropic of Cancer, and the Tropic of Capricorn. The latitude can easily be determined through the length of the day, the distance from the sun, and the guiding stars. Knowledge of longitude, on the other hand, requires the exact time at which the ship is located, and the time at which the ship stood at a location whose longitude is known. This is quite a complicated matter, so I suggest you read the book for detailed information.

The point is that efforts have been made to produce an accurate nautical clock. A nautical clock tells you the time and location of where one is standing. Knowing when and where you are allows you to travel anywhere in the world. Without the clock the age of navigation might never have arrived. Nor would the encounter between the East and West have taken place sooner. It would be safe to say that the East first came across the West upon the arrival of Francisco Xavier, a Spanish Jesuit missionary, in Japan in 1549. Thirty three years later in 1582 a group of Japanese boys went on the so-called Tensho Mission to Rome, the beginning of formal recognition of one another.

It is interesting to see what came as a medium that linked the two worlds: the clock. Resource abounds to support such claim. Among the treasures stored in the Toshoku is a gold table clock manufactured in Madrid in 1581. The clock is said to have been a gift from Viscaino to Tokugawa Ieyasu. The wish to receive clocks as a gift from Westerners appears to have been common among Asians during the 16th and 17th centuries. Ruggieri who entered China in 1582 writes as follows:

> As the viceroy appeared hesitant, the judge presented several eyeglasses to the viceroy saying it was my request, saying "The priest will return and present a beautiful steel clock to you once he recovers from his illness." The viceroy seemed delighted to hear that I had remembered my promise and told the judge to make sure I bring a clock on my next visit. It took a long time for me to recover during which the viceroy even wrote me a personal letter to remind me to bring the clock.

The viceroy knew that Father Ruggieri had an alarm clock. He might have sent for Fr. Ruggieri precisely because of the clock since clocks in China in those days were extremely rare. I believe time has come. We have nothing to loose by trying but everything to lose by not.

The viceroy here refers to Jin Seo of Gwangdong and Guangxi. Jin Seo allowed Fr. Ruggieri to enter the country out of greed for the clock. So in December 18, 1582 Fr. Ruggieri leaves Macao and sets his foot on China with a watch and a prism made of Venetian glass as gifts. Fr. Ruggieri writes the following emotional report:

> Behold the grace of God! Entering China, a feat finally achieved after forty years of plight suffered by numerous Jesuit priests beginning with Fr. Francisco Xavier. What was thought as extremely difficult, and even impossible at times, has come true so easily. It's like we're dreaming or enchanted by magic.

The clock first introduced by Westerners brings about significant change in the Chinese society. Fr. Mateo Ricci who later came to China made a list of presents to offer to the Emperor of the Ming Dynasty in 1600. The list, of course, included an alarm clock and glass. The world Atlas is another gift worth mentioning. Jesuit missionaries were granted permission to enter the palace only on two occasions - to repair the alarm clock and to draw the world map. These two items from the West were accepted by the obstinate East. The East understood perfectly well how the modern age came to existence - through navigation aided by these two items. The clock and the map teach us the concept of "now" or the "present times." The East and its people were naive in a way, unable to perceive the despair felt by Yi Sang who realized that there was no way for him to escape from the siren signaling noon.

The world map developed by Mateo Ricci was introduced to Joseon in 1603 through Lee Gwang-jeong, envoy to China. The alarm clock took a bit more time to enter Joseon in 1631 by Jeong Du-won who received the clock as a gift from Fr. Rodriguez, a Jesuit priest, who was on a mission to Christianize Joseon. Included in the gifts was Mateo Ricci's world map. The Jesuit priest to form ties with the highest ranking figure in Joseon was Adam Schall.

Adam Schall introduced the Western world to Joseon's Crown Prince Sohyeon, who was forced to stay in Beijing by the Qing Dynasty as a hostage. Sohyeon later returned to his home country in 1645, along with gifts such as books and items from Adam Schall. One can easily guess that the alarm clock and the world map were included in the gifts.

For this reason, Koreans routinely visited the Catholic church whenever they visited Beijing since the 17th century. Pak Chi-won wrote about his visit to the grave sites of Mateo Ricci and Adam Schall in *Yeoha Ilgi*. Lee Deok-mu wrote in *Ibyeongi* about his failed attempts to climb up the tower on the rooftop of the church. The main purpose of the visit was to watch new gadgetry from the West rather than to quench one's curiosity on Catholicism. In *Dongranseobpil*, Pak Chi-won talks about the string instrument and the alarm clock from Europe. His first experience with the instrument took place at Hong Dae-yong's home June 18, 1772. Hong Dae-yong understood the nature of the gadgetry well. In *Eulbyeongyeonhaengrok*, his account of his visit to Beijing, he says,

> I went ahead and pressed the post a couple of times and feigned to perform a song and dance number at which Ryu Song-ryong slightly smiled. [...] I asked to see other interesting things and Ryu Song-ryong asked me to follow. We came out the gate and reached a house on the West to find a hidden alarm clock there.

This is the part where Hong Dae-yong visits a Catholic church. There he got to play the pipe organ and observe the interiors of a clock tower. Hong Dae-yong first came to Pak Chi-won's mind as he first came to see gadgets. Hong Dae-yong's interest in the pipe organ and the interior of the clock tower stems from his experience of actually making an alarm clock. He met a scientist named Na Gyeong-jeok in 1759 during his visit to Naju. There he made an alarm clock and a celestial globe. The globe they made resembles a great deal the sphere held up by Atlas at the Rockefeller Center International Building on New York City's Fifth Avenue, the one Dava Sobel saw with his father. The sphere on Atlas' shoulder represents the scientific order and the world of eternal repetition which was what the East absorbed from the West. The alarm clock represented all of this.

4.

Gadgets from the West including the alarm clock introduced repetitive movement to Korean society. This accompanied with it a linear perspective of history. According to such perspective the world operates under the mechanism of cause and effect which was precisely what positivists in Korea learned from Mateo Ricci and Adam Schall. Christianity and communism were ideas based on such rule of cause and effect and were introduced to Korea as the perceptual version of Western gadgetry. Intelligentsia in Korea expressed as keen an interest in such philosophical gadgetry as they did alarm clocks. Unlike machines or gadgets, however, philosophy tend not to work under a uniform mechanism because there is no way to confirm the cause and effect on an individual level.

I wrote a short story titled "Pleasantry Not Quite Finished" which tells a story about the globe Pak Chi-won brought from his trip to Beijing. The globe which became a family treasure in the Park family shed light on world politics and revolutionary ideas in the minds of then teenagers such as Kim Ok-kyun, Hong Young-shik, and Park Young-hyo. The globe did not simply show the natural order per se, but a source of change to create a new world and to do away with the old order. Ten years later they start a revolution. The revolution, of course, fails and those who attempted to modernize the nation were either brutally murdered or exiled. On the night of the revolution, Allen, a Christian missionary* made a house call to treat Min Young-ik, a conservative who was attacked. No Chun-gyeong, his interpreter who stayed behind took *The Gospel of Matthew*, a banned book at that time, to his home, read it and became a devout Christian overnight. The conservatives became more receptive to Allen and his ideas after the incident and Allen established the first Western hospital Jejoongwon at the home of Hong Young-Shik who was murdered after the revolution failed. Spreading Christianity through medical service unfolds in Korea afterwards.

Two things drew my attention while I was researching this story. One was that the globe Pak Chi-won brought from Beijing played an important role in producing the first Korean Christian as well as spreading Christianity in the country. The other was that the world order represented by the globe and envisioned by Kim Ok-kyun, Hong Young-shik, and Park Young-hyo failed to materialize on an individual level. The gadgetry or social system of the West that so fascinated Koreans had little effect on the individual lives of Koreans but brought about huge changes on a social level. Korea has evolved nonstop since the 19th century. Korean society was eager to learn the world of cause and effect and has succeeded to a large extent.

On an individual level, however, the rule did not work as efficiently. As the right-wing extremist in Japan put it, perhaps the Japanese colonial rule did indeed open the door to modernization for Korea. Modernization for individuals, however, has been painstakingly slow. The only cause and effect that seemed to work in the eyes of the Korean people in the early 20th century was the law of the jungle. Neither the alarm clock nor the globe offered a glimpse to the order of the universe. If the law of the jungle, or imperialism, is the ruling order of modernization, how is it different from ancient times? Koreans in the 20th century, therefore, actually experienced a setback from the days of Hong Dae-yong, Pak Chi-won, and Lee Deok-mu and witnessed the survival-of-the-fittest aspect of the law of cause and effect. The frustration felt by Yi Sang as he stood in the garden on Mitsukoshi was a recognition of such absurdity which was effectively expressed through the oppressiveness he felt watching the clock. The law of cause and effect, which is sometimes regarded as a blessing by some, is therefore unjustifiable.

Throughout the 20th century, Koreans have done their best to create a world where the principle of causation is governed by natural order rather than by the law of the jungle. Such attempt was made through internalizing Christianity and the philosophy of communism. From a humanistic view point good people get rewarded. At the other end of the spectrum is the attitude, "Succeed if you want to get back at others!" Such is the natural conclusion when we apply the mechanism of the alarm clock, the pipe organ, the elevator, the escalator and the repetitive movement to the history of individuals. In the world of modern mechanized society it is taken for granted that good people should get rewarded. That's what the law of cause and effect says. Nonetheless, the mechanism didn't work properly when applied to individuals. In this respect, the government's effort to review our history in the new millennium is timely. I see this as an effort to introduce modernity to the lives of individuals in Korea, to create a society where the law of cause and effect draws identical results not only for society but also for its members. This would be our final step towards completing the process of modernization. It would also establish a sound identity for Koreans lost in the chaos of war amid the law of the jungle during the past 100 years.

But as a writer, I see this from a viewpoint different from that held by politicians. I am not interested in rationality. Nor am I concerned with good people being rewarded or the history of the law of causation. I am interested in things that are irrational and coincidental. Not in the clock that keeps accurate time, but in the clock that ever so procrastinates in the personal lives of individuals. Yi Sang expressed his interest in the continuous repetition of modern life as "standing right in the middle of the sky I pulled out my watch which told the accurate time. No matter how hard I tried to convince myself that the watch is not younger than me or that I am not older than the watch, I simply couldn't convince myself and thus I ended up smashing the watch on the ground." I feel that it is my duty to salvage those tempted to smash their clocks. I believe such individuals can be understood through the vision of hope I project, the hope that procrastinates unlike the clock in the modern era.

Ernst Bloch once said that human beings live to realize one's hopes. Unlike the relentless ticking of the clock, the time we govern sometimes goes fast and sometimes slow. The escalator and pendulum that fascinated me, the rooftop garden and the clock that infatuated Yi Sang, the alarm clock that captivated the heart of Pak Chi-won, and the Christianity and communism that cast a spell on Koreans under the harsh Japanese colonial rule, all these movements can be understood in the human context. People discovered a small possibility to realize their hopes in such regular movement and such infatuation changed their lives permanently. In most cases, people grew more unhappy. The hour we've been waiting for wasn't the siren that rang at high noon to tell us it's time for lunch but the budding of the wings that we do not possess today. Literature is a genre that lauds such wings to understand individual hopes and console those waiting for their dreams that have yet to be fulfilled. Thus modernity from a literary point of view is different from that viewed from a historical, political or economic perspective.

I am currently planning on a new novel. It's a story of a Korean boy during the Joseon Dynasty whom Céspedes took to Japan. Céspedes was the first Jesuit priest to enter Korea. The boy, known as the son of one of Joseon's highest-ranking officials, attended a seminary under the wings of Céspedes and went to Beijing in 1614 to seek a chance to return to Joseon. His attempts failed and he went back to Japan where he died a martyr. The idea for the novel had been in my mind for a long time, but I was never sure if such a person really did exist. During a recent visit to Japan, after much trouble, I finally laid my hands on a book titled, *El Martirologio Del Japón, and in it, I was able to find his name. In Italian it said "KAŬN Vicente S.J.[46] - coreano - noble, quemodo vivo,"* followed by a brief introduction of the person. I felt as if I was finally granted permission to write a story about this person who burnt at the stake at Nagasaki in 1626.

The logic goes as follows. As with many Koreans in the 20th century the boy had no control over the course of history. Many historical factors played a role in his life from the time he became a Jesuit priest to his martyrdom, and his life took a course that he had not intended. What would have happened had he successfully returned to Joseon? His personal life may have been salvaged to some degree and the fate of Joseon might have been different. But neither took place. The Catholic church regard him as the first priest from Joseon, but as an individual his life barely had any historic implication. If we eliminate the title that has little to do with his personal life such as "the first priest of Joseon," how are we to understand this person? I believe I can understand his life through the hopes and dismay I experience in my daily life. When we look through the lens of time as a personal concept rather than as a modernistic concept, the concept of time perceived by Yi Sang, for example, is not much different from what I perceive as time.

I therefore come to the conclusion that modernity from a literary point of view is individual. Literature is about understanding people, accepting life as it is no matter how absurd it may seem, and understanding the mentality and physical sense of others through my feeling and sense. As long as we're humans, we're all the same, living in the same era. That literature is created individually and that it is read individually have great implications. When we stand alone, we live synchronously. When we understand our own fate, we are living in the same era. Our life is nowhere close to the repetitive movement of the gadgets that fascinates us. Rather it is closer to the river flowing along its path. Sometimes we stumble and sometimes we briskly pass through. But we always go on. That is why I myself and writers before me have all been attracted to machines or gadgets at least once in our lifetime and also precisely why we have the urge to break away from the spell. When we feel isolated we are truly living in the modern age. Solitary individuals can be read by one another. And this is exactly where literature finds its starting point.

Translated by **Kim Hye-young**

*Copy editor's note: Horace Allen was the first missionary/physician from America in Korea. The hospital he founded is now known as Yonsei's Severance Hospital.

Session VIII

Peace and Difference: Gender, Race, Religion

Writing for Peace

Ngugi wa Thiong'o

As a writer, more so, one from Kenya, Africa, I cannot be indifferent to the issues of peace and war. My father escaped conscription into the First World War by faking an illness. Whenever he went for a medical exam, he would chew some herbs to raise his body temperature. Hundreds of African conscripts died in the German East African Campaign against the British. If he had gone to that war he might have met the same fate and I might never have been born. As it is, I was born in 1938, at the start of the Second World War in which I was later to lose my brother, a British soldier fighting for the King, as they used to sing. The war ended only to see Kenya plunge into another war, this time, a war of anti-colonial resistance to end the British settler occupation of more than fifty years. This was the Mau Mau war that broke out in 1952, during the same period as the Korean War. Independence came in 1963 but it was an Independence that came in the midst of the Cold War that made many of the newly independent African countries become battle grounds of the East and West.

Still we were full of hope at what then looked like the dawn of a new era in Africa and the world. There were a few warnings that all was not well and it may have been these that prompted me, as a young writer, in fact then just a college student, to write a paper entitled, *"Kenya: The Two Rifts,"* which was published in *The New African*, a new literary journal that was first published in the early sixties.

In the article, I argued that the new Kenya, like many African countries, had to find a way of overcoming two rifts that I then saw as undermining the stability of new Independence. There was a possible rift between the ethnicities that made up the country, often rooted in regional uneven development, a heritage of colonial practices. But I saw another rift, which later became the subject of my fiction, between the new elite who wielded power and the general population, particularly the working majority. I wrote as if these rifts were obvious and hoped that we would develop an economy, political practices and cultural values and policies that would narrow the two rifts between the different nationalities, and between the social elite at the top and the mass of poor peasants and workers below.

Looking back, I am not so sure from the point of view of the two divisions, whether the world of my childhood was all that different from the world of my children today. True, the colonial world is a thing of the past. The Cold War that saw so many dictatorships thrive, largely because they were supported by the West and seen as loyal allies, is also in the past, at least in form. And the world has seen the most incredible feats of achievement thanks to new technologies that make commodities for a fully fed, fully clothed and housed world possible. The human adventures and breakthroughs in space are also breathtaking. From the point of view of those travelers in space, our earth is truly one. The information technology is also bringing the world together, making regions, hitherto removed from each other, look like neighborhoods.

But the world, seemingly on the verge of a breakthrough in terms of what is possible for uniting humans, is threatened by the two rifts that I once wrote about, which have now become a global phenomenon. I am concerned that in the economic, political and cultural map of the world, a handful of Western nations control over eighty percent of world resources, both human and natural. The world is indeed divided between a handful of creditor nations and hundreds of debtor nations. The irony is that through debts and debt servicing, these poor nations have become net exporters of the capital they so desperately need for their own development. The gap between the wealth of a few 'have' nations, largely grouped around G8, and the poverty of 'have not' nations, largely located in Africa, Asia and South America, is increasing.

But there is in every nation another rift between a minority of social classes who control and consume over eighty percent of the resources within a nation and the majority of social classes within the same nation who scrape the bottom of the barrel. The gap between the rich and the poor has dramatically increased to an alarming magnitude over the post-Cold War era. The figure of the beggar and the homeless found in the street corners of even the most advanced nations is an image of our times. The fastest growing sector in nearly all the nations of the world is the prison population and every nation should do a soul searching before it points an accusing finger at other nations.

What is alarming is not only the existence of the two divisions between and within nations, but a growing culture of their acceptance as norms, even desirable at times as the inevitable consequences of progress and modernity. The result is inverted values. Humans are there for progress but progress is not there for them. We are creating a world in which capital has the freedom to move quickly across the borders of nation states, even making a mockery of such borders, but we erect racist barriers to the movement of labor. In a world that looks as if it is increasingly becoming one, racist and ethnic intolerance has increased. Is it any wonder that there have been massacres of innocents in the name of ethnic cleansing?

There is an increasing deification of the market as the sole arbiter of human economic practices. The deity shows pleasure to his true worshippers by increasing their profit and displeasure by withholding profits. The deity has even disowned all his other sons and left only one, a most intolerant capitalism. The IMF, the World Bank and even the World Trade Organisation, have become like temples and those who depart from the tents of worship are excommunicated. Capitalist fundamentalism and the forces it unleashes becomes a threat to the very modernity its earlier more tolerant form had created. Fundamentalism is when a system, any system, claims that there is only one way of performance and in this case the Market seems to say that there is only one way of worshipping it, through privatization and the abandonment of any social control to the practice of capital.

I see this situation of the two divisions as creating a very unbalanced world, a very dangerous world, a very unstable world, for when nations, big and small, refuse to address and confront the two issues, they will be very busy looking for causes of national and global instability elsewhere.

There are at least three possible responses to the possibilities of peace in the situation of the two divisions. There is the conservative approach – peace through the preservation of the status quo. This is "peace" erected on slavery and it is peace only to the oppressing class or nation. The absurdity of this approach to peace was best articulated by Tolstoy when he talked of the man who is carried on another's back and who will vehemently protest his willingness to do anything to help his victim, everything that is, except getting off his back. The advocates of mere aid-giving are in this category. The basic question is not that of aid or lack of aid to the underdeveloped world, but that of getting off their backs so they can develop a national base for their economy, politics and culture and from which they can interact with other nations and peoples.

There is finally the radical response. This calls for a total transformation of the systems of inequality and oppression in every nation and between nations. Modern industry, science and technology were they not directed toward maintaining inequalities (imagine the billions spent on nuclear and conventional arms!) could transform the lives of millions on earth. As it is, we are now in a world of contradictions. Human technology and ingenuity has created an endless frontier in space and, has created life in genetics, and yet human greed has decreed that there be poverty and disease on earth. We have the means to save life and yet we sit on heaps of weapons of mass destruction pointing an accusing finger at everybody else but ourselves. Poverty between and within nations is no less a weapon of mass dissatisfaction. Insecurity haunts the streets of even the most heavily armed nation. The prison population is the most rapidly growing sector in the wealthiest of nations. I, myself, do not believe that peace is possible in an imperialist dominated world.

Literature provides us with images of the world in which we live. These images shape our consciousness to look at the world in a certain way. Our propensity to action or inaction or a certain kind of action or inaction can be profoundly affected by the way we look at the world. Writing for peace should at the very least mean raising human consciousness to an uncompromising hatred of all exploitative parasitic relations between nations and between peoples within each nation. We must all struggle for a world in which one's cleanliness is not dependent on another's dirt, one's health on another's frailty, and one's welfare on another's misery. Peace is only possible in a world in which the condition of the development of any one nation is the development of all. Globalisation of greed and the means of human destruction should be met with the globalisation of the creed of sanity and human creativity. Now more than ever in human history, communities of different races, faiths, cultures, need to talk, to claim responsibility for their common future rooted in the notion of the sovereignty of the people of the earth.

Writing for peace should mean a constant reminder to humans that we live on the same earth and that any stockpile of weapons of mass destruction by any nation, big or small, is an act of war against the future of humanity. Let all nations turn those weapons into ploughshares. The earth is our communal father and mother as well as its future, and peace is the only guarantor of that common future, our common dream.

Speaking to Silence: Writing Women's War Experiences

Cho Uhn

1. Prologue

As a sociologist, I have been mostly doing fieldwork, thus I hesitated when I was invited to write a paper for the panel "Peace and Discrimination: Gender, Race and Religion" in this writing for peace literature forum. The hesitation is partly due to the fact that this is a "literature forum" but more due to the fact that peace, writing and gender are problematic crossing areas over which my personal and academic concerns are agonizing and no clear thread has spun out of it yet. Therefore, this forum is a space in which my perplexing and not fully developed concerns will be revealed. Instead of approaching the issue of gender, writing and peace theoretically, I will attempt an ethnographic writing on the issue, using personal experience and observation.

I came to read how poor our imagination was regarding peace in the Epilogue of *Women and War (Jeonjaeng kwa yeoseong)*, a collection of oral testimonies of women's experiences during the Korean War and the Vietnam War. The writer of the epilogue, Kim Eun-shil, mentioned an episode during her seminar on women and human rights.[1] She suggested that everyone close their eyes and imagine a world with no violence. At the time, one activist raised a question, "Why do we always conjure up things like flower-covered hills, children playing on those hills, and peaceful skies when asked to imagine peace?" She lamented our shallow

1) Kim Eun-shil, "Sangsangsok-ui pyeonghwa wa hyeonsilsok-ui pyeonnghwa" (Peace in Imagination and Peace in Reality), in Kim Hyun-a, Jeonjaeng gwa yeoseong *(Women and War)* (Yeoreum eondeok, 2004).

imagination and superficiality.

Her question brings us to the question of how we can define peace. If we equate peace with the absence of war, then how does war end? Does the end of a war mean when the opponent surrenders or when the sound of gunfire ceases? Or, is the end of a war defined as no more tears and pain? These questions suggest that we must contextualize peace in concrete terms of war. I contemplate and problematize the issues mentioned above and think that "writing for peace" cannot be different from writing war experiences.

The war is not over on the Korean Peninsula. We have been living for more than fifty years since the war came to a halt. The metonym in Korean for the Korean War is *yuk-i-o**, or 6/25, the day when the war broke out. When truce was declared, over ten million families were separated. In South Korea alone, there were two million casualties, two hundred thousand widows, and one hundred thousand orphans. Missing civilians totaled 303,212 and approximately one million people were killed. The South and the North have since been under constant military threat and have lived with the danger of imminent war. Peace for us is a fantasy-like illusion.

One of the ways in which to survive was to forget and to keep silent. This was not just a simple forgetting and silence, but a method of survival by being incorporated into one-sided silence, one-sided memory, and one-sided narrative. In other words, we have been living in the memory produced by the victors of war, men, and a nationalist imagination in which militarism, anti-communism, pro-Americanism, capitalism, and a patriarchal system became everyday culture. Women have been surrounded by stories the state and men created and relinquished their own memories and desires, accepting and expending stories produced by men and the state. Silence, similar to memory or discourse, is a ground where the mechanism of power relations of society works, and also the ground where new explanations are required at every historical juncture.

The studies of women who survived the Korean War emphasize silence and omission as an important "remembering process." An anthropologist who fifty years after the war studied a so-called red village, "journeying to the past," came to find that war widows excluded stories about their husbands and the time of the people's committees. Women who lived through that period said, "How can we possibly talk about everything that happened during that time?" "What's the point of talking about it now?" "It sure was a despicable time." They did not want to talk. Scholars who collected oral testimonies from former comfort women stated that without reading what has not been spoken, these women's lives could not be fully understood. The scholars expressed that they could not claim to have adequately recorded these women's narratives of deep psychological trauma without having followed pauses and silence. In this sense, silence had been embodied in these women's bodies.

Gendered silence is a topic that one cannot avoid in discussing women and war, as well as a theme that has not been touched upon for a long time. In the context of war, a woman's body is not an individual's but is occupied and destroyed by various symbols and signs. Stories of "defiled women" are silenced. In South Korean society, "stories about women's war experiences" could not be articulated. Recognizing a "problematic situation" suggests that narrativizing silent women's stories is not completely unrelated to expanding peace imagination.

2. Speaking to Silence and Speaking in Silence

1) Remembering and Mothers in War Memories

Studies on the history of the Korean War through oral testimonies began recently. These studies point out that many women who experienced the Korean War possess "mounds of stories" which they could not speak about. These women expressed that they were not able to talk, but even if they were placed in a situation where they could, no one would ask them to speak. These women said, "Who would want to listen? Even my children won't listen."

I am from the generation with memories of the Korean War. I grew up being warned constantly not to "speak a word outside." In South Korean society, where a tradition of disclosing private experience in public space is not established, I contemplated how to unfold personal memories and what kinds of methodologies to use. After much deliberation, I decided to write a novel entitled *House Made of Silence* (*Chimmuk-euro jieun jip*, 2003).

After the publication of *House Made of Silence*, many people who grew up being told "not to speak a word outside" and hearing "stories that were secretly whispered inside the home" but "secrets everyone knew" brought stories to me that they were not able to openly bring up. In their remembering process, "mother's stories" were always present. One woman in her seventies sent me a letter saying that she could finally tell her story. She said that her husband left home during the Korean War and became a "mountain man," meaning a partisan. At the time she was pregnant and went to her relative's home in the midst of gunfire. She gave birth to a son. Three years after the war ended, her husband returned with one leg missing and the other leg injured. "He could neither walk nor stand." The day her husband died, only his artificial leg returned home. The tone of her letter was rather unemotional. She used an epistolary style, a letter to her husband on the anniversary of her husband's death, but the stories she wrote she had never told anyone. Her son sent me a short email saying, "I am delighted that my mother has finally opened up to tell her story which she has never told anyone."

Shortly afterwards, I met her in person. Instead of talking about her husband she told me about her father who went missing the morning of the Yeosu-Suncheon Rebellion (October 19, 1948). After three months and ten days, she went to a police station to claim his dead body, which had been temporarily buried for ten days. When the Yeosu-Suncheon Rebellion occurred, she was seventeen years old. Her mother was near her time of childbirth. Since she was the first daughter of five children it was her responsibility to take care of her younger siblings and to claim her father's dead body. Her mother rushed to get her married off since she herself may die from giving birth. So she was introduced to a man who could support her siblings and got married. It was the man who became a partisan and disappeared to return with one leg missing three years later.

One of the readers was a man in his thirties, who seemed far away from war trauma. He told me about his uncle who went missing during the war. Since his grandmother got remarried this uncle had a different last name. His grandmother was a well-known novelist, but she had never made her story into a novel. Another letter was from a twenty-four year old university student in her senior year. She sent a letter saying that her mother was the first daughter of a poor woman who became a widow at the age of twenty-three during the war and introduced herself as a daughter who spent her childhood under the roof of her stepfather as her mother's "lump." Such stories are common in oral testimonies of war experiences.

One of the Japanese translators of *House Made of Silence* told me of her rather uncommon personal experience. She did not mind revealing her stories using her name. Hwa-su is a second generation Korean-Japanese. Her father was a first generation immigrant, her mother an illegal resident in Japan. Hwa-su's father had crossed to Japan during the Japanese occupation. Her mother was born in Osaka, but returned to her hometown on Jeju Island after liberation. In her late twenties, Hwa-su's mother illegally entered Japan. Since she needed a residence card she married her father, who was then twenty-one years older and had a wife and five children on Jeju. Five years later they got divorced and Hwa-su left Japan and returned to Korea with her father. She lived with her father's first wife and children. Hwa-su's father took pity seeing her mistreated by his wife, thus he took Hwa-su to Seoul and settled there.

Hwa-su's father decided to remarry realizing that his daughter needed someone during her adolescent period. He married a college-educated woman ten years younger than himself. At the time the new wife had a daughter of her own who was a college student in the Japanese language department. The reason why she married Hwa-su's father was because he had offered to help her own daughter with her study in Japan. The four of them became a family and lived together for some years to immigrate to South America at her stepmother's insistence. Several years later Hwa-su's father divorced her stepmother and passed away soon after. They lived as a family once, but now they were scattered and separated. Hwa-su's stepsister now lives in the United States and her stepmother in Korea. Hwa-su has returned to Japan where she has been living since.

While translating *House Made of Silence*, Hwa-su remembered her stepmother, whom she had long forgotten. Heavy silence that enveloped her stepmother and portions of stories that she had heard came to her mind. Her stepmother mentioned in passing about her brother and Marxist books that he had read. Hwa-su did not know that she would recall her stepmother in this manner whom she lived with less than ten years. She had never remembered her and she did not even know that she had remembered her at all. Her stepmother's stories were pieced together like a jigsaw puzzle.

Hwa-su searched for her stepmother's whereabouts in South Korea. When she told her why she had contacted her after ten years of silence, her stepmother began telling her the story. Her stepmother was in her seventies. She said that her family was labeled as "red," thus she could not find a job and could not get married. Her daughter was born out of wedlock. That was why she wanted to leave South Korea after she married Hwa-su's father. After Hwa-su's stepmother told the story, she was grateful for asking, which her real daughter did not even want to hear. She thought she was going to leave this world without telling anyone her story. But now that she was relieved to tell the story and was grateful for it. Then Hwa-su's stepmother said, "I wonder if you would know? The meaning of suffering … trampled life that could not be restored …"

2) Absent Stories of "Sisters"

Who records whose stories is an important task. In this gendered South Korean society, everything is gendered. War is not an exception. To this day, war has been planned by men, carried out by men, and recorded by men. Despite the fact that women too are war victims and survivors, their stories have been erased from the official war documents. And the Korean War and women's stories are mostly recreated and represented by male writers.

In South Korea, male writers who were born around 1940s and those who experienced war in their teens predominantly wrote stories on the Korean War and the division. Writers such as Kim Won-il (b. 1942), Hyon Ki-yong (1941), Hwang Sok-yong (1943), Yi Mun-yol (1948), Cho Jong-rae (1943), Yi Ch'ong-jun (1939), Han Seung-won (1939), Yi Dong-ha (1942), Yun Hunggil (1942), Yi Mungu (1941), and Kim Jooyoung (1939) all experienced the Korean War while in their teens. These writers were praised for creating a space in which to remember the war and the division, exposing a fissure between ordinary life and a false division myth represented by anti-communism and nationalism. Their ceaseless effort to remember the war and the division through "fearful eyes" and "boyhood recollections" signified that the subject of the division was close to being called "fate."

However, female writers of the same generation are difficult to find. Not only are female writers of the same generation difficult to find, but even if there are, they tend to avoid the subject of the war and the division. Pak Wan-so, the only female writer who has continuously dealt with the themes of war and division, is an exception. She was born in 1931. She was a college student, not in her teens when the war broke out. Why do women writers who experienced war in their teens not write about their experiences? Why do they not attempt to remember or explain the war and the division through "girlhood recollections"? Where are the stories of the sisters among those male writers who persistently recounted stories on family history?

Recently I received a letter from a woman in her fifties. Her husband has been living with painful memories of his father who was killed during the Korean War and of his mother who was thrown into the ocean when she followed a leftist who told her he would arrange a meeting with her husband. In her letter she wrote, "My husband, before he enters his hometown village, circles around the vicinity. He massages his chest, then he is finally able to enter." At the end she added, "My youngest sister-in-law lives with the pain of not having gone to school. It took me twenty years to empathize with her. To compensate for what she has missed, I calculated the cost of education from elementary to high school and gave her the money. As I handed her the money, I told her that nothing can be done about the past. With this money she has graduated from high school. I smiled in an attempt to make up for all those years. My husband insisted on continuing with his education; he has received his doctorate degree. What about a woman? It is distressing, but whom can we blame? The country? The ideology? As a woman, my heart went out to her."

These few lines may help us understand why there are not many war stories about women by women themselves. If the male writers' sisters who experienced war in their teens were able to write stories, they might have written completely different stories, about war and the family even if they had experienced the same family history. Then, women would not have been portrayed in war memories mostly as sacrificing mothers, prostitutes, talkative fools, and vain women. When a family became completely fragmented and impoverished, a boy was sent to school and a girl had to support her younger or older brother. The stories about families narrated by male writers metamorphosed into stories of the nation and "the image of family undergoing hardship signifies the loss of the nation." Taking this into consideration, the conception of a strong mother and mythologized motherhood is not strange or uncommon at all.

3) Speaking in Body: Comfort Women Are Speaking

The stories of former Korean comfort women and the writings about them are topics that cannot be avoided when discussing issues concerning gender and writing for peace. At the same time, how to present and approach the comfort women issue is an important yet an extremely difficult task. The moment one utters comfort women as the topic of his or her writing, it is difficult to avoid feeling guilty and burdened.

The word "comfort women" began circulating in the public arena in 1991 when an old woman who was sixty-seven years old at the time revealed herself as a former "comfort woman" with the help of two female scholar-activists. They demanded the Japanese government unveil the truth forty-five years after the end of the Pacific War (Korean War). Not only did the Japanese government attempt to cover up the history of comfort women so too did the

South Korean government. According to one study, between 100,000 and 200,000 Korean women were forced into sexual slavery. These women were offered to the Japanese soldiers as "royal gifts from the emperor." However, stepping forward as a witness was not easy for these women. Among countless victims, it took forty-five years for one witness to come forward to testify.

Testimonies by comfort women reveal politics of gendered silence. One of the reasons why they could not speak about their experience was because no one asked them and they were not given any chance to speak out. Even when they were placed in a situation to speak, they could not easily open themselves up. Speaking about their experiences was too painful and too difficult. Even after half a century, these women in their sixties revealed themselves as former comfort women, yet they could not easily express their trauma.

One woman mustered up the courage to speak out because she no longer had any family members left. Another woman reported secretly fearing that her children would find out. Even in the case where a woman decides to speak, knowing that her secret would be revealed to her neighbors and family members, remembering was a painful process. After she gave her testimony, she said she could not sleep at night. She would be shaken up remembering those days, and could not sleep even if she took sleeping pills.

These women were not even equipped with a proper language to express "mass rape." One woman expressed violation as "I was assaulted" and another woman "I did that thing." Another woman even said, "I accepted customers." These women did not have the language to express and represent their experiences. They were confused and embarrassed not being able to express different parts of their body when they were describing how their body was violated. Scholars who compiled the testimonies of comfort women pointed out that these women's narratives are not complete without reading into what has not been expressed. Without reading their silence and pauses, we cannot claim to have understood their deep traumatic memories. They speak in silence or speak with their body.

People who lived through the colonial era all knew about comfort women, nevertheless the subject was not discussed. It did not attract much attention from the literary realm either. Prior to the public testimony, only two stories on comfort women were available. Kim Jeong-han's novella *A Letter from Okinawa (Okkinawa-eseo on pyeonji)* was published in 1977; five years later *My Mother's Name Was Korean Whore (Emiireum-eun Josenbbi yeotta)* by a woman writer named Yun Jung-mo. These two stories were published before the comfort women issue became a public discourse. After the former comfort women's testimonies were publicized in 1991, no notable literary works dealing with the issue appeared. After Kim Sun-deok gave her first public testimony, more than two hundred former comfort women came out. Collections of their testimonies based on interviews were published one after another. Documentary videos such as "The Murmuring 1" (Najeun moksori 1), "Habitual Sadness" (Najeun moksori 2), "My Own Breathing" (Sumgyeol), and "Silent Voices" (Chimuk-ui sori) were made available for the public to make them aware of the issue. Yet, no important literary works were produced.

What does it mean to write stories about these women who experienced such dramatic events in their lives, more dramatic than a novel? What kind of writing is required to represent and unfold complexities of their lives and their trauma? These questions precisely problematize whether gendered subalterns can speak. It is interesting that writers living in South Korea where comfort women testimonies emerged cannot easily write about them. However, Korean-American writers have produced acclaimed works. In particular, Nora Okja Keller's *Comfort Woman* (1997) and Chang Rae Lee's *Gesture Life* (1999) have been lauded as literary successes. Putting aside literary analyses, these writers began working on their book as soon as they heard the stories, which is an interesting area to be explored.

3. Writing Women's Stories: Purification Rite for Peace

If writing for peace is about making people become aware of the pain, the suffering of the weak, and expanding the sensibility to resist violence, then retelling war stories, writing counter memories that challenge the orthodox history, and breaking the women's silence certainly are the subjects for writing peace. Writing memories of those who have been excluded from the orthodox historiography of war, in particular, reconstructing women's memories and writing women's war experiences, signifies restoring a "usable past" for our subjectivity. The remembering process becomes even more meaningful when it is connected to the process of healing. For women, "not speaking" and being "unable to speak" was a mechanism and their "wisdom" for survival, but silence does not mean healing or resolving the problems. Healing begins when these women are able to speak freely. In this sense, women writing their war experiences signifies a "rite of purification for the dead."

In South Korean society, women in war are subalterns who do not have their own language through which to articulate their traumatic experience. The question then is whether gendered subalterns can speak in the realm of writing women's stories in the context of war. Only recently have we encountered collections of oral testimonies by subalterns. The women's war experiences are represented in a collection of oral testimony, as well. How to write on the topic of subalterns is an important task and an area we need to challenge. The reason why we direct our attention to women's subjectivity is because they have been victimized over and over again; they are the victims of war culture and ideology and are treated as the "other." Looking at war through the eyes of women and interpreting and recording women's experiences filtered through their points of view will elucidate how their experiences have been denied and marginalized. Using the women's language to identify violence as violence and creating a language to resist that violence can help create counter-memory and gain strength. Peace can then materialize.

Writing women's war experiences is still problematizing terrain to bring more question than answers: What is a critical and revolutionary method of storytelling that shakes silence? What does it mean to disclose gendered silence and problems of remembering? What does it mean to record and interpret war memories from the women's points of view? What does writing mean in this context? What is important here is politics rather than the form in which to express their experiences. Writing women's war experiences does not mean that only content matters. Here, writing women's war experiences demands experimenting with feminine/feminist writing. Experimenting with crossing over genres and forms collapsing the boundary between fiction and nonfiction is also required. Revealing women's silence and remembering is a significant area that enables reconstruction of a center and a territory in which we can extricate ourselves from war culture. The reason why we need to pay attention to their language and to the sensibility of a marginalized group is that their sensibility is critical and concrete. The politics of women's writings concerning war experiences and memories is a challenging area, not only in the South Korean literary realm, but it is an unavoidable ground in writing for peace.

Translated by **Jennifer Lee**

*Copy editor's note: the Korean War by date started in 6/25; yuk-i-o, literally six-two-five.

Peace and Difference:
Gender, Race, and the Universal Narrative

Margaret Drabble

When writers are asked to address the subject of 'writing for peace' they assume that they should declare in favour of peace and against war. They also assume that women, in general, are supposed to be more pacific by temperament than men. I am happy, as a woman writer, to assent to both those propositions. But from this first point of bland agreement onwards, we are, if we are honest, plunged into possibilities of disagreement and conflict. Despite all the lip service we pay to peace, we do not seem to be making much progress towards it. The world is not a safer place or a less divided place than it was five years ago, at the time of the first Daesan conference. In practice, it is not clear that we all prefer peace to war.

Many philosophers and political theorists have argued that the condition of war is more natural than the condition of peace. The Canadian neuroscientist, Steven Pinker, provocatively claims in his recent book *The Blank Slate: The Modern Denial of Human Nature* (2002) that there has never been a human society that has not been violent and aggressive. All societies, however simple, however evolved, however amply provided with the means of subsistence, are aggressive. Warfare is natural, peace unnatural. This is because violence is hard-wired and programmed into the genes of man. Not, perhaps, into the genes of woman– but into man. Man is by instinct a war-loving creature. Peace is not a universal value. Peace is an artificial condition, artificially maintained.

One of the writer's tasks is to use words carefully, and to notice when others are using them for propaganda purposes. Large, broad, abstract words like 'peace' and 'freedom' can be used for different purposes, and with very different meanings. George Orwell in

Nineteen Eighty Four (1948) showed us how words can come to mean their opposites, but what we now call the "slipperiness" of words was recognised long before Orwell and Derrida. One of the most telling quotations ever made about peace comes from the Roman historian Tacitus, writing in the first century of the Christian (or Common) era. Tacitus describes the (unsuccessful) invasion of Britain by Julius Caesar and his Roman legions, and he puts into the mouth of a defending patriotic Briton an impassioned speech in favour of repelling the Romans, which ends with the famous attack on Roman imperialism: 'The Romans are unique in being as violently tempted to attack the poor as the wealthy. Robbery, butchery, rapine, with false names they call Empire; and they make a wilderness and call it peace.'

So the power of naming, the conquering power of false naming, has been recognised for at least two thousand years.*

To an invading conqueror, peace can mean a repressed and docile people, whereas to the conquered, it means disenfranchisement. This is as true of cultural invasion as it is of military invasion. In the field of literature, the foe now is not only state censorship– though this still exists in many parts of the world, and there are many Korean writers who have suffered imprisonment because of their work. There is another foe, in the form of invasive mass consumerism, which threatens independent art and literature. It does not censor, it invades, as an alien algae invades an ocean, spreading itself and suffocating native indigenous species. What looks like peace can be the death of difference, the triumph of sameness– a kind of cultural wilderness, where all artistic and cultural distinctions are levelled, or survive in a mutant commercial form, as a kind of airport art, as a version of kitsch.

So I will tread carefully, as I enter the dangerous territory of gender, race and difference. Gender and race are divisive issues– so divisive that the word 'race', proposed for inclusion in the title of this paper, has now become almost unviable, and I thought for some time of substituting the slightly less incendiary term 'nationality' for 'race'. Indignation rises at the very sight of the word 'race'. (I wrote a draft of this paper in a hotel in Philadelphia, on a street called Race Street: the very word looks provocative, on a street sign, or on the page). The existence and nature of racial characteristics and sexual characteristics have been the source of the most impassioned and inflammatory debates– they are the 'hot buttons' of the genetic debate about human nature. The word 'difference' is loaded with danger. Are men and women equal, equal but different, or are they, as some feminists have argued, not different at all?

To some, any acceptance of difference involves acceptance of discrimination and (potentially) of continuing subjugation– the acceptance of some being more equal than others, as Orwell put it. Are Asians different from Africans? Are the English different from the French, the Koreans from the Japanese, the Australians from the Canadians, and if so, in what sense are they different, and how and where, in what forum and in what language, are we allowed to discuss the differences? And what on earth does the ubiquitous word 'Caucasian' mean, as a racial or ethnic classification? Is there any neutral territory where we can meet to discuss difference without coming to blows? Are there any universal values which we can claim, in this post-Enlightenment, post-modern era of multiculturalism and relativism– or has the very notion of the Enlightenment concept of universal human nature and culture been abandoned? President Bush may believe in it, but his endorsement is not very reassuring.

Maybe it is better to accept that we are different, and mutually incomprehensible, and that attempts to understand the opposite sex or to understand other cultures are doomed to failure. (I wonder how that common English phrase, 'the opposite sex', translates into other languages, and whether 'opposition' implies a kind of programmed conflict.) Maybe it is better to stay safe in our own culture, and build high walls around it. Better to remain partitioned, divided. Attempts to cross borders can easily be made to look like aggression, invasion, appropriation. Good fences make good neighbours, said the poet Robert Frost, as every American schoolboy knows. Maybe we should build more fences, not try to visit one another. Peace lies in isolationism. Or so a defeatist might argue.

Let me in turn be provocative. I believe that the issue of gender is not as dangerous as it was ten years ago. It is no longer a battlefield. Feminism, feminist theory, and women's literature have been accepted, and women's studies have taken their place as an important discipline. In much of the world, women have created opportunities and achieved a degree of equality and representation that would have been unimaginable a hundred years ago. This is not lip service: it is a fact. To be sure, there is not yet full equality of income and opportunity, and issues of discrimination are raised almost daily, usually by women but sometimes by aggrieved men. At a meeting I attended recently in England a male author protested strongly about the discriminatory nature of the British Orange Prize for Fiction, which is open to female authors only. (The Orange Prize, sponsored by the Orange telephone network, was founded in 1996, to redress a perceived gender imbalance in awards made for the older and more traditional literary prizes.)

Is the Orange Prize a Ghetto Prize, which encourages rather than discourages discrimination? This is a fair question, but it is the kind of question that will continue to be asked until a sense of equality is achieved. Until then, we will go on counting. In the *Proceedings* of the first Daesan conference, published in 2002, there are 30 participants listed, 26 male, and 4 female. Winners of the Nobel Prize for Literature now number 100, of whom 7 have been women– but we should note that of those seven women, four have been elected within the last fifteen years of the prize's history. And we must also remember that equality is not a matter of prizes, because literary prizes, however powerful as symbols, are a lottery.

By and large, these gender issues no longer arouse intense bitterness. The sisterhood has won the fight. There may be internal power struggles and factions within the sisterhood, as Masao Miyoshi acknowledged in his paper on *Literature, Diversity and Totality* five years ago. He agreed that the literary discourse of feminist studies may be splintered by factionalism or exploited by opportunists, and most of us can think of occasions when factionalism has broken out into academic warfare. Not all women are pacific by temperament: some are highly combative– including, when provoked, myself– and the phrase 'post-feminism' is still contentious. But the movement towards fuller recognition of women's cultural and legal status is, I believe, irreversible. For example, it would be unthinkable, now, in Europe or the United States, to compile a work of biographical reference without an attempt to include a balanced representation of women. In revising *The Oxford Companion to English Literature* for the year 2000, I as editor went out of my way to seek overlooked women authors from earlier periods, and was able to draw on a rich new field of feminist scholarship. Similarly, the new *Dictionary of National Biography*, published in Britain in 2004, made great efforts to include more female lives. So did the *Encyclopedia of Life Writing*, edited by Margaretta Jolly, published in 2002: this two volume work also makes a determined effort to be international, and includes entries on writers from many minority languages, including Korean.

As novelist and as editor I have been fortunate to live through an era when women writers have enjoyed increasing respect, and more opportunities to meet one another. The notion of sisterhood, although it is still met with ridicule in some quarters, is not an empty concept. It exists across the divides of race and nationality and culture. In Asia, in China, in Australia, in Europe, in North and South America, I have met women who were fellow readers and fellow writers, and who have shared with me a fund of common experience and a sense of solidarity. We have been able to recognise one another as friends, allies, colleagues. It was a great pleasure to meet here in 2000 Park Wan-Suh, and subsequently to read her work in translation. This solidarity has not been separatist and sexually exclusive– for most of us also read and admire male authors, and do not discriminate against them– but it does represent a special kind of bonding. We have common interests, common subject matter, and these are now firmly established as a necessary and legitimate part of literary creativity and intellectual discourse.

I believe, optimistically, that the progress of women's emancipation is irreversible. The dark warning in Margaret Atwood's dystopian novel *The Handmaid's Tale* (1985) where women are returned to sexual subjugation and male dominance, will not come to pass. But I feel less optimistic about questions of race, nationality and culture. Here, the fault lines seem to be growing deeper and more dangerous. The world is on heightened alert, and the forces of Orientalism and Occidentalism are more and more violently opposed. Five years ago, many references were made here to Edward Said's enormously influential work, *Orientalism*, and there was much discussion of the ethics and literature of post-colonialism. Edward Said is dead now, but the issues he raised are tragically unresolved. He argued for peace through justice and enlightenment and mutual understanding, but what we have witnessed since his death is a growth of violence, and the triumph of the men of war on both sides.

This line of argument is too dispiriting for me to pursue further: we can all imagine the consequences of our failure to resolve these issues peaceably. There is no point in playing Cassandra, and crying doom. We writers must continue to try to negotiate the problems of multicultural discourse, and to edge our way towards cultural peace and enrichment rather than embittered cultural warfare or a flattened cultural desert.

A meeting such as this gives writers an opportunity for peaceful exploration and interchange. It gives us a rare opportunity to make connections. The English novelist E. M. Forster, in his novel *Howards End* (1910), published four years before the outbreak of Word War One, provided us with the watchword 'Only Connect', and his great novel of cultural misunderstanding, *A Passage to India* (1924), illustrates how wise he was to urge us to do so, and how long and slow the journey to connections between races and cultures would be. Some post-colonial scholars and theorists have made mock of Forster, saying that he 'orientalised' India, and used Asia as a sexual tourist, but these theorists are wrong, and their analyses are partisan and partial. They miss the sombre nature of his Forster's warnings. Zadie Smith, one of Britain's most prominent young multicultural novelists, has praised Forster's explorations of the issues of race. He was a pioneer in the realm of cultural contact, not a profiteer.

Connecting is a slow process, even in the digital age where Korean technology has been so innovative. The Daesan Foundation promotes Korean culture, and it promotes translations into Korean of classic works from other languages. Its multicultural agenda is committed to the crossing of borders. This is a laudable aim, but like all progressive ideas it is beset with difficulties. Introducing cultures to one another is not a simple matter, as the whole history of Orientalism illustrates. Translation may be viewed not as a peaceful negotiation, spreading cultural understanding and mutual respect, but as an act of conquest. The English language itself, as some Koreans writers and scholars have pointed out, is invasive, aggressive, and dangerous. The effects of its current dominance of the Internet are not always beneficial.

Nevertheless, most of us believe that the way forward is through contact, not through isolationist policies and building higher fences. We must believe that, or we would not be here. The bold initiative of the Seoul Conference 2000 may have had many unknown consequences, but its effect on me personally was potentially devastating. It changed my life, and its fall out affected me profoundly during the past five years, and in ways that my hosts can hardly have foreseen. I would like to speak briefly here about the ways in which Writing Across Boundaries affected me and my writing life.

My most recent novel, *The Red Queen: A Transcultural Tragicomedy* is set partly in Korea, and it was originally inspired by my reading the memoirs of the Crown Princess of Korea, who died in 1815 at the age of 80. Her husband died in 1762, but she lived to tell and re-tell his story. I would never have come across this work, in its excellent translation by Professor Haboush, had it not been for the Daesan conference. This story is well known in Korea but not in the West, and I have had to think long and hard about the reasons that compelled me to re-tell it. Some of those are given in the novel and its prologue, and I will not repeat them all here. I was gripped by this narrative, which seemed to me to have a Shakespearean tragic power. It leaped across the borders of time and space, from past to present, from East to West. I felt as though I was reading *Hamlet* or *Macbeth* for the first time, without knowing the ending. The story unfolded for me with obsessive power, and would not leave me. I felt it belonged uniquely both to its writer, and to the world. It was a universal drama. How could this be, when its author during her long life was virtually imprisoned within the palace compound? How had she managed to communicate so directly with a reader who knew nothing of the culture in which she had lived? My novel explores these issues, and attempts to discuss the proposition of the possibility of universal human nature, and of the universal story.

My research into Korean culture, art and literature was, inevitably, superficial. Nevertheless, by reading various versions of the Crown Princess's story, and by trying to understand both her context and her triumph over that context, I became sensitised to Korean references, Korean artefacts, Korean attitudes. My ignorance remains enormous, but at least my curiosity was aroused. I counted Korean references wherever I went. The meetings of East and West have become a fashionable field for scholarship and art history, and the Silk Road a useful and popular metaphor for cultural diffusion. In the autumn of 2004, the Victoria and Albert Museum in London mounted a highly praised exhibition entitled *Encounters: the meeting of Asia and Europe 1500-1800*, which I eagerly attended, although my official 'research' was over, and my novel already published. Imagine my disappointment to find that Korea was represented by one artefact only, amidst a profusion of images from China, Japan and India. Even I, from my very limited knowledge, felt I could have made suggestions to fill that gap.*

To return to the question of the universal narrative, and bonding powers of feminism: the Crown Princess's story, in reaching me and the western readers to whom I hoped to transmit it, crossed from Confucian Korea during the Joseon dynasty to twenty-first century secular Britain. But it did not cross the border of gender. The Crown Princess was a woman, and she wrote as a woman. Maybe that is one of the reasons why she spoke to me so directly. In her narrative, amidst her description of courtly intrigue, factionalism, and violent historical events, she mentions that when she was a child she envied her cousin's red silk skirt. That little splash of colour illumines her narration brilliantly. It is a stroke of narrative genius. Why did she mention it? Did she know that it would authenticate her voice and her witness for centuries to come?

Five years ago, in a brilliant paper on *The Global Market and Literature in the Non-Western World*, Professor Kim Uchang discussed the relationship of Korean literature to 'world literature'–

and by 'world literature', as he says, we usually mean the Western tradition. Here he addresses the contemporary writer's problems with great insight– and an insight that pierced me the more keenly because he uses the egalitarian new convention of the female pronoun, 'she' for 'he', throughout his essay. I quote a paragraph which describes very precisely the working writer's often conscious dilemma:

> One wonders if in any tradition a writer would really bother to write unless there is this possibility of reaching out to universality while remaining paradoxically true to her own unique sense of things. If she presumes too much on this possibility, she is likely to become prophetic, vatic or didactic, but if she remains totally her individual self, she would just be the teller of true stories of a confessional kind (though permeated through and through with stereotypes and clichés furnished by society).

This is profound, and pertinent. The Crown Princess indeed managed to reach out to universality, and to remain true to her own unique sense of her life, her self, and her story. Her story is true and confessional, but it is more than that. It is because she reached out into universality that I was emboldened to adopt her story. I do not know if I had either a right or a duty to do so. But I am convinced that her story belongs to world literature, and that my re-telling it from a twentieth century western perspective no more damages its integrity that do modern dress performances of Shakespeare in Britain, or Shakespearean dramas adapted by Japanese, Chinese, Korean or Indian playwrights or film directors.

Nevertheless, I recognise that the adoption of plots is a highly contentious topic, and it is not always acceptable to plead the rights of the universal narrative. If adopting plots is contentious, how much more so is the adoption of babies. The twentieth century section of my novel includes a section that embodies and dramatises current anxieties about the ethics of cross-cultural adoption of children. Attitudes to adoption itself have changed very greatly in recent decades, in most Western countries, echoing greater sensitivity to the rights of the adopted child and its rights to know its biological parents.

In the old nature-nurture debate, it used to be held that nurture would prevail over nature in most cases, but we no longer believe this: geneticists have demonstrated that nature is far stronger than we used to think, and that even twins separated at birth and reared in different families retain strong psychological as well as physical resemblances. This is the stuff of drama– perhaps one of the best known British adaptations of the plot of the adoption trauma is Mike Leigh's moving film, *Secrets and Lies* (1996). And we remember that the drama of Oedipus unfolded because he was given away for adoption at birth. I suspect that every culture has its adoption myths and legends.

If all adoptions are contentious, how much more so are those that cross the borders of race and nationality– (as in *Secrets and Lies*). These transcultural adoptions are more strictly regulated in the West that they used to be, and now it is almost impossible for a white British couple to adopt a British-born baby from a different ethnic group. The image of predatory parents purchasing and forcing culturally conditioning upon infants from what we used to call the Third World has also been modified, though the practice continues. Five years ago, Elaine Kim in her paper on *Blackness and American Identity in Korean American Literature* discussed the cultural problems of mixed race protagonists in fiction, and alluded to the problems of adoption: 'Thousands of Korean children have been adopted by American families during the past 35 years. Until recently, the adoption story has been one of white American generosity, compassion, and largesse. But now, adoptees are growing up and beginning to speak back in English' (p.301).

My novel is a mixed race novel, questioning its parentage and its rights. It was for this reason that in the second half of the novel I introduce into this largely Korean story an adopted Chinese girl orphan. The image of this child sprang irresistibly into my imagination, as I thought, because of a deeply affecting (though for me casual) real life encounter with such a child. But, watching for the second time recently Zhang Yimou's great film *Judou* (a film which was itself influenced, I suspect, by the novels of Emile Zola and Thomas Hardy) I noted that I had for years also carried in my memory the image of the small, determined, angry illegitimate baby boy in that film, who grows up to avenge himself upon his legal father, his biological father, and his mother. At the back of my mind must have been a query about the legitimacy of adoption, and of the right of adoptees to call for revenge. Sometimes, when we think we are writing for peace, we may be writing for war. Again I ask myself, does that mean that we should risk nothing, and stay at home, in our own square mile of well trodden territory, behind our well built fences? We do not wish to be accused of 'Orientalising' in our literature, or of Westernising' our adopted babies. Perhaps it is safer to take no risks, to exercise self censorship.

As Professor Kim Uchang recognises, the writer is in search not only of the personal, the unique, the detail, the difference. The writer is also in search of similarities, connections, and parallels. What we have in common as human beings becomes more interesting as we grow older, and as, with the acceleration of history, borders become more permeable. It is the balance between these two quests, these two impulses, that demands our hardest effort as artists, and as moral beings. There is a danger that the cross-fertilisation of material and the search for a universal story can end in blandness. We make a bland story and call it an archetype, just as we can make a desert and call it peace: we may include all ingredients, and create a fusion cuisine than has no distinct flavour.

We can see this process in progress in the work of the distinguished Chinese film director I cited earlier, Zhang Yimou, whose latest film, *Hero*, has had much popular success in the West, and was clearly aimed at a global market. *Hero* and its successor, *House of Flying Daggers* are martial arts movies, trading on the box office success of Ang Lee's *Crouching Tiger Hidden Dragon*. Hero is of great visual beauty, but the story line is so simplified that it does not reach the dignity of a universal archetype. Zhang Yimou's earlier films, *(Red Sorghum, Judou, Raise the Red Lantern)* reach universality because they are culture specific, and full of authentic detail. *Hero* lacks authenticity because it aims too narrowly for the universal, and thus converts into kitsch. This is the paradox with which the working artist must contend.*

And, as a paradoxical parenthesis– how strange it is that Taiwanese-born Ang Lee's film version of Jane Austen's *Sense and Sensibility* has proved to be perhaps the best, the most English, and the most authentic of all Jane Austen adaptations. Here is a work that effortlessly crosses boundaries of race and gender, and has pleased the most discriminating of Austen's admirers. The workings of cultural transfusion and dispersal are deeply mysterious and unpredictable.

So, to conclude: I believe that the future is already committed to gender equality. The task now is to recognise that only by embracing the multicultural may we hope to sustain a lasting and flourishing peace. Edward Said, a Palestinian who lived and worked in New York, wrote in English, and is read round the globe, aptly symbolizes the urgent need for cultural understanding and mutual respect. We must reach out, and make connections, and we should not reject the tentative overtures of others to connect with us, when they are made in good faith. Differences need not perish through contact: they can flourish, and produce remarkable new growth. Connection need not be conquest, and peaceful co-existence depends on effort on all sides. Foreign territory is not necessarily enemy territory. Good fences may make good neighbours, but artificial barriers and borders create hostility and paranoia. We must recognise the difference between a neighbourly fence and a brutally fortified frontier.

November 5, 2004

*Note: The Bush doctrine holds that 'moral truth is the same in every culture, in every time, in every place'. From this innocent-sounding universalist proposition, the Bush doctrine slips into a proclamation of the right to use pre-emptive force to establish this universal moral truth. It then concludes with the proposition that 'all peoples have the right to determine their own form of government'. The logic of this circular argument is that of the Roman Empire. 'They make a wilderness and call it peace'.

*Note: A search of the *Dictionary of National Biography* (Oxford University Press 2004) for the words 'Korea' and 'Korean' produced 181 results. Of these, over 90% referred to the activities of British nationals who had been engaged in or were writing about the Korean War. The rare exceptions were a handful of travellers, such as Isabella Bird, or missionaries, or experts on ceramics. These statistics speak for themselves.

*Note: I have not see Quentin Tarantino's kung fu movie, *Kill Bill*, which incorporates Japanese, Chinese and Spanish dialogue: I conform to the pacific female stereotype in being unable to watch Tarantino's excessively violent films.

Gender Discrimination and Below the 38th Parallel: Living in False Peace and in False War

Kim Seung-hee

1. Women Born into a Discourse of Gender Discrimination

No human being is born a clean slate. We are always born into a certain established culture, in other words, into a certain environment. The environment forms that culture and restricts our consciousness, actions, and dreams. For Korean women born in the 1950s, the male-centered Confucian value system has been one of the discourses degrading women.

When I was young, I remember seeing a framed motto at my friends' homes and stores that read "Familial harmony accomplishes all things." This phrase shows that in a traditional society, a harmonious home was most valued. The discourse of a harmonious home makes perfect sense if humans are predicated to be domesticated beings, but seen from a gender perspective, it is a repressive discourse on women. The underlying meaning of "Familial harmony accomplishes all things" is that in order to maintain a peaceful home, women's silence and sacrifice are absolute necessities. The discourse of "Familial harmony accomplishes all things" in a traditional society functions as a mechanism to oppress women's tongues, ears, eyes, hands, and feet. The motto "Familial harmony accomplishes all things" was framed and hung on a wall and women have existed only in silent smiles.

Women are becoming framed pictures.
Like framed still life,
they are silent and peaceful;
like framed family mottos,

they are peaceful and dignified.
Women are quietly selling off their souls.
Made beautiful to make men dream,
pasted over a wallpaper mat,
turned quietly into a framed "Familial harmony accomplishes
all things,"
women hang unnoticed on the wall of the back room.

Could Mona Lisa's smile really be a laugh?
Or perhaps crying?
Is her smile forgiving?
Or does it show betrayal?
I have no way of knowing,
but I can feel the pounding force of a terrifying volcano
under her dark breast,
beneath her mesh clothing, like a shadow.
The volcano—hot as the kitchen of a witch,
that male fantasies cannot make beautiful
or stuff—
makes her smile
in a strange, eternal terror.

She is undefinable,
neither holy woman nor witch.
The great painting of an eternal tornado
can neither be framed nor conquered
as only a mother,
as only a wife.
Love is punishment to a woman.
But a woman is punished
to become a goddess through love.
She frames eternity herself,
commanding the world as her backdrop,
and stands stall.
(From "Between Saint and Witch")

Mona Lisa, wearing black clothes, smiles under the frame

"Familial harmony accomplishes all things." Although it is not certain whether Mona Lisa is smiling or crying, something is disconcerting, as if she has the volcano Mt. Vesuvius hidden in her kitchen. Peace is serene yet insecure and ambiguous below the 5000 watt high voltage cables.

Proverbs such as "Men cannot live with a bear but can live with a fox" and "If the hen clucks, the house is ruined," are male-centered discourses that became shackles restraining women and subverting their desires. How many women have knelt down within the walls of Confucian discourses, deprived of their dreams? Women became martyrs in the religious realm and also became incapacitated in the cultural domain.

2. "The World of Propriety" and Cultural Lies

In a culture where the self is excluded as the "other," establishing subjectivity is like encountering an unknown situation and questioning "why?" Therefore, the social persona and the signification of desire, which is the unconscious, clash violently. One of the reasons why we find the disintegrating self in poems by women poets can be understood in a similar line of reasoning. The unconscious is an impulsive energy that questions and doubts consciousness and is a negative strength that attempts to dismantle a symbolic system of cultural order. The poetics of skepticism in a male-centered society de-centers the male-centered symbolic system when viewed from women's perspectives and works actively in the realm of feminist literature.

Sandra M. Gilbert and Susan Gubar stated that seeing from women's perspective itself is an act of questioning, challenging, doubting, and dismantling the established order. Therefore, it is possible to discuss feminist poems in terms of a poetics of skepticism. This skepticism begins with looking at traditional values that are considered natural or proper with a "skeptical viewpoint." Women poets have vigorously articulated or expressed through texts that things people have considered to be natural are in fact unnatural and even unjust. Therefore, poems by female poets are "poetics of women's skepticism." Women have gained a "will to doubt" unconsciously or pre-consciously, and this will is their attempt to reexamine and reevaluate "lies of consciousness." Feminist literature demystifies lies of consciousness and attempts to reread texts. Women's literature is like looking at "cultural lies" through a magnifying glass and discovering symbols of gender discrimination in the "World of Propriety."

Conflicts produced in a gender discriminating culture are closely tied to the need to reexamine the patriarchal "World of Propriety" we are living in.

When I wake up in the morning, the world is there;
when I wake up in the morning, the World of Propriety is
there.
The World of Propriety properly exists,
and the World of Propriety is properly there.

Why is the World of Propriety always there,
as if where it should properly be?
The World of Propriety is there so properly
that no one can peel away its thick skin:
it is properly there.

Who created the World of Propriety?
The World of Propriety must have been created by proper
people,
people who are capable of creating it properly,
people who would be proper even if they did create it.

Therefore, the World of Propriety is, of course, right.
Because Propriety is always right, of course.
If you were to peel away the skin of the World of Propriety,
you would be hit by the hand of Of Course and be kicked out.
The hands of Propriety are invisible hands, and
yet why are they so properly the hands of Of Course?

In the World of Propriety, I am the only one who is not proper.
I am forever unfamiliar with the World of Propriety

and cannot trust the words of the World of Of Course either.
The World of Of Course, does not
like me at all.

The World of Propriety tames the World of Of Course,
And the World of Of Course tames our world.
Sue the World of Propriety!
Sue the World of Of Course!
The occupying force of sand comes nearer, day by day,
the World of Propriety into which our feet sink all day long.
Not knowing whether we are dead or alive, we trudge with all
our might,
for the heaviest battle in the world is to fight against it.
Before the sand of Of Course sets in concrete
and the prison of Propriety swallows the whole world,
I wish I could hold Propriety and Of Course in my hands
And gobble them up! Chomp! Chomp!
("The Heaviest of Struggles in the World 2")

The "World of Propriety" is constructed with concrete and, therefore, cannot be easily torn down or transformed. One of the most difficult battles is a battle with the "World of Propriety." Common sense always wins. Since taking sides with common sense gives us a sense of security and peace, most people learn to accept common sense as natural and proper. However, women poets need to debunk cultural lies of the "World of Propriety." Through this process they will question their own culture, disagree, and sometimes become bleeding sacrificial offerings.

Everyday we find obituaries in the newspapers. Yet, we do not realize that obituaries are a perfect example of a male-centered Confucian value system that buttresses Korean society and its desire to erase women's existence from the face of the earth. The reason why we do not realize this is because we take it as a natural phenomenon. I wrote two poems regarding newspaper obituaries. One is about the disappearance of an individual; the other is about women in the context of Confucian patriarchal ideology.

Kim Geum-dong (Director, Seoul District Prosecutors Office), Kim Geum-su (Chief Doctor, Seoul Ch'odae Hospital), Kim Geum-nam (Manager, Political Affairs Section, Saehan Newspaper) father's death, Pak Yeong-su (Executive Director, Oseong Products) father-in-law's death—Kim Geum-yeon (Professor, Department of Home Economics at Sehwa Womans University) father's death, Ji Sang-ok (Professor of Political Science at Samsung University) father-in-law's death, Jason Lee (Korean-American, Business) father-in- law's death=on the 7th at 3:30 pm at Severance Hospital, Sincheon. Hearse departs at 9:00 am. 364-8752. Burial ground, the family graveyard.

By the way, who died?
("Korean Way of Death")

Reading this obituary, it is difficult to determine who died. There is no way of knowing the name of the deceased, what he did, or how he died. This obituary tells us who his sons are and their social status and his sons-in-law and their social status. Since the names of three sons-in-law are mentioned, it is obvious or apparent that the deceased is survived by three daughters. However, there is no mention of the daughters' names, except for one daughter, Kim Geum-yeon, who is a university professor. Korean obituaries are like a family tree, delineating men's power networks. Rather than the three daughters who are his own flesh and blood, his sons-in-law are given prominence. Two daughters who are not socially active have been elided. This is the absolute Confucian centered value system. Can we truly say that this obituary is paying respect and mourning for the dead?

Obituary

Yi Sang-jun (Director, Goldline), O Hui-yong (Director, International Family Practice), Son Hui-jun (Namhan Broadcasting), Kim Mun-su (Professor, Dongseo University) mother-in-law's death=In the afternoon on the 4th at Samsung Seoul Hospital. Hearse departs on the 6th at 5:00 am.

People are missing.

Five even!

Maintaining the dignity of a martyr culture,
Gently covering the mouth with a handkerchief is the

Romantic story of a family of phallus god
("Korean Way of Disappearance")

In this poem, there are five invisible characters secretly hidden. It is clear that the mother-in-law of these powerful men is the deceased, but her name is not mentioned anywhere and the daughters' names are missing, too. The lies of gender discrimination in Korean society are written in daily newspapers as if it is natural. An obituary like this demonstrates that if we women are not married to a powerful husband, we will be one of many who will become a missing person.

3. Living like an Onion under the False Peace

There are times when unsaid lies can be truly beautiful. This beauty then is transmitted as established social morals and customs. Looking at cultural lies with doubts or suspicion can be read as a relationship between a married man and woman similar to that of the relationship between the United States and Mexico or between the imperialist and the colonized.

Mexicans say
God is too far away and
America is too close

Women say
God is too far away and
men are too close
("Love 2")

A priest marches waving a censer and
a soldier follows with a sword,
thus begins imperialism

A bride marches waving a bouquet and
a groom follows with white gloves on,
thus ends the wedding

Is it not true that
behind all marriages is imperialism wearing white gloves?
("Love 5—Love Wedding")

There is a saying that "Behind all marriages is imperialism wearing white gloves." This analogy compares the subjectivity of married women with colonial subjects. "Becoming colonial subjects" means discarding one's self and accepting the other. Even in a love marriage between a man and a woman, a power relationship is formed unconsciously and a hierarchy of gender intervenes. That power relationship is similar to that of the United States and Mexico. A power relationship and a gender hierarchy oppress a "nature of love." Regardless of the love of young married couples for each other, the couples suffer due to gender roles created and demanded by culture. A culture that takes gender discrimination as "natural" plays the role of an assailant disrupting and breaking peace of love.

I wrote five linked poems entitled "Peace Diary." What I have expressed in these poems is not limited to the experiences of Korean women. Rather "Peace Diary" is related to existential circumstances of all married women in this world. Television channels are turned on endlessly. My internal existence is cut into pieces and the time passes like an onion being peeled off, fluttering away in the world of fragmented images seen through different channels on the television. If there is peace, it is only a grotesque peace like a "headless body and bodiless head" connecting briefly. Women's existence vanishes like bubbles in this busy everyday life.

Is life like that?
After dinner, as I sit sloppily on a folding chair
peeling onions,
My seven-year-old daughter is stubbornly
flipping here and there through the channels.

Click, click: the screen changes rapidly.
In one scene an actress of delicate and innocent beauty,
mouthing something unintelligible,
is crying under an umbrella;
in another, a detective is investigating a
murder mystery;
in yet another, two rock singers, a young man and a woman
dressed in astronaut's suits,
are singing "O, Palestine, Palestine"
and fill my vision with the stage
of the universe,
filled with fantastic minerals.

O, my body without a head!
O, my head without a body!
Consolation:
the day is growing ominously dark.
Just as no one comes to rescue me,
neither do I go to rescue anyone.
Glancing at the screen jumping from one to another,
I busy my hands peeling onions.
I cannot figure out who the bad guy is
or who the good guy.
So I try watching the detective again.
Just then, a naked woman steps out of
a luxurious bathtub and begins to wash her beautiful hair
in a fragrant commercial for shampoo.

Is life really like that?
In the midst of busily peeling an onion,
I suddenly stop to look
for the onion,
but the onion has disappeared for good:
only the skins are piled up on my lap,
like shreds of faint memories.
This haphazard assembly governs my life
and thus, while floating and flowing

beyond the TV, beyond this world,
beyond the parentheses,
my body without a head
and my head without a body
meet each other as if by some unlucky karma;
a vicious peace!
("Peace Diary 1")

There is a saying that what is most personal is most political. For Koreans, the word "peace" is a dangerous word closely related to political and historical explosions. I was born during the Korean War. Before I was born, my grandparents, who were landowners, were killed by their tenant farmers, who had become followers of leftist ideology. From the mother's womb, I witnessed blood and experienced grief. After I was born, the truce agreement was reached on July 17, 1953. Since then we have been living under the false peace, meaning the "suspended war." Living below the 38th parallel, the symbol of suspended war, and living with fear that this false peace can be destroyed any time, made us realize the meaning of a life of violence and impermanence. In Korean, there is a phrase *"motae sinang,"* (literally, having religious faith from one's mother's womb) which means growing up in a Christian family or a Christian environment. Children who are born in this day and age are born not with "faith" but with "fear." For people who are born with fear, peace is understood as something that is unattainable, never experienced, and a place where they cannot return, like the Garden of Eden. Peace can be more insidious than destruction and explosion in the state of suspended war.

4. Blossoming Peace like Popcorn Popping in a Microwave Oven

We, the armistice generation, are instilled with a consciousness of "transient race" and "fugitive," living with fear that the war has not ended but been temporarily suspended and living crammed below the 38th parallel with landmines. The middle of the peninsula is teeming with landmines. We have not once believed that peace will continue on this land and this land will last forever when South

Korea and North Korea are face to face in hostility.

In the late 1970s, I worked as a journalist for a literary journal. I visited the home of a distinguished writers, husband and wife, both of whom were writers. The moment I walked into the courtyard, I realized the place was untidy. When I entered the living room, I saw bundles strewn about here and there. The atmosphere of the room was that either they had just moved in or they were about to move. I asked the wife, "Are you moving soon?" She answered, "It's been twenty years since I came down from North Korea, but I couldn't break the habit of living like a refugee. If war breaks out, we need to pack everything, right? That's why we have these bundles spread out here and there." Listening to her explanation, I realized that living below the 38th parallel is a life of exodus. Korea is not an island but for the generation who were born during the war and living during the ceasefire, Korea is like an island. Now we can come and go via sea routes to China and Russia, but during the Cold War, due to the wall of ideology and the 38th parallel, we could not even take a step toward the continent. Therefore, the Korean Peninsula was an island.

In my short story entitled "A Gray Whale's Sea Journey," I wrote about living in a space under the ceasefire line:

> I am thinking about Korea in this far away place in California. Korea is like a traditional Korean sock. The ankle of a sock is coiled tightly with threads so that inside the sock is a life where a move to the continent is prohibited. Inside the sock is muggy and fetid and the air is bad, too. Life inside the sock below the ankle, giving off a foul smell and no way of letting the foul smell escape, ends up hating each other.

People living below the 38th parallel with landmines are like swarming insects. They live a precarious life like they are below the guillotine wondering when the blade will hit. From time to time, poets go mad and lose themselves in despair. Or, they openly express their anger toward history as a form of escape and put up a resistance. They also have coped with the suspended war and the false peace of the "guillotine above their head."

The sun
life
death and
I

A musician is like a matchstick
wearing
a mad red hat

Somewhere in a musical score
mines are buried
I know

Before the curtain falls
Let's search for an exit.
("A Sad Quartet")

For people knowing that there are landmines and wondering when these mines will explode, peace is anxiety running through their veins like the 5000-watt high voltage cable. This kind of peace is truly "vicious." In *1984*, George Orwell wrote, "Peace is war, freedom is slavery."

This precarious situation continues today. The dynamics of the international political situation surrounding the two Koreas continues. In this situation peace is nothing but false and vicious, a stifling masochistic tension. Waiting for an imminent war below the 5000-watt high voltage cable ceasefire line is similar to a feeling of exhilaration of self-abandonment where the entire bodily nerves tingle with a numb sensation, boredom, and abnormal nervousness.

In the afternoons when I make popcorn,
I must say that I am awfully bored.
From the horizon in the east
to the horizon in the west,
the stretch of sky is filled as if with laundry.
At noon, once, when I was unemployed,
I emerged from the backdoor of a darkened theater

and was pierced by the numerous death needles of the sun,
shot all at once;
a quiet annihilation
like that shortly after Hiroshima.

"In a saucepan or deep kettle (preferably non-sticking), put half-a-teaspoon of table salt and one-quarter cup of shortenining or cooking oil."

I take out a big, deep-frying pan, turn on the gas range all the way up, and drop two dollops of margarine into the pan. The margarine shudders a while, then spreads out its white hair and dies quietly.

"Heat the oil until it smokes, then toss in two kernels of corn. Continue to heat until they pop."

Following the instructions, I throw the two kernels of corn into the heated pan and give it a try. Like the death of the thirteenth month, the hard kernels of corn blossom and pop with pure-white smiles. They hatch in abundance, to light up the butterflies that twinkle under the roofs of Seoul.

"Cover the bottom of the pan with a single layer of corn. Put in an additional one-third cup of corn and stir or shake the pan."

I quickly turn the bag of popcorn inside out, pouring the corn into the pan, put the glass lid on tight, and quietly watch the wonder of cooking. Ji-won Kim was the woman who wrote, "Cooking according to the directions of a cookbook is peace." It makes her happy, she said, as she has no responsibility. Thumping the clear-glass cover with their whole bodies, the kernels rise up like white flowers in full bloom, like love for the whole world, like enlightenment, like liberation.

"Continue shaking until the popping has finished, then turn off the heat."

I lift the lid and with a big wooden spoon I stir
the piping-hot popcorn blossoms—a bouquet of them, as light as ether—
and put them on a large platter painted blue.
Among the sweet smells of these tempting petals,

a parade of lanterns buoyantly pink
brushes by, as on the day of Buddha's birth.
On the bottom of the large pan,
a few kernels of unpopped corn
look back at me, in gloom.
Well into the lethargy of the afternoon,
their despair and mine
grapple for a moment
as if in an immoral love affair.

I lift my head
to cool my heated breath:
in the dirty-laundry sky of Seoul
my copy of the diary of Hae-cho
hangs like a mushroom cloud in a documentary.
Oh, my! How I wish it would rain tomorrow!
("Peace Diary 5")

People born after the 1950s spend their lives under the perilous 38th parallel. The 38th parallel governs and oppresses everything and suspends everything. We know this is true if we think how our personal freedom and peace were compromised and restricted during the Cold War and by the authoritarian regimes. As mentioned in the poem above, peace under the ceasefire is painful, like kernels popping in frenzy inside a microwave oven. A closed microwave oven door has pushed the Koreans into a dead end street after the armistice. In this extreme situation, in both domestic and international politics, peace is perseverance and self-destruction. Of course from this situation, Catholic suffering, Buddhist salvation, and nihilistic freedom can emerge. However, this is similar to popcorn kernels popping, blooming like flowers, a dangerous explosion of peace. Living under the precarious high voltage cables in gender discrimination and below the 38th parallel, the peace we can enjoy is the moment when the kernels pop and turn into flowers. Is it too cynical or paradoxical to call this peace?

Translated by **Jennifer Lee**

Session IX

Varieties of Western Modernity

The University, the Universe, the World, and "Globalization"

Masao Miyoshi

I. Where We Are

The first two words in the title look connected, and in many serious ways they presumably are in our time. But according to the OED, the word "university" made its appearance around 1300—without a direct and explicit relationship to the idea of the "universe," which began to circulate at a later date. The Latin word for the university, *"universitas,"* meant a community and the early medieval university was often a semiformal community of students and teachers. The *"studium generale"* was also a common term, that is, a generally and "universally"—not locally—authorized degree-granting institution, a guild, throughout Christendom. The Pope was its ultimate authority. The "universe" as we employ the term in our secular age had to await the arrival of humanism and enlightenment, centuries later, with modern cosmology. The history of the university in Medieval Europe was significantly different from its modern version, as I will elaborate later on.[1)]

The relationship between the ideas of the university and of the universe (or even "universal") has never been a stable one throughout history. In fact, even today's university is organized and operated in such a way that the two ideas seem to be significantly remote. In this paper I'd like to examine in what way the university and the universe (and the universal) are, and should be, connected today as we think about them from the perspective of our current

1) For the history of the university in medieval Europe, the most helpful publication is *A History of the University in Europe*, ed. Walter Buegg, Vol. 1, *Universities in the Middle Ages*, ed. H. De Ridder-Symoens (Cambridge University Press: Cambridge, 1992). Throughout this paper, I often depend on the so far published Volumes I, 2, and 3 of this Cambridge *History*. Vol. 4 (that treats 1945-the present) is yet to be published.

economic, social, and environmental "globalization," another word associated with the universe. The consideration of such topics together is hoped to offer suggestions for the future of the now defunct discipline of the humanities.

Let me start out with "globalization." By now a thoroughly over-used but still abused term, globalization was a "new" development, at least during the early 90s, striking some people as a hopeful consequence of the end of the Cold War. Believers celebrated it as true cosmopolitanism, worldwide prosperity, utopia. Big corporations were in the forefront of the welcoming party. They would cast a wide net across national borders, and this seemed to promise an unprecedented great catch. Unlike those directly involved in business and international relations, academic and intellectual critics were wary and skeptical.[2)]

As things have unfolded since, it is clear that globalization, a version of "free trade," is an intensified form of capitalism with brutal results for a large segment of the U.S. as well as the world population. With the collapse of the Soviet economy and the triumph of neoliberalism, industrial and financial capital expanded enormously and circulated both widely and rapidly. Not just capital, but production, markets, and consumption also grew immensely. Communication, information technology, travel, and tourism—that is, "exchange" in a wider sense—also increased at a phenomenal pace. At the same time, as we have also come to understand, globalization did not evolve *globally* at all; it was ruthlessly selective

2) See *Global Culture: Nationalism, Globalization, and Modernity*, ed. Mike Featherstone (London: Sage, 1990); Roland Robertson, *Globalization: Social Theory and Global Culture* (London: Sage, 1992); *Global Visions: Beyond the New World Order*, eds. Jeremy Brecher, John Brown Childs, and Jill Cutler (Boston: South End Press, 1993); Richard J. Barnet and John Cavanagh, *Global Dreams: Imperial Corporations and the New World Order* (New York: Simon and Schuster, 1994); William Greider, *One World, Ready or Not: The Magic Logic of Global Capitalism* (New York: Simon and Schuster, 1997; Saskia Sassen, *Globalization and Its Discontents* (New York: The New Press, 1998); Justin Rosenberg, *The Follies of Globalization Theory* (London: Verso, 2000); *Global Capitalism*, eds., Will Hutton and Anthony Giddens (New York: The New Press, 2000); James H. Mittelman, *The Globalization Syndrome: Transformation and Resistance* (Princeton: Princeton University Press, 2000); Joseph E. Stiglitz, *Globalization and Its Discontents* (New York: Norton, 2002); Leslie Sklair, *Globalization: Capitalism and Its Alternatives*, Third Edition (Oxford: Oxford University Press, 2002). And of course, there are many others. However, it should be noted that despite these reservations, few scholars and intellectuals refused to enjoy the benefits of "globalization" such as an enormous increase in cross-border traffic and exchange.

in expansion and out-sourcing. Only the rich and trained benefited from the increase in production and circulation. Labor suffered heavily as workers lost jobs—the "benefits" that at times reached low-wage regions were often temporary and miniscule, and the workers were placed under brutal working conditions. The poor have been unable to move, stranded geographically and economically. Globalization, maximally exclusive and maximally profit seeking, has led to two important developments, and another, more local but to us as relevant, event: One, an unprecedented gap between the rich and the poor; two, an extraordinary environmental deterioration; three, changes in the nature and function of higher education and culture. The three developments are closely interconnected. The one lesson people have learned from "globalization," albeit at an unimaginably high price, is that everything that happens anywhere is inescapably interconnected, positively or negatively, with everything else and to every other place in the world°™climate change, food production, starvation, human rights violation, fashion and fad, violence, academic freedom, political suppression, war, arts, epidemics, consumption, poverty, wealth, or fundamentalism.

To begin with the gap between the rich and poor, it has dramatically widened both among and within nations. Today, 1.2 billion people in the world live on one (ppp) dollar a day, and nearly three billion people live on two dollars a day or less.[3)]

The gulf between the richest and the poorest nations and regions has also risen immensely. It is difficult to remember that around 1800—before the Industrial Revolution—today's first world and the third were substantially the same in wealth or the ratio was at most less than two to one. During the nineteenth century the gap began to widen: by 1880 the per capita income of the first world was double

3) There are numerous book-length studies on the subject, among which I find the following books helpful: On intra-U.S. inequality: James K. Galbraith, *Created Unequal: The Crisis in American Pay* (New York: Free Press, 1998), Kevin Phillips, *Wealth and Democracy* (New York: Broadway Books, 2002), and Lawrence Mishel, Jared Bernstein, and Heather Boushey, *The State of Working America, 2002/2003* (Ithaca: Cornell University Press, 2003). As to international inequality, Kenneth Pomeranz, *The Great Divergence: China, Europe, and the Making of the Modern World Economy* (Princeton: Princeton University Press, 2000). *The State of Working America* has also an excellent chapter on "International Comparisons."

that of the third; by 1913 the ratio was three to one; by the mid twentieth century it was five to one. As late as 1970, a mere thirty-five years ago, the gap was only seven to one.[4)]

In 2003, at the beginning of the twenty-first century, the ratio of the per capita GDP of the richest countries (Luxembourg, Norway, Switzerland, or the U.S., ppp adjusted[5)]) to the poorest, the sub-Saharan countries, for instance, is 90 to 100 to one, and these figures are becoming nearly meaningless year by year. (The figures change, of course; so does the ranking.) The ratio of 100 to 1 is as hard to understand fully for those who live in the first world as it is to imagine what it is like to live on a dollar or two a day. On the other hand, the poor are well aware of how the rich live, if not in real life, through television, films, and the Internet that have spread everywhere even in the remotest regions.

Within the United States, the gap at the end of the 1990s is about the same as during the Gilded Age, that is, a period preceding the Depression when the inequality in wealth was the greatest in history. The top one percent currently owns 40.1% of national assets, whereas its percent share of American income was 15.8% in 1997. Black households remain poorer than Hispanic and white families. According to a recent report from the Pew Hispanic Center, the median white family in 2002 had assets (home, automobile, cash, etc.) of $88,000, whereas the Hispanic family had one 11th of that amount ($8,000), and the black family had one 14th (a little over $6,000). One third of black families and 26% of Hispanic families had zero assets or were in debt, whereas 11% of white families were in the same predicament. Since 1996 the white family grew richer by 17%, and the Hispanic by 14%, while in the black family wealth fell by 16%.[6)] The assets of the richest compared to the median families throughout history are also interesting: in 1790, the ratio was 4,000 to 1; in 1890, 370,000 to 1; in 1940, 850,000 to 1; and in 1999, 1,416,000 to 1.[7)]

---

4) These figures are from Eric Hobsbaum, *The Age of Empire* (New York: Pantheon, 1987), p. 15. David Landes gives slightly different figures in his *The Wealth and Poverty of Nations* (New York: Norton, 1998), pp. xx and 194. See also Pomeranx, *The Great Divergence*.

5) A recent OECD announcement. *The Economist*, January 22, 2005, p. 104.

6) "Study Says White Families' Wealth Advantage Has Grown," The New York Times, October 18, 2004.

7) Kevin Phillips, *Wealth and Democracy*, p. 38.

Some might argue that the widening gap in wealth distribution is not solely a result of globalization. James K. Galbraith, for one, argues that rising inequality is a result of "bad economic policy" that is, caused by economic, or more specifically "monetary" policy, and he considers globalization a matter of "secondary"[8] importance. Obviously, he is right. Policy changes in the seventies had serious consequences. But the monetary policy of Paul Volcker or Alan Greenspan is also a response to general economic conditions in the world. Besides, Galbraith ignores a similar trend occurring in most other countries where the monetary policy of the United States is not applied. For the foreseeable future, the chances of reversing the trend look less than dim throughout the world.

Government could mediate the domination of the economy by big corporations. In a democratic society, elected officials are presumed to represent all citizens. And yet in the United States now, corporate power has bought and absorbed not only small local business on the Main Streets, but has also grabbed political power in every branch of government. Congress has no will of its own at present and is at the mercy of a White House closely allied with corporate interests. Even the bureaucracy in the executive branch is not responsible to the citizens but solely to the president, as if he were a monarch, as can be seen from Bush's cabinet appointments. Similarly, the judiciary is increasingly answerable to presidential interests. Thus the domestic goals of George W. Bush's second term are privatization of the Social Security system, further reduction of taxes for the rich, the reorganization of the republic into an "ownership society," which in plain terms means a radical reduction or elimination of the safety net for everyone except the rich and the corporate. Environmental regulations are unenforced and dismantled. What is striking about the United States now is that despite the dynastic concentration of power and wealth among the very few, the majority of the people are not showing any sign of resentment or resistance. While the Bush "mandate" was very slight, and the actual vote cast for Bush in the 2004 election was far less than one third (59. 2 million) of the entire voting-age population (well over 200 million), the President can push his

8) *Created Unequal*, pp. 8-9.

agenda—including the unjustified and unpopular war in Iraq°TMwith breezy insouciance, and the citizens either vote against their own interest, or stay home in abject apathy.

Internationally, many of the poorer economies pay more for debt service than for education and health in spite of the devastating spread of HIV/AIDS, making the rich in the north even richer. It is self-evident that for the poor—nearly half the human population—to survive, richer countries must make contributions as well as offer debt relief. In fact, 147 heads of state gathered in 2000 to adopt the Millennium Development Goals that included cutting extreme poverty by half by 2015, and to that end the rich nations agreed in 2002 to donate 0.7% of their GNPs every year. As of now, however, only five nations (Sweden, Norway, Denmark, the Netherlands, and Luxembourg) have fulfilled the promise. The United States gives 0.15% of GNP at present, the lowest in ratio of all the OECD countries. (Most Americans seem convinced that their country is one of the most generous nations, but that is simply erroneous. Even including private contributions—0.06% of GNP—the U.S. donations rank side by side with Greece, which gives the second lowest share, 0.21%.[9]) The donation of 0.7% of GNP is such a trifle as to be meaningless in terms of even the barest possibility of creating a truly "global" economy.

The second serious impact of the "globalized" economy is an alarming environmental deterioration resulting from a totally unprecedented growth of material production and consumption. I don't need to go into detail here about the by now indubitable list of changes that have been taking place on the planet. Depletion of

9) The United Nations Millennium Project is the most comprehensive and up-to-date source of information regarding the world poverty. Jeffrey D. Sachs, the head of UNMP, announced an ambitious and detailed plan to end extreme poverty and save millions of children within a decade in January, 2005. Daphne Eviatar, "Spend $150 Billion Oer Year to Cure World Poverty," The New York Times, November 7, 2004, Nicholas D. Kristof, "Land of Penny Pinchers," The New York Times, January 5, 2005, Celia W. Dugger, "U.N. Proposes Doubling of Aid To Cut Poverty," The New York Times, January 18, 2005, and Maggie Farley, "Ending Extreme Poverty Is Realistic, Economist Tells Us," The Los Angeles Times, January 18, 2005. Of course, the success of the project entirely depends on the contributions by wealthy nations. Doubling aid means from 0.25% to 0.5% of GNP. For comparison, one might remember that the Marshall Plan of 1949-52 gave 2.0% of GNP for the rebuilding of Europe (and the European market for the U.S.).

natural resources, including fossil-based energy sources; accumulation of industrial and biological waste; toxic contamination of the atmosphere, ocean, soil, and, especially, aquifers; the loss of eco diversity; violent and frequent hurricanes and tornados; deforestation and desertification; climate change and flooding; ozone-layer depletion; epidemiological crisis; hunger and famine; excessive urbanization and decline in the quality of life. These developments affect each other: that is, some are causes and effects of other developments. This is perhaps only a partial list, and range of the damage may be even wider. More important, we may have already waited too long. Even if humans change their behavior now, it may already be too late, as some environmentalists have pointed out.[10] I will return to this topic later in connection with future possibilities.

Let me move on to the third, and more limited, development within the "global" economy, the university, which I paired with the universe in my title. For a while after the 60s, the students and faculty believed that the university was traditionally an autonomous

10) World Commission on Environment and Development, *Our Common Future* (New York: Oxford University Press, 1987), Alan Durning, *How Much Is Enough?* (New York: Worldwatch Institute, 1992), Herman E. Daly and John B. Cobb, Jr., *For the Common Good* (Boston: Beacon Press, 1994), Herman E. Daly, *Beyond Growth* (Boston: Beacon Press, 1996), Martha Wackernagel and William Rees, *Our Ecological Footprint: Reducing Human Impact on the Earth* (Gabriola Island: New Society Publishers, 1996), Eric A. Davidson, *You Can't Eat GNP: Economics As If Ecology Mattered* (Cambridge, Mass.: Perseum Publishing, 2000), Partha Dasgupta, *Human Well-Being and the Natural Environment* (Oxford: Oxford University Press, 2001), Lester R. Brown, *Eco-Economy: Building an Economy for the Earth* (New York: W. W. Norton, 2001), Peter Singer, *One World: the Ethics of Globalization* (New Haven: Yale University Press, 2002), Lester R. Brown, *Plan B: Rescuing a Planet Under Stress and a Civilization in Trouble* (New York: W. W. Norton, 2003), Spencer R. Weart, *The Discovery of Global Warming* (Cambridge, Mass.: Harvard University Press, 2003), Martin Rees, *Our Final Hour: A Scientist's Warning: How Terror, Error, and Environmental Disaster Threaten Humankind's Future in This Century—on Earth and Beyond* (New York: Basic Books, 2003), Paul Ehrlich and Anne Ehrlich, *One with Nineveh: Politics, Consumption, and the Human Future* (Wasington, DC: Island Press, 2004). *David Goodstein, Out of Gas* (New York: W. W. Norton, 2004), Paul Roberts, *The End of Oil: On the Edge of a Perilous New World* (New York: Houghton Mifflin, 2004), Ross Gelbspan , *Boiling Point: How Politicians, Big Oil and Coal, Journalists, and Activists Have Fueled the Climate Crisis—and What We Can Do to Avert Disaster* (New York: Basic Books, 2004), Donella Meadows, Jorgen Randers, and Dennis Meadows, *Limits of Growth, The 30-Year Update* (White Rivers Junction, Vermont: Chelsea Green, 2004), James Gustave Spech, *Red Sky at Morning: America and the Crisis of the Global Environment, A Citizen's Agenda for Action* (New Haven: Tale University Press, 2004).

place where scholarship was freely and independently pursued. This faith did not last long. As the tide of the neoliberal economy rose, the original ideal was replaced by the idea of accountability and that, in turn, was replaced by accounting. Furthermore, it is accurate to say that the university had never been really autonomous, from the very beginning of its history.

During ancient Greece, the Sophists who were the main stream of higher education taught for profit, charging an enormous tuition to the sons of the rich who wanted practical training for statecraft, which presumably these teachers could provide.[11] Socrates did not charge any tuition because he wanted to teach only those he found attractive.[12] Plato was wealthy enough not to demand compensation, but he, too, was devoted to the training of the philosopher king in the service of the state.

When the modern European university was established, during the medieval period, its objective was to serve the prince and the bishop. The university was not organized to discover "universal" truth, but rather to promote the "absolute" truth of the church, according to which those on the peripheries and margins were heathens and heretics to be simply dismissed, ignored, or suppressed. During the Renaissance the universities remained conservative and hostile to new ideas. The neo-humanists as well as new scientists had to meet in "academies," i.e., private homes and patrons' palaces outside university campuses. In the Enlightenment, Reason, or the universal truth, appeared to dominate, as Immanuel Kant's last book, *The Conflict of the Faculties* (1798) demonstrates. But even Kant, as both scholar and administrator, accepted the structure of the medieval institution. Furthermore, he did not challenge the authority of the Prussian prince over intellectual matters. By the time Schiller, Fichte, von Humboldt, and Schleiermacher became the intellectual leaders of Germany, the idea of the university was thoroughly nationalized, first as a resistance to Napoleon's occupation of Germany and then developing into nationism and nationalism alongside the general

11) H. I. Marrou, *A History of Education in Antiquity*, tr. George Lamb (Madison: The University of Wisconsin Press: 1956), pp. 48 ff.

12) "Lysis," Plato: *The Collected Dialogues*, ed. Edith Hamilton and Huntington Cairns (New York: Bollingen Foundation, 1961), pp. 146-147. See also Marrou, pp. 30, 44, and 45.

European nation-state formation.

In the nineteenth century, it was the nation-state in need of justification of its colonial and imperial projects that aggressively promoted state ideology through higher education and culture (as J. A. Hobson powerfully argued in 1902, at the height of British imperialism). This nation-statism constructed the humanities and social science disciplines that were centered on the idea of nations administered by the states. From arts to music, philosophy to literature, economics to anthropology, history to geography—higher education was deeply implicated in nationism, if not nationalism. As the industrial revolution advanced, the state of course supported it. The disciplinary division of learning was a condition of specialization and professionalization. At the same time, "discipline" also meant behavioral control, submission to rules and authority. To learn was to become a disciple of a master, and any defiance had to be restrained and punished. Similarly, the disciplinary borders were guarded and the invaders forcibly repelled. Disciplinary separation was supposed to protect scholarly expertise, but in fact it guarded the privilege of a guild. At the bottom of the humanities—and, more generally, of intellectual and vocational training as a whole—lay this construction and reinforcement of the power and authority of the state that supported the guild system. During WWII the mobilization of scientists was crucial to the U.S. victory. Defense research was assigned to the laboratories in and around the universities. The Manhattan Project was the most conspicuous example. During the Cold War the work of scientists was far more expanded and deeply integrated into state projects. The discipline of area studies was invented to guide the state in understanding how to control foreign, especially "remote," counties. National defense played a central role in the development of science and technology, social science and the humanities alike.

"Globalization" has changed much of this nation-state centrality. Now the state is in the service of corporations, especially huge transnational corporations. The state still funds much of university research, both private and public, with taxes paid by the citizens, but the products of such assistance are made available to

13) See my "Ivory Tower in Escrow." (See note 15 below.)

corporations in the form of patents—with the researchers (now called "inventors") and the universities sharing the profits. Since the passage of the Bayh-Dole Patent Act of 1980 especially, research universities and corporations have increasingly merged their goals and activities, raising serious problems of conflict of interest and commitment.[13] Research is not the only aspect of corporatization. The students, another product of higher education, are increasingly trained in practical skills, treated just like any other commodity, and the students are eager to participate in the transaction.

Corporations have also taken over the management of culture. "Culture" is neither a critical activity nor a community practice or expression anymore, but a stimulant for a diffuse desire for consumption, which aims at generating and expanding markets. Thus the humanities are not exempt from corporate encroachment. The curriculum is dominated by the idea of utility. National art, national music, national literature, national history, in short, disciplines in the nation-state-based humanities, no longer energize or inspire students and scholars. Consumer culture triumphs in the name of popular culture. Of course, the state as the administrator of the now weakened and blurred nation is as powerful as ever, but its operation is unapologetically dedicated to business interests. Ditto for creative arts. Novels and poems are still being written, of course, but they are more often than not commercial activities. Further, there are far fewer "serious" readers, critics, and reviewers, as often reported in the media and elsewhere.[14] Literary studies are supplanted by cultural studies that sprang up with "globalization"—and with the rise of theories of difference and identity politics. But even cultural studies are beginning to show signs of exhaustion.[15] Fine arts, too, are rapidly being absorbed into decorative and ornamental design.

---

14) There are numerous books on the decline of literary culture, of course. To take random examples, Andre Schiffrin, *The Business of Books* (London: Verso, 2000), Gabriel Zaid, *So Many Books* (Philadelphia: Paul Dry, 2003).

15) I have written a good deal elsewhere on the corporatization of the university. See, for example, "Sites of Resistance," *boundary 2*, Vol. 22, No. 1 (Spring 1995), 61-84; "Globalization, Culture, and the University," The Cultures of Globalization, eds., Fredric Jameson and Masao Miyoshi (Durham: Duke University Press, 1998), 247-270; "Ivory Tower in Escrow," *boundary 2* (Spring 2000), vol. 27, No. 1 (Spring 2000), 8-50; "Turn to the Planet: Literature, Diversity, and Totality," *Comparative Literature,* vol. 53, no. 4, (Fall 2001), 283-297.

Corporations are no less determined to keep departments of learning and knowledge separate from each other. Discipline (control and training) as practiced by corporations is more effective and thorough than by nation-states. Their instruments are of course different. In addition to "the church, the press, the schools and colleges" that J. A. Hobson listed as the tools of imperialist Britain,[16)] advertisement and careerism are now most conspicuous. Advertisement is omnipresent in everyday life. And all performances in life are now directed to self-promotion. Information is nearly always mixed with promotion or advertisement; universities and colleges encourage it, too—institutionally, academically, and personally. Commodification is so complete that any traveling is now thought of as tourism.[17)] (In several countries a governmental office administers culture and tourism together, as if they were identical.) Finally, discipline works most effectively by turning every specialization and profession into an exclusive and autonomous territory that rejects any inspection and intervention by outsiders. In the humanities as in sciences, scholars are expected to know their own fields and little else, thus virtually prohibiting any general criticism, either of politics, economy, culture, or society.[18)] Fragmentation is so thorough that few realize even the extent of fragmentation itself.

To briefly summarize my picture of "globalization" and its calamitous effects: One, the ever widening gulf in the distribution of wealth and power; two, the environmental catastrophe that is about to visit the planet or already here; three, the transformation of the university as a learning place into a corporate system, and of learning into intellectual property and entertainment. Paradoxically, however, these three disasters might, just might, offer humanity and the planet an unsuspected chance for confronting all these crises in an interconnected fashion.

---

16) *Imperialism* (Ann Arbor: The University of Michigan Press), p. 216.

17) Carolyn Cartier, "Touristed Landscapes/ Seductions of Place," *Seductions of Place: Geographical Perspectives on Globalization and Turisted Landscapes*, eds. Carolyn Cartier and Alan A. Lew (London: Routledge, 2005), pp. 1-19.

18) See, for instance, Carl R. Woese, "A New Biology for a New Century," *Microbiology and Molecular Biology Review*, Vol. 68, No. 2 (June 2004), 173-186. See also James Lovelock in endnote 25 below.

2. Hope Born from No Hope

As I turn to the possibility of entertaining hope in the age of "globalization," I must warn myself that my argument is built on the assumption that the utter hopelessness of this moment, paradoxically, might allow us to begin to imagine some space of hope. Thus, much of what I argue here as the place of hope in relation to the worldwide economic inequity, environmental crisis, and corporatized university is actually not much more than a repetition of what I have presented as the dark moments in history. I am aware of this, but this hope born from hopelessness is far more convincing—at least to me—than the optimistic, wishful, and unachievable options thrown around by, for example, a surprising number of environmentalists.[19] Of course we should vote for politicians who are dedicated to the restoration of equality both nationally and internationally. Of course we must curb consumption and production and preserve natural resources. Of course we should regulate corporations. Of course we should restore the spirit of criticism and cultivation. But how? And where do we begin?

Let me first discuss the environmental problems. Awareness of the crisis began in the early 60s with the publication of Rachel Carson's *Silent Spring*. There were occasional attempts by various U.S. administrations and other governments to face the problems. There were even a few success stories later, such as the halting of the depletion of the ozone layers in the last several years. The current Bush administration, however, radically changed the environmental policy. Bush and his Vice-President ignore the risks facing the entire world in favor of business profits, especially those of the energy industry. The Clinton-Gore regime, too, chose their favorite data and figures in the process of policy making, but they did not edit, revise, fabricate, and conceal major scientific

19) Paul and Anne Ehrlich's *One With Nineveh* (see note 10) is a pessimistic description of the environmental crisis. Toward the end of the book, however, they propose some recommendations. They suggest, for example, political reforms including amendments of the Constitution, prohibition of corporate contributions to political campaigns, new anti-trust laws, etc. Even worse than those fantasies is their proposal of placing the governance of the U.S. "in the hands of carefully selected and monitored specialists" like the Supreme Court and the Federal Reserve System! (pp.299ff)

20) See the IPCC website.

assessments and their own official reports. The nearly universally respected Intergovernmental Panel on Climate Change third assessment report of 2001[20] was dismissed out of hand, and the existent EPA and Energy Department rules and policies have been either ignored or altered. Before the 2004 election, forty-eight Nobel laureate scientists signed a protest against George W. Bush concerning environmental issues.[21] The Environmental Sustainability Index report of January 2005 (compiled by researchers at Yale and Columbia Universities) ranks the United States 45th of 146 countries studied. So how could this extremely hostile anti-environmental policy of the United States give any space to hope for the recovery of the earth and its inhabitants?

My hope—a bizarre word in this context—my hope is that precisely because of Bush and Cheney's incomprehensible irresponsibility and ignorance, even among industrial managers and financial leaders one can begin to see signs of unease and distrust about this administration's policies. As a New York Times headline puts it, "Going For Broke Could Break Bush."[22] Some, though not many, corporate managers are beginning to devise strategies on their own to cope with the imminent risks as well as with their clients' fear. George Soros' active efforts in environment and development are well known. The oil industry and OPEC are of course unlikely to change their course, but even in the oil industry the CEO of British Petroleum now insists the company's name is BP, "Beyond Petroleum." Royal Dutch Shell Oil is investing a large sum in alternative energy resources. To take a few more examples, American Electric Power, the largest electricity generator in the United States and a top emitter of carbon dioxide, has pledged to reduce emission from its plants 10 percent by 2010. Chevron is enforcing stringent environmental rules in its local operations in Indochina, as reported by Jared Diamond. Even General Motors says it has achieved its target of a 10 percent reduction in North

21) Andrew C. Revkin, "Bush VS. The Laureates: How Science Became a Partisan Issue," The New York Times, October 19, 2004.

22) Nicholas Confessore, February 6, 2005.

23) Mark Landler, "Mixed Feelings as Kyoto Pact Takes Effect," The New York Times, February 16, 2005, and Jared Diamond, Collapse: How Societies Choose To Fall or Succeed (New York: Viking, 2005), pp. 446-452. The city of Portland has decided to embrace the Kyoto Protocol on its own, and many corporations seem being attracted to the city.

American plant emission from 2000 to 2005.[23] Of course, BP or Chevron is not environmentally friendly, nor are the products of General Motors adjusted in mindfulness of their environmental effects. They all continue to explore and exploit on a huge scale for oil and natural gas. Yet the companies are beginning to recognize that serious efforts, not just public relations, help their business. While Detroit (including General Motors) persists in manufacturing SUVs and Hummers and the White House continues to give them its blessings, German and Japanese manufactures are committed to producing alternative fuel cars and cutting carbon dioxide and other greenhouse gas emission. This is not necessarily out of environmental concern, but may well be a profit-motivated project. They believe that the alternative energy-operated automobile has a good future prospect. The technology developed as they manufacture hybrid or electric cars can be sold later as intellectual property. The U.S. auto industry will be buying patents from Germany and Japan rather than oil from Saudi Arabia!

Perhaps more important, economists are beginning to examine seriously how to internalize the "externalities." That is, those factors that have been consistently excluded from consideration in the manufacture process such as environmental costs and "non-economic" factors are being brought into the purview of economics. One remembers that only a few years ago, Lawrence H. Summers, now the President of Harvard, then the chief economist of the World Bank, dismissed the introduction of ecology into economics as "worthless."[24] Of course, Meadows and others, Herman E. Daly and John B. Cobb, Jr., Eric A. Davidson, Lester R. Brown and others have been thinking about the ecological economy for several decades (see endnote 10). But more recently, even the mainstream economists (not "environmental" economists) are beginning to discuss ecological and environmental issues.[25] There is little doubt

24) Herman E. Daly, *Beyond Growth*, pp. 6-7.

25) Kenneth Arrow, Partha Dasgupta, Lawrence Goulder, Gretchen Daily, Paul Ehrlich, Geoffrey Heal, Simon Levin, Karl-Goran Maler, Stephen Schneider, David Starrett, and Brian Walker, "Are We Consuming Too Much?" *Journal of Economic Perspectives*, Vol. 18, No. 3, Summer 2004, 147-172.

26) Few recall that John Stuart Mill thought about the "stationary state" economy in his early book, *Principles of Political Economy* (1848), *Complete Works*, ed. J. M. Robson (London: Oxford University Press, 1965-91), vol. 3, 706-756.

that if economics is integrated with ecology, the whole structure of production and consumption, growth and stasis,[26)] including the pricing and wage-setting system will have to be fundamentally altered. And a changed structure will also have to consider the quality of life. What is a good life, what do we live for, what do we really want—topics that have been forgotten and have not been raised often for generations. And this re-organization of studies and thoughts may well lead to a general shift in people's attitude toward the earth's health.

While the "global" economy is not global, the environmental crisis is truly global. The rich will continue to try to escape from pollution and contamination, and they can afford to design an escape. But exclusive and permanent escape is an absurd illusion. The global linkage of the environmental crisis is in fact the key to my hope. Once people realize that there is no way avoiding the omnipresent crisis, even the rich will be forced to face it. How soon the encounter is going to take place, and in what way—that is a more crucial question, contingent on other developments in the economy and society.

Thus this logic of true globality seamlessly leads to the second critical aspect of the neoliberal economy, the have/have-not division that now splits the world. Moral injustice is obvious to nearly everyone, but the ethical discourse that has continued ever since the emergence of poverty several thousand years ago at the invention of agriculture promises very little at this point. The well to do will ignore the sufferings of the poor as long as they can keep distant from them and as long as they can keep the poor under control. However, when the poor reach a breaking point (which they are rapidly approaching), they will try to close this gap with rage and force. One quarter or more of the human population now has no clean water and decent food and shelter, and the number is getting bigger, as has been described earlier. They know very well how the rich live, in obscene opulence and wastefulness.

The bridge over this gulf will take various forms. Hunger and deprivation breed diseases and epidemics (such as HIV/AIDS, Ebola, Marburg virus, avian flu (H5N1), West Nile Virus, and many others). Few people would intentionally spread epidemics, but epidemics do break out even in developed regions. And the rich cannot quarantine all the poor and sick forever. There are too many planned and unplanned contacts between the disparate groups. To survive, the poor need to, for example, clear tropic woods and rain forests, and often they burn trees and bushes. At times, the fire spreads out of control as it did in 1997 in Southeast Asia and in 1991 in the Gulf War. The smoke and ashes traveled far on both occasions, reaching Hawaii and beyond. As the poor in Brazil destroy tropical forests for raising cattle, settlements, or other uses, the pharmaceutical and agricultural companies in the first world lose the vast profits they might make from the acts of biopiracy.

Perhaps the most precipitous form of the encounter is what preoccupies the leaders of the United States and United Kingdom at present: terrorism. It is easy to dismiss terrorism as a criminal and self-destructive act of radical Islamist fanatics, crazed and contagious, which will exhaust itself in time. But terrorism is perhaps better understood when placed in the context of the confrontation with the hegemonic economy by the desperate oppositions who have neither high-tech weaponry nor state support. Lester Pearson, a former prime minister of Canada, once said: "A planet cannot, any more than a country, survive half slave, and half free, half engulfed in misery, half careening along toward the supposed joys of almost unlimited consumption. Neither our ecology nor our morality could survive such contrasts."[27)] He said this in 1969, and during the 36 years since, the conditions of the poor have far worsened in comparative and absolute terms. If the view of terrorism as a confrontation of the disconnected halves is right, the only conclusion is that such terrorist attacks will not be likely to cease until the halves are connected. Since terrorism is not a state project, developed nations have no way of waging a conventional war against it, as they can witness daily in Iraq, Afghanistan, Israel, and elsewhere. Nuclear bombs and Tomahawk missiles will be useless in terrorist, guerrilla, or insurgency warfare. Am I arguing, then, that terrorism is an effective solution of the twenty-first century global contradictions? I don't believe that. Terrorism is unacceptable; innocent civilians should not be

---

27) Paul Ehrlich and Anne Ehrlich, *One with Nineveh*, p. 234.

wantonly murdered. One does recall, however, that after the First World War, the idea of "total war" prevailed, and all citizens of an enemy country were presumed to be enemies. In Dresden, Hamburg, Nanjing, Hiroshima, Nagasaki, and Tokyo, mass murder of civilians was committed repeatedly during WWII. And few have condemned these mass slaughters as war crimes or violations of human rights. It seems inevitable that the rich will remain in fear of terrorist attacks on their comfort and security, as long as they refuse to abandon the monopoly of wealth and indulgence and to share the earth's plenitude with the rest of the world. The current U.S. policy of the "global war on terror" means a fundamental transformation of the economy and law into an undefined security system (anywhere, anytime, and anywise). And it is more than likely to induce more terrorist assaults as well as endangerment of democracy in the United States itself. The point then is the restoration of wealth equality in the entire world to the conditions that prevailed before the nineteenth century. The planet as a whole, its population in its entirety, is finally emerging as the only viable imagery for all of us.

The third consequence of the global catastrophe is less significant in scale, although it is immediately relevant to those who live and practice in the university in the industrialized countries. The importance of culture and the humanities as tools for the nation-state projects lasted well into the mid twentieth century, as I have already mentioned. The decline began with fundamental skepticism about the idea of totality, authority, and centrality alongside the decline of nation-statism. It was replaced in a fairly brief period by the ideology of difference, especially as the old colonies began to gain independence. Edward Said's anti-Orientalism was one of the movements emanating from this challenge, joined soon by gender, ethnic, and popular-culture studies, which were advanced in the spirit of justice, equality, and liberation. Difference and diversity have been axial for several decades by now. What has gradually emerged from this initially liberating movement, however, is social and intellectual fragmentation. Socially, it coincided with the neoliberal development, as has been discussed, for instance, by David Harvey in his *New Imperialism* and forthcoming

Neoliberalism. Intellectually and institutionally, it has encouraged and has been encouraged by the emphasis on specialization and professionalization. Now totality is being avoided if not outright dismissed. And culture, too, is no longer matter-of-factly accepted, as its activities and products become absorbed into the commodity market, or operate as residual hegemonic state symbols. The neoliberal economy also converted the university and the museum into professions, businesses, and corporations, and careerism further isolated and atomized disciplines and scholars. The sale of the museum and the university may in itself be not a catastrophe.[28)] (Nor is it entirely new.) Yet the way today's scholars, artists, and writers of different "kinds" (in gender, ethnicity, class, and discipline) have ceased to talk together, discuss together, or even disagree together, despite their own powerful desire for integral transdisciplinarity, is dispiriting as well as egregious.

The abandonment of the humanities is evident in several ways. Preferring applied sciences (especially, bio-medical technology), engineering (information technology, e.g.), and business administration for their majors and fields of specialization, fewer students now enroll in humanities departments and the courses they offer. The graduate application has been decreasing. Those who persist and receive the doctorate have difficulties in finding employment. Those few who manage to land jobs face another difficulty, sooner or later, in publishing their dissertations, a requirement for tenure that stubbornly survives. It is a thoroughly familiar story.

What is still not widely acknowledged is that PhDs who finally convert their dissertations into books (that are likely to sit unread in the university library shelves) become so tired of their specialized subject matters, especially if they are literary, that as soon as they have an opportunity, they try to flee from them. Those in literature may well move on to film studies, or to fiction writing, or beyond the territory of arts into social and historical events, psychological

28) There have been numerous studies concerning the place of the museum in contemporary culture. To name just a few random scholars, Hal Foster, Tony Bennett, and Miwon Kwon have been raising important issues. See also a special section on "Museums," The New York Times, March 30, 2005, as well as my "Leere Museen: Endzeit? Die globale Kulturindustrie und die Chancen der Kunst," *Lettre International*, No. 47 (December 1999), 84-88.

questions, or political economical investigations. Brighter students especially crave fresh and comprehensive studies. In other words, "transdisciplinarity" describes the actual aspiration and practice of an increasing number of young, and also older, humanities teachers and scholars in higher education. For evidence one only needs to glance at university press catalogues. The category of literary studies has nearly vanished from many. What has taken place is, though publicly denied and not openly admitted, the erosion of departments, disciplines, and professions. Integrative and holistic learning that involves the totality of the complicated fabric of life and the world is increasingly more desired, though again, not openly acknowledged. One notes a marked lowering of the walls that surrounded academic humanities research throughout the twentieth century.

(A word of caution is needed here regarding "interdisciplinary" (as against "*trans*-disciplinary") studies. Recognizing the intellectual demands for studies that cut across departmental borders, university administrators have been encouraging an arrangement of "interdisciplinary" studies by organizing conferences, programs, centers, and institutes. In these gatherings, experts from different fields get together to discuss urgent and attractive topics. In itself a salutary attempt, this project nonetheless falls short of serious achievements. First, these forums are always temporary. After assembling for a limited period, the participants head home to their separate departments where the same conventional disciplines dominate. Hiring, promoting, and firing are all carried out in the discrete units as if nothing had happened to disciplines, and the interdisciplinary gatherings were just a pleasant memory—like a summer camp. Serious studies belong to a profession, specialization, that still rejects contamination by other disciplines. "Interdisciplinarity" is finally a self-contradiction, a deception.)

Environmental deterioration also demands that the planet be understood and experienced as a commonality that belongs to every single being on earth. Here globalization is a compelling actuality. Knowledge and understanding about it, too, ought to be global, or universal, and inclusive. Economics cannot externalize environmental factors: pricing needs to be fundamentally restructured. History and geography cannot neglect paleontology and geophysics; it must discard its narrow preoccupation with the brief development of human civilization, not to say regions and nations. History ought to think about the future as well as the long pre-human past. The humanities discipline that was once sustained by the idea of the nation-state can now seize this moment of despondency and reorganize itself around the planet and the universe, the ultimate cohesive totality as the central imagery.

Environmental sustenance cannot be considered without rethinking social totality. This time, in other words, the need for a radical social and class reformation is not just ethical or political, but a biological and psychological necessity for everyone, which even the richest in the world cannot dismiss any longer, however averse they might be. The environmental totality consists of a multitude of differences. Far from being vulnerable to totalitarianism, this commitment to totality is integrated with the recognition of individualities, singularities, and their interconnectives. This environmental integrationism does not forget the world, the planet, and the universe, unlike the fragmentary principle of difference and identity. Also unlike the principle of difference or the out-dated nation-statism, the world, the planet, and the universe—as well as all the genes—is a stirring and inspiring commonality on which people, artists, writers, scholars, and scientists can work together in a truly transdisciplinary endeavor.

Environmental totality demands that knowledge and learning remain undivided and inclusive. Here James Lovelock's eccentric idea of "Gaia" might be instructive. First of all, Lovelock pursues his studies at home in a Devonshire farmhouse with no connection with a university or research institution. He says he needs to be alone so that he can avoid "peer review," which for him means self-imposed inquisition or surrender to authority, expertise, or gentility. His goal is to be free to range over all the disciplines of science. Transdisciplinarity is a precondition of his "geophysiology" that considers the planet a vast living organism, "Gaia." Gaia, the totality of the evolving planet contains all the species and their environment in interaction with one another. The humans in it are merely one species among others, and the life of the earth extends far back into its beginning—long before the evolution of micro organisms, plants, and animals, not to say humans. Such a comprehensive perspective requires today's environmentalism to be reconsidered. How do we live with Gaia?

> It is always from the action of individuals that powerful local, regional, and global systems evolve. When the activity of an organism favors the environment as well as the organism itself, then its spread will be assisted; eventually the organism and the environmental change associated with it will become global in extent. ... If we see the world as a superorganism of which we are a part—not the owner, nor the tenant; not even a passenger—we could have a long time ahead of us and our species might survive for its "allotted span."[29)]

His rejection of anthropocentricity is both invigorating and liberating. Of course, one should be cautious lest his antihumanism should lapse into political indifference and historical ignorance. Further, his argument that Gaia theory and the "human values of kindness and compassion are not inconsistent" (p. 240) is not quite persuasive. And yet his denial of the planet as an inorganic object and disapproval of scientific disciplines as autonomous and discrete is something we ought to take seriously in our attempts to rethink the future of the humanities.

Another approach to inclusive totality I am proposing here was articulated by Felix Guattari in one of his last books, *The Three Ecologies* (1989). His project is neither an escape plan of the rich to green "Nature," nor is it sustainable-environmentalism, a plan to maximize exploitation of the planet just short of its irrecoverable destruction. Guattari's version of integral ecology, which he calls "ecosophy," is concerned with a reformulation of totality that demands a clear understanding of what it is that we produce and consume socially, environmentally, and mentally. What do our

---

29) *The Ages of Gaia: A Biography of Our Living Earth* (New York: W. W. Norton, 1995), p. 239.

products do for us in this post industrial capitalism which he calls "Integrated World Capitalism"? Isn't so-called production merely another name for consumption, destruction? Ecosophy is a fundamental reexamination and reorganization of social ecology, environmental ecology, and mental ecology, and a project to reformulate intellectual and human orientation. Guattari calls it "ethico-political articulation between the three ecological registers (the environment, social relations, and human subjectivity)."[30] Ecosophy must distance itself from the old political, religious, and intellectual commitment. Instead of being a discrete discipline, it will be a "multi-faceted movement" (p. 68). He then goes on to conclude:

> it should be understood that the three ecologies originate from a common ethico-aesthetic discipline, and are also distinct from the point of view of the practices that characterize them. Their different styles are produced by what I call *heterogenesis*, in other words, processes of continuous resingularization. Individuals must become both more united and increasingly different. The same is true for the resingularization of schools, town councils, urban planning, etc. (p. 69).

To sum it up, the earth will have to be understood as inescapably interconnected. For living with the planet, sharing—while being respectful of true singularization—is our only choice. And the world, the globe, the universe, and all the living things must constitute the base of our studies and investigations, in fact, of our consciousness itself. The university°™and the world that contains it°™could be a happier place, if it were reorganized around this idea of planetary commonality and totality.

Of course, all this argument—whether by Lovelock or Guattari—is conducted at a highly abstract level. Some might

30) Felix Guattari, *The Three Ecologies, trans. Ian Pindar and Paul Sutton* (London: The Athlone Press, 2000), p. 28. See also Gregory Bateson, *Steps to an Ecology of Mind: Collected Essays in Anthropology, Psychiatry, Evolution, and Epistemology* (Chicago: The University of Chicago Press, 2000). There are a few helpful essays in its continuation, *Sacred Unity* (Hampton Press, 2004).

dismiss it as impractical and aloof. As a counter-argument, I might submit that there is an actual institution called the College of the Atlantic in Maine, which offers only one degree in "human ecology." The college not only reuses and recycles nearly everything to make daily life as waste-free as possible, but its teaching is completely centered around human ecology. I confess that my knowledge of the institution is only through its catalogue as it is on the Internet. It may very well be still in the process of exploration and self-definition. But I can easily see that it suggests the possibility and practicality of such a reorganized curriculum. As the environmental danger intensifies every moment, it gives us some comfort that the reorganization of knowledge and learning is not just a dream, but a workable plan, however modest its beginning might be now.[31)]

31) Katie Zezima, "All Is Recycled, Except for the Graduates," The New York Times, June 4, 2005.

My Encounter with Western Modernity

Kim Kwang-kyu

The topic I was originally asked to discuss was "The Diversity of Western Modernity." Vast arrays of books are available on the various aspects of European modernism, and since I lack the ability to discuss the wide spectrum of the subject, I will instead talk about my own experience, focusing on my encounter with Western modernity.

I have a bad habit of reading everything in sight whenever I have a moment to spare; the nickname "bookworm" has trailed me for as long as I can remember. All of us are inundated with an avalanche of reading material. The number of pages in the newspapers has increased, magazines have become thicker and thicker, and books on all sorts of topics are being published in mind-boggling quantities. I find myself flooded with everyday reading material, not to mention the more serious literature that is my main interest. Even if I were able to spend the whole day reading, I would still feel that I wasn't keeping up. From time to time, my family has to physically restrain me. My wife and daughter grab the book I am reading, snatch away my reading glasses, or cover my eyes with their hands. They implore me to give my eyes a rest.

The best way to give one's eyes a rest is to close them, but keeping one's eyes closed is, for me, too closely associated with sleep and death. As long as I keep my eyes open and try to read something, I feel that I'm still alive. Looking back at my own past, I can say that the entire course of my life consisted of a series of reading experiences. When I was young, I grew up reading other people's works, and as a teacher I spent years teaching my students what and how to read. Now I write and publish books for other people's eyes. My nickname – the bookworm – has come to define my life, not just my occupation.

When I was a tiny bookworm, in the early 1950s, very few books were available for children and young adults. In a country devastated by the Korean War, where getting enough food to eat was the pressing concern of the day, little priority was given to cultural education or to the pleasures of reading. School textbooks consisted of mimeographed material on yellowish recycled paper, and even comic books – the passion of all teenagers – were hard to come by. At the time, we could only rent comic books and works of fiction from a few shops that specialized in lending out reading material. This was of course before the advent of television and not every household had a radio. The single cultural pastime available to us was to borrow books and read them at home over the weekend. The erratic electric supply frequently left us with no power at night and during such blackouts, people would have to read by candlelight, or with the aid of a petroleum or more traditional oil lamp. I can remember reading novels, belly-down on a warm floor, vaguely aware of the shadows of people and furniture dancing in the flickering light and of the sounds of itinerant vendors hawking their homemade buckwheat snacks outside the window – but surely reading was a luxury few people could have enjoyed. The books I remember reading at this time include Yi Gwang-su's novel *The Soil* and his historical novel *Crown Prince in Hemp*, Yeom Sang-seop's novel *Three Generations*, Hong Myeong-hui's multi-volume novel *Yim Kkeokjeong*, Sim Hun's novel *The Evergreen*, and the Chinese classics *Romance of Three Kingdoms* and *Outlaws of the Marsh*. It was by reading popular realist novels that I stumbled into the world of literature.

When I was in middle school and then high school toward the end of the 1950s, I read voraciously, if indiscriminately. I remember how my parents were once summoned to my school after a teacher caught me reading a novel that had caused a social uproar when it was first serialized in the newspaper. The novel was about a love affair involving a married woman, a topic deemed shockingly immoral at the time.

The first collection of world literature appeared in Korean translation in 1958. Though I was poor, I still managed to save enough of my pocket money to begin buying one volume of the collection at a time. The first literary work in translation I bought was Franz Kafka's "Metamorphosis (Die Verwandlung)." Existentialism – ever so fashionable at the time – fanned the vanity in this literature-loving youth, and pushed me to buy the book in question. This astonishing work proved to be a turning point in my reading career, for it departed from the grammar of realism to which I had been so accustomed.

"As Gregor Samsa awoke one morning from uneasy dreams he found himself transformed in his bed into a gigantic insect." I had never read any story that started so abruptly. Kafka's short story is about a man who suddenly turns into an insect, dies amid his family's neglect, and is thrown into the trash. I simply couldn't agree with the opening premise—that a human being could have transformed into a beetle. In my mind, before anyone could metamorphose in this way, the reader at least deserved a plausible explanation. How could a story begin after such a sudden metamorphosis took place? Despite this unexpected beginning, however, the story developed in such realistic detail that I couldn't put it down until I reached the tragic ending. It was by no means an enjoyable story, a great departure from the glamorous tales I was used to reading. These tales were stories about brave heroes who moved around the world competing with each other, tales about righteous robbers who punished corrupt government officials and helped innocent citizens, or tales about young men and women who managed to seal bonds of love despite every obstacle imaginable. Why in heaven's name had Kafka written this work of fiction? With what little ability I had acquired in Korean classes to appreciate the finer points of literature, I found myself dumbfounded. Whenever my eyes caught sight of this slender volume in the corner of my bookcase, I was depressed. Following the old saying that one can understand anything if one reads it 100 times, I flipped through the pages of this book over and over again. Though I never found a good answer to my question, the very discovery of such a story proved to be a powerful shock to me, and afterward I gradually drifted away from historical novels, love stories, and all popular fiction with a realistic bent. This was, one might say, the point when my own literary metamorphosis took place.

Before I met Kafka, my taste – as was the case with most teenagers – was attuned to works of realism that were written with the aim of enlightening people. Plays struck me as far more plausible than operas, and movies truer to life than theatrical performances. I found it strange when two singers in an opera broke out into a duet, singing about two different things, or when an actor in a play embarked on an aside in front of his interlocutors, for I lacked the basic perception that these constituted an agreement of stage, a form of art. It never occurred to me that all the scenes in a film were virtual images, created through staging, shooting, and editing. I thought about novels in a similar way. I liked stories in which plausible protagonists appeared and helped unfold a storyline that resembled real life. Although I had learned from the textbooks that literature was a product of fiction and imagination, I failed to understand it completely. I had yet to comprehend that art is the creative process of constructing something that exists neither temporally or spatially. At this stage of my life, I preferred Tolstoy's novels when it came to foreign literary works. The shock I felt upon encountering Kafka can be likened to someone accustomed to Schubert's string quartets listening to Schönberg's atonal style for the first time, or to someone used to beautiful impressionist paintings standing in front of an unconventional abstract painting for the first time. To me, this jolt of modernism was a real eye-opener. It took me a long time, however, to absorb this shock and to digest it as my own experience. It was only in my early 30s that I developed the insight that enabled me to understand what Kafka wrote at the age of 29.

The protagonist Gregor Samsa has three family members: his father, his mother, and his younger sister. When Gregor, who once supported the family, can no longer make a living now that he is an insect, all the members of his family must go out and find jobs. His father works as a bank messenger, his mother embroiders for money, and his sister makes a living as a saleswoman. They do not even consider Gregor the insect a part of the family any more, and gradually they come to treat him as a monster. As his family members adjust to their new reality, a change takes place inside each of them. Nevertheless, the internal world of Gregor the insect remains unchanging. Judging from the psychological descriptions and the free indirect discourse (erlebte Rede), which reveals his innermost thoughts, it is clear that Gregor himself keeps – until the very moment of his death – the self-consciousness of a good-natured, hard-working salesman who cares deeply about his family.

It is possible for anyone to have a similar experience. Let us imagine that a person who supports his family is seriously hurt in a traffic accident. In the beginning, his entire family will take care of the head of the household and they will do everything they can to restore him to his former condition. But if he becomes an invalid and loses his ability to work, and is expected to spend the rest of his life bedridden, the family's attitude will gradually change. They will have to go out into the world to make money, and with the subsequent internal change that inevitably takes place, they may very well come to regard him as something troublesome to have around, indeed no different from an insect. The invalid, in turn, will realize that he is an object of abhorrence and avoidance within the family, someone who is undermining his family's peace and prosperity. If he kills himself or succumbs to his illness in the wake of this realization, his family will breathe a sigh of relief and perhaps take a walk outdoors, just as Gregor's family does after his death. The family can then get on with their lives.

Even in cases that are not so extreme, anyone who has spent significant time taking care of an elderly parent would certainly nod to the truth embodied in this old Korean saying: "It is hard to find a filial son after a parent's long illness." We may say that Kafka is showing the archetype of all such experiences in human life from the stance of the metamorphosed Gregor.

Reading Kafka's other works, I found myself once again wandering in the mist of uncertainty. The scenes described in *The Castle* (Das Schloss), *Amerika*, and *The Trial* (Der Prozess) were simply marks on a map called German literature, a place where I could not personally visit. Meanwhile, I was unexpectedly drawn to two small lawsuits. For the first time in my life, I had to present myself to the court and consult with a defense lawyer, thereby experiencing firsthand the true hassle of having to participate in a trial.

Joseph K, the protagonist of *The Trial*, is inexplicably arrested by some unfamiliar men on the morning of his 30th birthday, spends a harrowing year running here and there to defend himself against a charge about which he has no information, and eventually he is executed on the eve of his 31st birthday. If the reader relies on the usual method of studying a text, it is difficult to comprehend what the strange trial is all about and how it actually leads to K's execution. Before I even attempted a literary analysis, however, I could feel what the work as a whole, despite its ambiguity, was trying to get across, for I had experienced firsthand how alienating the seemingly clear-cut process of a trial could be for ordinary people – a process consisting of an attention to the minutest of legal points, the presentation of evidence, the prosecutor's summary, the argument of the case on behalf of the defendant, and finally the verdict.

It took me more than the first 30 years of my life to realize the simple truth that life is an accumulation of experiences, and that the creation and appreciation of literary works are ultimately based on and conveyed through experience. This is how I began to see the structures of Kafka's other works that attempt to illustrate our reality.

Kafka's story *Amerika* is a commentary on industrialization, capitalist society, and an economic structure that promotes mass production and mass consumption, as well as a portrait of the lives of citizens who live in a dense metropolis with a population of 10 million. The story presents an archetype of life for modern men who live anonymously in the chaos of modernity.

The land surveyor K, in Kafka's *The Castle*, is thrown into an ambiguous space of duality between the ideal and the real, dreams and lived reality, absolute transcendence and relative limitation, religion and everyday life, God and man. He neither reconciles the two sides nor narrows the gap between them. When I read this story I felt that K was the very portrait of myself, stuck in an epistemological rut, unable to make any progress in my understanding of the world.

When I stumbled upon this quite scholarly approach to literature and gained insight into Kafka's world, I felt as though I had caught a glimpse of a fundamentally new way of perceiving literary art. I came to understand that opposing divisions in aesthetics – realism versus modernism, extreme naturalism versus avant-garde surrealism, purposefulness versus aesthetic autonomy – were in fact useless oppositions, for each of these artistic methods sought, by a means of words, sounds, colors, and movements, to depict the experiences of human beings with both physical and spiritual lives.

Before I came upon Albert Camus' comment – "The whole art of Kafka consists in forcing the reader to reread." – I had already gone over his works several times. One might say that Kafka's magic lies in his ability to keep the reader flipping the pages of his stories that are far from enjoyable to read. His prose is crafted with such simple words and such a dry style that one might even say his vocabulary is meager, and that his sentence structure is terse, almost monotonous. A detached narrating voice and highly accurate descriptions work together to provide a lucid presentation of details, and sometimes this precision drives the narrative to the verge of comedy. Let me quote the passage in "Metamorphosis" when Gregor Samsa, the insect, attempts to open the door of his room:

> Slowly Gregor pushed the chair towards the door, then let go of it, caught hold of the door for support – the soles at the end of his little legs were somewhat sticky – and rested against it for a moment after his efforts. Then he set himself to turning the key in the lock with his mouth. It seemed, unhappily, that he hadn't really any teeth – what could he grip the key with? – but on the other hand his jaws were certainly very strong; with their help he did manage to set the key in motion, heedless of the fact that he was undoubtedly damaging them somewhere, since a brown fluid issued from his mouth, flowed over the key and dripped on the floor. . . . As the turning of the key progressed he circled round the lock, holding on now only with his mouth, pushing on the key, as required, or pulling it down again with all the weight of his body. The louder clock of the finally yielding lock literally quickened Gregor.

This is a detailed narration of how the insect crawls from the bed to the door, holds a key in its mouth, and finally turns it to open the door. The appearance and behavior of the metamorphosed Gregor are discussed vividly on several occasions in the story. Even after finishing the work, however, the reader fails to form a clear picture of the insect in his mind. Kafka's distinct technique is to render this ambiguous, fantastic form with an utterly precise, realistic style. We may say that it is a combination of realism and modernism. Herein lies the existential inevitability of Kafka's literature.

When "Metamorphosis" was published in Leipzig in 1915, the publisher wanted to use an illustration of an insect on the cover. Kafka, however, expressed strong objections, saying that it was impossible to give shape to his insect. What he meant by this was that the realistically depicted external reality was a metaphor of an internal world and at the same time a symbol of existence. This is the reason why Gregor Samsa's metamorphosis cannot be turned into a drawing, why it cannot be composed as a musical piece, or why it cannot be adapted into a play or a movie; it can only be read as a literary work. This gives us a hint as to why literature itself must exist.

My encounter with Kafka's stories proved to be my baptism into Western modernism, though I wasn't aware of it at the time. I had already become a bespectacled bookworm by this point, for my eyes had deteriorated as a result of a constant struggle over tiny words in dictionaries, frequently perused in an effort to understand and translate foreign works.

I don't remember exactly when I first encountered poetry. Publishing books of poetry must have been more daunting at the time, considering that there was no market to speak of for novels, with people borrowing them from lending shops. When I was in middle school, I borrowed a book of poetry and copied some of the poems as part of an assignment, making an anthology of my own. Several of Kim So-wol's poems were in this book. Looking back, it is likely that that this old book was a copied edition of *Azaleas* (1925). It was at this time when I first read Kim's representative works written in the first half of the 1920s (when he was in his early 20s), including "Golden Grass," "Ah, Mother and Sister," "Azaleas," "Road Away," "Unforgettable," "The Cuckoo," "Mountain Flowers," "Parents," "Calling the Spirit." Without making any effort, I soon committed them to memory.

Shall I say,
I miss you?
and now I miss you.

Shall I go on?
Yet
One more time . . .

Crows over that mountain, crows in the field
Caw at the sight
Of the setting sun.

Flowing water
River water in front, and in back
Gurgling: come on hurry up, okay I'm coming.
It flows and flows but still keeps on flowing.

It was enjoyable to recite this poem, because it spoke intimately to my youthful spirit, and the three-foot poetic meter in Korean enhanced the fun of the poem. Written by Kim So-wol, who occupies an unrivaled position in the history of Korean poetry, it is a good example of traditional lyrical poetry.

Although it is classified as a new genre of Korean poetry in the early part of the 20th century – in other words as modern poetry – it is a far cry from Western modernity in view of its folksong-like language and romantic sentiment. I came to realize this distance after getting acquainted with modern German poetry during my undergraduate days. In a German poetry class I took in the early 1960s, expressionist poems were included on our reading list. I cannot forget my shock at encountering for the first time these representative works of German literary modernity. A good example is the poem "Schöne Jugend" in Gottfried Benn's Morgue and Expressionist Verse (Morgue und andere Gedichte), a book of poetry published in 1912.

A fine childhood

The mouth of a girl who had long lain in the reeds
looked so chewed up.

When we broke open the torso, the esophagus was so full of holes.
Finally in a bower under the diaphragm
We found a nest of young rats.
One little sister rat lay dead.
The others were living off liver and kidney,
drinking the cold blood and enjoying
a fine childhood.
And find and fast was their death too:
we threw the whole bunch into water.
Oh, how those little snouts squeaked!

Der Mund eines Mädchens, das lange im Schilf gelegen hatte.
sah so angeknabbert aus.
Als man die Brust aufbrach, war die Speiseröhre so löcherig.
Schliesslich in einer Laube unter dem Zwerchfell
fand man ein Nest von jungen Ratten.
Ein kleines Schwesterchen lag tot.
Die andern lebten von Leber und Niere,
tranken das kalte Blut und hatten
hier eine schöne Jugend verlebt.
Und schön und schnell kam auch ihr Tod:
Man warf sie allesamt ins Wasser.
Ach, wie die kleinen Schnauzen quietschten!

I was still shaky when it came to the salient linguistic features of German poetry, because grasping the grammatical meaning of this poem itself was a struggle. Yet, it was the first time that I had ever come across such a poem. The reader's expectations – set up through the title and the first phrase, "the mouth of a girl" – are confused in the second line, and then completely shattered from the third line on. The cold medical tone of the poem describes the process of a postmortem examination conducted on a drowned person. The narrator relates how "the esophagus was so full of holes" when they broke "open the torso," and how "finally in a bower under the diaphragm" they found "a nest of young rats" "living off liver and kidney." While the drowned person is merely a material object, the rodents living off that object are the subject of the poem. The poetic self, who observes this perverse relationship between dead girl and feeding rats, indeed defines himself in relation to these rats. A literal translation of the original text gives us "one little sister rat" and "young rats." The narrator refers to the period of their inhabitation as a "fine childhood," and even follows this with an exclamation of regret, "oh," in the last line. Turning a body touched by death – once seen as the completion of life or a returning to God – into an object inhabited by rats can be seen as not only blasphemous to the human soul, but also as contrary to the very spirit of art at the time, which advocated the pursuit of truth, goodness, and beauty. Even in the tradition of German poetry, this was without doubt a terrible provocation. It goes without saying that a comparison with Kim So-wol's poem, which was written some 10 years later, made me realize that a great gap existed between the West's modern lyrical poetry and contemporary Korean poems. More than anything, the German poem shattered my conception of lyrical poetry, because it was certainly not the kind of work that readers would enjoy reciting over and over again to commit to memory.

The best way to appreciate Kim So-wol's poem "Road Away" is to recite it, rather than reading it silently. Even though it is normally experienced in printed form, everyone tacitly agrees that it is good material for recitation. On the other hand, Gottfried Benn's "A Fine Childhood," despite the inherent rhythm of its metered verse, is far from a satisfying text to read aloud. It is a poem to be read silently; and since its power lies in the imagery it conjures up in the mind, the work is easily understood in silence. We may say that it is a new type of poem that severs itself off from the tradition of literary recitation, a tradition implied by the word "Lied," meaning song. These songs were handed down from generation to generation, as is evident by the titles of old epic poetry, such as *Nibelungenlied*. With this new method of dismantling traditional poetry, an entirely new tradition was established. Instead of reciting these poems by playing up the rhythmic characteristics, as is the case with Kim So-wol's poem, we have no choice but to read them silently or to murmur them to ourselves.

Murmuring is a distinct act of discourse, somewhere between "speaking" and "reciting." We could even say that it is the last remaining method of reading literary texts out loud, these literary texts that are themselves gradually being pushed to the fringes of experience in an era of science and technology under capitalism. Murmuring may be a way of speaking that is the farthest from social communication or economic benefit, in that it does not serve the purpose of clearly conveying specific intentions. When people murmur, they are either completely ignored or criticized for not speaking clearly. Nonetheless, such responses have little impact on the act of murmuring. It is an attitude that ignores others, or that seems to say, "Who asked you to listen?" Although it is very difficult to live this way, there are a handful of people who choose to live their entire lives murmuring. They are none other than poets and writers of the world. When this murmuring – the very opposite of practical statements found in the discourses of politics, economics and social affairs – reaches an extreme, the gap between literature and reality, and between writers and readers, widens even further, impeding the conveyance of meaning and ultimately all communication.

We find signs of such a phenomenon in Kafka's stories and Benn's poems. If this is to be summed up as "modernity" – on the basis of certain characteristics evident in such literary works – we should not give it a completely negative evaluation. Even though the method of expression in this new trend of literature has lost realism's function of clear discourse and often collapses into an ambiguous murmuring, it is a form of discourse that reflects the turbulent times of drastic change and a society that has splintered into alienated groups. Concomitant with globalization, this trend has crossed the boundaries of the West and has spread throughout the world. In my case, however, I make efforts in my own way to prevent my murmuring from becoming an incomprehensible monologue.

Translated by **Yu Young-nan**

Opening a View - from and to Language

Erling Kittelsen

To be in the act of writing does not have to do with psychology or literature in itself, but with the threshold in your own mental space for language. You stand there when you want to express yourself. You do not necessarily stand there when you want to understand. I believe in a universal, holy, resistant language which covers and explains what is hidden. An anchor for the ray which shall relate your inner self to a maelstrom of changes in the world; an attempt to enlighten knots which will arise if everything continues. You throw light on your own foot and enlighten on behalf of others. To call the resistant ray introvert – without a relating ability, which is often done in the money – orientated and communication-fanatic Western world, – is to say that the individual has no place in the collective. It just means that the cliché of the individual should fit in with the cliché of the collective. In the world as a cliché it falls together with the forced collective dream. Our time is introvert, lacks a view from and to language, but breakings are happening.

I will describe modernism as a *condition* in the Western societies - seen from my Northern angle. We invented literary modernism in order to get rid of our empires, our cruelties, our heroes, our classics, our self-celebration, our self-censorship. We invented modernism in order to find a more common and earthbound and at the same time absurd form of language. I cannot tell how far we have come, but the questions related to modernism are being contradicted by a variety of expressions. We move in our own direction with God and everything. We enter with a more personal form, our choices, the will is ours, the will which is choosing us. Our beliefs, the object of belief become a complicated area.

Every expression has its limits. Idiocy comes into existence when one applies one's own criteria on other forms. How can an author be liberated to become a listener and to be a person who just reveals what he or she knows and understands; how can one take away the shadowing inseparable ties to economy, politics and media in order to avoid being gagged by an unspoken convention. Inside this it is, of course, possible to do our work as it should be done and overshadow the need of other living literary forms and interpretations. But the scope is being narrowed, the literary interest diminishes in the perspective, one must ask where the thirst actually is situated. If the author does not manage to establish a dialogue with the inner self and between the different parties, then what?

When profitability is in question it is aiming for a conclusive way of *thinking*, more than earning money. Art has to touch upon this aim. We think that we choose something "easy", for reasons of economy, but something else might have been better with the same amount of efforts if we have awakened and could manage to care more for the things that might come later, to keep the space open for a wide range of art and literary forms. Instead we have economy as a form of thought and culture in the very heart and core of art and literature, and this happens not as a result of censorship, but as a result of a marginalization of the literature and other cultural expression forms lacking calculable profitability. It is a fight for a platform. It should look like as if those forms will disappear in their own order. It is taken for granted that these forms will speak only to the especially interested and that it is not necessary that they should be made into the professional mainstream in the theatre, the literary institutions and publishing houses. This, however, will lead to the collectivity losing its critical skills. Everything is allowed, but people as a whole are supposed to be shielded from the experiments and critical minds. Majority's voice will be heard all the time, the opinion poll where the questioner has decided all the premises. Those able to frighten the fiend on the open field, will be thrown out from the war. They will hold on somewhere else. Your disobedience, the things that hold your inner self up, the beam of light that does not fit in the codes, which are the free key needed to come along in this society – in tough enough societies this beam is able to survive in the collective underground. In good societies it will come to the surface. In Western societies, however, this sense is muted and it has to accept by and large a life in an exclusive know – all niche.

The Western world has needed modernity the most. Abundance and wealth are merely phenomena on the surface and new forms and structures emerge which give other ways to perceive the world. Questions are being asked and new critical and experimental poetry has been created, and allows itself to wonder with the help of language codes probably never before seen in the world. – Or, reality is being turned upside down and let loose in the basement, in the renovation of language that gives new entrances to our problems; it is less important to have a core, it is enough to consider you "in". The known world is being perceived from another side, in a free form, in another language – and can take you into another profundity.

Time is to sustain in the imagery until we are together with more than it can depict. We can live within what has already happened, but not yet has come to the visible surface. How do we give it the language, we share something before it is expressed, does it lie as a seed, everywhere, following its inner logic. This inner collective strives for another structure and a common acceptance.

In East Asian poetry the poet's meditation and withdrawal have two aspects; he/she contemplates social life *and* the inner self. The poet takes care in silence of the collective inner self and offers what he/she thinks the society should accept. Western authors and readers experience this literature as a reminder of the relations between inner and outer phenomena and the sudden (inner) understanding which also concerns the outer world. We lack – or have lost – an anchor in our own world of concepts, for silence as a gathering element in a collective sense that meditation also brings us out. We use East Asian poetry as an alibi for letting this loose in ourselves. We must, however, find this anchor within ourselves, in our own culture, and thus with a bigger core, can meet others and not only accentuate the differences with them or imitate them.

For postmodernism, as it is understood and developed as a tendency, no elements are superior, they work together and supplement one another, the aim is to enlarge the area. In this way it remains for example the interpenetration philosophy (the Avatamsaka School) of Buddhism, but it might contain fear of the vertical perspective, everything should fit in, it can stand in dialectic relations, be harmonised with each other, spread out, change places and value, be redistributed in absurdum... An unplaced element runs free, things are both free and closed, and there is no compulsion (and consequently no freedom), no surprise (everything might happen). What is unplaced can confusingly become the core. I would dare to think core, that it finds its way to itself apart from the systems which hold it and quarrel about the truth, the simplicity, the economy, the profitability, the depths, the superiority and the ideas we may die or kill for. Not mentioned is *where* the crisis dwells (only the cliché), no-one dares to meet face to face.

We have been entertained and bored and so cool in our good, postmodern spirit. We have belonged to the avant-garde and played football with the core, designed it and let it fall apart in fear of the enemy: the established, conventional, conservative, god-believing and opportunistic literature. God is, of course, interesting in a social context: the suffering mystic with a preference for social prejudice and the characteristics of anxiety and pain. But the God as being, however, will not accept any paraphrases unless the ghosts of metaphysics turn up. It is better to keep away from the core (the mystic's inner life) *or* let it run freely. Even in daylight the being of God is gloomy. Only emptiness should be vessel for God's possible image. The image should be made as simple as possible, that would be the safest thing literary and philosophically (and certainly an indication that one is a real mystic). One does not, then, separate or distinguish between the metaphysical and the image which reproduces the image (upon which the metaphysical is built); an image which is pulled out of the surface (after a bath) and thus tears down the situational ethics, the image we hold for one another; love and fulfilment at the same time. Fulfilment is an impossible word to use here, the word has been handed over to the enemy, the vessel can just be filled up like emptiness can be filled up when we keep it open. We cannot believe we control the made-up universe as well.

The being of God is bewildering. The source has been cut off because someone has taken its place, someone we do not like is stuck there, and we do not appreciate the source they use. The outer opponent often reveals an inner contradiction. We are not able to tell the ambiguities apart. We do not encounter the resistance where it is, but mix it together and let everything speak through the outer frame or we let it stay in the inner self. What do we lose? Also in our text: tensions, telling distances between the levels, parallelisms, camouflage, taboo (only if it is revealing itself in the visible conflicts). We lose the latent drama between the inner and outer elements. Everything is permitted as long as it does not surpass the superficial interpretation codes.

Our (national) poet laureate, Henrik Wergeland, has in his main work *Creation, Man and Messiah*, described a mythical universe where spiritual beings mix with historical persons. To me this universe belongs to an inner universe integrated in Wergelands own self. The mythological elements seem so random (the seriousness lies behind the curtain), and we cannot call this a metaphysical work. His poetry, so concerned with the society and the spiritual world at the same time, have been close to the people, but just this work nearly nobody read because of its seriousness. May be it would be a puppet-play in China. I was asked to write a play as an answer to Wergelands work. "What is it about", somebody asked. "Distances", I said. Open it at any place, and you can find how it deals with distances. The core here is not Wergelands or mine, but we have an overlapping domain and from here the text is singing.

The core exists, but not independent of the subject. No core is pointed to, and how can you, when you are inside of it? The subject guarantees the core, it could be the subjects core, it could be the core in itself (which the subject relates to), this does not probably make any difference, it is just words. The point is that the core cannot be dissolved into fragments (and then be put systematically or disorderly together). The core cannot be controlled or be alluded to. It exists, the rest are words which must be sharpened in order to retrieve their shine in the superficiality's mirror. This is the opposite of the myth of Narcissus in which man views and falls in love with his image in the well. In our aspect it is the human being who rediscovers his own image on the surface, the collective also finds itself on the surface, but does not only live there. The ego is dissolved in the self to the benefit of the self in the collective. The subject relates to a sum, the core point where the parts interrelate. The subject understands subjectively, or objectively – or believes so. There is no ready-made core one can relate to critically or in unproblematic ways. The core may be God, but the name is in the dark. The taboo exists in some place. I search under the cover, ask about the tolerance in the room and utter the unwanted words with the actor's ordinary voice and cannot find the situation, only a standpoint (why something is being said), and words that emerge as other words in the audience. Perhaps we dare not move out, and we cling to the story. The place becomes place just by liberating us from the outward actions, your place comes to you, it gathers below you, there is no other place to stand, the situation has lost its grip, it is an image, we can read images and let there be situations and the opposite. We must let the standpoint (not only our own visions) come. You are a hostage; you also are in another place.

"What about our old gods from Northern mythology", I asked myself. Do they represent a standpoint or should they rest in peace, either as non-existent (and not good enough in relation with other mythologies) or as a ready-made ware, a value we got into possession and, among others, use in our national advertisement, mostly as Vikings' beliefs, where the war-like and rough come into focus? The problem is that we have made taboos and prejudices of it all: the Vikings and their cruelties and violence are in focus. Our oldest poetry we have surrounded with a taboo. Something about the label from Christianity, at the same time it shall fit the national promotion. I was preoccupied with this taboo myself. Should I write in a culture with such deadlocked relations to its written sources, this was, of course, possible in the free spirit of modernism, but I looked under the cover and studied the Poetic Edda and scaldic poetry (more than 1000 years old) in the light of the reasons I found for the refutation of the one-sided reading method, which again opened the room for free speculation. Would not it be better to come into dialogue with other sides of this poetry? Another world actually emerged, and the most surprising aspect was that details I knew from earlier wound into each other and created other platforms for understanding. One example: They speak about a war between two groups of gods, emphasis in different sources put on the peacemaking ceremony where a hostage exchange is administered. They are not hostages in a threatening way, but the opposite; they guarantee that peace will continue, a premise is that the two groups of gods intermingle. The peace ceremony is in focus in the sources, not the war. Additionally it shows that phenomena as exile, hostage, deposit and marriage between different groups of gods take place under the surface of official events. Dimensions of the world hinge into one another and if one does not succeed in strengthening it, the chaos powers must be tied up and the main gods will eventually fall due to their own actions. Even if female powers and chaos representatives are being called "evil" by interpretations and translating authors, this word does not exist in the oldest poems. The world is kept together with a legislature which all parts must accept.

I translated a famous Edda-poem (Voluspá) from old Norse and wrote an answering poem to each of the 64 stanzas and named the dialogue *SHE (1989) Conversation with our ancestors* and my poetic answer of today displays an interpretation of the stanza and what I, from my point of view, was moved to say! The strength of the old Norse poetry lies in my opinion in the ability to see the wholeness from several perspectives; the Gods, the Dwarfs, the Giants etc. The mythology itself depends on the breakthrough from groups or individuals; you can compare it with the Korean poetry from the same period. This ability lies deep in the language itself, the words, so to say, have a consciousness about their own standpoint. Exactly this aspect I find as being disregarded because of other priorities when we mediate the Poetic Edda Mythology. Even Snorre – he wrote both our kings' history and a mythological textbook in the 13th C. – was an epic author without a feeling for the great-great grandmothers haiku, in the Poetic Edda. In the following time the tendency has also been to see and understand the mythological connection between images in order to create mono-structured stories and tales. The mythological image itself – as a poetic and philosophical starting-point – has been driven into the shadows to the advantage of total explanation (this goes for my view upon both text and mythological theory).

The word as something *being within* can build on a surety °© at the same time it may not get into market-driven framework of understanding. This is in itself a huge challenge for literature; think about the problem of autism, genius etc. Will those things they possess ever reach the surface? The most radical thing you can do in the Northern hemisphere today is to demand space for your inner life or a scholarship in order to be able to receive the world, to understand as much as possible, one will ask: What is this person's purpose here? Is there a "hatchway" in the system which perhaps could foresee that she/he in the longer run could be the most important person of all? If this person were healthy and law-abiding, then it would be worse. In such a case, hospital or prison would be the only solution. In another culture this person would be seen as a wise man, a shaman, monk or a member of a council and taken care of by everyone. In our culture she/he is on the bottom of the society and a threat against those ideas with which we build our world.

A concept almost emptied of all meaning in my own country, is *culture*. The word has been thinned out and means no longer a counterforce to commercialism. The word has just become a category baked into the system. But *culture* is more than a product; it means constant, incessant change, undercurrents and room for dialogue. If it just becomes a product it will be connected to Value – and culture really is the opposite, it is what binds together and develops fractions and in that context it brings and includes values. What then when a culture develops negative sides, violence, war and superficiality? We have been accustomed to the fact that it is culture too, especially so after one had abolished the concept of *culture* in a protest against Value conservatism. It is easier to stretch the word when the culture sits tight, when it at one point stands unmoved 10 or 1,000 years. Then we need the concept of culture to put things into order! This would be as important in Norway today as it was to understand the labour movement back in time. This labour movement has not managed to continue or develop its social democratic perspective with the help of concepts adequate today. It comforts itself as all others with the money-ideological perspective. As simple as that. And as difficult, as we have many other wishes, needs and dependencies than to develop our culture. We say that a human being is cultured when she/he is tolerant, open-minded, self-integrated and distinct in her/his behaviour. We need a concept to understand all this and other aspects of our own cultural situation. Every culture will – irrespective of religions, political systems, mentality – cherish openness, politeness and a more precise knowledge about its own basis by developing its cultural elements, in order to both encounter other cultures, disclose censorship and understand its own sides. The opposite would mean a plug in the mechanics of social structure. The very distribution key between the ability to meet others and to understand yourself has stopped to move. To find out what happens we need a cultural concept which is intact, useful and depth-seeking. It is no use making language empty when it can be instrumental. Even "modernism" and "postmodernism" are used for any convenient situation. We must look for entrances instead of lamenting the conformist ideology's lack of concepts. Strength will be emancipated if we leave this area which will hypnotize us.

To me modernity has meant to go into what I think is lacking. One could say: To hell with communication if we are to speak together. It means to search for a language form, which does not seek the domination, but awakens the language in the other. And it might mean to be supplemented by another voice as was the case in the conversation with Voluspá (Poetic Edda) and also two other dialogues I have had with old Norse literature. New entrances to my own cultural heritage have also opened up for dialogues with other linguistic areas; I have joined skilled philologists in languages far from my own and given translations of poetry in Norwegian. Here the two people from different cultures are forced to think about the same things. I may believe in this on a larger scale as well. Let the two conflicting parties talk about culture and not mention politics and they will have to listen to voices that cross their areas.

We become real through what is foreign, what is not authentic (from our place), what we do not immediately reach. If we exist for what is intact and expand our world from that point, we will never reach what is space. We expand our core and control it, but we will never be seen. Society may sense us, analyse us, but realization fails. The Western mentality is stuck in this perspective and becomes more and more aware of that fact. If we continue to exist for ourselves as the real thing, we sustain our own richness and feed our ideologies – also our fairytales and understanding – before we actually are seen, before we stand out in space. Literature should be the expert to articulate and invite in necessary wisdom, and be able to stand on the outside *and* see further.

A figure in a text in Western literature is usually interpreted from his/her character, role and attitudes. In the East a lot of characteristics will easier allude to inner realties. We lack two different logics; one being identical with what the person feels superficially, another logic lives and must live in order to live in the consciousness. It is a special feature of the modern Western thinking and culture that this separation shall be taken away and the reasons for these logics made into one. Imperialism, communism and capitalism have not exactly increased the possibilities for thinking through all this. Depths often become locked rooms lifted up in broad daylight by spiritual cranes, everything must up and out, be solved or stamped by psychology and religion. We cannot move independently from the surface without phenomena as fantasy, poetry, absurdity, ecstasy; phenomena which relate to the other as normality and lack the parallel world's preciseness and clarity in both language and content. Literature has had its phases in unambiguity's (so far as form and basic understanding are concerned) iron grip. The need for a surrealism is not surprising, a theatre of the absurd (with language renewal) and a social realism (with content metamorphoses). Eventually, postmodernism, which will liberate us from modernism without promising any future. Time dresses with space and embraces all the possible worlds. We hold our breath a short moment, wind caresses our cheek... This is why it is silly to prolong this phase of postmodernism when with the next breath we will have entered another era where we must revive subject and the core in a completely different manner.

Renaissances have an aspect of re-conquering, in our context it is important to allow the two causalities, which never can describe one another or fulfil one another, but can only be in dialogue. Not everything needs to be expressed on the surface; although it has been never so manifold, or, for drama, a recognizable situation; that inner life and belief get its meaning when performed in the outer frame. Actually, inner life can concern the interest of the collective. How can we develop a vocabulary and means for this type of cognition, religious life, meditative life or lunatic life independent of what the surroundings maintain, i.e. inner life as if it is basis, even emptied of an aspect of justice? What does it mean that this is focused, what is it that really matters? In the rich Scandinavian societies it is almost prohibited or impossible to resign, to leave the system. This has been made impossible by a bureaucracy. From outside it is a standstill, from inside it is either a standstill or a concentration which pushes everything else aside. We have psychiatric terminology for living in two worlds independent of each other. But what if this is chosen, without an alibi, in order to reach your goals? Then – it is an example of a condition for which there is no terminology. Transferred to a poetics we must take into consideration what literature should not lock out as much as what it positively should reveal. People have their inner lives, that is what they have, they have their own private dreams, it is not so interesting – even if the media try to exploit them – they also have a deeper longing and passion, almost hidden, why don't they grab it? Or is it too dangerous for today's thoughts about what is negative and positive, good and evil? We are being woven in – or we weave ourselves in tight. This place seen from outside can be a sort of prison and we see ourselves as sitting there, rightfully or wrongfully. One could liberate oneself from this place, or let it come to us. This is something that must be solved inside the web, where you do not see yourself from the outside, where you are stuck, where you cannot draw a boundary, but accept more, where you are more than what is being pictured, where you compromise between being a prisoner and a prison guard. We have to be aware. Our courage is undisputable *inside* the frame.

Poetry is translucent. The plot is a moveable picture, the intrigue is a scaffolding for the plot, it raises a room, something else happens, the text gets a place to sing from, the foot has been set down, it is necessary, it is sung from the place it is sung from, it is sung from where replicas, actions or situations come into existence. It is not necessary to twist one's inner self, be brilliantly creative, solve all movements; there is a place from where the text sings, time aspects cross the room, we are several places, we are real, we look at our starting point in a huger image where we shall come to existence.

From the place where the text sings, we are free. The text is free and uses whatever possible words for what is known. The core is where it is to be found. Not in the heart of ideology, the religion, the metaphysical world, the erotic life or the situation, but where the subject intervenes with the wholeness which is huger, where the subject stands for this wholeness, from where it is being sought a place to sing.

The text is free and should not strive for depicting wholeness in the space as some sort of summary, essence or rearranged truth. Nevertheless, it tries to - in a language conscious way - to articulate parts of it. The wholeness includes the standing point. The text wants the audience to participate – and from their core feelings give their own language images - in the building of a safer world as Gods, Dwarfs, and Giants.

A poetics *wishes* maximal tolerance and maximal possibility for the person to also have a solid place, a place to stand (from and to language).

Facets of Modernity

Choi Yun

Before approaching my theme of modernity, I would like to reflect first on the relationship between modernity and the topic of our conference, "Writing for Peace." Considering the relationship between modernity and writing for peace, one might think a peaceful resolution of conflict would be the principal theme discussed. Upon further reflection, we might take into account two different aspects of this relationship: how modernity has hindered and helped peace.

When modernity's postmodernism arrived in the West, people had no interest in literature or need that literature could fulfill. People believed literature could not solve problems of the world, like ending war or sustaining hope. To some extent, the sentiments persist to this day, but is there any truth to these kinds of feelings? Another important characteristic of contemporary modernity has to do with how it has affected human experience of reality. In spite of how interconnected our world is, life has become more compartmentalized for human beings, and so lessened.

What I want to discuss is different from modernism—not the age of modernism or its tangible outcomes. What I understand as modernity is the whole of things engraved in the mind that caused the tangible outcomes we recognize as modernity. This same structure originated modern literature. The difference between modernism and modernity is that modernism was a time when literature flourished in quality and quantity, but quickly lost prominence, particularly in the West. Modernity, however, remains to this day.

Modernity originated in the West, has gone through a number of changes, countless experiments and failures, and to date is a system of multifaceted but refined practices and ideologies. Modernity is a complex stratum of technology and theory systems, none of which has ever been completely unified. I think modernity's process of evolution in Western civilization was inevitable. By examining this inevitability, it is possible to plan and compensate for stages of evolution in a given society. No doubt, in the case of modernity, the changes have been in part born out of responses to necessity.

Through the growth of technology in the West, the modern age developed effectively, and modernism spread throughout the globe. Modernity began with an irresistible, non-reducible force. Universal standardization, modernity's chief pursuit, had an explosive effect on the world. The effects of standardization were so overwhelming that when reflecting upon the changes, the thought of one uniform world was frightening to those of a critical mind.

We who live in Asia notice the surprising influence of Western modernity every day. The traits of modernism have become well known in the world; the ubiquity of this knowledge is one of the traits of modernity. Just as light and sound do not move at the same speed, however, the trends of Western modernity are different from what has taken place in Korea.

Our conference may be a welcome opportunity for me to examine what Western modernity has meant to me, a writer born in Korea and writing in Korean. I have always put off such self-reflection as if it were difficult homework, and because it involves considering so many contemporary Korean writers with their individual differences. In broad terms, I would like to first trace the meaning of modernity in the period of history I have lived, while at the same time questioning modernity. Second, as a non-Western writer, I would like to consider Western modernity and its future in the West with respect to our theme of Writing for Peace.

Modernity as a Critical Reflection of Language and Culture

I was born in the year and month of the signing of the truce agreement for the Korean War. My infancy took place in a landscape of reconstruction. I grew up as a literature student in the rhythm of the Korean economy's modernization. I learned about the West by studying abroad in France from the late seventies to early eighties, and after this time, I continued to travel frequently between Korea and France. I belong to a generation that spent its college days in scenes of anti-dictatorship demonstrations so violent that schools had to be closed every semester.

The dictatorship penetrated into the time-space daily life of people; in Korea, we call this period "The Era of Renovation." Unawares, a willingness to criticize had formed in the minds of us students. This willingness led to a self-possessed, liberal skepticism that was important in the face of suppression.

The uniqueness of Korea in the seventies was due in part to the nation dedicating itself to adopting Western techniques of modernization. Korea's political and social problems were not much different from other developing countries that begin a process of modernization. "Industrialize Our Country into the Modern Age" was a slogan of the times; one could see signs advocating intense economic modernization everywhere. It was an expensive modernization that caused a lot of suffering and sacrifice among people.

After our independent nation was established, Korea eagerly consumed as much of the West as possible in the process of modernization. It was a voracious consumption. I think the eagerness to consume Western modernization will not continue as strongly as it has without constant encouragement and motivation, including the ongoing political and economic support from the West. The fervor for Western influences was born from a particular historical situation in Korea, and inspiration drawn from Western human rights movements. Korea's present circumstances are different now, and the Western influence is no longer needed as it once was.

Influence from the West became more pronounced after the Japanese colonial period had ended. The Japanese had attempted to annihilate the Korean national identity. Perhaps because our liberators were from the West, Western influences on Koreans were enticing and persuasive, suggesting a new symbiotic relationship at that time.

The surging importation of Western modernity took place during my youth. To say that Korea was where Korea's own unique modernization was constructed is not so plain and simple. A strong resistance to everything that confined, hindered, prohibited, and suppressed was the fundamental emotion of literature students during the time. Modernization took place while a dictatorship served as background noise. Throughout the early modernization Korea undertook, I thought it natural to want to experience Western culture in its place of origin—not the Korean version of modernity, but where it originated.

The most important thing modernity has meant to me, as a woman is that it gave me a sense of respect. I was born into a family that valued Korea's traditional Neo-Confucianism, and so it was not easy to live as a woman. I also inhabited a conservative patriarchal society that did not have discussions on topics of gender. I grew up with a few friends who contemplated gender issues as I did. The moment a girl who reflects upon these issues becomes an adult, she may experience alienation from her culture. The special women I knew all possessed the same curiosity about the possibilities life could offer, and chose to act in similar ways. Their curiosity naturally brought to their attention words like democratization, rationality, and equality—the things that have provided the foundation of western modernity. These kinds of discoveries led to young people, not only culturally oppressed women, dreaming of a new visionary future.

Of course, there was no easy place where one could go and simply open a box and observe "modernity." Modernity has taken different forms according to nation and culture. I think when one asks questions with a critical mind, one begins to understand Western modernity.

There were three differences between Korea and the West at the outset of their respective processes of modernization. Korea had no tradition of Christianity as Western modernity did. Korea quickly created the infrastructure necessary to begin its era of modernization, whereas the West had approximately one hundred and fifty years to do so. There was also no subversion or revolution on a national scale by Koreans for the sake of better governance. We know this sort of event is a precursor for the improvement of human rights. In these respects, there was not much in common between the historical context of modernization in Korea and the West.

I met modernism in my youth. It was a powerful influence in my life. It led me to look with a critical eye on my culture, its history, and language. From my own experience, I believe Western modernism has played or continues to play a role, no matter how strong or weak the pressure, in most of human civilization.

Though pragmatically different, Korean and Western literatures have especially achieved a kind of harmonious mixture in Korea. This came about in part because Western literature was a global movement. It had inter-regional humanitarian appeal, familiar themes, encompassed advanced sciences and technologies, and had the propensity unique to Western literature to surmount boundaries of language and culture. Since the advent of modernism, the development of science and technology has continued to grow beyond boundaries and limitations of physical communication. Western literature, in contrast, has overcome boundaries of nations, regions, religions, and race.

In the West, modernity and the literature of modernism might be the two most important events that have ever occurred. All through modernism, literature grew in more ways than any other period in human history. Realms of humanity and literature were explored that previously had not been. Especially in literature, an impetus for liberty gathered which expressed itself as a means to and experiment in removing every oppressing limit on human thought. Respect for liberty, human rights, individuality, and freedom sometimes became a form of tyranny during modernism. Liberty occasionally killed human beings in the name of freedom, and curtailed human rights in the name of human rights.

Generally, the ideals of humanity were explored by literature in the modern age. Visionary propositions—the desire to explore ideas through literature—make this period of writing even more precious. For non-Western countries that read this literature, they learned that modernism encompassed extremely dynamic properties. These countries eagerly explored modern humanism and conceptions of progress in modernity. There was a willingness to be self-critical and reflective, which to this date is practiced in non-Western countries.

For literature, the most important thing that occurred during modernism was the growing awareness of the many properties and functions of language. All manner of questions about the relationship between men and language were posed by literature. More than any other era, human beings valued the capacity of language to surprise. The unanticipated outcome of scientific research on language was also profoundly important to literature. The modern age truly can be called the age of language.

Language became a starting point for literature in the modern era. The language in literature gained a kind of equivalency to human reality. With regard to not only literature but also all human activities, language was the most important topic of the previous century.

Modernity's process of development through modernism advanced to the point of comprehending the delicacy of the mind. This comprehension was so much more than what was known before. Language began to have meaning beyond words, the conception of beauty changed, and extreme experiments with language established new precedents. Functionality, complexity, different ways of ascertaining value, and properties of language were explored more in the twentieth century than the previous two. It is ironic that the number of readers of this new language in literature declined when the possibilities of language were more fully explored than any previous age in literature.

My personal experience with Western modernism is relevant to how I learned about modernism. When I began to learn of Western literature, Western modernism was a smooth and easy influence I could acquire compared to my real life, where exploring new ways of living was so difficult in my conservative Confucian family. Both Korean and Western literature commingled in my personal reading experience: Yi Kwang-su, Kim Dongni, Chae Mansik, Yi Sang, Flaubert, Dostoyevsky, Faulkner, and Kafka lived together. This was not due to any similarity in their writing, but because Korean literature found itself practicing methods of modern literature. Koreans who were interested in literature naturally had to read literature from the West.

Writing by Koreans and Westerners of the previous generation was strange to me. There was a meaning found in the writing that surpassed the range of my young emotions. This was unusual given the youth of Korea at that time could find themselves in new circumstances almost hourly. Until now, the landscape of Korean literature has changed as rapidly as Korean society has, and that change has been almost constant. It has been shown that Korean modernism, including its literature, has gone through changes faster than anyone could have anticipated. When modernism began in Korea, the literature of the time changed so much as to seem bizarre compared to the literature of the previous generation.

The influence of Western modernism played a critical role in my reading of dated Korean views on language and literature. At first, I could not completely separate myself from Korean classical literature, the morality of Korean traditional culture, or the Confucian sway over the Korean language. As I began to change, I experienced all three of these influences as oppressive. The traditional characteristics of Korean literature prevented me from approaching the true nature of human life from any point of view or sense of accuracy. These traditional characteristics had to be overcome. The traits of modernism I experienced through Western literature served as an important mirror for me. The mirror showed a way out of my burdensome influences so I could pursue my own perspective.

As my literary aspirations grew I made declarations like: "From public person to individual person"; "From a closed, self-sufficient system of meaning to one exposed to the outside"; "A true system of objectivity distanced from familial sentiment"; "From a literature of meaning wherein the pursuit is a publicly defined purpose to that of honest expression."

When Western literature broadly began to influence Korea, the situation in Korea was, at the outset, different from the West, as I have described above. There was an urgent need to reflect on this new Western literature with a calm mind. Korean literature of the time was the supreme tool for personal expression. It was widely available, and could uniquely enter the arena of history's ongoing evolution with regard to human rights, even though literature as a discipline never actually explores the marvelous worlds of humanity.

Literature of that time in Korea could not be free from the crisis of the divided peninsula and unnecessary dictatorship. It was in the seventies and eighties that Korean literature intervened in the unfolding of Korean history with a direct language. The Korean language in literature became a powerful, aggressive, and enlightened force for social reform and it expressed a sense of urgency for our Korean race. Compared to the old lyric tradition of Korean literature, this new use of language was fresh and had a sense of purpose in those days. The innovative craft in language was an important beginning that helped Korean literature flourish, leaving behind the scars of our country's dictatorship.

Since the beginning of Korea's new modern literature, which began with novels like Lee, In-jik's in the early 20th century, how many works of literature that followed emphasized the "strength" of the Korean identity? Without a distinctive rhetoric or aesthetics of power, it would have been difficult for Korean literature to leave the fetters of its troubled history behind. Even so, the energy that makes our literature strong and unique is not different from the masculine energy of Western modernity. This Western energy has influenced Korea's discourse of resistance.

The agony I experienced was that my writing was not a departure from the contemporary aesthetics of the time. I had to rise above this contemporary writing as well as accept it. I have always believed that literature should continually evolve when it describes our constantly changing world. My writing was groping in the dark, but also progressing—it was not simply a necessary tool for the times.

As time passed, my interest focused on the possibility of a different kind of literature—one less heroic, beyond the use of literature as a means to an end, and a modest literature free from authoritarian fantasies and distractions. I believed this new kind of literature could find a place in the Korean literary tradition. The idea of writing the kind of novels typically written or read by women was strange to me; I am referring to novels that had an attitude of consoling, comfort, safety, or lyrical sentiment. I had the same feeling towards literature that was straightforward, had aggressive masculine power, or outright challenged such power. Running away from these trials, fearing the potentially long struggle, or spending time trying to determine how well a new piece of writing works was to others a dereliction of my duty as a writer. I, however, was interested in a different kind of trial and struggle. And isn't every bit of progress made in literature the result of change? Every genre of literature is the sum of its contents, and can legitimately provoke the reader to ask questions. Between the orbits of materialism and the human spirit, literature always intersects with civilization to break new ground. Western modernism revealed to me many examples of form prioritized over content in those early writing years of mine. A style emphasizing cooperation between form and content became a new alternative for those writers exploring technical avenues.

Western modernism introduced Koreans to a new aesthetic standard that had been absent from non-western writing. Non-Western literati considered this new aesthetics a criterion for determining the value of a given piece of literature's modernity. It should not necessarily have been like this.

The Second Dilemma of Modernity

In literature, everything having to do with modernity became treated more attentively than in other fields. This was because an important conflict in literature brought about Western modernity's expansion. Language is the most important thing in literature; in no other field does language have such a presence. As I have said before, the ideas of modernity grew in the name of universal standardization through phases. This was due to a cross-cultural consensus. The process of creating a literature with the characteristics, questions, or appearance of modern Western literature instilled a slow growth of different literary styles in the world. Western literature came to be called "modern" in Korea, as it had been in other countries. When something is called "New Literature" in Korea, it typically suggests a style combining tradition with a Western literary motif, and a style suited for that motif. Similarly, the literature of several non-Western countries was ushered into the age of modernity. These were important changes for Korea.

Literature has become what Goethe dreamed—a global community. This is a natural outcome of modernity. Communication is one quality of literature that is universally valued. I often ask myself whether literatures of the world are becoming alike, just as the streets in Asian cities are becoming covered with advertisements from multi-national corporations. The essence of literature has a commonality that rises above individual differentiation. It is the reason why we, though not the same, come together to share ideas when we first meet.

At first glance, when literatures appear to have a sense of correspondence at the end of a trend, it is often the outcome of a new technical approach to language and genre. Inquiries into language have already diverged from questions of life and language. Genre is no longer a method for analyzing the world, but a skill. In the name of diversity, valuation of literary aesthetic standards disappeared in modernism as the range of possibilities became exhausted. So many experiments with literature and language carried out in the twentieth century have turned into variations of duplication. The word "universality," which now has an almost antique feeling, might fade into a more precise authoritative meaning regarding progressive stages of a given culture's development.

In this century, the function of language has been thoroughly investigated by Western civilization. The language of world literature has also been methodically examined. The world community because of problems with universal standardization has not yet agreed upon the value of this study. Though it is desirable and beneficial to agree on a universal human nature, deciding on how to name a thing so that it can be understood throughout the world requires a universal standardization to first take place. This is also true when deciding on how to make a meaningful assessment.

Literature is enjoying a new popularity in our age of globalization, and so literature has new universal standards. To discuss the morality of language and genre is now outdated in our global community of literature, but the universal standards in our postmodern age have neither rational authority nor significant beauty. This is in contrast to how modernism began.

Universal standards of culture and civilization came to non-Western countries like Korea in a way that was completely superficial, measurable, wasteful, offensive, and from misguided imagination. Most countries in the world are offended by how their respective cultures have been homogenized. This is certainly the case for Korea and other non-Western cultures that have mostly developed in isolation. We can observe in our daily life the qualities of this imperfect universalism in ideology, technology, economics, and how human beings consume on every continent of the world.

Literature may be the last field to resist or lay low the present trend of globalization in the world. The problems of language being a sign representing cultural identity or structures of the mind have become more important to the core of literature in today's postmodern age. If distinction, unusualness, character, identity, culture, language, and difference are emphasized even more as modernity unfolds, it demonstrates that a tendency toward global standardization does not necessarily lead to quick advancement. After stages of cultural growth where difference, distinction, and unusualness are emphasized in discourse, these changes are considered as established truths and have a political necessity.

Despite this, in the name of difference the world continues to suffer from discord worse than any other time in history. Endless competition and war among regions, races, and ethnic groups shows that problems remain in this era of globalization we all live in. Everyday in the world's news we clearly see problems that people still have not surmounted. Ethnic conflicts on the African continent, political negotiations in the Mid East or even along the ceasefire line of the Korean Peninsula—the evidence of human struggles born from difference abounds.

Chaos resulting from these situations has no substance for those who see language as the last bastion of defense against global standardization. Certainly, a small ethnic culture and its language may be like an island estranged from the world, resisting what otherwise is universally accepted. The presence of islands like these on the map of culture insists on the necessity of difference because of the characteristic nature of literature. Literature places great value on the uniqueness of individuals in our global culture.

In this vortex of standardization and difference, I ask myself a question. Does the regional and national uniqueness of a literature's language endure because of its power to resist standardization, the most dangerous aspect of modernity? If not, is it because such a small language or culture may grow into a neglected field of study if it is not already? Could such a situation for a culture's literature be connived as a necessary evil of the world or perhaps even be the reason for not resisting standardization? Everywhere in the modern world standardization and difference in literature seem to coexist, though a precarious state of balance is maintained. We find this ironic situation everywhere in the world; it has no regional preference.

I cannot help sensing a threat that formed at the end of modernism. This force resembles an ever-growing perpetual-motion machine. It is the reason why uniqueness coupled with diversity in literature has become a form of resistance—it creates its own new standards of coherence. The capacity to resist global standardization is the reason why literary language penetrates the superficiality of universalism. Resilient literature cuts across layers of the human soul, deeper than practical or scientific surfaces.

Is there a need for human beings to be rid of every inconvenience? I believe some difficulties in human life should be protected, kept, and perhaps celebrated. Literature has a duty to make room in the culture of universalism as it rises like a tide. Literature, through its uniqueness, monitors universalism. This quality literature possesses can, by itself, resist the onslaught of standardization. When universalism respects difference, at least in literature, it naturally enters the realm of writing for peace.

Translated by **Heo Tae-young**

Session X

Commonality of East Asian Cultures: Past, Present and Future

Moyan | There Can Be No Common Feature Without Individual Character

Park Yeemun | Social Responsibility or Poetic Obligation

Choi Won-shik | The Construction of A Common Language of East Asia

There Can Be No Common Feature Without Individual Character

Moyan

I am a Chinese writer who can understand no foreign language. I have only read a few Korean and Japanese literary works translated into Chinese and I only know a couple of Korean and Japanese writers. Thus, it is a truly difficult task to talk about the common features of East-Asian literature or to reflect on the East-Asian literature of the past or to assess current East-Asian literature. As a Chinese proverb says, it is like a dog that bites a high mountain, and as such so I do not know what to say here.

In my opinion, in order to discuss the common features of East-Asian literature, one should have great professional learning and should have deep knowledge about the geography, history, language, culture and customs of the East-Asian area. Upon this he or she could then compare East-Asian literature and then try to find the common features in that category. However, I am not endowed with such a knowledge and I am not gifted in that field, so therefore I am going to talk about some topics in connection with Chinese literature through only my own life experiences and writings. From my point of view, there leaves no room for doubt that Chinese literature is an important component of East-Asian literature and international literature. Chinese writers are part of a trend flowing in one direction on the current of world literature together with the global economic system. This situation is not different from the problems which the writers of the East-Asian area are experiencing.

Of course when we talk about the history of literature or about the content expressed in literary works, or discuss referring to the genealogy of literature and literary succession, the works of each country can be said to have their own characteristics. In other words, East-Asian literary works express their own individual character. I think it natural that we begin to study the character of the literature of each country in order to study the common features of East-Asian literature. I think that the purpose of studying the common features of East-Asian literature is to preserve and develop the individual literary character of each country.

The character of modern Chinese literature is closely related to the big events that happened in the recent and modern history of China. For instance, long-lasting wars, delaying time in vain, the violence that renders its witnesses shocked, starvation ferocious enough to make people mad, and a whole nation's religious mania on the verge of mental derangement all had a tremendous impact on the spirit of the contemporary writers, and this has been expressed repeatedly in many literary works. Besides these, just as the literature of every country has its own original form, so China has the heritage of its brilliant history, culture and literature. For example, the poems of the Tang period, the lyrics of the Sung period, the music of the Yuan period and the novels and comedies in the Ming and Ch'ing dynasties are dissolved in the blood of the writers and poets like a genetic factor. This has developed continuously for a long time and the contemporary literature manifests the distinctive Chinese characteristics. Of course, a genuine literature has the peculiar character of the world literature from the moment of its birth. In other words, a good work of literature, irrespective of what language it was written in, necessarily has common literary features and becomes a part of world literature.

Ordinarily speaking, we Chinese call the literature from the establishment of the People's Republic of China in 1949 up to now "Chinese contemporary literature." Chinese contemporary literature has walked along a tedious and winding path. The literature of the thirty years from 1949 to 1979 was treated as political material and was exploited as an instrument of political propaganda. Owing to the position of rank and the limitation of the ideology of the political party, the freedom of writers' creative writing and their horizon of literary expression were narrow and the writers' talent was suppressed. Accordingly, the literature of the period lost the common features of the world and East-Asian literature and was little more than propaganda of little value.

To my knowledge, Chinese contemporary literature in the genuine sense started in 1979. At that time, literary liberation and ideological liberation had been in progress simultaneously and the chains embodied in the slogan "Literature Works for the Politics," which had restrained Chinese writers for so many years, were cut. The liberated writers raked up the taboos one by one through their literary works and drew from the grudges in their hearts and articulated the resentment of the people. It was a coincidence with a historical event, and such a coincidence caused Chinese contemporary literature to take back unprecedented reputation and honor.

However, the literature in those days was relatively immature and of a clearly political bent and had a comparatively crude artistic character. With the onset of the 1980s, society gradually opened and taboos were dug up one by one. At this time writers began to be interested in the artistic character of literature and to research this aspect. During this period a large quantity of literary works of the Western world were translated into Chinese. As a result, numerous Chinese writers were awoke and they boldly began to imitate or refer to the Western works.

I started my literary career in 1985 with a novel named *A Transparent Carrot.* I had written a couple of novels before that time, but they were not popular among readers and I felt it difficult to write creative works. In my mind was a bugbear of finding a creative method that combined the so-called revolutionary realism with revolutionary romanticism. What was most difficult for me at that time was that I had no particular subject to write about. In the early 1980s, I was able to come in touch with some Western literary works such as William Faulkner's *The Sound and the Fury*, Gabriel Marquez's *One Hundred Years of Solitude*, Kafka's *The Metamorphosis*, Kawabata Yasunari's *Snow Country* and the like. After I read these books, I felt as if I had just awoken from a dream. I wondered why I could not realize earlier that a novel could be written that way. If I had discovered that earlier, I might not have been tortured with anxiety in search of the materials of a novel. I could have found similar subjects in my hometown and in my childhood and anywhere else. Those subjects are much the same, aren't they? Since then, having thrown away those books, I began to write my own novels.

I was successful in Chinese literary circles and was acknowledged by the readers because I could realize much from William Faulkner and Gabriel Marquez and established "Gaomi Dongbeixiang," which means "the Republic of Literature." Before that time, what tormented me most was that I had no subjects to write about. I often ransacked magazines and newspapers distractedly in the search for materials for novels and even ran about countryside villages and collected materials by visiting a factory. But once I returned home, I felt my head empty and I found myself unable to write a single letter on the manuscript paper. After that, in my novel entitled *A White Dog, A Swing and Its Seat*, I unconsciously wrote the following sentence. "There was a big white dog in Gaomi Dongbeixiang and, with the lapse of several generations, there was no purebred dog to be found."

Immediately after that, I felt that my visual field suddenly grew light and the mountains and streams of my hometown, the cultural climate and tender heart, the particular history of my family members, my needy life of twenty years, the folklore and the past episodes conveyed from mouth to mouth by the hometown acquaintances . . . all those things realistically came across my mind one by one just like Ali Baba, having cried out the spell "Open Sesame!" was suddenly spiritually awakened and opened the gate of the cave where the forty thieves had hidden their treasures. Numerous characteristic figures began to flash before me, competing with each other, talking about their own story to each other, desiring to be figured as characters in a work of fiction. At that time, I began to write hastily as if a poor person had suddenly obtained great wealth. The time when I had nothing to write about came to an end and now I was faced with too many topics to write about. I am a weak and timid person in real life, but when I write a fiction, I have a strong will and such courage that I am afraid of nothing.

From the moment I took Gaomi Dongbeixiang as my own space

for fiction, I felt like a beggar that had become a king of a country. All things in that place were ruled by my words and all the people, regardless of sex or age, were driven hard by me. If I attempted to kill a person, he could hardly keep his life, and if I intended to keep a person alive, he could never die. I was as happy as I could be as a writer. I could create Heaven and Earth and direct with my chin at my will and my Gaomi Dongbeixiang encompassed the whole world. It was the whole world and I was able to use everything as though they were my own possessions.

For the past twenty years my literary conception has passed through many changes. The only thing to which I have consistently held fast is the matter of individualization, which means that of creative writing and works. If I were a creative writer, I should essentially stick to the independent character of a person. It can be maintained when we keep enough distance from the current and style of the times.

Any creative writer will carefully look into a thing that can be the subject matter of a literary work, but the subject matter, unlike that of the masses, is depicted on the basis of a life that is rich in marked individuality. A language which a writer uses is naturally the language to which he belongs and should be distinguished from the language which other people use. A creative writer has a peculiar point of view to accomplish things and this is certainly not the same as the peculiar point of view of other people.

I think that a creative writer must not evaluate or judge a character or an incident of a novel at his convenience. But when he makes a literary criticism, it would seem that he should use critical criteria which are not identified with popular customs. Like this, the individualization of creative writing is emphasized here, and as a result the situation seems to have lost partiality. But we can hardly regard it as literature without any partiality. Of course I do not consider the golden mean, fairness and propriety to be the only good attitude which a writer should keep firmly in mind. It is a drawback of man to follow a certain trend or a crowd. Even though some people are disciplined in a group by compulsion, not all of them will lose their individuality. However, the huge inertia produced by the discipline in a group will push us to the edge of a violent current of the group, and our voices, having been buried in a loud chorus, will be rendered inaudible and feeble.

The chorus of a crowd is most important in our social life. But a singer who possesses a peculiar value will desire to produce his own peculiar voice which will not be lost in the sound of the crowd. Likewise, an ambitious creative writer will want to create his own work that is distinguished from the works of other people. Of course, I do not wish to say that the so-called individualization of a writer means that a work is seemingly against reason or that it seizes on trivial subject matter. The individuality of a writer should express his independent thought and personality in proper order. It is essential that in any situation or system he maintain his posture against it and that his thought and his personal independence be preserved. The writer will neither belong to any power or any group nor will he submit to any profit group or power. Likewise he will not use his creative work as a means of flattery.

The individualization of a work is naturally established on the basis of the writer's independent thought and personality. Of course, there will be no individualization of a work without the individualization of the subject of creative writing. I imagine the individualization of a literary work means that, first of all, the writer's disposition needs to be characteristic. Here, it needs something abstruse in terms of psychology and genetics and those fateful factors can seldom change. As a matter of fact, we can find numerous characteristic persons, but it would seem all the characteristic persons cannot become writers.

Next, when we take a look at the individualization of a literary work, there is an inseparable relation with the individualization of the writer's life style, and this constitutes a foundation. The writer's independent growth environment, the peculiar situation of his life and his unique experience of survival become the factors of the individualization of a work. Generally speaking, the writers who left monumental works underwent different experiences from those of ordinary people, which we can possibly say to be their destiny. What I mean by being destined here is that it should be experienced in later days and that it will be of no service with only the basic factor.

Suppose that you disguise yourself as a beggar and go begging on the street. You can obtain nothing but a physical and superficial experience. It will only be a response to the outside world and you will never have any deep feeling in your mind. However ragged you may be and even if you are bitten by a vicious dog and are dripping with blood, you would never forget that you are a writer and that you have only disguised yourself as a beggar.

The writer's acquired characteristic life also works as an important factor in literary creative writing. For instance, the geographical environment of the district where you are living, the cultural education you receive and the people with whom you have been socializing while growing are the factors that are to be decided before you grow to be a writer. Once you become a writer, those are the factors that will decide the fundamental features of a person. Your later situation and your effort may naturally become a factor in the matter of creative writing, but it is only a partial factor and not the fundamental one.

In such a situation most people cannot avoid being discouraged, but all efforts, being made in terms of individualized creative writing, seem to be fundamentally useless. This is surely a cruel reality, but even in the presence of many invariable factors, I think we can finally preserve and express our own individuality under the stimulation and consideration of the outside world.

So far as I know, in connection with the outstanding East-Asian literature, many excellent characteristic writers have been writing creative works. In order to pursue individualization, we must start from the reality of our people and our own hometown as well as from our country. And then we should make our way to the wider world and learn positively from foreign writers. Looking back on our own people once again, we must write a great many creative works. Among the East-Asian writers, there is a common feature of the writers of each country. After we study the common features of East-Asian literature, we should try to write characteristic works respectively by avoiding writing similar styled works. We can say that this is genuine literature.

A genuine literature is necessarily expected to manifest the abstruse and mysterious soul of mankind, but the manifestation of the abstruse and mysterious soul of mankind means neither the common feature of East-Asian literature nor that of world literature. Accordingly, East-Asian writers must emphasize and display individualism in order to realize an East-Asian common character. And when the creative works of East-Asian writers achieve concrete individualization, they will certainly be studied as the literature of the East-Asian region and through this way will occupy a high position in this tough world of literature.

Translated by **Moon Jung-il**

Social Responsibility or Poetic Obligation
(A Critique of the Marxist Conception of Literature)

Park Yeemun

Preface: Writing in the Primitive Age

Technological and scientific advancement has reached a stage where it has come to backfire, plunging mankind into catastrophic dangers. The Iron Curtain, drawn by the Eastern European nations that came to symbolize ideological and power conflict, crumbled overnight. The world hoped that harmony would come to replace conflict, peace to replace war, so that the international community would become home to civilized beings, not savages. The world, however, presents a quite different picture after a quarter century. Despite technological accomplishments we find ourselves exposed to a greater degree of political and social violence and fear stemming from aggravated conflict, wars, terrorist attacks such as suicide bombs. It is imperative for us to overcome such crises to restore peace from war, cooperation from conflict, reason from violence, civilization from savagery. Such is the most pressing challenge which warrants collective attention from mankind. Our obligation to seek a solution to the challenge calls for action which is, in turn, participating in reality. Taking part in resolving social ill is characterized as "categorically imperative."

But how exactly are we supposed to participate in society? That would depend on individual capacity and occupation. Then how are we as people involved in creative writing or creators of works of art to carry out our responsibility as members of society and take part in the real world? What are our obligations as poets, if I may narrow the term for the sake of convenience? What should we produce in the face of world demand for writing for peace?

Karl Marx's quote "The philosophers have only interpreted the world, the point, however, is to change it" readily comes to mind. Marx's belief is based on the view that the role of philosophy lies not in discovery of objective truth of the existing world, but in social reform towards a world we hope for. We call this "participatory philosophy." The logic applied to Marxist participatory philosophy can be used to create a "participatory literature" which asserts the responsibility and obligation of poetry to contribute to social reform and a better world for mankind.

However, is this truly viable? If the roles of philosophy and literature lie in changing the world, and thus, literature to become "participatory literature," what form should it take? As an answer to these questions, I will first discuss the relationship between civilization and language; second, that between existence and language; third, that between social responsibility and the poetic obligation of the poet; and finally, which types of writing can truly fulfill writing for peace.

I. Civilization and Language

1. Language as the Background of Civilization

Civilization is a strategy devised by humans to raise their quality of life. It is also a technical device and conceptual structure. History of mankind corresponds with the development of civilization and the history of development. Civilization has evolved since the primitive ages when human life and that of chimpanzees were hardly distinguishable to reach today's advanced hi-tech era where we are able to conquer the universe, decode the mystery of life and manipulate it at our will.

What is civilization? It is the product of language. Language renders life to culture, the concept and "meaning" of the world. Its outcome and incidents are exposed to humans and their consciousness to become objects to be described. Humans control the objective circumstances in which they are situated, make plans for the future, choose how to react based on such circumstances, and can develop their lives in a creative manner. Language, or the artificial symbol system that is unique to humans, serves as the starting point and the end point to enable humans to communicate their perceptions and consciousness. Language transforms physical nature into culture and the physical phenomenon into "meaning." The human being does not hold any value nor express its body, soul, inner or outer world outside the boundary of language.

2. Language: Its Bright as Well as Dark Side

What meaning does civilization, the product of language, hold in the lives of humans? Is it a blessing or misfortune? Advance or setback? The answer is seemingly evident. In this day and age when human civilization has successfully come to devise sophisticated means to control, conquer, manage, and manipulate nature, man has succeeded in propagation of its species, longevity, material prosperity, health, and high quality of life. Civilization, thus, undoubtedly comprises the concept of progress.

Recently, however, people have grown to realize that "progress" is only one facet of civilization. The bright side of civilization invariably produces shade which appears to grow darker as time goes by. As Freud and Marcuse had pointed out a century ago, the blessings of civilization have continued to demand payback. The price to pay is the fundamental and natural repression of the body and life on an instinctive and sensitive level. Had it not been for the pain of such repression, civilization would not have existed. In other words, without sacrificing the "Pleasure Principle," or the 'immediate fulfillment of the Eros,'a basic motivation of life, civilization would not have come to exist.

The problem, however, lies in the fact that the price to pay has risen too high. Had the hi-tech science civilization not been invented, mankind might not have had to worry about the possibility of the end of mankind due to war of mass destruction, terrorist violence, destruction, conflict between individuals, classes, regions, and race, environmental pollution, and destruction of the ecosystem. Civilization has revealed its ugly side - violence and repression in place of peace and happiness, a curse rather than a blessing. It has come to disclose its true color, much like Ouroborus, the snake eating its own tail.

What is the reason for such unavoidable two extremes of

civilization? The search for the answer should begin from the paradoxical functions of language.

II. Being and Language

1. Language and Cogitation

Language enabled man to perceive, recognize, and explain nature as an objective target, to observe and reflect on oneself, to engage in the improved construction of rational cogitation, and to choose one's action in a logical manner. Language must precede cogitation which, in turn, is a precondition of civilization. Language is the background and the underlying structure of cogitation and civilization. If civilization is the world unique to man, language is the source and essence of civilization. Man and civilization sans language are nothing more than concepts contradicting each other. Existence is recognized only through language. Language is the catalyst that forms the relationship between nature and man, as well as the force behind the creation of mankind. Heidegger once said language is "das Haus des Seins." Through the magical powers of language, phenomena and objects buried in obscurity and darkness have emerged under a category of concepts such as "God," "sky," "sea," "human," "dog," "wind," "tree," "refrigerator," "atomic bomb," "computer," or "book," while concepts that can neither be perceived nor understood were named, "goodness," "wickedness," "truth," "falsehood," "beauty," or "ugliness." Civilization is a conceptual transformation of the objective existence, nature, and the world following the above mechanism and the product of human effort to categorize and name objects through language.

Means with which the concept of existence is dug from human subconsciousness include objective and scientific method of recognition and explanation, while poetic language is expressed in a subjective manner. The outcome manifests itself in different ways - writing as scientific description and theory and writing as poetic expression and literature. Either way the outcome is to express an object outside the boundary of recognition and to conceal its existence. Language unearths "existence" hiding deep inside human consciousness and helps humans recognize and describe it.

Existence can be described in an objective manner using scientific language or in a subjective manner through poetic language. The two types of writing come in different forms, the former as descriptive and theoretical writing and the latter as poetic and literary writing. Either way, existence comes to light and, at the same time, conceals itself through writing. For words representing perceptive existence such as "god," "sky," "earth," "man," "dog," or "computer," as well as those describing conceptual existence such as "good/evil," "beauty/ugliness," or "truth/false" are nothing but concepts rather than perceptual entities, unlike the concrete objects these purport to describe.

Such an argument indicates that recognition of the world through the formation of a relationship based on contact and access with objects is impossible without breaking away from or keeping distance with, in other words, distortion or concealment of the existence. Discovery of truth by gaining access to existence is a distorted view due to separation from the existence. No linguistic representation or recognition is totally free from the intrinsic paradox and conflict of writing. Truth contains falsehood from the beginning, and vice versa. Existence also holds falsehood that was created by the linguistic distortion which operates on concrete existence before linguistic representation. While language can be the torch lightening the truth, it is also a violent force that invariably distorts existence. Without language, however, humans can no longer be. Language is like the hands of King Midas who was enslaved by the greed for gold.

King Midas was content to have possessed the magical powers to turn everything into gold at the touch of his hand. But he soon finds out that such powers can turn against him and destroy him. He needed food to live and had to touch the food to do so. The food, however, would instantly turn into gold at his touch. We who cannot but seek the truth of the universe are in constant search for the truth and have no choice but to resort to the use of language, much like the hands of King Midas. The challenge is whether humans can avoid the mistakes made by King Midas and reach the gold of unfolding the truth of existence without distorting the existence itself.

As a last resort, we categorize the use of language into "scientific" and "linguistic" in order to complement the shortcomings of one another. The writings manifest themselves as distinguishable types of writing - objective and subjective description. Such division is omnipresent in all language rather than being limited to specific language groups. This is not a coincidence but rather an unavoidable outcome. Language has struggled to overcome its intrinsic and unavoidable paradox. The struggle is in part Pascalian and part Sartrean - the former represents humans who exists as part of nature and at the same time who recognize and show awareness of nature while the latter reflects humans who can never become free of the impossible desire to become perfect and resemble god.

2. The Paradoxical Desire of Humans, Sartre's View of Human Existence and Heidegger's Diagnosis

Based on Sartre's theory of human existence, the struggle which has become an integral part of humanity is a conflict between his stance as etre-pour-soi and etre-en-soi, the former reflecting the need for man to set nature as a target of conquest for practical reasons as an entity separate from nature, and the latter reflecting man's attempt to inevitably keep a distance with nature and the attempt to break away from the logically resultant isolation and restlessness by simply remaining as an object. Based on such premise, man's attempt to resolve such paradox is understandable and inevitable. The conflicting view of the world is manifested by two contrasting writing styles.

The existential structure of humans, also called Homo loquens due to their linguistic properties, has all but obliged man to connect with nature and the outer world only through the use of language. Thus, man cannot but devise a scientific language that aims at utilizing the object of description and a poetic language that gears to exposing the truth of the object. The insatiable desire on the part of humans have developed civilization as a functional devise to continuously and faithfully satisfy the need of humans. In the process of satisfying the ever-expanding ambition the existence, nature, and the world have been exploited at an accelerating pace, resulting in the rapid advancement of scientific language and the cognition of the scientific world. In contrast, poetic language today, or the cognition thereof, has been in retreat, barely noticeable.

Why is this becoming a problem? If such a trend is attributable to the dominance of fetishism, why is the desire to fulfill materialistic needs becoming an issue? The answer to resolving the conflict between the scientific and poetic language can be sought through Heidegger's critical analysis of the history of Western philosophy.

According to Heidegger, post-Socrates philosophy is void of the essential truth of 'der Sein,' while obsessing with the superficial truth of the fragmental 'die Seienden.' The misstep of Western philosophy neither stems from its scientific viewpoint nor its poetic view of the world. Heidegger's view is that as long as man exists as Homo Loquens, he/she does not have the freedom to choose one over the other. The core of the issue is that the dominance of the scientific world view over the poetic view has expanded and we are now at the stage where such dominance has become almost complete. Truth by post-Socrates standards is not the presence/aletheia of existence, but rather a product of fragmented concepts which can be used as tools through the process of rational abstraction. The rapid scientific and technological development has not only instilled a sense of emptiness not only to the Western hemisphere but to the entire world. Nihilism which destroyed the spirit and suffocated the vitality of mankind is a corollary of exploiting nature for the use of man and the dominance of scientific language over poetic language for this purpose.

Now how are we to overcome this crisis unfolding in 21st century civilization?

3. Scars from Science and Poetic Cure

Existence as a tool for realizing objectives set by man works within the framework of rationality between human and that exists at present in a concrete form (anwesen). Scientific cognition and description are created when man mobilizes symbols, or languages that allow humans to intellectually conquer and control through logical description, explanation, systematic categorization and recognition within the artificial conceptual framework such as "sky," "mountain," "animal," "man," "dog," "toothbrush," "shoes," and "computer," etc. From a scientist's viewpoint, anything outside such frame of recognition or concept does not exist. Thus the conceptual framework for existence proposed by traditional post-Socrates existentialism or modern scientific technological circles has little to do with existence itself, but rather an abstract structure of existence filtered through a rational network of artificially constructed concepts.

Existence, nature, the world, individual objects and perceptions are a single entity that defies all attempts to distinguish or categorize one from the other. Existence, nature, the world, and individual entities discussed by scientific language are not existence in the true sense. Rather they are nothing but ideally manipulated concepts construed by linguistic violence.

Then what kind of language is used by the poet in describing existence, nature, the world and "sky," "mountain," "animal," "man," "shoes," and "computer," etc.? All languages, in a sense, attempt to transform the concrete to the abstract in a logical manner. If linguistic intervention is intrinsically violent, the outcome would no doubt be violent and distort the object being described no matter who uses the language, including the poet, albeit different in severity when used by scientists. Such a rule has no exceptions because the violence and distortion of existence is something language cannot shed due to its nature.

Even though we admit that the scientist and the poet use the same too, that is, language, and thus poetry and science operate in identical mechanism, their intentions and functions are in stark contrast to each other. If scientific language is the result of sacrificing poetic language, poetic language uses language to cure the ailment and pain of existence inflicted by linguistic violence and distortion of both scientific and poetic languages. Poetry is neither language blurting out sweet beautiful and titillating senses nor decorative language aiming to seduce the senses by painting the world with sensational colors. Poetry pursues truth of objects just like science. The difference is that poetry tries to catch the original state of an object itself, yet to be conceptualized or verbalized, not with a view to render practical value to the object as in the case of science.

Such attempt is paradoxical because poetry must overcome its limitations using the exact medium it is trying to overcome. As was mentioned earlier by Sartre, the ultimate goal for man is to exist as etre-pour-soi, or an independent being and etre-en-soi, an object that has no autonomous powers. The objective of poetry is also paradoxical, just like the paradox raised by Sartre regarding final goal of humans. While poets are fully aware that his/her objectives will never be attained, the poet cannot give up. It is because poets are also human. It is the poet's dream to encounter the original state of a single existence, nature, and the world before they are compartmentalized into abstract forms by reason, before they are conceptualized by language. No poet, rather no human can ever be free from such desire. Such desire is especially strong for the poet. Just like Icarus who knew he would eventually crash to the ground, poets fly up towards the sun spreading their wings called language. The ultimate role of poetry, then, is to cure language of its defects via language, to rectify the distorted existence created through inevitable violence inflicted by the poet attempting to recreate an object.

Despite the paradox and defect intrinsic to poetic language, Heidegger asserted that it is poetry rather than science or philosophy that represents undistorted existence in its original shape, that true cogitation comes not from philosophical cogitation based on reason but from poetic cogitation beyond the reach of reason, that the most profound thinkers were not scientists nor philosophers but poets, and that the profoundest cogitation on der Sein were carried out not by rationalistic philosophers such as Socrates, Plato, Aristoteles, or Descartes but by poetic philosophers including Anaximander, Heraclitus, and Parmenides.

Based on Heidegger's reflections on language, the defender of existence is not the scientist nor the philosopher but the poet, the resting place of existence, therefore, lies not in scientific theory nor philosophical system but the poet's nest. Reflections on the function of poetry applies universally to all forms of literature and art. The literary circle cannot remain immune to the growing influence of commercialism which forces literature to play up to the taste of the general public and to succumb to the popular demand for vulgar material. In the process, the writer degrades him/herself with rhetorical products for entertainment. Despite the changing trend with the times, the fundamental role of poetry, literature and art remains unchanged.

III. Social Responsibilities and Poetic Obligations

1. Marxist View of Participatory Poetry, Literature and Art

How are poets, writers, and artists to engage in creative activities, and what kind of creation should they produce in a world where political, military, social, moral, and ecological violence is expanding at an alarming rate? What is the relationship between their social/moral responsibility and poetic/cultural obligation? As a member of society and part of history, no poet, writer, or artists can be free of such questions. How can a poet or a novelist contribute to the peace of his/her community as well as all mankind? This question should always be in the minds of poets, writers, artists, philosophers, scholars, and professional intellectuals. This question asks to what degree professional intellectuals should carry the burden of moral responsibility to participate in social issues and to be involved in improving the world.

The radical criticism by Marx towards conventional philosophy and philosophers mentioned at the beginning of my talk can also be applied to traditional creative writing, literature and art. If Marx held a participatory philosophy his views toward literature or art can be summed up as participatory literature or participatory art. Marx's participatory philosophy was realized in the form of "Socialist Realism" in the socialist revolutionary government of the former Soviet Union, literature as engagement by Sartre's existentialism, the proletariat literature theory of Japan and Korea in the 1930s, Marxist/leftist literature after the Korean war, the participatory literature movement of Korea in the 1970s and 1980s after the Korean war, literature for the general public, ethnic literature, and the reunification literature movement.

What does it mean, then, for poetry, novels, and art in general to participate? What does "participation" mean exactly? It means forming a relationship with a certain group, getting involved, and sharing the pain as well as the joy in the reform process of that group. Thus the role of participatory literature is to engage in literary writing which contains direct and active action related to social issues with a view to resolve and reform various social issues, big and small, fundamental and peripheral. Action functions under the premise that it is a value that is chosen and demands realization. If participation cannot but be ideological and thus political, poetic, literary, and artistic participation also must constitute a part of ideological and political action.

The "Socialist Realism" of the former Soviet Union has asserted the need not only for scientists and philosophers but also poets, writers, and artists to contribute to the inculcation of the public the disparity of capitalism, to the reform of the existing immoral society, and ultimately the creation of a just and equal society free of exploitation through scientific research, pursuit of philosophical truth, writings and art works in line with values established by the communist regime. The socialist realism literature of Korea in the 1970s and 1980s has expanded at an explosive rate as part of the social participation campaign of the people, the general public, reunification literature, culture and art in the literary and cultural arts circles. Social realism in the former Soviet Union and North Korea branded poets, writers, artists, philosophers, and scientists who were either opposed to or critical towards Marxist or Leninist ideology reactionary elements and purged them. In South Korea artists who were not completely in agreement with the ideology emphasizing nationalism or reunification were stigmatized as feudalists, anti-nationalists, anti-reunification, conservatives, reactionaries, or rightists and were the target of ridicule and disdain. Victims of such movements often found themselves unable to be established as artists during this time. Sartre's "Participatory Literature" is no different from social realism in that it denies the unique value of literature and asserts the need for literature to subjugate itself under political ideology. One discrepancy is that while Marxists put the realization of a communist society which guarantees justice and equality to mankind in the forefront among its highest value, Sartre aims at "securing and expanding the freedom of man," or the "existentialism of humanity."

2. Issues Surrounding 'Engagement' of Poetry, Literature, and Art

Is participation, or Marxist social reform or Sartre's existentialism, a unique role of poetry, literature, or art? The problem is that it is not. While philosophical theory can change the world, it is only one mode of recognizing and understanding the world. It cannot, in itself, become a means to function as an action plan nor can it change the world or society. A toothpaste, for example, can also be used to scratch an itchy spot or brush off the dust on shoes in addition to its original function of brushing teeth. The same goes for philosophy. While philosophy can be and has been used in numerous occasions as a tool for achieving economic, political, social, and ethical goals as well as discovering and recognizing truth, such functions are anything but unique functions of philosophy. There is a clear difference in logic between recognition itself and actions taken based on recognition. The realm of poetry, novels, and art works may and has frequently been used as tools to justify certain political ideologies or existing regimes of the ruling poser. However such functions are certainly not their essential roles. Words are neither agricultural products, manufactured goods, bulldozers nor bullets. Words are simply words void of any physical powers.

The value of poetry, novels, and art lies in the critical re-examination of ideology of power and the ruling system and, in some cases, resulting in its overturn rather than their functional utility to serve political, economic, and ethical values. In the process everything is viewed from a different and new perspective and, if possible, from an angle that reflects its essence and truth.

Classic literature did not earn its status through its political ideology or ethical values. Nor are great poets, writer, or artists and their works of ethical loftiness and progressive ideology granted their laudable status automatically. And there is considerable evidence to support this claim. The fundamental value of poetry, novels and art works lies not in offering ideological or emotional pleasure to the readers/audience. The true value of poetry, novels, and art works lies not in giving pleasure or comfort to readers but to illuminate or express through language or writing the world, society, man, and his/her experience in its original form before undergoing the conceptual manipulation process that either defied description through language or was hidden behind language. As was previously mentioned, such illumination and expression is the fundamental role of poetic, literary, and artistic language. While literature may serve as a tool for social reform of a particular ideology, it is neither a sufficient nor a necessary condition.

The question of whether literature should take active part in social issues has resulted in dichotomized positions of various names - participatory literature vs. pure literature, Marxist realism vs. bourgeois escapist literature, and nationalistic/proletariat literature vs. universal literature. To answer the question, we would first have to lay down the differences in two fronts.

First is the differentiation of political participation in the social sector and intellectual/spiritual participation on an individual level. To insist only the former constitutes true participation as does participatory literature is simply dogmatic.

The second is related to whether literature is an action plan for social reform based on a particular political ideology, a means of entertainment that meets the public needs, or a means to uncover the fundamental truth through intuitive recognition of existence, nature and the world. As with everything else, literature can perform all of the above. However, the unique role that can be performed only by literature would be the latter two rather than the first. Many areas other than literature may carry out the first role, while the other two are indigenous to literature. If not, there is little reason to justify the need for literature as one type of writing. Literature exists to meet the demand that cannot be fulfilled by any other type of writing. The fact that literature is a ubiquitous type of writing that can be found in any society in the world shows that man is continuously undergoing inner struggle regarding existence of self that is more instinctive, fundamental and personal than political or social reform. It also reflects the fact that man is in constant need for resolving such issues. The poet, writer, or artist who mainly deals with personal and inner existential drama largely remains outside the realm of public, social, and political matters.

Poetic, literary, and artistic participation, therefore, symbolize the sincerity and thoroughness of poets, writers, and artists who deal with themes unique to them. Unlike what supporters of participatory literature, socialist realism, nationalist literature, or Marxist literature think, literature participating in the world in a real sense does not lie in serving a particular political ideology. On the contrary, real participatory literature resists and criticizes such political and ideological pressure, lending sharp critique to images of existence, the world, and the true image of humanity distorted by abstraction of a particular ideology. Such literature and writing is true to its proper domain and "participatory literature" in the true sense. Such is the fundamental, original and sincere role of literature which helps human to become more humane as homo loquens.

From the viewpoint of the object subject to description, all forms of writing are inherently violent and repressive in that writing attempts to render abstractness to a concrete object and to hold it under a conceptual frame. Man as homo loquens, nevertheless, cannot break away from such restrictions. Man has continued to use such violent and repressive language to overcome the linguistic limitations and gain access to existence, nature, and the world in its original form. Man cannot free him/herself from the need to express and to explore internally and intellectually such experience. Thus came to existence poetry, literature and art. No other form of expression has resisted against violence in a fundamental level to convert conflict between man and nature, and among languages to peace more than poetry, literature and art. Poetry for poetry's sake only can represent such intentions.

Conclusion Poet as Citizen or Citizen as Poet?

1) Conflict between Citizen and Poet

We all have civil and moral obligations to contribute as part of a community to solving problems be it facing the society we live in or mankind. Then what exactly are the responsibilities of the poet, novelist and the artist who are professional writers?

Two different answers come to mind. First, as a poet, novelist, and artist, I can establish rules and take responsibility. Or, I can act as a citizen or a member of the society before being a poet. I can assert that I have the obligation to engage in the particular type of writing called poetry no matter what happens around me, be it a riot or a war - poetic writing is one mode to resist and overcome violence and oppression on a fundamental level.

And the other option? I may choose to do away with writing poetry, no matter how much I cherish the experience and decide to join the crowd in the streets, or go to the frontline to fight, asserting that such is my obligation and responsibility. Korea literati in the 1970s and 1980s would object to the former, criticizing it as a distorted form of "pure literature" and a morally cowardly "escapist literature." Those calling for "pure literature" or "independent literature" would brand "participatory literature" as anti-poetic and anti-literary pseudo-literature which subjugates literature under political authority.

Who is right? I would side with the latter. The former denies the unique role of poetry, novels, literature, and art, and refuses to separate its ideological, political and functional roles. Such denial is a fallacy since its argument is based on denying the very existence of "literature and art" expressed in the form of writing and symbols and the unique standards on which writings have been assessed.

2) Dilemma of Choice and Existential Decision

Then is the poet to exert his/her effort in producing poetry, turning a blind eye to the urgent and concrete difficulties, violence, oppression, injustice, and wrongdoing prevalent in society? Not necessarily. The poet can decide one's stance through objective comparison of two options - the value of one's poetry in a short-term vs. long-term view, microscopic vs. macroscopic view and the value of discarding writing, participating in social, political, and ethical issues that has little to do with poetry.

Those opting for the latter position have, in a sense, already given up writing "poetry" and, in turn, are expressing political and ideological values in the form of "poetry." At the risk of sounding paradoxical, true participatory poetry, literature, and writing are, in fact, anti-Marxist in that engaging in faithful poetic and literary writing can resist linguistic violence committed by ideology, conceptualization, theory, and science by destroying such language through writing. If such writing can be categorized as "pure," participatory literature and writing for peace in the true sense begins from faithfully adhering to pure literature and poetic creations. To produce the truest form of literature, the poet, writer, and artist are obligated to engage in the most poetic and literary writing and to perform their roles with the utmost sincerity.

This is not to say that the poet, writer, and artist must always adhere only to one's role under all circumstances. As was mentioned above, depending on his/her view of the world and values, one might give up poetic, literary, or artistic writing to plunge into the world of politics, ideology, economy and military and participate in the ideological arena, market place and the frontline for one's cause. Which position should one choose? No one can provide an answer. It depends on the thoroughly thought-out decision of the poet, writer and the artist. There is no paradox in these two truths. The poet is free, depending on the circumstances, to choose based on one's decision and live as a poet or live as a citizen.

Translated by **Kim Hye-young**

The Construction of A Common Language of East Asia

Choi Won-shik

1. The Korean Peninsula in the Age of Invisible War

If we are to say that the collapse of the Berlin Wall (1989) was the symbol that signaled the closing of the twentieth century, the September 11 terror (2001) was the shocking sign that opened the twenty-first century. As the socialism of the twentieth century (Leninism and its variants) rapidly declined, together with the diffusion of this kind of disillusionment, capitalism came to be praised as "the end of history," and the movement of capital, which attempts to develop on a commercial scale not only the far-flung regions of the globe but also that of the mind, is now sweeping the whole world under the name of globalization. When the brake of socialism that had steadily restrained the world of capitalism ceased its operation, like a majestic emperor, the hegemony of America became magnificent. And then a new form of terrorism, impregnated by globalization, demolished classical terrorism in a single stroke. As the gigantic flash struck America suddenly like a ghost, her illusion was acutely cracked. We are reminded that Immanuel Wallerstein[1)] pointed out the radical surfacing of East Asia (China or Japan) under the prospect that the dismantlement of the Soviet Union would accompany the degeneration of America. Even though the Soviet Union in the age of cold war commanded a partial hegemony together with America, America and the Soviet Union might be thought of as companions in the twentieth century, collapsing together if one side falls. The terrorism of September 11

1) Immanuel Wallerstein, *The End of the World as we know it: social science for the twenty-first century*, translated by Baek Seung-wook (*Changjak-gwa-bipyeong*, 2001), p. 82.

might be an important sign of that. In the proper America of the sacred and inviolable country that had never been exposed to an external attack, and what's more the Tower of Babel of capitalism in the heart of New York, the so-called Twin Towers were demolished in a roaring sound by cold-hearted terrorists. The incident revealed the modern revelation with a voiceless outcry from the innocent sacrificed souls.

Immediately after the incident, the Bush administration of America proclaimed "a war against terror" and dashed toward invisible enemies like a Don Quixote. However, America, which had plunged into a war against Iraq (2003), following a war against Afghanistan (2001), displayed her weakness in terms of hegemony. With the support of only England, and despite the opposition of the traditional alliances, America rapidly broke down the Hussein regime and proclaimed the close of the war in high spirits—but the war is still going on. After a lapse of two years since the proclamation of the termination of war, the early prediction that the Iraq War would be a second Vietnam War has proven true, as indicated by the unfortunate situation in which the number of American fallen soldiers is over one thousand. When we think of the irrational move of a one-sided strategy as the expression of weakness, not that of strength, we are afraid that America, which is driving the whole world into an invisible war, may also be another counterpart of the terrorists.

The one-sided strategy of America assigned North Korea to "an axis of evil" (2002) and drove the Korean Peninsula and Northeast Asia into a crisis of flux. The Korean Peninsula and Northeast Asia before the September 11 terror was on the verge of establishing a new base toward a twenty-first century of reconciliation and cooperation, having parted from the tone of the twentieth century, which was stained with conflicts and disputes. With the advent of the age of the post-Cold War, the southern triangled alliances (South Korea, Japan and America) and the northern triangled alliances (North Korea, China and the Soviets), which had stood face to face, were slowly softening. South Korea, which had passed through military dictatorship and entered a new democratic stage, and North Korea, where the succession of the Kim Il-Sung regime had proceeded, began to cooperate with each other and there was a growing tendency toward peaceful unification. The June 15 Pyongyang Proclamation, established in the year prior to September 11, was a dramatic milestone. The two Koreas, having washed away their long hostility, frankly recognized the impossibility of a one-sided unification strategy which they had confirmed through the Korean War. Both sides decided to grope for a way to peaceful unification, keeping in mind the common features of the South's confederation of provinces and the North's rudimentary federal system. The kernel of the proclamation was that both sides chose gradual progressionism on the basis of stable construction instead of a rapid unification strategy, which might be a seed of new dispute. Both sides experienced the Korean War's start as a civil war and easy expansion to an international war, and as such realize the partition of the Korean Peninsula is a potential powder keg that can lead the whole area into the terrible disaster of war. The proclamation is a message of peace upon which fly doves over the whole area as well as over the Korean Peninsula by disorganizing the root of disputes. However, America's war against terrorism directly after September 11 made North Korea a potential attack objective, and Northeast Asia is showing sings of returning to the status before the June 15 proclamation. As symbolized by the visit to Pyongyang by Koizumi, Japanese Prime Minister (September 2002), Japan had begun to pursue a definite autonomy from America but returned to the bosom of America on account of the North Korean nuclear crisis (October, 2002). Even China, in secret, joined America, which had tried to safeguard the single pole system and heeds the preservation of its own "empire" through the progress of the work of Northeast Asia. Taking advantage of the horrible terrorism in the Republic of North Ossetia that occurred just before the third anniversary of the September 11 terror, Russia also followed the containment offensive strategy of America. As the Strong Three around the Korean Peninsula imitated America, the relationship between South and North Korea suddenly stagnated.

How can we escape from this crisis? Now is the time when we feel keenly the necessity of all citizens' solidarity for peaceful movement across the boundaries of each country, avoiding some perilous factors that America's one-sided doctrine may cause and for the sake of peaceful abandonment of North Korea's nuclear weapons programs. Fortunately enough, the American one-sided doctrine restored again the peaceful movement against war, which had almost disappeared. A real peaceful movement began to burn for the first time in Korea on the occasion of the fiftieth anniversary (2003) of the armistice with the high spirits of the waves of a peace movements all over the world. Thinking of the brilliant lighting of candles to pray for the welfare of the Korean Peninsula and the world, the unification movement opened a new way to communicate outside of the text of a one-state doctrine on the Korean Peninsula. Combining the unification movement and the peace movement, the Korean attempt at a new movement devoted to the reconciliation of South and North, the solidarity of East Asia and the construction of an international peace system, ardently needs the deep understanding of the writers and intellectuals of the world. The theme of the International Literary Forum in Seoul on this occasion is "Writing for Peace." I hope that the scene of writers and intellectuals from around the world gathering to discuss "Writing for Peace" will be a humble stepping stone toward the solidarity of the citizens of the world to bring peace, which has slipped backward since September 11, into Northeast Asia.

2. The Korean Peninsula and Its Neighbors

The geopolitics of the divided Korean Peninsula is acute. When you consult a map of East Asia, China, adjoining the Korean Peninsula, comes in sight first. Of course, China reaches beyond the range of East Asia. China, which lies on the very long borderlines with Northeast Asia, Southeast Asia, Southwest Asia, Central Asia and Russia, is a kind of empire which has a long history. The People's Republic of China, located in the center of Asia, is concerned with all its frontiers, especially paying keen attention to the eastern region of China, the only opening to the long coastline. In the meantime, the eastern coastline, which China made an axis of development since its reformation and opening (1978), is a dangerous district that could lead to the fragmentation of the empire. This coastline was the invasive route through which modern Europe and America and Japan, the military spearhead of imperialism, rendered the empire of Ch'ing a paper tiger and is still today an area where the worldwide empire of America and its subordinate partner of Japan are facing each other as respective enormous powers. In this regard China has the feature of two sides, as a part of East Asia and crossing over the range of East Asia. China, which had crouched for a long time after the Opium War (1840-42), is now one of the most powerful East Asian countries. It is dreaming of the revival of the empire of China and it is observing the height of the waves of the Pacific Ocean very closely.

Russia is another empire bordering the Korean Peninsula. The central part of Russia is Europe but it would not be too much to say that the domination of Mongolia molded Russia, and Russia is a country which has a strong Asiatic character from its birth. There is an old joke that goes "Scratch a Russian and you find a Tartar,"[2] which means that Russia has maintained the succeeding character of the Mongol empire. Having broken free of "the yoke of Mongolia" in 1480 after the reign of Peter the Great from 1682 to 1725, Russia rose as an empire and crossed Siberia, "the calm land,"[3] through the invasive route of Mongolia. Russia made the Maritime Province of Siberia (Primorsky Krai) its territory in 1860 according to the Beijing Treaty and finally arrived at the border of the Korean Peninsula. The appearance of "the Empire of Winter" in East Asia aroused a deep sense of crisis all over the area. Not only China, which had a long borderline with Korea, but also America was trying to access the continent from the sea, and Japan joined the procession in preventing Russia from advancing southward. When the Soviet Union manifested an intention of joining the liberation movement of the East Asian people after the Russian Revolution (1917), China seceded from the line for a time. However, when the Soviets commanded a strong hegemony together with America after World War II, an ideological dispute (1956) between China and the Soviets gained momentum with Khrushchev's criticism of Stalin

2) Ruth Benedict, *The Chrysanthemum and the Sword: Patterns of Japanese Culture*, Boston: Houghton Mifflin Company, 1989. p. 290.

3) Sibir, the origin of Siberia, means "the calm land" in Mongolian.

and finally developed into a large-scaled border dispute (1969). A fissure came to appear between the two countries again. Seizing this opportunity, the United States had China secede decisively from the Soviet Union by means of ping-pong diplomacy (1971). The United States of America, foreboding the defeat of the Vietnam War, commanded a high-level strategy of reconciliation with China instead of giving up Vietnam. The reconciliation between China and America possibly could constitute a small post-Cold War signal, which led to the dismantling of the Soviet Union. Since then the Russian influence on East Asia has rapidly declined, but after the appearance of the Putin government, the catch-phrase of which is the reconstruction of a strong Russia, the situation is changing. Russia has regulated her identity as "“he bridge between Europe and Asia" and has been trying to restore her lost influence on East Asia ever since her collapse.

Unlike China and Russia, which share a border with North Korea, Japan and America across the sea, which do not border the Korean Peninsula, are exercising deep influence on this area through South Korea. We already know that Japan, which was reared as "the Military Police of Asia" by the imperialism of Europe and America, colonized the Korean Peninsula and Manchuria and finally invaded China. However, her dream to be an empire was frustrated as a result of the defeat of the Pacific War (1941-45).

After World War II, America entrusted Japan to manage East Asia and presented herself for the management of this area on the axis of Japan. America had lost the continent due to the success of the Chinese Revolution of Mao Tse-tung and narrowly secured South Korea from the Korean War (1950-53), and was now meddling in the state of Vietnam again. Ho Chi Minh's forces of North Vietnam defeated French troops and, on the occasion of the Geneva Convention (1954) which allowed North Vietnam to be governed by the communists, began to step into the state of Vietnam in the place of expelled France and participated in the war actively by sending ground troops from 1965. When Vietnam was unified by the Hanoi government in 1975, American troops came to tread in French troops' steps. If we can say that the Korean War was the first war that America did not win, then the Vietnam War was the first war in which America was defeated. In the United States of America's long process of reconstructing the anti-communism net encircling East Asia, Japan, which was selected as an enormous rear supply base, was successful in reconstruction, stepping on the ruins after the war under the umbrella of security from America. The success was due to the choice of America, which fostered Japan as her subordinate partner as the cold war intensified in East Asia. We need to heed the fact that Korea was able to spur its economic development owing much to the special procurements of the Vietnam War. This would be a stepping stone toward surpassing North Korea. As the Korea-Japan Agreement (1965) was contracted under the lead of America, America drew closer to the triangle of Korea, Japan and America. All these installations made America a winner over the Soviets in spite of its successive failures in East Asia.

Despite the advent of the post-Cold War age, East Asia is still unstable. The relationship between China and Taiwan can drive that of China-America – "neither friend nor enemy" – into a serious conflict at any time. Compared with relatively stable China and Taiwan, the Korean Peninsula is very fluid, because the non-symmetrical character is spreading due to the obviousness of the character. Nevertheless, the Korean Peninsula, which is the last divided country on Earth, still cannot dissolve the hostile opposition perfectly. Why is it that the Korean Peninsula is different from Vietnam, which achieved successful reunification at the end of the Cold War? It is because the geopolitical conditions of the Korean Peninsula, surrounded as it is by empires, are much more rigorous than those of Vietnam. If we can say that Vietnam is the southeast gateway of East Asia, then the Korean Peninsula is the northeast gateway of East Asia. Unlike Vietnam, which has only a northern border with China, the ill-fated Korean Peninsula is surrounded by the big four countries of the world, as was pointed out above. Unfortunately enough, Northeast Asia is one of the most heavily armed areas with the Peoples' Army of China, the Far East Army of Russia, the Self-Defense Forces of Japan and the Pacific Army of America stationed in Japan and Korea, including the concentrated military power of South and North Korea. How can we exclude the anti-peaceful factors from the insecure Korean Peninsula standing face to face with the supreme firepower at the border of the cease-fire line? That is the question. The Korean War has not come to an end even now after a lapse of over a half century since the cease-fire. In other words, the war is still going on even though combat was temporarily suspended under the agreement of the countries concerned. Moreover, since South Korea was against the cease-fire and was excluded from the conclusion of its agreement, South Korea is far from a treaty of peace to bring the state of war to an end.

In spite of this situation the reason we have been able to maintain a state of risky peace for more than half century is due to the lessons of the hot battle of the Korean War. Both sides have in common in their minds that it is impossible for the measures of war to alter the divided state of the Korean Peninsula, as we remember that we returned to a divided state again even after having experienced a severe international civil war. Nobody wants the Korean Peninsula to be returned under the domination of one of the big four countries around it. Since then, America and the Soviets tried to make South and North Korea a showcase in which they displayed their respective strengths through the non-military competition of systems. In this economic war North Korea was successful in reconstruction at the beginning after the war, but since the 1960s, South Korea leaped to affluence around the semi-peripheral area in terms of economic development. We can find that the paradox of the Cold War is breathing here. After the Korean War, East Asia has been constantly stable while South and North Korea have basically maintained the status quo in a hostile coexistence.

In the meantime, entering into the post-Cold War age, the Korean Peninsula and its peripheral area have been progressively destabilized, because the division of the Korean Peninsula is showing a sign of change. With China rising and South Korea advancing, North Korea is faltering. The fight of force in order to gain an advantage over the others is in full swing in the alteration of the status quo of the Korean Peninsula, which is a post of strategic importance to both continental powers (China and Russia) and the oceanic powers (Japan and America). Even in this crisis, the one-sided doctrine of America is restrained because East Asia is one of the most active economic axes in the world now. China, which strongly wants the maintenance of the status quo of the Korean Peninsula and will guarantee her economic growth, is taking the role of North Korea as a supporter and will depend on the fact above all that South Korea now realizes herself to be the greater victim of the crisis than at any other time.

3. Another East Asia

Why do we talk about East Asia? In other words, why are we dreaming of another East Asia? It is based on the wish for a permanent peace in East Asia, through the transformation of a hostile co-habitation into a harmonious co-existence of South and North Korea. The discussion of East Asia,[4)] raised at the entrance of the post-Cold War age, is testing "critical regionalism" as the golden mean across nationalism and globalism by establishing the Korean Peninsula (South and North Koreas), China (Taiwan, Hongkong and Macau), Japan (and Okinawa) as a unit of thinking or as that of analysis. The discussion of East Asia is a planning for peace in order to escape from the East Asia of the twentieth century that experienced repeated conflicts and hostility, having been involved as the guests of America and the Soviets, who brought the Cold War after the arrival of the West. Of course we do not mean to beautify the image of East Asia before modern times, because even at that time Korea, China and Japan experienced numerous severe conflicts, evolving around the Korean Peninsula. But the conflicts of the times were not habitual, unlike those after the arrival of the West. What is more, as the ghost of communism commanded its strong magical power over this area in the face of imperialism, the disputes came to take on much more complex aspects. In this regard, we must remember that the buds of the discussion on East Asia were shot out at that time in front of "the common crisis." At the beginning of the destructive threat of the West, the discussion on

4) Choi Won-shik, "The Discussion of East Asia as a Design of the Whole World Divided into Three." Toward the Northeastern Community, *Dong-A Ilbo-sa*, 2004. pp. 9-24.

East Asian solidarity was raised in the above three countries respectively. Now it is a matter of common knowledge that the discussion of solidarity was dispersed due to Japan's metamorphosis into advance guard points. Of course, we can hardly attribute the dissipation to Japan alone. If Korea and China had actively reformed the old system into the new state of affairs, they might have prevented the miserable war in which not only the invaded country but also the invading ones became victims. Discussions about East Asia are proceeding toward planning for discussions about the solidarity of Asia, frustrated one century ago in terms of criticism. As was pointed out above, the discussions on East Asia are not exclusive regionalism, namely, "the construction of East Asia by the East Asian people" held up by Japanese imperialism, but a critical regionalism which even America and Russia are seriously considering. The critical regionalism can abundantly communicate with the reality of internationalism. East Asia, where advantages and disadvantages are entangled on the axis of the Korean Peninsula, is an unintelligible Gordian Knot. The situation is too grim for the knot to be wisely untied with only nationalism and regionalism. Lee Gang-guk said as follows shortly after the Liberation of August 15, 1945:

> The people of Joseon were not able to liberate themselves with their own strength in spite of their bold and obstinate fight against Japanese Imperialism. ... The fact that the people of Joseon enjoyed the pleasure of liberation from the epoch-making victory of the democratic United Nations was a matchless joy to them and must be a matter of eternal regret at the same time.
>
> The international element in connection with the liberation of Joseon forces her to be restricted internationally in the solution of the problems of Joseon. … The solution of the problems of Joseon always can be understood and expected as only a part of the international and democratic solution of post-war problems.[5)]

Because the liberation or division of the Korean Peninsula was

5) Lee Gang-guk. The Construction of Democratic Joseon, *Joseon Inminbo-sa, Dept of Public Welfare*, 1946. p. 110.

achieved internationally, the solution of its problems also should be done internationally. This grim insight is valid even now. Discussions about how to construct a peaceful system in East Asia on the axis of the peaceful foundation of the Korean Peninsula are also the product of internationalism in anticipation of globalism.

Owing to the attempt to pass over the past approach of a one-state doctrine, the criticism is raised that any discussion of East Asia is a very naive one on the post-nationalism that underestimated the Cold War structure, which still exists in this area.[6)]

If the discussion of East Asia brings up nationalism as only an object of dismantling, it deserves criticism. In reality, there are some that belong to this category. I think that the nationalism should be overcome fundamentally, but we are not to deny the property (nationalism) now when the hierarchy of the world system is operating sternly, with core, semi-periphery and periphery. Rather, even for a smooth dismantling of the hierarchy, the work of establishing a proper country, where the welfare of the general public is soundly embodied, is the kernel. The dual working of embodying nationalism and passing over it can be said to be the discussion of East Asia. And the discussion of East Asia never underestimates the Cold War structure, still a factor in this area. The discussion of East Asia is the planning of a post-Cold War version of East Asia, in that this discussion was raised in order to break through the reality still burning as East Asia's Cold War legacy even as post-Cold War waves travel worldwide.

To begin with, we must provide a clue of communication by calling out the East Asia suppressed in us in order to build up East Asia as a critical regionalism. It is prerequisite that the common works of Korea, China and Japan, which have been confined in the mutual ignorance of the segregated domination by the West, should realize their ignorance and make their understanding abundant. The discussion of East Asia is against the Western doctrine outwardly in that the discussion has an aspiration to watch the modern times of the West from the origin by training this point of view. However, inwardly, it draws a line from the Asianism of Japan that imitated the

6) Choi Jang-jip. "The Ideological Base of East Asian Community" *Asia Research* vol. 47, Book 4 Korea University, Asiatic Research Center. 2004, pp. 106-107

Western doctrine conversely. As we know, the Asian doctrine of Japan, now reduced to the demonstration of "the Co-Prosperity Sphere of Great East Asia," is nothing but a variant of anti-Eurocentric Eurocentrism.[7)] Because of the dark shadow of the Asian doctrine issued from Japan, an argument for spreading the concept of the whole of Asia rather than only East Asia has been carefully raised.[8)] To be sure, this concern needs to be fully respected, but the question lies in that East Asia is also regarded as "an imagined community." "One Asia" may be a structure which the West has imagined, but East Asia can hardly be regarded as "an imaginary community" to the effect that East Asia operated the regional system as a sphere even before modern times. On the contrary, the Asian doctrine of Japan, based on the imperialistic desire for ruling in order to newly organize this area as an advance guard of the West, can be said to be near the "imagined community." In connection with this, I have no objection to extending and intensifying the understanding about Asia, but I am cautious with regard to the suggestion that East Asia be extended to all of Asia. I believe it is essential that we restore the discontinued common historic memory of East Asia after the shock of the West and make use of it as an imaginary resource for proceeding toward another East Asia.

4. The Discovery of a Common Language

Virginia Woolf once expressed her frustrations by saying, "There was no common language prepared for her to use"[9)] outside the masculine mode of sentences for a long time and today the writers and intellectuals of East Asia are experiencing similar difficulties. When East Asian writers and intellectuals speak or write about East Asia, they are surprised to find that they are lacking a common language or sentences to communicate with. This means something more than that they cannot but use English as a common language. Even when we speak and write in Korean,

---

7) Immanuel Wallerstein, op.cit, p. 251

8) Yamamuro Shinichi. "Asian Doctrine and Asiatic Understanding of Japan." *The Recognition of East Asia of East Asian Modern Intellectuals*, Seong-gyun-gwan University, Daedong Cultural Research Institute, 2005. pp. 85-87

9) Virginia Woolf. *A Room of One's Own* 1929, translated by Oh Jin-suk (Sol, 2004) p. 144

we find a number of traces of the languages of the West, starting with English. It is no exaggeration to say that the Korean language of today is Korean outwardly, but it is a kind of language that has a deep color of translation of Western languages or those processed in Japan. This very situation makes the people of East Asia stammer when they try to speak about East Asia.

We are looking at East Asia with the eyes of the West; like a stranger. For example, when we want to know about Japan in Korea, the easiest reference book to choose is *The Chrysanthemum and the Sword* by Ruth Benedict. Interestingly, the book is instructive in terms of understanding Japan and also instructive to understand Korea, which experienced Japanese colonization. According to the plot of the book, a matchmaker cooked up a false situation, pretending to meet people by chance, to arrange a wedding in the presence of the parents of two families. The fact that this kind of custom has its origin in Japan is a typical case.[10)] Nevertheless, we cannot readily agree with the American claim[11)] that the book became "an immediate classic" as soon as it was published in America in 1946. As the author made clear, in June 1944, when the defeat of Japan in the Pacific War appealed to people's sense of reality, this book[12)] was written at the request of the American Government as a report of an anthropologist for the immediate performance of war and the establishment of the occupation policy for post-war Japan. We cannot forget that the book is a thoroughly West-centered text in which Japan was alienized with America as the standard. The book, written with a fervent hope to know Japan, "the most alien enemy,"[13)] vividly shows that knowledge is based on the social psychology of domination and conquest. Moreover, the female anthropologist author never visited Japan.[14)] Accordingly, she chose the method of

10) Ruth Benedict. op.cit, p. 120

11) Ezra Vogel, Forward, Ruth Benedict, op.cit. p. ix

12) Ruth Benedict, op.cit. pp. 4-5

13) Ruth Benedict, op.cit. p. 1

14) Ruth Benedict, *The Chrysanthemum and the Sword: Patterns of Japanese Culture* translated by Kin Yun-shik and Oh In-seok, Eulyu-munhwasa 1992, "Preface of the Translators" p. 4. The translators highly evaluated this point by saying "This book proved the possibility that the research of learning without witnessing its objective directly can be more strict." Can it be so? In case of this book, this point can be regarded to be the disproof of a colonialist text.

interviews instead of first-hand research. The survey, however, was not survey-styled any more. This book was edited under pressure, as if prisoners of war were being examined or criminals investigated.[15)]

In this book Benedict twice mentions Alexis de Tocqueville (1805-59). As we know, though Tocqueville was born of a noble family that suffered during the French Revolution, he supported the revolution later and went over to America in 1831 to examine the American prison system at the request of the French government. He left an excellent report entitled, "Democracy in America." Benedict imitated the posture of Tocqueville consciously or unconsciously in this book. Just as an American-born noble young man from the Old World observed the unfamiliar America, so she investigated an unfamiliar island country that fearlessly challenged America as an anthropologist of the New Continent, which succeeded to European hegemony. For all that, the approach to the deep-rooted hierarchy of Japanese society, referring to the insight of Tocqueville who evaluated American democracy based on "the equality of conditions" as a choice in the future, seems to be a bit complicated. In the situation where a defeated Japan approved the authority of America, she rejected the assertion of a section of America that the America-styled principle of equality be adopted and said as her conclusion, "Meantime Japan will have to rebuild her self-respect today on her own basis, not on ours."[16)] This statement that affirms the hierarchy of Japanese society in terms of the viewpoint of Darwinism shows the original form of the American occupying policy of post-war Japan. America chose to make use of the mended Emperor system for post-war Japan. With regard to this, Tocqueville makes a distinction from Benedict. While he has a view of America as the future of the world with his eyes wide open, she looks at Japan thoroughly from the position of America. For her, America is an unmovable North Star.

In the meantime, Japan chose Korea as the object of satisfying

15) E. Vogel, op.cit. p. x. Vogel complimented the thoroughness of Benedict, but for my part, the interview is appalling. When we recollect the Japanese-Americans who were persecuted in America during the Pacific War, it is much more so. They were actually treated as potential spies or enemy prisoners of war.

16) Ruth Benedict. op.cit. p. 150

her resentment. While Japan was preparing for the occupation of a colony, all through the period of occupation and up to this time, Japan's reports about Korea were always dotted with distortions, though there had been some exceptions. Korea in turn seeks revenge against Japan lest Korea be defeated. Some books, which have sensational titles like *No Japan* Exists have been published. This kind of foolish chain is rampant in East Asia. A number of works on China which copied the West's imagination about China, an empire with a long history, had a number of absurd fancies about the countries around her. We are, as it were, in a state where we willingly surrendered to the separated occupation of the West while the Orientalism of the West was copied unlimitedly in East Asia.

This state of things obstructs communication in East Asia. The writers and intellectuals of East Asia before modern times were bilingual. Even if they were leading their lives in their mother tongue, they had the memory of cultural history in common by using Chinese characters in common as a medium of mutual communication. Confucianism, which originated from China and Buddhism, which was spread from India, are universal religions of East Asia. The existence of these religions made the life of the common literary language take deep root in the whole area. It was due to this very common literary language that the discussion of Asian solidarity was raised in the beginning of modern times, because the common literary language had been alive even though its tradition had become feeble. After the collapse of the Sino-centric system, as the tradition of the common literary language became weak, East Asia fell into keen competition to make the imagination of the West its own. Where can we find a way to build "a common house" in East Asia and overcome this mutual non-communication? A language represents "a house of existence." It is high time for us to share our wisdom for the creation of a common language. Of course I do not mean to return to the common literary language of the days gone by. Taking all the better struggles into consideration which each country of East Asia experienced while passing through the twentieth century, let us discover a common language that can cope with "the common house" of East Asia on the basis of those traces. And then, on the basis of the common memory of East Asia, in the common work of creating a common language and sharing experiences that we obtained through collisions against the West after modern times, namely, making another East Asia, the site for the genuine peace of East Asia to nest—not the negative peace of cease-fire, but the positive peace of guaranteeing the welfare of all East Asia, which will become wider than ever before.

Translated by **Moon Jung-il**

Session XI

Technological Change and the Globalization of Communication

Jean Baudrillard | LA DIASPORA MENTALE DES RESEAUX

Kim Seong-kon | Film as a Cultural Text

Robert Coover | Literary Hypermedia and the Cave

Kim Young-ha | Tsunamis, Kundera, Kafka and a Few Thoughts

LA DIASPORA MENTALE DES RESEAUX

Jean Baudrillard

Nous ne sommes plus aliénés, nous ne sommes plus menacés par l'Autre dans notre identité, nous sommes au contraire dans un système d'identification totale, et menacés d'une déperdition totale de l'autre. Le Reality Show, la Réalité Virtuelle grandissante, hégémonique sont autre chose que le "spectacle", qui laissait encore place à une prise de conscience critique et à un travail du négatif, à la contradiction et à la démystification. Qui dit aliénation dit toujours désaliénation possible. Tandis qu'ici, il n'y a ni mystification ni dépossession. Nous sommes au contraire en possession de toute l'information virtuelle, et nous ne sommes plus spectateurs, nous sommes désormais acteurs de la performance virtuelle, et de plus en plus intégrés dans son déroulement collectif. Nous devenons tous des électrons positifs, et alors que nous pouvions affronter critiquement l'irréalité du monde comme aliénation et comme spectacle, nous sommes sans défense devant l'extrême réalité de ce monde, devant cette positivité sans réserve, devant cette perfection virtuelle. En fait, nous sommes plus aliénés qu'aliénés – aliénés à la puissance deux, parce qu'au-delà de toute désaliénation possible.

C'est cela la forme nouvelle de la terreur - deterrence - auprès de laquelle les affres de l'aliénation et du spectacle étaient bien peu de chose.

C'est le délire identitaire : celui de notre individualisme contemporain.

Le néo-individu post-moderne n'a rien à voir avec celui de la belle époque, le héros de la subjectivité aux prises avec lui-même et avec le social. Le héros de la singularité radicale selon STIRNER est bien mort. Et même l'individualité "self-directed" selon

RIESMAN a disparu de l'horizon du social comme de celui des sciences humaines. Le néo-individu est au contraire le produit le plus pur de l' "otherdirectedness" : une particule interactive, communicationnelle, en feed-back perpétuel, branché sur tous les réseaux. Chacun est prêt à se constituer en micro-particule autonome. Pourquoi pas ? L'heure est à l'invention quotidienne de nouvelles particules. Pourquoi les innombrables particules de nos sociétés ne revendiqueraient-elles pas chacune leur identité et leur "charme" personnel ? Evidemment ça donne un ensemble chaotique, où la liberté n'est plus que la résultante du choc des particularités - donc plus du tout un problème philosophique.

Cet individu n'en est pas un du tout. Ce n'est pas un sujet. C'est un repenti de la subjectivité, de l'appropriation héroïque de soi. Il ne songe qu'à l'appropriation technique du moi. Il est converti à la religion sacrificielle de la performance, de l'efficacité, du timing, du morphing et du zapping - liturgie bien plus féroce que celle de la production - sacrifice sans appel aux divinités de l'information, de la communication et des réseaux.

Nulle religion n'a jamais exigé autant de l'individu en tant que tel. C'est la pire des religions, puisqu'elle récupère toute l'énergie libérée par l'effacement des religions traditionnelles. C'est un intégrisme nouveau, celui des circuits intégrés. Et pour que les circuits soient bien intégrés, il faut que les individus soient désintégrés. Par rapport à cet holocauste volontaire, les quelques résurgences de religiosité ou d'intégrisme traditionnel sont négligeables. Les effets de religieux ne font que masquer la métastase proprement religieuse d'une société entière dans le culte du virtuel et des réseaux.

Cet individualisme "post-moderne" n'est pas né d'une problématique de la liberté et de la libération. Il est né d'une libéralisation des réseaux et des circuits asservis, c'est-à-dire d'une circulation et d'une diffraction individuelle des ensembles programmés – chacun ressuscitant pour lui-même, dans son micro-univers, le spectre de l'ensemble (on peut parler ici de "spectralité" dans le double sens du terme). C'est en quoi cet individu fait masse, et fait masse à lui seul. C'est le devenir-masse de l'individu, ou le devenir-individu de la masse. Alors qu'il y avait, entre le sujet et la structure sociale, une opposition, une dialectique vive et distincte, il n'y en a plus du tout entre l'individu et la masse, dont la relation n'est plus qu 'aléatoire et statistique.

"Liberté" et "libéralisation" sont absolument opposées.

La liberté se joue dans l'espace symbolique du sujet, où il est confronté à sa propre finalité, à son propre destin. La libération, à l'image de celle de l'énergie, se joue dans un espace quasi physique, illimité, où chaque fonction, chaque individu est porté à la limite virtuelle de ses possibilités, et même au-delà. C'est pourquoi la liberté est une forme critique, qui confronte le sujet à sa propre aliénation et à son dépassement, tandis que la libération est un processus exponentiel, qui mène à une réaction en chaîne. La liberté est une idée et une métaphore, la libération, elle, en est la réalisation effective, et donc aussi la fin. Mais de toute façon, nous ne sommes plus ni dans l'une ni dans l'autre, ni dans la liberté ni dans la libération, nous sommes dans la libéralisation, c'est-à-dire dans l'échange généralisé, où le problème de la liberté ne se pose même plus, où il ne peut plus être posé.

La pathologie qui s'attachait au corps métaphorique, avec sa division et son refoulement, ne joue plus dans la phase métastatique. Or le corps proliférant, celui de l'obèse, du cancer, du clone, est une métastase, une excroissance, ce n'est plus une scène, et le phantasme et le refoulement ne valent plus pour lui (non plus, mais à l'inverse, que pour le corps de la métamorphose). Il n'y a plus d'inconscient en quelque sorte, et c'est la fin de la psychanalyse. Mais sans doute le début d'une autre pathologie : on connaît cette mélancolie clonique et chronique (qui est celle aussi des ordinateurs) des êtres divisibles à l'infini, des êtres in-sexués qui procèdent non plus par génération, mais par démultiplication, non plus par croissance, mais par excroissance, non plus par séduction, mais par trans-duction (celle des corps devenus réseaux et qui circulent au fil des réseaux). On connaît cette mélancolie de l'être et de la société narcissique - narcissique par indivision et par indéfinition - à laquelle l'analyse ne peut plus rien. De toute façon, la psychanalyse n'a quelque chose à dire que dans le champ de la méta-phore, qui est celui d'un ordre symbolique. Elle n'a rien à dire ni dans celui de la métamorphose, ni, à l'autre extrême, dans celui de la métastase.

La fragmentation, c'est l'éclatement d'un ensemble.

Le fractal, c'est l'expansion indéfinie d'une même forme élémentaire. (Mandelbrot). Comme dans l'hologramme, où chaque détail est la matrice virtuelle de l'ensemble. Les multiples clones d'une cellule-mère sont un ensemble fractal. Devenu indivisible (au contraire du sujet divisé), l'individu ne peut plus que se démultiplier lui-même au fil des réseaux. C'est la diaspora mentale des réseaux.

Par rapport à la règle symbolique fondamentale (la relation duelle), l'individuation est déjà une dérégulation. Le multiple et le fractal, la dispersion et la dissémination des identités, c'est la dérégulation totale.

Même effet, même processus de fragmentation, de fractalisation indéfinie de la matière : on est passé de la substance et des ensembles organiques des corps, à travers l'atomisation progressive, à des structures de plus en plus élémentaires : les atomes, puis les molécules (molaire et moléculaire), des corps aux corpuscules de plus en plus infimes, jusque dans l'infinitésimal. Aujourd'hui la subdivision sans limites des particules – telle qu'on peut dire (c'est la seule certitude) qu'il n'y a pas de stade référentiel définitif de la matière, du monde-objet.

Pas davantage de limites à la subdivision infinie du sujet, de l'être humain. Ventilation dans l'infinitésimal - résultante de tout le mouvement analytique de la modernité (l'art a reflété, et souvent même anticipé sur cette molécularisation, cette abstraction progressive des éléments simples, comme sous l'effet d'une bombe à fragmentation de la réalité) tel qu'il n'y a plus non plus de stade référentiel définitif de l'être humain.

Même chose pour l'image, pour le corps, pour l'espace, qui n'est plus là qu'à l'état fragmentaire et discontinu.

Même chose avant tout pour le temps. D'abord réglé, cyclique et ritualisé, celui du sacrifice, de l'éternel retour - puis "libéré", il devient continu, linéaire, historique, chronologique (il s'autonomise comme dimension transcendantale, ce qu'il n'était pas lorsqu'il était inséparable de l'événement rituel). Il devient "réel", mesurable, infini, celui de la durée et de la mémoire.

Première révolution du temps : sa libération, suivie d'une deuxième, la notre, qui est en même temps une réinvolution, dans la mesure où il disparaît virtuellement dans le "temps réel" - diaspora et dissémination du temps dans l'instantanéité et la simultanéité de quelque chose qui n'est même plus le présent, mais une succession discontinue d'instants sans mémoire, de particules de temps qui s'effacent dans leur opération même - diffraction, temps fractal là aussi.

Il y a longtemps que l'information a franchi le mur de la vérité pour évoluer dans 1'hyperespace du ni-vrai-ni-faux - puisque tout y repose sur la crédibilité instantanée. Ou plutôt l'information est plus vraie que le vrai, puisqu'elle est vraie <u>en temps réel</u> - c'est pourquoi elle est fondamentalement incertaine. Ou encore, pour reprendre la théorie de Mandelbrot, on peut dire que, pas plus dans l'espace de l'information que dans l'espace historique ou dans l'espace fractal, les choses ne sont plus à une, deux ou trois dimensions : elles flottent dans des dimensions intermédiaires. Donc, plus de critères de vérité ou d'objectivité, mais une échelle de vraisemblance.

Vous lancez une information. Tant qu'elle n'a pas été démentie, elle est vraisemblable. Et, sauf accident, elle ne sera jamais démentie en temps réel, donc elle restera toujours crédible. Même démentie, elle ne sera plus jamais absolument fausse, puisqu'elle a été crédible. Contrairement à la vérité, la crédibilité n'a pas de limites, elle ne se réfute pas, puisqu'elle est virtuelle. Nous sommes dans une sorte de <u>vérité fractale</u> : de même qu'un objet fractal n'est plus à une, deux ou trois dimensions, mais à 1, 2 ou 2, 3 dimensions, ainsi un événement n'est-il plus forcément vrai ou faux, mais oscille entre 1,2 ou 2,3 octaves de vérité.. L'espace entre le vrai et le faux n'est plus un espace de relation, mais un espace de distribution aléatoire.

On pourrait en dire autant de l'espace entre le bien et le mal, entre le beau et le laid, ou même entre la cause et l'effet. Même la sexualité évolue aujourd'hui dans une curieuse dimension intermédiaire - ni masculin ni féminin mais quelque part entre les deux - la différence sexuelle est de plus en plus fragile. Le principe d'incertitude ne relève pas seulement de la physique, il est au cœur de toutes nos actions, au cœur de la "réalité". Cette situation erratique, cette dérive, cette incertitude généralisée entraîne tous les faits et les événements vers un stade qu'on pourrait appeler "météorologique". Qui n'est plus celui de l'imprévisibilté naturelle des éléments, mais celui d'une indécidabilité seconde, issue des progrès même du calcul et de l'information.

Ainsi nous avons fait un virage de causalité, un virage de responsabilité, comme on fait un virage de cuti. L'une et l'autre, comme l'espace chez Mandelbrot, sont devenue virales et fractales. La responsabilité n'est pas morte, elle est devenue virale - la vérité n'est pas morte, elle est devenue virale et insaisissable - la maladie même est devenue virale. Jusqu'à la sexualité, qui flotte aujourd'hui dans une drôle de dimension interstitielle, ni masculin ni féminin mais quelque chose entre les deux, 1,2 -1,7. Plus de définition sexuelle, donc plus de différence sexuelle à proprement parler. Le principe d'incertitude est au cœur même de la vie sexuelle comme de tous les systèmes de valeur.

Venu du fond des sciences, et de l'indistinction du sujet et de l'objet, il s'est propagé partout, en abolissant la distinction du bien et du mal, du vrai et du faux etc. Plus de critère ni d'indice de distinction : le virus est l'hypostase de l'indifférenciation des valeurs, de leur contamination respective et de leur dispersion par dissémination fractale. C'est notre péché originel à nous, exactement inverse de l'autre, celui d'Adam et Eve, qui relevait de la connaissance du bien et du mal. Notre malédiction à nous vient de l'impossibilité de distinguer le bien et le mal, le vrai et le faux. Nos ancêtres étaient tombés dans l'angoisse morale de la distinction, nous sommes tombés dans la panique immorale de l'indistinction. Et notre entrée dans l'ère du virus pour méconnaissance et confusion des termes de la valeur fait écho de très loin à l'expulsion de nos ancêtres du paradis terrestre pour cause inverse de connaissance du bien et du mal.

En effet, avec cette perte d'immunité de la valeur, avec cette profusion et cette dissémination fractale de la valeur, toutes les infections mortelles, tous les virus qui ont dormi dans nos cellules, se réveillent sous le coup de la crise ! Et notre impuissance vis-à-vis de cet état de choses est bien pire que l'antique responsabilité morale du bien et du mal qui pesait sur les consciences.

Nous sommes régis désormais dans tous les domaines par un principe d'incertitude - qui est au cœur même du virtuel. Mais une incertitude qui n'est plus celle de la précarité, de la fragilité objective des conditions d'existence - ni celle qui résulte du conflit, du déséquilibre des valeurs, mais une incertitude radicale, paradoxale, que j'appellerai de troisième type, et qui résulte, au fil de la mondialisation, dans un excès de tout, de disponibilités, d'information, d'interaction, d'interconnexion. C'est le profil de l'échange généralisé, qui est aussi celui d'une réalité intégrale, d'un monde en voie de totalisation virtuelle, en même temps que de dérégulation totale. Et quand je parle de dérégulation, je ne parle pas tellement de celle, libérale, des marchés et des flux de capitaux, que de celle, symbolique, qui est la perte de la règle fondamentale.

Or la règle fondamentale est celle de la dualité, de l'altérité et de la distance.

Et c'est celle-là qui est partout en voie d'écrasement dans une confusion et une promiscuité généralisée.

Nous avons dévoré non seulement la distance qui séparait toutes les parties du monde, la distance géographique - non seulement la distance temporelle qui séparait le passé du futur, vers une sorte de collision instantanée du temps qui s'appelle le temps réel, mais la distance mentale qui nous séparait de notre propre image, et jusqu'à la distance métaphysique qui nous séparait de la vérité et de la réalité.

Nous avons dévoré notre propre image, notre propre vérité et notre propre réalité.

L'ayant dévoré, nous sommes donc dans une situation de réalité intégrée, de réalité intégrale, sans distance et donc sans transcendance - dans une promiscuité totale avec nous-mêmes..

C'est ce qu'on appelle aujourd'hui l'individu, celui qui ne se divise plus - résultat de cette collusion, de ce collage avec lui-même, qui fait qu'il dispose intégralement de lui-même, et ne sait plus ce qu'il est. Le fait que chacun se pense aujourd'hui comme individu est déjà, quand on y réfléchit, une dérégulation fantastique.

Promiscuité, immersion, confusion, dévoration - fin du pathos de la distance.

Avec Internet, les gens s'immergent dans leur propre cerveau, en fait ils dévorent leur propre cerveau, ils le digèrent, et l'opération mentale devient une opération interactive.

Vidéo, écran interactif, multimédia, Internet, réalité virtuelle : l'interactivité nous menace de partout. Partout ce qui était séparé est confondu, partout est abolie la distance : entre les sexes, entre les pôles opposés, entre la scène et la salle, entre les protagonistes de l'action, entre le sujet et l'objet, entre le réel et son double. Et cette confusion des termes, cette collision des pôles, fait que nulle part il n'y a plus de jugement de valeur possible : ni en art, ni en morale, ni en politique. Par l'abolition de la distance, du "pathos" de la distance, tout devient indécidable. Jusque dans le domaine physique : la trop grande proximité du récepteur et de la source d'émission crée un effet Larsen qui brouille les ondes. La trop grande proximité de l'événement et de sa diffusion en temps réel, crée une indécidabilité, une virtualité de l'événement qui lui ôte sa dimension historique et le soustrait à la mémoire. Nous sommes dans l'effet Larsen généralisé. Partout où opère cette promiscuité, cette collision des pôles, ça fait masse. Jusque dans le reality show, où on assiste, dans le récit en direct, dans l'acting télévisuel immédiat, à la confusion de l'existence et de son double. Plus de séparation, plus de vide, plus d'absence : on rentre dans l'écran, dans l'image virtuelle sans obstacle. On rentre dans sa vie elle-même comme dans un écran. On enfile sa propre vie comme une combinaison digitale.

A la différence de la photo, du cinéma et de la peinture, où il y a une scène et un regard, l'image vidéo comme l'écran de computer induisent une sorte d'immersion, de relation ombilicale, d'interaction "tactile", comme disait déjà Mac Luhan de la télévision. Immersion cellulaire, corpusculaire : on entre dans la substance fluide de l'image, pour éventuellement la modifier. Tout comme la science s'infiltre dans le génome, dans le code génétique pour transformer le corps même. On se meut comme on veut, on fait ce qu'on veut de l'image interactive, mais l'immersion est le prix de cette disponibilité infinie, de cette combinatoire ouverte. Ainsi du texte, de n'importe quel texte "virtuel" (Internet, wordprocessor) : ça se travaille comme une image de synthèse, ce qui n'a plus rien à voir avec la transcendance du regard ou de l'écriture. De toute façon, dès qu'on est devant l'écran, on ne perçoit plus le texte comme texte, mais comme une image. Or, c'est dans la séparation stricte du texte et de l'écran, du texte et de l'image, que l'écriture est une activité à part entière - jamais une interaction.

De même il n'y a que dans la séparation stricte de la scène et de la salle que le spectateur est un acteur à part entière. Or tout concourt aujourd'hui à l'abolition de cette coupure : immersion du spectateur dans le spectacle, Living théâtre, happening. Le spectacle devient convivial, interactif. Apogée ou fin du spectacle? Quand tous deviennent acteurs, il n'y a plus d'action, il n'y a plus de scène. C'est la mort du spectateur en tant que tel. Fin de l'illusion esthétique.

Autre forme d'implosion : le retour-image. La réalité intégrale, c'est que tout fonctionne en circuit intégré. Quand tout ce qui peut se produire a son immédiat retour-image. Mai 68 et les transistors sur les barricades. On ne fait plus rien sans se voir entrain de le faire. Même l'ironie fait partie du mécanisme. Promiscuité immédiate de l'écran de contrôle, dans notre tête aussi.

Encore une fois ce n'est pas une représentation, c'est une circonvolution des choses qui fonctionnent en boucle, qui s'abouchent à elles-mêmes comme la bouteille de Leyde, qui se télescopent elles-mêmes, qui se suturent et se saturent.

Réalité parfaite, au sens où elle est réalisée de part en part (perfectum) - où tout se vérifie par collage et confusion avec sa propre image. Ce processus affecte très généralement l'univers visuel et médiatique, mais aussi la vie politique et intellectuelle, la vie quotidienne et individuelle, nos gestes et nos pensées. Cette réfraction automatique d'elle-même touche jusqu'à notre perception du monde le plus naïf et le plus naturel. Partout, le retour-image, qui scelle en quelque sorte toute chose par une mise au point sur elle-même, par une simulation automatique d'elle-même, est comme le virus de notre (post)modernité. Le retour-image court-circuite le regard, court-circuite la représentation, doublant en quelque sorte les choses à l'avance et interceptant leur déroulement. Recouvrant toutes choses du voile de leur mise en scène - phénomène particulièrement sensible dans l'univers photographique, où les êtres et les choses s'affublent immédiatement d'un contexte, d'une culture, d'un sens, d'une idée d'eux-mêmes, désarmant toute vision, et créant une forme d'aveuglement, que dénonce Raphaël Sanchez Ferlosio : " II existe une terrible forme de cécité dont bien peu s'aperçoivent : celle qui permet de regarder et de voir, mais pas de voir d'un coup sans regarder. C'est comme cela qu'étaient les choses auparavant : on ne les regardait pas, on se contentait de les voir. Aujourd'hui tout est emprisonné de duplicité, aucune impulsion pure et directe. C'est ainsi que la campagne est devenue "paysage", c'est à dire, représentation d'elle-même..."

Dans ce sens, c'est notre perception mène, notre sensibilité immédiate, qui sont devenues esthétiques. La vue, l'ouïe, le toucher, tous nos sens sont devenus esthétiques, dans le pire sens du terme. Toute vision nouvelle des choses ne peut donc résulter que d'une déconstruction de ce retour-image, d'une résolution de ce contre-transfert qui obture la vision, afin de rendre le monde à son illusion radicale (celui-ci étant sans retour, sans image et sans retour-image).

II faut bien distinguer ce processus de confusion avec sa propre image, du processus de la représentation, où nous nous différencions au contraire de notre image, et entrons dans une forme ouverte d'aliénation, et de jeu avec elle.

Le miroir, l'image, le regard, la scène ouvraient précisément sur toute une culture de la métaphore.

Les machines ne produisent que des machines.

Ceci est de plus en plus vrai à mesure du perfectionnement des technologies virtuelles. A un certain niveau de machination, d'immersion dans la machinerie virtuelle, il n'y a plus de distinction homme/machine : la machine est des deux cotés de l'interface. Peut-être même n'êtes vous plus que son espace à elle - l'homme devenu la réalité virtuelle de la machine, son opérateur en miroir.

Cela tient à l'essence même de l'écran. Il n'y a pas d'au-delà de l'écran comme il y a un au-delà du miroir. Les dimensions du temps lui-même s'y confondent dans le temps réel. Et la caractéristique de n'importe quelle surface virtuelle étant d'être là d'abord, vide, et donc susceptible d'être remplie par n'importe quoi, à vous d'entrer, en temps réel, en interactivité avec le vide.

Les machines ne produisent que des machines. Les textes, images, films, discours, programmes, issus de l'ordinateur, sont des produits machiniques et ils en ont les caractéristiques : artificiellement expansés, liftés par la machine, films truffés d'effets spéciaux, textes truffés de longueurs, de redondances, dues à la volonté maligne de la machine de fonctionner à tout prix (c'est sa passion à elle) et à la fascination de l'opérateur pour cette possibilité illimitée de fonctionnement. D'où le caractère fastidieux de toute cette violence et cette sexualité pornographiée, qui ne sont qu'effets spéciaux de violence et de sexe, même plus fantasmés par des humains - pure violence machinique qui ne nous touche plus. D'où tous ces textes qui sont comme l'œuvre d'agents virtuel "intelligents" dont le seul geste est celui de la programmation, le reste se déroulant selon des critères automatiques. Rien à voir d'ailleurs avec l'écriture automatique, qui elle jouait du télescopage magique des mots et des concepts, alors qu'ici, ce n'est que la déclinaison automatique de toutes les possibilités.

En avant le design machinique du corps, le make-up du texte et de l'image. Cela s'appelle la cybernétique : commander à l'image, au texte, au corps, de l'intérieur en quelque sorte, en jouant avec le code ou les modalités génétiques. C'est d'ailleurs ce fantasme de performance idéale, du texte ou de l'image cette possibilité de corriger sans fin, qui provoque chez l'opérateur ce vertige d'interactivité avec son propre objet, en même temps que le vertige anxieux de n'être pas allé jusqu'aux limites technologiques de ses possibilités. En fait c'est la machine virtuelle qui vous parle, c'est elle qui vous pense. Y-a-t-il d'ailleurs dans le cyberespace la possibilité de découvrir réellement quelque chose ? Internet ne fait que simuler un espace mental de liberté et de découverte. En fait, il n'offre qu'un espace démultiplié mais conventionnel où l'opérateur interagit avec des éléments connus, des sites établis, des codes institués. Rien n'existe au-delà de ses paramètres de recherche. Toute question est assignée à une réponse anticipée. Vous êtes l'interrogateur en même temps que le répondeur automatique de la machine. A la fois codeur et décodeur - en fait, vous êtes votre propre terminal. C'est ça, l'extase de la communication.

Il n'y a plus d'autre en face. Plus de destination finale. Le système tourne ainsi sans fin et sans finalité, et sa seule possibilité est celle d'une reproduction et d'une involution à l'infini. D'où le vertige confortable de cette interaction électronique qui agit comme une drogue. On peut y passer sa vie entière, sans discontinuer. La drogue elle-même n'est jamais que l'exemple parfait d'une interactivité folle en circuit fermé.

Pour vous apprivoiser on vous dit : l'ordinateur n'est jamais qu'une machine à écrire, plus pratique et plus complexe. Mais c'est faux. La machine à écrire est un objet parfaitement extérieur. La page flotte à l'air libre et moi aussi. J'ai un rapport physique à l'écriture. Je touche des yeux la page blanche ou la page écrite, ce que je ne peux faire avec l'écran. L'ordinateur, lui, est une véritable prothèse. Je suis avec lui dans un rapport tactile et intersensoriel. Je deviens moi-même un ectoplasme de l'écran. D'où sans doute, dans cette incubation de l'image virtuelle et du cerveau, les innombrables défaillances qui affectent les ordinateurs et qui sont comme les lapsus de votre propre corps.

Par contre, le fait que la priorité soit celle du réseau et non celle des individus, implique la possibilité de s'y dissimuler, de disparaître dans l'espace impalpable du virtuel, et ainsi de n'être nulle part repérable - ce qui résout tous les problèmes d'identité, sans compter les problèmes d'altérité. Ainsi l'attraction de toutes ces machines virtuelles vient sans doute moins de la soif de données et d'information que de la possibilité de se dissoudre dans une convivialité fantôme. Forme planante qui tient lieu de bonheur : elle vous donne tout, mais subtilement elle vous dérobe tout en même temps. Le sujet y est en quelque sorte parfaitement réalisé, mais quand le sujet est parfaitement réalisé, il devient automatiquement objet (il devient identique à lui-même), et c'est la panique.

Collusion de tous les espaces, de toutes les temporalités, de toutes les identités dans l'univers virtuel - c'est comme dans les rêves : plus de négatif, plus de distance du négatif, tout est possible en même temps, rien n'est opposé, tout est juxtaposé. Et ça, c'est la négation du temps. Car le temps est ce qui fait que tout n'est pas possible en même temps. Or, avec le temps réel, c'en est fini de cette altérité du temps, de cette altérité des instants les uns aux autres.

C'est aussi du même coup la négation du langage – car le langage, c'est justement ce qui fait qu'on ne peut pas tout dire en même temps. Avec l'informatique et le digital, c'en est fini de cette fonction d'articulation symbolique du langage, c'est-à-dire tout ce par quoi le langage est bien plus que ce qu'il signifie. Tout ce qu'il y a en lui d'absence, de vide, et en même temps de littéralité, est éliminé dans l'alternance digitale du 0/1, tout comme le négatif dans l'image de synthèse. Il ne reste que la mise au point exclusive sur ce qu'il signifie - et ça, c'est la réalité intégrale du langage, autrement dit sa réalité virtuelle.

Le 0/1, c'est aussi la mort du signe. Car ce langage intégral n'est même plus fait de signes - le signe et la représentation en ont disparu. Or, c'est quand l'échange du signe et de la réalité devient impossible, que celle-ci, en quelque sorte laissée à elle-même et devenue insignifiante, devient exponentielle et prolifère à l'infini. On a affaire à la fois à la réalité intégrale du langage et à une désignification brutale.

On dit communément que le réel a succombé à l'hégémonie du signe, des images, du simulacre. Bref, que la réalité a succombé à l'artifice. (C'est cette analyse qui sous-tend tout notre concept de Société du Spectacle). Il faut inverser toute cette analyse aujourd'hui parfaitement vulgarisée, et dire exactement l'inverse : nous avons perdu le signe et l'artifice au profit du réel absolu. Nous avons donc perdu à la fois le spectacle, l'aliénation, la distance, la transcendance, l'abstraction - tout ce qui nous séparait encore de l'avènement de la réalité intégrale, d'une réalisation du monde immédiate et sans appel.

Disparition du simulacre en tant que tel, qui caractérise un stade ultérieur de la simulation : celui d'un plus réel que le réel, d'un hyper réel.

Or, qu'est-ce qui rend l'échange possible, sinon la transcendance abstraite de la valeur ?

Qu'est-ce qui rend possible l'échange de la langue, sinon ta transcendance abstraite du signe ?

C'est tout cela qui est aujourd'hui liquidé, pulvérisé. La valeur comme le signe sont affectés de la même dérégulation vertigineuse. Non pas le réel, mais le signe, et à travers lui tout l'univers de la signification et de la communication, subit la même dérégulation que celle des marchés (elle a sans doute même précédé celle du marché mondial).

Le miroir du Signe est brisé. Le stade du miroir en général est dépassé. On est au stade de l'écran. Et on ne revient pas de l'autre côté de l'écran.

Cette réalité parfaite, à laquelle nous sacrifions toute illusion, comme au seuil de l'enfer on laisse toute espérance, est bien évidemment une réalité fantôme. Elle est évidemment d'un autre monde et, au détecteur de mensonge, si on pouvait les y soumettre, la réalité comme la vérité avoueraient qu'elles n'y croient pas. C'est comme un membre fantôme : la réalité a disparu, mais nous en souffrons exactement comme si elle existait encore. Or, comme le dit Achab dans Moby Dick : "Si je ressens les douleurs de ma jambe, alors qu'elle n'existe plus, qu'est-ce qui vous assure que vous ne souffrirez pas les tourments de l'enfer, alors même que vous serez mort?"

Ce sacrifice n'a rien de métaphorique, il tient plutôt de l'opération chirurgicale - qui tire en plus d'elle-même une forme de jouissance ."L'humanité, qui jadis avec Homère avait été objet de contemplation pour les dieux olympiens, l'est maintenant devenue pour elle-même. Son aliénation d'elle-même par elle-même a atteint ce degré qui lui fait vivre sa propre destruction comme une sensation esthétique de premier ordre." (Benjamin).

C'est contre ce monde devenu tout entier opérationnel, objectif et sans alternative, que se développe le déni de réalité, le désaveu de réalité. Si le monde est à prendre en bloc, c'est alors qu'on le refuse en bloc. Il n'y a pas d'autre solution. C'est un rejet semblable au rejet biologique d'un corps étranger. C'est par une sorte d'instinct, de réaction vitale que nous nous insurgeons contre cette immersion dans un monde achevé, dans le "Royaume des Cieux", où la vie réelle est sacrifiée à l'hyper réalisation de toutes ses possibilités, à sa performance maximale, un peu comme l'espèce est aujourd'hui sacrifiée à sa perfection génétique. Notre abréaction négative résulte de notre hyper sensibilité aux conditions idéales de vie qui nous sont faites.

Il faut rendre sa véritable signification à la révolution du Virtuel, contre ses acteurs et ses défenseurs mêmes, qui réduisent paradoxalement le virtuel à une problématique réaliste. C'est la même péripétie qu'avec la révolution macluhanesque du médium, où on est passé à côté de la véritable mutation médiatique en réduisant le médium à une simple technique instrumentale. D'ailleurs on est passé de la même façon à côté de la révolution technique en général, en réduisant justement la technique à une simple technique.

Ainsi sommes-nous en plein réalisme technologique, sociologique, politique, idéologique du Virtuel. Le mode d'emploi du virtuel, le bon usage du virtuel, l'éthique du virtuel, la politique du virtuel, la démocratie virtuelle - c'est-à-dire en faisant passer toutes les catégories traditionnelles sur le virtuel, sans rien changer à leur définition et à leurs principes de base. C'est ça qu'on peut appeler le réalisme : tous les postulats sont revus et corrigés en fonction du virtuel, sans être du tout remis en cause à partir du virtuel.

Or la spécificité du virtuel est de faire événement dans le réel contre le réel, et de remettre en cause toutes ces catégories du réel, du social, du politique, de l'historique - tel qu'il n'y a plus d'événement de tout cela que virtuel. Autant dire qu'il n'y a plus de politique que virtuelle (et non pas une politique du virtuel), il n'y a plus d'histoire que virtuelle (et non pas une histoire du virtuel), plus de technique que virtuelle (et non pas des techniques du virtuel), plus d'économie que virtuelle, plus de catastrophe que virtuelle (et non pas de catastrophe du virtuel).

Réinterpréter le Virtuel à travers toutes ces catégories qu'il liquide, c'est à peu près le même contresens que de réinterpréter la science dans les termes de la théologie, comme il a été fait pendant deux siècles, pour ne pas voir que la science mettait fin à la théologie - ou de réinterpréter les média en termes politico-marxistes, pour ne pas voir que c'en est fini du déroulement de l'histoire avec l'entrée en scène de l'information etc...Que c'en est fini de la réalité avec l'entrée en scène du Virtuel - mais que c'en est fini aussi de la réalité du Virtuel lui-même.

Le Virtuel nie sa propre réalité en même temps que celle de tout le reste, et il est repris par un jeu dont il ne détient plus la règle (personne ne la détient). C'est comme dans le jeu de la pierre, du ciseau et de la feuille : toujours l'un triomphe de l'autre dans une spirale infinie. Il n'y a pas de stade suprême de l'intelligence, et ce n'est certainement pas celui de l'Intelligence Artificielle.

Matrix : naïf, la Réalité Virtuelle - c'est un comble – y est traitée réalistement. La simulation est traitée comme constat, au lieu d'être une hypothèse. Les réalisateurs la transforment en phantasme visible. Or l'indistinction du réel et du virtuel, comme celle du bien et du mal d ' ailleurs, est bien plus subtile que ça.

Ballard : " II n'est plus possible de partir du réel comme donnée et de fabriquer de l'irréel et de 1 ' imaginaire. Le processus serait plutôt inverse : ce sera de mettre en place des situations décentrées, des modèles de simulation et de leur donner les couleurs du réel, du banal, du vécu."

Mais, finalement, peut-être faut-il se poser tous ces problèmes en d'autres termes que ceux de l'aliénation et du destin malheureux du sujet. C'est au fond cette viralité, cette virtualité sans frein, cette emprise du virtuel qui nous y invite. Nous sommes en pleine pataphysique, c'est-à-dire de tout ce qui a outrepassé ses propres limites, de tout ce qui a outrepassé les lois de la physique et de la métaphysique. Or la pataphysique est ironique, et l'hypothèse qu'on peut faire sur tout cela, c'est qu'en même temps que les choses sont arrivées à un stade paroxystique, elles sont arrivées à un stade parodique.

Peut-on avancer l'hypothèse qu'au-delà du stade critique, du stade héroïque de la philosophie (qui est aussi celui de la métaphysique), il y a un stade ironique de la technique, un stade ironique de l'histoire, un stade ironique de la valeur ?

Ceci nous délivrerait enfin de la vision heidegerienne de la technique comme effectuation et stade ultime de la métaphysique, ceci nous délivrerait de toute nostalgie rétrospective de l'être, au profit d'une gigantesque ironie objective de tout ce processus technologique - ce qui ne serait pas loin du snobisme radical, post-historique, dont parlait Kojève.

Film as a Cultural Text

Kim Seong-Kon

Introduction
1. The Crisis of the Humanities

As the age of electronic media approaches, it looks as if we are heading toward a grim future where the humanities will no longer be appreciated and literary studies will be obsolete in colleges. Certainly, that would be a dreadful nightmare for all the teachers and scholars in the humanities, not to mention humanity itself. And yet, that is precisely what's happening on university campuses right now.

While this may seem like hyperbole to some, to those in the humanities witnessing such changes or their incipience, it is a compelling, relentless reality. Since the last decade, students' interest in the humanities has been in considerable decline. One of the indicators of this radical change is the sharp decline in enrollment figures in the humanities, especially in European languages and literature, such as French, German, Russian, and Spanish.

Professors in the departments of European languages and literature thus envy English professors, for English is still undisputedly one of the most popular fields in the humanities. Nevertheless, the latter is well aware of the fact that even for English departments, the situation is not as rosy as it used to be and there is nothing to be sanguine about.

"What're you reading these days?" If you ask this question to one of the English major undergraduates in Korean universities, expecting to hear such big names as Shakespeare, Joyce, or Hemingway, you will surely be disappointed. The typical answer you will hear must be: "Mostly law books. I'm busy preparing for the bar exam."

You may directly ask them, "Not interested in English literature?" Then they will immediately reply, "No. You can't make money with literature, can you?"

Indeed, money is the reason why so many students prefer law school, business school, or medical school these days. Exasperated, you may ask the class, "How many of you are interested in literature anyway?" Then you may see only one hand or two timidly rising among 35 students in your class. What the other 34 students are doing in the English Department simply eludes us. What we know is that few undergraduates take courses or major in literature these days, and that phenomenon unfortunately results in fewer jobs and fewer graduate students in the field of literature.

When I was in college back in the 1960s, it was a shame to say that I had not read Shakespeare, Joyce, or Hemingway yet. Today, it is a shame to admit that one has not read *The Lord of the Rings*, or has not seen the movie version of it yet. You would feel almost guilty if you had not read *Harry Potter* yet. Indeed, popular novels and Hollywood movies have successfully replaced once-flourishing serious highbrow literature and completely occupied the imagination of college students today. Under the circumstances, the crisis of the humanities and the death of literature seem imminent.

It is precisely in this context that the humanities and literature turn to 'cultural studies' that emphasizes the interrelationship of ethnic identities, gender studies, postcolonial studies, and film studies. This means that the humanities and literature are now almost always explored and discussed in relation to their cultural and social implications, hegemony, ideology, and history. In many countries this cultural approach seems to succeed, at least partially, in bringing students' interest back to the humanities and literature.

2. Pop Culture vs. High Culture: 'Beauty and the Beast'

Jerry Griswold of San Diego State University once came to Seoul to present a paper on American popular culture entitled, "America's Beauty and the Beast." He talked about in-depth psychological interpretations of the so-called "beauty and the beast" movies, such as Jack Nicholson's *Wolf*, Tom Hanks' *Splash*, and the television drama, *Beauty and the Beast*, not to mention the Walt Disney animation with the same title.

Listening to his presentation, I came to think of the possibility of applying his title to a wider symbolic meaning; it occurred to me that the unlikely love and marriage between "beauty and the beast" could become a superb metaphor for the ultimate reconciliation between highbrow and lowbrow culture today. Only if highbrow culture (beauty) had the courage to kiss lowbrow culture (the beast), the latter might turn into a handsome prince! Then we may be able to celebrate the birth of truly idealistic middlebrow culture.

Like Belle in *Beauty and the Beast*, belles-lettres today has become a helpless captive locked up in a magnificent castle of the ugly but powerful beast (movie industry, television network, or the Internet). And the only way for literature to escape from the enchanted castle seems to be to embrace the beast that will eventually bring forth a splendid metamorphosis of the ugly thing in disguise. Only the power of a pure girl's kiss can turn the beast into a charming prince. The seemingly incompatible couple finally reconciles and brings a happy ending.

Likewise, another odd couple—printed media and electronic media—can also reconcile and be complementary for each other. Indeed, film in our century serves many of the purposes that literature has always served. For example, literature is an excellent cultural text and an important social document, and so is film. Both of them reflect our collective hopes and fears, and record our social life and milieu. Hollywood movies, too, always provide indispensable materials for the scholars of American literature and culture, whether domestic or foreign.

In his essay, "Stupid Cross-dressing Killer Werewolves," Jerry Griswold wrote: "If you want to understand America today, where would you begin? You might, for example, go to the theater and watch movies Americans like to see. Why? Movies are our shared dreams, the dream life of our culture. Up there on the big screen, you can see the themes and issues we are struggling with."

Griswold also maintained that in 1994 Americans were preoccupied with the idea of "category (boundary) breakdown," and

American movies produced that year faithfully delineated it. For example, in *Forrest Gump* the distinctions between stupidity and cleverness break down, in *Mrs. Doubtfire* the distinctions between male and female break down, and in *Wolf* the distinctions between human and animal break down. I would add that the above movies also reflect other characteristics of the times, such as parody of history, weakening image of man, and a wish to restore the repressed wild spirit, respectively.

Nevertheless, there are some people who think that Hollywood movies, which are helplessly popular, are playing to the lowest common denominator, and thus cannot be intelligent or decent enough to complement literature. They are only half-right. There may be some low-grade movies, to be sure. Yet, movies are much more than special effects or stunts, and there are a number of great movies that have already become classics.

There are others who firmly believe that movies will eventually cause the death of literature. On the contrary, exhausted literature may be replenished, and the moribund humanities can be rejuvenated, thanks to film. John Sullivan assures us that such a pessimistic belief is totally groundless: "In the 1950s, many thought that television would be the death of movies. Instead, it became a secondary source of income. After a movie's original run, it could be sold to television, with the right to screen it alone fetching millions of dollars. The advent of cable and satellite TV and in-home video machines have reopened up yet more markets. A movie now is sold four different times: first theaters, then in video, then on cable, and finally on broadcast television." Then, why worry? Film can be a reliable partner of literature in this age of electronics and new media. Mark Shechner writes:

> Contrary to popular myth, film has been the salvation of fiction, not its downfall. I would go farther and say that the current health of American fiction is dependent almost entirely upon the motion picture industry. I don't know the figures, but it ought to be clear that fiction in itself is not a moneymaking venture without subsidiary rights. There just aren't enough readers to go around in America. Writers require audiences, and

there is no writer who is wholly unaffected by the pressure of contemporary taste, or lack of same.

Will the humanities eventually die out, as the print-oriented old generation does? The larger question may become: "If we lose the humanities, will we lose our humanity? And if so, what will replace it?" In fact, it is more likely that the humanities and, more specifically, literature will simply be recast on an alternate stage, but for such a production to succeed, to draw an audience, it will take the leadership of not one, but many directors.

Literature and Film

1. The Other Side of Reality: 'The Matrix'

Mass culture theorists have argued that films are the product of industrial and ideological processes that eventually shape their form and content, the ways in which they are consumed by audiences. They take the film text as the starting point for scrutinizing the processes of its production, distribution and consumption by the dominant culture. But that theory has been criticized by more contemporary Cultural Studies theorists who take film as a serious and significant cultural text.

In this chapter, I shall discuss the ways in which literature and film are interrelated; how film texts could provide us with what literary texts used to do as a cultural text, how literature could collaborate with film to draw wider audience, and how writers can embrace the world of images and sounds. I will also discuss how contemporary literary theory is reflected in contemporary film texts.

In the past, the reality people perceived was rather simple and stable. The distinction between good and evil was crystal-clear, and human prejudice, too, was far less complex. Today, however, reality seems ever more inscrutable and illusive, and all distinctions between good and evil, between truth and untruth, between the real and the imaginary seem rapidly disintegrating.

Perhaps that is why contemporary moviegoers enormously like the movie *The Matrix* (1999) and its sequels *The Matrix Reloaded* (2003) and *The Matrix Revolutions* (2004), all of which vividly delineate the nightmare landscape of the so-called "post-human era." Watching *The Matrix*, we come to realize that what we perceive as reality may be a simulation, that is, a virtual reality computer program designed by some supernatural beings or A.I. (Artificial Intelligence) to keep the humankind under control. And that realization, even though it is only a hypothesis, has fundamentally altered our consciousness and lives for the past few decades.

At first, Neo in *The Matrix* is skeptical about the truth Morpheus ('the dream god') reveals to him. "What is real? How do you define 'real'?" asks Morpheus, "If you talk about what you feel, what you can smell, taste, and see, then 'real' is simply electrical signals interpreted by your brain." Indeed, MIT professor Marvin Minsky once said: "The brain is just hundreds of different machines connected to each other by bundles of nerve fibers."

Reality is hallucinatory and the mind is an illusion. That means the mind, nothing but a physical phenomenon, is no more than the interactions among the brain's numerous neurons. Now this is a stunning blow, to be sure, to those who firmly believe that reality is a fixed entity because it means that we may now live in a dream world, not in reality. "The present reality exists now only as part of neuro-interactive simulation that we call the Matrix," insists Morpheus, "You've been living in a dream world, Neo."

The Matrix is a computer-generated dream world built to keep an entire race of humankind under control. In *The Matrix 2* the perception of the present is even more complex, and the vision for the future is even bleaker. Returning to the source of the Matrix, for example, Neo encounters the Architect ('the Creator'), who discloses the terrible truth that even the messiahs and the saviors including Neo, and even the Oracle herself are only part of the program. That is to say, all of them are simply irregularities in the program that will be ultimately taken care of. Even the painful choice of humans whether or not to fight the Matrix is part of the program!

What, then, can we do about it? There seems nothing much we can do. Only love seems to be able to cure the wounds and bring hope back to our desolate world. In *The Matrix 2*, indeed, the love between Neo (One) and Trinity (Three) restores so many things they have lost including the latter's life.

In that sense, *The Matrix* seems to reflect Judeo-Christian faith with its messianic and Superman visions. And yet, one can find in *The Matrix* and its sequel a strong resonance of Chuang Tzu's philosophy which perceived the arbitrary, unstable boundary of the real and the unreal as early as the 3rd century, B.C. In *The Matrix*, then, the East and the West harmoniously co-exist to seek a third possibility.

"Why does it feel more real when I dream than when I am awake?" asks Karl Popper (it parodies the philosopher with the same name) in *Animatrix*, a Japanese animation subtext of *The Matrix*. He asks: "How can I know if my senses are lying?" The correct answer may be: "You never know." Jean Baudrillard has already warned that we now live in a world where images and simulation predominate over reality. How, then, do you know the world is not just another simulation? What makes you so sure that you are right?

As a superb cultural text, *The Matrix* serves as a profound insight into and a powerful criticism of the contemporary society in which we now live. And like a literary text traditionally does, it effectively alters our consciousness and weltanschauung, opening our eyes to the other side of reality that has been largely unknown to us.

2. Pride and Prejudice: How to Read 'X-Men'

Ever since Pandora opened her fateful box, human beings have exercised hatred, bigotry, jealousy and prejudice against others. In the twentieth century alone, we have witnessed such tragic incidents as the Holocaust, the Killing Fields, and Apartheid caused by Nazism, Marxism, and racism, all of which considerably expedited the annihilation of human civilization.

Meanwhile, more than one-third of the entire population on earth suffered from imperialism in one way or another, and Americans experienced the devastating effects of McCarthyism in the 1950s, which has been appropriately called a modern day witch trial.

“Both industrial capitalism and Marxism are creeping horrors,” boldly announces Thomas Pynchon in his critically acclaimed novel, *The Crying of Lot 49*. “I saw the best mind of my generation destroyed by madness,” cries Allen Ginsberg in his celebrated poem, “Howl.” The two disillusioned writers remind us that human history is full of wars, intriguing conspiracies, and ideological clashes that result in massacre, genocide and fascism.

Bryan Singer’s film, *X-Men*, vividly renders the nightmare landscape of a society plagued by blind prejudice against and groundless fear of those who are different. *X-Men* and its sequel, a movie adaptation of the comics with the same title, depict a world divided by normal humans and mutants, which resonates with the Square and the Freak from the 1960s.

The movie is set in the “not too distant future” when mutants endowed with extraordinary powers live among normal humans. During the next step of human evolution, the number of mutants increases and an anti-mutant groundswell builds throughout the world. A McCarthyesque U.S. Senator Robert Kelly proposes mutant registration laws that can control, manipulate, and subjugate all existing mutants.

This is all too familiar, because the pattern mirrors the same process in human history: strangers begin living among us; we fear them; soon someone launches a crusade to mandate a law to control them. The result is sometimes a war, and other times, a horrible genocide.

Confronting this worldwide hysteria, the ‘evil’ mutant leader Magneto, a Holocaust survivor who is gifted with extraordinary powers, decides to wage war upon humans and destroy them completely. It is highly symbolic that the movie begins at a Nazi concentration camp in Poland, for the main theme of *X-Men* is the human prejudice that is persisting, if not flourishing, worldwide. And it is ironic that the little Jewish boy who was a victim of racial prejudice has become a man of extreme prejudice and hatred.

On the other side is the ‘good’ mutant leader Professor Xavier, an immensely powerful telepath who runs a private school for young mutants. Xavier and his followers (they are the *X-Men*) choose to assist humankind and seek peaceful co-existence, even though humans discriminate against them. They want to stop a potential war between humans and mutants, and yet, the war between 'evil' mutants and 'good' mutants is inevitable.

It is into this complicated situation that two new mutants, Rogue and Wolverine stumble. A barely pubescent teenage girl, Rogue's is able to absorb the energy or the life of anyone with whom she comes into contact. Her sense of isolation and frustration is beyond imagination, because she is completely cut off from the basic human exchange of affection. Wolverine has a metal-reinforced skeleton and razor-sharp claws, along with miraculous healing powers. He is like a lone wolf, half-human and half-machine with horrendous temper. Both of them are attracted to each other, and soon find themselves in the center of a tug of war between Magneto and Xavier.

'X-Men' means 'unidentified men.' They may live among us at this very moment, sometimes as foreigners, and other times as minorities. The movies, *X-Men* and *X-Men II*, are a powerful reminder that many of us still abhor the idea of 'difference' and hold strong bonds to something that is similar, whether it is religion, race, ideology, opinion, or sexual orientation. If we see *X-Men* only as visceral entertainment, not as a film designed to resonate afterwards, we miss so many precious messages in it.

As W. H. Auden once said, "Many misunderstandings arise, not over concrete points, but over a failure to recognize certain presuppositions or attitudes which we all make, according to our upbringing, in such a way that we cannot imagine anybody taking any other one." Yet, we are still shunning the unfamiliar, out of groundless fear and prejudice. We should be ashamed of ourselves indeed.

3. Political Correctness: 'The Human Stain'

Robert Benton's new film *The Human Stain* is mesmerizing audiences with its powerful criticism of and profound insight into contemporary society through the portrait of a man embroiled in a web of social intrigue and hypocrisy. Based on the novel by Philip Roth, this exceptionally fine film is a scathing indictment of the new Puritanism called 'political correctness' and the old bigotries that continue to plague contemporary American society.

Coleman Silk, a 71-year-old professor of classics and dean of Athena College, is a powerful man at the height of his carrier enjoying fame and prestige in academia. Suddenly, he falls from grace, his professional career shattered, after being falsely accused of racism by political foes; he had referred to some students, who never attended his classes, as 'spooks,' by which he meant 'specters.' However, as they happened to be African-American, he is subject to allegations of racism, because 'spooks' is also a slang expression for 'Negroes.'

Hopelessly victimized by academic jealousy and intellectual fashion, Coleman is unjustly forced to resign from the college. Since the fiercely feminist professor Delphine Roux is the one who poignantly indicts him, the issue is too sensitive for anyone to want to get involved or offer support. Even the African-American professor Coleman hired turns his back on him, saying, "Sorry, Coleman, I can't be with you on this." Shocked by the heartrending news, Coleman's wife dies from a heart attack.

With his life, career and reputation in ruins, Coleman retreats from society to a secluded wood. Here he gains insight and a kind of renewal through two meaningful relationships: one is with a novelist called Nathan Zukerman, who has also retreated to the woods and the other is with his 34 year-old lover Faunia Farley, who also lives in a remote location outside of town. Coleman intrigues the blocked writer Nathan with his extraordinary life story, and comforts the lonely Faunia who suffers from psychic trauma. All of the major characters in this movie are alienated, victimized, and psychologically wounded as a result of the prejudice and bigotry of others.

Through flashback, the movie then reveals an astounding truth; even though Coleman appears to be white, he is, in fact, a colored man from an African-American family. He was careful never to disclose this truth, not even to his wife, and so lived with the cancer of a lie for fifty years. Initially, he was naïve about social reality, which he pays for bitterly when he brings his white girl friend Steena to his home. He asks her, "How would you like your coffee?" to which she replies, "Black is fine." The irony is that black is not fine with her when it comes to heritage. Discovering Coleman's ethnic background, Steena leaves him without reservation, saying, "I love you, but I can't do this, Coleman."

Perhaps one way to see *The Human Stain*, then, is as a story about racial 'passing' (for white), perceiving Coleman not as a liar but as a man of unflinching courage and uncompromising dignity who tries to reinvent himself. But his 'passing' inevitably entails dishonesty, tragedy and despair. When Coleman plans to marry another white girl, Iris, he decides to hide his ethnicity and tells her that his parents are dead.

Later, finally confessing his dark secret to Faunia, Coleman laments, "I want to be free. But I became a prisoner instead." Coleman's relationship with Faunia is symbolic, in the sense that he has finally removed his mask of hypocrisy and armor of social accruements — a white man, a famed scholar, his Oxford education — to reveal his true identity to an almost illiterate janitor. Unlike Steena, Faunia stays with him to the end, to his last moments in a car accident on a snow-covered, 'white' road.

The whole irony of *The Human Stain* is that so-called politically correct people falsely accuse a man of something for which, in a sense, they themselves are actually guilty, ruining him with their groundless moral superiority and bigotry. Looking at Korean society today, one cannot but help feeling that the same thing is happening in our country, too. Beware! Inspired by self-righteousness, political correctness can easily become a dictatorship of 'thought police' that will ruthlessly bind us.

4. Tyranny of the Absolute Truth: 'Minority Report'

On the other hand, Steven Spielberg's breathtaking and intriguing film, *Minority Report*, vividly illustrates how important minority opinions are in any decision-making process. This futuristic film set in 2054 begins by presenting a Utopian crime-free world controlled by a special police unit called the Department of Pre-Crime. It is a seemingly perfect world, but it soon turns into a nightmare because the system behind it ignores minority opinions.

The film focuses on John Anderton, head of the Department of Pre-Crime, who has reduced the murder rate to zero by operating three genetically engineered precognitive women called "Pre-Cogs." As the three psychic visionaries have the unusual ability to foresee crime scenes, the police can be dispatched to arrest the would-be perpetrators before they actually commit the crime.

Anderton's confidence in the precision of the "Pre-Cogs" is unswerving. He has never had the slightest doubt about the credibility of their reports. Then, suddenly, the psychics predict that Anderton himself will murder a man he does not even know. Once the hunter, Anderton now finds himself being hunted by his own police squad. Only then does he consider that the fail-safe prescient visionaries could be wrong, and so could his own beliefs.

"Most of the time, all three Pre-Cogs see an event the same way," Lois Smith, who has implemented the "Pre-Cogs" program, tells Anderton. "But once in a while, one of them will see things differently than the others."

"Why don't I know about this?"

"Because the minority reports are destroyed the instant they occur, for "Pre-Cog" to function, there can't be any suggestion of fallibility."

"Are you saying I've haloed innocent people?" asks Anderton.

"I'm saying that every so often those accused of a pre-crime just might have an alternate future," answers Smith. .

This is somewhat of an eye-opener for Anderton. He now knows the Pre-Cogs can be wrong, and realizes that obtaining the suppressed minority report is the only way for him to avoid an inevitable arrest and execution.

Interestingly, in Spielberg's film Anderton's unswerving confidence that he is doing the right thing stems not so much from his sense of justice as from a personal psychic trauma. He is a man traumatized by his past, plagued by a sense of guilt that he could not prevent the kidnapping of his young son from a public pool years ago. Driven by his own personal conflicts, he acts with an absolute conviction that he and his world are in the right. That is, until he is awakened to another reality.

Then, what about decision makers—if not their persuaders—in

any country, are they acting to satisfy a grudge or sooth some personal psychic trauma under the pretense of social revolution? If so, what damage could this error cause? One can be sure that there are people among us who are hopelessly sublimating their personal conflicts or jealousies into a grand and justifying social cause. They join the ranks and roar with the crowd, but this means minority voices are silenced, ignored, and finally vanished. Where are the likes of Justice William Douglas or Earl Warren who courageously stood against all pressures and threats? Let minority opinions be heard, unless we stumble into a totalitarian society.

5. Aliens among Us

In the United States foreigners are called 'aliens.' It is a term that appears on most legal and official documents concerning foreigners. If you have to line up somewhere, you'll need to stand under the 'aliens' sign unless you have a U.S. passport or a green card. One may feel very uncomfortable when referred to as an 'alien,' especially with all of the connotations and images the word conjures up. It brings to mind all of those movies featuring aliens that, in particular, can steal identity.

John Carpenter's masterpiece of horror, *The Thing*, is an example, whose creeping horror is partly derived from the distrust and paranoia that develops among close friends and colleagues working on an isolated Antarctic station. These scientists unknowingly allow an alien into their midst that had emerged from a space ship found frozen in ice. The alien lives by taking over the form of other living things, and, before long, begins killing and taking over the identities of individual scientists one after another. The problem for survivors is to determine who among them remains human and who has become alien. Their camaraderie collapses as distrust, paranoia and hostility take hold.

The same parable of human paranoia can be found in Don Siegle's celebrated cult classic, *Invasion of the Body Snatchers*. In this haunting movie, carnivorous aliens invade a small town in California, bringing with them egg-like pods that give birth to dehumanized replicas of the town's folk. Suddenly, people start to discover that beloved friends and family are not the people they used to know. They look the same, but in fact emotionless replicas have replaced them. How would you cope in such a nightmare situation, where even your friends, colleagues or closest loved ones could not be trusted?

These movies can be interpreted as more than just thrillers. On another level, the alien presences in them are metaphoric of the foreign ideologies, paranoia and evil that can infiltrate human society, destroy social harmony, change identities, and turn people against each other. These are precisely the kind of infiltrating forces we can see at work in Korean society today. As Korean society rapidly transforms, it seems to be transforming some of its people as well, with many of these transformed creatures doing a remarkable job of disguising themselves as one of us." Of course, the changes to people are less obvious than what we see graphically represented in 'alien' movies but they are no less insidious.

Are the people you talk to genuine? What is their true identity? Consider the television series, "V", where aliens disguise themselves as humans and live among humankind. In this vision, it was impossible for people to know who was alien unless the outer layer of skin they wore was peeled off and their characteristic reptilian features exposed. Here is another metaphoric representation of the society we now live in: on the outside, things might appear to be the same, but beneath the skin there could be a reality of unearthly proportions. This society is becoming ruled by outer appearances, where inhabitants are often not what they seem, and, as a result, it is becoming an isolated reality where trust is difficult to maintain. People are less inclined to communicate freely, wary of to whom they speak.

Then who is most at risk in being exposed to such 'alien' influences? Think back to the 1980s, Korean parents were appalled by a nightmare reality whereby their loving children, after being brainwashed at school, turned into leftist activists. They found themselves confronted by fiercely politicized offspring who would sharply criticize them for being bourgeois and conservative. "Who is this person!" cried parents at that time, "This is not the son I used to know!" These circumstances are being revisited in Korean society today with parents suspecting ill of their children and teachers suspicious of their students. Yet we just stand by and helplessly watch radical teachers brainwash our children, turning the classroom of our future citizens into an incubator for future 'aliens.'

Another Sci-Fi movie that is metaphorically very close to home with regard to this is *Faculty*. In this film a swarm of parasitic aliens take over the bodies of the teachers of a school and then try to control the students. Young students, however, courageously revolt against the alien-teachers, refusing their bad influence and finally manage to destroy them. Will we see such a happy ending to what has developed in Korea? It will certainly be like a horror movie if the 'aliens' among us end up infecting the whole country. In *Invasion of the Body Snatchers*, human replicas are produced while people sleep. Then, it is time to wake up before those we cherish have turned into something we no longer recognize.

Conclusion: Literature in the Age of Electronic Media

Ever since the advent of television and computer, there has been a rumor that the novel is dying, if not already dead. Leslie Fiedler in fact announced the death of the novel in 1963 and subsequently published a book appropriately entitled, *What Was Literature?* Louis Rubin, Jr. joined in to spread the news with his book, *The Curious Death of the Novel* in 1967, and, in that same year, the prominent postmodern novelist John Barth wrote his monumental essay, "The Literature of Exhaustion," lamenting the end of the novel. If the situation seemed terminal then, what about now, given the massive proliferation in the use of personal computers?

Marshall McLuhan once noted that print-oriented novelists are perhaps doomed to perish, as electronic media and computer games are becoming the dominant medium. Indeed, many young people don't seem to bother reading novels now; they're too busy with electronic gadgets; they seem to prefer surfing the Internet rather than reading a book, clicking the mouse rather than turning a page. And often what they seek is not so much profound knowledge as quick tidbits of information. Not surprisingly, some writers –

resigned to the trend – now seem to write fiction for the sake of other writers. In any case, they are often faced with the reality of 'publish and perish' rather than 'publish or perish.' Is literary fiction destined to become an obsolete genre to be preserved in a museum like an extinct species?

Not just yet, thanks to the Harry Potter series. Like a magic spell, it brought new life to the world of literary fiction and brought young people back to the printed medium. Together with that, the epic movie version of Tolkien's *The Lord of the Rings* introduced the uninitiated to the literary origins of the tale. Now we see the likes of Matthew Pearl's gripping debut novel, *The Dante Club*. Set in post-Civil War Boston, this erudite and intriguing novel explores early American literary history through a complex murder investigation. When a series of gruesome murders are committed in Boston, imitating some of the most terrifying torments found in Dante's "Inferno," well known Bostonian writers of the Dante club team up to pursue the murderer.

Against this background, a cultural war takes place in this novel. On the one hand, the Dante Club represents those who were struggling to overcome both cultural aristocracy and parochial nationalism at the time. On the other, is the so-called Boston Brahmins at Harvard, believing only in a Latin and Greek heritage, and exerting pressure on the Dante Club to prevent the influence of Dante on the American cultural landscape. (To them, Dante was as low and unworthy as any foreign immigrant arriving at Boston harbor.) Also, somewhat aligned with them, Emerson and his followers were maintaining a cultural independence from Europe to such an extent that they were unwittingly stumbling into the intellectual quagmire of nationalism.

Thus the novel presents a broad perspective on the American cultural scene of this period, bringing to life the intellectual issues and dilemmas of 19th century American society. A splendid blend of fact and fiction, real life and imagination, *The Dante Club* is a captivating thriller with lofty literary themes and references that will satisfy the most learned of readers. This book, in particular, will have a strong appeal to Korean readers, for it mirrors some of the problems of contemporary Korean society – our own cultural conflicts: the confrontations between stubborn conservatives and radical nationalists; the urgent need for a wider, global perspective; and the problems created by people so obsessed with their cause that they think they can do anything. *The Dante Club*, is an example of what we are beginning to see more of these days, a novel that dissolves the boundary between literary fiction and popular fiction. These kinds of books are selling well, too.

At the top of bestseller lists is the equally fascinating, *The Da Vinci Code*, by Dan Brown. Coincidently, like *The Dante Club*, it also features portraits of those who stubbornly believe that they are the harbingers of absolute truth and also those who kill indiscriminately according to their religious convictions. It is also a blend of fact and fiction, producing an amazing reinterpretation of Western religious history. While investigating an enigmatic murder at the Louvre, two scholars unfold some of Western civilization's greatest mysteries, such as the secret of the Holy Grail. In doing so, they end up uncovering an alternative history of Jesus Christ.

In the age of film when film is mightier than literature, literary works tend to emerge as a form that could be read like studio treatments and thus could be easily converted into film. Those literary works often are so sketchy and vacant in their language that they just seem to wait for a filmmaker to fill in the blanks with appropriate images. *The Da Vinci Code* looks like a studio novel and thus may be criticized for that matter.

Yet these two recent novels are an indication of a new standard being set in the world of literary fiction – books that can appeal to the masses and yet remain above a low brow, pulp fiction classification. Moreover, those new novels are capable of bringing back readers to literature, while competing with electronic media that are prevalent in our times.

As long as writers continue to produce novels of sophistication and entertainment like *The Dante Club* or *The Da Vinci Code*, it is unlikely that the novel will die out. For now, it is flourishing once again, even in the age of high tech electronic media.

Literary Hypermedia and the Cave

[Brown University Literary Arts:
http://www.brown.edu/Departments/Literary_Arts/hypertext.htm.]

Robert Coover

I wish first of all to thank the Daesan Foundation for its efforts on behalf of Korean and world literature, and to acknowledge the important theme of this forum. I am here as a representative of the most bellicose nation on earth, one that believes problems can be resolved by instruments of shock and awe, a ruthless destructiveness made possible by advanced technology, to talk about new art forms made possible by advanced technology. The technology I use is, however, associated not with domination but with equal access networking, not with conflict but with communication, not with muscle but with mind. I don't underestimate the military and corporate uses made of this new digital technology, nor the potential threats to our freedom in and on it, but I do believe that the digital world is our current reality, the river we are all swimming in, and we must, as thinkers, artists, doers—as citizens—do all we can to jump in and keep our heads above water and resist all efforts to pollute or divert or monopolize or rule that river …

Does digital technology pose a threat to traditional literature? Of course it does. The book is a cumbersome and expensive thing, contrasted to the weightlessness of light. And it requires a sizable audience in order to survive, and if that audience moves, as it is moving, toward the Internet, then the book and thus literature as we know it is in danger. But the digital revolution is, I am afraid, a real one, and irresistible. If literature is to be rescued from oblivion, then writers and artists must enter into this new domain and see what they can do about finding a place for it…

PROLOGUE:

The impact of new technologies upon literature is both profound and negligible. Negligible in the sense that our oldest known narrative of any length, the Gilgamesh Epic, hacked out on clay tablets by the heirs to the inventors of writing itself, is still readable and can still touch us, and the same of course can be said of pre-Biblical, Biblical, and ancient Greek narrative and poetry, and of ancient Chinese literature as well. Indeed there are those who will argue that these great works have never been surpassed, and that all subsequent writing amounts to little more than footnotes to the original classics.

But it must also be said that changing technologies continually reshape the very nature of the artistic enterprise. The dominant narrative forms of recent times, the novel and the movie, for example, would not have been possible without the technologies that created, not so much the forms themselves, as the new audiences toward whom artists directed their endeavors, some translating the classic modes into the new technologies, others exploring the new technologies for new forms appropriate to them, Miguel de Cervantes being a classic exemplar of the latter.

Now, once again, in this era of the digital revolution, the audience is moving on into new realms, and consequently so are the authors and artists. As with the previous technological transitions, the book lives on in a more or less recognizable form within the new computer-driven technology, [and] at the same time totally new forms are emerging. Whatever one might feel about these changes, they cannot be ignored. It was an awareness of the irresistible and irreversible power of the digital revolution that provoked me into creating the Brown University hyperfiction workshops a decade and a half ago, so that, together with bands of young graduate and undergraduate students, we might begin to explore and understand the new electronic media as creative writing spaces. In that respect, as, now, Cave writers, we are no different from the cave artists of Altamira—a new medium presents itself: you see what you can do with it.

HYPERFICTION:

…So it was that, fifteen years or so ago, we began developing a new kind of writing at Brown University, based on what was then a very arcane concept, hypertext. Now we all know what hypertext is, using it daily in our Web interactions, but back then it was still a strange and mysterious concept. We called our pioneer experimental courses "hyperfiction workshops," and at first used a hypertext authoring system built at Brown in the late 1980s, based on earlier attempts dating back to the mid-1960s, called Intermedia, and when Intermedia died, we turned to a new software called Storyspace, this new storytelling and lyric generating medium being generally acknowledged as a further development of what was being called, for lack of a better term, postmodernism.

Our students created hundreds of hyperfictions and hyperpoems using these authoring systems, including the notorious collaborative Hypertext Hotel. **[Hypertext Hotel "Front Desk" plus some links: http://www.hyperdis.de/hyphotel/1347.html.]** Students could enter the Hotel at will, open up new rooms or services, create characters, interact with characters introduced by others, launch events, meditate on the architecture, alter narrative trajectories begun by others, use the house phone or organize programs in the grand ballroom. In the early days the young authors tended to gravitate to the bars, though swimming pools, golf courses, hair salons, chapels, day care centers, and rooftop bordellos also opened up. This was one of the first truly interactive group fictions, a predecessor to the games and chatrooms of later years using avatars and story creation, though it was dependent upon a local server and limited largely to text, that being all that memory could handle.

[Shelley Jackson's "Patchwork Girl" on CD-ROM.] This was the classic era of text-rich hypertexts, and one of the most intricate and elegantly composed of these pre-Internet hyperfictions was Brown University graduate student Shelley Jackson's classic *Patchwork Girl*, a kind of self-reflective hyperfictional parody of Mary Shelley's *Frankenstein*. The very choice of the central metaphor of Patchwork Girl, the patching together of a new body, whether of flesh or text, from linked fragments of other bodies, also of flesh, also of text, once dead, now given new life, new form, if somewhat strange and "monstrous," was alone a stroke of genius. **[Tour begins.]**

The important new thing here is the - link, the ability to escape the page-turning mechanism of the bound-book technology and enter into the possibility of webworks of multilinear interactive fictions and poems, created in part by the navigational choices of the reader, something made possible only by the computer. All existent literary art can be moved into the computer, but literary art peculiar to the computer cannot be moved out of it. Thus, in part, its power.

Patchwork Girl is divided into five linked sections, and one of these is the raiding of the graveyard for body parts—and for the stories attached to their previous owners. Thus, from the outset, this patching together of a physical body from disparate but harmonious parts was linked to a similar patching together of story materials, the body becoming text, text body, a traditional theme given its true hypertextual configuration with this multiply coded, larger-than-life patchwork girl …

TEXTS:

Assembling these patched words in an electronic space, I feel half-blind, as if the entire text is within reach, but because of some myopic condition I am only familiar with in dreams, I can see only that part most immediately before me, and have no sense of how that part relates to all the rest. When I open a book I know where I am, which is restful. My reading is spatial and even volumetric. I tell myself, I am a third of the way down through a rectangular solid, I am a quarter of the way down the page, I am here on the page, here on this line, here, here, here. But where am I now? ...

You could say that all bodies are written bodies, all lives pieces of writing.

LITERARY HYPERMEDIA:

All this was happening back before the invention of Windows and the laptop computer in the days of slow modems tethered to the mainframe, back when hard-drive and floppy memory was still measured in kilobytes. That meant, since sound and graphics took up too much memory, the early experimental electronic writers, like those we've seen, worked almost exclusively in text. Moreover, most of the current software for generating sound, graphics, and motion graphics had not yet been invented, the use for such tools being too limited for commercial development.

But then, suddenly, along came—not the Internet exactly, for it had been there all along—but the browsers and interfaces that made the Internet visible and widely accessible. Almost overnight it seemed, together with the new IBM Windows applications, the boom in laptop computers with expanded memory along with CD-ROMs and ZIP drives, the invention of Netscape and other browsers, the creation of HTML and Java and VRML and rapidly improving hypermedia, there came the sudden worldwide rush to the Web. The impact upon communication, expression, commerce, sex, politics, indeed all forms of human exchange, has been truly phenomenal, and one senses that that impact is only beginning to be felt.

And electronic writing, soon to be known as literary hypermedia, began to look and sound quite differently: **[Young-Hae Chang's Dakota: http://www.yhchang.com/DAKOTA_KOREAN.html.]** You must all know this exhilarating piece, since Young-Hae Chang Heavy Industries is based here in Seoul, and indeed Young-Hae and her collaborator Marc Roge are here in the audience today. "Dakota" intentionally avoids hypertext and interactivity, graphics and motion graphics, photos, illustrations, even color, leaving viewers simply with sound and black-and-white text (they write in three different languages, by the way), but all those other elements are now available and many Net artists like to use them all.

[Talan Memmott home page: http://memmott.org/talan/.] Talan Memmott, for example, does his own programming, and consequently no other hypertexts out there, if we can still call them hypertexts, look quite like his. **[Lexia to Perplexia.]** For many young writers today, learning to program is like learning to read and write—an elemental compositional tool. Though each individual work by Memmott is relatively self-contained, they interlink in many ways, above all thematically, creating a larger ongoing opus of which they are each a part of a still developing whole. A vision of a sort, forming itself. **[Berth of V-Ness.]** There are story lines and characters, some of which reappear from work to work, but these traditional narrative elements soon disappear into an embracing project of self-reflection and self–examination, the "self" here being more that of the form itself, than that of the author. It is as though Memmott is seeking to think as the machine thinks, his intricate and elegant designs, precise and classical, being a way for that character, that ghost in the box, or beyond it, to dress itself up for spectators. **[Lux Bronzino.]**

> **[Camille Utterback's "Text Rain": http://www.camilleutterback.com /textrain.html.]**
>
> Those of us who are writers and readers tend still to privilege the word, for, in our perversely archaic love of storytelling and poetry, we cherish still the peculiar qualities of text, its intimacy, subtlety, vast expressive range and, through its very transparency, its power to stimulate thought and imagination, and then to reflect upon what it has done. It is true that the whole world is a text to be read, but it is also true that written literary text, standing alone on the tablet, the parchment, the page, the screen, is a unique and wondrous thing, nor so fragile as one might fear. Indeed, after a rough time of it for awhile, lost in all the hot hypermedia inventions of early Web days, it is not only making a comeback on its own, but is invading other media like fine arts and film.

This piece, "Text Rain" by Camille Utterback and Romy Achituv, is an interactive installation in which participants use their bodies, to lift and play with falling letters that do not really exist. The participants stand or move in front of a large projection screen on which they see a mirrored video projection of themselves in black and white, combined with a color animation of falling letters. Like rain or snow, the letters appears to land on participants' heads and arms. The letters respond to the participants' motions and can be caught, lifted, and then let fall again. If a participant accumulates enough letters along their outstretched arms, or along the silhouette of any dark object, they can sometimes catch an entire word, or even a phrase. The falling letters are not random, but form lines of a poem about bodies and language.

[Noah Wardrip Fruin and Camille Utterback's "Talking Cure": http://www.studiocleo.com/cauldron/volume4/confluence /wardrip-fruin/ .]

Net artist and electronic writer Noah Wardrip-Fruin, who received his MFA at Brown a year ago and is now working on his Ph.D. in New Media Studies, collaborated with Camille on an interesting installation piece called *Talking Cure*. Noah is teaching the Cave Writing workshop this year in my absence, and has several other works on, or described on, the Web. *Talking Cure* uses the story of Anna O, a patient of Joseph Breuer, who gave to Breuer and Freud that infamous idea of psychoanalysis, or talking cures. Anna's snake visions are interwoven with imagery from the Gorgon Medusa. The reader or viewer has a microphone into which she can speak and add further text. The sound environment is a collage of all of these. Reading is accomplished with bodily movement. The reader sits in front of a video camera that displays her image on the screen as text. There are three colors, three layers of text, and words spoken by the viewer replace one of these layers. The video clip was shot at a large symposium where other things were going on nearby and the voice over is somewhat lost, but it gives some idea of how the piece works.

[ELO Website, News, Directory: http://www.eliterature.org/.]

There are literally thousands of works of literary hypermedia out on the Net or accessibly by way of it. There are several ways to locate them, there are curators everywhere, but one good one is through the Electronic Literature Organization, created at Brown during a 1999 conference on literature and technology, and now based at UCLA in California and directed by a professor at the University of Iowa. One service they provide is their directory of available works of digital literature …

[John Cayley's "What We Will": http://www.z360.com/what/index1nn.htm.]

John Cayley's "What We Will" won the 2001 $10,000 Electronic Literature Organization poetry award. Cayley, who runs a book distribution company in London specializing in East Asian books of art, is a frequent visitor to Brown, where he has been developing literary projects in the virtual reality environment of Brown's Cave, about which more in a moment. This is his lyrical, melancholic Web-based work, "What We Will." While still driven by text, now as voice over, John used QuickTime Virtual Reality, or QTVR, to create this hyperpoem. Is this a narrative, a movie, or a poem? Many have already answered this. It is both all and none of the above. It is web art.

[Jeffrey Shaw's "Legible City": http://www.jeffrey-shaw.net/html_main/show_work.php3?record_id=83#.]

In this groundbreaking work of 1989, *Legible City*, by Jeffrey Shaw and Dirk Groeneveld, the viewer rides a stationary bicycle through a simulated 3D representation of a city—the actual ground plans of Amsterdam, Karlsruhe, and Manhattan are used—in which the buildings have been replaced by letters, forming a readable text. Thus, cycling through these cities of words is a journey of reading. The handlebar and pedals of the interface bicycle give the viewer interactive control over direction and speed of travel. Shaw likes to move the physical real world into the virtual environment, and he does that here through the physical effort of cycling. A small monitor screen in front of the bicycle shows a simple ground plan of each city, with an indicator showing the momentary position of the cyclist. In the Amsterdam and Karlsruhe version, the letters are scaled to the same proportion and location as the actual buildings they replace, resulting in a transformed but exact representation of the actual architectural appearance of these cities, or at least their skylines. The virtual Manhattan version does not have that feature, but is more interesting hypertextually, as it contains eight separate fictional storylines to cycle through.

CAVE WRITING: IMMERSIVE VIRTUAL REALITY:

[Brown University Cave Homepage: http://graphics.cs.brown.edu/ research/cave/home.html.]

...Which cycles us right into the full immersive virtual reality of Brown University's Technology Center for Advanced Scientific Computation and Visualization, popularly known as "The Cave," one of several in the world, but the only one so far invaded by writers. It is, as its homepage says, an eight-foot cubicle in which high-resolution stereo graphics are projected onto three walls and the floor to create an immersive virtual reality experience. Special hardware and software, including head and hand sensors, keep track of the positions and movements of a person entering that environment, changing the images in the Cave in a way that allows the visitor to feel wholly immersed in the virtual space. It is, in short, a wow experience.

Though a facility built by scientists for scientists, the Brown Cave presented itself as an exciting new medium for writers. Just as we tested the future of literature on the screen and the Internet in our hyperfiction workshops, the challenge here was to see how the literary word might fare in immersive virtual reality, convinced that virtual reality would inevitably be recognized as a viable narrative medium, along with film, books, theater, and electronic writing. **[Cave Writing home page: http://www.cascv.brown.edu/cavewriting/.]** To get our foot in the door, we proposed a kind of scientific project to (1) introduce the word, both as visual text and as voice over, (2) augment the sound potential and work to develop positional or directed sound, and (3), using our decade or so of experience in hypertext, construct sophisticated narrative movements to complement the spatial ones presently in use.

This was accepted, we brought a lot of new ideas into the Cave as well as new life—I mean, our pieces are *fun*—and now we're an integral part of the facility. Over two dozen different projects have been launched during the three active semesters of the workshop and three shorter research periods, in which text itself becomes the hard real thing in a world of simulacra. The little demo film I am going to play shows only a handful of the projects attempted so far, and none of the fifteen or so from this year. **[Slide show of Cave photos.]**

Of course, the film cannot deliver the experience of immersive virtual reality. For one thing, so as not to get a double image, we have to run the Cave in mono while filming, which means you are simply looking at four films running simultaneously on the four flat screens. In the stereo scenes, shot during actual Cave demos, you will see double images, which the viewers in the Cave will be seeing through their glasses as single images at various distances and directions from them—including right in front of their noses, as you'll hear. In the opening sequence, showing one scene from "Hypertable," the user is confronted by a virtual wooden table and a number of virtual boxes; he literally picks up one of the little boxes with his glove and sets it on the table, whereupon it explodes around him …

Video: The Cave Writing Workshop. 3 minutes.
See script below.

Screen (see script below): Will close with an eight-minute video of this award-winning Cave project:

"Screen," which was presented at SIGGRAPH 2003, is an experiment in interactive Cave reading, using only text, voice over, and reader movement. It is, in effect, though brief and unlike anything ever seen before, literature as we've always known it. This is the whole film, with which this talk concludes.

SCRIPT of Cave Video:
Cave Writing is an advanced electronic writing workshop, moving off the screen, to explore the artistic potential of text, sound, and narrative movement in immersive 3-dimensional virtual reality. What might be thought of as adventurous experiments in spatial hypertext. It represents a new way of thinking about and working with language that has all the power of film and theater, the intimacy of screen and book, and the direct interactivity of real-life encounters.

The workshop projects, collaboratively developed by teams of writers, artists, 3D modelers, electronic music composers, and creative computer programmers, have ranged from playful exercises as simple as puns and riddles to intricate poems, dramatic theatrical events, and complex narratives. One finds oneself in effect inside the book or play, able to interact intimately with it, uncovering hidden texts, sometimes helping to create the poem, scene, or story one is reading and hearing.

Here for example in a piece called "Screen," presented at SIGGRAPH in 2003, a haunting meditation upon memory and the loss of memory, the reader, confronted with the disintegration of a series of remembered tales, is drawn interactively into the effort to save them, engaging in a direct kinesthetic language confrontation that is utterly different from anything that has been attempted before, and one that is important for scientific visualization as well as for the liberal arts.

And in this piece, an interpretive voice-over reading of a memorial poem by A. R. Ammons, the user/reader is swept along in an experience that incorporates all three of the primary objectives of the workshop: to introduce (1) text, both visual and audio, and (2) positional sound, and (3) to create navigational structures more akin to narrative than to traditional spatial exploration.

It moves from the vastness of outer space through green forests, fractal spheres and Petri dishes with animated microorganisms, to the quiet interactive engagement with old family photos with their ghostly presences from the past. For the first time, the reader is literally immersed in literature …

Script of frame narrative of "Screen":

In a world of illusions, we hold ourselves in place by memories. Though they may be but dreams of a dream, they seem at times more there than the there we daily inhabit, fixed and meaningful texts in the indecipherable flux of the world's words, so vivid at times that we feel we can almost reach out and touch them.

But memories have a way of coming apart on us, losing their certainty, and when they start to peel away, we do what we can to push them, bit by bit, back in place, fearful of losing our very selves if we lose the stories of ourselves.

But these are only minds that hold them, fragile data, softly banked. Increasingly, they rip apart, blur and tangle with one another, and swarm mockingly about us, threatening us with absence …

[The three "story" screens in the center of the piece tell tales of virtual experiences triggered by memory. The first screen tells the story of a woman, waking, imagining that the lover who has left her is in bed with her; the back screen is told by a man who senses his dead mother's fingers in his hair, cutting it; the third screen is a woman's waking remembrance of a room at her grandmother's house. Depending on the time remaining, we may fast forward through some of these three stories.]

[END] We stare into the white void of lost memories, a loose scatter about us of what fragments remain. No sense but nonsense to be found there. If memories define us, what defines us when they're gone? An unbearable prospect. We retrieve what we can and try again…

Tsunamis, Kundera, Kafka and a Few Thoughts

Kim Young-ha

There was this article in *Newsweek* I was flipping through while flying over the Pacific. Stuart Weinstein, the scientist on duty at the Pacific Tsunami Warning Center (PTWC) at 3:00 on a quiet, Sunday afternoon, saw a sharp rise in the tide gauge on Cocos Island in the Indian Ocean, south of the Sumatra Islands. At first it read 8.0 on the Richter scale. Earthquakes of this size were rare, but as its epicenter was far from the islands, he filed a report stating that there would be no significant damage. From then on, information about the earthquake continued streaming into the center in Hawaii at thirty-minute intervals, and the estimated size of the earthquake quintupled to 8.5. He and his colleagues called the station chief, Charles McCreery, and informed him. But by that point, it was too late. The tsunami had already swept over the northern Sumatras, and instantaneously several thousand people had lost their lives.

Over the next week, angry emails piled up in McCreery's mailbox. "You fool," they read. "Hotel phone numbers are listed right on the Internet. Like anyone else, you could have found the phone number and warned them." This kind of thing. McCreery blamed himself. "Now that I stop and think about it, that would have been a very good idea." But bypassing the chain of command and directly calling the hotels in Phuket was easier said than done. And there might not be many high-class hotel managers who, on a beautiful Sunday morning, would believe a call from a scientist on the other side of the world and send their guests packing. In spite of this, McCreery remains racked with guilt and has vowed to do whatever it takes to construct a tsunami early warning system.

Here's the thing in the article that struck my interest. From the other side of the world, the United States, armed with satellites and cutting-edge technology, was forecasting the outbreak of the tsunami. But it was unable to get any warning to the first-class hotels in Phuket, which are connected by Internet and dish antennae to the global network. After the tsunami, however, those emails blaming the PTWC scientists were delivered quite quickly and precisely, and in large numbers.

I got off the plane and met my wife, who was waiting for me, in the lobby of the Incheon International Airport. My wife told me of yet another tsunami, which in this case had swept over Korea. A certain advertising firm had conducted interviews with entertainment reporters and created detailed files on hundreds of entertainers who were being considered for use in advertisements, she said. The files included movie and TV stars, fashion models, and so on. In them were reports on their potential for future development, level of popularity, acting ability, etc. The problem was that the file also included the rumors and gossip surrounding each entertainer. It was hardly likely that a file this hot would stay under wraps for long. Naturally, it leaked out (the source is still unknown; perhaps we'll never know), and in just two days it had spread over the entire country. Even Internet users in Japan, China, and the United States were able to read it. It spread through blogs and instant messengers. The entertainers were described variously as gigolos, spoiled brats, violent maniacs, and as the mistresses of top politicians and CEOs. Whether these things were true or not was meaningless in the face of this tsunami of information. The public prosecuted them, but without trial, and the judgment was handed down along with the indictment. Unconditional guilt! The more you deny, the heavier it becomes. The public's wrath was quiet but strong. The resplendent fame of the celebrities, which had been lording over them, came crashing down.

Small movements of communication which begin quietly and secretly but cause a massive ripple effect naturally cause us to think of chaos theory and the butterfly effect. But these aren't enough. We can't help but asking: What is the meaning of something as meaningless as this having such a rapid and wide expansion? What is literature to do in the face of this sort of information tsunami? Is it enough to find a butterfly flapping its wings, or should it stand far back and record the development from the wings to the tsunami?

And then there's another sort of communication. In Milan Kundera's *The Joke*, Ludvik, the main character, sends a postcard to his girlfriend Marketa, whose utter seriousness about everything and infatuation with the Communist Party's training program has gotten under his skin. The sending of a silly postcard from a Stalinist-controlled university town in Prague was a fatal thing in those days. But what he'd written was simple. "Optimism is the opiate of the masses! The stench of stupidity emanates from sound minds. Long live Trotsky!—Ludvik." This postcard, sent to tease his girlfriend who so loved the training center, which controlled sound minds, got him branded a Trotskyite. He was hauled off to the military and worked in the mines. The more he tried to clear up the unjust accusation, the further his descent into hell. In the end, he was forced to recognize that the charge that he was a Trotskyite with remnants of liberalism was more real than his actual self, and that it was closer to his real nature than he himself was. He was unjustly accused, but as a result of the accusation, the charge became reality. Like computers of the future which evolve on their own, the charge establishes its own justification, like a self-fulfilling prophecy. In any event, somehow the postcard Ludvik sent left he and his girlfriend's possession, becoming the property of the party and the state, and he was branded an enemy of the revolution. His friends deserted him, and he was exiled to a distant place, alone. *The Joke* is a novel that is attached as a footnote to a single postcard. Postcards are delivered quickly, but life lasts a long time. Perhaps this postcard was not communication between Ludvik and Marketa, but rather between a single person and the system (if in fact this sort of thing can also be called communication). Even if its message is delivered after having been translated, amplified, and distorted.

Novels have been having a love-affair with postcards for a long time. Postcards are a cheap, light, and carefree medium. Postcards in novels, unlike those in life, arrive calmly and then change the fate of some individual. Postcards usually come flying back from the past. From friends, family, or lovers parted with long ago, or perhaps from the character's subconscious. At first glance, this communication seems unilateral, but if you think about it, by the end of the novel you often find that inside the recipient there was something that had been waiting for it, or perhaps even actively demanding it. In Yun Dae-nyeoung's novel *Fishing for Sweet Fish* Communication*, the main character receives a postcard. It was signed "Sweet Fish," and on the front was the Edward Curtis photograph "Hopi Indian." The character had once given a collection of Curtis' photographs to a woman as a present, and he'd also written a newspaper article about fishing for sweet fish. "No doubt you have a memory of meeting and parting with a certain woman," read the postcard. The main character went out to meet the senders of the card at the designated meeting place, a café called the Telephone. As the name signifies, this novel was a product of the age of postcards and telephones. A secret organization called Fishing for Sweet Fish Communication used both phone calls and postcards to lure the main character to their underground meetings. Sweet fish are spawners, returning to their birthplaces to lay eggs, and this was a place where those in denial of reality and wishing to return to the past got together and got drunk and high off hallucinogens and booze, and the enjoyment of their own inner wounds.

For Dae-nyoung Yun, the means of communication are not important. Together with the development of technology, the types of communication depicted in the novel have gone from postcard to telephone, telephone to computer networks, and computer networks to the internet. But there's no great change in the fundamental essence. A message suddenly comes to a person who's been living a quiet, peaceful life, and that message is connected to some long-repressed past trauma or action. He goes to meet the people who sent him the message, and in the end finds himself in a situation from which there is no escape.

This sort of communication stands in contrast to the tsunami variety. Its speed of diffusion is slow, and it doesn't indiscriminately wash over everything. Only at the start are they similar, in the sense that they both begin quietly and secretly. But inside, information tsunamis are filled with incredible destructive force. The destructive energy, however, is hampered by time and space. The closer to the center, the greater the shock, and the further away, the safer things are. On the other hand, Kunderaesque communication is not greatly affected by distance. It knows its target, and whether or not the sender is aware of it, it usually hits it and arrives with precision. Like a control tower and a pilot giving signals back and forth and landing an airplane gently down on the runway, the sender and recipient are already connected. So when the message takes off, it has already arrived. The destructive force doesn't start from the epicenter, but from an entirely different dimension. To use Freudian terms, you could say it's determined in the realm of the unconscious.

One day, in 1996, I was on my way to my publisher's to look at a revision. I got off at Chungmuro Station and was about to transfer to Line Four and head north. I was standing in line, waiting for the train that would be there any minute. But then I noticed that there was an attractive, stylish young woman waiting to get on the subway going in the same direction as I was. The train came, and we got on at almost exactly the same time. There were no seats, so both of us had to stand. Armed with big, shiny earrings and a hip sense of fashion, the woman, who had no interest in the likes of me, was focused entirely on herself, nodding her head from time to time for no apparent reason. While I was watching her out of the corner of my eye, the train mercilessly raced on, and in a few minutes it was my stop. I wanted to say something to her, to meet again and have a cup of coffee when we had more time, but it wasn't easy to just go up to someone and start a conversation in a public place like a subway. I fumbled around in my pocket. My hand grabbed hold of a rather heavy object. It was my beeper. That was just at the time that beepers were becoming popular, and so the price had fallen to about twenty or thirty thousand won. If people called, they could leave their phone number or a simple message. It was a strange sort of communication medium. Uni-directional in one sense, but bi-directional in another, you used a pay phone or some other phone to call the number on your screen. I had to give my beeper to that girl, I thought. Give it to her as I got off the subway. And tell her that I'd call soon, so please hold on to it. That way I could finish my meeting with the publisher and give her a call. She didn't know the beeper's number, so she'd just be waiting for my message.

But that was all just my imagination. The beeper remained quietly in my pocket. It was simply communication inside of a daydream, if you want to put it that way. And that night I went home and wrote that daydream as a short story. It was a story in which a girl who'd been given a beeper on the subway found it difficult to throw away, and the guy who'd given it to her wasn't able to page her quickly. All the contents in the story, however, occurred inside their imaginations.

In this sort of situation, when communication is only possible inside one's imagination, or when it's being mediated by a beeper limited to receiving messages from only one direction, there is no destructive energy, and there is no discreet correspondence between the two sides of the communication. It disappears quietly, like ink dropped in water. And so it seems unlikely that it could result in any big social repercussion. On a Stalinist campus even a far milder act than this can bring on catastrophe, but that sort of amplification is difficult to imagine in a large city like Seoul, highly developed by capitalism. Seoul has turned into a gigantic sponge. Things soak in, leaving no trace. It's no longer a city where fates are changed by a single poem, or a single placard.

For example, people periodically go up the railing of the Han River Bridge and cause a disturbance with their threatened acts of suicide. And there are also some cases in which people go up to the high railing and tell people to go and find their wives, who've run off, or beg them to get them out of some difficult situation they've been unjustly thrown into. During the three years from 2000 to 2002 there were 349 such disturbances, and in 2003 there were fourteen people who actually jumped. The police oiled the arches on the bridge, but they didn't succeed in reducing the number of people who go up there and shout to the world. Since 1917, when the bridge was built, the number of supplicants to suicide has not been small, and it's been a headache for the authorities. When they climb up the arch, firemen, ambulances, and fire trucks arrive, and the traffic is controlled. The cars back up and people crane their necks to get a look. If it lasts a long time reporters come and turn it into a story, but that's all. It's nothing more than an event. Since

1917 there's been a surprising amount of development in the means of communication, but the bridge is still busy. To stretch it a bit, you could say people are lining up. It's not that they're going to the bridge because they don't have home phones, cell phones, and the Internet. They yell, and someone responds, but in fact no real interaction exists there.

This sort of sponge-like communication, in which even though you call there is no response, or even if there is it is only possible in the realm of imagination or invention, is easy to find. And when you run up against this sort of false communication, you come to meet Kafka. Joseph K, the main character in Kafka's *The Trial*, is charged in court without having committed any crime. The people handling the case come looking for him at his house and at his bank. He's never able to learn the nature of the charge against him. And as he goes around trying to prove his innocence, he only makes more serious mistakes. No one, not even his uncle, who he goes to see with his concerns, or the people around the court pay any attention to what he has to say. They just rattle on with their own talk. The novel is comprised of an infinite number of conversations, but not a single one of them has any meaning. The only thing that is clear is that he has been accused. That's all he was informed of, at the very beginning, like some command from God. Here, the fact that Joseph works in a bank holds deep significance. An employee, who's been recognized as being quite talented in a place that's something like the heart of capitalism, receives a message from the court, which is a highly organized, and thus an incredibly secretive government body. Perhaps if the situation in the novel continued and this were Seoul, Joseph would ultimately feel tempted to climb the Han River Bridge. The proof of Joseph's innocence is endlessly delayed. It could have been no other way. From the beginning, it had been utterly impossible.

In my short story "Whatever Happened to the Guy Stuck in the Elevator?," written in 1999, one morning, the main character's razor breaks, and he's only able to shave half his face. It's time to leave for work, and so he has no other choice but to throw on his clothes and make a dash for the elevator, but of all things, the elevator's broken. He races down the emergency stairs nearby, but on the sixth floor he discovers there's someone stuck in the elevator. The elevator had gone up with him stuck in it, and it was now stuck between floors. So there were just two legs hanging out between the elevator and the ceiling. The main character promised the legs (not the person!) that he'd send help soon, and told him to hold on for just a few minutes. But there was no security guard on the first floor. Intending to call 911 soon, he went to the bus stop, but the pay phone at the bus stop was out of order. He asked the people around him if he could borrow their cell phones, but they had a hard time believing his story about a guy stuck in the elevator. They refused to let him use their cell phones, of course. A few minutes later, the bus he'd gotten on was in an accident, and the police came. He told the police who'd come for the accident about the guy in the elevator, but they were annoyed with him. They did check their radios, but as there'd been no special report, they ignored him. Finally, after a long series of complications, he arrives at work and calls 911. It was already noon. The 911 receptionist was suspicious about the fact that he was so far away from the place of the accident he was reporting. In the 911 control room, the caller's location is precisely shown. And his statement that the accident had happened around 8:00 increased her suspicion. His attempt to report the accident ultimately ended in failure. That night, he returned home and asked the people in the elevator with him whether by any chance they knew what had happened to the guy who'd gotten stuck in the elevator that morning. Everyone shook their heads and avoided him. Finally, unable to learn anything, he took a shower and went to sleep.

In this story, a variety of means of communication—beepers and cell phones, wireless radios, the emergency button in the elevator—make their appearance. But the type of communication attempted by the main character is Kafkaesque, and everything starts going wrong. This somewhat foolish guy gives every person he meets a long, tedious explanation of the situation in his request for help, but they have a hard time believing him, as he doesn't even have a proper shave. As time goes by and he becomes increasingly nervous, his behavior becomes more and more inappropriate, and he makes everything worse.

Korea's highly advanced communication system doesn't accept accident reports in which the time and place don't match with that of the accident. The guilt the main character feels for not keeping his promise mingles with the pressure he feels of having to get to work and do his job, and it sends him into a panic. This system looks as if everything is running smoothly and perfectly, but just one slip can be fatal. We know that the expressionless people who ride the buses and subways every morning, and do everything as if they are machines look very carefully for some order in the system, and are used to it. Break out of that pattern, even just a little, and you'll see just how unkind the system is, and just how hostile things are outside it.

We're living in a world in which tsunami, Kundera, and Kafkaesque modes of communication all coexist. Of these, the mode with the greatest connection to the development of technology is the tsunami mode. Its explosive force is huge, and it expands at great speed. But if the question is whether the Kafka or Kunderaesque modes are more humane, the answer is no. As in the examples above, all three modes either distort, suppress, or amplify as they attempt to convey human messages, and in the end drag humanity into crisis.

What's clear is that technological development is still unable to solve this problem. It doesn't even show the slightest sign of doing so. So, where is literature? Where is literature situated amongst these three different sorts of violent communication? Let's go back to the first question. Is literature to observe these phenomena and convey them as they are? Or can it become some sort of escape route or shelter?

Sometimes, albeit cautiously, I'm seized by the hopeful notion that literature has already constructed new channels of communication capable of confronting the destructive ones, and that perhaps precious things, however small, are coursing through them. And so that perhaps, separate from the indictment and criticism of the destructive aspects of communication, literature may provide a secret, hidden garden within itself which may only be enjoyed by those in possession of it. Dostoevsky's *Notes from the Underground*, John Coetzee's *Disgrace*, or Charlotte Bronte's

Jane Eyre are incapable of providing any help to their readers in terms of improving their own communication. But in that respect, they're no different from advanced technology. These works simply depict characters who confront the breakdown in communication and preserve their own self-esteem, and thus say to their isolated readers that they are absolutely not alone, nor have they been for a very long time.

In terms of this function, there may be no great difference between Stephen King and Joseph Conrad. Varieties of isolation are as broad and vast as the diversity of humanity itself, and any type of literature is capable of establishing a secret channel of communication with any particular individual. This function, as impossible to prove as it is to deny, is the place that's been granted to literature. Like monks in the Middle Ages, and on into the future, we will continue, from this underground cave in which nothing can possibly be proven, to communicate with those who transcend both time and space.

*Translator's Note: The Korean word for sweet fish is homonymous with a word that means "secret language used between members of a tightly-knit group."

Translated by **Jason Rhodes**

Session XII

Ecology, Sustainable Growth and Literature

Gary Snyder | Writers and the War Against Nature: Those Who Love the World

Jang Hoe-ik | Environmental Issues Reflected in Science and Literature

Vera G. Galaktionova | Heroes of the New Literature: Spokespersons of National Interests or an Ideology of Globalization?

Writers and the War Against Nature: Those Who Love the World

Gary Snyder

I grew up in the maritime Pacific Northwest, on a farm north of Seattle where we kept a hen flock, had a small orchard, and tended dairy cows. My uncles were loggers, merchant seamen, or fishermen.

After college, where I studied anthropology, literature, and East Asian culture, I had no choice but to go back to working in the woods and at sea. In the late fifties I spent nine months working in the engine room on an American-flag oil tanker that hired me out of the port of Yokohama. I was a member of the National Maritime Union, had my seaman's papers, and it wasn't hard to pick up a job in almost any port of the world. That ship kept me at sea for a continuous nine months. Two things touched me deeply on that job: one was the stars, night after night, at every latitude, including way below the equator. With my little star book and red-beam flashlight I mastered the constellations of the southern hemisphere. The other was getting to know the birds of the ocean. I loved watching the albatross — a few of those huge graceful birds would always be cruising along behind our ship, trailing the wake for bits of food. I learned that a Wandering Albatross (of the southern hemisphere) might fly a million miles in one lifetime, and that it takes a pair of them almost a year to raise one chick. Night and day, they always followed us, and if they ever slept it seems it was on the wing.

Just this January, a study was released describing the sudden decline of albatross numbers worldwide. It even rated an editorial in the *New York Times* (January 20, 2005). Their sharp decline is attributed to much death by drowning. The long-line fishing boats lay out lines with bait and hooks that go miles back, dragging just below the surface. An albatross will go for the bait, get hooked and be pulled down to drown. As many as 100,000 a year are estimated to perish in this way, enough to threaten the survival of the species if it keeps up. What have the albatross, "Distinguished strangers who have come down to us from another world," ever done to us? The editorial concludes, "The long-line fishing fleet is over-harvesting the air as well as the sea."

Out on the South Pacific in 1958, watching the soaring albatrosses from the stern of a ship, I could never have guessed that their lives would be threatened by industrial societies, turning them into "collateral damage" of the affluent appetite for ahi, maguro — tuna species — (my own taste too). Yet this is just a tiny, almost insignificant, example of the long reach of the globalized economy and the consumer society into the wild earth's remote places. A recent book on global logging and deforestation is titled *Strangely like War*. What is happening now to nature world-wide, plant life and wildlife, ocean, grassland, forest, savannah, desert — all spaces and habitat — the non-human realm of watersheds and ecosystems with all their members, can be likened to a *war against nature*.

Although human beings have interacted with nature — both cultivated and wild, for millennia, and sometimes destructively so, it was never quite like "war." It has now become disconcertingly so, and the active defense of nature has been joined by a few artists and writers who have entered the fight on "the wild side" along with subsistence peoples, indigenous spiritual leaders, many courageous scientists, and conservationists and environmentalists worldwide.

There is a tame, and also a wild, side to the human mind. The tame side, like a farmer's field, has been disciplined and cultivated to produce a desired yield. It is useful, but limited. The wild side is larger, deeper, more complex, and though it cannot be fully known, it can be explored. The explorers of the wild mind are often writers and artists. The "poetic imagination" of which William Blake so eloquently spoke, is the territory of the wild mind. It has landscapes and creatures within it that will surprise us, it can refresh us and scare us; it reflects the larger truth of our ancient selves, both animal and spiritual.

The French anthropologist Claude Levi-Strauss once said

something like "Art survives within modern civilization rather like little islands of wilderness saved to show us where we came from." Someone once said that what makes writing good is the wildness in it. The wildness gives heart, courage, love, spirit, danger, compassion, skill, fierceness and sweetness — all at once — to language. From ancient times story-tellers, poets, and dramatists have presented the world in all its fullness: plants, animals, men and women, changing shape — speaking multiple languages — intermarrying — traveling to the sky and under the earth. The great myths and folktales of human magic and nature's power were our school for ten thousand years. Whether they know it or not, even modern writers draw strength from the wild side.

How can artists and writers manage to join in the defense of the planet and wild nature? Writers and artists by their very work "bear witness." They don't wield financial, governmental, or military power. However, at the outset they were given, as in fairy tales, two "magic gifts": One is "The mirror of Truth." Whatever they hold this mirror up to is shown in its actual form, and the truth must come out. May we use that mirror well! The second is a "Heart of Compassion," which is to say the ability to feel and know the pains and delights of other people, and to weave that feeling into their art. For some this compassion can extend to all creatures and to the world itself. In a way nature even borrows the voices of some writers and artists. Anciently this was a shamanistic role where the singer, dancer, or storyteller embodied a force, appearing as a bear dancer or a crane dancer, and became one with a spirit or creature. Today, such a role is played by the writer who finds herself a spokesperson for wild, non-human entities communicating to the human realm through dance or song. This could be called "speaking on behalf of nature" in the old way.

Song, story, and dance are fundamental to all later "civilized" literature. In archaic times these were unified in dramatic performance, back when drama and religious ceremony were still one. They are reunited today in the highest and greatest of performance arts — the grand scale of European opera, the height of ballet, the spare and disciplined elegance of Japanese Nô theater, the grand and almost timeless dance-and-story of Indonesian

Gamelan, the wit and hardiness of Bertolt Brecht's plays, or the fierce and stunningly beautiful intensity of Korean Pansori performance. Performance is of key importance because this phenomenal world and all life is of itself, "not a book, but a performance." I will say more about performance a little farther on.

For a writer or artist to become an advocate for nature, he or she must first stumble into some connection to that vast world of energies and ecologies. Because I was brought up in a remote rural district, instead of having other kids to play with I had to entertain myself by exploring the forest surrounding our farm, observing the dozens of bird species and occasional deer, fox, or bobcat; sometimes hunting, sometimes gathering plants that I could sell to herb-buyers for a few pennies, and camping out alone for several days at a time. Heavy logging was going on in the nearby hills. Even as a boy I was deeply troubled by the destruction of the forests and the careless way that hunting — both water fowl and deer — was conducted.

At fifteen I got into the higher mountains of the Cascade Range in Washington State, starting with the ridges and high meadows around the snow-covered volcano called Mt. St. Helens, or *Luwit*, a 3000 meter peak just north of the Columbia River. Here is what I discovered back then, and finally chose to write about in my recent book *Danger on Peaks*.

Climbing the Mountain

> Reaching the summit, I thought — west coast snowpeaks are too much! They are too far above the surrounding lands, there is a break between, they are in a different world. If you want to get a view of the world you live in, climb a little rocky mountain with a neat small peak. The big snowpeaks pierce the realm of clouds and cranes, rest in the zone of five-colored banners and writhing crackling dragons in veils of ragged mist and frost-crystals, of pure transparency in blue.
>
> Mt. St. Helens' summit is smooth and broad, a place to nap, to sit and write, watch what's higher in the sky, or do a little

dance. Whatever the numbers say, snowpeaks are always far higher than the highest airplanes ever get. I made my petition to the perfect shapely mountain, "Please help this life." When I tried to look over and down to the world below, there was nothing there.

And then we grouped up to descend. The afternoon snow was perfect for glissade, and leaning on our stocks we slid and skid between cracks and thumps into soft snow, dodged lava slabs, got into the open snowfield slopes and almost flew to the soft pumice slopes below. Coming down is so fast — Still high we walked the three mile dirt road back to the lake.

Atomic Dawn

The day I first climbed Mt. St. Helens was August 13, 1945.

Spirit Lake was far from the cities of the valley, and news came slow. Though the first atomic bomb was dropped on Hiroshima August 6, and the second dropped on Nagasaki August 9, photographs didn't appear in the *Portland Oregonian* until August 12. Those papers must have been driven in to Spirit Lake on the 13th. Early the morning of the 14th I walked over to the lodge to check the bulletin board. There were whole pages of the paper pinned up: photos of a blasted city from the air, the estimate of 150,000 dead in Hiroshima alone, the American scientist quoted saying "nothing will grow there again for seventy years." The morning sun on my shoulders, the fir forest smell and the big tree shadows; my feet in thin moccasins feeling the ground, and my heart still one with the snowpeak mountain at my back. Horrified, blaming scientists and politicians and the governments of the world, I swore a vow to myself something like "By the purity and beauty and permanence of Mt. St. Helens, I swear I will fight against this cruel destructive power and those who would seek to use it, for all my life."

The statement in that 1945 newspaper saying that nature would be blighted for decades to come outraged me almost as much as the destruction of innocent human life. I was already a youthful conservationist/environmentalist, and after that I went on to be active in the anti-war movement as a student, and struggled against the use and proliferation of nuclear weapons. At the time it seemed as though these efforts were naive and hopeless, but we persevered

During my university years I was studying the philosophies and religions of the world. I learned that the most important single ethical teaching of the Buddhist tradition is non-violence toward all of nature, *Ahimsa*. This seemed absolutely right to me. In the Abrahamic religions, "Thou shalt not kill" applies only to human beings. In socialist thought as well, human beings are all-important, and with the "labor theory of value" it is as though organic nature contributes nothing of worth — Later it came to me "green plants doing photosynthesis is the ultimate working class." Nature creates the first level of value, labor the second.

Then I read translations of Buddhist texts from India and China. The Dao De Jing and the Zhuang-zi texts helped broaden my view. I read the Lun yü — the Confucian "Analects" — and saw how the Master called for Etiquette in regard to nature, as well as human society (7.27). These studies brought me to the thought that almost all of later "high civilization" has been a sort of social organization that alienates humans from their own biological and spiritual heritage.

While I was laboring in the forests most of my fellow loggers were Native Americans of the Wasco and Wishram tribes of Eastern Oregon. From them I learned that it was possible to be a hunter and a fisherman with a deep spiritual attitude of gratitude and non-violence.

Eventually I re-entered college as a graduate school in East Asian Languages at the University of California at Berkeley, and finally got a chance to go to East Asia. I lived for a while in a monastery in Kyoto Japan and studied with a Zen teacher in the Rinzai (Chinese *Linji*) tradition. I took the precepts under my teacher, who told me that "Of all the precepts, the First Precept is most important and contains the others: *Ahimsa*, Non-harming, Cause the Least Possible Harm." To live with that precept is a challenge — he once said to me "How do you not harm a fence? How would you save a ghost?"

I lived in Japan for ten years, partly in the monastery but also in my own little house, and supported myself by teaching English conversation to Japanese company middle management people. I asked my adult students, "Why are you so intent on learning English?" They answered, "Because we intend to extend our economic influence worldwide, and English is the international language." I didn't take them seriously. Today that company, Matsushita Electric, is worldwide.

In my spare time I hiked in the local mountains, learned East Asian plants and birds, and started seriously reading scientific books on ecology and biology. All those essays analyzing food-chains and food webs — this was a science, I realized, dealing with energy-exchange and the natural hierarchies of various living systems. "When energy passes through a system it tends to organize that system," someone wrote. It finally came to me that this was about "eating each other" — almost as a sacrament. I wrote my first truly ecological poem, which explores the root nature of various human foods:

The Song of the Taste

Eating the living germs of grasses
Eating the ova of large birds
the fleshy sweetness packed around
the sperm of swaying trees

The muscles of the flanks and thighs of
soft-voiced cows
 the bounce in the lamb's leap
 the swish in the ox's tail

Eating roots grown swoll
  inside the soil.

Drawing on life of living

clustered points of light spun
    out of space
hidden in the grape.

Eating each other's seed
    eating
  ah, each other.

Kissing the lover in the mouth of bread:
    lip to lip.

This innocently celebratory poem goes straight to the question of conflict between the ethics of *Ahimsa*, non violence, "respect for all beings," and the necessary lives of indigenous peoples and Native Americans I had known. They still practice ceremonies of gratitude, and never present themselves as superior to other life forms. *Ahimsa* taken too literally leaves out the life of the world, and makes the rabbit virtuous but the hawk somehow evil. We must see the organic world as a great feast, a *puja*, to which we are the invited guests, and also, sooner or later, part of the meal. We can be grateful for that. We can enter into the process, but with gratitude and care, not an arrogant assumption of human privilege. This cannot come from "thinking about" nature; it comes from a being *within* nature.

There are plenty of people of influence and authority in the churches, in industry, the universities, and high in government who still like to describe nature as "red in tooth and claw" (a line of Albert Tennyson's) — a fundamental misunderstanding — and use it as part of the justification for the war against nature.

I would now like to propose some simple definitions: The English word "nature" is from Latin *natura*, "birth, constitution, character, course of things" — ultimately from *nasci*, to be born. It connects with the root *nat* which is connected with birth, so we have nation, natal, and na-tive. The Chinese word for nature is *zi-ran*, (in Korean *Jayeon*), meaning "self-thus." Although in common English and American usage "nature" is sometimes used to mean "the outdoors" and set in opposition to the realm of development, the word nature is best used in its specific scientific sense, referring to the physical universe and its rules, the "laws of nature." In this use it is equivalent to the Greek *physis*. In other words, nature means "everything." The agricultural, the urban, the wild mountains and forests, and the many stars in the sky are all equally phenomena. "Nature" is our reality.

Cities and agricultural lands however are not "wild." *Wild* is a valuable word. It is a term for the free and independent process of nature. A *wilderness* is a place where wild process dominates and human impact is minimal. Wilderness need not be a place that was never touched by humans, but simply a place where wild process has ruled for some decades.

The wild is self-creating, self-maintaining, self-propagating, self-reliant, self-actualizing, and it has no "self." It is perhaps the same as what East Asian philosophers calls the Dao. The human mind, imagination, and even natural human language, can also thus be called wild. The human body itself with its circulation, respiration, and digestion is wild. In these senses wild is a word for the intrinsic, non-theistic, forever-changing natural order.

Ecology, another key word, has Greek *oikos* as its main root, with the simple meaning of "household." It referred originally to the study of biological interrelationships and the flow of energy through organisms and inorganic matter. In recent years it has become a popular synonym for "outdoor nature" in popular usage. I prefer to use it closer to the original meaning, with an emphasis on the dynamics of relationship in wild natural process. (I presented these definitions more fully in my 1990 book *The Practice of the Wild.*)

The field of ecological study embraces questions of population rise and fall, plant and animal succession, predator-prey relationships, competition and cooperation, feeding levels, and the flow of energy through ecosystems — and this is just the beginning. I have learned a great deal in my work on the forest issues of western North America over the last few years from people in the field of "Forest Ecology" (sometimes with the help of my older son Kai Snyder, who is a professional scientist). I have come to better understand the dynamism of natural systems, the continuous role of disturbance and the unremitting effects of climactic fluctuations. The "human ecology" aspect of the ecological sciences helps us understand the role that human beings have played as members of wild nature, and how the interconnectedness of the entire planet requires that we take care of this place we live. It tells us what "sustainable" means, and that modern humans must again become members of the organic world.

The organic life of the planet has maintained itself, constantly changing, and has recovered from several enormous catastrophic events as well over hundreds of millions of years. Now we are realizing that the human impact on air, water, wildlife, soil, and plant life is so extreme that there are species becoming extinct, water dangerous to drink, mountains with mudslides but no trees, the exhaustion of fossil fuels underground, and soil that won't grow food without the subsidy provided by petroleum. As we learned over time to work for peace instead of war, so now we must also work for a sustainable biological, existence, an alternative to the prospect of continually dwindling resources and rising human populations.

One can ask what might it take to have an agriculture that does not degrade the soils, a fishery that does not deplete the ocean, a forestry that keeps watersheds and ecosystems intact, population policies that respect human sexuality and personality while holding numbers down, and energy policies that do not set off fierce little wars. These are the key questions.

Many of our leaders assume that the track we're on will go forever and nobody will learn much; politics as usual. It's the same old engineering, business, and bureaucracy message with its lank rhetoric of data and management. Or, when the talk turns to "sustainability" the focus is on a limited ecological-engineering model that might guarantee a specific resource for a while longer (like grass, water, or trees) but lacks the vision to imagine the health of the whole planet. The ethical position that would accord intrinsic value to non-human nature, and would see human beings as involved in moral as well as practical choices in regard to the natural world, makes all the difference.

"As …a dewdrop, a bubble, a cloud, a flash of lightning, view all created things." Thus ends the *Diamond Sutra*, reminding us of irreducible impermanence.

Sustainability cannot mean some kind of permanence. A waggish commentary says "Sustainability is a physical impossibility. But it is a very nice sentiment." The quest for permanence has always led us astray — whether building stone castles, great walls, pyramids for the kings, great navies, giant cathedrals to ease us toward heaven, or Cold-War scale weapons systems guaranteeing "mutually assured destruction." We must live with change, like a bird on the wing, and doing so – let all the other beings live on too. Not permanence, but "living in harmony with the Way."

The albatross, all nineteen species of them, are companions with us on earth, sailing on their own way, of no use to us humans, and we should be no use to them. They can be friends at a distance, fellow creatures in the stream of evolution. This is fundamental etiquette. Legislation from the governments regarding fisheries in the sea or deforestation in the mountains would help enormously.

So, back to those key questions, what would it take? We know that Science and the Arts can be allies. We need far more women in politics. We need a religious view that embraces nature and does not fear science; business leaders who know and accept ecological and spiritual limits, political leaders who have spent time working in schools, factories, or farms and who still write poems. We need intellectual and academic leaders who have studied both history and ecology, and like to dance and cook. We need poets and novelists who pay no attention to literary critics. But what we ultimately need most is human beings who love the world.

One time in Alaska a young Koyukon Indian college student asked me, "If we humans have made such good use of animals, eating them, singing about them, drawing them, riding them, and dreaming about them, what do they get back from us?" I thought it an excellent question, directly on the point of etiquette and propriety, and putting it from the animals' side. I told her "The Ainu say that the deer, salmon, and bear like our music and are fascinated by our languages. So we sing to the fish or the game, speak words to them, say grace. We do ceremonies and rituals. *"Performance is currency in the deep world's gift economy."* The "deep world" is of course the thousand- million-year old world of rock, soil, water, air, and all living beings, all acting through their roles. "Currency" is what you pay your debt with. We all receive, every day, the gifts of the Deep World, from the air we breathe to the food we eat. How do we repay that gift? Performance. "A song for your supper."

I went on to tell her that I felt that non-human nature is basically well inclined toward humanity and only wishes modern people were more reciprocal, not so bloody. The animals are drawn to us, they see us as good musicians, and they think we have cute ears. The human contribution to the planetary ecology might be our entertaining eccentricity, our skills as musicians and performers, our awe-inspiring dignity as ritualists and solemn ceremonialists — because that is what seems to delight the watching wild world.

Gift Economy, what's that? That might be another perspective on the meaning of ecology. We are living so to speak in the midst of a great potluck feast to which we are all the invited guests, and we also are eventually the meal. The Ainu of Hokkaido, when they had venison for dinner, sang songs aloud to the deer spirits who were hanging about waiting for the performance. The deer visit human beings so that they might hear some songs. In Buddhist spiritual ecology, the first thing to give up is your ego. The ancient Vedic philosophers said that the gods like sacrifices, but of all sacrifices that which they most appreciate is your Ego. This critical little point is the foundation of yogic and Buddhist *askesis*. Zen Philosopher Dogen famously said, "We study the self to forget the self. When you forget the self you become one with the ten thousand things." (There is only one offering that is greater than the ego, and that is "enlightenment" itself.)

The being who is willing to give away her enlightenment is called a Bodhisattva. In some of the Polynesian societies the Big Person, the most respected and powerful figure in the village, was the one who had *nothing* – whatever gift came to him or her was promptly given away again. This is the real heart of a Gift Economy, the economy that would save, not devour, the world. (Gandhi once said, "For greed, all of nature is insufficient.") Art takes nothing from the world, it is a gift and an exchange. It leaves the world nourished.

Poems, novels, plays, with their great deep minds of story, awaken the Heart of Compassion. And so they confound the economic markets, rattle the empires, and open us up to the actually existing human and non-human world. *Performance* is art in motion; in the moment; both enactment and embodiment. This is exactly what nature herself is.

Soaring just over the sea-foam
riding the wind of the endless waves
albatross, out there, way

away,   a far cry
down from the sky

9 February 2005

Environmental Issues Reflected in Science and Literature

Jang Hoe-ik

Environmental issues have recently become a subject of particular interest. The severity of the problem is part of the reason, but literature has also played an important role in creating and promoting public awareness. If we entrust science with the role of accurately perceiving the problems generated by the destruction of the environment, then it is the responsibility of literature to bring the problem into the popular consciousness.

I will discuss three seminal works which have raised environmental awareness: Rachel Carson's *Silent Spring* (1962)[1), Daniel Quinn's *Ishmael: An Adventure of the Mind and Spirit* (1992)[2) and Jean Giono's *The Man Who Planted Trees* (1954)[3). Although all of them contributed significantly to the fundamental issues, there are certain differences in their perspective regarding our civilization. While Carson maintained a basically optimistic view of civilization, Quinn presents a perspective rather critical to our civilization. Jean Giono, on the other hand, reveals a man who returns to nature, transcending civilization itself.

These differences in perspective are not simply based on personal opinion, but fundamentally related to the writers' views on the nature of life. To understand the present environmental issues appropriately, we need to have a new perspective on life and man's position within the realm of life. I will elaborate certain points on these regards.

We also need to listen to our inner voices coming from a deep

1)Rachel Carson, *Silent Spring* (London: Penguin Books, 2000).
2)Daniel Quinn, *Ishmael: An Adventure of the Mind and Spirit* (New York: Bantam, 1992).
3)Jean Giono, *The Man Who Planted Trees* (Boston Shambhala, 1999).

unconscious province. In the long evolutionary processes, we might have accumulated certain knowledge of this domain. What we need to do now is to bring this dormant knowledge to the surface. I believe literature is one of the ways which will enable us to recognize and awaken this consciousness. In this regard, it is particularly worthwhile to examine Jean Giono's *The Man Who Planted Trees*, which depicts a character returning to the simplicity of nature, severing ties to civilization.

Silent Spring Awakens Environmental Consciousness

Most people become aware of environmental problems through experiencing them firsthand and feeling them on their own skin. But before they can actually feel or take notice, serious damage may have already been done. Environmental damage may not easily be understood without keen scientific reasoning, and only the scientists specializing in the field can find their causes and effects. We may thus come to realize that what began as beneficial measures to better our lives may instead invite danger.

The majority of scientists are perhaps not well equipped with effective means to inform the general public of the problems. It may not be possible to make the general public understand by using the language of science. Another language, specifically, that of literature is required. Therefore, writers must be proficient in two skills: one, to accurately understand the situation through the rational reasoning of science; two, to be able to express ideas through prose. Writers must awaken our consciousness, not only intellectually but also emotionally concerning the facts and dangers that we cannot recognize and feel in everyday life.

One classic example is Rachel Carson's *Silent Spring*. As a biologist, Carson had a broad knowledge of chemistry, ecology, pharmacology, and medical science. She collected data concerning the effects of pesticides and various chemicals being widely used. After she thoroughly examined and understood the dire results, she described her findings using an ordinary yet eloquent and lyrical prose:

> There was once a town in the heart of America where all life seemed to live in harmony with its surroundings. The town lay in the midst of a checkerboard of prosperous farms with fields of grain and hillsides of orchards where, in spring, white clouds of bloom drifted above the green fields ....
>
> Then a strange blight crept over the area and everything began to change. Some evil spell had settled on the community: mysterious maladies swept the flocks of chickens; the cattle and sheep sickened and died. Everywhere was a shadow of death. The farmers spoke of much illness among their families ....
>
> There was a strange stillness. The birds, for example–where had they gone? Many people spoke of them, puzzled and disturbed .... It was a spring without voices. On the mornings that had once throbbed with the dawn chorus of robins, catbirds, doves, jays, wrens, and scores of other bird voices there was now no sound; only silence lay over the fields and woods and marsh.[4)]

Around this time DDT was a popular pesticide, and the above paragraph was sufficient to alarm people. After the publication of Silent Spring, the use of DDT was prohibited in the United States and many national nonprofit environmental organizations and grass roots organizations were established. Senator Gaylord Nelson suggested that President John F. Kennedy go on a national conservation tour and his effort to conserve environment eventually led to the founding of "Earth Day" on April 22, 1970.

Carson did not stop at warning of the dangers of pesticides and chemicals. She proposed a biological prescription for exterminating harmful insects, suggesting alternatives.

> A truly extraordinary variety of alternatives to the chemical control of insects is available. Some are already in use and have achieved brilliant success. Others are in the stage of laboratory testing .... All have this in common: they are biological solutions, based on understanding of the living organisms they seek to control, and of the whole fabric of life to which these organisms belong.[5)]

4)Carson, pp. 21-22.
5)Carson, p. 240.

Her suggestion differed from those of environmentalists. She was not proposing to simply replace highly poisonous chemicals with less poisonous or not poisonous ones. Rather she was advocating the need to convert to a new form of cultivation on the basis of a fundamental understanding of life. She wrote, "We stand now where two roads diverge .... The road we have long been traveling is deceptively easy, a smooth super–highway on which we progress with great speed, but at its end lies disaster. The other fork of the road–the one 'less traveled by'–offers our last, our only chance to reach a destination that assures the preservation of our earth."[6)] Carson emphasized the fact that there was a new road on which people had not yet trodden.

Ishmael Touches Upon the Origin of the Problem

In *Ishmael: An Adventure of the Mind and Spirit*, Daniel Quinn locates the origin of the problem in agricultural life. Quinn introduces a gorilla, Ishmael, who has learned to speak and to understand human civilization. Through Ishmael, Quinn critiques the civilization that deviated from the natural evolutionary process ten thousand years ago: "In order to accomplish anything, man had to settle down in one place where he could get to work, so to speak. I mean that it was impossible for him to get beyond a certain point living out in the open as a hunter–gatherer, always moving from place to place in search of food."[7)] Thus, man had to become an agriculturalist; this was the major turning point. Quinn speaks through the voice of Ishmael:

> Man was at last free of all those restraints .... The limitations of the hunting–gathering life had kept man in check for three million years. With agriculture, those limitations vanished, and his rise was meteoric. Settlement gave rise to division of labor. Division of labor gave rise to technology. With the rise of technology came trade and commerce. With trade and commerce came mathematics

6)Carson, p. 240.
7)Quinn, p. 68.

> and literacy and science, and all the rest. The whole thing was under way at last, and the rest, as they say, is history.[8)]

He uses the analogy of a man who crashes an aircraft attempting to fly without having completely understood the mechanisms of flying. Ten thousand years ago, man designed a craft named "civilization" and pushed it off into the open air.

> At first all was well. In fact, all was terrific .... They felt wonderful, exhilarated. They were experiencing the freedom of the air: freedom from restraints that bind and limit the rest of the biological community. And with that freedom came marvels–all the things you mentioned the other day: urbanization, technology, literacy, mathematics, science.
>
> Their flight could never end, it could only go on becoming more and more exciting. They couldn't know, couldn't even have guessed that, like our hapless airman, they were in the air but not in flight. They were in free fall, because their craft was simply not in compliance with the law that makes flight possible.[9)]

Here Quinn is talking about the "laws of aerodynamics" which make flying possible. What are the laws of nature that man needs to know in order to understand how to stop the free fall? These are the basic laws of ecology: "In the natural community, whenever a population's food supply increases, that population increases. As that population increases, its food supply decreases, and as its food supply decreases, that population decreases. This interaction between food populations and feeder populations is what keeps everything in balance."[10)] Man has defied this law and has changed these circumstances.

> You've killed off your competitors for the game, but your game has competitors as well–competitors for the grasses. These are your competitors once removed. Kill them off and there'll be

8)Quinn, p. 69.
9)Quinn, pp. 107-108.
10)Quinn, p. 13.

> more grass for your game.
>
> The more competitors you destroy, the more humans you can bring into the world, and that makes it just about the holiest work there is. Once you exempt yourself from the law of limited competition, everything in the world except your food and the food of your food becomes an enemy to be exterminated.[11)]

This leads to the destruction of the ecosystem. According to Quinn, after the invention of agricultural development, in following the civilizational process, ecological destruction was inevitable.

Does this mean man must return to being a hunter–gatherer, return to the time before the agricultural revolution? Quinn does not say so. Gorilla, Ishmael, says "What I've been at pains to give you is a new paradigm of human history …. Your task is not to reach back but to reach forward." He asks,

> "You're an inventive people, aren't you? You pride yourselves on that, don't you?"
>
> "Yes"
>
> "Then invent."[12)]

This is the answer Quinn throws out. He arrives at the root of the problem but leaves the answer to the imagination of the reader.

New Understanding of Life

There is one significant difference between Carson and Quinn. Carson does not blame civilization itself. Rather, she argues that the way in which we approach civilization is wrong and must be rectified. In contrast, Quinn seems to posit civilization itself as the root of the problem. Carson follows the existing viewpoint that acknowledges the special position that man has been placed within the ecosystem, and Quinn addresses the more fundamental problem. Then, how are we supposed to approach the problem? A new way of understanding life and human beings is required.

---

11)Quinn, pp. 131-132
12)Quinn, p. 250.

First, we must realize that we have misunderstood the concept of life. We usually suppose that there is something characterizing "to be alive" within every living being, and call it "life." But if we examine more closely, it becomes evident that this conception of life is based on our insufficient cognition.

Suppose, for instance, I hold a broken branch from a willow tree. Is this branch alive? I think we need to call it alive. Otherwise, how can we explain later when this branch is planted and grows to become a normal tree? What about a desiccated branch? If this too is treated and planted properly, it may grow to become a tree. How far, then, can we extend this idea of "alive" to this dried branch?

In the movie *Jurassic Park*, we see the extraction of dinosaur DNA from fossils and the cloning of living dinosaurs. This movie certainly suggests only the possibility of such events. But considering that modern science cannot completely ignore such possibility, and it is only a matter of technique rather than principle, can we really insist that there is no life in this fossil? If we regard this fossil as having life, then the concept of life we have had so far changes drastically. When a person dies, we assume his or her life has terminated. But if we accept a fossil as having life, then we must say that a dead person, mummified and then fossilized for several millions of years, still has life.

Inside this dried branch or dinosaur DNA is an important element that constitutes life. When combined with certain other external factors, perhaps it can be revived. However, it is not appropriate to say that such element inside this branch or fossil has life. Such element, devoid of all external factors, does not exhibit any trait that can normally be called alive. It is, therefore, misleading to think that there is "something" inside this branch or fossil that makes it a living being. The reason why this broken branch comes to life again is not because it has "life" in it, but because it can combine with suitable elements outside and exhibit certain features we normally call alive.

"Life," taken as something charactering to be alive, is not something inside a supposedly living being, but is a characteristic manifested when that being is combined with certain outside factors, which together with that particular being make living possible. We would not want to say an elephant's leg or trunk alone is alive. Only when the leg or trunk is connected to other parts of the elephant, we call the whole thing alive. Then a problem arises. An elephant cannot survive without food, air, and a suitable climate. In other words, it alone cannot be alive. Then what is the true "living elephant"? When can we say that a thing is "truly alive"?

In order to answer these questions, we must first examine whether there is an entity that can sustain its living completely without any external support. If we can indeed find such an entity, then we can say life is located inside this entity. To find such an entity, we may simply enumerate all items necessary for our survival and add them up. Once we reach a point where we no longer have anything necessary for our existence, then the totality of such items will form the desired entity. This is the true "living elephant," and will contain "life" in truest sense. This is, in fact, the minimum possible range of system exhibiting life phenomena without any external support. Such an entity needs to have a name, and for the lack of better choice, I have called it "global life" *(onsaengmyeong)*.[13] Denoting the grand total of self-supporting life phenomena as a single entity, "global life" can formally be defined as the minimum self-sufficient unit of life.

All other living entities like organisms and cells lead a dependent existence, and can be characterized as "alive" only when suitable relationships are maintained with the rest of global life. Such a dependent entity in the global life can be called an "individual life" *(natsaengmyeong)* in contradistinction with "global life." We see here why it is so difficult to identify "life" as something inside the "individual life" alone. As we saw with the example of the broken branch, the subsistence of "individual life" is as much critically depended on the connection with its "co–life" (*posaengmyeong*—the rest of global life beyond a particular "individual life") as on something inside it. The misconception of life as "something inside the individual life" not only costs us the full meaning of life, but also makes it hard for us to grasp the role

---

13)H.I. Zhang, "Humanity in the world of life", Zygon: Journal of Religion and Science 24, December 1989, pp.447~456. Also in Zhang Hwe Ik, *Sam kwa onsaengmyŏng* (Life and Global Life) (Seoul: Sol culpansa, 1998).

and importance of "co–life."

Then, what shape or form does "global life" actually have? This can only be seen through the investigation of how far physical conditions extend vitally to make the phenomena called "life" possible. This investigation should be based on the best knowledge presently available and, therefore, the answer is necessarily tentative. I will not go into details, but it can be argued that a global life is realized under the following conditions: 1) A star-planet system, like our sun and earth, is formed, allowing a steady flow of energy from star to planet due to the temperature difference between them; 2) With certain material richness on the part of planet, a sophisticated system, like our ecosystem, composed of auto-catalytic subsystems evolves, transferring certain amount of stellar energy into the free energy of its own. So far, the only known instance of such a global life is our own, framed on our sun-earth system, which was born some four billion years ago and has grown richer and richer ever since.

Among many features exhibited in life thus formed, the most marvelous is that the "consciousness," which recognizes itself as the subject of living, emerges from inside this life system. Consciousness has a very special property that it can never be recognized from outside. Suppose an extraterrestrial being with perfect intellectual ability appears and examines our life, this alien may understand life as a phenomenon as perfectly as science allows it, but there would be no way of experiencing our consciousness by itself. The experience of consciousness can only be available to a being that possesses corporeal body within the life system. The concept designated by a conscious being to itself is the so-called "I."

Position of Human Beings within "Global Life"

What sort of material mechanism is necessary within this global life for this subjectivity called "I" to appear? This is a difficult question to answer unless we can incorporate every possible material configuration as our body and feel it subjectively, but it seems reasonable to assume that this stage of consciousness is possible only when a sophisticated nervous system like the human brain is provided. Once we acknowledge this, we may say that human beings occupy an extremely interesting position within global life. Being one of many "individual lives" in global life, a human being is not much different from other "individual lives." But the human being stands apart from all other forms of "individual life," because it is the only being to be conscious of "I" as a subject and also to comprehend the whole scope of life it belongs to.

We usually consider this "I" as being confined to our possessed individual body. If we require, as a criterion for self-identity, the interconnection and unification of our nervous information network, we can safely associate this "I" with our body, since the central nervous system is composed of the nerve cells within the body. But as our interests and information channels extend to the entire society and to the entire global life, our consciousness can expand as well. This means that "I" can ultimately be extended to the "I" of global life.

One of the reasons why we cannot easily accept this wider "I" is because we cannot sense this identity as "my life." We cannot easily extricate ourselves from our deeply ingrained notion of life as something within "individual life." But once we properly understand the notion of global life and realize that one's life can be fully life only when it is identified as global life, it becomes much easier to identify "I" with the "I" of global life. Likewise, the "body of global life," namely, the material substance that constitutes global life, becomes, in a more profound sense, "my body."

Once we accept this point of view, the position of human beings within global life can be compared to the position of nervous cells within a human body, and the human culture, in its collective sense, to the central nervous system. This means that we are awakening as a global "self" through the working of collective human culture. Alternatively, it can also be said that global life, after four billion years of existence without consciousness, finally awakens itself to be a self–conscious being. Like man becoming self–conscious after certain developmental stages, global life is now being awakened through the help of human beings. This certainly is a significant event. As man cannot think of returning to life without sel–consciousness, it is also inconceivable for global life to return to the state of no consciousness. From this time forward, global life is expected to remain conscious and lead to a life with its own subjectivity.

Is "Global Life" Healthy?

There is one serious problem, however, concerning the state of "global life": Is it really healthy? "Global life" is a living body in a genuine sense of life, and therefore, is susceptible to disease and even to extinction. There is no authority, certainly not a "global life doctor," who can diagnose it. But it is widely suspected that it might be healthy. Various circumstantial evidence suggest that the health of "global life" has severely been damaged, and we human beings are the culprits. We have not only distorted the normal physiology of "global life," but might possibly be an agency leading to its eventual demise.

It is analogous to the case of cancer cells in a living body. Cancer cells are not external intruders but integral parts of our body. For some unknown reason, however, they have forgotten their assigned function and multiply without control. They subsequently obstruct normal function, ultimately inviting death. Human beings likewise occupy and inhabit major portions of global life, obstructing its normal function just to thrive and populate it with more humans.

Look at, for instance, our rapid increase in population. For a long time, men were threatened and subsisted only barely. But from about forty to fifty thousand years ago, they managed to maintain and enjoy a relatively stable existence. Human beings, now spread throughout the world, maintained balance with the ecosystem through primitive living as a hunter–gatherer. The world population was maintained around four million during this time up to ten thousand years ago, and it seems reasonable to interpret this population as what the native ecosystem could provide sustenance for.

After the agricultural revolution, which began around ten thousand years ago, however, the population increased exponentially. At year 0, it was 100 million and by 1000 A.D., 350 million. In the year 1900 it had increased to 1.6 billion and recently exceeded six billion. This indicates a 1500–fold increase since the hunter–gatherer era during which the ecological balance was maintained.

This phenomenon, as Quinn has indicated, occurred as a result of the agricultural revolution that brought great disturbance to the ecosystem. There are, however, counter argument that this increase in population might be part of healthy development of global life. In the case of the human body, an infant's brain develops with abnormal rapidity before birth. This can be seen as a transitional phenomenon to provide for the growth of extraordinary nervous system required for human mental and physiological functions.

Can the increase in human population in the ecosystem be similarly interpreted as a transitional but normal growing process forming "mental" faculty for global life? A positive answer would be possible if we can guarantee the health of today's ecosystem. But, as mentioned above, there are many visible symptoms indicating otherwise. Many wild animals and plants constituting the body of global life have lost their habitats and are on the brink of extinction. According to the estimation of biologist Edward O. Wilson, every year 27,000 species of wild life are being destroyed. If this continues, 1,000 years from now all species will be extinct.[14) This is a grim diagnosis for the global life, which has existed for 400 million years and has 500 million years more to exist on this planet up to the time the sun ceases burning.

Are There Alternatives?

We find difference in the viewpoints of Carson and Quinn. Carson argued that we had only recently embarked upon the wrong road, whereas Quinn claims that we set out upon the wrong path 10,000 years ago. It is therefore safe to conclude that some time after 10,000 years ago the normal physiology of global life began to turn into a morbid one, but the exact time and moment may be revealed only through a more reliable diagnosis of global life. Such a diagnosis,

14)Edward O. Wilson, *The Diversity of Life*, (Cambridge: Harvard University Press, 1992), p. 268; Edward O. Wilson, *The Future of Life,* (New York: Alfred Knopf, 2002), pp. 98-102. This calculation is based on the assumption that the estimated number of species presently existing is about thirty million.

based on proper conception of life and understanding of its inner mechanism, would indicate what action corresponds with normal physiology of global life and what the proper ways to cure it are.

We need, in particular, to reconsider the meaning of "production." We cannot live without consuming material goods, and for these goods, we have to participate in production. But the "production" does not mean making something from nothing. It simply means the process in which a part of "global life" transfers to another. The question is whether or not this process of transference accords with the normal physiology of global life, and whether or not such is appropriate for healing it. For this, we can make use of the ecosystem of 10,000 years ago as a reference point. Taking this as a prototype, we can judge that the less distorted from and the higher dependent upon the natural ecosystem (rather than on human factors), the closer to the "normal physiology." And the direction to reduce such a gap would be the direction to recovery of it.

It is of secondary importance to determine how far such effort must proceed. More urgent is whether we are in the right direction or not. Our present economic principles in which demand encourages supply and supply encourages demand in turn certainly run counter to healing "global life." Calling for "sustainable development" while retaining these "economic principles" is like hoping for improved health while encouraging the cause of the disease. The prevailing understanding of the situation as an "environmental problem" seeking remedy from "sustainable development" is fundamentally flawed.

We here encounter a grave difficulty. We seek a solution in direct opposition to the mainstream. One responsibility of literature is to bring this to our consciousness. Can we accomplish it before it is too late? No one yet seems to have an answer.

Finding Solace in *The Man Who Planted Trees*

Jean Giono's *The Man Who Planted Trees* comforts us. Compared to the other two works mentioned, at least on the surface, Giono's work does not openly problematize environmental issues. This piece was published before these issues became a public concern. Furthermore, there is no evidence suggesting that the author himself was well aware of this problem, scientifically or philosophically. Yet, this work illustrates a person who is pulled by an unknown force to bring an ecosystem to life.

The narrator sets out on a journey to a vast wasteland once inhabited but now desiccated with only wild weeds growing. He finds a man who plants trees after days of wandering in utter exhaustion with no water:

> I thought I glimpsed in the distance a small black silhouette, upright, and took it for the trunk of a solitary tree. In any case I started toward it. It was a shepherd .... The man spoke little .... The shepherd went to fetch a small sack and poured out a heap of acorns on the table. He began to inspect them, one by one, with great concentration, separating the good from the bad .... There he began thrusting his iron rod into the earth, making a hole in which he planted an acorn; then he refilled the hole. He was planting oak trees. I asked him if the land belonged to him. He answered no. Did he know whose it was? He did not.[15)]

This man named Elzéard Bouffier, maintaining his livelihood with only several sheep, is laboring to bring this deteriorated place to life. No one has asked him to do it, nor does anyone even recognize what he is doing. Bouffier does not even try to find out whose land this is. He has become one with nature.

After the narrator's initial encounter with Bouffier, he returns years later to find trees growing and the river flowing again.

> Creation seemed to come about in a sort of chain of reaction. He did not worry about it; he was determinedly pursuing his task in all its simplicity; but as he went back toward the village I saw water flowing in brooks that had been dry since the memory of man. This was the most impressive result of chain reaction that I had seen. These dry streams had once, long ago, run with water. Some of the dreary villages I mentioned before had been built on the sites of ancient Roman settlements, traces of which still

15)Giono, pp. 4-17

remained; and archaeologists, exploring there, had found fishhooks where, in the twentieth century, cisterns were needed to assure a small supply of water.

The wind, too, scattered seeds. As the water reappeared, so there reappeared willows, rushes meadows, gardens, flowers, and a certain purpose in being alive. But the transformation took place so gradually that it became part of the pattern without causing any astonishment.[16)]

Men had destroyed nature, but it was being restored by one man. This old man did not even realize the significance of what he was doing. He only knew this was what he needed to do.

In the direction from which we had come the slopes were covered with trees twenty to twenty–five feet tall .... Peaceful, regular toil, the vigorous mountain air, frugality, and, above all, serenity of spirit had endowed this old man with awe–inspiring health. He was one of God's athletes. I wondered how many more acres he was going to cover with trees.[17)]

Here we find a ray of hope. Giono shows that men not only destroy nature but that deep inside they have this desire to restore what they have damaged. It is comforting to know that we try to find problems and attempt to rectify them. More comforting, however, is the fact that we instinctively carry out some healing action even without consciously recognizing the problem as a problem. Artificial attempts at problem solving invite risks of failure. But if our natural tendency spontaneously directs us toward it, a higher possibility of accomplishment is expected. Can literature help awaken this deeply seated nature in us, then there is room for hope.

Translated by **Jennifer Lee**

16)Giono, pp. 27-30.
17)Giono, pp. 36-38.

Heroes of the New Literature: Spokespersons of National Interests or an Ideology of Globalization?

Vera G. Galaktionova

The question asked by this essay's title has a straightforward answer, but requires a discussion of pertinent information. Dorofej from Askalon, an orthodox philosopher who lived from the late sixth to early seventh centuries, had an interesting idea I think is important. It is represented geometrically by a circle with radii focusing into the center, which is God. A man on the circumference comes nearer to a person he cares about on the circumference only by removing one of the men in between them and closing the diameter of the circle. Those who move along the radii to the center all move closer and closer to each other, even if they don't know each other.

Since the first century, Christianity has offered ways to generate friendship, peaceful co-existence, and mutual respect, but has never espoused conflict. People who follow basic religious teachings—prohibitions against murder, theft, sexual deviance, jealousy, greed, and the pursuit of wealth for its own sake—observe the general commandments of all religions. Worshipping the golden ox of materialism is considered by those of a strong spiritual faith as an impermissible evil; it threatens a man's soul, the people around that man, and the world.

The modern world's policy of globalization also has its own ideology. A golden ox is at the center of this ideology. People who move to the center by accumulating capital pursue the ox and come closer to each other, but their lives and tight-knit communities are against the commandments of the world's religions. Money is quickly accumulated only when commandments are trespassed against or completely violated. Instead of respecting life, "kill anyone who thinks differently" is the doctrine followed. The entertainment industry, for example, earns its prosperity by exploiting sexual desire. The rich envy the richer, and the poor admire both. Believers in the ox think that those who devote their lives to a higher principle of truth are unwise, while those who accumulate wealth are most worthy of respect.

These problems of humankind have newly fallen upon Russia as it attempts to join the global economy. Competition for assets and resources and their quick conversion into cash has become more important than human welfare or any other matter in the country. The figures are astonishing. I could describe the details of the timber industry in the Russian Tigar Forest (the lungs of the globe), the quality of air in the world, the slow death of Lake Vaikal, or how the great Volga River is now a slow moving pond polluted by dirty tributaries. It would not be productive to do so. One may struggle for a cause like these and not give in, but the results will still not be successful. If one is successful, the victory is not complete, is temporary, and often local. The destruction and disruption of nature results from a blind pursuit of individual desire to accumulate wealth. Human beings destroy themselves, and consequently the world of nature that surrounds them.

I have recently completed a novel titled *Calm on the Eve of May 4*. It was published in the 2004 November and December issues of "Moscow," and since its publication, the novel has generated some heated controversy. The main theme of the novel is a loss of tradition, national community, and the human soul. It shows how human beings cause destruction inadvertently because of their actions. The protagonist of this novel was educated as a professional electrician, but he later becomes a successful businessman. The novel plots his interactions with his old school friends, one of whom is a reanimator—a person who brings those near death back to life—and another who is a pathologist. The pathologist believes the death of body and soul is a blessing. The characters come together to discuss the possibility of revitalizing the protagonist's dying wife, whose name is Ljubov'. Ljubov' means, "to live" in Russian.

The first sentence begins, "Ljubov' is far away now, on another side of life. She is in a coma and calm, cradled, as it were, between Heaven and Earth." The protagonist disassociates himself from this situation, though he must place his full attention on her needs for her to survive. This is the question to be explored: under these circumstances, what will he do?

Later, the novel describes an important condition of the landscape in this way:

> This summer in the Nura River, as it
> calmly flowed through the steppes, pale,
> large, and slow-moving fish appeared.
> They were like the fish described in the
> Apocalypse. They swam peacefully in
> clear water along the warm shores, as if
> no different from any ordinary fish. Their
> tails were transparent, as if having no
> skin, scales, or bones. The fish began to disintegrate; their
> tissues floated away
> from their bones, twitching in places.
> Fishermen were shocked by this grotesque
> spectacle. They jerked their hooks from
> the water, the worms near death, wriggling
> like question marks ....

The situation of the land and the fish is personified in the character of the protagonist. As the protagonist begins to change, he reflects on his circumstances, culminating in these thoughts:

> If the world is a reflection of the soul,
> ruined but alive, it would have to be obliterated pulverized and
> scattered.
> If the world were obliterated, it would be
> useless for people to talk to each other
> as if they cared.

The essential matters of the protagonist's life rise before him, and he must find answers to the problems he faces. He should come into balance with his life, but his inability to connect with his life makes it difficult. He realizes, though, that people do share conversations with one another, and the world is not in shattered pieces. The protagonist takes hope in this, and consequently his soul.

The novel is about the hard-fought transitions the protagonist, an anti-hero, undergoes. He was a hateful man before his wife's coma. He only pursued his own interests and had abandoned any devotion to the quality of his life. His heavy personality, however, comes from a cruel inheritance. The man is the son of the chief of a relocation camp, where Russians massacred Russians. The fratricide was a result of ethnic conflicts. Generally speaking, ethnic conflicts should be resolved by the descendants' strength of will. Some ethnic conflicts may be overcome in the contemporary moment they occur, but others reappear after a period of concealment. The story connects these ideas to the protagonist as he tries to resolve three parallel conflicts: the upheaval in Russian society, the haunting ethnic conflict that took place in his father's camp, and the terminal condition of his wife.

The process of dissolution of the human soul or a country's people has its own inertial force. For this reason, the protagonist must be free from his inability to connect with the world—purified, as it were—otherwise, that lack of connection will cause self-destruction.

The protagonist responds to his inability to connect with his life; he tries to find a way to usurp his lack of connection with the world and his own spiritual humanity. The protagonist, a man who once worshipped the golden ox, comes to worship the ways of God; he once harmed his country and people, but after his change works to protect them. The novel suggests that when the protagonist is ready to know his own soul as inseparable from the world, the causes of evil on earth will disappear.

Recent research from the Russian Laboratory on the Human Brain was a significant help to the writing of my novel. A theory by Professor Bekhtereva states that the world is interactive—activities of the brain also change the world. Impulses we feel, experience, and pursue occur in our real surroundings. These occurrences can influence a decision to pursue God or the golden ox.

Our contemporary times differentiate individual engagement with reality in extreme and dangerous ways without any mediation. On one side, there is the destruction of everything and the tyranny of money, while on the other side, there is the resurrection, revival, and rebirth of love for selfish reasons.

The Soviet Union caused disharmony and de-evolution as a means to achieving globalization. Every republic of the Soviet Union advanced independently down the road of the golden ox. After the fall of the Soviet Union, however, conditions for God and friendship arose. Orthodox Christian commandments—no murder, theft, or corruption, respect for parents—coincided with teachings of world religions, as found, for example, in the Koran.

Soviet communism used religion to overcome theoretical atheism. It required the best teachings on religion from Soviet ethics. The morality of the creators of communism was presented as a set of the most religious commandments selected from a variety of religious traditions. This was done for the sake of improving relationships among societies by using their shared values as a system of government-sponsored religious commandments. Avva Dorofej's ideology, for example, became a new system of government-sponsored religious doctrine in eastern Soviet-era nations. If a structure of power arises similar in ideological content to the triune of the New Testament, the Koran, and communist moral doctrines, and it has a direct impact on governmental decisions, then a kind of solidarity will in fact have been born. Such a birth may gradually overcome humanity's ever-present will to destroy.

The tragedy that followed the dissolution of the USSR left twenty-five million Russian and ten million native speakers of Russian out of Russia. Every border of the former Soviet republics now divides our people. Incredibly, a law was passed making it difficult for Russians from old republics to obtain their rights as Russian citizens; Russians who registered in the old Soviet republics before 1992 lost their citizenship. For Russian refugees, this law was a form of fratricide and betrayal. To this day, many of them die before my eyes without any aid from their country.

Defenders of human rights remain silent because they, the defenders, have no immediate impact on Russia. Year after year, the conflict in Chechnya has continued to claim the lives of Russia's most productive age group because they were left behind. The disbanding of the USSR and the weakening and exhaustion of Russian people has brought the world many benefits, but disbanding the government has had a price paid by the blood of innocent people. Is any of this truly the will of God?

Am I actively opposed to globalization? No. Civilizations on earth have always undergone changes born from the evil of the world, but it is also true that every such movement has a current of self-annihilation; globalization will destroy itself. The people whose activities are involved in movements like globalization also consume themselves. Despite these circumstances, the number of people from the circumference to the center (God) will continue to increase. Those who follow the natural laws of nature do not approach one another by scientific technology, but a strong will.

The heroes of my novels have traces of self-destruction in their souls. The traces are a reflection of the destructive tendencies in the world. My novel expresses it this way: "if the world has pain, so must the human soul." In my novel, the abnormal incandescence of the sun often represents catharsis. The impetus of fate that is yet to be fully realized, or lives that end before sinning—both of these metaphorically return to the sun. The irritation of the sun influences how people repent sins that are fratricidal; it punishes and enlivens people with their previously misdirected energies. This happens in the novel because every evil is fratricidal. Surplus energy of the sun metaphorically punishes living things, and this widens the scope of human discernment—perception is clarified. There is scientific evidence for these interrelations between the sun and human beings that I will presently discuss.

The Cosmic Pulse of Life by A. L. Chizhevsky and *Bio Sphere and Noos Sphere* by V. I. Bernadsky discuss the effects of activities of the sun and natural rhythms of the earth and cosmos on human beings. According to their research, human beings affect nature only in terms of the physical and chemical.

Nature is, however, essentially moral and divine. I believe nature will respond to human immorality and damage done to divinity in a way that is more serious than currently predicted. A scientist in the future discovering that the sun reacts to our human emotions will not surprise me.

Chizhevsky acknowledges the influence of ancient Chaldean wisdom on his book, *Geliotarakasiya*, when he states:

> If the earth and all living things on the earth had merely an organic structure ... serious damage at the basic physical-chemical level would cause the organic realm of the earth to be profoundly disrupted.

Nature is not, however, one-directional. If the basic physical-chemical level of nature has an influence on organisms, then organisms also have an affect on the physical-chemical level.

I have been to a district in Chernobyl called 30 Kilometrvaya. Officially, it is an uninhabited radioactively polluted district. Leftovers of plutonium, strontium, and cesium damaged the district after the reactor explosion. It had been a beautiful landscape for thousands of years. I wrote about this in my work, *Dark Non-fiction, White Russian Land*, collected in *Wind in the Empty Century* (Moscow, 2000). Though people lived only fifteen kilometers from the dead district of 30 Kilometrvaya, they would not leave their dangerous land. They continued to breed cows, drink contaminated milk, and collect radioactive strawberries and mushrooms.

These people told me no radioactivity was measured near the Orthodox icons in their district. I had no opportunity to confirm this. Observers of the situation did confirm that the youth of Gomel suffered more than the religious old people who came back to their hometowns after the explosion. Gomel was less polluted by radiation and is more than thirty kilometers from Chernobyl. The old people's bodies were more contaminated by radiation than the young people, but the old people continued to farm the land of 30 Kilometrvaya, and live. They were able to do this through prayer. Their bodies did not suffer from any physical-chemical damage, though they had been more exposed to radiation than the younger generation who lived further away.

Thirteen years after the explosion I had the chance to go to 30 Kilometrvaya and meet many hard working old people. Their faces glowed with endless patience and good cheer. Their hospitality and kindness was astonishing. This is a clear example of how spiritualism can overcome organic destruction of the human body.

Chizhevsky demonstrated that the activities of the sun can improve and evolve relations between groups of human beings and influence cycles of revolution in culture. I'd like to emphasize here that the law of the pendulum is the oldest and truest. The evolving supernatural energy of people does not disappear into nature. There is no doubt that nature responds to the spiritual growth of human beings.

That we follow the ways of God is a blessing to earth. It is not a matter of individual faith. To violate religious commandments and abandon what is divine, or to pursue monetary benefits in a manner suited to animals will result in surprising, undesirable, and pervasive consequences. This is because nature is a clear, timeless system of interdependence.

Bernadsky has a theory for what he calls the "psycho sphere," as opposed to what we know as "biosphere." This theory originated with the English oceanographer John Murray in the early twentieth century, and then Tiehard de Chardin named it "*noos* (reason) sphere," using noos instead of psycho. Both terms referred to the idea that "all living things" had a quality of spirituality.

It is already late in our contemporary moment to mention the problem of water pollution on earth. We need a new philosophy for survival—a philosophy to correct the terrible crimes of civilization. My intention is to properly change the misguided direction of civilization's development.

N. Zarubina, a Russian philosopher who studies the character of "money-driven men," wrote in the December 2004 issue of "Moscow,"

A money-driven man can stand no obstacle
to his egotistic, inexhaustible pursuit

> for competitive advantage that heartlessly
> violates or circumvents moral norms. A
> money-driven man is intolerant. He is
> aggressive and creates conflict. He uses
> every economic, social, and environmental situation for his own
> benefit. Nature is
> only an object without spirit or identity
> to him. It is only a source for resources
> or necessities. The money-driven man does
> not care how much he damages nature.

Such money-driven men are driving globalization. They pressure men interested in managing their own land through their own vision. Men who want to manage their land with heartfelt respect view nature and culture as national assets. Money-driven men exploit land, but "managing" men preserve it for posterity.

How does nature respond to the cruelty and bestiality of money-driven men? How does the universe respond to people who believe, "We dominate you because it is in your best interest," and then bomb places like Serbia and Iraq? What happens when the law of the pendulum swings to the other side? It's not surprising to see honest Americans leave America in short order. They escape from a system that destroys and attacks the self. Nature's response will come on a surprisingly unexpected scale. Everything has an influence on everything.

It is heartbreaking that we, the inheritors of great literature, should witness the art of literature rent into pieces as a commonplace event in Russia. Literature that is born from deformed, cheap ideas tramples down profound, well-crafted and cultured language, and the possibility of such great writing overflowing bookstores. The effect of literary pollution on the spirit of readers is another environmental catastrophe. We can fight against oil pollution by ships, but how can we calculate the damage done by vulgarity, derisiveness, and tastelessness? Writers who are driven by money and fame have no interest in national history or fate because of ignorance, and they thrive because of the basest emotions of their readers. Generally, the protagonists of new literature have no sense of societal purpose; they chat, drink, and fight. They do not love. They have only sexual liaisons. The most important purpose to their lives is to be rich.

Globalization requires standardization. It destroys diversity of culture and language, and lowers the standards of the human spirit. Money is an important tool of globalization because money has no interest in good, bad, virtue, or sin. Money, the criterion of all modern action, structures and prematurely ripens literature. It deforms the faceless and immoral. It does not revive the human spirit but annihilates it. Instant literature, no more than a relief from stress, earns a lot of money.

Russia, with an expensive system of education, is entering a civilized world of culture, but now is the time when everything should be honestly called by its true name, isn't it? Shouldn't a highly developed civilization serve as an exemplar of a highly evolved world morality? The way of modern men from the circumference, to the radii, to the center of the golden-ox circle, is a way of suicide. There should be no one so foolish as to commit offenses by tearing down all the things of nature on earth for the sake of competitive advantages.

It is a somewhat cheerless experience to read Bernadsky, even though he believed in human reason and theories of the biosphere and *noos* sphere. Bernadsky was convinced that nature should be developed with a visionary earnestness. In his defense, Bernadsky did criticize how men have used reason inspired by nature to cause damage to and hold supremacy over nature, thereby destroying the biosphere. Bernadsky also acknowledges the harm men do to themselves by these actions.

As an intellectual, Bernadsky wrote,

> Civilization forgets the relationship
> between human beings and other living
> things. Men try to make the existence of civilized human beings
> separate from
> nature's world of living things.

By inquiring into these interrelationships, it is apparent that the obstacles separating humanity and nature may be split into pieces and finally fall away.

Bernadsky could not anticipate the rise of men so greedy, removed from nature, and free from moral structure. He could not anticipate how synthesized by civilization and anti-nature these men would think, how they would come into existence and pursue world power. These men achieve their aims through economic and political struggles, forcing others on the planet to follow their wills.

Bernadsky sounds like an objective scholar doesn't he? I agree with him then that there should be an attempt to eradicate problems of greed in the world and exploitation of nature. The problems and exploitation will end when we insist that human beings live inclusively with nature.

Endnotes

Alexander Chizhevsky (1897-1964)
Russian biophysicist who founded heliobiology.

Vladimir Bernadsky (1863-1945)
Russian naturalist and philosopher who founded geochemistry, biogeochemistry, and radiogeology.

John Murray (1841-1914)
English Oceanographer. A citizen of St. Petersburg who graduated from Edinburgh University, Murray joined the exploration of the globe on the ship *Challenge* in 1872.

Tiehard de Chardin (1881-1955)
French paleontologist, philosopher and theologist. Lived in China from 1923 to 1946. He found Peking Man.

Translated by **Heo Tae-young**

Session XIII

Poverty and Stratification of the World

Thomas Brussig | Armut und Krieg Heute

Gong Sun-ok | A Poor Writer in the Age of Globalization

Armut und Krieg Heute

Thomas Brussig

Sehr geehrte Damen und Herren,

Mein Name ist Thomas Brussig. Ich komme aus Deutschland, aus Berlin. Ich bin aufgewachsen an der Nahtstelle des Kalten Krieges, und zwar auf der falschen Seite, also im Osten. Die Angst vor einem Atomkrieg gehörte zu meinem Aufwachsen. Mit dieser Angst war es seit Gorbatschow vorbei, und bis ich die Einladung zu dieser Konferenz bekam, hielt ich es für ausgeschlossen, daß sich nach dem Ende des Kalten Krieges wieder Schriftsteller aus aller Welt treffen, um sich über das Problem des Friedens auszutauschen.

Wenn wir Einfluß nehmen wollen, dann geschieht das zuerst über unsere Bücher. Doch die Erfahrung lehrt, daß kein Buch gezielt Einfluß nehmen kann. Das Schöne an unserer Branche ist ja, daß immer wieder Zufälliges und Überraschendes geschieht. Die größte Wirkung geht immer von den Büchern aus, die ihre Wirkungen auf eine unvorhersagbare Weise entfalten. Um es salopp zu sagen: Ein Buch, das nicht mindestens von drei Verlagen abgelehnt wurde, kann nicht unsterblich werden.

Die zweite Möglichkeit unserer Einflußnahme besteht darin, in Interviews oder Aufsätzen Zusammenhänge einleuchtend und klar darzustellen, in üb erzeugenden, griffigen Worten. Da stehen wir in direkter Konkurrenz zu Politikern oder Journalisten, die durchaus die entgegengesetzte Meinung vertreten. Wenn es die Worte gäbe, die den Krieg verbannen könnten, dann wären sie schon ausgesprochen – zu groß ist die Sehnsucht der Menschen nach Frieden. Es gibt in jeder Sprache großartige und zugleich sehr einfache Lieder und Gedichte, die auch immer populär sind. Und obwohl jeder diese Lieder und Gedichte kennt, kommt es immer wieder zu Kriegen. Wenn die Trompete zum Angriff bläst, dann ist es, als wären all die klugen, richtigen Worte, die die Krieg verabscheuen, nie gesprochen worden. Es gibt Umstände, da ist das Wort schwach und unbedeutend.

Warum ist das so?

Es gibt offenbar ein Geheimnis um den Krieg, vor dem wir, die den Frieden wollen, machtlos sind. Diesem Geheimnis wollen wir in diesen Tagen auf die Spur kommen, und ich bin gebeten worden, etwas über kriegerische Konflikte im Licht von Armut und sozialer Schichtung zu sagen.

Der Ansatz, der einen Zusammenhang zwischen Armut und Krieg herstellt, hat in der deutschen Politik eine gewisse Tradition. Willy Brandt, der deutsche Bundeskanzler von 1969 bis 1974, danach als Vorsitzender der Nord-Süd-Kommission ein bedeutender Entwicklungspolitiker, sagte 1980: „Die Geschichte hat uns gelehrt, daß Kriege Hunger nach sich ziehen, aber weniger bewußt ist uns, daß Massenarmut ihrerseits zum Krieg führen oder im Chaos enden kann. Wo Hunger herrscht, kann Friede nicht Bestand haben. Wer den Krieg ächten will, muß auch die Massenarmut bannen." Im Januar dieses Jahres sagte der deutsche Bundespräsident Horst Köhler: „Ohne weltweite Armutsbekämpfung wird es für uns langfristig keine Sicherheit geben und auch keine politische Stabilität. Und deshalb ist Entwicklungspolitik die beste Konfliktprävention. [...] Zwischen Sicherheit und wirtschaftlicher Entwicklung besteht ein Zusammenhang. Das ist fast schon eine Binsenweisheit."

Die Statistik gibt Horst Köhler recht. Von den 18 bewaffneten Konflikten, die im Jahre 2002 beobachtet wurden, fanden immerhin 17 in Ländern statt, deren jährliches Pro-Kopf-Einkommen unter 755 Dollar betrug und die damit nach Einteilung der UN zur untersten Einkommensgruppe gehörten.

Ich glaube, wir sind uns dennoch alle einig, daß ungleich verteilter Reichtum nicht die Ursache von Kriegen sein kann. So wie Menschen unterschiedlich sind, ist auch ihr Reichtum unterschiedlich. Es ist sogar so, daß das Ziel der Nivellierung von Lebensverhältnissen, das sich gern als „soziale Gerechtigkeit" tarnt, oft mit Gewaltanwendung verfolgt wird. Denken wir an das Terrorregime der Roten Khmer in Kambodscha: Das Ziel der

Abschaffung aller sozialen Unterschiede ging einher mit der Ausrottung ganzer Klassen und Schichten – und eingeführt wurde die „Armut für alle". Nun sprachen weder Horst Köhler noch Willy Brandt wohlweislich nicht davon, daß eine wie auch immer geartete „soziale Gerechtigkeit" Kriege und Gewalt bannt und Sicherheit schafft. Ich will die beiden Herren nicht absichtlich mißverstehen oder ihnen etwas unterstellen, was sie nicht gemeint haben. Sie meinen, daß die Überwindung von Armut nicht nur Wohlstand, sondern auch mehr Sicherheit einbringt. Leider teile ich nicht die Zuversicht dieser beiden von mir so hoch geschätzten Herren. Gewiß, es gibt einen Zusammenhang zwischen Armut und Gewaltkonflikten – aber keine simple, direkte Kausalität.

Denn so überzeugend der Zusammenhang von Armut und Kriegen auf den ersten Blick scheint – ich kann keinen zwingenden Zusammenhang erkennen. Beginnen ärmere Länder einen Krieg gegen reichere Länder? Ja. (Der Irak greift 1990 Kuwait an.) Beginnen reichere Länder einen Krieg gegen ärmere Länder? Ja, passiert ständig. Beginnen schwächere Länder einen Krieg gegen überlegene Staaten? Ja. (Japan greift 1941 die USA an.) Beginnen stärkere Länder einen Krieg gegen schwächere Staaten? Ja, passiert ständig. Beginnen ungefähr gleich arme Länder Krieg gegeneinander? Ja. (Iran und Irak in den achtziger Jahren.) Beginnen ungefähr gleich wohlhabende Länder Krieg gegeneinander? Ja. (Deutschland und Frankreich in den beiden Weltkriegen.) Überfällt ein großes Land ein viel kleineres? Ja, passiert ständig. Überfällt ein kleines Land ein viel zu großes Land? Ja. (Israel Ägypten im Sechstagekrieg.) Sie sehen: Ob ein Staat arm, reich, groß oder klein, hochgerüstet oder fast wehrlos ist, spielt letztlich keine Rolle. Ebensowenig wie die Staatsform: Diktaturen führen Krieg gegeneinander oder gegen Demokratien – und umgekehrt. Nur daß entwickelte Demokratien gegeneinander Krieg führen – da fällt mir kein Fall aus den letzten 50, 60 Jahren ein.

Es gibt drei aktuelle Thesen, die sich mit Kriegsneigung befassen.

Die erste These: Demokratien führen gegeneinander keinen Krieg. Wenn wir an Jugoslawien denken, stimmt das nur bedingt – die kriegführenden Staatsgebilde waren zumindest auf dem Papier

Demokratien. Doch tatsächlich war zumindest in Serbien ein autoritär gesinntes Regime an der Macht. Daß unter Demokratien keine Kriege ausbrechen, mag daran liegen, daß es der Alltag in Demokratien ist, Lösungen auszuhandeln, einen Konsens zu erarbeiten, Kompromisse zu schließen. Daß „der andere" eine andere Meinung hat und eigene Interessen verfolgt, und das beides zu achten und zu schützen ist, ist ein Gedanke, der am Anfang der Demokratie steht. Und solange Reden möglich ist, wird Gewalt verabscheut und als Mittel der Auseinandersetzung abgelehnt – nicht nur von Pazifisten. Darüber herrscht Konsens. Daß Demokratien gegeneinander keine Kriege führen, hat insofern mit dem Armutsproblem zu tun, daß sich nur relativ wohlhabende Länder Demokratie leisten können.

Die zweite These klingt fast wie ein Widerspruch zur ersten: Demokratien haben die Tendenz, gegen Nicht-Demokratien Krieg zu führen. Komischerweise fällt mir zu dieser These vor allem eine Demokratie als Beleg ein. Aber warum haben Demokratien, und besonders eine, die Tendenz, gegen Nicht-Demokratien Krieg zu führen? Bei Samuel P. Huntington kann man lesen: *Der Konflikt zwischen liberaler Demokratie und Marxismus-Leninismus bestand zwischen Ideologien, die bei aller Unterschiedlichkeit die höchsten Werte zumindest scheinbar miteinander teilten: Freiheit, Gleichheit und Wirtschaftswachstum. Ein traditionaler, autoritärer, nationalistischer Russe dürfte ganz andere Werte haben. Ein westlicher Demokrat konnte mit einem Sowjetmarxisten eine intellektuelle Debatte führen. Dasselbe mit einem russischen Traditionalisten ist ihm praktisch unmöglich.* Wenn also Demokraten nicht mehr die Möglichkeit einer irgendwie gearteten Verständigung mit Nicht-Demokraten haben, wenn jegliche Basis einer Verständigung fehlt, dann wird es kritisch. Möglicherweise ähneln Demokratien – besonders eine – dem fünfjährigen Thomas, der auf dem Spielplatz zu Henry sagte: „Wenn du nicht mein Freund sein willst, dann hau ich dich so lange, bis du mein Freund sein willst." Wenn Demokratien – besonders eine – mit einem anderen Staat überhaupt nicht reden können, dann – so zumindest würde Huntington die zweite These deuten – führen sie Krieg, um überhaupt miteinander reden zu können. Es hängt mit dem

Selbstbewußtsein der Demokratien zusammen, daß sie das eigene Modell für das überlegene halten – und da meine ich tatsächlich alle Demokratien und nicht nur eine. Demokratien sind auch da noch stolz auf ihre Demokratie, wo schon längst kein Grund mehr besteht. Und obendrein gibt es eine Demokratie, die militärisch sehr effektiv operieren kann. So, wie es beim Fußball heißt „Geld schießt Tore" kann man hier sagen „Geld gewinnt Kriege". Ich persönlich kann diesem Interventionismus wenig abgewinnen. Solange es nicht Anzeichen gibt, daß sich die Menschen in bestimmten Regimes tatsächlich wehren, solange sie nicht selbst in ihrer eigenen Angelegenheit aktiv werden, muß ich deren Angelegenheit nicht zu meiner machen. Zuallererst müssen die etwas riskieren, die etwas zu gewinnen haben. Denn je größer die Gefahren waren und je höher der Preis war, der für die eigene Freiheit bezahlt wurde, desto kostbarer erscheint sie dann auch, wenn sie da ist. Wer Freiheit und Demokratie installiert, ist dazu verurteilt, sie zu einem Erfolgsmodell zu machen.

Die dritte These besagt: Die größte Kriegsneigung besteht in den sogenannten failed states, also zusammengebrochenen Staatsgebilden, wo die Armut in soziale Desintegration umschlägt. Es gibt keine Rechtssicherheit und keine staatliche Gewalt mehr, ebensowenig wie verläßliche Instanzen. Es ist hier auch nicht mehr der Staat, der Krieg führt, nicht mal eine Partei mit einer irgendwie politischen Zielsetzung. Dies ist interessant und beängstigend zugleich, denn hier geschieht etwas, das man in Europa zuletzt im 17. Jahrhundert erlebte, im Dreißigjährigen Krieg. In den Gesellschaften der failed states erleben wir eine Entstaatlichung des Krieges oder, anders gesagt, eine Privatisierung des Krieges. Die Protagonisten jener Kriege sind nicht mehr Staaten, die gegen Staaten Kriege führen und schließlich Frieden schließen. Die Protagonisten jener Kriege sind der Söldner, der Kindersoldat, der Warlord und der international vernetzte Terrorist. Deren Kriege beginnen nicht mit einer Kriegserklärung und enden nicht mit einem Friedensvertrag. Diese Kriege schwelen vor sich hin, dauern lange, scheuen die Kriegsentscheidung hinaus und halten sich an keinerlei internationale Regeln der Kriegsführung. Es sind Kriege der Plünderungen, der Verwüstungen, der Massaker und

Vergewaltigungen. Es sind keine Kriege mit Fronten, Schlachten, Truppenbewegungen und Kriegsgefangenen. Diese Kriege haben so wenig mit dem zu tun, was wir unter Kriegen verstehen, daß wir sie schon gar nicht mehr Kriege nennen sollten; eher Gewaltkonflikte oder kriegerische Gewalt. Es ist ein sehr alter, schon überwunden geglaubter Typ des Krieges und Typ des Kämpfers, der da auf die Welt zurückkehrt. Mit modernen Kriegen haben diese Kriege nichts zu tun. Kriegsgefangene werden, wenn sie nicht sofort getötet oder so schwer verstümmelt werden, daß sie nie wieder kämpfen können, als Geisel genommen und gegen Geld wieder freigelassen. Dieses Schicksal erfahren meist die Gefangenen, hinter denen ein potenter Staat steht. Insofern ist es vom Standpunkt des Rechts und der Logik völlig verständlich, daß die Guantanamo-Häftlinge nicht den Status von Kriegsgefangenen haben: Diesen Status gewähren die kriegführenden Parteien gegenseitig den Gefangenen der anderen Seite. Derlei Abmachungen zwischen Feinden leben allein von ihrer Gegenseitigkeit. Was jedoch, wenn Gewißheit besteht, daß sich der Feind nicht an die Regeln hält? Was, wenn der Feind ein schwer greifbares, unlegitimiertes Etwas ist? Das Wesentliche an Regeln ist, daß sie für alle gelten. Gelten sie nicht für alle, dann gelten sie für keinen.

Wir sind hier aber plötzlich auf ein Phänomen der neuen Konflikte gestoßen: Unsere Welt ist zunehmend von *asymmetrischen Kriegen* geprägt. Es stoßen immer weniger Staaten und ihre Armeen aufeinander, sondern privat finanzierte Banden und Haufen, die in den *failed states* im Vakuum der Macht operieren. Es ist für die hochgerüsteten und modernen Armeen der Demokratien ein schwer zu kalkulierendes Risiko, sich in eine solche Region zu begeben und Ordnung zu schaffen (was, und das ist kein Zufall, mehr nach Polizeieinsatz denn nach Krieg klingt). Geld gewinnt zwar Kriege, nur dürfen auf der eigenen Seite keine Opfer zurückbleiben – was übrigens auch eine Asymmetrie der neuen Kriege darstellt: Die eigenen Toten haben für Staaten eine viel verheerendere Wirkung als für Privatarmeen. Ein Staat schuldet den Hinterbliebenen Erklärungen, er muß vor den Angehörigen den Tod eines Soldaten begründen können.

Ich sage gleich, daß ich im weiteren Verlauf meines Vortrages nie wieder so dicht an den Zusammenhang zwischen Krieg und Armut kommen werde wie in den failed states. *Jedesmal, wenn ich zum Busbahnhof nach Abidjan* [die eigentliche Hauptstadt der Elfenbeinküste] *fuhr*, schreibt der US-Politologe Robert D. Kaplan, *war das Taxi umlagert von Scharen junger Männer mit unruhigen, radarartigen Blicken, die ihre Hände durch das Fenster streckten und ein Trinkgeld dafür wollten, daß sie mein Gepäck trugen – auch wenn ich nur einen Rucksack hatte. In den Städten sechs westafrikanischer Länder sah ich überall ganz ähnliche junge Männer, haufenweise. Sie waren wie freie Moleküle in einer sehr instabilen sozialen Flüssigkeit, einer Flüssigkeit, die deutlich kurz vor der Zündung stand. – „Weißt du", sagte mein Freund der Minister, „in den Dörfern Afrikas ist es absolut selbstverständlich, an jedem Tisch beköstigt und in jeder Hütte beherbergt zu werden. Aber in den Städten funktioniert diese kommunale Existenz nicht mehr. Du mußt für deine Beherbergung bezahlen und zum Essen eingeladen werden. Wenn junge Männer erkennen, daß sie sich mit ihren Beziehungen nicht über Wasser halten können, dann gehen sie verloren. Sie schließen sich anderen Migranten an und rutschen geradewegs in die Kriminalität."*

Kriegerische Konflikte, die in Zusammenhang mit Armut stehen, werden also nicht wegen Armut geführt, sondern in Armut. Und so wie der Staat machtlos ist, ist auch die Literatur machtlos: Können Sie sich vorstellen, daß Sie einen von denen, die ihre Hände durch das Fenster strecken, mit Ihren Büchern erreichen?

Wenn *failed states* in einem Sumpf aus Armut, Rechtlosigkeit, Korruption und Gewalt versinken, dann heißt die Therapie nation building. Damit ist gemeint, Polizei und Verwaltungen aufzubauen, eine allgemein respektierte und breit legitimierte Autorität zu installieren, eine Rechtsordnung zu schaffen und einen Staat zum Leben zu erwecken, der sich für die Belange seiner Bürger verantwortlich fühlt. Im nation-building könnten die wohlhabenden Demokratien ihre Domäne finden.

Denn es ist ja nicht die Tatsache gefährlich daß Konflikte existieren. Gefährlich wird es, wenn Gewalt als selbstverständliches und legitimes Mittel zur Lösung von Konflikten betrachtet wird. Nicht Konflikte sind das Problem, sondern die Art und Weise ihres

Austrags. Und es ist leider so, daß in armen Gesellschaften, in *failed states* gar, keine Institutionen existieren, die Konflikte friedlich regeln und schlichten können. Schwache Staaten verfügen häufig weder über allgemein anerkannte Verfahren der Konfliktbewältigung noch über ausreichende Mittel, die wenigen vorhandenen Konfliktbewältigungsmechanismen auch durchzusetzen. Das ist solange kein Problem, solange es traditionelle, nichtstaatliche, aber wirksame Instanzen des Interessenausgleichs, der Schlichtung, der gewaltlosen Konfliktbewältigung gibt. Doch wehe, die Tradition zerbricht! Aus diesem Grund kann die Formel gelten, daß Armut nicht zwangsläufig den Ausbruch von Gewalt nach sich zieht, aber daß arme Gesellschaften tendenziell anfälliger sind für den gewaltsamen Austrag von Konflikten.

Und dennoch ist es eine Illusion, daß sich Kriege dadurch bekämpfen lassen, indem die Armut bekämpft wird. Es war eine der bittersten Erfahrungen der Entwicklungshelfer, daß ausgerechnet Ruanda, das als ein Musterbeispiel für Entwicklungshilfe galt, zum Schauplatz eines entsetzlichen Völkermordes wurde. Es ist sicher nicht verkehrt, die Armut zu bekämpfen – aber die Bekämpfung von Armut ist kein Allheilmittel bei der Bekämpfung von Kriegen. Friedens- und Konfliktforscher beklagen, daß selbst die humanitäre Hilfe in Flüchtlingslagern, die die Elenden der Elenden mit dem Nötigsten versorgt, das Sich-Hinziehen von Gewaltkonflikten befördert, da diese Flüchtlingslager von den Kriegsparteien als Rückzugs- und Rekrutierungscamp gesehen wird und nicht selten durch gewalttätige Gruppierungen humanitäre Hilfe abgezweigt wird – als Preis dafür, daß wenigstens ein Teil der Hilfe an ihr Ziel gelangen darf.

Es gibt tausend gute Gründe dafür, etwas gegen die Armut zu tun. Wir können die Armut bekämpfen, weil uns schlecht wird, wenn wir im Fernsehen Hungernde sehen, wir können die Armut bekämpfen, weil wir im Urlaub kein Elend sehen wollen, wir können die Armut bekämpfen, weil wir Menschenfreunde sind, wir können die Armut bekämpfen, weil wir Flüchtlingsströme verhindern wollen, wir können die Armut bekämpfen, weil wir Konsumenten für unsere Produkte wollen – aber wir dürfen nicht glauben, daß es keine Kriege mehr geben wird, wenn es keine

Armut mehr gibt.

Die Bekämpfung von Kriegen ist ein eigenes Problem, das eine eigene Aufmerksamkeit erfordert. Es droht, so formulieren es Konfliktforscher, häufig dann der Ausbruch von Gewalt, wenn bestimmte Bevölkerungsgruppen eine relative Minderung ihrer Chancen, eine Verschlechterung ihrer Lebensbedingungen und Partizipationsmöglichkeiten erfahren oder wenn sie vom Fortschritt ausgeschlossen werden und wenn sich diese Trennung entlang ethnischer oder religiöser Trennlinien abspielt. Also: Selbst wenn Armut in einer Gesellschaft erfolgreich bekämpft wird, kann dies zu Konflikten führen. Nämlich dann, wenn die Armutsbekämpfung Unterschiede macht und die Erfahrung neuer Ungerechtigkeit hervorbringt. Deshalb sind besonders auch dynamische Gesellschaften von Gewaltausbrüchen bedroht, denn wo es Gewinner gibt, da gibt es – ja, nicht unbedingt Verlierer, aber da gibt es auch jene, die sich benachteiligt, betrogen, Zu-kurz-gekommen fühlen. Die Dynamik so zu gestalten, daß sie nicht zu gewalttätigen Eruptionen führt, ist hohe Staatskunst.

Wenn Armut tatsächlich die Ursache für Kriege wäre, dann müßten wir erleben, wie der Reichtum mal kurz und gewalttätig umverteilt wird. Aber das erleben wir gerade nicht. Gewalttätige Konflikte dauern neuerdings lange und gehen mit einer stetigen Verelendung einher. Die Konfliktlinien verlaufen entlang ethnischer oder religiöser Grenzen, aber nicht entlang der sozialen Schichtung. Trotzdem sprechen alle Konfliktforscher von einem Zusammenhang oder einer Korrelation zwischen Armut und Krieg. Vermutlich ist jedoch nicht Armut die Ursache von Kriegen und Gewalt, sondern potentieller Reichtum – und je stärker der potentielle Reichtum im Kontrast zur gegenwärtigen Armut steht, desto höher ist die Gefahr eines Ausbruchs von Gewalt.

Der Krieg in den Armutsregionen ist extrem billig. Er wird mit leichten Waffen geführt, insbesondere mit Kalaschnikows – also mit Waffen, für die keinerlei Ausbildung notwendig ist. Landminen und Mehrfachraketenwerfer sind weitere Waffen, die in den neuen, billigen Kriegen zum Einsatz kommen. Panzer sieht man nur dann, wenn sie im Lande zurückgelassene Überbleibsel des Ost-West-Konfliktes sind, Bombenflieger und Düsenjets gibt es in den neuen

Kriegen überhaupt nicht. Die Kämpfer sind, wenn überhaupt, nur nachlässig uniformiert, als „Militärfahrzeuge" dienen Pick-ups. Es gibt keine Staatlichkeit, die die Kämpfer besolden und unterhalten muß; durch Plünderung und Raub sorgen die Kämpfer selbst für ihren Unterhalt. Das Bedrohliche dieser neuen Kriege ist, daß aufgrund ihrer geringen Kosten viele Kriegsherren in der Lage sind, diese Kriege auch zu führen und mit sehr wenig Geld eine fürchterliche Truppe aufstellen können. Zwar wird diese Truppe niemals gegen hochgerüstete Armeen auch nur den Hauch einer Chance haben – aber um Massaker unter der Zivilbevölkerung anzurichten und ganze Landstriche jahrelang im Griff der Angst zu halten – dazu reicht es allemal.

Schauen wir auf die Ökonomie der neuen Kriege: Während sich die klassischen Staatenkriege immer weniger lohnen, weil die eigenen Verluste eines Angriffs selbst bei erfolgreichem Kriegsverlauf nicht aufgewogen werden können, sind die neuen Kriege für die mächtigsten der Beteiligten lukrativ. Hier bringt die Gewalt den Warlords mehr ein, als sie kostet – zumindest kurzfristig, und die langfristigen Kosten haben andere zu tragen. Ja, die Rückkehr des Warlords ist ein zuverlässiges Indiz dafür, daß sich der Krieg wieder lohnt, jedenfalls dann, wenn er mit leichten Waffen, billigen Kämpfern und vor allem mit lukrativen Anschlußmöglichkeiten an die großen Geschäfte der globalisierten Wirtschaft geführt werden kann. Die Warlords treten nämlich auch als Schutzpatron für verschiedenste Geschäfte auf, an denen man außerhalb der Gebiete, die sie unter ihre Kontrolle gebracht haben, ein Interesse hat: Sei es die Vergabe von Schürfrechten oder die Lizenz für die Ausbeutung von Bodenschätzen, seien es skrupellosere Geschäfte wie Drogen- und Menschenhandel (der meist in Zusammenhang mit Prostitution steht), sei es die Lagerung giftiger, radioaktiver oder sonstiger hochproblematischer Abfälle oder der Export von Edelhölzern. Der Staat, den sie mit Kalaschnikows, billigen Kämpfern und Pick-ups lokal oder regional entmachten, ist zu schwach, um sie an ihren Geschäften zu hindern.

Ein Zusammenhang zwischen Armut und Kriegen ist auch dann zu entdecken, wenn man sich für die Menschen interessiert, die kämpfen. Die meisten von ihnen sind arm – sei es nach ganz allgemeinen Maßstäben, sei es, daß sie, sofern sie aus reichen Gesellschaften kommen, dort zur Unterschicht gehören. Gerade für Kämpfer, die aus armen Regionen und bitterarmen Ländern entstammen, bietet Krieg, so paradox das klingen mag, eine sichere Lebensgrundlage. Der Krieg bietet eine Zugehörigkeit zu einer Gemeinschaft, die Waffe sichert Respekt und natürlich auch die Macht, das Nötigste und auch etwas darüber hinaus an sich zu reißen – Statussymbole, Geld, Schmuck etc. Lieber die Hand an der Waffe als bettelnd durch das Fenster eines Taxis gestreckt. Der Krieg bietet Abenteuer und Abwechslung. Der Krieg bietet das Gefühl, für etwas da zu sein, eine Aufgabe zu erfüllen. Und geht der Krieg erst länger als ein Jahrzehnt, dann wird es für die Kämpfer dieses Krieges immer unmöglicher, sich ein Leben außerhalb dieses Krieges vorzustellen. Dann ist Krieg zur Lebensweise geworden.

Die Armut der Kämpfer ist keine Domäne der *failed states*. Auch die regulären Soldaten der US-Armee entstammen fast ausnahmslos den Unterschichten. Der freiwillige Dienst in der kämpfenden Truppe bietet ihnen etwas Geld und die Chance, im Falle einer Eignung in den Reihen der Armee aufzusteigen. Auch Qualifizierung und Zugang zu ansonsten unbezahlbarer Bildung ist ein Motiv für den Kriegsdienst in der US-Army. Doch da der Dienst in der US-Army nicht ungefährlich ist und eine Garantie für das Überleben z.B. im Irak nicht gegeben werden kann, muß man sich fragen, in welcher Lebenslage ein Mensch ist, der sein Leben aufs Spiel setzt und das Risiko des Sterbens in Kauf nimmt.

Der Bandenkämpfer und der einfache US-Soldat haben noch mehr gemein: Sie kämpfen in Kriegen, die sie innerlich kalt lassen. Sie würden, wenn sie die Chance hätten, etwas anderes, etwas Sinnvolles tun. Immer, wenn ich Lebensgeschichten dieser Krieger lese, denke ich, schon bevor das Leben an dem Punkt angelangt ist, an dem sie zur Waffe greifen: Mit denen willst du nicht tauschen.

Es gibt vermutlich eine Art von Armut, die fatalistisch macht und Menschen in eine Verzweiflung treibt, in der sie zu allem bereit sind. Wer das eigene Leben nicht mehr liebt, der ist zu allem bereit. Das hat nicht unbedingt etwas mit materiellem Reichtum zu tun. Ich möchte mich für die nun folgenden Gedanken schon im voraus entschuldigen; ich bin Schriftsteller und verfüge über eine blühende

Phantasie. Wir können seit über 20 Jahren ein Experiment beobachten, dem sich China unterzieht: Dort wird, was nicht unvernünftig ist, aber im Gegensatz zur Tradition steht, vom Staat die Ein-Kind-Ehe propagiert – und auch mit drastischen Lenkungsmaßnahmen begleitet. Da nun aber männliche Nachkommen höher im Kurs stehen als weibliche Nachkommen, sind die Ein-Kind-Familien zumeist Familien mit einem Jungen. Der chinesische Staat produziert mit den besten Absichten, nämlich der Bevölkerungsexplosion Herr zu werden, einen beträchtlichen Jungenüberschuß. Wenn die Jungs groß werden, wird es eine Konkurrenz um die knappen Mädchen geben. Der chinesische Staat, der diesen Jungenüberschuß mitzuverantworten hat, muß nun ein überzeugendes Lebensmodell für ledige Männer bieten – anderenfalls lebt diese Gesellschaft mit einer Art von Spannung, die schwer auszurechnen ist, und die jene Art von Verzweiflung und zu-allem-entschlossen-sein nährt, die an Kriegen schuld ist. Heute hoffen wir nur, daß all die Männer, die keine Frau finden, hinter dem sagenhaften chinesischen Wirtschaftswachstum stecken. Gibt ja überall auf der Welt Männer, die lange im Büro bleiben. Nur haben die chinesischen Workoholics keine Frau, die auf sie wartet.

Aber was, wenn sich die neue, zutiefst untraditionelle Idee der Ein-Kind-Ehe so breit durchsetzt wie staatlich gewollt und zugleich die Tradition des „wertvolleren" Jungen bestehen bleibt? Und wenn die ledigen Männer nicht alle zu Millionären werden? Wenn es nicht gelingt, ein überzeugendes Lebensmodell für den chinesischen Single zu bieten? Dann entsteht in der chinesischen Gesellschaft eine Art von unberechenbarer Spannung, die sich auf unberechenbare Weise entladen wird, entladen muß. Ob das ein Krieg sein wird, kann ich natürlich nicht sagen – aber ich glaube, daß in derartigen Konstellationen die Sehnsucht nach Frieden durch andere, sehr berechtigte Sehnsüchte, übertönt wird. Wenn der Mensch an den Punkt kommt, an dem er glaubt, daß sein Glück nur noch durch einen Krieg machbar ist, dann ist er auch bereit, diesen Krieg zu führen. Und wenn viele Menschen sehr ähnlich fühlen, dann sind sie die freien Moleküle in der sozialen Flüssigkeit, die Robert D. Kaplan beobachtet hat. Daß Krieg zuallererst Unglück, Tod und Leid produziert, wird in Anbetracht des eigenen Unglücks vergessen.

Ich habe soeben einen Krieg erklärt, der nie stattgefunden hat und von dem wir alle natürlich hoffen, daß es ihn niemals geben wird. Aber das Beispiel zeigt vielleicht, wie vertrackt das Problem ist. Denn die Bevölkerungsexplosion ist in vielen extrem unterentwickelten Ländern eine Ursache der Armut. Die chinesische Entwicklung gibt jedoch eine Ahnung davon, daß entschiedene Maßnahmen der Armutsbekämpfung die Gesellschaft eben nicht friedlicher machen, sondern ein neues Bedrohungspotential hervorbringen.

In Europa blicken die Friedens- und Konfliktforscher voller Sorge nach Asien. Es werden historische Parallelen mit Europa zu Beginn des 20. Jahrhunderts gezogen, also der Zeit vor dem Ausbruch des 1. Weltkriegs. Der ferne Osten ist eine Region, die sich sehr dynamisch entwickelt. Die raschen Veränderungen im Kräfteverhältnis schüren einerseits Ängste, schaffen andererseits aber auch Chancen, die mit Überschätzungen der eigenen Stärke einhergehen. Dazu kommt, daß die Staaten Asiens zwar technologisch ultramodern werden, aber das Wachstum nicht unbedingt nutzen, auch die Demokratie zu entwickeln. Daß die unglaubliche technologische Dynamik keinen Niederschlag in der geistigen und moralischen Entwicklung findet, sehen auch wohlmeinende Konfliktforscher Europas mit großer Sorge. Natürlich ist es auch in der westlichen Welt so, daß die moralisch-geistige Entwicklung dem wissenschaftlich-technische Fortschritt hinterherhinkt. Aber der Westen hat seine selbst verursachten Katastrophen schon erlebt – sei es das Grauen des ersten Weltkrieges, dem jahrelangen Krepieren in einer zerschossenen Landschaft, sei es die industrielle Tötung von Menschen im Holocaust, seien es die Flächenbombardements des 2. Weltkrieges.

Natürlich kann ich in Korea einen Vortrag zum Thema Armut und Gewaltkonflikte nicht halten, ohne die Frage in die koreanische Sitution zu übersetzen: Wenn der nordkoreanische Staat eines Tages zusammenbricht – sind dann im Zuge des Transformationsprozesses Gewalttaten zwischen Nord- und Südkoreanern zu befürchten?

Für die deutschen Friedens- und Konfliktforscher grenzt es an ein Wunder, wie die Transformation Mittel- und Osteuropas und die Auflösung der Sowjetunion vonstatten ging. Gemessen am

Zerstörungspotential verlief die Transformation fast reibungslos. Ein jahrelanger Krieg auf dem Balkan, mehrere Kriege im Kaukasus – aber gemessen an der dramatischen Umwälzung von Lebensperspektiven der Millionen und Abermillionen Mittel- und Osteuropäer und in Anbetracht der millionenfachen Verarmung – 30 % der Russen leben heute unterhalb des Existenzminimums – entspricht die kriegerische Destruktivität nicht dem angestauten Konfliktpotential. Ganz abgesehen von der jahrzehntelangen Unterdrückung, aus der ebenfalls noch viele Rechnungen offen waren, die ebenfalls nicht in Gewalttätigkeiten mündeten. Insofern widersprechen die Fakten vielen von dem, was ich heute gesagt habe. Die Realitäten widersprechen dem Wissen über die Realitäten – zugunsten der Menschlichkeit. Das ist ein kleines Wunder, denn wir sind von den barbarischen Potentialen des Menschen schon einiges gewohnt. Ich kann aus eigener Erfahrung sagen, daß dieses Wunder nur möglich war, weil die Losung „Keine Gewalt" ein allgemeiner Konsens war. Um es ganz zugespitzt zu sagen: Als ich im Oktober 1989 zu der Demonstration ging, auf der ich mit dem Schlimmsten, nämlich einem Massaker rechnen mußte, hatte ich zwei simple Vorsätze. Erstens: Ich will mich nicht töten lassen. Zweitens: Ich will niemanden töten. Aber ich ging zu dieser Demonstration, weil ich es nicht mehr ertragen konnte, so weiter zu leben wie bisher.

Dieser Gedanke der Gewaltlosigkeit war tief im Volk verwurzelt, über die politischen Anschauungen hinweg. Es gab Soldaten und Polizisten, die scharfmacherische Befehle verweigerten, hohe Offiziere, den den Befehl zum Ausrücken aus der Kaserne nicht weitergaben, es gab Eliten (Pfarrer, Provinzfunktionäre und vor allem Künstler mit hoher Reputation), die an den kritischsten Tagen gewalttätiges Vorgehen gegen Demonstranten abwendeten, indem sie sich mit den Machthabern über einen Minimalkonses der unbedingten Gewaltfreiheit verständigten. Daß die Demonstranten durch ihr besonnenes Verhalten die Staatsmacht nicht provozierten, sondern zeigten, daß sie die Forderung „Keine Gewalt" auch an sich selbst stellten, beförderte ebenfalls den friedlichen Verlauf dieser Umwälzung. Viele Demonstanten, insbesondere Frauen, sprachen die

Bewaffneten direkt an, redeten auf sie ein. Der Konsens der Gewaltlosigkeit hielt auch dann, als die Kräfteverhältnisse umgekehrt waren, als die alte Staatsmacht und die verhaßte Stasi entmachtet waren.

Die Frage ist also, wie man die Losung „Keine Gewalt" in die Köpfe der Menschen bekommt, obwohl diese Losung allen machtpolitischen Instinkten widerspricht. Und obwohl Gewalt immer wieder als schnelle und beste Lösung propagiert wird, gerade in Filmen, in der der ehrliche Rächer mit all den Schurken aufräumt. Ob die Formel „Keine Gewalt" in Korea eine Chance hat, weiß ich nicht – dazu kenne ich Korea nicht gut genug. Ich weiß, daß der erfolgreichste koreanische Kinofilm eine Fraternisierungphantasie zwischen nord- und südkoreanischen Soldaten erzählt, die sich monatelang heimlich an der Grenze treffen und ihre Ähnlichkeit entdecken. Dieser Film kann nur deshalb so erfolgreich gewesen sein, weil er bei Millionen Koreanern einen Nerv getroffen hat – die Sehnsucht nach Verbrüderung und einem friedlichen Miteinander. Ein hoffnungsvolles Zeichen. Ich weiß aber auch, daß der koreanische Film, der letztes Jahr das Festival in Cannes gewonnen hat, die Bebilderung einer privaten Rachephantasie ist. Kein hoffnungsvolles Zeichen. Und ich weiß auch, daß die Koreaner ihr Fußballteam mit dem Schlachtruf „Kämpfen!" zum Sieg treiben, daß sie also, mit anderen Worten, das Spielfeld zum Schlachtfeld machen. Auch kein hoffnungsvolles Zeichen. Na gut, immerhin haben die Koreaner fair gespielt. Aber vielleicht lag das ja nur an ihrem holländischen Trainer. Die Holländer sind bekanntlich die pazifistischsten Pazifisten überhaupt – und damit haben sie übrigens auch eine beschämende Erfahrung gemacht. Ich muß mich stoppen, denn ich beginne schon wieder von meinem Lieblingsthema, dem Fußball, zu reden.

Möglicherweise sind Sie mit meinem Vortrag unzufrieden. Zusammenhang zwischen Armut und Krieg – ja, irgendwie schon, aber so genau kann man es auch nicht sagen. Deshalb will ich zum Ende einige Klarheiten festhalten, die sich bei dem Thema schließlich doch ergeben.

Erstens: Man kann nicht einfach sagen, daß Armut zu Gewalt führt, aber man kann klar sagen, daß Gewaltkonflikte zu Verarmung führen, auch wenn natürlich nicht jede Armut auf der Welt ihre Ursache in Krieg und Gewalt hat. Aber Krieg und Gewalt bringen immer wieder ohne jeden Zweifel Armut hervor. Nicht nur durch Zerstörung von industriellen und landwirtschaftlichen Kapazitäten oder der Infrastruktur, durch die Vernichtung menschlichen Lebens. Krieg geht oft einher mit Flüchtlingskatastrophen. Ganze Landstriche werden unbewohnbar, Familien, Dorfgemeinschaften, ganze Stammesgesellschaften oder Völker lassen all ihr Hab und Gut zurück und versuchen an einem unbekannten Ort, ein neues Leben zu beginnen. So werden halbwegs funktionierende soziale Verbände zerschlagen, Schulen und Krankenhäuser fehlen zunächst an den neuen Orten – die Verelendung ist programmiert. Wir sollten uns das pauschale Urteil verkneifen, daß die Bekämpfung von Armut die Welt sicherer macht. Aber daß Kriege die Welt ärmer machen, ist und bleibt eine traurige Tatsache.

Zweitens: Kriege gehören zu den raren sozialen Phänomenen, die einigermaßen vorhersagbar sind. Kriege brechen also nicht plötzlich aus, wie ein Feuer oder eine Krankheit. Kriege sind eher wie Gewitter. Es geht der eine Zustand in einen anderen Zustand über. Konfliktforscher haben eine Art Frühwarnsystem entwickelt – Indikatoren, die auf einen Kriegsausbruch hinweisen. Zum Beispiel ist Kriegshetze in den Massenmedien eines dieser Indikatoren – also ein simpler, ganz leicht zu beobachtender Indikator. Grenzkonflikte und Streitigkeiten um Territorialfragen sind ebenfalls ein Indikator.

Drittens: Gibt es irgendein Parameter, das sich überall dort findet, wo Kriege und Gewaltkonflikte beginnen? Die Antwort ist – Ja!

So hat ein deutsches Friedensforschungsinstitut eine interessante Entdeckung bei der demographischen Situation von Aggressoren ausgemacht: Kriegerische Gesellschaften sind in der Regel jung. Sie haben einen hohen Anteil von unter-25jährigen. Also: Gesellschaften, deren Bevölkerung im Hooligan-Alter ist, drohen selbst zu Hooligans zu werden. Und es gilt die Umkehrung: Gesellschaften, deren Bevölkerungsstruktur überaltert ist, sind die friedfertigsten. Klar, welcher Rentner prügelt sich schon.

Damit muß ich enden. Es tut mir leid, daß ich nicht vor Sie hintreten konnte, mein Manuskript überm Kopf schwenken und dazu rufen konnte: “Ich hab sie, die Formel! Ab morgen gibt es keinen Krieg mehr!" Im Gegenteil: Ich glaube, daß wir unruhigen Zeiten entgegengehen und daß uns insbesondere die nichtstaatlichen Gewaltkonflikte in Zukunft noch stärker beschäftigen werden. Wir stehen am Anfang einer unheilvollen Entwicklung, und ich habe keine Ahnung, wie die zivilisierte Welt ihrer Herr werden kann.

Vielen Dank für Ihre Aufmerksamkeit.

A Poor Writer in the Age of Globalization

Gong Sun-ok

Prior to becoming a writer

To be perfectly honest, this is the first time I've ever tried my hand at writing a "paper" to be presented and discussed at a forum. When I was first approached about my possible participation, I drew a complete blank as to how one goes about writing such a piece. In fact, not only did I have no idea how to begin writing, I'd never even attended this kind of literary forum. Still, it occurred to me that something honest and true to life might be enough; it was that thought that gave me the courage to begin writing. In a way, this paper of mine may turn out to be less a discussion of a specific issue, as befits a conference setting, and more a catalogue of my life to date, a kind of "story of days past." And it's a story on the tiresome old subject of struggling with poverty, too. To be honest, even as I was writing my first novel, I had no idea whether the novel I was writing was actually a novel or not. I wasn't sure what, exactly, made a novel a novel and just assumed that any 'story' would do. After all, don't the *Shimcheong-jeon* and the *Chunhyang-jeon* show us that the body of a novel is, when all is said and done, a story? Wherever you go in this country, ten out of ten people who have been through rough times will all tell you the same thing: "If you turned my story into a novel, it'd take more than a hundred volumes." That was all I knew about novels. Then one day, even though I knew so little about novels, a kind of craving welled up inside me. This was back when each day was a repetition of the last – the life of a factory worker. Upon my graduation from a high school in Gwangju, I was accepted to the Korean department at Chonnam University. At the end of the first semester of my first year, however, I was forced to drop out. The reason? Poverty. Back then, students would quit school to experience the real world and be "on site," going to work in factories or on farms. For me, however, dropping out had nothing to do with a desire for "on site" experience; school had simply become too difficult to fund any longer. To be honest, even this attempt of mine to attend university was in itself beyond my family's means.

After I dropped out of college, I held a number of different jobs. The kind of work available to a woman in her twenties with only a high school diploma, however, was quite limited. You could become a factory hand, a department store clerk, an accountant for a small business, or a bus attendant. There was another alternative, too, if these options didn't work out, but that path can remain unnamed. The city bus lines considered high school graduates to have too much learning to employ as attendants, so I became a long-distance express bus attendant. Twenty years ago in Korea, women my age, women in their twenties with only a high school education had only one way to escape their exhausting existence as clerk, accountant, or attendant: marriage. My marriage, however, proved to be a mere continuation of the struggle with poverty, albeit in a different shape. The lucky ones might meet a "white collar" college graduate, but most of us ended up with men whose lots in life were much like ours. At the time, however, I did not know that this was the case. Small wonder, then, that novels about riding the "elevator of desire" were so popular in those days among women in their early twenties. At least the fact that we had our high school diplomas allowed us the comfort of dreaming about marrying a college graduate, even if it was only through a novel or television soap opera. (In reality, many of my friends from back home who left their parents as young girls in elementary or middle school to go work in the factories of the city eventually married men they met at their factory.) One thing is certain: there is nothing new about the popularity of today's 'Cinderella fantasy' soap operas among young women despite (or rather, because of) this recession of recessions. If, in theory, a perfect distribution of assets was attained in this world and "class divisions" became themselves impossible, then these stories, too, could not exist. These novels and soap operas endlessly promote the fantasy of "crossing class divides" while simultaneously helping to solidify those same divisions in actuality.

My marriage ended in divorce. A new divorcée, I had two children by my side. The road ahead was looking bleak. Poverty, so familiar to me ever since childhood, was once again by my side and there seemed to be no way to escape it. Employment opportunities for a high school educated divorcee saddled with children were, of course, even more limited than those open to high school educated 20-something young women. My options were: insurance lady, yoghurt delivery lady, cafeteria lady, and factory lady. With my two children in tow and no clue what I was doing, I set out for Seoul. One morning, during my third year working at the Guro Industrial Complex, I woke up to find my hands so swollen that I couldn't uncurl my fingers. Staring down at my curled, immobile fingers in despair, I asked myself whether, today, too, would have to be spent at the factory repeating the same motions over and over again all day long. It occurred to me that I could no longer live like this. The money I made at the factory went to day care for the kids, with barely enough left over to cover the rent and just enough food to keep us from starving to death. More than anything, though, it was the hunger for a kind of 'spiritual life' that became impossible to endure. By spiritual life, I mean a life that does not revolve around repeating the same motions every day in a factory – a life, in other words, that is "creative." I coveted a life in which I might create something different each day instead of manufacturing the same product, day in and day out. My life denied me this, and I was lonely. It was clear that I was living a life that cut me off from the rest of the world. Perhaps it was this craving, this awakening that first led me to start writing. Perhaps it was my earnest desire to communicate with the world that led me to write.

Where is this place in which I now stand?

Even now, it feels strange every time someone addresses me as "teacher." After all, if I'd stayed a factory worker, I would be known as "Auntie Button-sewer," or maybe "Auntie Number Three Sewing Machine Sun-ok." And those aren't the only options: if I'd worked in a cafeteria I would now be the "Rice Lady" or "Side Dish

Lady," and if I delivered yoghurt I'd be the "Yoghurt Lady,"… Instead, simply because I am a middle aged "aunt" who happens to write for a living, I am addressed by the world at large as "teacher." That is how I see it.

One day, someone asked me:

"Teacher, how did you become a writer?"

"Well, I switched careers because the money I made from writing was better than what I made working in the factories."

I'm not sure if my words seemed strange or just outright absurd, but they did visibly bewilder my companion. The person who asked me the question was a poet with a college diploma. They do say that these days, people without college diplomas are harder to find than those who have them; well, in the case of writers this seems to hold doubly true. To become a writer one must have at least graduated college, taken several years of intensive writing classes, and tasted the bitter cup of failure a time or two after entering the spring literary contests. Someone who has gone through all this, perhaps, might deserve to be called "teacher." To be so cavalier and call it "switching careers"! What an insult to writers, to literature itself! – I suppose this may be the reaction of some.

Then again, the reason I still find it embarrassing to be addressed as "teacher" simply because I am a writer – or, in other words, simply because I switched careers from Sewing Machine Lady to Writer Lady – is not necessarily because I neither attended college nor took intensive writing courses. It is not because I never even entered a piece in a spring literary contest, instead finding myself suddenly transformed one day from Sewing Machine Lady to author. It is because, I think, of the fact that so little has actually changed in the transition from life as the Sewing Machine Lady to life as a writer. The natural next step in such reckonings is a calculation of wages: so, how much do I, "the writer," earn in an average month these days?

That said, the subject I was asked to discuss was "poverty and the broadening class divisions of the world," a subtopic of this forum dedicated to "Writing for Peace" – and here I am, unsure whether what I have written, or rather, testified, is even relevant to the task I was given. All I know is that I wish to explore this place in which I now find myself. By revealing this place in which I now stand, I hope to find a starting point from which I can branch out into more universal territory.

So, returning to the topic of this "place" of mine, I must confess that even now, I cannot say that I have completely escaped poverty. I automatically equate every word I write with the sum I will be paid in its stead. There is no difference between this and the calculations I made back when I still sold physical labor, estimating how much my work was worth. Today I am simply a "laborer who writes," yet another day-laborer with no security or benefits. This country offers no social security to its writers. Of course, the same goes for this country's farmers, laborers, and much of the general working classes. I am a member of one of the lowest rungs in the class system of this country: an impoverished writer-laborer. And it is this true identity of mine that leaves me embarrassed every time I find myself being addressed as, and responding to, the name "teacher."

Of course, it is true a much larger variety of money-making opportunities are open to me now, as a writer, than back when I worked with a sewing machine. Once I write a piece, as long as the editor doesn't reject it, I am paid for the manuscript. Sometimes I am even paid to lecture. Invitations to lecture, though, always leave me a bit distraught. What will I possibly be able to say? What is it that these people want from me? (That there are people who would invite me, with my lack of formal learning and nonexistent understanding of literature in general, simply because I am a writer!) It is an embarrassing situation but, from time to time, when the pay is too good to turn down, I do set out on such "business trips." I try, self-deprecatingly, to think of this as just a "little something on the side." After all, let us be honest. When a so-called writer, particularly one who writes full-length fiction, finds oneself writing small (often considered "throwaway") pieces for newspapers and magazines, when one must scrape a living together from these small articles and essays rather than one's novels – well, to say that this does not sadden us would be an outright lie. (Still, in this time of economic recession, I suppose one should be grateful for what one does get.)

Whenever I receive a check for a newspaper column or magazine story, or maybe as payment for a lecture, the people in my life, from my many neighbors to my flesh and blood, all have something to say.

"Thank goodness for this ability to write, this talent of yours," they say.

Ah, now let us discuss the people in my life. I am a worker whose hard labor involves writing 'throwaway' words. My brother-in-law does his hard labor in a factory, loading bricks. He and I are both laborers; the only difference is the form of our toil. By this reasoning, I myself and all those around me are now, and have always been, manual laborers. My sister works in a grocery store, a job that pays by the hour. Not long ago, she was fired for requesting overtime pay. Every phone call from my sister starts in exactly the same way.

"Do you have work these days?" she asks.

For people who feed themselves each day with that same day's wages, life is divided into two categories: "days with work" and "days without."

It is only when I say yes, I am quite busy, that she lets out a sigh of relief.

"It's good to be busy," she says. Because saying you are not busy is tantamount to saying you are "jobless" or "unemployed."

Looking at their lives, you see what is essentially an endless series of "crashes." There simply is no way for them to escape their impoverished state. My sister goes on: "In a year I work 365 days. And you know, working like this used to be enough to keep us afloat and even save a little on the side – but the strange thing is, these days it's a struggle just to keep food on the table."

What can this mean? Working full time and still struggling to make ends meet? This is what they call the "working poor." My parents, who both passed away long ago, used to always say to us children: "Don't you kids live off the dirt like I've had to; you be sure to become someone who makes a living with a pen."

Despite their wishes, however, my parents did not have the means to educate their children. As I mentioned before, even I, the only member of our family to ever darken the doorway of a university building, was eventually forced to drop out. It's true that

I do make a living with my pen, just as my parents hoped I would. On the other hand, as I am far from being a "bestselling" author, it is also true that I still do not enjoy the kind of life my parents ultimately wanted for me. Can it be that a means of escaping this poverty simply does not exist when it comes to me and mine?

I once read a book called *The Reproduction of Labor and Class in an Industrial Society*. Below are two case studies that were described in that text.

> My child will graduate from SunHwa Arts Middle and High schools and go on to study music at Seoul National University. It's difficult to find employment in Korea, so going abroad to study is a must. By the time my child returns from studying abroad, she will be an accomplished pianist. As for other aspects of my child's future, Gyeongbok Elementary School, where she is currently a student, and SunHwa Arts Middle and High schools are all good schools with good students, so I don't think there is any danger that she might make the wrong kinds of friends or be negatively influenced in some other way. She's a very clever girl to begin with, so she'll do very well and make a fine life for herself. We are willing to do whatever it takes to help our child and provide her with everything she needs.

> The only things our boy seems to like are computers and video games. Well, they say that in this day and age, being good at computers is enough to make a living, so I guess we'll let him study and do what he likes. It's his life and he's the one who's going to have to live it, and it's not as if anything will change because I think they should. If he wants to continue his studies, we'll help him to do that .... It's not as if we could make him do it even if he decides he doesn't want to. Already he's become belligerent, talking back all the time, and it's only likely to get worse. For now, we'll put him in high school and if he wants to go to college, we'll do what we can to send him.

Of the two situations detailed above, which comes closest to the reality in which I and my children, my relatives and their children, and my poor neighbors and their children all find ourselves? Clearly, our situation is a closer match to the second example than the first. It is not that I find the second scenario to be terribly frightening in and of itself – what scares me is that our society is so distinctly divided into two groups, one that represented perfectly by the first scenario and the other by the second. What scares me is the reality of how accepted, how imbedded this division is becoming. What can a writer do, living in this kind of reality, particularly a writer such as myself, who works with a pen but ultimately lives no differently than her parents who worked the earth? Must I accept this distinctly divided reality simply because I have no other resources? Or must I somehow find a way to resist? What can a writer do?

I grew up in a situation where my parents did not structure my life for me, beginning to end, ahead of time; indeed, they were sometimes unable to give me support even when I needed it. Today, I myself am in a situation where I cannot structure my children's lives for them or guarantee my support whenever they may need it. As such, as an individual in such a situation, I see that I am living a life that is completely in keeping with my one inheritance: poverty. A so-called writer in this society's class system, I myself am clearly living a life that occupies the very bottom rung. The only thing I, as a writer, can do in this situation is write – and since a work cannot help but reflect the life led by its author, it should come as no surprise that my writing cannot help but reflect my life and the lives around me, that I cannot write any other way.

My sister, my sister's husband, the people in our lives – these so-called "manual laborers" all say the same thing. Just as my parents used to, they tell me that I must write their story. Write the stories of people who have nothing, they say. If your writing turns away from our lives, they say, you will only be deceiving yourself. I don't have the "talent" for writing, they say, so I can't write it; you must write it for me. Because of this I feel a kind of "pressure" that I must tell the stories of those who do not themselves have the "talent" necessary to find a way to share their lives with the world. There is one thing I know for certain: my writing will never be able to change their lives, to help lead them in a better direction. Still, many people going through rough times listen to or sing popular songs to help soothe their troubled hearts; all I hope is that my writing might play such a role. That, I hope, is the place in which I stand as a writer. Even if I fail in the role of direct spokesperson, I hope, at least, to be a writer who never turns away. In other words, I will honestly examine the situation in which I find myself. In this context, let us reflect on how lucky we are to have writers such as Hwang Seok-yeong and Jo Se-hui, who provided this world of shackles and adversity with literary masterpieces that gave honest, exact insights into the lives they lived in this country, into the pain, the true nature of their times.

How must I, a writer of these times, live my life? What kind of literature should I write?

Some time ago I was contacted by a literary organization based outside of Seoul. They were compiling a volume of works on the theme of "poverty," and they wished to include a piece from me. I'd had few opportunities to write fiction in 2004, making a living by spending most of my time writing about a dozen "small pieces" each month to be published here and there. One of these projects was an internet column I wrote four times a month as part of a weekly government briefing managed by the national press office. (Unfortunately, the biggest factor in my decision to write this column was the relatively high pay.) It is difficult to face the harsh reality of being a novelist who does not, or rather, cannot write novels, and must depend instead on columns and essays to make a living. Nevertheless, the problem of supporting my family is immediate and impossible to ignore. Even though I cannot shake the feeling that each column I write wears away a little bit more of my literary sensibilities, I am unable to turn down requests for these "little pieces," these projects that fail to inspire me as a writer. Each time, I comfort and make excuses for myself:

"My parents, too, never shirked work they found unpleasant – they had to make a living. Not only did my parents do it but countless people in this world have endured and, even in this very moment, continue to endure endless insults and humiliation in order to survive."

After all, didn't the artist Park Su-geun once paint portraits of American soldiers in order to support himself?

In any event, it was this thought alone that helped me to endure life even as I felt the wearing away of my "literary spirit." I had written several small pieces during the course of these ruminations on the topic of "poverty," and this was the reason the literary organization came to contact me. They wished to republish these pieces in their compilation and needed my consent. Initially, I couldn't help but question their request – were there so few writers writing about poverty in this day and age? I couldn't believe that they wanted to use such short, hard articles written not in the form of regular prose but as a newspaper column .... Yet, according to the editor, it is difficult to find work by contemporary Korean fiction writers that addresses the "impoverished reality" of our times.

I once heard someone say something that I found completely impossible to understand. This baffling statement was someone's opinion that any writer who hoped to make a living should never write critically about the present age; that the more miserable the real world became, the more glorious one's words should be; that the more base and mean the real world became, the more beautiful one's writing should be; that, ultimately, this was the only way a writer would be able to survive the in the real world .... When I replied that I simply could not understand what he meant by this, the speaker replied that this was why I would always be a poor writer. If, in a base, miserable world, one writes prose that is neither glorious nor beautiful, will one's work be 'meaningless' to the countless masses already condemned to spend their days living out that same base, miserable reality? Where, then, must a writer who writes such prose go to find meaning? What, exactly, constitutes beautiful prose, beautiful literature?

In the wake of the globalization and "new liberalist" frenzy that swept across the world, as well as the IMF intercession that took place during that time, it is as if an actual typhoon had swept across the land – in every place you look there is yet another scene of "poverty" and "need." A father overwhelmed by the task of raising his children stops his car along the road and throws not just one but both his children into the river, like a pair of dolls. A baby born to a destitute couple is laid, like a blanket or a pillow, inside a dresser drawer and later discovered to have starved to death (in this age of obesity-related illness). Driven to despair by poverty, an entire family commits suicide by poison, all together in a motel room. A packed lunch delivery system is designed to help keep poor students fed throughout the school vacations, but it is soon discovered that the lunches are not fit for human consumption. Children with healthy, living parents line up outside orphanages. All those credit cards our government allowed for so long to be issued at will – a part of their plan to stimulate the economy – have been used by ordinary people strapped for cash, paying off one card with another, accumulating debt. Now bankrupt and delinquent, these people have nothing left to spend and the lower-class economy has collapsed. The stores they used to frequent, the local neighborhood Chinese restaurants and soup stalls are all teetering on the brink of ruin; restaurant owners are throwing down their kettles and crying out that they just "can't take any more" ....

There has also been an increase in the rate of crimes caused by the ever-widening gap between rich and poor. People for whom life itself seems like a living hell, with day after day offering them nothing but wrath and rancor and sadness – these people are taking their hellish lives, they are taking the wrath, rancor, and sadness that comes from their impoverished existence, and they are unleashing it upon the fuzzy target of an unspecified majority. The subway fire in Daegu, the murder of the rich, elderly couple, the incident where one person pushed another onto the rails of a subway station .... This is all that life holds for ordinary people, for poor people; at the same time, the lives of those at the very top of our society fail to inspire hope in the hearts of the poor. If anything, their examples inspire despair. We must have growth to have distribution, they always say. It seems that this country is perpetually in need of further growth. It is a country not yet ready for the distribution of wealth – not ever, always, thirty years ago, and thirty years from now, either. In the midst of all this the poor must live out their lives of frustration, living on simply because dying is not an option. And in this life, in order to eat, to survive, they must always be ready to endure whatever insult or humiliation may come their way.

When this country was a colony belonging to its neighbor, any self-aware writer with a conscience and a sense of social consciousness would have felt stifled. Any such writer would have felt the same under the military dictatorship as well. And now, in this country that still has not been able to resolve the issue of reunification, the "tyranny of the capitalist powers-that-be" are strangling the poor, the laborers, the farmers, the small city businesses – all in the name of "globalization." Jobs are becoming less and less stable as outsourcing and part-time positions grow in popularity and agrarian communities are descending into panic as they are driven into a state of waste, no longer knowing what they should plant or tend. Adults spend sleepless nights wracked with money worries, some surrendering to despair and ending their own lives while others desert their families to live, homeless, on the streets. Children, too, often end up leaving the competitive atmosphere of school and taking to the streets, the next step in a childhood already so rife with sadness. All over the neighborhoods of Guro-dong and Garibong-dong, now full of communal living quarters for immigrant laborers from China, were once temporary shelters that catered to these street children. Where are all these children now? They roam the streets, unable to attend school because their parents, too deep in credit card debt to register their identity with the government, have no official address to provide. It would seem that the children provided with the "unsound packed lunches" were actually the lucky ones. There are people who may ask what is universal about the kind of poverty that actually prevents a child from attending school. There are those who do not believe the unbelievable stories that so often arise from conditions of extreme poverty. But this reality exists, in truth, as clear as day.

In the words of Arundhati Roy, the author of *The God of Small Things*, writing fiction "is a way of seeing, of making sense of the world." I hope to truly see the reality that is the "sad dizziness" of my country, to make sense of a world where some children cannot go to school and live on the brink of starvation while other children have parents with enough money and power to make anything possible – I hope to distill all this into a novel. As long as I make my living as a writer, I will not seek out opportunities designed simply to maximize profits from book sales. I will simplify my life as much as possible and turn my purified gaze outwards to examine and make sense of this complicated world. People who live in poverty, those people who despair as one escape route after another becomes blocked, those who hope to live in peace despite their impoverished state – I will never write a single line that ignores their plight.

Arundhati Roy has also said that it is a writer's duty to help find a way to understand actions carried out in the name of globalization which may be difficult to comprehend for those armed with nothing but common sense .... Writers must communicate what it is to lose your work and human dignity, to lose your future and your past.

We must find the elusive answer to the question of what, exactly, it is that continues to make poor people poorer. Even as we try to make sense of this complicated world, we must also "protest" most violently. That, I believe, is the most meaningful act a writer can undertake in this formidable age of globalization.

Contributors

Foreign Participants
Domestic Participants

Appendix I

Prospectus

Appendix II

The 2nd Seoul International Forum for Literature:
Seoul Declaration of Peace

Foreign Participants_

Jean Baudrillard

Sociologist, cultural critic, and theorist of post-modernity. Born in 1929 in Reims, France, he studied at the University of Paris (Sorbonne), and taught at the University of Paris X, Nanterre. He was also Scientific Director at the University of Paris IX, Dauphine. He was associated with Roland Barthes, to whose semiotic analysis of culture his first book, *The System of Objects* (1968) was indebted. It examines, as *Consumer Society* (1970), the psychological imperatives of consumption in an advanced capitalistic economy. Other titles of his works include, *The Mirror of Production*, *Symbolic Exchange and Death*, *Seduction*, *Simulacra and Simulation. Fatal Strategies* and *The Illusion of the End.*

Bei Dao

Poet, essayist, novelist. Born in 1949 in Beijing, his early poems were a source of inspiration during the April Fifth Democracy Movement of 1976. He has been in exile from his native China since the Tiananmen Square massacre of 1989, during which time he was in Berlin. He has taught at the University of California at Davis and is currently the Mackey Poet in Residence at Beloit College. Among the English translations of his works are *Old Snow* (1991), *Forms of Distance* (1994), *Landscape Over Zero* (1996), *Unlock* (2000), *Blue House* (2000). *Midnight's Gate*, a collection of essays, has recently been published.

Wolf Biermann

Poet, dramatist, essayist, song-writer, translator. Born in Hamburg, Germany, in 1936, he settled in the German Democratic Republic in 1953 and studied Political Economy, Mathematics and Philosophy at Humboldt University, Berlin. In 1963 his first play, *Berliner Brautgang*, was banned. An active contributor at different newspapers, he has been awarded Berlin's Fontane Prize (1969), the Georg Buchner Prize (1991) and the National Prize of the German National Foundation (1998).

Thomas Brussig

Novelist and dramatist. Born in 1965 in Berlin, Germany. Brussig studied sociology before going on to study drama and film. His first novel, *Wasserfarben* (Watercolors), was published in 1991 under a pseudonym. His novelistic account of the fall of the Berlin Wall, *Helden wie Wir* (1995, Heroes Like Us), has been adapted into a award-winning stage play and film, and translated into numerous languages. He also wrote the screenplay for the film *Sonnenallee*, based on his novel *Am krzeren Ende der Sonnenallee* (1999, At the Shorter End of Sun Alley). The novel *Wie es leuchtet* (How Bright It Is), was published in 2004.

Robert Coover

Novelist. Born in Iowa (U.S.) in 1932, he studied at Indiana University, Southern Illinois State University and the University of Chicago. His first novel, *The Origin of Brunists* won the 1966 William Faulkner Award. He is the author of fifteen books of fiction, including *The Universal Baseball Association, Inc., J. Henry Waugh, Prop.* (1968), *The Public Burning* (1977), *Spanking the Maid* (1981), *A Night at the Movies* (1987), *Ghost Town* (1998) and *Stepmother* (2004). He taught at a number of universities, including the University of Iowa and Brown University.

Margaret Drabble

Novelist, biographer and critic. Born in Sheffield (U.K.) in 1939, Drabble studied English at Cambridge. She became an actress and worked for the Royal Shakespeare Company at Stratford-upon-Avon before her first novel, *A Summer Birdcage*, was published in 1963. She has published several novels, including *Jerusalem the Golden* (1967), *The Waterfall* (1969), *The Needle's Eye* (1972), and *I* (1975), as well as a trilogy *The Radiant Way* (1987), *A Natural Curiosity* (1989) and *The Gates of Ivory* (1991). After her visit to the first Daesan Writer's Forum in 2000, she wrote and published *The Red Queen* (2005), inspired by the memoirs of an 18th-century Korean crown-princess and in part by the author's experience of modern Korea.

Vera Grigorievna Galaktionova

Novelist. Born in 1948, Galaktionova Graduated from the Maxim Gorki Literary Institute in Moscow. Her works focus on Chernobyl, regional disputes in Karabakh (along the frontier between Azerbaijan and Armenia), divisions within the spiritual unity of Russia, the collapse of the Soviet Union and hostilities between different ethnic groups, and the historical mechanisms underlying these social divisions. Her works include *The Mighty Cross*, *The Winged House*, *On Buyan Island*, and *Quiet Night*.

Robert Hass

Poet. Born in 1941 in San Francisco, California, Hass majored in English Literature at Stanford University. He served for two years (1995-7) as Poet Laureate of the United States. An active translator, he currently teaches English Literature at UC Berkeley. He collaborates closely with Gary Snyder and other writers on environmental issues. His books of poetry include *Sun Under Wood* (1996); *Human Wishes* (1989), *Praise* (1979), and *Field Guide* (1973). He is currently a Chancellor of The Academy of American Poets.

Hasumi Shigehiko

Critic. Born in Tokyo (Japan) in 1936, Shigehiko majored in French Literature at the University of Paris. He is a film critic, critic of symbolic culture, and a specialist in French literature. He has taught at the University of Tokyo, at which he is now an emeritus professor. His publications include *The Invention of Mediocrity*, *Antitheory of the Japanese Language*, and *Mnemonic Devices in Cinema*, and *Film Lunatics: Here, There, and Everywhere.*

Erling Kittelsen

Poet, playwright, and author of children's books. Born in 1946 in Oslo, Norway, he studied philosophy before published his first volume of poems, *Vile fugler* (Wild birds, 1970). He is currently involved in a number of projects designed to translate poems written in Chinese,

Arabic, and Latvian into Norwegian. His plays include *Abiriels love* (Abiriel's lion, 1988) and *Pa himmelen* (In heaven, 2000).

Jean-Marie Gustave Le Clézio

Novelist. Born in Nice, France in 1940, he received Prix Thophraste Renaudot for his first novel, *Le Procs Verbal* (Interrogation) in 1965. Between 1967 and 1970, he lived with a tribe of Embera Indians in the Panamanian jungles. He taught literature at the University of New Mexico and translated Native American myths. In 1978, he published *Mondo et autres histoires* (Mondo and other stories). He has published over 30 books, including *La fievre* (1965, Fever), *Le deluge* (1966, The flood), *L'extase materielle* (1967, The material ecstasy), *Chercheur d'or* (1985, Gold seeker), *Desert* (1987, Desert) and *La quarantaine* (1995, Quarantine). His latest novel is Revolutions (2003, Revolutions) He returned to Nice in 1996. Other works include *Trois villes saintes* (Three sacred cities), *Hasard* (Chance), and *Poisson d'or* (Goldfish).

Tibor Méray

Novelist and journalist. Born in Budapest (Hungary) in 1924, Méray studied Latin literature and worked as editor of a literary review before he went to North Korea as a military news correspondent during the Korean War. He spent fourteen months there and witnessed the signing of the 1953 Armistice at Panmunjom. He supported the Hungarian Prime Minister Imre Nagy in his opposition to Stalinism and after the 1956 Hungarian Uprising took refuge in Paris, where he currently heads the Hungarian Human Rights Commission. Among his publications are *Reporting from Korea* and *The Truth on Germ Warfare*.

Masao Miyoshi

Thinker and essayist, Miyoshi is currently an Emeritus professor, University of California at San Diego. Some of his recent works include reflections on the humanities in an increasingly capitalist university. Major works include *The Divided Self: A Perspective on the Literature of the Victorians* (1969), *Accomplices of Silence: The Modern Japanese Novel* (1975), *As We Saw Them: The First Japanese*

Embassy to the United States (1860) (1979), *Postmodernism and Japan* (1989). More recently, he has published shorter articles or co-edited volumes with multiple contributors. Recent papers include "Japan Is Not Interesting," (2000), "Ivory Tower in Escrow," (2000), and "Turn to the Planet: Literature, Diversity, and Totality" (2001). He participated in the First Daesan International Forum in 2000.

Moyan

Novelist. Born as Guan Moye in 1956 in rural Shandong, northeastern China, he has adopted the *nom de plume* Moyan, meaning "don't speak" in Chinese. At the age of 20, he joined the People's Liberation Army. He has authored nine novels and published over 70 short stories in the past 22 years, many of which has been translated into other languages. The film version of the novel, *Red Sorghum*, won first prize in the Golden Bear awards at the Berlin Film Festival in 1988. His most recent work, *Forty-one Bombs*, (2003) focuses on the problem of modern China's rampant corruption. Works that have been translated include *The Garlic Ballads, Shifu, You'll Do Anything for a Laugh, The Republic of Wine* and *Big Breasts and Wide Bottoms.*

Oe Kenzaburo

Novelist. Born in Japan in 1935, Oe graduated from the Department of French Literature, University of Tokyo. Published his first novel, *Bud-Nipping, Lamb Shooting*, in 1958. Beginning with *A Personal Matter*(1964), other works are rooted in traditional stories and myths but relate them to life in the modern world, such as *The Silent Cry* (1967) and *M/T and the Wonders of the Forest* (1986). He completed the publication of his trilogy *The Flaming Green Tree* in 1995, just after he received the 1994 Nobel Prize in Literature. His next novel was *Somersault* (2003). In the 1970s he gave support to the campaign protesting the imprisonment of the Korean poet Kim Ji-ha.

Orhan Pamuk

Novelist. Born in Istanbul, (Turkey) in 1952, he studied at the Institute of Journalism at Istanbul University. After studying architecture in Istanbul Technical University his first novel, *Cevdet Bey and his Sons*

(1982), won the Orhan Kemal Novel Prize. His historical novel *The White Castle* (1985), extended his reputation abroad. Other works include *New Life* (1995), *My Name is Red* (2001), and *Snow* (2004). His novels are rich with allusion to old Sufi stories and traditional Islamic tales. He has recently published a book about Istanbul, a city that fascinates him. He is the country's best-selling author and his books are now translated into 20 languages.

Luis Sepúlveda

Born in Chile in 1949, Sepúlveda was imprisoned in 1979 by the Pinochet regime while still a student, for more than two years. While exiled, he first traveled in South America, founded theatrical groups in a number of countries, then took part in a UNESCO research project on the impact of colonization on the Amazonian Indians. The result was his first novel, *Un viejo que leia novelas de amor* (The old man who read love stories). Other works include *Diario de un killer sentimental seguido de Yacare* (Diary of a Sentimental Killer), *Desencuentros* (Failed Meetings), *Nombre de torero* (Name of a Bullfighter) and *Mundo de fin del mundo* (The World at the End of the World).

Gary Snyder

Born in 1930 in San Francisco, California, Snyder was brought up in Oregon and Washington State. He received his BA in anthropology at Reed College, Portland, in 1951. He studied Oriental languages at Berkeley (1953-6), was associated with Beat writers such as Ginsberg and Kerouac, lived in Japan (1956-64), and later studied Buddhism. He currently teaches literature and 'wilderness thought' at the University of California at Davis. He has been described as an eco-poet and an eco-warrior. His main publications include: *Riprap* (1959), *Myths & Texts* (1960), *Mountains and Rivers Without End* (1965), *Turtle Island* (1974), *Axe Handles* (1983), *The Practice of the Wild* (1990, prose), and *No Nature*(1993). He won a Pulitzer Prize for Poetry in 1975 for Turtle Island, and his No Nature became a finalist for the National Book Award in 1992. When Snyder published *Mountain and Rivers Without End* in 1996, he was awarded more than five major prizes.

Ngugi Wa Thiong'o

Novelist, essayist, and playwright. Born in Kenya in 1938, he studied English Literature in Kampala, (Uganda), then went for graduate studies in England. As a novelist Ngugi made his debut with *Weep Not, Child* (1964), the first novel in English to be published by an East African author. *The River Between* (1965) was based on the Mau Mau Rebellion (1952-1956), as does *A Grain Of Wheat* (1967). In 1980 Ngugi published the first modern novel written in Gikuyu, *Caitaani Muthara-Ini (Devil on the Cross)*, rejecting the use of English in truly African writing. Ngugi's critical works include *Decolonizing the Mind* (1986) and *Moving the Center* (1993). He left Kenya in 1982 to live in self-imposed exile. He is Distinguished Professor of English and Comparative Literature and Director of the International Center for Writing and Translation at the University of California at Irvine.

Domestic Participants_

Paik Nak-chung

Critic, scholar. Born in 1938 in Daegu, Paik studied English literature at Brown University and Harvard. He is currently Emeritus Professor in the English department of Seoul National University. Founder and editor-in-chief of *Changjakgwa bipyeong*, a major organ of political dissent in Korea since 1966, he has published a number of books of literary criticism and recently on the politics of the divided Korea: *On seeing modern literature, Korean literature and world literature, Shaky structures of division*. Has received the Simsan Award, the Daesan Literary Award, the Yosan Literary Award, the Manhae Prize etc.

Bok Koh-ill

Novelist, poet. Born in 1946 in Asan (South Chungcheong Province), Bok studied economics at Seoul National University, and began his career as novelist and poet in 1987. His publications include volumes of fiction and poetry: *Beneath a red moon, Village outside Camp Seneca, Lullaby for my wife as she grows older* and other titles. Much of his writing concerns political and social issues.

Cho Uhn

Sociologist, novelist. Cho was born in 1946 in South Jeolla Province. After studying English at Seoul National University, Cho went on to do graduate studies in social sciences at the University of Hawaii. She is now a professor in the social sciences department of Dongguk University. Her published books include *Half an experience half a voice*, and *091012 "study hard?"* Cho has also published a collection of short fiction, *House built of silence.*

Choi Jang-jip

Political scientist. Born in 1943 in Gangneung (Gangwon

Province), Choi completed undergraduate and graduate studies in the political science department at Korea University before graduating from the University of Chicago and becoming a professor in the political science department of his alma mater. He is currently the head of the university's Study Center for Asian Problems. He has published *Theory of Korean democracy, The Korean workers' movement and the state*, and *Democracy after democratization.*

Choi Won-shik

Critic. Born in 1949 in Incheon, Choi completed undergraduate and graduate studies in the Korean department of Seoul National University, and began his career as a critic in 1972, and is currently a professor in the Korean department of Inha University (Incheon). His publications include the following volumes: *Logic of Korean literature, For a productive dialogue, In search of modern Korean literature*, and *Repatriating literature*. He is a regular contributor of the *Changjakgwa bipyeong*. Received the Daesan Literary Award.

Choi Yun

Novelist, translator. Born in 1953 in Seoul, she studied in the Korean department of Sogang University, and French literature at the University of Provence, (France). She is currently teaching at the French department of Sogang University. After her first publication, the novella *There one flower blooms soundlessly* in 1988, she has published several novels, including *Person with gray eyes*, *Clearing in the forest*, *Flower fragrance with thirteen different names*, and *Mannequin*. She also translated the series of Korean literature published by Actes Sud in France, including works by Yi Mun-yeol and Yi Cheong-jun. Her novels have received the Dongin Literary Award, the Yi Sang Literary Award; her translations have received the Republic of Korea Translation Award and the Daesan Translation Award.

Gong Sun-ok

Novelist. Born in 1963 in Gokseong (South Jeolla Province), Gong studied Korean language and literature at Chonnam University. She began her literary career by publishing the novella *Seeds of fire* in the literary journal *Changjakgwa bipyeong*. She has published several collections of short stories: *Bloom, daffodils, One fine world*, as well as novels: *Thirty left behind in Austria, Come into the millet field, Red quilt*. She was awarded the Award for Young Artists.

Hwang Ji-woo

Poet. Hwang was born in 1952 in Haenam, (South Jeolla Province). He studied in the department of Aesthetics at Seoul National University and philosophy at Sogang University (Seoul). Throughout his career beginning in 1980 he has published several collections of poetry: *Even the birds are leaving the world, Lotus in a crab's eye, Sea gleaming as night falls*. He has also published a drama, *May bride*. Has received the Kim Su-yeong Literary Award, the Hyeondae Literary Award, the Soweol Poetry Award, and the Daesan Literary Award.

Hyun Ki-young

Novelist. Born in 1941 in Jeju Island, Hyun studied English at Seoul National University. Hyun began his literary career when his short story *Abeoji*, (Father) which won the New Year's Literary Award of *Donga Ilbo*. He has published a number of novels, including *Suni's cousin*, *One spoon on the earth*, and *Sea and wine glass*, among others. Has received the Hankook Ilbo Literary Award, the Manhae Literary Award, the O Yeong-su Literary Award. He is currently serving as the head of the Korean Culture and Arts Foundation.

Hwang Seok-young

Novelist. Born in 1943 in Shenyang (Manchuria), Hwang studied philosophy at Dongguk University. His first work was published in 1962, but *Pagoda* received the prize in the New Year's Awards of the *Chosun Ilbo*. He has published a number of novels: *Strange land, Jang Gil-san, Ancient garden, Guest, Sim Cheong*, among others. He received the Manhae Literary Award, the Danjae Award, and the Daesan Literary Award.

Jang Hoe-ik

Environmental activist. Jang was born in 1938 in Yecheon (North Gyeongsang Province). He studied physics at Seoul National

University, and at the state universities of California and Louisiana. He is now Emeritus Professor in the physics department of Seoul National University. His publications include: *Science and meta-science, Living and total life.*

Kim Kwang-kyu

Poet. Kim was born in 1941 in Seoul and studied German language and literature at Seoul National University and the University of Munich, (Germany). He is currently teaching in the German Department of Hanyang University (Seoul). His first poems were published in 1975 in the review *Munhakgwa Jiseong*. Since then he has published eight collections of poems, including *The last dream to affect us, Nothing of my own, but still, When first we met*. He has received the Nokwon Literary Award, the Kim Su-yeong Literary Award and the Daesan Literary Award. His poems have been translated into several languages.

Kim Seong-kon

Born in Jeonju, Korea in 1949, Kim Seong-kon is a literary critic and Professor of English at Seoul National University. He has taught at Pennsylvania State University, Brigham Young University and the University of California, Berkeley as a Visiting Professor. Formerly Dean of the School of Language Education and Director of the American Studies Institute at Seoul National University, the founding President of the Korean Association of Literature and Film, and President of the International Association of Comparative Korea Studies, he is currently President of the Korean Association of Modern Fiction in English and a Visiting Scholar at Harvard University. His publications include *Literature and Film*, *Korea in the Multicultural Age, Cultural Studies and the Future of the Humanities*, and *Reading Culture through Film.*

Kim Seung-hee

Poet, novelist, scholar. Kim was born in 1952 in Gwangju (North Jeolla Province). She studied English and Korean language and literature at Sogang University, where she is now a professor. Her first novel, *On the way to Santa Fe*, was published in 1994. She has published several volumes of poetry: *Concerto for the left hand, A smile speeding down falling rain*, and *Men don't know*. She has also published other works of fiction, including the novel *A bird with a slightly heavier left wing*.

Kim Yeon-soo

Novelist. Born in 1970 in Gimcheon, (North Gyeongsang Province), he began his literary career with the publication of poems in the review *Jakgasegye*; since then went on to publish a number of novels: *Twenty, Goodbye Yi-sang*, and *When I was still a child*. He received the Dongin Literary Award, the *Jakgasegye* Literary Award, and the Daesan Literary Award.

Kim Young-ha

Novelist. Born in 1968 in Hwacheon, (Gangwon Province), Kim studied business at Yonsei University. He began his literary career in 1996 by publishing *Meditation on a mirror* in the magazine *Review*. Since then, he has published a number of collections of short stories: *I have the right to destroy myself, What happened to that man stuck in the elevator?* and two volumes of essays: *Fishing for corbina fish* and *Post-it*. His first volume was translated into French; a number of his stories have been translated into English. He has received the Dongin Literary Award, the Isan Literary Award, and the Hyeondae Literary Award.

Kim Uchang

Critic. Born in Hampyeong in 1937, Kim studied at Seoul National University, Cornell and Harvard University. He taught at Seoul National University, State University of New York and Korea University where he is now a Professor Emeritus. His publications on literary criticism, art history and social analysis include: *The Poet in Time of Need, Studies in Aesthetic Reason, Towards Rational Society, Politics and the Life-World, Landscape and Mind*. He received the Seoul Award for Cultural and Artistic Criticism, the Palbong Award for Literary Criticism, and the Daesan Literary Award.

Ko Un

Poet, novelist, translator and essayist. Born in Gunsan (North Jeolla Province) 1933, he first began to publish his poems in the late 1950s. His first volume of poems, *Transcendental sensibility*, was published in 1960 when he was a Buddhist monk. He has published about 140 volumes of poems, novels, essays, and translations from Chinese, including 20 volumes of *Maninbo, Songs for tomorrow, South and north, Late songs*, the novel *Hwaom-gyeong*, and studies poets Han Yong-un and Yi Sang.

Oh Jung-hee

Novelist. Oh was born in 1947 in Seoul and studied creative writing at Seorabeol Arts College. She received the New Year Award from the *Joongang Ilbo* for her first work *The toy shop woman*. Her published work includes; *The Garden of Childhood*, *Spirit of the Wind*, and *Bird*. She has received the Yi Sang Literary Award and the Dongin Literary Award.

Park Yeemun

Poet, critic. Born in Asan (South Chungcheong Province) in 1930. Park studied French at Seoul National University and Paris-Sorbonne (France) and philosophy at the University of Southern California. He has published several volumes of poetry including *Charles River under snow, Butterfly's dream*. His collections of essays include *Dreams of literature and language, The road not yet finished*, and *Ardor of a happy nihilist*.

Yu Jong-ho

Critic. Yu was born in 1935 in Chungju (North Chungcheong Province). He studied at Seoul National University, State University of New York and Sogang University. He is currently Distinguished Professor in the Korean department of Yonsei University. His volumes of literary criticism include: *Disordered declaration, Pleasure of literature, What is literature?, Rereading Korean poets, Before and after my liberation*. Yu received the Seoul Award for Cultural and Artistic Criticism, the Republic of Korea Literary Award, the Pyeongun Literary Award, and the Daesan Literary Award.

Prospectus_

The Daesan Foundation and the Arts Council Korea are planning to hold the Second International Forum for Literature in May, 2005. The First Forum, with the theme of "Writing Across Boundaries" was held in September 26–28, 2000, with the participation of many distinguished writers from abroad and home, we would like to believe, with a huge success. The theme of the Second Forum will be "Writing for Peace," which we consider to be of a particular pertinence at this period of world history.

One would think that a world, rapidly becoming one, should hold high hopes for peace and prosperity for humanity as a whole, but one cannot deny that prospects of increased conflict and misery loom equally large, What is the role literature can play in the globalizing world if it is to move towards an order of peace and prosperity?

This is the central question we would like to consider. Immense task ahead for peace and prosperity would lie above all in the practical realms of international politics, economy and other negotiable hard issues. However, an enduring ground for peace will be laid when there develop mutual recognition and understanding among the peoples of different societies and cultures, and among persons of different backgrounds and beliefs—not only through images and news available in the media but at the level of serious and truthful communication in authentic human plurality and universality. Literature has a privileged role to play in preparing this ground. Only with the development in the deeper and truthful communication of humanity, the practical task of peace could be justly and properly oriented.

The Forum will discuss various issues related to peace and the role of the literary form of human communication in world peace: ideals of peace in different traditions, cleavages and conflicts in the global community of humankind, the relationship between the West and the rest, the multiple realities of the world, the impact of Western modernity on the world, the changing conditions of the mode of existence of literature and their significance in the literary form of human communication across boundaries of cultures and persons.

Issues related to the question of peace are of profound concern to all the peoples of the world, but the study of the question of peace has a particular urgency to the people and writers of Korea who feel they live under the threat of a potential conflict of global scale due to the tensely divided condition of their country.

We cordially invite your contribution to this international forum on the question of writing for peace in the globalizing world.

The 2nd Seoul International Forum for Literature

Seoul Declaration of Peace

Today, at the dawn of the 21st Century, we witness with dismay the nations of the world still being ravaged and threatened by wars, acts of terrorism, and other forms of violence bringing about destruction of life and environment. The threat of nuclear, chemical and other weapons of mass destruction hangs over the heads of humanity. Fanaticism, political ideologies and cultural chauvinism feed into politics of war and violence. Also responsible is the lack of a sense of human solidarity.

We, writers taking part in the 2005 Seoul International Forum for Literature, believe that war is failure of reason and admission of incompetence. Conflicts among nations must be settled peacefully within the framework of international law.

To abolish war, we must condemn political, ideological, and religious doctrines that support it. We must do away with aggression, bigotry and self—centeredness, and advocate perseverance, endurance and compassion. Peace is a product of long patient work. We must call upon those who are in charge of the fate of their nations to work together in order to uphold peace throughout the world.

We must strive to ensure for all humanity justice, equality and freedom from persecution, pain and suffering. Perpetual poverty defines life in some countries; people starve and suffer from malnutrition and lack basic necessities. Without narrowing the widening gap between the haves and have—nots, further conflicts are inevitable.

Lasting peace depends on the healthy condition of life on our planet. We must look carefully into the causes of the extinction of animal species and the degradation of the environment. Our resources are being depleted and devastated. Toxic waste is released to pollute the air. Corruption, greed and hasty profit—making go unchecked. Concerted efforts are necessary to restore the health of the earth.

We call on the peoples of the world to support movements and programs to:

1. Abolish war as an instrument of international politics.
2. Work for global disarmament, and for the prevention of nuclear proliferation.
3. Increase aid to the poorer nations in the world.
4. Abolish discrimination and ensure the equality of rights and benefits for all in society.
5. Demand equitable labor policies and practices, and make them enforceable across nations.
6. Respect the rights of all minorities.
7. Protect and preserve the environment for all sentient beings.

We are fully aware that we are meeting in a country artificially divided for more than a half—century and still threatened by nuclear war. We hope there will soon be a peaceful resolution for problems caused by the division of the country and the tension that still persists. Also, as a special problem related to it, we would like to ask for international support for the preservation of the DMZ wildlife zone in Korea, an ironical product of the unfortunate division as it is.

We call upon all nations to put pressure on their governments to adopt policies for a peaceful global community. We know that our voices alone are not going to dramatically change the present or future of the world. But we will not be silent to become accomplices of those causing the pains and sufferings of their fellow creatures.

Let us work for peace in the world altogether. Also, we understand that peace means work of moral commitment, dialogue, forgiveness and reconciliation.

* Participating writers at the 2nd Seoul International Forum for Literature issued a 'Seoul Declaration of Peace' to appeal for world peace. The Declaration aims to be a tool in international politics, calls for the eradication of war, the end of nuclear proliferation, global disarmament, abolition of social injustice for all humankind, including rights to equality and freedom of choice, seven clauses proposed for all people living on this earth. 17 international writers and 61 Korean participants signed the Declaration of Peace, a total of 78 individuals.